The Soldier and the Changing State

BUILDING DEMOCRATIC ARMIES IN AFRICA, ASIA, EUROPE, AND THE AMERICAS

ZOLTAN BARANY

PRINCETON UNIVERSITY PRESS
PRINCETON AND OXFORD

Copyright © 2012 by Princeton University Press
Published by Princeton University Press, 41 William Street,
Princeton, New Jersey 08540
In the United Kingdom: Princeton University Press, 6 Oxford Street,
Woodstock, Oxfordshire OX20 1TW

press.princeton.edu

Library of Congress Cataloging-in-Publication Data

Barany, Zoltan D.
The soldier and the changing state : building democratic armies in Africa,
Asia, Europe, and the Americas / Zoltan Barany.
p.   cm.
Includes bibliographical references and index.
ISBN 978-0-691-13768-1 (cloth : alk. paper) —
ISBN 978-0-691-13769-8 (pbk. : alk. paper)
1. Civil-military relations—Case studies. 2. Armed Forces—
Reorganization—Case studies. I. Title.
JF195.B37 2012
322'.5—dc23   2012004497

British Library Cataloging-in-Publication Data is available

This book has been composed in Sabon

Printed on acid-free paper. ∞

Printed in the United States of America

1 3 5 7 9 10 8 6 4 2

IN MEMORY OF OLD FRIENDS,

FRANCIS E. McINTYRE (1923–2010)

AND

CAROLYN M. HOLBROOK (1959–2011)

CONTENTS

ACKNOWLEDGMENTS

⫞⫟

This has been a big book to write in terms of the learning, thinking, reading, writing, and field research it required. I have received assistance from many quarters and I am elated to be at the point where I can thank those who deserve to be thanked.

At my academic home, the Department of Government at the University of Texas, I have been the beneficiary of a large contingent of first-rate comparativists from whom I continue to learn. I am especially grateful to Robert Hardgrave for several lengthy conversations about India and Pakistan, Ami Pedahzur for his long-standing enthusiastic support and assistance with the tables, and Kurt Weyland for sharing with me his impressive Latin American address book and for his advice about how to structure the project. Conversations with colleagues elsewhere directly influenced the book's development. Tom Bruneau urged me to consider Guatemala as a third case of post-praetorian rule in Latin America, Larry Diamond to think about Indonesia in the Asian context, and Scott Mainwaring to contemplate El Salvador as an interesting post–civil war example. Some colleagues are also responsible for increasing my work-load and thereby, hopefully, making the book better and more comprehensive. In particular, Nancy Bermeo convinced me that I really needed to include "post–civil war" as a separate category and, thus, an additional chapter. And, in the end, I surrendered to Paul Bolt's good-natured insistence that I would not do the book justice if I did not have a chapter on Asian states after military rule.

I cannot possibly list everyone who talked to me about their countries or regions of expertise and helped to make my field research more productive, but I must express my gratitude to John Abizaid, Felipe Agüero, Surachart Bamrungsuk, Mwesiga Baregu, Anton Bebler, Walter Bgoya, Edgardo Boeninger, Henri Boshoff, Tom Bruneau, Carlos Cáceres, P. R. Chari, Stephen F. Cohen, Constantine Danopoulos, Francisco Fernando de Santibañes, Thanos Dokos, Maria Espona, Claudio Fuentes, Hiroshi Fujikawa, Jorge González, Mark Gose, Wilfried Heinemann, Dale Herspring, Aida Hozić, Goran

Hyden, Mihail Ionescu, José Miguel Izquierdo, Gurmeet Kanwal, Faroz Khan, Choong-nam Kim, Lilian Kinghazi, Senad Kljajić, Cristián Labbé, Len le Roux, Marcus Mietzner, Jongryn Mo, M. G. Molomo, Ian Murray, Laurie Nathan, Walter North, Abillah Omari, Marina Ottaway, Ioan Mircea Pascu, Martin Rink, Arun Sahgal, Indria Samego, Richard Samuels, Ross Sanoto, Thomas Scheetz, Werner von Scheven, Jörg Schönbohm, Annette Seegers, Narcís Serra, Jowuno Sudarsono, José Manuel Ugarte, Thanos Veremis, Sebastián Vigliero, Larry Watts, and Jorge Zaverucha. Given that in quite a few countries the subjects I was researching are considered sensitive, I was not surprised that a fairly large number of people—politicians, diplomats, and military officers—spoke to me on the condition of anonymity. They know how much I appreciated their willingness to help me.

In nearly every country I traveled to I was extensively briefed by the knowledgeable, well-informed, and helpful civilian and especially military personnel at U.S. embassies. I can confirm from personal experience that the multilingual, multi-degreed, and intellectually sophisticated officers exist in significant numbers in real life, not just in Robert Kaplan's books. Though in line with State and Defense Department policy they had to speak to me without attribution, I want to thank them as a community of professionals who made a major contribution to my research.

Some of the talks I gave about various portions of the book generated probing questions and useful suggestions from the audiences. I want to especially thank my hosts at Kansas State University, the Universidad Adolfo Ibáñez in Santiago, the Universidad de las Américas in Quito, the Universities of California (Berkeley and Santa Barbara), Florida, Miami, and Oklahoma, several venues at the University of Texas, the U.S. Air Force Academy, the U.S. Naval Postgraduate School, and the panel organizers at the 2008 Triannual Armed Forces and Society Conference in Santiago and the 2010 convention of the International Studies Association.

A project of this magnitude requires substantial resources and time. For over a decade now I have been privileged to hold the Frank C. Erwin, Jr., Centennial Professorship that has covered much of the research and travel expenses. In addition, the University released me from teaching obligations for the spring semesters of 2009 and 2010, allowing me to roam the globe and work on the manuscript full-time. Visiting positions at the East-West Center in Hawaii in 2006 and at the University of Edinburgh in 2007 provided pleasant and stimulating environments to work in. I am especially thankful to the Hoover Institution for selecting me as a W. Glenn Campbell and Rita Ricardo-Campbell National Fellow and the Susan Louise Dyer Peace Fellow in 2007–2009. Michael McFaul facilitated my appointment and David Brady made me feel welcome. Conversations with a number of people at Hoover—especially Bruce Bueno de Mesquita, Larry Diamond, and Mike McFaul—helped shape the book.

I heard someone say that "a good friend will visit you in jail but a *great* friend will read your manuscript." If true, I am lucky, for many friends and colleagues agreed to comment on my work. First of all, I am grateful to the four scholars who read the entire manuscript. Daniel Chirot has been a source of encouragement, criticism, and insight from beginning to end. We talked about the project as I was planning it, then Dan read the chapters as they were being written and again, shortly before submission. Harrison Wagner actually *wanted* to read the manuscript; his comments, in turn, compelled me to rethink parts of the book. Bruce Bueno de Mesquita and Adam Przeworski were generous with their time as well and offered numerous incisive suggestions. I am also indebted to colleagues who commented on individual chapters: Donald Abenheim, Felipe Agüero, Oren Barak, Thomas Bruneau, Constantine Danopoulos, Hiroshi Fujikawa, Eugene Gholz, Robert Hardgrave, Dale Herspring, Feroz Khan, Evan Laksmana, Len le Roux, Herman Lupogo, Rohan Maxwell, Marcus Mietzner, Laurie Nathan, Abillah Omari, Sarah Phillips, Martin Rink, Richard Samuels, Thomas Scheetz, Werner von Scheven, Narcís Serra, Charlie Thomas, and Jongseok Woo.

This is my second project entrusted to Chuck Myers. He again confirmed his reputation as an editor who cares deeply about the books he works with and makes them better by offering sensible and informed suggestions and selecting expert reviewers who write the kind of reviews one hopes for: challenging, critical, and constructive. Many thanks also to Beth Clevenger for overseeing so efficiently the manuscript's metamorphosis into book form.

The two most important people in my life have only a vague idea of what is between the covers of this book. Nevertheless, Patti and Catherine tolerated my frequent and lengthy travels, bizarre work schedule, and absentmindedness with only sporadic grumblings. When we are apart, I count the days, and often the hours, until our reunion. The next project will have fewer case studies and will require much less travel—and that's a promise!

I dedicate this book to the memory of two friends who played a central role at different periods in my life and passed away while I was in the final stages of writing. I shall always remember them with affection and gratitude.

The Soldier and the Changing State

Introduction

⊰ ⊱

On May 23, 2003, Order No. 2 of the Coalition Provisional Authority, the U.S.-dominated transitional government that oversaw postwar Iraq in 2003–2004, disbanded the entire Iraqi armed forces. This was a controversial decision for a number of reasons. While the Ba'ath regime was uniformly hated in Kurdistan and amongst the population in southern Iraq, the military—a conscript army with a large proportion of Shia Muslim draftees and Sunni officers—had enjoyed considerable sympathy and respect in the rest of the country.[1] The dismissal of the Iraqi army created an alarming security and public safety vacuum; produced a large pool of trained, armed, humiliated, and desperate men for whom joining the anti-American insurgency became a logical choice; and destroyed the only national institution in a deeply divided society, an institution that could have actively participated in postwar reconstruction. Indeed, Order No. 2 has been called "one of the greatest errors in the history of U.S. warfare."[2]

It was the abolition of the Iraqi army that motivated me to write this book because it aroused my curiosity not so much about what went wrong in Iraq but about the challenges and necessary conditions of building and rebuilding armed forces that would become the loyal servants of democracies. Order No. 2 raised a number of questions regarding the military in changing political environments. Is there ever a good reason to dismiss an entire army? How should democratizers treat the traditions, histories, and cultural factors of the old army? What political-institutional safeguards can state-builders utilize to ensure the military's reliability? How important are military elites' political preferences in determining the outcome of regime change in general and of democratic consolidation in particular?

MAIN ARGUMENTS AND QUESTIONS

Developing civil-military relations that are marked by the army's steadfast support of democratic rule is an indispensable prerequisite without which the democratization project itself cannot succeed. The regular armed forces are one of the most important institutions states maintain; this is especially so in the case of nondemocratic polities. Because the majority of such states enjoy little popular legitimacy, they must rely on the agents of coercion of which the most powerful and comprehensive is the military establishment. What to do with these institutions in a democratizing sociopolitical environment? How to build a democratic army—that is to say an army that supports democratic governance, *not* one or another political party? One quickly realizes that the answers to these questions largely depend on the sort of political and social foundations upon which democratic armies are to be built. .

I started to read what has been written about armies and democratization and found very little that deeply addresses the questions that have arisen about Iraq and militaries in other states experiencing profound political change. A number of leading democratization scholars recognize the imperative of creating democratic armies and accept it as a critical condition of democratic consolidation but they seldom identify let alone discuss the principal issues involved. For instance, Adam Przeworski writes that the army must be placed in an "institutional framework of civilian control over the military [that] constitutes a neuralgic point of democratic consolidation"[3] but does not engage the subject further. Robert Dahl argues that wherever military and police forces exist they should be controlled by civilians, and their civilian controllers themselves must be subject to the democratic process, but aside from brief reflections on the military and democracy in ancient Greece and Rome, he does not develop these insights.[4] And Dahl, like other major figures of comparative politics who study democratization, does not locate an army supportive of democratic rule as a crucial prerequisite of democratization. In the late 1980s and early 1990s, with a large number of countries democratizing, Nancy Bermeo, Alfred Stepan, and others observed the "surprisingly little attention in the transition literature" to the study of the military.[5] Since then the situation has not changed drastically.

To be sure, there are many studies that describe defense reform in different democratizing states. Some more ambitious works, mostly edited collections by groups of authors, have analyzed the same process on a larger scale, comparing the democratization of military establishments in two or more countries of the same region. Insightful single-country and regional analyses like these are indispensable building blocks of an even more general study that aspires to understand democratizing armies and civil-military relations across regions. In short, the scholarly and more popular literature on democratization is both wide and deep, but no broad, cross-regional comparative study exists that explains how armies and civil-military relations are transformed to serve democratic rule.

Although he has not written such a work either, the shadow of Samuel Huntington looms large over this endeavor, for no other scholar practicing the art of general comparative politics was more aware of the central role of the armed forces in the modern state. Actually, three of Huntington's classic studies are directly relevant to my book. *The Soldier and the State*[6] remains, more than fifty-five years after its publication, *the* landmark statement on modern civil-military relations, one of my key substantive concerns here. The notion of political development is central to the question of what happens to armies during regime change and state formation, so I felt compelled to re-read *Political Order in Changing Societies.*[7] The book in the Huntingtonian oeuvre that speaks most clearly to this volume, however, is *The Third Wave: Democratization in the Late Twentieth Century,*[8] the only general assessment of democratization that places the importance of democratizing armies in its proper perspective. Although merely twenty-some pages of *The Third Wave* deal exclusively with the armed forces, throughout the book its author is sensitive to the various challenges that confront those attempting to democratize the military establishment. Huntington did not systematically examine the various political contexts in which democratic armies may be built and he did not produce a comprehensive comparative study evaluating the record of democratizers in these areas, but these were not his objectives.

In sum, there is a long-standing, yawning hole both in the academic and the policy-oriented literature concerning the evolution of military politics in changing states. Only a broadly comparative study that encompasses the different political environments and geographic regions in which democracies may take root can generate the proper appreciation and explanation of the critical necessity as well as the tasks and challenges of building democratic armies. My goal is to fill this gap and to answer some of the important questions that occurred to me as I watched America's efforts in Iraq unravel after the abolition of the Iraqi army.

In this book I will make three principal arguments. First, my central claim is that *democracy cannot be consolidated without military elites committed to democratic rule and obedient to democratically elected political elites.* Put differently, *the political preferences of military elites determine whether democratic consolidation is possible.* "Good" militaries are a necessary, if insufficient, condition of democratization. Regimes undergoing systemic political transitions are particularly vulnerable to domestic instability and threats posed by foreign actors. Whether fledgling democracies encounter dangers that originate from within or from abroad, they need armed forces that obey the commands of the emerging civilian authorities. All polities require at least the passive support of their military elites; for transitioning states, however, this need is even more acute.

Second, *building democratic armies is more difficult to accomplish in some contexts than others. The political and socioeconomic settings in which democratic armies must be built are different and thus pose dissimilar*

challenges to those crafting democratic armies and civil-military relations.
Though this point may sound fairly obvious, it ought to be made in view
of the insistence of some experts that seeking to build a universal theory of
democratization and civil-military relations is a worthwhile pursuit.

Third, *numerous generalizations* can *be made to help understand the
transformation of military politics in different environments* (say, in the
wake of civil wars or after communism). *Nevertheless, providing substantive and useful explanations for civil-military relations in such diverse political and socioeconomic environments is virtually impossible for a general
theory.* "It would be cruel to recall," the French political scientist, Alain
Rouquié, observed, "the number of carefully documented theories and definitive judgments that history has suddenly refuted and destroyed."[9] The
great diversity in empirical experiences discourages ambitions of devising
"grand theories" beyond my main contention that military elites decisively
influence the course of democratization. In the field of civil-military relations we should champion theoretical flexibility and support a variety of
approaches with more modest claims but enhanced utility.

Democratization and, thus, the building of democratic armies, usually
commences in response to a major change that shocks the political system and
sets it on a new path. The pivotal event may have been a long time coming
(such as the British hand-over of its colonies to native peoples) or triggered in
response to exogenous causes (such as the beginning of democratic transition
in foreign, often neighboring, countries). Scholars of historical institutionalism refer to these events as "formative moments" or "critical junctures," when
the path of an organization or institution is set, confirmed, or changed.[10]

In this book, I consider three contexts that follow such formative moments: after war, during regime change, and following state formation. I will
study each of them in two different settings, as I shall refer to them in the
balance of the book. Wars, particularly the two kinds of wars I privilege in
this study—cataclysmic wars such as World War II, and civil wars—typically
upset the status quo and induce major political changes that include the rebuilding of the armed forces. In the case of major wars, I am addressing the
losing side, the country that suffered a devastating defeat. Regime change
is another principal reason for building new armies. The old authoritarian
regime—here I look at military and communist regimes—was, by definition,
supported by antidemocratic armed forces that must be reformed in order
to be the servants of the emerging democratic political order. Finally, state
transformation poses another sort of demand for a new military. The two
subcategories of state transformation I take up in this study are those following colonialism, when a former colony becomes one or more independent state(s), and after (re)unification or apartheid, when two different po-

litical or social entities are joined. Let us briefly consider the three contexts, six settings, and twenty-seven cases of the study.

I. War
    A. Following total defeat in *a major war*: Germany, Japan, and Hungary
    B. After *civil war*: Bosnia and Herzegovina, El Salvador, and Lebanon

II. Regime Change
    A. After *military rule*
        1. in Europe: Spain, Portugal, and Greece
        2. in Latin America: Argentina, Chile, and Guatemala
        3. in Asia: South Korea, Thailand, and Indonesia
    B. Following *communism*: Slovenia, Russia, and Romania

III. State Transformation
    A. After *colonialism*
        1. in Asia: India, Pakistan, and Bangladesh
        2. in Africa: Ghana, Tanzania, and Botswana
    B. Post-*(re)unification* and *apartheid*: Germany, Yemen, and South Africa

Some key disparities between these environments appear even at first glance. For instance, after defeat in a major war, outside power(s) took on the responsibility to build new armed forces. External influence was also considerable in the postcolonial and post–civil war cases, but in the others the project of building democratic armies was managed mostly internally. And, of course, integrating parts of East Germany's armed forces into the West German *Bundeswehr* and establishing an army free of racial discrimination after white supremacist rule in South Africa presented challenges not experienced elsewhere. The number of contexts might be further increased or subdivided but they are broad enough to present most of the different challenges political, military, and civic elites face as they attempt to democratize their armed forces and, more generally, military politics.

In order to focus the inquiry, I pursue explanations to three general questions:

1. Which pre-democratic settings (state-socialism, colonial rule, etc.) are more conducive to the successful democratization of military politics and why?
2. Should democratizing states dismantle what exists (the old army) first and build from the ground up or should they attempt to integrate the old structures and personnel into the new? Under what conditions?

3. What are the main variables (conditions, policies) that encourage
   the development of democratic civil-military relations and which
   ones impede it?

Clearly, it is not possible to answer these queries without detailed knowledge of the relevant countries and their armed forces. In particular, we need
to understand the role of the armed forces in the fall of the old regime
and how that role influenced the military's post-transition behavior. What
are the specific issues encountered while building new armed forces in the
given political setting that are different from other settings and cases? What
are the concerns unique to the particular countries examined? Under what
conditions can civilian authorities utilize the armed forces in a domestic
contingency? What institutional arrangements have been implemented? Are
outside actors important in shaping the new army—and if so, in what way?
We will be able to answer these queries in the conclusion.

Obviously, it does not make sense to consider *all* these variables in every
case, and concerns that are essential in one context may be irrelevant in
another. On the whole, though, these questions will help to train our sights
on issues that matter and to focus on particular problems, such as where
country X went wrong and what requirements for constructing democratic
armies were absent in country Y, thus preventing its democratic development. At the end of each empirical chapter I summarize my findings in a
table that systematically evaluates the relevant variables for the three countries in that particular setting.[11]

CASE SELECTION AND CHRONOLOGICAL COVERAGE

To evaluate the arguments and to engage the questions I seek to answer, I illustrate them using the experiences of countries in different contexts. Above
I identified three of these (after war, regime change, and state transformation) and six settings—that is, postwar, post–civil war, postpraetorian, postcommunist, postcolonial, post-(re)unification/desegregation—but elected to
write nine case-study chapters for a couple of reasons. First, after World
War II so many states in different regions of the world endured military
rule or became independent that it seemed like shortchanging the subject
to restrict the analysis to single postpraetorian and postcolonial chapters.
Second, military regimes and colonial administrations (even by the same
colonial power) were very dissimilar in different regions and so were the
regimes that followed them. Therefore, I decided to devote separate chapters

to postpraetorian Southern Europe, Latin America, and East Asia, and to postcolonial South Asia and Sub-Saharan Africa.

In selecting the individual cases I wanted to do justice to both methodological rigor and flexibility, though in some cases the decision was dictated by sheer necessity.[12] In any event, my main concern was to introduce the reader not only to "crucial" cases but also to portray some outliers whose atypical experiences enrich the analysis in different ways.[13] For each chapter, then, whenever possible, I chose two main examples that demonstrate the range of experiences—that is, cases that may be considered either successes or failures *or* that produce similar outcomes for different reasons and in different ways. So, for instance, on the one hand, my cases for the postwar context are West Germany and Japan, two political systems in which firm civilian control over the new armed forces was successfully established, but, despite the many similarities of these two countries, there are important differences. On the other hand, for the postcolonial South Asian setting, India and Pakistan practically offered themselves as obvious choices given that they possess a parallel historical background of imperial rule and yet have turned out so differently. Furthermore, I chose to expand the analysis by looking at a third case in every setting whenever possible. Although I devote less attention to these "secondary" cases, I conclude that they exhibited certain atypical attributes or their experiences were more distinctive and thus looking at them yielded new insights and expanded our comparative vistas.

In the postwar context, I selected Hungary as a secondary case because of its interesting features and drastically different experience from Germany and Japan. While Hungary was Hitler's last ally, major domestic political forces there keenly desired a democratic future after the war. Nonetheless, the decisive role regarding the future of the Hungarian state and its armed forces was played by a foreign power, the Soviet Union, and the Hungarian experience with the USSR provides an interesting contrast to the two primary cases of the chapter. It shows how different outcomes can be when the state that dominates the reform of the armed forces is not a democracy—as the United States and its allies in the German and Japanese cases—but a totalitarian dictatorship.

I decided to study how new armies were built in post–civil war environments in three relatively well-known and recent cases: Bosnia and Herzegovina, El Salvador, and Lebanon. Differences in the causes of these civil wars, in their paths to the peace treaties, in the involvement of foreign states and organizations, and in their political traditions all suggested appealing opportunities for substantive comparison. In particular, I wanted to consider a case in which the civil war that preceded democratization was based on ethno-religious divisions (Bosnia and Herzegovina) and another where the hostilities were produced by political and socioeconomic disparities (El Salvador). Lebanon presented itself as an intriguing secondary case for a number of reasons, most obviously because there exists, aside from the regular military, another armed force in the country, Hezbollah's army, that is viewed as legitimate by a large part of the citizenry.

In the next section of the book we will study the reform of civil-military relations in settings following regime change. We will start with Southern Europe, which had three praetorian or military-dominant polities in the post–World War II era. Though neither Spain nor Portugal was what many experts would call typical of military rule, each was governed by long-lasting authoritarian regimes at roughly the same period of time. In both Iberian states the military was a highly influential political institution for decades, and democratization posed challenges comparable to those in other post-praetorian regimes. The Greek colonels' brief reign is a classic example of military rule and seemed like an appropriate secondary case.

In the Latin American context, Argentina was an obvious choice of a military regime that compiled a poor record of governance and a terrible legacy of human rights violations. On the other hand, both the Chilean and the Brazilian generals were in a strong position when democratization began: they built up reasonably strong economic records, they retained the support of a significant part of the electorate, and, consequently they were in a relatively advantageous bargaining position when negotiating their own withdrawal from politics. Because of these similarities, dropping one of them (Brazil) and including, as a secondary case, the more unusual example of postpraetorian army-building in Guatemala promised to augment the analysis. In the same vein, South Korea and Thailand are cases that show what can go right and wrong, respectively, with the democratization of civil-military relations while Indonesia, for a number of reasons, offers valuable lessons quite different from the other two countries.

Since 1989 nearly three dozen postcommunist states have attempted to build democratic armies. I selected Slovenia and Russia as my primary cases, and Romania as a secondary one. Slovenia epitomizes the postcommunist success story in many ways, including the establishment of democratic armed forces, while Russia, following a couple of hope-filled years settled on an authoritarian political track, a trajectory well traceable from the civil-military-relations aspect as well. Both of these states were part of larger federations but while Slovenia was the smallest of the former Yugoslav republics and had to sit idly by as Serbia divided strategic assets, Russia was the largest member of the Union of Soviet Socialist Republics and in position to set the terms of splitting property and equipment. Romania's experience is unique because it signifies the only instance where the collapse of state-socialism in a unitary state was accompanied by large-scale violence with the army's participation and where political elites succeeded in constructing democratic civil-military relations in spite of some false starts and setbacks early on.

The third context we will be studying is the transformation of not just the regime but the state itself. We will consider two main categories of state change, the emerging new independent state in the wake of colonialism on the one hand, and the integration of two political entities, two former states in the case of unification or reunification and of two or more social groups following the apartheid regime on the other. In South Asia, Bangladesh appears to be a logical secondary case given that it was a part first of British India (along with India and Pakistan) and, after partition until 1971, Pakistan itself. This distinctive background practically begged for an explanation of the trajectory of post-independence Bangladeshi military politics. In the chapter on postcolonial Africa I settled on countries that were under predominantly British colonial rule—both to facilitate library and field research and to enhance their comparability with the South Asian cases. I selected Ghana, which endured a variety of praetorian governments, and Tanzania, which has never been subjected to military rule. I decided on Botswana as my secondary example because it had a very different experience both with British rule and with developing an army after independence, given that it did not have one until 1977.

In terms of transforming military establishments after the unification of two states, the choices were clear: Germans and Yemenis became the citizens of one state following decades of separation during the Cold War. (While Germany was reunified, the Yemeni case is one of unification, since no unitary Yemeni state existed prior to 1990.) The profound differences between these two cases undoubtedly render them less comparable than might be desirable. Still, issues such as how political elites approached processes of reunification and how they dealt with the dominant position of one military force versus the much weaker other divulge interesting contrasts. I included South Africa in this chapter because while nothing like the unification along the German or Yemeni lines took place there, in an important sense South African society and its armed forces were brought together. In this respect, then, all three militaries were integrated, although, to be sure, in rather different ways. Even though the South African case cannot offer a strictly comparative dimension, it may nonetheless reward our attention with insights of a different sort.

I placed all my cases in the post–World War II era. I could have chosen different historical periods—say, some nineteenth-century Latin American countries for the postcolonial setting or the United States for the post–Civil War context—but it seemed prudent to embrace the one major commonality among an all too disparate set of states. All of my cases were affected by the Cold War and its aftermath one way or another. Another variable I considered relates to the time period for the treatment of individual case studies. Clearly, to cover the entire democratic era of Germany or Japan would make little sense as it would not significantly contribute to the book's objectives. Even cursory treatments of the case studies' entire post-transition histories would result in a tome that no publisher would want to publish and, quite possibly, no reader would want to read. What I am particularly concerned with is the process of establishing armies in changing polities and not the history of civil-military relations in any given state.

The matter to resolve, then, was how to establish a cutoff point, that is to say, where to stop the narrative. Such a date offers itself quite conveniently in some cases (say, NATO's membership invitation to Slovenia and Romania) but in other settings it is not nearly so evident. For instance, the end of the 1971 Indo-Pakistani War and the subsequent resignation of President Yahya Khan seems a reasonable juncture at which to conclude the story on Pakistan, but in 1973, Prime Minister Zulfiqar Ali Bhutto introduced important reforms that have affected Pakistani military politics ever since. India, on the other hand, firmly established a legal and institutional environment for its civil-military relations soon after independence in which no transformative changes have transpired for decades. Setting a hard and fast rule to standardize coverage (such as the first decade of democratization) would be a disservice to the analysis; it makes more sense to consider the issue on a case-by-case basis.

OBJECTIVES AND CAVEATS

This book features twenty-seven case studies and my main ambition is not to reveal astounding new findings about individual countries to experts who spent their careers studying the military politics of, say, Japan, Portugal, or Tanzania. Entire volumes have been devoted not only to the military politics of each of my case studies but in many instances to various aspects of the civil-military relations of that case. Naturally, I am building on the accumulated wisdom of my past and contemporary colleagues as it is imparted in their books, articles, and in our discussions. Rather, I have two main objectives:

First, I want to show that building democratic civil-military relations may be the most fundamental prerequisite of the transition to and the consolidation of democracy. Along the way I hope to offer the reader concise accounts of the post-regime-change military politics of my cases. Second, through the case studies, I want to illustrate how different the political contexts are when democratic armies are built, so that the reader can appreciate the divergent tasks and challenges for political and military elites. To be sure, we will identify several patterns among the three different contexts and across geographical regions. For example, we will learn that drawing the legislature into deliberations on defense affairs usually improves civil-military relations or that the out-going military government's record will go far in determining the generals' bargaining position vis-à-vis the civilian successor regime. Still, at the end of the day, I agree with Narcís Serra's contention that "no theoretical model exists which can explain these kinds of processes and anticipate outcomes."[14]

I also wish to state at the outset what is beyond the aspirations of this book. Within the framework of this study, I do not have the opportunity to concentrate on important matters like defense doctrines, strategies, tactics, weapons systems, debates on nuclear weapons and their proliferation, or alliance politics except to the extent that they directly bear on the democratization of military politics. The field of civil-military relations is rightly considered to be at the intersection of comparative politics and international relations but since in most democratization processes domestic political considerations outweigh international ones, even in the case of democratizing military establishments, I view this book primarily as a contribution to comparative politics.

Two terminological caveats need to be entered here. I am well aware that, strictly speaking, "democratic army" may sound like an oxymoron since armed forces are inherently hierarchical and nondemocratic institutions. Military personnel do not vote for their superiors, and their compliance with orders is seldom optional. I want to underscore that by "democratic armies" I mean *armies that are supportive of democratic rule*. Similarly, when I speak of "democratic civil-military relations" I am referring to the triangular nexus between state, society, and the armed forces that rests on democratic principles. Second, for stylistic reasons I use the terms "army," "armed forces," and "military" interchangeably. In instances when I refer specifically to the army as the land-based force—as opposed to the air force, navy, or some other branch of service—I make that unambiguous.

Finally, I am mindful of the ideological partiality of this book. To say that "more democracy is a good and desirable objective" is to take an ideological position. I make no apologies for taking this position and I wish to register my pro-democracy bias at the outset.

A Road Map to the Book

Chapter 1 invites the reader to think seriously about the armed forces as an institution, its place in the state, and its role in politics and society. To understand how democratic armies may be developed and the complexity of the tasks and challenges involved, we ought to be acquainted with the armed forces as a political institution and civil-military relations as an important component of the universe in which the myriad of political and societal interactions occur that make up politics in the modern state. This is a vast subject and the scope of the chapter does not permit an exhaustive examination of many arguably relevant issues. My objectives are limited to sorting out the essential normative, theoretical, and empirical concerns pertaining to the building of democratic armies. The principal dilemma a potent military force poses for the state—it has to be strong enough to protect the state and yet it must not be tempted to destroy the state—already occupied thinkers in ancient Greece. I will briefly explain what they and their successors elsewhere thought about the matter, note some germane theoretical contributions to the study of military politics and democratization, and then outline the basic standards and institutional arrangements of democratic civil-military relations.

Chapters 2 through 10 are empirical chapters organized by the three contexts that provide the impetus for democratization. In these chapters my goal is to explain how democratic armies are built and civil-military relations are developed in a wide variety of environments, to contrast the experiences of individual countries, to assess the differences between the six settings, and to find answers to the questions posed above. I did not impose on myself a unitary chapter outline because I wished to save the book from turning into a dreary checklist and to allow the topics and specific settings to influence the layout of individual chapters. Having said this, in all the chapters, I summarize the main contours of military politics prior to the beginning of the transition process so we can have a sense of their points of departure. Furthermore, I offer a background sketch on the particular cases so that once the analysis moves to specific questions, the reader will be familiar with the essential attributes of the countries in question.

For the most part, the empirical chapters consist of comparative analyses of civil-military relations structured by the relevant research questions. I try to find the answers to some of the same questions (e.g., is there institutionally balanced civilian control over the armed forces? are there organizations of politically independent expertise on defense issues?) in every chapter, though to a degree the issues I take on are specific to the given context. For instance, deciding what traditions to maintain from the legacies of the colonial army would be a relevant concern in the newly independent states of Africa and South Asia but not in postpraetorian Latin America. In the last part of each empirical chapter I will reiterate the main differences and similarities between the individual cases, how we can account for them, and, as noted above, sum up our findings in a comparative table.

In the conclusion I want to compare not so much the individual cases but, rather, to learn from the contrasts that have emerged from the six different settings we examined. In other words, my objective is to draw all the strings together and summarize what we have learned from the book. I will review what we have discovered about the importance of the armed forces as a politically relevant institution of the modern state, the major findings yielded by the comparative analysis, and the lessons they hold for democracy activists and policy-makers. I conclude with a set of policy recommendations that those interested in the democratization of the armed forces and military politics should find valuable.

CHAPTER 1

What Does a Democratic Army Look Like?

⚐ ⚑

The principal foundations on which the power of all
governments is based (whether they be new, long-established
or mixed) are good laws and good armies.
—Machiavelli, *The Prince*[1]

There is no organization more important for the survival of the state than its armed forces. For millennia, communities have relied on armies for protection, for conquest, and for less obvious functions, such as conveying their strength and commitment to defend and advance their interests. Yet, many people, even those interested in politics and governance, have little understanding of the military as an institution charged with a country's defense. Where does the army fit in the organizational structure of the state? What are politicians' expectations of the armed forces? What are the military's responsibilities to the state and to society? What does a democratic army look like and how can we tell it from a nondemocratic one?

This chapter invites the reader to think seriously about the armed forces as an institution of the modern state, as a part of society, and about the relationships between them. I begin with a brief inquiry into how major thinkers in times past viewed the army and how key elements of military politics have changed through modern history. In the following part I briefly discuss some of the useful theoretical contributions that inform the study of civil-military relations and democratization in different political environments. In the rest of the book I tell the stories of how different countries went about democratizing military politics, so it is going to be helpful to have a gauge against which their records can be measured. To that end, in the third section I outline the indispensable components of democratic military politics in terms of institutional arrangements and relationships, and present the major aspects of the societal side of civil-military relations. In doing so, I explain the functions and obligations of society, the state, and the armed forces.

ARMIES, STATES, SOCIETIES: LOOKING BACK

What is the fundamental difference that sets apart sovereign states like Brazil from provinces like British Columbia and cities like Bangkok? All three entities feature political systems complete with separate executive, legislative, and judicial branches, they all tax their residents and, in return, provide services for them. What makes them so different is Brazil's right, indeed obligation, to protect its citizens with a military force whose function is to fight foreign enemies. For Max Weber, "the monopoly of the legitimate use of physical force" (*Gewaltmonopol des Staates*) is part of the very definition of the modern state.[2] I agree with Adam Przeworski who contends that the state actually possesses only the monopoly to *license* different bureaucracies—the armed forces, various police agencies, intelligence services, border guards, etc.—to bear arms.[3] This is an important distinction because establishing effective civilian control signifies different challenges depending on the armed organization in question. (In this book, however, we are only concerned with the regular military—including its branch services, the army, navy, and the air force.)

In the formative period of ancient Greek and Italian city-states and, much later, in the medieval towns of Italy, the early centralization of state administration and the organization of those economically competent to bear arms, equip, and train themselves allowed those states to rise and prosper.[4] Affluence, in turn, enabled ancient and medieval cities to bolster their military force that could be used to defeat the private armies of wealthy enemies and thereby further increase state power. The state's strength—projected through its military force—then might be put to good use not only as a protective device against external enemies but also to expand its territories and influence.[5] Most of the principal dilemmas of civil-military relations were articulated by philosophers and political thinkers as early as in ancient Greece, because the fundamental problem of military politics is as logical as it is eternal: the state needs the armed forces for its own protection, but the same forces, owing to their monopoly of the tools of large-scale violence, also present a potential threat to the state's very existence.

The question "who will guard the guardians?" (*Quis custodiet ipsos custodes?*) was first posed by the 1st–2nd century AD Roman satirist Juvenal—to show the impossibility of imposing a moral code on women when the enforcers themselves are corruptible—and has been frequently invoked to acknowledge an age-old political dilemma.[6] The crucial challenge for politicians is to ensure the unconditional obedience of the military while at the same time allowing it sufficient autonomy to successfully discharge its functions and execute its missions. The army must be strong enough to prevail in war but conduct its own affairs so as not to destroy the society it is intended to protect. Moreover, the military should use society's resources only to the extent justified by the threat confronting the state and must not extract state assets merely to increase its own strength.[7]

The armed forces may be considered the quintessential Weberian rational organization that is bound by rules that unambiguously lay out standard operating procedures, rewards for compliance, and punishment for disobedience. As Samuel Huntington pointed out, the military as a state institution is shaped by two forces: a functional imperative stemming from the threats to society's security, and a societal imperative arising from the social forces, ideologies, and institutions dominant within society.[8] The army is an inherently political institution: there is no such thing as an apolitical military. The state or, more broadly, the constitutional order of the state, needs the implicit support of the armed forces. This leads us back to my definition of the "democratic army," that is, a force supporting not one political party or another but the principle of democratic governance. Put differently, civil-military relations in mature liberal democracies are based on the submission of officers to civilian authority not because the officers necessarily agree with or respect politicians but because they value, above all else, a democratic order that cannot exist without the civilians' control of the armed forces.[9]

The political role of the military as a controversial issue already surfaced in ancient Greece. Many of the leading political figures in Athens, like Pericles, Nicias, and Alcibiades, were generals whose political power was based both on their leadership of the army *and* on their ability to persuade the Athenian assembly to support their proposals. An excellent example of this is Thucydides' description of how Pericles, aided by his celebrated oratorical skills, in effect "sold" the Peloponnesian War to the Athenian assembly.[10] Military intervention in politics emerged as an important issue in imperial Rome. Indeed, the terms "praetorianism" and "praetorian rule" originate from the Roman praetorian guards—originally a detachment of bodyguards used by emperors—who began to play an increasingly bloody and ambitious political role in the first century AD. They removed Emperor Gaius (Caligula) in AD 41, were key participants in the Pisonian Conspiracy in AD 65, killed Emperor Galba in AD 69 (within the context of a civil war), and may have been involved in the murder of Emperor Domitian in AD 96.[11] No wonder that Roman politicians occasionally thought it prudent to bribe the army camps around the capitol in order to make sure that the soldiers' attention stayed firmly on professional concerns.[12]

In *The Republic*, Plato considered the necessary attributes of soldiers toward citizens and enemies. In the well-known "just city" speech the relationship between soldiers ("guardians") and the citizenry is treated extensively as Socrates explains that guardians "must be gentle to their own people, but hard for the enemy to deal with. Else they will not wait for others to destroy the city but will destroy it themselves first."[13] Another important point is the clear recognition that officership and soldiering require sophisticated skills and, therefore, professional education. In order for "matters of war to be well performed," Socrates contended, the guardian "should have the most freedom from all other pursuits, for he requires technical knowledge and the greatest diligence."[14] The need for professionalism was appreciated even earlier in China and is a major theme in the writings of Sun Tzu (6th–5th century BC). Indeed, the very concept of the "General Staff" originated in China's Warring States period (475 BC–221 BC).[15] Early strategic thinkers, like Sun Tzu II, thought soldiers should be "organized by homeland for the sake of the inner cohesion of a unit."[16] As in Athens, fairness, integrity, and benevolence were considered important attributes of fine generals in ancient China.[17]

There are, to be sure, numerous significant differences between ancient and modern democracies. In Athens, as I alluded to above, the most important military decisions were made by a public vote of citizens to whom generals could (and did) speak directly. There and in other Greek city-states the distinction between the army and the rest of the citizenry was blurrier than today because at one point nearly all free citizens had to perform military service. In Republican Rome, too, all citizens were made eligible for entry into the army in 107 BC with the removal of property requirements for military service.

The goodness of government was considered of paramount importance from the perspective of martial determination. In ancient China, for instance, the morality of the imperial government, specifically of the sovereign, was considered so significant that it was believed to be one of the five fundamental factors of war. If "Tao," or moral influence, was the guiding principle of governance, then, Sun Tzu explained, soldiers would accompany their leaders "in life and unto death without mortal peril."[18]

Nearly two thousand years later, the importance of the sovereign's active engagement with his army was clearly understood and emphasized in the writings of that famous Florentine political philosopher, diplomat, poet, and playwright, Niccolò Machiavelli. The point is evident in his repeated warnings in *The Prince* that "A ruler, then . . . should pay attention to nothing aside from war, military institutions, and the trainings of his soldiers"; that "the prime reason for losing power is neglect of military matters"; and that "a ruler must think only of military issues, and in time of peace, he should be even more occupied with them than in war."[19]

Machiavelli also tackled the weighty issue of whether armies should be staffed by citizens or contracted foreigners. Like many other medieval city-states, Florence had traditionally depended on a citizens' army. By the beginning of the fourteenth century, however, the reluctance of ever more prosperous citizens to bear arms had forced city fathers to turn to mercenaries for protection. The *condottieri*—the word actually means "contractors" in Renaissance Italian—often proved more dangerous to their civic employers than to the enemy because of needlessly prolonging campaigns for larger payoffs, threatening to retire at the hour of crisis, and so on. Not surprisingly, Machiavelli was an early champion of the popular militia.[20] Still, three centuries later he was criticized by the Prussian military thinker, Carl von Clausewitz—who otherwise praised Machiavelli's "very sound judgment in military matters"—and others for denying that war needed to be either civic or moral and, especially, for discounting the significance both of the individual soldier and the need for military professionalism.[21] In Machiavelli's *The Art of War*, Fabrizio Colonna, the Papal Captain declares that

> I should not so much consider the nature of their [military] profession as the moral virtue of the men, and which of them could perform the most services. For this reason, I should prefer to choose husbandmen and men who have been accustomed to work in the fields as men more useful in an army than any other kind of person.[22]

Notwithstanding Machiavelli's uncharacteristic myopia on this point, the notion that officership was a *profession* has been a perpetual theme of the literature on the military from, as we have seen, Plato onward. Weber maintained, for instance, that the reason that best explained the success of the numerically small French and British troops that colonized India in the late 1700s was not their superior firepower—Indian armies were well equipped with cannons and often with muskets—but their organizational excellence, methods of drill, and rigorous battlefield discipline.[23] The signal weakness of India, on the other hand, was its military tradition that honored the exploits of the individual rather than of the unit.

By this time, the British had also benefited from civil-military relations in which generals considered political intervention anathema to their profession. Civilian rule was last supplanted by military force in Britain during the English Civil War (1642–51) between parliamentarians and royalists. The former, led by Oliver Cromwell, overthrew the monarchy and replaced it with parliamentary authority—first the Commonwealth of England (1649–53) and then the Protectorate (1653–59) under the personal rule of Lord Protector Cromwell and, after his death in 1658, of his son, Richard. Cromwell introduced a new kind of army that in its entire conception and organization constituted a major advance toward modern professional militaries. The personnel of his New Model Army consisted of full-time professionals

rather than part-time militiamen; it was intended for service anywhere in
the country rather than tied to a garrison or a particular region; levels of
discipline were high; promotions were based on merit; and, perhaps most
importantly, officers were professional soldiers who did not have seats in
either the House of Lords or the House of Commons and, therefore, were
not linked to any political or religious faction among the parliamentarians.[24]

The great innovation of the French Revolution was that it introduced
masses of ordinary people—rather than mercenaries and individuals selected for their martial skills—as participants of war. Indeed, the modern
form of conscription emerged in the French Revolution, when the government utilized its power to press able-bodied men into military service for a
limited period of time. As Clausewitz noted, "Instead of governments and
armies as heretofore, the full nation was thrown into the balance."[25] Soon
many countries adopted this practice to bolster their military power, to reduce the cost of warfare, and to be able to maintain a standing army even
in peacetime, and, not incidentally, to create a sense of common identity
particularly in ethnically and regionally divided states.

Clausewitz was a student of Gerhard von Scharnhorst's, the first minister of war and chief of the General Staff of Prussia (1808–10) and, no less
importantly, the founder of the world's first modern institution of military
higher learning, the *Preußische Kriegsakademie* (1810). Prussia was unique
in the first half of the nineteenth century because the authority of the king
as Supreme War Lord was not challenged by a parliament and thus he could
continue to isolate the military from constitutional politics. While Cromwell's army was strongly influenced by profound ideological and religious
undercurrents, in Prussia a more uncontaminated professionalism became
institutionalized. Increasingly, career advancement in the Prussian army was
based on merit instead of family background, and as Huntington pointed
out, the by-product of the rise of nationalism was the concept of "a nation
in arms" and its corollary of a national army in which, according to an 1814
law, all male citizens were obligated to serve for five years (three on active
duty, two in the reserves).[26] In other words, about two centuries ago the
armies led by aristocrats and staffed by mercenaries began to give way to
armies led by professional officers commanding conscripted men.

In his posthumously published *On War (Vom Kriege)*, a monumental
work on the nature, theory, and strategy of war, Clausewitz also laid down
some of the essential principles of modern civil-military relations. Military
officers must always be subordinate to civil authority and ought not participate in politics. Political activism, Clausewitz claimed, would undermine
their professionalism, would create unnecessary cleavages within the officer
corps, and would distract them from their responsibilities. Rather, he con-

tended, officers should be politically neutral and guided by statesmen whose job it was to know the "big picture" and to provide the armed forces with clear directives and policy objectives. A successful minister of war does not have to be intimately familiar with military affairs but he must be aware of the capabilities and limitations of his forces and must be willing to listen to and carefully consider the opinion of expert military professionals. As Huntington summed up, for Clausewitz

> the military profession exists to serve the state. To render the highest possible service the entire profession and the military force which it leads must be constituted as an effective instrument of state policy.[27]

By about 1800 several major West European states—Britain, France, the Dutch Republic, Prussia—and the United States accomplished what North, Wallis, and Weingast call "consolidated control of the military." They all established state control over all military resources and assets of the country and "a set of credible conventions that determine how force is used," though, to be sure, in different ways.[28] Early nineteenth-century Prussia was an absolute monarchy and Prussian officers swore fealty to the kaiser, not to a constitution or a representative body of the population. During the short-lived Weimar Republic (1919–33) members of the Reichswehr pledged their loyalty to the constitution, but soldiers of the Third Reich (1933–45) once again swore allegiance to an individual, Adolf Hitler, a point that illuminates why civilian control over the armed forces is hardly a sufficient criterion of democratic military politics. Democratic civil-military relations can only exist in democratic states: civilian oversight does not mean democratic control of the armed forces; it is merely one of several essential prerequisites of democratic civil-military relations.

At its inception, the relationship between the state and the armed forces in the United States was strongly affected by the British tradition of military non-interference in politics. When General George Washington dispersed his army and declined the offer of sovereign authority following the conclusion of the War of Independence, he became a modern Cincinnatus—the general in ancient Rome who, after defeating foreign enemies, rejected the dictatorial powers extended to him and returned to his farm—as he set the highest standard for his successors.[29] In the more than two centuries since, the institutional arrangements of American civil-military relations have undergone many changes along with the armed forces themselves but they have always retained their democratic character.

The government of the United States has never been in any danger of being overthrown by the military but the absence of a coup does not mean U.S. civil-military relations have been without problems. Even a most perfunctory survey of the post–World War II period reveals that a commanding general was guilty of insubordination (Douglas MacArthur during the Korean War), a serving chairman of the Joint Chiefs of Staff publicly advocated views that were at variance with those of civilian leaders (Colin Powell in 1992), and a top commander and members of his staff made derogatory comments about U.S. policy and policy-makers to a journalist (Stanley McChrystal in 2010). But again, it is important to put things in their proper perspective. As Richard Betts noted, "[i]n American civil-military relations the water never gets chin-deep. In the worst of times, it splashes up toward knee level. Our feet are always wet, but the water rarely gets above our ankles."[30]

In any event, the tensions in American military politics are hardly unique in long-established democracies. In particular, extraordinary circumstances tend to create fertile ground for breakdowns in civil-military relations. For instance, the French top brass mounted two coup attempts during the Algerian War of Independence (1954–62) to protest what they considered inadequate political support for their campaign against Algerian rebels. The army leadership and right-wing elements organized a putsch in May 1958 that set in motion the events that led to the creation of the Fifth Republic. Three years later, French generals in Algeria organized a coup d'état that was intended to oust President Charles de Gaulle and establish an anticommunist military junta.[31] This coup did not have a chance because it did not enjoy the support of conscripted soldiers let alone that of the larger society.

My intention with this brief sketch of the changes affecting the state-military nexus through the centuries was to illustrate three important points. First, the fundamental issues of civil-military relations have been discussed and debated since the very beginning of organized states. Second, civil-military relations have undergone a long evolutionary process reflecting changes in societies, political systems, and warfare itself. And third, the military politics of even long consolidated democracies can use improvement and refinement.

USEFUL THEORIES OF CIVIL-MILITARY RELATIONS

The field of civil-military relations is situated at the intersection of two disciplines, political science and sociology, though it also benefits from insights drawn from history and regional studies. It is an area of social science that has produced many valuable theoretical contributions, normative guides, and empirical analyses but not a grand theory that can account for the myriad divergent cases and patterns. More than five decades after its publication, Samuel Huntington's *The Soldier and the State* is still the unsurpassed standard for civil-military-relations scholars, the book that has influenced the way we think about military politics, and the one no college or academy courses on the subject can ignore. Huntington asked simple and important questions and provided persuasive answers to them. It is worth remembering the political and historical context—some of the most tension-filled years of the Cold War, in the mid-1950s—that provided the backdrop for his theorizing. Huntington believed that in order to be effective, soldiers had to be different from their fellow citizens whose main values derived from liberalism. The military, he argued, must remain isolated from both society and politics and retain and guard its professional autonomy.

In contrast, Morris Janowitz, a sociologist and another formative scholar of the field, argued in his classic *The Professional Soldier* that in the post–World War II context the military ought to move closer to society, embrace civilian values as much as feasible, and become open to professional reform and new organizational techniques.[32] While for Huntington honor, loyalty, and duty were the defining characteristics of the professional soldier, Janowitz insisted that "in a democratic society it is highly inappropriate for honor to be the sole, or even the dominant value of the professional military cadre."[33] Janowitz believed that the essence of civilian control of the armed forces consisted of improved assessments of military performance. He did not fully appreciate the gravity of and direct impact on civilian oversight by the variety of potential institutional frameworks. If Huntington was accused of neglecting to protect democratic values, then Janowitz was faulted for failing to protect the democratic state.[34] At the end of the day, Janowitz did not offer an alternative theory explaining how civilians ensure their control over generals, and his answers to the key issues of civil-military relations were basically quite similar to Huntington's views.

Notwithstanding its multifaceted contributions, *The Soldier and the State* is of little help when thinking about the armed forces in processes of democratic transitions. An oft-repeated criticism of Huntington's work is that it is "ethnocentric" and offers little insight into the workings of military politics in settings other than the United States.[35] Huntington's purpose was to lay out a theory of civil-military relations pertaining to established democracies but since the present study is mainly concerned with states that are *transitioning* into democratic regimes, some of the central issues Huntington focused on are clearly less relevant. In the last half-century many important contributions have been made to civil-military-relations theory but most of these primarily pertain to military politics in the United States.[36] What among them is useful from the perspective of democratic transitions?

The timing, strategy, planning, and execution of coups and the conditions that motivate them has been the topic of a substantial theoretical literature.[37] "Military influence," the range of institutional behavior that falls between the extremes of violent coup d'état and the army's full compliance with its civilian masters, has proven more difficult to theorize about, however, even though it is perhaps the most important concern of civil-military-relations scholars. One of the key problems is that accurately measuring the gradations between the two end points of the coup/no-coup spectrum is extraordinarily difficult given the complexity of cases and the number of potential explanations and their varying importance relative to one another.

Nonetheless, several scholars have devised instruments for this purpose. In the early 1960s Samuel Finer formulated a simple six-point scale to evaluate the modes of the military's political intrusion:[38] (1) normal constitutional channels; (2) collusion and/or competition with civilian authorities; (3) intimidation of civilian authorities; (4) threats of noncooperation with, or violence toward, the civilian authorities; (5) failure to defend civilian authorities from violence; and (6) the exercise of violence against civilian authorities. Finer ordered these behaviors into three categories: influence (1–2), blackmail (2–4), and displacement/supplantation (4–6). A quarter-century later Alfred Stepan came up with an alternative to Finer's scheme, listing eleven "military prerogatives," spheres—such as the army's constitutionally sanctioned role in the political system; its relationship to the chief executive, the government, and the legislature; and its role in intelligence, police, state enterprises, and the legal system—where the army as an institution assumes the right, formal or informal, to exercise control over its own internal governance and to play a role in extra-military jurisdictions within the state apparatus that are germane to its interests.[39] Though Stepan's "low-moderate-high" scale does not permit a nuanced appraisal of military influence, it provides a useful framework for thinking analytically about military participation in politics.

Narcís Serra conjures up a seven-stage process of transition to democracy as the military's autonomy and political intervention are gradually diminished, proceeding from the control of political power all the way to democratic civil control over the armed forces.[40] Stepan's and Serra's work, centered primarily on Southern Europe and Latin America, is most directly relevant to democratizing states that are emerging from military rule but less pertinent to political environments where the armed forces traditionally held modest political power. Risa Brooks's recent work on the political strategies generals might pursue in democratic states—such as public appeal, politicking, and alliance building—is illustrated with examples from

American civil-military relations but can also be a useful tool for a more general study of the subject.[41]

Efforts to generate grand theories of military politics often yield valuable insights but cannot achieve their goals owing to the infinite variations among individual cases.[42] For instance, Michael Desch, in *Civilian Control of the Military*, argued using a structural theory of civil-military relations that "the strength of civilian control of the military in most countries is shaped primarily by structural factors, especially threats, which affect individual leaders, the military organization, the state, and society."[43] The book includes several useful case studies that support the theory, but they seem to have been selected, as political scientists would say, on the dependent variable, that is, cases that would not fit the theory were neglected. Moreover, as Jongseok Woo has argued, the causal logic of external and internal security threats versus civilian control is at odds with Desch's arguments, suggesting that high threats lead to the presence of a politically influential military whereas low threats lead to a politically inconsequential army.[44] Finally, Desch tends to give short shrift to cultural, historical, and other relevant factors that could be useful in explaining why some threat environments are actually structurally indeterminate.

The best theoretical work in civil-military relations has targeted and often succeeded in realizing more modest goals. These include, among numerous others, Brian Taylor's explanation for the absence of military coups in Russia, Harold Trinkunas' illuminating account of the different transition experiences of postpraetorian regimes in Latin America, and Rebecca Schiff's theory of concordance, which offers a unique and creative method of elucidating the differences between South Asia's postcolonial armies. Andrew Cottey and his coauthors made a useful contribution to the study of democratic transitions in postcommunist states by differentiating between "first generation" (structural reforms to establish a democratic framework) and "second generation" (filling the framework with substance and providing for the effective management of the armed forces and defense policy) civil-military relations reforms.[45] Serra, who is not just a scholar but—as Spain's long-standing defense minister conceived and implemented a slew of reforms in 1982–91—also a practitioner, convincingly argued that military reform must not be isolated from the process of transition or general democratic reform in which it is embedded and offered a new conception of defense reform outlining its multifaceted components.[46] Their work—as well as that of several others—informs this study and will be helpful in explaining the diversity in military politics around the world. In this book I approach civil-military relations by looking at all three sides of the issue (the state, the military, and society) and with a keen awareness of the role of foreign actors.

The ultimate measure of a theory is its *usefulness* in illuminating diverse phenomena. The principal shortcoming of most general theories of military politics is nearly always oversimplification: the neglect of significant cultural, historical, and environmental factors without which the nuances of civil-military relations of a given state cannot be fully understood and appreciated. The variety of settings, conditions, and explanatory variables stacks the odds strongly against the emergence of powerful and general theories of civil-military relations. As the military historian Richard Kohn noted, "in the end, there are no cookbook recipes for civil-military relations, as diverse and unexpected as they can be."[47]

BASIC STANDARDS OF DEMOCRATIC CIVIL-MILITARY RELATIONS

In modern democracies military politics should be understood as a set of relationships between a set of institutions. The institutions belong to one of the three sides of the civil-military relations triangle: state, society, or the military itself. The branches of government are the most important state institutions in the equation. They can be broken down further to the chief executive (president and/or prime minister), the cabinet, government ministries, and the various agencies of the executive branch that deal with defense and security matters. Parliament and its committees, and the specialized organizations that serve them, are the key institutions that constitute the legislative side.

The societal side is at times neglected in writings on military politics even though obviously there can be no state or army without society itself. Perhaps the reason for this occasional disregard is that until relatively recently, society's role in the civil-military relations was largely limited to spawning officers and soldiers. In democracies, however, public opinion and societal agents such as the media and nongovernmental organizations (NGOs) have gradually emerged as influential components of politics, including military politics.

The armed forces constitute the third side of the civil-military relations equation. Although in most armies the majority of uniformed military personnel are conscripted or enlisted soldiers or noncommissioned officers (NCOs), the study of military politics is primarily concerned with professional officers whose specialty is the management of violence (as opposed to enlisted men whose expertise is the application of violence).[48] The officer corps makes up the elite of the military profession; its highest-ranking members represent the military as a whole as they articulate the army's views and convey its needs to the state and society. By its very nature the military cannot be a democratic organization given its unambiguously hierarchical institutional structure, corporate culture, and top-to-bottom decision-making and implementation processes. As in other professions, the military officer's responsibilities increase with every consecutive promotion. Unlike in other professions, the officer's responsibilities will likely include accountability for the job performance, well-being, and, in combat, the life of an ever larger number of persons and their equipment under his/her command.

A distinction should be made between two key entities of the defense establishment. The ministry of defense is an institution of the state and its top manager, the minister, is a member of the cabinet, while the General Staff is the highest echelon of the professional armed forces that facilitates defense planning and the bidirectional flow of information between the high command and the individual units. Its leader, the chief of the General Staff, is the military's top uniformed officer. This is, more or less, the standard institutional structure in liberal democracies but, of course, there are departures from it. For instance, in Japan and Germany—states where at the time of the new armed forces' inception concerns about the resurgence of militarism were high—the army remains in a far weaker institutional position. In this section my goal is to acquaint the reader with some of the elementary issues of civil-military relations in modern democracies that will accompany us in the balance of this book as we learn about states' efforts to build democratic armies.

Civilian Control Shared by the Executive
and Legislative Branches

Civilian control of the armed forces is the most fundamental principle of military politics in democracies; without it, democratization cannot succeed. In its simplest form, society's elected representatives and leaders ensure that soldiers' attention is fully occupied by their professional concerns, that they do not interfere in political life, and that they provide expert advice to politicians when it is sought. The military's political involvement must be limited so that only members of the armed forces who possess the most expertise and experience on a given issue—usually the highest-ranking officers—interact with politicians. These interactions should take place through regularized channels and be transparent to all as long as military secrets are not compromised.

Military and foreign policy must be made by politicians. The debate on alternative policies and approaches is framed by civilians who enlist military experts as advisers as needed. Once politicians reach their decisions—with or without the assistance of military experts—armed forces personnel do their utmost to implement them. It is entirely possible that military officers understand the given issue better than their civilian superiors; still, they must execute civilian orders even if they disagree with them. Quite simply, civilians have the right to be wrong; soldiers, on the other hand, do not have the right to be insubordinate.[49]

Clearly, there is inherent tension and even conflict between politicians and officers. Neither perfect amity between the generals and their civilian masters, nor an obsequiously, unquestioningly obedient top brass is the proper measure of good civil-military relations.[50] Military leaders—their confidence bolstered by expertise and experience—would be foolish if they did not try to use their influence to sway civilians to decide in favor of the armed forces' preferred course of action. In a pluralistic political system, some conflict is not only inevitable but, in fact, desirable.[51] It suggests that both politicians and military leaders are doing their jobs. This built-in tension in civil-military relations requires constant engagement, monitoring, and interaction and compels politicians to keep an eye on and try to better understand the armed forces. When senior officers enjoy great prestige and possess advanced bureaucratic skills, when they believe that their capacity to fulfill their missions may be at risk, or when they doubt the competence of the civilian leadership, politicians can face great obstacles in exercising their authority.[52]

What most readers remember from *The Soldier and the State* is the two contending approaches of civilian control over the armed forces that Huntington called "objective" and "subjective." *Objective civilian control* is appropriate for advanced industrial democracies where militaries are highly professional organizations that acknowledge the limits of their professional competencies and accept civilian supremacy in foreign and military policy decisions. The state, in turn, views soldiers as the guardians of society, recognizes them as highly skilled professionals who abhor political interference, and endows them with significant autonomy in conducting their affairs—such as training, education, and the promotion of all but the highest ranking officers—thereby minimizing civil-military conflict.

Subjective civilian control, on the other hand, is more appropriate for political environments that are either undemocratic or where democracy has not been around long enough to generate sufficient trust between the state and the armed forces, where the army has a history of political intervention, and where it has not attained a high degree of professionalism and may be tempted to turn its gaze from the barracks to the state house. To prevent that from happening, the state closely supervises the military and uses its various agencies—such as domestic/military intelligence, auditing services, etc.—to ensure that soldiers are not engaged in independent activities that might run counter to state policy. In other words, in this kind of political environment the state achieves its goal of extending comprehensive controls over the armed forces "by civilizing the military, making them the mirror of the state."[53]

Objective civilian control achieves its end "by militarizing the military, making them the tool of the state."[54] Put differently, objective control depicts "good" civil-military relations where the officer is trusted by the state to mind his/her own business, as it were. Subjective control, in contrast, suggests "bad" civil-military relations where the officer lurking at the corridors of political power is viewed as a perpetual menace. Huntington's critics who point out that some highly professional armed forces, such as those of Pakistan and Turkey, regularly intervene in national politics tend to overlook his proviso that the correlation between higher levels of professionalism and fewer instances of political meddling hold only for consolidated democracies.

In time, institutions gain or lose influence vis-à-vis one another, and the nature and extent of civil-military relations reflects the shifting balance between the strength of political institutions and the political strengths of the military.[55] Civil-military relations—and, by extension, civilian control issues—are affected by a number of other factors, perhaps most importantly the external and internal threat environment the state and military faces. In the absence of foreign and domestic threats, the military might be less averse to meddle in politics or prone to shirk its duties to society, issues that Michael Desch and Peter Feaver have carefully considered and written about.[56] The paradox of objective control, as Richard Kohn noted, is that the development of military professionalism goes hand in hand with the diminution of the state's oversight of the armed forces.[57] This might not present a potentially perilous problem in robust democracies but would be a major risk to the fragile democracies just emerging from one or another sort of authoritarian regime that this book is largely concerned with. A serious shortcoming of the early civil-military relations literature was that it put excessive emphasis on the notion of civilian control but was relatively little bothered by the attributes of the state that was doing the controlling. This continues to be an important contemporary issue given the spread of authoritarian politics by democratic means. Even a cursory look at the "electoral authoritarian" regimes in Africa, the former Soviet Union, and Latin America suggests that while civilian control may be the key issue in established democracies, there is far more to military politics that should hold our interest.[58]

An important criterion of democratic governance is that civilian control over the armed forces be *balanced* between the executive and legislative branches of government. As Robert Dahl wrote, "the civilians who control the military [and police] must themselves be subject to the democratic process."[59] The legislature debates foreign policy and defense issues and ought to have the power to call on members of the executive branch and the armed forces to testify before it in open or closed hearings. Issues may include a broad spectrum of matters ranging from reporting progress made in a war, the acquisition of weapons systems, the expansion or reduction of periods of conscription, to appropriate levels of defense burden sharing within an international alliance. In democracies parliamentarians enjoy the opportunity to advise or otherwise convey their opinions to the executive branch. The lawmakers' most significant impact on the armed forces, however, is their debate, vote, and monitoring of the implementation of the defense budget, and their deliberation and adoption of laws regulating military-security issues.

Within the legislature, defense-related committees and their staffs are the key players because they exercise actual civilian oversight and are the loci of military expertise. There might be several such parliamentary committees—for instance separate committees in the lower and upper houses and for armed forces and foreign affairs—and their membership might overlap to some extent, especially in a legislative chamber with a relatively small number of deputies. It is important that defense committees provide a real alternative to the voice of the executive branch on security matters. This is not always easy because the executive branch often enjoys better access to information and may attempt to compartmentalize or isolate pertinent information from lawmakers.[60] If members of defense committees possess real, practical, up-to-date knowledge of pertinent issues, they are far more likely to be consulted by the executive branch than if they do not.

The constitutional design of a state might favor the presidency or parliament in assigning authority and obligations.[61] There is no hard-set rule as to whether "parliamentary" or "presidential" regimes are more conducive to successful democratization because different environments (e.g., political cultures, histories, relative weights of institutions like political parties) produce different institutional settings. In many instances of failed democratization, the problem lies not in the distribution of authority among institutions but the lack of commitment and discipline of political institutions to play by the rules. In most cases the day-to-day management of military forces and civilian control are most effective when exercised by the ministry of defense (as distinct from the general staff), which is a part of the executive branch and is overwhelmingly staffed by civilian personnel.[62]

There can be no robust civilian oversight without strong political institutions. Fledgling democracies, where the military has a tradition of political intervention and retains extensive political and economic influence, face an especially dangerous and difficult challenge.[63] Strong, stable party systems, free and fair elections, a broad transparency of political processes—especially regarding financial matters—will ensure the popular legitimacy and political influence of the executive and the legislature. The best preventive medicine for the military's political intrusiveness is effective democratic governance and what Juan Linz called "loyalty" to the democratic system on the part of all major political actors.[64]

The Chain of Command

The military's chain of command and the political institutions' areas of responsibility over the armed forces must be codified for all potential scenarios (peacetime, emergencies, war). In most democracies, the head of state is the military's commander-in-chief, and the civilian minister of defense is responsible for the army's day-to-day operation. Selecting a defense minister who possesses a measure of expertise or at least some demonstrated interest in defense-security matters and international affairs signals to the armed forces that the state takes them seriously. Ideally, the defense minister and his ministry are integrated into the governmental power structure, enjoy the confidence of the president/prime minister, and are willing to defend the legitimate professional interests of the military. Although the ministry is a part of the executive branch, its relationship with the legislature is exceedingly important because in democracies the parliamentary functions of formulating defense-related laws and overseeing defense budgets have a direct bearing on the armed forces' well-being. It is important that chains of command *within the armed forces* be clearly spelled out and potential ambiguities eliminated. The top-ranking uniformed person of the military—the chief of the General Staff or whatever designation he/she may hold—should be subordinate to the *civilian* defense minister, a cabinet member who represents the government in the armed forces and the armed forces in the cabinet.

The main purposes of the defense ministry are to structure the relationship between the elected civilian leaders and the armed forces command, to define and allocate responsibilities between and among civilians and uniformed personnel in the ministry, to maximize the effectiveness of its employees and the efficient use of resources entrusted to it by the state.[65] The minister—in conjunction with the president and/or prime minister and other cabinet members—formulates defense-security policy and identifies the roles and missions for the various components and units military. She/he and the senior staff of the ministry must also maintain appropriate relations with other ministries. For instance, a good nexus with ministries of finance or foreign trade might facilitate timely disbursement of funds and acquisition of materials from abroad. Just as essential for democratic governance is the defense ministry's constructive relationship with the legislature and, to a lesser extent, with NGOs, the media, and foreign partners. Of course, there are many local varieties of institutional arrangement produced by historical events, political customs, or convenience. What is important is that the chain of command privilege civilians, be clear, codified, and respected by all pertinent institutions.

The Use of the Armed Forces

Since a critical objective of civilian leaders is to prevent the armed forces from interfering in domestic politics, the conditions under which the military may be used internally must be specified by law. Generally speaking, in the modern democratic state the only legitimate internal role for the army is to provide relief after natural disasters.[66] The military is ideally positioned to fulfill this goal—which can also increase its societal esteem—given its manpower, transportation capability, and equipment (e.g., heavy machinery for tasks like bridge building, demolition, and infrastructure reparation). In particular, the armed forces should have no role in anti-drug-trafficking and -manufacturing policies because such activities inevitably increase the likelihood of corruption, and besides, such activities should be the responsibility of internal security forces. In a similar vein, soldiers should not participate in domestic programs such as rural development or policing functions that might foster their politicization. States that maintain paramilitary organizations, gendarmeries, militias, national guards, and so forth must clearly regulate the use of such organizations. The constitution must be clear about both the sort of domestic tasks permissible for the armed forces to take on and the conditions necessary for their deployment.

In a democratic state the wartime use of the military must also be unambiguously regulated by the constitution. Ordinarily, the power to declare war and states of emergency rests with the legislature or, at the very least, the executive must obtain the parliament's approval. The deployment of troops with or without a formal declaration is an important constitutional issue pertaining, in particular, to presidential powers and has been widely debated. In the United States, for instance, it was settled only in 1973 with the War Powers Resolution, which clearly defined how many soldiers could be deployed by the president and for how long without legislative approval. In Canada, however, the declaration of war is still entirely an executive prerogative—while Parliament has been consulted, it has never claimed the right to declare war or to say when it has to end or how it should be conducted.[67]

Budgetary Oversight

The executive and legislative branches must share exclusive fiscal responsibility over defense expenditures. Parliament's authority to prepare, enact into law, disburse, and scrutinize the military's management of the budget is its most powerful tool for controlling the armed forces. The budget process ordinarily commences in the defense ministry where military and civilian personnel ascertain what the ministry's requirements are for the following year. The defense minister then submits the ministry's budget proposal to the cabinet where further deliberations take place.

The government then presents the budget to the legislature where the debate that is most important to democratic civil-military relations takes place. In democracies the executive branch provides the legislature with as detailed a breakdown of the military's budget as possible, to allow thorough scrutiny. The only exception should be items whose discussion might compromise military secrets, but even these ought to be assessed by members of the parliamentary defense committee(s) who are sworn to secrecy. It is critical at this point that lawmakers receive accurate information from independent defense experts who can fairly evaluate the claims and requirements of the defense ministry. Once the legislature approves the budget, it still has the important obligation to ensure that monies are disbursed by the defense ministry as originally stipulated. For the sake of effective civilian control the armed forces must not have independent access to financial resources and must not be involved in business activities.

Minimizing the Military's Prerogatives and Political Activism

The international relations scholar Hans Morgenthau wrote that "A completely neutral armed force within the state is a contradiction in terms."[68] In fact, a democracy should not aspire to a politically neutral military but to one that is firmly committed to democratic governance. The armed forces must be depoliticized and its members must not play any political role other than exercising their civic right to vote. They must not run for, accept, or hold political office and should not appear at political rallies in uniform. The selection and promotion of the top military leadership must be controlled by civilians—ideally some combination of officials from the executive and legislative branches and again, ideally (but not necessarily!), following consultation with leading generals.

In virtually all authoritarian systems military officers enjoy numerous political and/or socioeconomic prerogatives. The aim of democratizers is to "roll back" the army's privileged status and establish armed forces that are the reliable, capable, and also valued and respected servants of the state and its citizenry. The military must become accountable before the law, obedient to and supportive of the democratic polity, and its professional responsibilities must be constitutionally regulated. As Feaver wrote, the armed forces should be staffed by the kind of individuals who are *inclined* to obey and the state should adjust the incentives of the military so that, regardless of their nature, they would *prefer* to obey.[69]

All too often the elites of newly emerging democratic regimes have little understanding of and/or interest in learning about the military as a professional organization. This is a costly mistake because it is in the direct interest of the state to maintain armed forces that are not only supportive of democratic governance but also capable of executing the missions politicians assign to them. It is important not only that the military stay away from politics but also that it be content with the conditions of service. Although in a democracy the army should not have to be bribed or appeased, if at all possible, the state ought to extend the armed forces high professional status through the provision of up-to-date equipment and decent salaries and benefits; to raise the social esteem of the military profession; to avoid intruding in the army's internal affairs—such as training and routine promotions—and, by all means, to avoid using the military as a tool in domestic political competition. A democratic state must honor the military's esprit de corps while preserving democratic values and respect for human rights within the military culture.[70]

Generals have the right to expect clear and sound guidance from the state. In postauthoritarian settings reducing the mission of the armed forces to the defense of the nation from its *external* enemies and banishing it from domestic politics is essential. It is the obligation of the political leadership to define the roles and missions of its armed forces. The primary roles of the military (defender of the state, provider of security in crisis zones as a peacekeeping force, fighting terrorism at home and/or abroad) changes rarely but its missions are dependent upon an infinite variety of circumstances.[71] Although in a democratizing state—especially one following military rule—the temptation to radically enfeeble the armed forces is often present, politicians must try to resist, as they have a special responsibility to ensure that the armed forces maintain their ability to defend the state. At the same time, the military's size should correspond to the challenges it might face. A state that maintains an unnecessarily large standing army and a bloated officer corps, is not only squandering resources but—depending on the political environment—might also be asking for trouble. If the officer corps shows symptoms of boredom or discontent, signing it up for international peace-keeping duties is a good way to make it feel both useful and appreciated.

The critical objective of democratizing states is to increase the armed forces' professionalism. This may be done in partnership with the top brass by devising an appropriate system of military training and education and by promoting an organizational culture of self-restraint, deference to the constitution, and recognition of the sacrifices society makes for its defense. Timing and sequencing are important and rushing these reforms—especially in democratizing states emerging from military rule—may well turn out to be counterproductive. In a political context in which the armed forces are threatened by aggressive civilian interference in their internal affairs, some changes might best be postponed or implemented gradually.

Independent Defense Expertise

The democratic state must promote civilian competence in defense matters because only equipped with this sort of knowledge can the legislature become an informed and adept overseer of the armed forces. Having such expertise in parliament as well as in NGOs and the media also prevents the executive branch from dominating the military sphere. Generating defense expertise is a time-consuming endeavor and is best tackled early. In many democratizing states there may be no reliable trainers or experts available to whom the education of new defense specialists can be entrusted. In such cases the assistance of institutions and trainers from abroad might be requested.

The Role of Foreign Actors

Laurence Whitehead was wrong when he wrote that "in peacetime external factors can only play a secondary role in redemocratization."[72] In fact, there is a demonstrable direct causal relationship between states' desire to gain membership in prestigious international organizations and their willingness to democratize in numerous areas, including civil-military relations and minority protection.[73] The leverage of external actors, such as NATO or the government of the United Kingdom, depends on the strength of the desire of political elites in democratizing states for what potential benefits these foreign actors hold (say, membership in the Atlantic Alliance or a security cooperation package, respectively). Obviously, if a state has only modest interest in making the sacrifices to attain the favors held by external actors then the latter possess little clout to affect policy outcomes in that state.

In the defense-security domain, most foreign organizations have traditionally focused their efforts on positively influencing the emerging civil-military relations in democratizing states. More specifically, the main thrust of democracy promotion efforts has been to stimulate firm and institutionally balanced civilian control over the armed forces in countries where the military often had been "out of control." While privileging civilian control in these environments certainly has been commonsensical, concerns such as defense efficiency (the rational use of limited resources) and military effectiveness (completion of tasks with the allocated resources and on time) have been often ignored.[74] Paying attention to these issues is important both in terms of national security and, in the long run, in terms of healthy civil-military relations.

The Societal Dimension

The societal side is just as indispensable a component of the civil-military relations triangle as are the state and the armed forces. Societal issues have become increasingly important since World War II and, even more so, in the last three decades. It is impossible to make informed judgments about whether a state is to have a conscript-based or a professional army without understanding public opinion regarding compulsory military service, demographic trends, and the education system. Let us consider some of the key societal issues democratizers must tackle.

Conscripts or Volunteers?

One of the basic questions regarding a democratic army is whether its soldiers are drafted or enlist voluntarily. Sound arguments can be marshaled in support of both conscription-based and volunteer armies. In states facing severe external threats, where military training for most citizens is considered socially desirable and strategically necessary, and where there is no overwhelming popular opposition to the draft, universal conscription is usually the preferred option. Democratic states must ascertain that the draft is fairly implemented and individuals whose personal or religious convictions forbid bearing arms or performing military service are given the option of unarmed service in the military or work assignment in some socially useful area (e.g., health care, eldercare, or education). Conscript armies tend to be less effective and require more resources on a per-soldier basis for the amount of military capability they provide; they often act as de facto training institutions maintained at the expense of defense modernization. Nonetheless, a major advantage of mandatory military service is that it can serve as a powerful agent of socialization by bringing together young men from disparate socioeconomic, ethno-religious, and regional backgrounds and help mold them into a real community through training and shared experiences. Draft-based militaries tend to attract more active societal scrutiny given that a large proportion of the citizenry will have served or had a relative who served in the armed forces. Furthermore, there is some evidence that mandatory military service—particularly in warring societies—leads to higher levels of political participation while volunteer armies tend to have the opposite effect on citizens' political activism.[75] All things being equal, conscript armies in which the burden of military service is shared more or less equally are the more democratic option.

Some experts, including Hans Morgenthau, had thought that drafted armies were superior because they could not be "an instrument of a *coup d'état* or of a counterrevolutionary policy because the draft army is, however incompletely, a reflection of the people at large."[76] Although the reasoning is logical, Morgenthau was mistaken. Conscript armies have been used against unpopular regimes by their commanders on numerous occasions—just think of the Romanian army in 1989 or the Tunisian military in 2011. The crucial issue Morgenthau neglected is the legitimacy of government. Precisely because conscripted soldiers come from society at large, if society views political elites as illegitimate, draftees will be unlikely to put their lives on the line for them. Professional or volunteer soldiers are self-selected, however, and do not constitute a representative sample of their cohort. Nevertheless, in a democratic society where the soldiers' conduct is governed by regulations approved by civilians, enlisted men will be no more likely than conscripts to follow an officer who issues an illegal or unconstitutional command. (It should be remembered that actions that threaten society nearly always originate with officers, in rare instances with NCOs, but hardly ever with regular enlisted soldiers.)

According to some experts the prestige of the military is based on societal approval.[77] Here, too, regime legitimacy is a crucial but often ignored aspect of the issue. An army can have an illustrious history and stellar martial traditions but if it serves an illegitimate regime it cannot count on public support. Another interesting normative question is whether the military as an institution should reflect societal values. Some scholars in the United States have argued that the answer should be a resounding "yes" lamenting what they have identified as a growing gap between the political and sociocultural values of civilians and military personnel.[78] Nonetheless, it is quite possible that what ordinary people want, above all, from their soldiers and officers is not so much that they mirror their own values but that they be effective professionals who unquestioningly support democratic rule, and that they abide by the constitution.

Ethno-Religious Divisions

It would seem beyond dispute that a democratic army should be equally open to individuals with diverse ethno-religious identities and regional backgrounds. Those who want to serve as professional soldiers should be judged by the same criteria. In some cases it might be wise to introduce policies that encourage the participation of underrepresented minorities. A number of additional questions must be sorted out in multiethnic and/or multireligious societies that do not have standard answers but, rather,depend on the particular setting.[79] For instance, should the state involve itself in cases where members of one ethnic or religious group are disproportionately represented in the officer corps not because of political manipulation but owing to one group's greater interest in the profession? Should soldiers be given the opportunity to serve in their own ethnic/religious region or should they—perhaps for purposes of societal integration—be stationed in ethnic/religious areas different from their own? Alternatively, should individual units be staffed by soldiers of different ethnicities and religion or should they share the same ethno-religious background? If we base our response on the Indian experience, we might well come up with different answers than if we consider Italy or Indonesia.

In deeply divided multireligious and multiethnic states or in post–civil war settings, democratizers interested in the cohesiveness of relatively small military units, such as a company, battalion, or even regiment, might choose to organize them by ethnicity and/or religion. Organizing single-religion units of the new Iraqi army during and soon after the hostilities between Shi'ites and Sunni would seem like a prudent way to proceed. It may be an acceptable first step toward the creation of a genuinely multiethnic military establishment that is characterized by ethnically and religiously integrated units. This ideal, however, is not easy to accomplish. Historically, there are relatively few cases of successful ethnic-racial-religious integration on the unit level. Success in this regard requires societal patience and, occasionally overt political interference, such as the July 1948 desegregation of the U.S. armed forces by President Harry Truman's executive order #9981.[80]

Gender and Sexual Identity

In recent decades a number of publicly debated questions have centered on the gender and sexual orientation of prospective soldiers. How far should the armed forces go to accommodate female soldiers? Should women be allowed to serve in combat positions? Should soldiers be forced to divulge their sexual orientation? Should the military open its doors to openly gay soldiers? The rule of thumb seems to be that in a democratic state the popular will should determine the answers to these questions. Societies, even democratic societies, often hold quite different values and support different approaches and thus it is hardly surprising that the citizens of Israel, the Netherlands, and the United States think differently about these issues.[81]

The Military as Social Laboratory

An important question is whether the armed forces should be used by the state to implement progressive policies that society considers controversial. The rationale is that while democratic polities enjoy only limited influence over their societies, they do control the armed forces. Consequently, the successful introduction of progressive but contentious social programs into the military might serve to eventually persuade the rest of society of their correctness. For instance, racial integration in the U.S. Army was begun long before mainstream society—especially in some regions of the country—was ready for it. The military became the first large organization in America where blacks were guaranteed equal opportunity to succeed. This policy was a resounding success both because it was "right" and because it enhanced the armed forces' effectiveness.[82]

The Media

In democracies the media are free to investigate and report on the armed forces, thereby acting as society's overseer of the army and as an important source of information about military affairs. Journalists must have sufficient access to the defense-security establishment without jeopardizing military secrets so that they can fulfill their responsibility to contribute to societal debates on defense reform, security issues, and foreign policy initiatives. The media's obligation for fair reporting is enhanced in countries that maintain volunteer armies where ordinary people may not have alternative ways to learn about defense issues. The press can also play a useful role by consistently monitoring and reporting on the armed forces thereby helping to prevent their physical and spiritual withdrawal from the larger community and ensuring sure that they remain a valued part of society.[83] Obviously, media organizations are responsible for accurate and substantive war reporting. Even in democratic polities, however, state pressure to broadcast a skewed version of reality will try the media's courage and independence.[84]

Nongovernmental Organizations

In democratic states—and, in some instances, nondemocratic ones—NGOs serve as an institutional locus of independent defense specialists, fulfilling an essential function in civil-military relations. Independent defense experts, who may work at think tanks, research institutes, or universities, produce policy-relevant research on military and security issues. Along with the media, it is their job to raise "fire alarms" if they discover anti-democratic activities in the defense-security establishment—such as corruption, political meddling, or irregularities with weapons acquisition. In many newly democratizing states there is a severe shortage of independent defense expertise. The reason is that in most nondemocratic regimes the military enjoys a monopoly of defense-related expertise and training and is keen to ensure that no public discussion of and education in security-relevant subjects takes place. Filling this vacuum quickly is a necessary task of the democratizing state.

WHY DO PEOPLE WITH GUNS
OBEY PEOPLE WITHOUT GUNS?

Having considered the nuts and bolts of civil-military relations, we can now ponder this, one of the eternal questions of politics that, as Adam Przeworski recently reminded us, we still do not have a satisfactory explanation for.[85] In 1923, when the Italian political scientist Gaetano Mosca wrote that civilian control over the military was "a most fortunate exception, if it is not absolutely without parallel, in human history," he might have been accurate but for some European and North American cases.[86] Given the many instances of successful democratization since then—which, of course, has necessarily implied success in establishing democratic civil-military relations—answering this puzzle might not be quite so daunting a task. Having learned from the case studies that follow this chapter—I shall point to some of them as examples as a teaser of sorts—I can offer explanations that, I believe, go a long way toward making us understand the reasons why militaries obey civilian power.

For millennia, the armed forces have taken power motivated by any number of specific desires that can be grouped into two general categories: their judgment that civilian rule was incompetent, corrupt, or both, and/or their view that the government did not sufficiently accommodate their material, professional, or strategic interests. At the same time one should not overlook the fact that soldiers might engage in politics at the *invitation* of civilian masters who believe the military's participation in politics will boost their regime's performance and/or stability (example: Tanzania after 1964). Nonetheless, that men with guns do consistently subordinate themselves to men without guns is so counterintuitive that Samuel Finer suggested:

> Instead of asking why the military engage in politics, we ought surely to ask why they ever do otherwise. For at first sight the political advantages of the military *vis-à-vis* other and civilian groupings are overwhelming. The military possess vastly superior organization. And they possess *arms*.[87]

Why indeed, would the military *not* interfere in politics? There is no one-sentence response to this complex question. In fact, there are four different keys to this puzzle. The first and second of these explain the generals' reluctance to get involved in politics in the first place either (1) because they are not inclined to do so or (2) because the state succeeds in preventing them from doing so.

1. *Commitment to civilian rule.* Military officers obey their civilian masters for the simple reason that they consider them the *legitimate* rulers of the state and believe this to be, quite simply, the right thing to do. They arrive at this realization as a result of professional and political socialization, tradition, and organizational culture. They are convinced that their responsibility is to subordinate themselves to civilians, the rule of law, and to refrain from participating in partisan politics.[88] This commitment is not contingent upon the manner in which the state and society treat the military. As Washington impressed upon the disgruntled troops contemplating action against the Continental Congress in 1783: "a soldier's sacrifice to the nation is first and foremost just that, a sacrifice" and the government's inability to compensate the army adequately did not give its personnel the right to rise against the people's duly appointed representatives.[89] Rather, the commitment of democratic soldiers is an absolute, a true dedication to the principle of civilian rule (examples: contemporary Germany, Spain, Japan, and other liberal democracies. Commitment to civilian rule does not necessarily mean commitment to *democratic* civilian rule. In fact, armed forces in authoritarian

states may be just as genuinely loyal to their civilian authoritarian rulers (examples: Imperial Japan, Soviet Union, postcommunist Russia, or the present-day Thai generals to their king) as their colleagues are in liberal democracies.

2. *Civilian control.* In this scenario the government possesses the capacity to keep the armed forces out of politics. Put differently, the absence of military interference in politics is explained not by the generals' reluctance to meddle—they may or may not have the inclination to do so—but by the state's ability to establish a system of control mechanisms that effectively precludes the military's political involvement. The agents of civilian oversight may include state-controlled rival armed organizations (e.g., presidential or republican guards, paramilitary groups), civilian and military intelligence agencies, political commissars, and the ruling party's branch organizations in the armed forces. Targeted personnel policies such as co-opting particularly loyal officers into the state bureaucracy, rewarding them with seats in the legislature, and the selective extension of privileges can enhance state control over military elites. The objective of these strategies is to thwart the officer corps' capacity to mount coordinated action against the state (examples: Nazi Germany, communist armies, Iraqi army under Saddam Hussein).

The third and fourth explanations for the absence of military involvement in politics are very different. In these cases the armed forces *have* participated in political life but relinquished their political power for one of two broad reasons.

3. *Failed at governing.* The generals decided to withdraw from politics because they were generally incompetent and widely unpopular rulers. Their ineffectiveness might have been manifested by economic downturn, enduring social conflict, defeat in war, or a combination of these phenomena (examples: Greece and Argentina after military rule).

4. *"Mission accomplished."* Military elites in this situation have willingly transfered political power to civilians for one or more of three reasons: (1) they ran the country and, according to their own criteria at least, accomplished their objectives; (2) they realized that their continued participation in politics would jeopardize whatever social esteem and institutional prestige they might enjoy; (3) they withdraw from politics owing to "governance

fatigue," that is, having grown weary of political responsibilities and wishing to return to the barracks or to abide by their pledge to call elections or a referendum and respect the results (examples: postpraetorian Chile, South Korea).

CONCLUSION

The course of democratic transition and consolidation is unique to the country that is experiencing it. There are many different political, economic, and social tasks to accomplish, and how they are approached is inevitably affected by country-specific factors. As we will see in this book, much depends on the point of departure, that is, what kind of regime precedes the democratization process and how committed political, military, and social elites are to democratic consolidation. Many postmilitary regimes, for instance, get stuck at levels far short of the ideal by allowing generals to retain influence over government policy and maintain a hand in the national economy. For states that begin the process of democratization with no functional armed forces in place—such as Germany after the fall of the Third Reich or Slovenia in the wake of Yugoslavia's collapse—the likelihood of quick progress is greater because they start, as it were, with a clean slate, more or less.

Three things ought to be kept in mind. First, democratization in general and the democratization of civil-military relations, in particular, are always gradual processes. Some countries—given their histories, specific socioeconomic and cultural conditions, and their political traditions—can democratize faster than others. The point is that democratic transitions should be considered successful as long as they continue to move in the right direction. Second, the conception of the ideal democracy and that of the ideal civil-military relations change as societies change. Military inventions, for example, have had a major impact on how soldiers relate to one another, how military organizations and service branches develop, and how the state's understanding of the military's range of possible missions changes. The sexual identity of soldiers or the involvement of nongovernmental organizations in military affairs were not issues that even the most democratic states concerned themselves with just a few decades ago. Societies change and with them the goalpost of the "ideal" is moved farther down the road.

Third, democracy is not some ultimate and clearly defined end result but an elusive goal that can only be approximated, constantly pondered, debated, and enhanced. The *process* of democratization will likely grind to a halt without necessary, though occasionally unseemly, political compromises.[90] The same is the case with civil-military relations: states, societies, and soldiers must strive to improve these even if they fall short of reaching perfection. Having said this, just because in some political contexts realizing the basic criteria of democratic civil-military relations—such as civilian supremacy over the military—seems more difficult than in others certainly does not justify relaxing principles or, as David Pion-Berlin advises, changing our definitions and analyses to "less normative and more analytical."[91] To the contrary: rather than lowering the bar, it is essential to maintain high standards against which progress (or relapse) can be measured. For the same reason, I also take issue with David Mares who argues that "civilian domination of the military is a normative and historical product of the European and U.S. experience rather than a prerequisite for democracy."[92] Without civilian supremacy over the armed forces—regardless of where it first took root—there can be no democracy.

For the democratizing state, creating the institutional framework of democratic civil-military relations is an urgent and indispensable task. Once it is accomplished, policy-makers and military leaders can focus on improving the armed forces' effectiveness and efficiency (except, of course, during conditions of war when this sequencing might have to be reversed). At its core, democratic civil-military relations require political elites who accept that the armed forces are legitimate tools of the state, who are willing both to pay attention to defense issues and to oversee the military without stifling its corporate identity, and who provide sufficient resources for defense so that officers and soldiers can adequately discharge their missions. Society should be ready to learn about security issues and make the necessary sacrifices for their own protection. And the military should concern itself with protecting the state and its people from external enemies to the best of its ability while, beyond a firm commitment to democratic governance, staying out of politics altogether.[93]

BUILDING DEMOCRATIC ARMIES
AFTER WAR

CHAPTER 2

After World War II:
Germany, Japan, and Hungary

⛬ ⛬

This is the first of the nine empirical chapters where we will look at how democratic armies have been built in various settings. This chapter is different from the ones that follow in two respects. First, though the emphasis is placed mainly on countries whose army was being built, as in the other chapters, in this postwar context, external actors played a more fundamental role than in most other settings. Second, while in our two main cases the intent of political elites and foreign actors was clearly to build *democratic* armies, in the case of Hungary, I want to show the crucial differences in military politics in a setting where a nondemocratic external power took control of a state against the wishes of the majority of local elites, in a society that desired a democratic future. In this chapter, then, we will learn about the democratization of civil-military relations in two erstwhile fascist dictatorships, postwar Germany and Japan,* whose armies had destroyed and terrorized large swathes of the surrounding territory. These are two paradigmatic cases of building *democratic* armies. Hungary after World War II, on the other hand, illustrates the trajectory of military politics in numerous European states where domestic political forces were defeated by the Soviet Union and its native communist puppets. The Hungarian case is also a good example of the particular approach to state-building that Moscow pursued in much of Eastern Europe in the first decade of the Cold War.

The war started by Germany and Japan ended with their unconditional surrender and left them physically and psychologically devastated, their elites humiliated and discredited, and their populations humbled and impoverished. The creation of lasting democratic regimes on the ashes of these

---

* In this chapter, unless otherwise noted, "Germany" denotes the Federal Republic of Germany, in other words, West Germany. Japanese names appear according to the Japanese practice of putting last names first.

dictatorships stands as the signal achievement of democracy promotion. An important part of this process was the building of the new West German and Japanese armed forces. We will follow the two armies from the end of World War II until 1960 and 1954, respectively, because by these dates it was clear that—some future developments notwithstanding—the commitment to democratic governance was uncompromising and unconditional in both settings. The year 1960 closed an important stage in the bilateral work on German rearmament between the United States and West Germany while in 1954 Japan's Self-Defense Forces were officially established. We will consider the evolution of Hungarian civil-military relations from the end of the war until the March 1953 death of Joseph Stalin, which is a suitable point to mark the consolidation of the Soviet-controlled communist regime and the completion of the armed forces' transformation.

In this chapter I make five key points. First, the unqualified defeat both countries suffered allowed those building the armed forces to start with a more or less clean slate—that is, they did not have to make major concessions to the ancien régime—that a less definitive victory might not have permitted. Second, the context of the Cold War had a strong impact on the rebuilding of these armies in a number of ways: that they were rebuilt at all, when, and how. Third, the rearmament of the Japanese and Germany armies was met with serious reluctance in many quarters in the United States and Western Europe. These misgivings, however, did not come close to the apprehensiveness of German and Japanese elites and publics about the issue. Fourth, the capable leadership of two people committed to democratic ideals played an important role. The two heads of government, Chancellor Konrad Adenauer and Prime Minister Yoshida Shigeru, were able stewards of their nations' interests and obtained the best deals possible under the circumstances. Finally, both the German Bundeswehr and the Japanese Self-Defense Forces had become strict adherents to the "democratic army" ideal adumbrated in chapter 1, so much so, that the legal frameworks in which they functioned constrained their ability to cooperate with their democratic allies in the international environment.

BACKGROUND: TWO DEFEATED STATES

Unlike many other countries we will learn about in this book, Japan and the Federal Republic of Germany were modern states with well-developed institutional frameworks, advanced industrial economies, and educated populations prior to World War II. During the Weimar Republic of the interwar period, Germans briefly experienced the benefits as well as the political turmoil that often accompanies nascent democratic regimes. The Japanese could look back on no democratic tradition; their emperor was surrounded by a reverence not extended to other mortals. Nevertheless, Japan, too, had a strong constitutional tradition dating from the Meiji restoration (1868–1912), and both countries built reliable and sophisticated civil service bureaucracies that could be counted on once postwar reconstruction commenced. In both societies the armed forces had traditionally enjoyed a great deal of political influence and freedom from close civilian scrutiny.

For generations, the loyalty of German and Japanese soldiers and officers was first and foremost to the king and later to the kaiser and the emperor, not to the nation or the constitution. The German military was mainly rooted in the Prussian army, perhaps the most effective and skilled military force of its time, which nonetheless espoused preindustrial values and defended anachronistic traditions.[1] After World War I the officer corps was divided between those striving to maintain the militarist code of the past and those who accepted the legitimacy of the nascent democratic order. In the interwar era the military failed to develop a deep-seated institutional loyalty to the Weimar Republic. Soon after Adolf Hitler came to power in 1933, officers and soldiers took the traditional oath to him personally, just as they had to the kaiser before 1918. In so doing they bound themselves to the man intent on sweeping away their traditions of tolerance and the moral limits to power.[2] Throughout World War II the German army, the *Wehrmacht*, remained a highly reliable and professional organization.[3] At the same time, the Wehrmacht debased the professionalism of its officers through Nazism—with the passage of time the army adopted more and more of National Socialism's ideological tenets—as well as its participation in genocide.[4]

Under Japan's old constitution the emperor nominally dominated military matters: as supreme commander he declared war, made peace, and concluded treaties. The veneration of the emperor was a universal trait of Japanese soldiers and officers who swore loyalty to him. At the time, his subjects regarded the emperor as a god who represented everything Japanese, and in this sense, he was equal to the nation and the constitution. The military's political influence was traditionally high although it became somewhat diminished in 1922–31 owing to the decreasing likelihood of war. Unlike in Germany, in Japan generals and admirals held important political offices: for instance of the thirty prime ministers leading the forty-two cabinets between 1885 and 1945, fifteen were military officers.[5] Field Marshal Yamagata Aritomo, one of the most influential among them, made sure that no government could be formed without military representation and, in 1912, set the precedent that the army could dismiss a cabinet.[6] In the 1930s the officer corps had increased their political influence and secured a robust presence in various forums, such as the Four-Minister Conference (attended by the premier, and the ministers of foreign affairs, war [army], and navy). The eminent political scientist Harold Lasswell rightly considered the Japan of the 1930s the archetypical garrison state.[7]

The main objective of Japanese military cliques was to curb the authority of the civilian government, which advocated friendly relations with Britain and the United States. Unlike in Germany where intraservice rivalry was mostly limited to competition for resources during the military buildup of the late 1930s, in Japan deep cleavages had developed between the army and the navy. This schism was manifested not only in institutional bifurcation—Japan, unlike Germany, had separate ministries for the two main services—but also in divisive rivalries that persisted through to the very climax of the war.[8] The leading admirals in government (Suzuki Kantarō, the last wartime prime minister, and Yonai Mitsumasa, the navy minister [and a former prime minister himself]) supported the Potsdam Declaration—the July 1945 statement of the Allies that outlined the terms of Japan's surrender—while the army's top generals opposed it and managed to carry the day. In the end, on August 12, 1945, both army and navy chiefs urged the emperor not to accept the surrender terms offered by the Allies. In short, there was a significant difference between the two states: while in Germany the military was strictly subordinated to civilian institutions, in Japan there was virtually no civilian control over the Supreme Command during the war.[9]

Demobilization

For several years after World War II the Germans and the Japanese—their countries now occupied by their erstwhile enemies—were "paralyzed by the political, military, and human failure of their nation" in the previous decade.[10] The Soviet Union quickly established its rule over what officially became the German Democratic Republic in 1949, while French, British, and American troops stationed themselves in the rest of the country. In Japan the United States—given its predominant role in that country's defeat—took responsibility for building the new state more or less single-handedly, and exercised unilateral control from the beginning.[11] Japan regained its sovereignty in 1952, West Germany only in 1955 when it entered NATO as a full member.

The first task of the U.S. occupation forces both in Japan and West Germany was the complete disarming and demobilization of the local armed forces, the abolition of all military organizations, and the prosecution of those proved guilty of war crimes. Japanese leaders asked General Douglas

MacArthur, the Supreme Commander of the Allied Powers (SCAP) in Japan, to permit them to temporarily retain separate ministries for the army and the navy to facilitate the discharging of nearly seven million men from the armed forces. Most of the released soldiers left for the countryside, where they faded into the impoverished and often hungry population. Postwar trials in Japan, China, and the Soviet Union culminated in prison terms for several thousand Japanese military personnel and the execution of two thousand officers. The demobilization of the Japanese officer corps was completed in October 1945, and the two service ministries were abolished a few weeks later.

The German military was also demobilized and thousands of its members were prosecuted for war crimes by international and German authorities. Several million German prisoners-of-war—in addition to many hundreds of thousands from other countries, including Japan—were used as slave laborers in the Soviet Union. Nearly 40 percent of them died there, over a million and a half were never accounted for, and the majority of those who survived were released only in 1953.[12] The vast majority of the approximately five million German POWs in Allied—excluding Soviet—custody were freed by the end of 1947 (fifty-six thousand perished while in captivity).[13]

The most controversial decision General MacArthur made was to save the emperor in order to maintain a semblance of historical continuity and stability in a society that was devastated by the war. MacArthur ensured that in Japan's new constitution the institution of the monarchy was upheld even if sovereignty was transferred to the people.[14] Retaining Emperor Shōwa and relying on the existing bureaucracy as much as possible meant not only that they escaped responsibility and punishment for their conduct during the war but also risked creating a public perception that they were somehow exonerated.

One of the reasons the rebuilding of the German and Japanese armies was so extraordinary was that the Allies—but, primarily the United States—and their German and Japanese colleagues were able to start pretty much with a blank sheet of paper. That is, the countries were demilitarized, the armed forces were disarmed, and the traditions and ethos of the old armies were thoroughly discredited. The widespread rejection of the past—remaining elements interested in reviving the military were easily marginalized—enabled native democratizers and their American supporters to start from scratch and enjoy the luxury of not having to mollify or appease any major political and military constituencies of the ancien régime.[15] It is important to underscore that West Germans constituted the leading force of democratization but they could not have succeeded without the political and security framework created by American civilian and military personnel.

The Impact of the Cold War and the
Reluctance to Rearm

By 1948 it became clear that America's reliance on its monopoly of nuclear weapons and economic aid to Western Europe would not be sufficient to protect European democracies. By this time the Soviet Red Army occupied much of Central and Eastern Europe, and Moscow's strategic interference in Greece, Turkey, Korea, and Iran had only been intensifying. The West was hopelessly outgunned in Europe. In 1948 there were only four Anglo-American divisions in Central Europe and practically no air force between the English Channel and the twenty-two Soviet divisions amassed just across the border in the Eastern Zone occupied by the USSR. In terms of military personnel, the disparity was 10:1 in the Soviet's favor.[16] The successful detonation of a Soviet nuclear bomb, their blockade of West Berlin, growing French involvement in Indochina that distracted Paris's attention from European affairs, the slow economic and military recovery and diminishing international clout of Great Britain, and cuts in the Truman administration's defense budget all compelled Washington to take a proactive approach to Western Europe's defense.

In his January 1949 inauguration address, President Harry Truman offered military assistance to nations willing to work with the United States to maintain peace. Between 1949 and 1960 over forty states received some $24 billion in American military aid.[17] The escalation of the Cold War required a collective security arrangement between North America and Western Europe. The greatest value of NATO's creation in 1949, as former Under Secretary of State Clayton Will wrote, lay "not so much in the unification of the defense strength of its members . . . but in the proof which it will give to the democracies themselves that they can effectively unite, freely and openly, for peace."[18] Commencing the Marshall Plan and organizing NATO were two of the three main ingredients of U.S. strategy in Western Europe. The third, and most controversial, was the rearmament of Germany.

Many Americans—especially in the armed forces leadership—believed, in spite of their uneasiness about seeing Germans in uniform again, that rebuilding Germany military capabilities was an indispensable component of Western Europe's defense. The most immediate and persuasive argument for Germany's rearmament, however, was the outbreak of the Korean War in June 1950. Policy-makers in Washington tended to see the North Korean invasion of the South as a Soviet test of Western democracies, not entirely unlike Hitler's challenge to them in the early and mid-1930s. The similarity between a divided Korea and a divided Germany was also hard to miss.

Top U.S. generals, like Omar Bradley, chairman of the Joint Chiefs of Staff, assumed a major role in convincing congressional leaders of the folly of opposing Germany's rearmament. Even Secretary of State Dean Acheson, a longtime opponent of remilitarizing Germany, conceded that Western Europe's defense would be hopeless without robust and eager German participation.[19] The Korean War affected Japan even more directly, and drastically altered its security situation. The United States was poorly prepared to fight a war in East Asia, and most of its troops in the region were tied down occupying Japan. Although the prospects of Japanese rearmament met only with disgruntlement among Japan's neighbors, they—in particular the Soviet Union and China, where communist regimes took power in 1949—were the West's antagonists and held no leverage. In any event, the imperative of Japanese rearmament was a direct consequence of the Korean War, a conflict Moscow and Peking initiated, supported, and participated in to spread communism and suppress democratic forces.

Understandably, West Europeans were even less enthusiastic about Germany's rearmament than Americans. As French statesman Jean Monnet wrote, "with World War II only five years behind us, the mere mention of a German army was enough to horrify Europeans, including the vast majority of the German people themselves."[20] West Europeans were doubtful about both the authenticity of Germany's democratic transition and America's long-term ability and commitment to control German fighting forces. France was particularly concerned. In response to U.S. plans for German rearmament, René Pleven, the French President of the Council (as the country's prime minister was called until 1958), countered with a proposal for a European Defense Community (EDC), a pan-European defense force as an alternative to Germany's integration into NATO. The most contentious issues regarding the EDC were the level of military integration and the size of the forces. Through much of the early 1950s the United States pressured the French cabinet to accept a larger German army than it was comfortable with. As the 1950s progressed, Washington and its European allies, now anxious to see Germany field a substantial army that could take part in Western Europe's defense, continued to make various concessions to Paris.

Monnet was correct: the last thing most Germans and Japanese—including a large proportion of the emerging political elites in both countries—wanted was to see their compatriots in uniform. Moreover, few West Germans relished the thought of taking up arms against their brethren in the Soviet Zone. Polls conducted in 1951 revealed not only that a majority of Germans opposed re-creating the German army but also that 27 to 55 percent favored giving precedence to German reunification over

European unification.[21] Nonetheless, between 1950 and 1954 public support for and opposition to German participation in a West European army had grown from 33 to 47 percent and diminished from 52 to 36 percent, respectively.[22]

In Japan the small minority supportive of rearmament was represented by nationalist politicians and former military officers. Their main argument boiled down to issues of sovereignty, namely that no independent country should have to put up with the stationing of foreign troops on its soil or rely on foreign armies for its defense. Some of the leaders of this movement were "Class A" war criminals—such as ex–foreign minister Shigemitsu Mamoru—who insisted that the responsibility for protecting Japan lay solely with the Japanese.[23]

THE REARMAMENT OF GERMANY AND JAPAN

The first step toward both German and Japanese rearmament was the creation of a centralized police force. Germany established a 25,000-strong national police organization in 1950, while Japan formed a 75,000-men "Police Reserve Force" barely two weeks after the Korean War broke out.

Enlightened and competent leaders can make a tremendous difference: both Japan and Germany were extraordinarily fortunate to have been guided through their formative postwar years by two politicians who steadfastly held up their nations' interests even in difficult situations when they possessed little leverage. Konrad Adenauer, West Germany's long-serving chancellor (1949–63) was a resolutely anticommunist and pro-Western democrat with a deep distrust of former generals and militarism. He recognized that West Germany held the key to the defense of Western Europe and that West Germany could survive only if it were closely integrated with it; he also understood that West Germany's geostrategic location strengthened its bargaining position. In 1949 Adenauer publicly declared that while he was against the creation of German national armed forces he was willing to consider Germany's participation within a European army.[24] He faced enormous domestic opposition to rearmament from political parties, pacifists, nationalists, certain religious circles, as well as from certain outspoken former Wehrmacht officers who could not be given a part in a new German military force, whereas others offered the administrative foundation for a contribution to a European army.[25] By advocating rearmament as part of Germany's reintegration into the Western world, Adenauer helped restore Germany's sovereignty and increase its security.

In 1950 Adenauer appointed a trade union chief and political ally, Theodore Blank, as "Commissioner of the Federal Chancellor for Questions Pertaining to the Increases of Allied Troops." The "Blank Office" (literally, *Dienststelle Blank or Amt Blank*) was the direct precursor of the West German Ministry of Defense, and its head, the first defense minister.[26] Blank thought the most difficult part of his job was to rebuild the armed forces' prestige, which denazification, reeducation, and the popular backlash against virtually anything connected to the military had effectively diminished. His staff included a number of former Wehrmacht officers, several of them aristocrats, who made enormous contributions to the new German armed forces, the Bundeswehr, in its formative stages. The military career of Count Johann-Adolf Kielmansegg—who was close to the Stauffenberg group that attempted to assassinate Hitler in July 1944—culminated in his posting as NATO Commander of Forces in Central Europe in 1966–68.[27] Along with Kielmansegg, Count Wolf von Baudissin, Ulrich de Maizière, and Adolf Heusinger played major roles in planning the Bundeswehr. Baudissin was a captain in the German General Staff when he was captured by the Allies in 1941. In time he became Commandant of the NATO Defense College in Paris and subsequently served the Alliance as Deputy Chief of Staff at the Supreme Headquarters Allied Powers Europe (SHAPE). During the war, de Maizière served as an aide to General Adolf Heusinger who himself became a military adviser to Adenauer. Heusinger was the Bundeswehr's first Chief of Staff (*Generalinspekteur der Bundeswehr*) in 1957–61; de Maizière, in turn, succeeded him in that position in 1966–72.

Fearing the loss of her sovereignty over political and military affairs in the wake of the loss in Indochina, in 1954 the French Parliament rejected the EDC, whose greatest champion was the United States.[28] Thus, after several years of intense negotiations, European reservations closed the door to the favored American option, the rearmament of West Germany in a European institution. In 1954–60 the United States and Germany worked on rearmament on a bilateral basis along with British and French aid. If anything, the experience demonstrated the difficulties involved in creating a new military organization even for a nation with as remarkable a military past as Germany.[29] In 1954 the West German Constitution of 1949 was amended to allow rearmament and to give the federal government exclusive jurisdiction over defense questions. The modified Constitution forbade preparations for any sort of aggression, defined "defense" as the fundamental function of the armed forces, and regulated in several articles the transfer from normal legal order into a state of emergency.[30] Importantly, only one parliamentary committee was constitutionally mandated, the legislature's defense committee. When the Bundestag, the West German parliament, ratified the Mutual Defense Assistance Bilateral Agreement in 1955, the last legal obstacle from equipping West Germany's armed forces disappeared.

Though German military planners considered rearmament a primarily political and strategic question, they were nonetheless eager to acquire the most modern weapons and to participate in the front lines of the West's defense. Armored divisions dominated their plans and they feared that in the American conception Germany's role was primarily as a source of infantry units, uncharitably viewed as cannon fodder. The first group of German soldiers—101 officers and NCOs—was commissioned on November 12, 1955, on the two-hundredth anniversary of the birth of General Gerhard von Scharnhorst, the great Prussian military reformer. Selected German personnel were sent to study in the United States and other NATO countries and to visit American installations in Germany. The goal projected for Germany in 1954 was to train, equip, and socialize a 518,000-strong army by the end of 1959. The expectations were, in hindsight, quite outlandish, which explains the disappointment of many U.S. policy-makers with the tempo of German rearmament in relation to burden-sharing in NATO. Members of Congress were particularly annoyed with the Bonn government's reduction in its payments for the stationing of American troops in Germany and slowing the pace of the Bundeswehr's growth at a time when the German economy was booming and U.S. balance-of-payment issues placed pressure on the dollar. Actually, even in 1967, Germany fielded no more than 460,000 troops.[31]

Though spirited public deliberation surrounded virtually all issues connected to the armed forces, few were more discussed than conscription. Defense Minister Blank, a steadfast proponent of the eighteen-month conscription, was a casualty of this debate which ended, in 1957, with the legislature's authorization of a twelve-month service period. Well before the Bundeswehr was established, the right to conscientious objection was enshrined in the 1949 Constitution. The proportion of young men who refused to serve in the armed forces had risen consistently and at a rapid pace.[32] Blank was replaced, in 1956, by an up-and-coming Bavarian politician, Franz-Josef Strauss, determined to put quality before quantity. In 1958–59 Strauss reorganized the Bundeswehr to adapt it to fighting in a tactical nuclear environment in accordance with the U.S. doctrine of massive retaliation and the pentomic division.[33] The proposed size of the forces was reduced from 500,000 to 350,000, and divisions—initially mimicking the larger American postwar divisions—were reorganized into highly mobile combined arms brigades capable of independent operations.[34]

Until 1955 all defense planners were civilians—even former Wehrmacht officers—in a sharp break from a past in which defense planning was the exclusive bailiwick of the General Staff. During the planning stages the Blank Office also invited academic experts and, of course, liberally drew on the expertise of American and other Allied personnel. In fact, the "overcivilianization" of the military sector was one of the grievances of some officers once the Bundeswehr was established in 1955. Whenever a dispute broke out between a civilian official and a uniformed officer in the ministry of defense in the first decade of the Bundeswehr, the latter virtually always lost regardless of the merits of the case. For this reason the military elites attempted to alter the chain of command—in which the highest ranking uniformed officer (the Bundeswehr's Chief of Staff) was subordinated to a civilian deputy minister of defense.[35]

Building Japan's Self-Defense Forces

The Japanese were lucky to have had Yoshida Shigeru as their prime minister in 1946–47 and 1948–54.[36] Yoshida's well-known contempt for the Imperial Army, his ardent pro-American and pro-British sentiments, and his serviceable English made him an ideal person for MacArthur and the Occupation Forces to work with. Although, like Adenauer, he was initially opposed to rearmament, in the end he opted for a strategy through which Japan would accept a new constitution and the security treaty because these would give his country freedom to devote its energies to economic development.[37]

Japan's Police Reserve Force (PRF) was separate from the framework of existing police organizations even if the initial recruitment was conducted by them. The first recruits were wartime irregular officers but, given the scarcity of available manpower, the ranks began filling with former professional officers up to the rank of colonel. These individuals were gradually removed from the purge lists maintained by the SCAP and in time began to obtain leading positions in the armed forces. The purge affected 210,000 Japanese—a much smaller proportion of society than in Germany (0.29 percent versus 2.5 percent)—and more than 167,000 (80 percent) of the purged were erstwhile military officers.[38] The Korean War contributed to changing societal attitudes that allowed for the mass depurging of former army and navy officers in October 1951: about four hundred of the newly depurged officers immediately entered military school, and many were subsequently sent to the United States for advanced training.

As with the Bundeswehr, the formation of the Japanese Self-Defense Force was the result of years of discussions and bargaining. Japanese politicians wanted to limit the size of their new army while the United States—eager to limit its own manpower commitment—was seeking a far larger Japanese force than Tokyo was comfortable with. Prime Minister Yoshida tried to keep that figure under 200,000 while U.S. Secretary of State John Foster Dulles asked for as many as 350,000 troops. A major difference vis-à-vis Germany, however, was that while hammering out the agreement with Japan, Washington could conduct negotiations unencumbered by cantankerous allies. Most plans for Japan's rearmament were made by former Japanese officers, not because of some diabolical scheme to return Japanese militarism, as many left-wing political forces knowingly claimed, but owing to sheer necessity: there were no Japanese citizens with training and expertise in military matters other than those who had served in the Imperial Army.

The negotiations, particularly on the Japanese side, were strongly influenced by Article 9 of the 1947 Japanese Constitution, perhaps the most renowned and controversial constitutional article in modern times. Article 9—inserted on MacArthur's personal instruction—stipulates that "the Japanese people forever renounce war as a sovereign right of the nation and the threat or use of war as means of settling international disputes." Furthermore, it declares that "land, sea, and air forces, as well as other war potential, will never be maintained" and "[t]he right of belligerency of the state will not be recognized."[39] With this extraordinary article, the Japanese and American drafters of the Constitution painted future Japanese policy-makers into a corner they have been trying to maneuver out of for over six decades. Nonetheless, when it was written, the constitutional ban on the exercise of collective self-defense was an effective method for Japan to avoid entanglements in American Cold War strategy.[40] Still, the resistance to changing the Constitution, combined with the realities of the Cold War and the post–Cold War world, has produced some tortured constitutional interpretations. In any case, for many Japanese, the presence of a quarter million of their uniformed compatriots training in military bases surely hinted at something unconstitutional.[41] Still, ordinary Japanese are little bothered by the issue, and, historically speaking, even the Japanese peace movement has focused not on Article 9 but on nuclear weapons and Japan's role as a peacekeeping nation.[42]

For Germany rearmament was primarily a political question that allowed Adenauer to integrate his country with the community of West European democracies. In contrast, for the Japanese who were building a democratic state in geographic isolation, rearmament was as much an economic issue as a political one. Prime Minister Yoshida wrote that rebuilding its armed forces was not an option Japan could contemplate on its own given that at the time it lacked the necessary wealth.[43] Significantly, rearmament was also a matter of timing for Yoshida: if Japan was to continue its cheap ride on American security guarantees, it would have to offer more of the collective goods that the United States was seeking.[44] As the Japanese economy grew, defense demanded an ever-diminishing share of the total industrial output—1.2 percent in 1954, 1 percent in 1960, to around 0.5 percent thereafter for the rest of the Cold War—and served to allay the fears of pacifists and leftists about Japan's impending remilitarization.[45] Yoshida brought together pragmatists, like himself, with the pacifists—appeased by the constitutional guarantees that Japan would never again become a great military power—allowing him to neutralize the extreme right side of the political spectrum.

The Peace Treaty of San Francisco was signed on September 8, 1951—on the same day the United States–Japan Security Treaty was also signed—and came into effect on April 28, 1952; with that, Japan regained its sovereignty. By this time all but about five thousand career military personnel had been released from purge restrictions.[46] In the same year the name of the PRF was changed to Security Force (SF) and that of its Headquarters to Security Agency. The Agency was placed directly under the Prime Minister's Office and was not given ministerial rank, but this time it integrated the coast guard, the Maritime Safety Agency (theretofore a part of the ministry of transportation). Following violent attacks from leftist political groups, the government sponsored two laws under which, on July 1, 1954, the Security Board became the Japan Defense Agency (JDA)—in effect, a defense ministry—and the newly named Self-Defense Force (SDF) (consisting of ground, air, and maritime self-defense forces) became officially recognized as "charged with the defense of the peace and the independence of Japan."[47] After much negotiation Japan agreed to field an army of 180,000; a navy of 16,550; and an air force of 7,600 with 558 fighting aircraft and 13,100 radar personnel.[48] By the time Yoshida left government in late 1954, his country had a large military establishment, defense expenditures had become a routine part of the budget, and air and maritime forces had been added to ground defense.

From the middle of the 1950s till the end of the 1960s four essential features characterized the SDF. First, its alliance, cooperative activities, and personnel relations with the United States had significantly deepened. Second, the dramatic recovery of Japan's economy had allowed the reduction of the relative burden of the SDF on the budget and made the development of facilities and weapons acquisitions possible. Third, domestic political stability had alleviated active societal opposition to the armed forces. Finally, with the passage of time, a generational change occurred, and the proportion of post–World War II graduates of the Defense Academy increased in the officer corps and advanced in rank.[49]

CONTROLLING THE ARMED FORCES

Germany

Postwar German politicians were keenly interested in ensuring that the military would be subordinated to the state and that civilians would thoroughly control the armed forces. Toward that end, the German legislature passed a number of laws that were designed to guarantee civilian control of the armed forces and the rights of citizens in uniform. Chancellor Adenauer believed that the federal government should keep the army firmly in hand—initially he even wanted officers to take an oath supporting his policy of Western integration—with the legislature's role primarily focused on developing the defense budget and supervising its disbursement.

Not surprisingly, this conception did not fail to alarm members of the legislature. They were aware of the civil-military relations problems of the Weimar Republic and feared that unbalanced executive control of the military could eventually result in its restoration as a semiautonomous institution. Parliamentary discussions centered on the concept of *Innere Führung* and on issues of tradition. Innere Führung—translated variously as "inner structure" and "moral compass"—was developed by military and civilian leaders, particularly Baudissin, to cultivate the "organic integration of the army into the democratic states; devotion of its leaders to the state and its constitution; identity of values in the army and in the democratic state."[50] According to this notion the new German soldier was a "citizen in uniform" not motivated by fear of the drill sergeant but by moral convictions and a desire to protect freedom and democracy. Adenauer himself often emphasized the need for German soldiers to be fully integrated into society. The concept of Innere Führung continued to evolve along with the changing sociopolitical environment. In the early 1960s it was defined by Ulrich de Maizière, a former Chief of Staff of the Bundeswehr as

> the duty of every military superior to educate soldiers who are capable and determined to defend freedom and the rights of the German people in a hot and a cold war against every aggressor. *Innere Führung* is based on the values of the Constitution, acknowledges the political situation, transfers trustworthy military virtues and experiences of the past into our modern time and takes into consideration the consequences of modern military technology.[51]

Equally important, the legislature established the new position of parliamentary defense commissioner (*Wehrbeauftragter*) to guarantee the rights of individual soldiers and to supervise the implementation of Innere Führung.[52] The post of the defense commissioner—as an organ of and responsible to the Bundestag—was initially viewed as controversial in the officer corps, but by the 1970s it had become widely accepted. Members of the Bundestag's Defense Committee were generally quite active in overseeing defense affairs and taking advantage of the prodigious information they received from the military bureaucracy. Overall, parliamentary deputies insisted that the Bundestag should enjoy substantive influence over the armed forces and they managed to accomplish this from the beginning, even before the armed forces existed.[53]

Still, the armed forces, as specified in the Constitution, were a part of the executive, and its primary overseers were located in that branch. The defense minister—acting under the guidelines laid out by the chancellor—was the person directly responsible for the military, including its weapons purchases, personnel policy, and training. In peacetime the Bundeswehr was overseen by the defense minister. When the defense minister was not present, the Chief of Staff of the armed forces reported to a special civilian deputy minister, called a State Secretary in the Defense Ministry (the *Staatssekretär im Verteidigunsministerium*).[54] In an emergency the war powers were transferred to the chancellor. Aside from the Chancellor's Office, the ministry of foreign affairs also participated in shaping external security policy. The top defense coordination body, however, was the Federal Security Council, a committee of federal ministers chaired by the chancellor. Although reforms in the 1960s and 1970s somewhat augmented the military's advisory role, they also reaffirmed the principle of civilian control.

In order to prevent the stratification and compartmentalization of the forces, the Bundeswehr did not have a general staff. Its most senior uniformed officers were the chiefs of staff of the army, air force, and navy, who reported to the Bundeswehr's Chief of Staff. The latter, however, was not a supreme commander but merely the senior military adviser to the defense minister. The Constitution (Article 9, Section 3) forbade the use of the military for domestic functions with the exception of assisting the state police and the border guards under extremely strictly regulated conditions. As we shall see in chapter 10, since the end of the Cold War this system of civilian control has been altered but its overall character has changed little.

Japan

Japan has never really had balanced or "normal" civil-military relations: either the military enjoyed a dominant role in the state or it was cowed into total submission.[55] In pre–World War II Japan there was essentially no civilian control of the armed forces. In the wake of World War II the Japanese government installed an institutional arrangement that was such an extreme variety of what Samuel Huntington called "subjective civilian control" that it has come close to institutionalized disrespect of the armed forces. In essence, professional military personnel are strictly supervised by a civilian bureaucracy that completely lacks military ethos and perspective; this arrangement has been enthusiastically endorsed by postwar Japanese political and economic elites.[56] At the core of this arrangement are the several layers of civilian institutions placed between the military and the government that virtually prohibit the access of military professionals to politicians. The Japanese Constitution does not specify the locus of military authority or the legal status of the armed forces for the simple reason that it categorically outlawed the maintenance of a military force.[57] Amending the Constitution would be quite difficult—it has never been done—because it requires a two-thirds majority in the Diet (the legislature) and ratification by a national referendum. Many Japanese constitutional scholars believe the adaptation is neither necessary nor desirable; in any case, individual laws can be amended and can also be ignored, along with the Constitution.[58]

Although security issues were often the subject of heated arguments in the Diet, the parliamentary oversight of the military-security realm was nowhere near as strong as it was in West Germany. In the absence of an effective system of legislative control, the Japanese parliament's oversight of the armed forces was mainly displayed in its annual approval of the budget as part of the Budget Law and its power to decide the dispatch of SDF forces. The Diet mostly created ad hoc committees for defense issues; it did not have permanent security committees until recently. There have been virtually no specialists on defense in the Diet, and most politicians seldom paid attention to security matters because they did not appeal to the voters. Expert advice to parliamentarians was provided first and foremost by the civilian staff of the JDA's Internal Bureau and especially its Bureau of Finance, whose professional assessment was informed by consultations with military officers. Given the many drawn-out legalistic debates over defense, the Cabinet Legislation Bureau—an elite body that oversees the legal aspects of government policy—also played a significant role in security policy.[59]

For fifty-three years, the Japan Defense Agency—in 2007 it became a ministry—was an underprivileged institution and the position of its head, the director-general, was clearly inferior to that of a minister. By law, the director-general (DG) was a civilian Diet member appointed by the prime minister. The DG selected the highest-ranking officers, including the chairman of the Joint Staff Council—a four-star general or admiral—and the chiefs of staff of the three services. Ordinarily director-generals and their deputies were temporarily transferred to the JDA from the ministries of foreign affairs, finance, or international trade and industry (MITI).[60] Surprisingly, one former director-general (in 1970–71), Nakasone Yasuhiro, a commissioned officer in the Imperial Army during World War II, was able to reverse the perception of his post as "one for time-serving ministers and lightweights."[61] Nakasone—who, in the 1960s was a leading voice calling for constitutional revision and an independent defense policy—had actually ascended to the pinnacle of Japanese politics and become prime minister in 1982.

Within the JDA responsibility lay in the hands of civilian decision-makers while the input of military men into defense policy was minimal. For the most part, bureaucrats from the three prestige ministries (foreign affairs, finance, and MITI) ran the JDA via decisions reached through informal interministry coordination that ensured both the assertion of their corporate interests—which, therefore, underscored Japanese national security policy—and the restrictions on the JDA's political autonomy. In the mid-1950s JDA officials and Prime Minister Hatoyama Ichirō lobbied for an additional political body to exercise general supervision over rearmament and defense policy. After a lengthy legislative debate, the National Defense Council—composed of six civilian cabinet members—was established in 1956; it is unclear how much actual influence this body has enjoyed.[62] Nevertheless, the JDA remained under the direct authority of the Prime Minister's Office, which exercised supreme control over and supervision of the SDF on behalf of the cabinet. Civilian control was also facilitated by the rivalry among the services. Officers assigned to various military institutions and installations—such as the Joint Staff College—were expected to be the representatives of their own branch of service. Active-duty military personnel were not allowed to engage in any political activity except voting, similarly to other employees of the government (Japanese law considers military officers ordinary public servants). Once retired, they could enter politics as some high-ranking officers did, though few succeeded in building prominent political careers.

Japanese officers did not question the concept of civilian control (*Shibirian Kontoororu* or *Bunmin Tousei*) which, at least in the beginning, was an entirely new idea to them. But it quite possibly went too far. The roots of the disagreements between the civilians and soldiers in Japan were similar to those in Germany, another extreme case of subjective civilian control over the military. Namely, civilian members of the Defense Agency believed that they must keep a steady eye on virtually all aspects of military affairs to prevent the recurrence of the prewar military's high-handed attitude, whereas uniformed officers viewed this kind of civilian control overly intrusive and disrespectful. Military officers had no opportunity to express their professional opinions on defense-security policy issues outside the SDF. No Japanese officer has testified before the Diet since 1959. Moreover, front-line commanders were required to seek permission before firing on an enemy—because of Article 9 of the Constitution—even if the enemy had already landed in Japan. Actually, a top officer was dismissed for suggesting he would not wait for such authorization.[63]

Even the Chairman of the Joint Staff Council (JSC), the highest ranking uniformed officer, advised the Director-General only in theory. In fact, not only could he not initiate decisions on behalf of the JSC but he did not even have direct access to the Director-General let alone the prime minister. The chairman of the JSC was actually merely an advisor to the JDA's civilian bureau chiefs. The chiefs of the services were at a similar disadvantage. For instance, if a chief of staff of a given service branch received a report from a subordinate commander regarding an external attack, he was to report not to the chairman of the JSC—who was out of the loop!—but to the head of the Bureau of Defense Policy who, in turn, reported to the director-general. The latter then reported to the prime minister.

West Germany's New Kind of Army

The challenge for West Germany was to build a new kind of army that did nothing to employ Germany's military past as a weapon against pluralism and human dignity. By 1955 West German society had developed a highly negative attitude toward all things military and was ready to thoroughly debate every aspect of the new Bundeswehr and ensure that it had as little in common with the Wehrmacht as possible. Political and military elites wished to develop an innovative interpersonal environment within the armed forces, hoping that "democratic" values would govern relations between soldiers and their superiors. They despised the unnecessary emphasis on uniforms and the abuses of the past that had obtained in many instances in the treatment of common soldiers. Baudissin recalled the humiliations of basic training and the barracks square in the Reichswehr of the 1920s and demanded the elimination of traditions and customs that did not match his notion of a "democratic" army.[64] He proposed, for instance, that soldiers be obligated to salute only their immediate commanding officers, that conscripts—unlike professional soldiers—not take an oath to the Constitution, that they only participate in a ceremonial ritual of obligation to the armed forces (less their conscience be conflicted), and that they, as "citizens in uniform" (*Staatsbürger in Uniform*) have political rights equal to those of officers and NCOs.

The idea that the Bundeswehr should be a *democratic* army—or, "an army in a democracy"—was of paramount importance to a West German society that was eager to learn from the political mistakes of the Weimar Republic and its soldiers. The existence of armed forces without deep-rooted loyalty to the democratic regime was widely regarded as one of these mistakes.[65] Civilian and military elites walked a tight rope between trying to develop a combat-ready military and limiting the danger posed by historical German traditions that seemed to threaten effective civilian control and military accountability.[66] Political education and training, a vital part of the overall training of soldiers, was instituted in order to deepen their sense of obligation as citizens to military service. Consistent with this notion, the soldiers' right to vote signified their status as citizens with civil duties. A major controversy surrounded the constitutional question of whether or not trade unions should have access to the barracks. After all, trade unions should be permitted to address the soldiers as citizens and employees. But, officers—particularly disbelieving former Wehrmacht officers—argued, "what happens if there is a war and the conscripts decide to go on strike?" or "if they decide they don't want to go on maneuvers?" In the end, a new soldiers' union, the *Bundeswehrverband* was allowed to be formed and it became part and parcel of life in the Bundeswehr.

Much care was taken at first that the color and cut of Bundeswehr uniforms bore no resemblance to those of the Wehrmacht. Initially no rank identification or service branch insignia was allowed on the jackets though after some controversy this was changed prompting one old soldier to sigh with relief, "At last the German soldier can be distinguished from a mailman or bell hop."[67] Ironically, the Wehrmacht-style field-gray uniforms were revived by socialist East Germany's *Nationale Volksarmee* in 1956.[68] Not surprisingly, most American military advisers believed that the Germans were going too far in worrying about soldiers' rights and "had perhaps swung too far to the extreme in their effort to eliminate the stiff, strict discipline and harsh extra-legal punishments of the past."[69] In fact, most U.S. Army officers had little regard for Baudissin and were, if anything, happy to recycle Wehrmacht officers who would otherwise have been persona non grata in the Federal Republic.[70]

After 1956 Germany moved rapidly to establish military academies and schools but American advisers at these institutions were unprepared for the disorganization, lack of service regulations, and established procedures despite years of planning.[71] Bonn's overly ambitious mobilization plan meant that things had to be accomplished in an unrealistically short time. The new soldiers' preparation was generally inadequate, not surprising in view of the fact that Germany had had no armed forces for over a decade. Only those who previously served in the *Bundesgrenzschutz* (border guards) were of partial exception because there they could practice some of their skills. The Bundeswehr hoped to recruit 1,135 veteran pilots but only 60 erstwhile pilots from Hermann Göring's Luftwaffe qualified (along with an additional two hundred to three hundred flight instructors). Almost all of the new air force's initial training had to be provided by American and British personnel.[72] The American-made weaponry that at this point made up much of the Bundeswehr's arsenal was a frequent sore point because there were not enough mechanics and technicians around, maintenance standards were generally poor, and spare and replacement parts were often unavailable. In addition, U.S. equipment was often inferior in quality to that of the vanished Wehrmacht. The difficult physical conditions in the ranks in the early years often conflicted with the ideology of defense ministry officials who insisted that harsh training undercut the appeal of Innere Führung.[73]

Breaking with the Past:
The Self-Defense Forces

The Japanese public's general reaction to the creation of the armed forces was disbelief, a sense that it must have involved something illegal. Like Adenauer, Prime Minister Yoshida Shigeru was well aware of the need for members of a defense force to form an organic part of a democratic state, to possess a sound knowledge not only of the technical aspects of their work but also of the world at large, and for the SDF to turn out officers "who would be sensible citizens as well."[74] Yoshida instructed military units to undertake rescue work following natural disasters in order to foster closer relationship between the solders and the population. He also encouraged military parades in large cities to improve public attitudes, but this policy backfired when bystanders yelled "tax thieves" and worse to the marchers. As soon as the SDF was established, the government commenced a rather bizarre propaganda campaign that intended to make the military look "cute" and "peace-loving"—by portraying soldiers on publicity posters as cuddly teddy bears dancing on warships and the like—to endear to population to it.[75]

When the Police Reserve Force was created in 1950, the monthly pay of ¥4,500—20 percent higher than the salary of a regular police officer—plus uniforms and food made the job so appealing that for the initial seventy-five thousand positions 328,003 men applied, including a village mayor from Shimane Prefecture.[76] This interest did not translate into any public esteem

for soldiering, however. There was never any disagreement between politicians and the public that conscription was unconstitutional; it contradicted
the articles on the right to liberty and the prohibition of involuntary servi-
tude and labor.[77] (The SDF Law did allow for a reserve force.) A 1958 poll
of 536 male middle-class and working-class high school students found that
out of twenty-three occupations, they ranked "soldier" nineteenth in terms
of prestige, twelfth by income, and twenty-second when the "importance
with respect to the functioning of society" was concerned. (Only "political
boss" received a lower rating).[78]

As in most other economic environments with rapidly expanding employment opportunities, the attraction of the military career to young Japanese
men had begun to diminish soon after the SDF was established. Antimili-
tarist and pacifist sentiments have always been prominent in postwar Japanese society, though volunteer associations supporting the SDF had already
sprung to life in the 1950s. Some of these were modest revivals of right-wing
nationalism, while others were innocuous social organizations located near
SDF bases and camps. Still, the popular contempt reserved for the SDF was
such that it encouraged its personnel not to wear their uniforms in public.
It was not until after the Cold War that soldiering became an acceptable occupation for middle-class Japanese, due in large measure to the SDF's very
respectable performance in international peacekeeping operations.

Just like the Germans, the Japanese put a premium on raising the standards of military education that also emphasized the importance of civic
virtues. The "Public Security University"—under the direct control of the
Security Board—enrolled its first students in 1953. By the time the first 337
officers graduated four years later it had been formally renamed the Defense
Academy. Among the graduates was Sakuma Makoto who would become
naval chief of staff in 1989. Sakuma recalled that "Our old textbooks were
destroyed after the war, and the new textbooks with 'democracy' in them
glittered our eyes. The value system had completely changed, and we wondered what was real."[79] For the first twelve years of its existence, the Defense Academy was led by President Tomo Maki who called on the cadets
to become "balanced human beings" and to "understand democracy" so
that they could become future leaders.[80] Two additional innovations also
attempted to eradicate the imperial legacy. First, all officers, regardless of
branch, trained together for four years so as to eliminate the rivalry that
had been such an important aspect of the imperial forces. Second, curricula emphasized science and engineering, which reflected reservations about
military education prior to the war that had stressed victory via spiritual
power and hand-to-hand combat.

THE SOVIETIZATION OF THE HUNGARIAN MILITARY

Hungary, Hitler's last ally, was liberated from the Nazis and a vicious native fascist dictatorship that had taken power only six months earlier by the Soviet Red Army on April 4, 1945, following a series of hard-fought, devastating battles.[81] From that day on, Stalin and the Soviet leadership—who viewed the country as a war trophy to be exploited for economic and strategic advantage—and their initially few local acolytes methodically extended their comprehensive control over Hungary's politics, economy, population, and armed forces.[82] The Hungarian experience, especially when juxtaposed with the German and Japanese cases, clearly demonstrates the difference that results when the foreign power driving civil-military-relations reform is not a democracy but an autocracy.

The 1945 Armistice Agreement, signed between Hungary and the Allies in Moscow, prescribed the creation of an Allied Control Commission (ACC) to supervise Hungarian political developments until the conclusion of the Paris Peace Treaty (in February 1947). Aside from its chairman, Marshal of the Soviet Union Kliment Voroshilov, the ACC's additional members were one general each from the United States the United Kingdom, and the Soviet Union. Although the U.S. State Department considered maximum American participation in the ACC important, the Anglo-American group proved wholly impotent in the face of Soviet machinations.[83] Hungary was quickly becoming Moscow's client state, and, given the Red Army's ubiquitous presence, there was little Hungarian society, let alone an American and a British general, could do. The Peace Treaty gave a stamp of legality to Soviet positions in Eastern Europe, including, of course, Hungary.[84]

At the end of the war the vast majority of Hungarians and the political forces representing them wanted to establish a democratic state. In 1945 the Independent Smallholders' Party (ISP) won the national elections—the last free elections Hungary was to hold until 1990—by garnering over 57 percent of the votes. The runner-up Social Democrats (SDP) with 17.4 percent also fared better than the Hungarian Communist Party (HCP) (16.9 percent), the only beneficiary of massive Soviet support. The ISP's intention to take the reins of power was vetoed by Soviet leaders, the true masters of Hungary's fate, who insisted that a coalition government be formed with strong communist presence. Notwithstanding virtually unlimited Soviet backing and electoral fraud of all sorts, in the 1947 general elections the HCP received barely 22 percent of the vote although the "Left-Wing Bloc" it managed to wrest control of garnered 60.8 percent of the ballots. In late 1947, however, Stalin unambiguously signaled to the international communist movement a drastic turn from the gradualist "popular front" strategy to seizing power outright, and the HCP was ready to oblige. In 1948, after three years of coalition politics, the HCP—aided by the assistance of Soviet intelligence agencies and nearly 200,000-strong occupation forces—eliminated its democratic rivals one by one, neutralized domestic opposition figures by deportation and imprisonment, and established a single-party dictatorship.

At the end of the war, many Hungarian Army officers did not return to their homeland—some units finished the war in Germany, Denmark, and Poland, fighting against the Red Army alongside the Wehrmacht—deserted, or were picked up and deported to the Soviet Union. The remaining officers were thoroughly purged at the HCP's insistence. Already in 1945, special committees were set up to investigate the professional and political records of officers. Of those who chose to subject themselves to the process, 27 percent of the generals and 22 percent of the officers were removed from the new army.[85] In 1946 the democratic parties agreed to the HCP's demand to expel additional thousands of officers from the military though many of them were recalled in late 1948, after a large-scale rearmament campaign—induced by the Yugoslav expulsion from the Soviet Bloc and the overall intensification of the Cold War—to fill up the armed forces. This measure was justified with reference to Lenin's own invitation to czarist officers to aid the Bolshevik effort in the Civil War.[86] Once officers loyal to the communists entered the army, nearly all of the recalled cadres were again dismissed. The point is that even these ruthless dictatorships—no matter how they deplored the soldiers of the old regime—considered it inexpedient to dismiss the extant armies (something the United States would do in Iraq in 2003).

The military clause of the 1947 Paris Peace Treaty allowed Hungary to organize a "democratic army" consisting of no more than 65,000 land force personnel and a 5,000-strong air force.[87] The escalation of East-West tensions, however, quickly led to intense Soviet pressure for the substantial enlargement of the Hungarian armed forces. Not for nothing was Hungarian Workers' Party (HWP, the HCP's post-1948 name) leader Mátyás Rákosi referred to as "Stalin's best pupil": he and the party elites did their utmost to comply with Moscow's demands. Between January 1949 and January 1952 the Hungarian army's size increased more than fivefold (from 41,500 to 210,400) while the size of the officer corps grew by over 1,000 percent. In addition, the ministry of defense employed 15,000 civilians in administrative and support capacities and 64,000 workers in the forty-eight factories (twenty-one of them were new) engaged in weapons production.[88] By the end of 1953, Hungary's military establishment had grown to nearly 500,000 men.[89]

Even during the three-year coalition phase, when democratic parties still existed and, in fact, played a significant though diminishing political role, the HCP treated the military as its own bailiwick and succeeded in shutting out democratic political forces from deliberations on national defense. In fact, as early as in October 1946 the Defense Committee of the ISP, the most influential democratic party, reported that "by now all key positions in the military are occupied by the communists."[90] By 1948 nearly all career military officers were members of the HCP. The communists routinely called their new armed forces a "democratic army" (*demokratikus hadsereg*) because, ostensibly, its soldiers served "the people"—hence its name, Hungarian People's Army (HPA, or *Magyar Néphadsereg*)—and not the old bourgeois-capitalist regime.

The Sovietization of the Hungarian armed forces proceeded according to a well-rehearsed blueprint overseen by thousands of Soviet military "advisers" deployed at all levels from the top echelons of the new defense ministry down to individual company-sized units. The advisers' primary function was to reorganize the HPA's supreme command along Soviet lines and to initiate and assist in the expansion of officer training. The Soviet advisers thoroughly controlled the process of the Hungarian armed forces' transformation into a military force imitating the Red Army in their training, indoctrination, tactics, and even uniforms, meals, and military commands.[91] In 1950 Soviet professional manuals, military regulations, and Codes of Service became compulsory. As a general rule, Hungarian officers were subordinated to Soviet advisers on every level and, in the 1948–53 period, the HPA was essentially integrated into the Red Army through its command structure and organization.

Naturally, a major effort of the regime targeted the extension of firm communist control over the military, a perfect example of the Huntingtonian "subjective" civilian control. The main thrust was the education and training of "political officers" who were assigned to every company and were supposed to ensure that troops were loyal to the Hungarian Communist Party and its Soviet masters. The political officers belonged to a new branch of the HPA, the Main Political Administration (MPA), charged with the overseeing the political-ideological indoctrination of personnel. The MPA and the various military and civilian intelligence services active within the armed forces were the most important instruments of political control. The MPA was a massive bureaucracy that included several secretariats to supervise various aspects of political life—agitation, propaganda, Marxist-Leninist education, publications—in the military. In 1948 political officers became co-commanders of their units—a Soviet practice that was abolished in the USSR during World War II due to its disastrous battle-field consequences—meaning that the orders of military officers were invalid if they were not countersigned by a political officer.[92] (In case of disputes, the political officer's word prevailed.)

Another effective tool of civilian (i.e., communist-party) control was the HCP's periodic purging of the military leadership. The initial purge, in 1947, was organized by General György Pálffy, head of the ministry of defense's Military Political Department, and directed at anti-communist activities in the armed forces. One familiar with the political history of the period is hardly surprised that within two years Pálffy himself was sent to the gallows for insufficient dedication to the communist cause. Further purges in 1949–50 resulted in the arrest, imprisonment, or execution of more than a dozen generals while military courts sentenced approximately 10,000 individuals in 1951; 6,500 in 1952; and 4,600 in 1953.[93] The HCP also established a number of overlapping defense-related committees to, in essence, spy on one another, thereby creating an atmosphere of institutional paranoia in the defense establishment. Some of these bodies operated entirely in secret while others were a matter of public knowledge. The party-state established several military academies to produce officers loyal to the regime. Selection criteria strongly favored the social classes of the HWP's preference. In 1952 the officer corps comprised 32 percent workers, 38.7 percent peasants, 16.8 percent employees, 9.9 percent tradesmen, and 2.5 percent intellectuals.[94] By 1948, 80 percent, by 1953, 91.3 percent of the officers had been trained after 1945.[95] Promising Hungarian officer candidates and higher-ranking officers were trained in the Soviet Union beginning in 1948; importantly, they were picked not by their commanders but by the MPA and the HWP's Personnel Department.

The top brass's political influence was insignificant. Some high-ranking officers did participate in a few important political decision-making bodies of the party-state but it is important to understand that their soldierly role was a distant second to their identity as communist-party functionaries. Already at this early stage of communist civil-military relations, the practice of placing prominent communist-party cadres in leadership positions in different areas of the state and economic administration even without any relevant expertise was firmly in place. In this period, the HPA's leaders often lacked even the most basic professional qualifications; they obtained their military posts owing to their standing in the communist party. In other words, political reliability was far more important than professional competence.

As in most other communist countries, the state bureaucracy was subordinated to the communist party. For instance, the defense minister, always a serving general, reported to the secretary of the HCP's defense committee. The legislature was a rubber-stamp body; its members, including some

top active-duty military officers, received their seats as a reward for political loyalty. (Elections, though regularly held, were meaningless as an expression of political preferences: the list of candidates consisted of a single
communist-party-nominee's name who was, in some cases, an HPA officer.)
The party controlled the military and its budget and no external civilian
experts—even if there had been any—would have been invited to inform deliberations. Significantly, the importance of all these arrangements paled in
comparison to the Soviet domination of virtually every aspect of Hungarian
political and economic life in the 1945–53 period. The HCP's leaders were
selected and dismissed at will by Stalin and his lieutenants, who maintained
dedicated telephone lines to their underlings in Budapest. The section chiefs
of the HCP's Secretariat conferred directly with their Soviet counterparts,
who were, in fact, their superiors. In Moscow's chain of command, Soviet
embassy staff played an important part, and ambassadors regularly consulted with members of the HCP Central Committee.

The dreams of Hungary's democratic politicians in the wake of World
War II remained just that. During the first decade of the Cold War, their
country became one of the worst dictatorships in Europe. After Stalin's
death and particularly in the early 1960s, domestic politics and economic
life had become gradually more relaxed. Nonetheless, Hungary's armed
forces remained firmly under Soviet control until the end of the Cold War,
and the basic characteristics of communist civil-military relations changed
little. The Hungarian People's Army was firmly controlled by civilians but,
of course, there was nothing democratic about Hungarian military politics.
Furthermore, the HPA was not a servant of the Hungarian people but of the
vastly unpopular communist regime and, ultimately, of the Soviet Union's
strategic interests. No wonder that the societal prestige of the military profession had plummeted.

CONCLUSION

Post–World War II Germany and Japan are perfect examples of "democracy
building" as they relate to a quintessential state institution, the military.
Aside from the numerous similarities, there are some interesting differences between the German and Japanese experiences of building democratic
armies after the war. I will mention just seven. First, the geographic situation
of the two countries was the source of important disparities. Germany, in
the middle of Europe, partitioned and surrounded by erstwhile enemies, and
on the very forefront of the Cold War was in a more central and exposed
position than Japan, an island nation surrounded by the Pacific Ocean. Sec-

ond, German foreign relations were dominated by Bonn's participation in international organizations such as NATO and various West European institutions. On the other hand, especially in the early postwar years, Japan's foreign affairs were overshadowed by its bilateral ties to the United States. In a like vein, West Germany was integrated into the transatlantic and West European security system whereas Japan was entirely reliant on the United States for its defense. Third, owing to its history and geostrategic position, the building of the Bundeswehr was preceded by a long series of multilateral talks while the decision to build the SDF was reached relatively quickly as a result of bilateral negotiations. In both cases, however, the United States, the same country that led the demilitarization of Germany and Japan, insisted on their rearmament.

Fourth, the U.S. was fearful of alienating its European allies, and initially eager to share the responsibility with them for rearming West Germany. Nonetheless, owing to their reluctance or outright opposition, building the Bundeswehr became an American project by default. Only after the program began in earnest, did French Prime Minister Pierre Mendès-France suggest that a multinational agency should distribute American aid. Secretary of State Dulles refused this impudent proposal—it was French opposition that killed the proposed European Defense Community in the first place—and insisted that Washington retain control of its own aid program.[96] In contrast, from the very beginning the United States had intended to oversee Japan's rearmament on its own. Fifth, while Germany defined its external security first in political and then in military terms, for Japan becoming an economic powerhouse, along with the prosperity and international leverage it implied, enjoyed precedence vis-à-vis any strategic or security consideration.

Sixth, German politicians were willing to amend the Constitution five years after it was enacted to permit Germany's rearmament, and, while the modification prohibited any type of aggressive action, it allowed the country to defend itself. In stark contrast, Japanese political elites have steadfastly refused to consider revising the Constitution. As a result, Article 9 has remained a huge political issue: How to "explain away" the existence of the SDF in view of the unequivocal constitutional ban on maintaining armed forces? The Japanese "solution" has consisted of a plethora of unfortunate and incredible rhetorical somersaults that make the government seem insincere and, to some, undemocratic.[97] Finally, while Germans had a very public discussion of the war and the role of the Wehrmacht, this kind of societal soul searching never took place in Japan. To be sure, Germans were pressured to deal with their war legacy by their neighbors and the progressive intellectuals who returned after the war, while the Japanese had no outside actors forcing them to come clean, certainly through 1954, the end of the period of our survey.[98]

Having seen the disparities, what generalizations can we now make about building democratic armies following massive defeat in war based on the similarities between the German and Japanese cases? First of all, a democratic foreign power, the United States, dominated the transformation of these military establishments and did not have to perennially seek consensus and settle for compromises with other countries. Second, the fact that both of these armies along with their countries were utterly destroyed and their societies demoralized at the end of the war made building their new states (and armed forces), starting from the ground up, easier than if their defeats had not been quite so conclusive. Third, the United States did not have to *create* institutions but rather to manage institutional refurbishing since both Germany and Japan had a history of modern institutions and constitutional traditions. Moreover, both possessed a large pool of capable civil servants (including soldiers) who could be returned to their jobs under U.S. occupation.

Fourth, their military traditions have made the politicians and the general public in Germany and Japan extremely averse to building armed forces that resembled the old defeated institutions. This overwhelming sentiment not only ensured the formation of military establishments disinclined to interfere in politics, but also guaranteed they would occupy a weak position in the institutional framework of the new states. Fifth, the widespread rejection of military traditions went so far that both the Bundeswehr and the Japanese military have suffered from excessive civilianization or veneration of civilian values that, particularly in the Japanese case, have been detrimental to military effectiveness.[99] To the extent that independent civilian expertise on defense issues existed in Germany and Japan after the war, this was the bailiwick of a group of former high-ranking officers who were far more influential in Germany than in Japan.[100]

Finally, military elites in postwar Germany and Japan were fully committed to democratic rule, but, in all fairness, they could not *not* be given the preponderant role of an outside actor whose main goal was to help establish a democratic state and to develop democratic civil-military relations. Clearly, U.S. political and military authorities would not have allowed personnel whose allegiance to democratic governance was in doubt near the new German and Japanese armies.

Do these generalizations hold for Hungary, which was similarly defeated and destroyed at the end of the war? The key difference, as we have seen, is that while the United States assisted Germany and Japan become democracies and helped them establish *democratic* armies, postwar Hungary was literally and utterly taken over by a seemingly omnipotent communist state whose objective was to establish a servile client state. Hungary had no independent politicians after 1948 and the views of its public were basically irrelevant in a totalitarian state. Still, there are some similarities to the German and Japanese cases to the extent that Hungary's near-complete defeat and destruction in the war also allowed a foreign power to oversee its military transformation, rearmament, and the building of new institutions pretty much from scratch.

In both of our main cases democracy-promotion was supported by a dedicated foreign state that was willing to commit significant manpower to the project, prepared to stay for the long haul, and ready to devote a great deal of money and materiel. (In other words, the three factors that were missing in the U.S. involvement in Iraq in the 2000s—manpower, long-term commitment, and money—were available in post–World War II Germany and Japan and virtually assured success.) The Soviet Union was similarly single-minded in its involvement in Hungary but its objective was the communization of the country. Moscow was entirely successful in turning Hungary into a satellite whose sycophantic ruling elites did their utmost to curry favor with Stalin and his lieutenants.

In the end, the Bundeswehr and the SDF had become uniquely German and Japanese institutions that were, to be sure, strongly influenced by American military thought and advice but certainly not determined by them. Although some civilian experts, including the noted scholar, Morris Janowitz, proposed that American advisers should actively promote democratizing the emerging German and Japanese military establishments, generals at the Pentagon decided against it.[101] They argued that America's army was the result of many decades of political, social, and cultural development and could not be "grafted onto" German or Japanese society. As Brigadier General John Oakes contended, "we make a great mistake when we attempt to make people over in our own image."[102] The U.S. military's contributions included providing a model, an example, of what democratic armies "looked like" in practice rather than in a textbook.

TABLE 2.1

After World War II: West Germany, Japan, and Hungary

	Country Period	West Germany 1945–1960	Japan 1945–1954	Hungary 1945–1953
Background	concessions to the old regime	no	no	no
	influence of the old military class	none, then moderate	none	none
State	main tasks	demobilization, disarmament, purge, rearmament, democratic indoctrination	demobilization, disarmament, purge, rearmament, democratic indoctrination	demobilization, disarmament, purge, rearmament, communist indoctrination
	civilian political leadership	strong, democratic, competent	strong, democratic, competent	strong, dictatorial
	civilian involvement in defense affairs	overcivilianization	overcivilianization	full civilian (party) control
	state approach to militarization	reluctant, cautious	reluctant, negative	native government has no say
	executive control	moderate, desires more	strong, ministry underprivileged, prime minister's office strong	full party-state control
	legislative oversight	strong, substantial, parliamentary, defense committee	weak	rubber-stamp, insignificant
	purges of military	yes (extensive), some of those vetted later return	yes (extensive), some of those vetted later return	yes, recurrent
	foreign influence	USA/W. Europe: very important	USA: decisive	USSR: decisive

TABLE **2.1** *(continued)*
After World War II: West Germany, Japan, and Hungary

	Country *Period*	*West Germany* *1945–1960*	*Japan* *1945–1954*	*Hungary* *1945–1953*
Military	interference in politics	none	none	co-opted by party-state
	domestic function	strictly regulated (virtually none)	military not officially recognized	protection of regime from domestic enemies
	advisory function	moderate to minimal	virtually none	none
	institutional attributes	no general staff	Joint Staff Council	extensive indoctrination
	effectiveness	constitutional constraints	constitutional constraints	no constraints, external control
	commitment to democracy	yes	yes	no
Society	independent civilian experts	some former/ retired officers gradually emerge as defense experts	very few, some former/retired officers	no
	military's prestige	low but increasing	low	low
	soldiers in society	"citizens in uniform"	separation from society	"communist soldier"
	conscription	yes	no	yes
Political system at the end of the period	consolidated parliamentary democracy	consolidated parliamentary democracy	communist dictatorship	

CHAPTER 3

After Civil War:
Bosnia and Herzegovina, El Salvador, and Lebanon

"Civil war" is a controversial concept in large part because civil wars are often thought of very differently by individuals fighting on opposite sides: the aggressors are likely to call it "civil war" while to those who are attacked such terminology suggests that all sides are equally culpable. Among the three cases I consider in this chapter, this notion was most apparent in Bosnia and Herzegovina, where many Bosniaks (Muslims) I interviewed took umbrage at my using the term "civil war" to describe the 1992–95 war in their country. After all, they said, "we were attacked by the Serbs and the Croats" and this was "a Serb war of aggression against Bosnia," pure and simple. I think of civil war, along with Stathis Kalyvas, as "armed combat within the boundaries of a recognized entity between parties subject to a common authority at the outset of the hostilities,"[1] regardless of who started it.

In this chapter we are going to learn about army building in three very different political environments that were nevertheless quite similar insofar as their brutality and intensity. The war in Bosnia and Herzegovina (hereafter BiH or Bosnia) was the shortest in duration and may be viewed in the context of federal Yugoslavia's breakup in the early 1990s. The opposing sides in BiH were set apart primarily by their religion (Muslim Bosniaks, Roman Catholic Croats, and Orthodox Serbs) and the regions they have traditionally inhabited. The antagonists of the Lebanese civil war (1975–90) were also differentiated by ethnicity, region, clan membership, religion (Shi'a and Sunni Muslims, Maronite Christians, and Druze), and political factionalism that was ignited, initially at least, by differing views of the Palestinian refugee population's militarization. In contrast, the civil war in El Salvador (1979–92) was based, first and foremost, on socioeconomic class identity. This was a conflict in the Marxist sense, a fight between marginalized and dominant social classes.

Our two primary cases are Bosnia and El Salvador. Although the objective in both countries was to develop a democratic army in the wake of the civil war, it has not been achieved fully in either setting. Our "good" case is the BiH, which has come far closer than El Salvador to building a democratic military. Although Bosnia continues to struggle with several fundamental political issues, from a narrow civil-military-relations perspective, it has been quite successful. In fact, I will argue that establishing a federal army has been perhaps the most impressive political achievement of the post–civil war era to date. Civil-military relations in El Salvador have also improved significantly but a number of issues that were left unregulated by the 1992 Chapúltepec Peace Agreement and additional concerns that have emerged since then have constituted problem areas. Lebanon, the secondary case in this chapter, is unique not just in the category of post–civil war army building but because it is an outlier in our entire group of twenty-seven cases in two important respects. First, in the first fifteen years after the civil war, a foreign army, Syria's, controlled some of Lebanon's territory and was instrumental in rebuilding the Lebanese Armed Forces (LAF). Second, aside from the state-controlled LAF, another local, contending or complementary (depending on the particular time and on whom one asks) and yet *legitimate* military force has functioned in the country: the large, well-equipped, and effective militia of Hezbollah, a Shi'a Islamist political and paramilitary organization. The chronological parameters of the case studies are from the three peace agreements that concluded the civil wars to the October 2010 elections in Bosnia, the end of the first year (June 2010) of Mauricio Funes's presidency in El Salvador, and Hezbollah's temporary takeover of West Beirut in May 2008.

In the first part of this chapter I trace the political process that led to the end of the civil wars in the BiH and El Salvador, and evaluate the peace accords. In the following section I look at how the new BiH and Salvadoran armed forces were built, the successes and the shortcomings of this process, and evaluate the continued role of outside political forces during this undertaking. In the third part the focus shifts to the rebuilding of the Lebanese Armed Forces and their coexistence with Hezbollah's military arm.

FROM CIVIL WAR TO PEACE IN EL SALVADOR AND BOSNIA

From the 1930s on, El Salvador's ruling economic and political class had counted on the army, the security and paramilitary forces, and the police to keep order and control the country's impoverished and marginalized peasantry. In 1979 junior military officers, fearful that the left-wing opposition organizations and parties would establish communist rule similar to that in neighboring Nicaragua, mounted a bloodless coup. The civil war was sparked by the assassination of Archbishop Óscar Arnulfo Romero as he was saying mass by extreme rightists in March 1980. In January 1981, the Farabundo Martí National Liberation Front (FMLN), formed by a number of left-wing groups just three months earlier, launched a guerrilla war against the government that was to last for over a decade, take the lives of seventy-five thousand people, and create over one million refugees.[2] The war was fought over ideology and economic inequality and against the dominance of an extraordinarily oppressive political class that refused political space for the opposition and was often unable to control the armed forces that did its bidding. This was a case of deficient civilian authority rather than of military domination but it meant that politicians often lacked the capacity to restrain the death squads and army units that committed, as a Truth Commission report later established, 95 percent of the serious violence throughout the conflict, primarily against civilians.[3]

Turning to the Balkans, during more than four decades of state-socialism the socially enforced ethnic tolerance had created an integrated, secular, and urban culture in Yugoslavia that seemed well positioned for democratization.[4] The breakup of the country began when it became clear that the leaders of Slovenia, Croatia, and Serbia preferred war to compromise.[5] In Bosnia the population in 1991 was composed of 47 percent Bosniaks, 31.4 percent Serbs (whose number was closer to 40 percent if one adds those who identified themselves as "Yugoslavs"), and 17.3 percent Croats.[6] The Serbs—and, to a lesser extent the Croats—had long been concerned about the significantly faster demographic growth of the Muslim community in relation to their own. Populist politicians, led by Slobodan Milošević, the Serb president, and Radovan Karadžić, the founder of the misnamed Serbian Democratic Party in Bosnia, skillfully manipulated popular sentiments and, aided by journalists and intellectuals, effectively spread nationalist myths to people whose insecurities had already been stirred up by the uncertainties of the political situation. The ensuing civil war claimed the lives of 57,523 soldiers and 39,685 civilians and rendered 2.5 million people homeless.[7]

The Peace Process

The Salvadoran peace process received a boost when Alfredo Cristiani of the Conservative Nationalist Republican Alliance (ARENA) won the presidential elections in 1989. The moderate and pragmatic Cristiani was willing to declare and defend his democratic principles and was clearly committed to ending the civil war. He was the perfect politician to begin the peace process. According to U.S. Ambassador William G. Walker, "No one to the left of Cristiani could have negotiated. No one to the right would have."[8] The time was propitious for other reasons as well. The end of the Cold War effectively darkened the prospects of financial and military aid both for the FMLN supported by the Soviet Union, Cuba, and Nicaragua, and for the government's forces bankrolled primarily by the United States. In addition, the downfall of international communism took the ideological wind out of the FMLN's sails. Finally, overall conditions in El Salvador had by this time terribly deteriorated not just because of the ongoing civil war but also owing to a devastating earthquake in 1986 and the declining world market price of coffee, the country's biggest export earner.

Following his election Cristiani let it be known that enduring peace would require not only the demobilization of the FMLN's forces but also the curbing of the political power traditionally held by the armed forces of El Salvador (FAES). This proposition was considered so radical that at first both the hardliners and the reformists of the political spectrum were skeptical of Cristiani's bona fides.[9] Nevertheless, his intentions to end the war were taken more seriously when he publicly acknowledged that the civil war originated in the injustice, repression, and social inequity that long characterized Salvadoran society. The first talks between the government and the FMLN took place in September–October 1989. Soon after, extremists eager to derail the peace process killed trade unionists and assassinated six Jesuit priests and their housekeeper and her teenage daughter. FMLN guerrillas retaliated by taking over the Sheraton Hotel in the capital, San Salvador. The international condemnation that followed these actions achieved its goal— the army's top brass were particularly sensitive to the outrage voiced by the U.S. Congress, which had the power to withhold military aid to FAES—and returned the parties to the negotiating table. Remarkably, then, the war began with the killing of one priest (Archbishop Romero) and ended with the murder of six others.

The road to peace was not a linear process in Bosnia either. A major milestone along the way was the March 1994 signing of the U.S.-initiated cease-fire, the Washington Agreement, between the Bosniak and Croat sides. The United States offered its support to Croatia's application for membership in European institutions and facilitated aid for the country in return for Croatia's acquiescence to an accord with Bosnia. The agreement that established the Federation of Bosnia and Herzegovina (hereafter the Federation) with two constituent peoples, Croats and Bosniaks, and a military alliance between them was directed against Bosnian Serbs. Croatian paramilitary groups and Bosniak army units continued to exist as separate entities but began to cooperate in operations against the Bosnian Serbs. In the summer of 1995 Croat and Bosniak forces (including Croatian forces from Croatia) set out to reconquer the territories that had been held by the Bosnian Serbs since 1992. Realizing that the tide had at last turned against them, Serb leaders now signaled that they were prepared to engage in serious peace negotiations.[10]

Both in El Salvador and in the BiH, foreign actors were primarily responsible for ending the war and negotiating the peace agreement. In the former, the military's growing dependence on American assistance, and internal pressures within the officer corps, had made it particularly vulnerable to the United States. When in the summer of 1990, talks bogged down over military reform issues, the U.S. Congress's decision to withhold half of the $85 million in military assistance earmarked for the following year was surely a factor in softening the position of the Salvadoran high command.[11] Although the shift in Washington's policy clearly contributed to ending the war, the United States had little credibility as a would-be peacemaker in El Salvador given its long-standing past support of the government and its armed forces.[12]

The heavy lifting in El Salvador was done by the United Nations after the organization's New York headquarters received requests to mediate in December 1989 and January 1990 from FMLN leaders and President Cristiani, respectively.[13] The mandate for the operation, United Nations Observer Mission in El Salvador (ONUSAL), was granted by the two warring sides and ratified by the U.N. Security Council. Established in May 1991 in the midst of civil war, it became one of the most successful U.N. internal peacemaking efforts since the Cold War.[14] Not that it was easy going. According to Álvaro de Soto, the U.N. General Secretary's Personal Representative in El Salvador, negotiations during the two-year peace process were "built brick by brick."[15]

In the BiH, in contrast, it was the U.S. government that played the major role in ending the war and getting the antagonists, literally and figuratively, to the peace conference near Dayton, Ohio. Once again, the most influential West European governments either passed the buck or were unable to settle and compromise on a course of action, even as the war with its attendant atrocities continued a few hundred miles from their borders. Once the United States committed itself to resolving the crisis, it stayed engaged and played a central role in ending the war. According to several Bosniak military officers and government officials I interviewed in 2009, if it were not for America's involvement, the war might still be going on.[16] The U.S. contingent was the lead component in the NATO-led force that the U.N.

Security Council authorized to provide security in the extremely volatile period between cease-fire and peace. As Robert Kaplan wrote, NATO's 1995 humanitarian intervention in Bosnia changed the debate regarding the Atlantic Alliance from "Should NATO exist?" to "Should NATO expand?"[17]

Chapúltepec and Dayton

On the last day of 1991 the Salvadoran government and the FMLN initiated a preliminary peace agreement negotiated by the two sides with observers from the Roman Catholic Church and the United Nations. The final document was signed in Mexico City's Chapúltepec Castle on January 16, 1992. The most important short-term impact of the agreement was a nine-month cease-fire that took effect on February 1, 1992, and was never broken. The Chapúltepec Peace Accords created a historic opportunity to radically transform civil-military relations in El Salvador: this was possibly its most important long-term outcome.

The Chapúltepec agreement outlined a specific plan for ending the war, demobilizing forces, reintegrating combatants into society, dealing with past human rights abuses, preparing for free and fair elections, and a number of other issues in nine chapters and several annexes.[18] The accord included several key provisions with respect to the armed forces of the FMLN and the government.[19] The FMLN's forces had to be dismantled by October 31, 1992, and the manpower of the FAES had to be cut by half—that is, down to thirty-one thousand—by 1994. The government's paramilitary National Police and Treasury Police forces would be absorbed into the regular army, and a new civilian police force with the participation of former FMLN combatants was to be created. The Salvadoran Civil Defense and the FAES's five American-trained elite battalions were to be dismantled. At the same time, all intelligence organizations, including the military's intelligence agency, were transferred to the authority of the president of the republic. An independent three-person committee was called to life to purge human rights violators from the officer corps, and a truth commission was instituted to investigate the worst cases of abuse. Furthermore, all political prisoners were to be freed.

It is important to recognize that Chapúltepec's success, just as the prospects of democratization in postmilitary regimes, hinged on the demilitarization of politics. The agreement reflected the determination of *all* parties— that is, critically important, including the government—to diminish the FAES's political clout and social autonomy by curtailing its force, structure, and mission (which was reduced to protecting El Salvador's borders). In doing so, the agreement not only terminated the civil war but also laid the foundations for El Salvador's transition to democracy.[20]

This is not to say that the Chapúltepec Peace Accord did not have some serious drawbacks or that it did not overlook a number of important and troubling aspects of military politics. Even though the FMLN initially took up arms under the banner of communism and to achieve some semblance of social and economic justice, in the end the peace treaty stipulated not a single recommendation or provision for economic reform. Although an Economic and Social Agreement was to be prepared by the FMLN, in the end the two sides took it off the agenda due to the urgency of wrapping up the peace treaty.[21] Though the greatest political price for the peace agreement was undoubtedly paid by the Salvadoran armed forces, it could have been forced to give up even more. The agreement failed to specify that the defense minister should be a civilian, and did not lay out a system of effective legislative control over the defense budget. It did not provide for executive control over the internal promotion of senior military officers. The settlement was also silent about whether or not active-duty military officers might continue to head state enterprises or agencies and whether the armed forces could retain their influence over telecommunications and water services. Thus, in all of these areas the FAES managed to retain a measure of autonomy even if Chapúltepec had severely curbed its overall influence in the country's political and social life.[22]

The Dayton Agreement that ended the civil war in Bosnia was a very different document occasioned by a very different situation and for a very different purpose. Negotiated in Ohio, the agreement was signed by the presidents of the Republic of Bosnia-Herzegovina, Croatia, and the Federal Republic of Yugoslavia (and witnessed by representatives of the European Union, Germany, France, Russia, the United Kingdom, and the United States) in Paris on December 14, 1995. The signatories committed to "the sovereignty, territorial integrity, and political independence of Bosnia-Herzegovina."[23] Aside from the main document, the Dayton accords—officially, "The General Framework Agreement for Peace in Bosnia and Herzegovina"—contain eleven annexes that detail the responsibilities of the Bosnian parties and the international agencies charged with monitoring implementation.[24] It also includes a Constitution annexed to the agreement that outlines the federal divisions of power between the national government of the BiH and the governments of the two entities, the Bosniak-Croat Federation and Republika Srpska (RS), the Serb Republic.

The Dayton Agreement was essentially a peace resolution focused chiefly on establishing a peacekeeping arrangement. Annex 1A, "The Agreement on Military Aspects of the Peace Settlement," created a multinational military Implementation Force (IFOR) composed of units from NATO and non-NATO nations to ensure compliance with the agreement and the implementation of its military annex. The signatories agreed to not just a cessation of hostilities but also to a withdrawal of foreign forces from Bosnia within thirty days. Those troops included, among others, a full brigade of mujahideen fighters registered as an independent unit within the Third Corps of the Bosniak army.[25] Moreover, the document prescribed the redeployment of Bosniak, Croat, and Serb forces, the deployment of IFOR, the creation of a Joint Military Commission (chaired by the IFOR commander and made up of local commanders and representatives), and specified the condition of prisoner exchanges. Annex 1B was concerned with regional stabilization and outlined confidence- and security-building measures as well as guidelines for regional and subregional arms control.

Croats and Serbs residing in Bosnia had a "mother country" to turn to for help, a country whose citizenship they could easily obtain, just across the border. Bosniaks, on the other hand, enjoyed no such security guarantee and thus signified the one group with a clear incentive to rearm and to use the peace settlement as a period to prepare for war. (In a scenario where Bosniaks should have had to defend themselves from a combined Croat-Serb campaign, they would have found themselves in a 1:12 force ratio.)[26] In order to remedy this situation and to win Bosnian President Alija Izetbegović's agreement to the settlement, U.S. negotiators added a special military assistance program called Train and Equip for the Bosniak-Croat Federation to address the Bosniak and Croat perception that they were and would be outgunned by the Bosnian Serbs.

Like the Chapúltepec Accords, Dayton also had a number of major shortcomings. Still, perhaps because of the inherently more difficult and volatile situation of the BiH—three nations in one country divided by religion and regional identity in addition to the all-too-fresh memories of a brutal war—Dayton's deficiencies are more serious and more difficult to resolve. While Chapúltepec created the basis for substantive democratization and military reform, in some respects Dayton "sowed the seeds of instability by creating a decentralized political system that undermined state authority."[27] While Chapúltepec brought the insurgents and the government together, Dayton, one can argue, froze the conflict in place and generated new sources of insecurity. Ambassador Richard Holbrooke, the primary architect of the Dayton Agreement, conceded that even though under the circumstances a better accord could hardly have been reached, it contained numerous flaws.[28] First of all, the agreement left two opposing armies in one country, one of them itself divided into two mistrustful components. Second, the framers of Dayton allowed the Serb portion of the BiH to retain the name, "Republika Srpska," which while possibly understood as a largely symbolic gesture at the time, could be seen by Serbs as encouraging future efforts for them to achieve autonomy. Third, arbitrary time limits for IFOR (one year) could have left the impression on Serbs that they might be able to outwait the enforcing powers.

In terms of its military conditions, the special Train and Equip program *appeared to* countermand Dayton's arms control provisions even though it stayed within the specified limits. To make matters worse, the United States asked Islamic states to be the program's primary underwriters thereby increasing the Bosnian Serbs' perception of vulnerability. Moreover, as Susan Woodward pointed out, the same program encouraged the militant wing of the Bosniak political spectrum "to entertain the prospects of an eventual military victory to liberate territory from the Bosnian Serbs."[29] Few observers would have disagreed with NATO's Secretary-General George Robertson who remarked in November 2000—that is, five years after Dayton—that if NATO were to leave, "violence would still be likely."[30]

Politics after the Civil War

In one fundamental respect both peace agreements were entirely successful: they stopped the wars, and armed violence did not return. Political life after Chapúltepec and Dayton was dominated by different issues in the two countries, stemming largely from the different roots—class based versus ethnoreligious—of the civil wars. In essence, some of the basic factors motivating men to fight were not resolved and have continued to dominate both daily newspaper headlines and the anxieties of political leaders.

In the March 1994 national elections, ARENA's candidate, Armando Calderón Sol won over the left-wing coalition's Rubén Zamora. By this time the FMLN had turned into an open, well-organized, and legitimate political party whose fighting force had long been demobilized. The elections were monitored by 863 ONUSAL observers in addition to 500 others and were declared "acceptable" though far from flawless.[31] Calderón's policies intended to bring about national reconciliation and the integration of former guerrilla fighters into civilian life, objectives he largely succeeded in accomplishing. After two more ARENA presidents, in 2009 Salvadorans elected an FMLN politician, Mauricio Funes, as their chief executive. An enormous success of Chapúltepec and of Salvadoran postconflict politics has been that one of the root causes of the civil war, the military's societal influence, has been virtually stamped out.

Since the peace agreement El Salvador's underlying social and economic problems have not been resolved. To the contrary, the liberal economic reform policies that international organizations like the World Bank and the International Monetary Fund have prescribed and funded enriched a small portion of Salvadorans, often those who were already well off, leaving the already poor and vulnerable segments of the population unaffected or worse off. An enormous problem not unrelated to issues of poverty and social justice has been the large-scale criminal violence that has replaced the civil war's political violence. The Mara gangs, transnational criminal organizations that originated in Los Angeles and are composed mainly of Salvadoran youths, have been heavily involved in arms and drug smuggling and distribution and criminal activities of all kinds, and have managed to penetrate Salvadoran political institutions, the judiciary, law enforcement agencies, and businesses.[32] Notwithstanding these serious defects, the long-term political prospects of El Salvador seem more favorable than those of Bosnia. In El Salvador a major factor in postconflict politics has been that internationally monitored elections have encouraged former adversaries to consider peaceful politics as a viable alternative to armed struggle.

In contrast, political liberalization in the BiH only reinforced the power of extremists, who, in any event, have never embraced compromise as a useful political approach.[33] Since 1995, Bosnian politics has been dominated by one basic and deep-seated issue that affects many federations. The Bosniaks are far more interested than the Bosnian Serbs in maintaining Bosnia-Herzegovina as a federal state. (The Bosnian Croats are somewhere in the middle.) Consequently, Bosniak political maneuverings are motivated by the desire to centralize state authority. Bosnian Serb political elites, on the other hand, are much less committed (if at all!) to the BiH, and their endeavors are centered on the objective to gain more autonomy. This underlying conflict in Bosnian politics is highly unlikely to change in the foreseeable future and was already apparent during the first postconflict elections, in 1996. The bottom line is that the BiH, as a country, really matters only to the Bosniaks because they, unlike the Serbs and the Croats, have no place else to go. In the meantime, a whole generation of Bosnians has been educated in different schools and has grown up with limited contact with members of other ethnic groups.

In spite of many warnings from observers, the international community—and particularly the Clinton administration—exerted considerable pressure on political elites in Bosnia to hold national elections in September 1996. As experts on the ground had predicted, elections held so soon after the cessation of hostilities consolidated the power of extreme nationalists opposed to ethno-religious reconciliation. Holbrook later admitted that "The election strengthened the very separatists who had started the war."[34] While the United States and other Western governments refused to influence the

proceedings in 1996, in subsequent elections they were publicly supportive of moderate candidates. No matter, ethno-nationalist parties have continued to sweep elections—notwithstanding the appearance of dozens of
new parties—and they thereby have managed to fill political institutions
with individuals ill disposed to ethnic cooperation. Voters have tended to
vote along ethnic lines regardless of the qualifications of candidates or their
stance on issues. A glimmer of hope materialized in the October 2010 national elections with the win of the Muslim presidency by Bakir Izetbegović,
son of Bosnia's wartime Muslim leader, ousting incumbent Haris Silajdzić,
an extreme nationalist.[35] Izetbegović is a political moderate, compared to
the available alternatives, and a proponent of dialogue and cooperation
among ethnic groups.

The political system of the BiH is based on a power-sharing arrangement
with substantial devolution of power and jurisdiction away from the central
government and toward the two entities, the Bosniak-Croat Federation and
Republika Srpska. Bosnia has a three-person presidency—one from each
of the three nations—with a rotating chair. Each of the three communities
elects five delegates to the legislature's fifteen-member upper house while
of the forty-two seats of the lower house fourteen are assigned to the RS
and twenty-eight to the Federation. Virtually every political office from the
presidency on down to low-level public-service appointments is assigned
according to an ethnic quota. Not surprisingly, political life is fraught with
cronyism, nepotism, corruption, and inefficiency. From the beginning, political elites in the RS stonewalled or delayed most federal efforts targeting centralization. After the International Court of Justice ruled in July 2010 that
Kosovo's declaration of independence from Serbia was legal, the RS revived
the idea of a referendum on secession from Bosnia.[36] Croats have repeatedly
voiced their interest in creating a "third entity," meaning an actual separation of the "Bosniak-Croat Federation." Bosnian Croat political elites have
been mostly silent about outright secession from the BiH, letting the Serbs
make the arguments for them.[37]

In many ways, the most important officials in the BiH since 1995 have
been the "high representatives." The Office of the High Representative
(OHR) is an ad hoc international institution created by the Dayton Agreement and charged with overseeing the implementation of civilian aspects
of the accords. The High Representative, who is also the EU's Special Representative in Bosnia and Herzegovina, represents the Peace Implementation Council (PIC) that is composed of fifty-five countries and agencies
that support the peace process. In 1997, PIC expanded the power of the
high representative to include imposing legislation and dismissing from

office any public official who impedes the implementation of the Dayton agreement and interethnic cooperation.[38] The PIC, which is to say, the international community, has tried to increase the strength of the central government, but, in the past five years, a lack of committed leadership and a willingness to appease the RS have rendered the OHR far less effective than it had been earlier.[39]

IMPLEMENTATION AND BEYOND: BUILDING THE BOSNIAN AND SALVADORAN ARMIES

The actual building of post–civil war armies differed sharply in Bosnia and El Salvador. Accomplishing this task was more difficult and took longer in Bosnia where a new army had to be created from the forces of three former antagonists. In El Salvador, however, the objective was to integrate some erstwhile FMLN combatants into the FAES, whose size simultaneously had to be reduced. Nonetheless, some of the basic tasks—such as demobilization, the destruction of excess weapons, the democratization of civil-military relations—were similar in both cases. In Bosnia, perhaps owing to the many still unresolved issues and shaky political stability, the building of the new Bosnian army stands out as the great success story of the past decade and a half. In El Salvador, due to the omissions of the Chapúltepec Agreement and more recent developments under President Mauricio Funes, the final result, in terms of civil-military relations, is less convincing.

The Hard Road to Success in Bosnia

A few weeks after the December 1995 formal transfer of authority from the United Nations Protection Force to IFOR, units of the latter began to supervise the demobilization of the Bosniak-Croat and the Serb armies in Bosnia, the transportation of weapons into storage sites, and the redeployment of forces on either side of the boundary lines. In a short time some 300,000 soldiers of the total 420,000 present at the end of the war were demobilized. The process did not go without some hiccups—for example, Bosnian Serbs were putting police uniforms on soldiers, an act expressly forbidden by the Dayton Agreement's military annex—but in the end it was accomplished more or less on time. The number of troops was further decreased in several stages. In 2002, for instance, 10,000 soldiers left the army of the Bosniak-Croat Federation and 3,500 the army of the Republika Srpska, effectively reducing the total military strength of Bosnia to about 20,000.[40] At the same time, the size of foreign peacekeeping contingents (IFOR [1995–96], then the Stabilization Force [SFOR, 1996–2004], then the European Union's EUFOR [2005–]) had gradually diminished from the initial 60,000 to 12,000 by 2003 and less than 2,000 in 2010.

Although during the first eight years after Dayton efforts to create a single Bosnian army led nowhere, this period was not without achievements in the security realm. In 1996, under strong pressure from Washington, the Muslim-Croat Federation established a joint defense ministry and military command in order to receive the benefits of the Train and Equip program.[41] A project run by the International Organization for Migration helped thousands of soldiers transition into civilian life. In the meantime, NATO organized numerous seminars and meetings—first held at the NATO school in Oberammergau, Germany, later in Sarajevo and Banja Luka in Bosnia—to facilitate reconciliation between officers who fought against one another during the war. Patient and considerate handling of this process by NATO and the gradual expansion of topics discussed began to mend the rift between the participants.[42] For much of this period the three armies remained dependent on foreign assistance. The entire funding of the HVO (the Croat forces in the Federation), for instance, came from abroad: 83 percent from Croatia and the rest from the United States.[43]

The reorganization of the army on the state level was opposed by the Serb member of the presidency, Mirko Sarović, in 2002. Soon after this disagreement, however, a scandal broke out—apparently the RS sold some of its excess armaments to Iraq in defiance of the U.N. arms embargo—which led to his resignation. This was followed by revelations of other incidents, such as illegal exports to Iraq by a company located in the Federation. This was the perfect window of opportunity for the OHR and other international actors along with supportive Bosnian elites to push for substantive defense reform. In January 2003 the Standing Committee on Military Matters—an institution established by the BiH Constitution that lacked purpose or staff until 2003, when, as a result of sustained pressure by and support from the international community, it began to coordinate the activities of the armed forces in the BiH—introduced "Five Pledges" that affirmed the objective of developing democratic civilian control over state-level defense and security institutions. The pledges, inspired by the BiH's foreign policy decision to pursue membership in NATO's Partnership for Peace (PfP), included such goals as strengthening the role of the presidency in the national security realm, creating parliamentary oversight of the armed forces, and restructuring the military in preparation for eventual NATO membership.

In May 2003 the High Representative established the Defence Reform Commission (DRC) with successive mandates to set up democratic, civilian, state-level command and control of the entity armies, to create the first post-war BiH Ministry of Defence and central military staff (2003), to implement the 2003 agreement and legislation (2004), and to establish a single military force in BiH (2005). In 2003–2004 the DRC was chaired by James Locher, a former U.S. Assistant Secretary of Defense; he subsequently co-chaired the DRC with the new BiH Minister of Defence until the end of 2004, when he was succeeded by the political adviser of the new NATO Headquarters in Sarajevo, Raffi Gregorian, a charismatic American, who went on to be Deputy High Representative in August 2006.

Based on these foundations, in 2003–2006, comprehensive defense reforms were implemented that resulted in a single army with a unified command-and-control structure.[44] The reforms were the result of intense negotiations between the Bosnian Serbs (who, fearful that the numerically stronger Bosniaks could overrun them, wanted to get rid of conscription), Bosniaks (who, fearing Serbia, clung to the idea of a mandatory draft), and Croats (who, given their relatively small numbers, supported a state-level army that would have equality in decision-making). Preparatory work proceeded in eleven working groups, with a co-chair each from the international community and from Bosnia, with altogether 120 experts working on the reforms. State-level legislation was passed by the BiH parliament to codify the first stage of having two entity armies under the BiH Ministry of Defence (MoD) and central military staff (2003), and the second stage when entity armies were replaced with a single state-level army (2005). By 2003–2004 all generals who served as such during the war were retired from the armed forces along with other high-ranking officers who did not pass SFOR's muster.

In all consequential personnel appointments in the defense sector, as in other areas of public life, ethnic quotas are utilized. The armed forces' commander in chief is the three-person presidency, which names generals and makes decisions regarding the deployment of military units. Decisions that are not approved by parliament within sixty days become invalid. The legislature monitors the entire defense establishment with the exception of intelligence. Its Joint Committee for Defense and Security was established in November 2003 and is composed of six members from each house of parliament. It has been one of the most proactive committees in the legislature with bimonthly meetings and frequent field visits. It deliberates and passes legislation, oversees the implementation of defense and security policy, and plays an important part in the periodic defense and strategic review. The legislature, through the Joint Committee for Defense and Security, controls and oversees the budget of the entire defense and security sector. Its budget hearings are attended by the defense minister and the Chief of the Joint

Staff. Committee members check all elements of the military's budget and make necessary changes.

The state-level MoD was established in early 2004 and the entity-level ones were abolished on January 1, 2006. The MoD operates as a civilian bureaucracy—its staff is made up of approximately 320 civilians and 60 uniformed officers—and exercises administrative control of the armed forces. The civilian minister has two deputies, all three coming from the different ethnic groups. The MoD is responsible for the management of the armed forces, implements all decisions pertaining to financial matters, and reports to the president and the Council of Ministers. Military personnel may turn to the ombudsman, an office maintained by the legislature, with their grievances. The Joint Staff (JS) has conventional military responsibilities. Aided by two deputies, its chief, the highest ranking uniformed officer of the land, is a three-star general who is the top defense counselor to the presidency. Although the MoD and the JS have often been at odds over several issues, they have not posed an overt challenge to civilian control, and the two have worked reasonably well with NATO and other international organizations. One source of frustration has been the lack of qualified professionals, a concern only exacerbated by the imperative of ethnic balancing.

The Bosnian armed forces—their size was stabilized at ten thousand uniformed personnel, one thousand civilians, and five thousand thus-far non-existent reservists—remain the largest multiethnic institution in the country. The duration of mandatory military service had been reduced repeatedly; by 2005 when it was abolished, it was down to six months. Since then the Bosnian army has been made up entirely of professional soldiers. No significant ethnic factionalism has been reported in the military, which is partly a result of careful ethnic balancing and the practice of reaching all consequential decisions based on consensus. For instance, officer recruitment proceeds according to a 45 percent Muslim, 38 percent Serb, 17 percent Croat quota. Each of the army's three infantry brigades is made up of three separate ethnically homogeneous battalions with ethnically mixed brigade headquarters and supporting units. The MoD signed an agreement with religious communities and provides services for the three major faith communities in the armed forces. Active-duty military personnel enjoy the right to vote but may not run for office, join political parties, or organize trade unions. Largely due to the enduring high-level unemployment, the army has had no trouble attracting or retaining personnel. Military education is being reformed with particular attention to bringing together personnel from different ethnic backgrounds. Given that Bosnia does not maintain a military academy, virtually all officers and NCOs have received some military training abroad, particularly in the United States, Germany, Austria, and Turkey.

Despite the general success story that Bosnia's post–civil war army has become, some problems remain. Although the defense establishment has maintained good relations with the media, there are few NGOs with a military-security focus and few independent security experts to advise politicians. At the same time, it is likely that owing to Bosnia's recent history, public awareness of defense issues is higher there than elsewhere. The pension system for retired military personnel is still based in the entities rather than on the central state level. Some perquisites of military personnel as well as the number of years of military service are not recognized in the RS the same way as they are in the Federation. The defense budget, at 1.28 percent of the GDP for 2010, is far too low to allow the investment and equipment purchases Bosnia needs to join NATO. Personnel costs claim 80 to 85 percent of military expenditures. The number of bases and other physical facilities was reduced from more than four hundred to sixty-nine, and the rest are being returned to the state, which is obviously a positive development. In late 2010 there were still some twenty-four thousand tons of small arms and ammunition, a legacy of the civil war, to be destroyed. This is an expensive and difficult undertaking, but delays perpetuate a potentially serious security concern.[45]

The ultimate objective of Bosnian defense reforms is gaining full membership in NATO. Bosnian political elites believe—just like their counterparts in other slowly developing postcommunist states, like Romania—that NATO membership will not only provide long-term security benefits but also will offer a stamp of international approval that can be converted into foreign economic investment and improved reputation abroad. Not surprisingly, then, NATO accession is considered of paramount importance, though, of course, it runs a distant second to ethnic/nationalist imperatives. In part to help Bosnia's chances, NATO has maintained a Peace Support Operations Training Center in Sarajevo, now run by a Bosnian colonel. Bosnia needs to develop a NATO-compatible defense doctrine and create new capabilities to engage in peace support operations. Toward that end, in recent years the MoD has sent observers to the Congo, Ethiopia, Eritrea, and Afghanistan (ten staff officers) as well as a platoon to Iraq to dispose of unexploded ordnance (up to 2008) and a platoon to NATO's International Security Assistance Force from early 2011 (plus approximately ten individual staff personnel from late 2009).[46] At their October 2010 meeting, NATO ministers agreed to grant the BiH a Membership Action Plan (MAP) to help the country advance toward membership in the Alliance. Before Bosnia can embark on the MAP process, however, it must remedy a long-standing concern and register military property (such as bases) belonging to the state and used by the defense ministry.[47]

Achievements and Deficiencies in El Salvador

As in Bosnia, international organizations continued to play a role in El Salvador after the peace accords. In fact, ONUSAL's mandate did not expire until the spring of 1995, and it played a significant part in creating a stable political and social environment in the country. More specifically, ONUSAL's military division, dominated by Spanish personnel, was responsible for monitoring the cease-fire, counting troops and war materiel, weapons collection and disposal, and overseeing troop movements, among other things.[48] ONUSAL was followed by a new United Nations Mission in El Salvador (MINUSAL)—under the authority of the General Assembly—for one year, mainly to show the flag and to confirm continued U.N. support for peace-building in El Salvador. (Since 2003, members of the FAES have participated in U.N. peacekeeping operations in Libya, Côte d'Ivoire, Haiti, and the Sudan.)

In El Salvador, as in Bosnia, the demobilization of the contending armed forces, one of the critical tasks of post–civil war army building, was not an uneventful process. Initially, the FAES resisted the implementation of some of the peace accord's conditions, particularly the demobilization of the National Guards and the Treasury Police. In the end, the army's manpower was reduced from 63,000 to 31,000 in 1993, a year ahead of schedule, and to 28,000 in 1994. Government and military elites readily agreed to demobilization for three reasons. First, most of the discharged personnel were soldiers powerless to protest. Second, many officers—particularly those suspected of human rights abuses by the Truth Commission—were moved to other jobs in government. Third, the continuation of U.S. military aid was an effective incentive for the FAES to follow the demobilization calendar.[49] After demobilization was completed El Salvador still had the highest per capita level of militarization in Central America (5.1 soldiers per 1,000 inhabitants compared with, for instance, 3.4 in Nicaragua and 3.2 in Guatemala and Honduras).[50]

The FMLN, on the other hand, protested against inadequate concentration and storage facilities, which were making its demobilization difficult, and government harassment of some of its fighters, for example forced eviction from lands they had long occupied. It took the intervention of U.N. Under-Secretary-General Marrack Goulding to settle the conflict between the FMLN and the Cristiani administration. Once 20 percent of the FMLN's forces were demobilized, the government agreed to several legislative changes that included, most importantly, provisions to recognize the FMLN as a legitimate political party in the final stages of its demobilization and weapons destruction.[51] As in Bosnia, the demolition of excess armaments and ammunition constituted a serious issue in El Salvador, particularly because a chance event brought attention to the FMLN's duplicity. In May 1993 one of the organization's illegal weapons storages exploded in Managua, Nicaragua, demonstrating that the FMLN intended to preserve some of its arsenal even though it was prohibited by the peace accord. Following further U.N. mediation between the predictably dismayed government, which wanted to revoke FMLN's status as a political party, and the FMLN, which now intended to affirm its bona fides by divulging the location of and destroying more than one thousand arms caches, the crisis was resolved.

These events only illuminated the underlying issue emblematic of post–civil war environments: the lack of trust between the former warring sides that usually takes a considerable amount of time to overcome. In the end, notwithstanding some more or less predictable problems, the peace process in El Salvador was not seriously challenged, as both sides remained committed to pursuing their political objectives peacefully. Salvadoran governments have eschewed extremist policies while the FMLN has been remarkably successful in "transforming itself from a clandestine operation into an open, well-organized party."[52] Reforming civil-military relations—more specifically, taking the military out of politics—was key to the negotiated settlement at Chapúltepec. Although several things have gone right, in part owing to the aforementioned omissions in the agreement, the institutional arrangements of Salvadoran civil-military relations leave a lot to be desired.

The president of the republic is also the commander in chief of the armed forces and is advised by the National Security Council. The eighty-four-seat Legislative Assembly is empowered by the Constitution to be permanently involved in defense issues. In practice though, the National Defense Committee, comprised of eleven members, does not control military expenditure in any substantive way. When activist legislators manage to "force" the defense minister to present the defense budget to them, they merely score pyrrhic victories because they lack the information to ask anything but the most perfunctory questions.[53] According to some experts, there is an implicit deal between the state and the military: the soldiers stay out of politics and, in return, the state takes very good care of them.[54]

The Ministry of National Defense executes the conventional defense ministry functions such as the implementation of government policy, the coordination of military activities, and the preparation of the draft defense budget. The defense minister also proposes promotions, appointments, dismissals, and so forth, to the president after consulting with the chairman of the armed forces' joint chiefs of staff.[55] The president does not have a free hand in appointing defense ministers because he is constrained by the high command that would not accept a civilian defense minister. All Salvadoran defense ministers have been high-ranking, serving military officers. Active-duty military personnel are neither entitled to vote nor to stand as candidates for elected political office (though their retired comrades have the right to both).

In contrast to the relatively transparent Bosnian army, the FAES as an institution has remained well screened from the general public but no more so than most Latin American militaries. As prescribed by the peace accords, the military high command was purged of human rights abusers—more than one hundred officers, including the defense minister and his deputy, most of the flag officers, and many colonels—through a primarily internal process. Many of those who had to leave the FAES were retired or reassigned to public-sector jobs. Even though in 1994 an entirely new Supreme Court took office, the judiciary has been reluctant to deal with human rights abuses dating from the civil war; in fact, only a small number of officers have ever been brought to trial.[56] Letting the perpetrators of human rights abuses go free not only ignores the victims, many of whom were illiterate and poor peasants, who did not have the clout or media access to protest, but also sends a message of impunity to contemporary criminal organizations. In 2010 President Funes announced the creation of a state commission that would propose measures for the moral, symbolic, and material reparations of victims.

Signs of growing military openness toward society began to appear in the mid-1990s. After 1994, the new High Command, led by Defense Minister Col. José Humberto Corado, was ready to engage civilians in dialogue concerning the army's future role.[57] Conferences were organized on civil-military relations, military officers lectured at civilian universities, and a new School of High Strategic Studies was established in 1993 that served the educational needs of not just military officers but of civilians as well.[58] The School along with a number of emerging NGOs began to provide society with independent civilian experts on defense issues.

Two additional and related problems raise questions about the overall health of Salvadoran civil-military relations. The first has to do with the internal role of the armed forces. According to the Chapúltepec Agreement, the FAES is constitutionally limited to external security operations (defense from external threats) and providing help in national emergencies (this was to denote natural disasters). At the same time, the peace accords dissolved all three national police organizations and replaced them with a new National Civil Police (PNC). Partly because of the escalating and enduring crime wave and partly owing to political maneuvers and turf wars, through the years the PNC has become a repressive organization that has been occasionally out of control.[59]

From our perspective this is particularly germane because Salvadoran presidents starting in 1994 have allowed FAES troops to be used in Joint Task Force units (GTCs) with the PNC. These detachments are composed of seven to fifteen FAES troops under the command of one or two police officers. Also in 1994 nearly seven thousand FAES soldiers were deployed in the countryside, ostensibly to make up for the vacuum created by the lay-off of four hundred corrupt counternarcotics agents. When opposition politicians raised the issue, the government responded that the operation was legitimate because crime in rural areas had reached emergency proportions.[60] In addition, FAES personnel have also worked in the security detail at the National Airport in San Salvador, have been used to intimidate protesters and as backup for PNC officers in crowd control operations, and have conducted roadblocks searching for gang members. To be sure, these practices stem not from FAES initiatives—in fact, the army leadership apparently is against them—but from orders placed on it by the executive and powerful director of the PNC.[61]

The second troubling issue has to do with the first year of Mauricio Funes's presidency. Even though a major achievement of Salvadoran politics since 1992 has been the removal of military influence from political life, Funes has made a concerted and successful effort to court the military's support. Perhaps mindful of the military action that unseated Honduran President Manuel Zelaya in 2009, Funes has empowered the FAES and has dangerously broadened its role. Rather than terminating the incorporation of military personnel into domestic police operations, Funes has actually expanded the practice in direct violation of the peace accords. In doing so, the president may have voluntarily restored some of the political influence the top brass lost in the 1990s. Nevertheless, this is a calculated political move that Funes may have been forced to make by the crisis in public safety, which shows no signs of abating: involving the military in the anti-Maras campaign was the answer to the widespread criticisms of his crime-fighting record. As a result, Funes has gained substantial political backing from the FAES leadership but, not unexpectedly, has undermined his own core support base in the FMLN.[62]

THE LEBANESE ARMED FORCES AFTER THE CIVIL WAR

Unlike most civil wars that are played out primarily in rural settings, Lebanon's fifteen-year conflict (1975–90) is an example of predominantly urban guerrilla warfare. The Lebanese civil war also shows the powerful psychological role revenge often plays in such hostilities. Observers have described it as a long and vicious cycle: "If one Christian died, then two Moslems were killed, and so on. . . . When we acted, moved by revenge, we generated the spirit of retaliation."[63] Although the Lebanese Armed Forces (LAF) did not disappear during the conflict, their strength was eclipsed by that of the several militias to which many of its soldiers defected. For much of the civil war, the mostly Christian-led LAF had a minor place in the power balance underscoring the diminishing authority of the central government.[64] By the late 1980s whatever remained of the LAF was divided into virtually homogeneous Christian and Muslim units.

The Ta'if Agreement

In contrast to Bosnia and El Salvador, for Lebanon, ending the civil war was not primarily the work of foreign actors although mediators from the Arab League, the United States, and especially Syria, played an important part. Rather, after a long and difficult learning process the opposing sides finally acknowledged that their ideal outcomes would not be realized, and that without substantive compromises their country would continue its descent into chaos. Following the September 1988 expiration of President Amine Gemayel's term, a transitional government took power until a new president could be elected.[65] The interim cabinet consisted of the six members of the Military Council and was headed by LAF Commander Michel Aoun, three Christians, and three Muslims representing Lebanon's main communities. Most Muslims and Syria, the neighboring state most influential in Lebanese politics, were unhappy with Aoun's appointment and backed Prime Minister Salim Hoss's rival government. Thus, a peculiar and unprecedented situation developed that split the government between two central authorities that were unrecognized by each other and controlled contending armed units that at times clashed. In the end, these precarious conditions actually promoted the desire for a political settlement on both sides.

In October 1989 surviving members of Lebanon's 1972 parliament met in Ta'if, Saudi Arabia, to deliberate a "National Reconciliation Accord." The goal of the Ta'if Agreement, signed on October 22 and ratified on November 4, was to end the long civil war, to politically acknowledge and accommodate the demographic shift in favor of the Muslim majority, and to reassert Beirut's authority over Israeli-occupied South Lebanon. Perhaps the most important part of the accord was its resolution to remove the numerous sectarian militias that had perpetuated the war but never gained widespread legitimacy. As in Bosnia, the assignment of political offices to certain ethno-religious communities was a feature of the Ta'if Agreement, though, to be sure, in Lebanon this had been a practice even before independence in 1943.

Ta'if transferred executive power from the president (Maronite Christian) to the cabinet and the prime minister (Sunni Musim) while the powers of the parliamentary speaker (Shia Muslim) were enhanced by extending his term of office to four years. These measures replaced the old Maronite-Sunni political alliance at the helm and replaced it, responding to opposition demands for curbed presidential authority, with a "multi-communal troika."[66] The commander of the Lebanese Armed Forces was to remain a Maronite Christian, and LAF itself would be assisted by Syrian units regaining control over South Lebanon within two years.

The Agreement was decisive in determining Lebanon's Arab identity, confirming its unity, and defining its new political system as a parliamentary democracy based on the principles of separation, balance, and cooperation among the three branches of government. The accord was likewise clear about supporting an economic model based on individual initiative and private property and about setting the abolition of political sectarianism as a fundamental national goal to be realized gradually.[67] In two important areas, however, the Ta'if Agreement left issues subject to future discussion. First, it did not and could not resolve the conflict between Israel on the one hand and Lebanon and Syria on the other. While the agreement aimed to legitimize Syria's military presence in Lebanon, it stipulated that Syrian forces would stay in Lebanon for a period of no more than two years, at which point a joint Syrian-Lebanese commission would decide whether their deployment should be extended and, if so, in which areas, in what strength, and for how long. Second, although the Agreement introduced as many as thirty-one constitutional amendments—they were approved by the parliament and signed into law in 1990—a number of questions regarding the nature of internal political reforms and their implementation were left unanswered. One important such issue is the potential mechanism, deadline, and actualization of the abolition of confessionalism—the proportional allocation of political power among a country's communities, whether religious or ethnic, according to their percentage of the population—the Agreement identifies as a national goal.[68]

Demobilization, Hezbollah, and Syria's Role in Lebanese Security

The first tasks following the Ta'if Agreement were to expand state authority over the entire territory of Lebanon and to demobilize the different militias still in existence. The majority of the militias demobilized willingly, particularly when they saw that the LAF began to deploy to the greater Beirut area as early as December 1990 and then continued this operation throughout early 1991. The LAF raided the bases of noncooperating militias, disarmed them, and collected their weapons, often with the assistance of Syrian troops. The LAF's success in decommissioning the militias enhanced its legitimacy in most quarters of Lebanese society. Nearly all armed groups were entirely deactivated by the deadline (April 30, 1991, as stipulated in the Ta'if Agreement). The progress the LAF made in extending its authority over the country was very gradual. In March 1992 half the army was stationed in South Lebanon, and by early 1993, the LAF enjoyed a strong presence in the densely populated areas of Beirut. Nonetheless, the last illegal ports on the Mediterranean did not come under its authority until 1994.[69]

The demobilization of the militias was promoted by the 1991 amnesty law according to which no one would be held accountable for crimes committed during the civil war. The law was something akin to state-sponsored amnesia and did not prevent relatives of the thousands of individuals who disappeared during the conflict to challenge it.[70] Still, after 1991 most militias had transformed themselves into legitimate political parties—much like the FMLN in El Salvador—and many of their erstwhile commanders had metamorphosed into prominent politicians. Therefore, prosecuting them would have been extremely costly in terms of the national reconciliation project. In Lebanon, as in many other contexts, the price of stability included letting the human rights violations of the past go unpunished.

In contrast to all other militias, Hezbollah, the Shi'a Muslim paramilitary organization, was allowed to continue. Given Hezbollah's proven record as a guerrilla fighting force, and in view of the Syrian and Iranian support it had long enjoyed, it was quite likely that, by the late 1990s, even if the Lebanese government had wanted to, it could not have rid itself of this militia. Quite simply, by this time the LAF was no match for Hezbollah's six thousand to seven thousand experienced and highly motivated fighters and its superior arsenal.[71] Furthermore, the diverse Lebanese political, social, and military elites concurred that the country's archenemy was Israel, and Hezbollah's uncompromising hostility toward Israel coupled with its effectiveness made it an invaluable strategic ally. The LAF and Hezbollah have viewed each other as legitimate fighting forces in the name of the broadly defined national interest. While there is an element of competition and mistrust between the two, especially in instances of overlapping deployments, they also have a record of cooperation and intelligence sharing on security operations.

Indeed, Hezbollah's participation in Lebanon's *political* life has been enthusiastically welcomed by state authorities. In fact, owing to the country's political power balance, Hezbollah has repeatedly found itself in a kingmaker position, most recently following the June 2009 elections.[72] In June 2011 Hezbollah became the dominant participant in the Lebanese government following a political crisis that began in January when the U.S.-backed central government was toppled after Hezbollah's ministers resigned to protest Prime Minister Saad Hariri's meeting with U.S. President Barack Obama. The new prime minister, Najib Mikati, is a wealthy businessman who enjoys Hezbollah's support.

Syria, always keenly interested in its western neighbor's affairs, mounted a full-scale military intervention in June 1976 during heightened concerns regarding Lebanon's potential disintegration. For the next thirty years, Damascus stationed 15,000–25,000 troops on Lebanese soil reaping political and strategic benefits commensurate with its investment. Following the Ta'if Agreement, Syria's influence only seemed to increase. According to some observers it was in complete control of Lebanon, which effectively became a Syrian colony.[73] Not surprisingly, Syria was ideally situated to put its stamp on the development of the post-Ta'if Lebanese defense sector. The May 1991 Treaty of Brotherhood, Cooperation and Coordination bolstered by the Syrian-drafted Defense and Security Agreement four months later served as the formal bases of Syria's clout in the Lebanon's security domain.[74] Damascus's influence was so pervasive that it entailed, for instance, making certain that if the commander of a given LAF unit was not pro-Syrian, his deputy would be.[75]

Syrian troops remained in the country far longer than anticipated by the signatories of the Ta'if Agreement. They left only after a gross political miscalculation by Damascus. Unhappy with Lebanese domestic politics after President Émile Lahoud's term expired and not being able to swiftly get their favored candidate into office, Syrian agents may well have been involved in the assassination of former Lebanese Prime Minister Rafiq al-Hariri in Beirut in February 2005. Subsequent mass demonstrations protesting excessive Syrian meddling in Lebanese politics and concerted pressure from the United Nations (its September 2004 Resolution #1559 called for "all remaining foreign forces" to withdraw from Lebanon) and the international community eventually persuaded Syria's President Bashar al-Assad to withdraw his troops.[76] In any event, Syrian elites soon realized that they did not have to keep thousands of troops in Lebanon to influence Lebanese politics.

Reforming the LAF

For fifteen years after the Ta'if Agreement the LAF did not have effective control of the parts of their country occupied by Syrian forces. The withdrawal of Syrian troops, completed on April 26, 2005, redefined the LAF's role. Although Damascus continued to hold some sway over Lebanese military affairs—it offered training and provided weapons for the LAF's campaign against the Fatah al-Islam organization in 2007—its overall role has diminished.[77]

The stipulations of the Ta'if Agreement regarding civil-military relations were implemented with few problems.[78] The president continues to be the "supreme commander" of the armed forces though the cabinet's authority in the defense realm was expanded to include declaring states of emergency, war and peace, general mobilization, overseeing all intelligence services, and approving high-level LAF promotions. The unicameral 128-seat parliament, through its Defense, Interior, and Municipalities Committee, was to execute all the usual functions including deliberating and overseeing the disbursement of the LAF's budget. Protecting the homeland and, when necessary, assisting the Internal Security Forces in the maintenance of public order are the LAF's basic functions. The army was to be unified and prepared so it could fulfill its national responsibility "in the face of Israeli aggression." These objectives have only partially been realized. The most important brake on the development of Lebanese civil-military relations, however, has been the continued existence of Hezbollah's military wing, a force free of state control.

The reconstruction of the Lebanese Armed Forces was one of the most important components of increasing the authority of the central state in post–civil war Lebanon. As in Bosnia, integrating all major ethno-religious communities into the armed forces was the crucial undertaking of the LAF's reform. What did Lebanese political elites do to eradicate the sectoral identity of army personnel and thereby increase their loyalty to the LAF as a national institution? First, in a relatively short time, virtually all commanders (brigade, battalion, company, and platoon) were extensively shuffled around different units. Soldiers and NCOs were also reassigned but following a more relaxed timetable. Second, the LAF leadership's objective was to set a 60:40 ratio between Muslims and Christians in each brigade and a 65:70 to 35:30 ratio among enlisted personnel in each brigade and battalion. Special forces, commando regiments, and the Republican Guard were assigned a 50:50 quota.[79] Former militiamen had the right to apply to the rapidly growing LAF (its size increased from about 25,000 in 1991 to 59,100 in 2010) but, in the end, only 6,645 of them, mostly Muslims, entered the LAF.[80] Actually, it was necessary to recruit Christians in order to maintain the ethno-religious equilibrium in the army. Between 1991 and 2004 the sectarian distribution of the officer corps shifted to 47 percent Christian and 53 percent Muslim, in concert with the growing proportion of Muslims in the country.[81]

Third, every six months each battalion was to relocate to a different region to avoid the cultivation of special links between individual units and districts. Given Lebanon's modest size (10,452 square kilometers or 4,015 square miles), this was not a particularly difficult initiative to put into practice. Finally, for the first time in the country's history, mandatory military service was introduced in order to promote the socialization and intermingling of Lebanese youth. Beginning in 1993, all males age eighteen were subject to a one-year service in the armed forces. Draftees generally made up about 25 to 28 percent of the 55,000–60,000-strong LAF. Conscription ended in February 2007; after fourteen years the government judged the LAF's integration a success and the draft no longer necessary.[82]

In one critically important respect the LAF has been quite successful. Since the Ta'if Agreement, the state media and the army's internal propaganda apparatus have been consistent in proclaiming that the LAF is a national army free of a sectarian identity and accountable only to the state. Military and civilian elites have portrayed the armed forces as being "from all of Lebanon and for all Lebanon," their pursuit of security impartial and in accordance with legal regulations. Within a few years, the government has succeeded. People have begun to look at the LAF as a symbol of unity and its leaders as the best hope to lead the country.[83] This institutional popularity is one of the main reasons for the success of two former army commanders, Émile Lahoud (1998) and Michel Suleiman (2008), in recent presidential elections. The LAF, like the Bosnian army, is widely considered the country's most representative national institution. In a July 2008 poll 76 percent of the respondents supported additional investment into the military.[84]

The LAF in Action and Inaction

In spite of obvious achievements, the LAF has suffered from three important civil-military relations problems, all rooted in its political environment. First, it remains a force with an insecure and weak command primarily due to the pull of political, sectoral, and regional loyalties.[85] The LAF has been hesitant to take action and is extremely risk averse lest it jeopardize the delicate cross-sectarian makeup of its ranks. Nonetheless, these traits might be viewed as strengths, considering that other armies in the Middle East and elsewhere are more willing to leap into action but often end up aggravating the situation.

Second, the LAF has to coexist with Hezbollah's military wing as one of the two armed forces in the country. While the LAF is considered legitimate by all sectors of Lebanese society, Hezbollah is seen as such mostly only by the Shi'a Muslim community. The state controls the LAF and recognizes the legitimacy of but certainly does not control Hezbollah. Hezbollah's exemption from being disarmed like the other militias in post-Taif Lebanon, complicates the reform and restructuring of the LAF. Third, on several occasions the LAF leadership has not followed the orders of the political elites. This does not necessarily mean that the LAF actually vetoed the orders of its civilian masters, because, apparently, these instances were handled tactfully and in consultation with the government. Still, this is hardly an acceptable practice in a functioning democracy.[86] Three examples, that also illuminate the first and second points, stand out.

First, during the February 2005 demonstrations occasioned by Hariri's assassination, LAF commander Michel Suleiman refused to turn the army against the protesters as ordered by the government of Prime Minister Omar Karami. Suleiman's action contributed both to the growing perception of Lebanese citizens that their armed forces were becoming a valuable part of the executive branch and, quite likely, to Suleiman's election as president in 2008.[87] Second, in the summer of 2007 the LAF led a three-month-long campaign against Fatah al-Islam, a radical Sunni Islamist terrorist group said to be inspired by al-Qaeda in the Nahr al-Bared Palestinian refugee camp in Lebanon. Prior to engaging the enemy—Fatah al-Islam provoked the hostilities, having attacked LAF—the army did not get proper authorization from civilian authorities and entered the refugee camp, something it usually refrains from doing. This was the most important armed conflict the LAF has been involved in since the Ta'if Agreement, and while the army roundly defeated Fatah al-Islam, the operation also revealed several chinks in the LAF's armor, such as deficiencies in cross-agency and cross-ministerial communication.[88]

Third, in May 2008, after telecommunications minister Marwan Hamade sought to tame Hezbollah's power by banning its private underground telephone system, whichmaintained nearly 100,000 numbered lines, the Lebanese opposition, spearheaded by Hezbollah, took control of most of West Beirut. The LAF became paralyzed and, along with the Internal Security Forces, simply stood by on the sidelines. Of the three alternatives in front of it—side with the government, side with Hezbollah, or do nothing—it chose the third. The main culprit, however, was a political leadership that was, perhaps understandably, so worried about splintering the country again that it decided to do nothing rather than to further antagonize Hezbollah and its supporters.[89] The May 2008 events also suggested that even with the $100 million U.S. military assistance (requested by the Obama administration for 2011) and even if the LAF were willing to engage Hezbollah in combat, the government's army will not be able to pose a credible challenge to Hezbollah in the foreseeable future.

The summer 2006 Hezbollah-Israel war also underscores the LAF's ambiguous status as Lebanon's protector. The LAF made no attempt to disarm

Hezbollah after its fighters attacked an Israeli patrol on the Israeli side of the Blue Line security zone. To be sure, the LAF was ill-equipped to do so, but its non-involvement confirmed the coexistence of two separate armies. During the thirty-three-day war in South Lebanon, the LAF once acted as a bystander, committing only a few symbolic acts against the Israeli Defense Forces (IDF).[90] The war resulted in a Hezbollah victory of sorts and allowed fifteen thousand LAF troops to be deployed in formerly Israeli-held South Lebanon. A national dialogue to deliberate whether or not Hezbollah should lay down its weapons was planned for that summer but indefinitely postponed mainly because the Hezbollah militia had once again demonstrated it was a more effective force to fight Israel than the LAF.

CONCLUSION

Building democratic armies after civil wars is a process that is quite different from building armies in other settings. Let us now consider what patterns emerge from our examination of the three case studies in this chapter.

1. *The role of international actors.* The very nature of civil wars necessitates an essential role to be played by extraneous political and, at times, military entities in ending the violence and resolving the conflict. It is no coincidence that all three peace accords we looked at were signed abroad and with the indispensable backing and participation of foreign negotiators (with the partial exception of Lebanon). Foreign actors usually also assume an important role in postconflict engagement. Just which international organization or foreign state might be the best situated to take a leading role in mediation depends on the specific context. International organizations considered impartial—like the United Nations or the Organization for Security and Cooperation in Europe and the Organization of American States—are clearly preferable to individual states. When international organizations are not equipped, willing, or capable of stepping in, neutral states or states with no particular stake in the country plagued by conflict are best to turn to. In some instances, however, the conditions may be so desperate that they can be ameliorated by almost any state and/or international organization willing and able to help.

International organizations, as we shall see again in chapters 4 and 7, also hold an important trump card: the key to membership. The long-term prospects of Bosnia are brightened by the fact that future membership in NATO and the EU provide, in theory, at least, substantial long-term incentives to political elites to sort out their differences and learn to get along. For states eager to advance economic development, domestic political legitimacy, and popular approval, obtaining membership in a prestigious club like NATO or the EU signifies great achievement. But post–civil war states can gain much from the assistance and support of the international community in many other ways, too. Attracting direct foreign investment, being invited to participate in multinational projects, gaining positive media notice abroad can be equally important and profitable. At the same time, it is also important that the foreign actor involved carry not just a carrot but also a stick, so that it is capable of deterring and, if necessary, punishing, noncompliance with treaty clauses and actions detrimental to reconciliation and political stability.

2. *The importance of peace agreements.* The peace accords that follow the end of civil wars are critically important in mapping and deciding future political, military, and social arrangements. Foreign intervention in the absence of a peace agreement is likely to trigger violent opposition by parties who value the pre-intervention status quo.[91] Peace settlements need to be comprehensive and to anticipate yet-unseen problems that might emerge (of civil-military relations and otherwise). The future political price to be paid for overlooking fundamental issues may be substantial. All three peace agreements we considered—Chapúltepec, Dayton, and Ta'if—had major flaws, mostly of omission and, to a lesser extent, of ambiguity. Nonetheless, it is important to recognize that at the time peace accords are negotiated, some issues might be too sensitive to deal with and some developments simply cannot be foreseen. It is useful to remind ourselves that the most important aims of peace agreements are to stop the fighting and quickly demobilize, even if the rest of the process will be messy and contentious.

3. *Encouraging domestic responsibilities.* Weaning domestic actors off their reliance on international organizations as quickly as practicable is an important objective of post–civil war environments. Just how soon foreign players might leave depends, of course, on the individual context. Shutting down the U.N. mission in El Salvador in 1996, merely four years after the peace agreement, was entirely appropriate just as fifteen years after Dayton, terminating the presence of international organizations would still seem hasty. Domestic actors, including civilian leaders and experts as well as NGOs can make a major contribution to demilitarization and demobilization. The prospects of defense reforms will be enhanced if carefully vetted local military elites are allowed to play a substantive role in their conceptualization, planning, and implementation.

4. *Demobilization and related concerns.* The demobilization of forces and the reintegration of erstwhile combatants into civilian life are two of the most pressing goals of post–civil war democracy builders. The terms of demobilization must be precisely outlined in the peace agreements. The

collection and destruction of excess weapons and ammunition are related tasks that, as we have seen in our case studies, are often very contentious. Owing to the lack of trust between former enemy forces, it is not surprising that they want to retain some strategic advantage or security guarantee that will enable them to resume fighting if necessary. Therefore, promoting transparency and building trust between the different sides through a variety of confidence-building measures implemented by impartial security institutions is critically important for long-term stability.

5. *Balancing personnel, promoting a national identity.* In post–civil war environments the need to balance public sector positions—from the chief executive and the army general to the postal employee and the corporal—between the various former enemy communities assumes great significance. Quotas are based on whatever issue divided the population and led to war, whether it was religion, ethnicity, regional origin, or social class. Apportioning jobs on the basis of identity may generate corruption and inefficiency but it is likely to go far in preserving peace. In the military realm putting ethno-religious quotas into practice is a similarly difficult endeavor that—as we will see in the contexts of postcolonial India, Pakistan, Ghana, and Tanzania—can be accomplished according to different methods and with varying levels of success. Nonetheless, fostering the creation of a truly national identity, particularly in the armed forces, is an important long-term objective. It seems wise to keep members of different ethnic and religious groups in separate units following a civil war and to integrate them gradually, progressing from larger to smaller elements as conditions allow. That is, first include different homogeneous battalions in a brigade, then different single-religion companies in a battalion, and so on.

6. *The need for gradualism.* Virtually every aspect of post–civil war politics demonstrates the need for gradualism. Given that in civil wars, by definition, the warring sides know each other, healing the rift between them is likely to take far longer than between strangers after, say, a war between different states. For starters, the amount of time between the realization of opposing sides that a cease-fire and peace settlement are desirable and the actual signing of a peace agreement may be considerable. True reconciliation between the erstwhile antagonists is nearly always a long process; indeed it might take generations. At the same time, it must be relentlessly pursued because as long as politics is about identity rather than issues, nationalist and extremist parties will enjoy an influential political role at the expense of political organizations with more substance-oriented agendas.

In sum, notwithstanding the profound disparities between Bosnia, El Salvador, and Lebanon, several common themes emerge regarding building armies after civil wars. Nevertheless, one is hard-pressed to pinpoint a common thread with respect to the post–civil war military elites' commitment to democratic rule. In militaries divided along ethnic and religious lines, one's group membership is likely to trump all other loyalties, though in time, particularly given favorable political and social developments, commitment to democracy may become more robust and, eventually, might even dominate other forms of identity. In the two relevant cases in this chapter, one may be a bit more sanguine about the BiH officer corps' allegiance to democracy than the LAF's. The problems in El Salvador are just as complex and include the army's increasing participation in police operations and their growing influence on domestic politics. Such qualms about the three armed forces' dedication to democratic governance are one of the main reasons one cannot call the three states consolidated democracies.

At the end of the day, the necessary involvement of outside actors, the imperative of demobilization along with the need for gradualism, the need for power sharing and ethno-religious balancing, all suggest that post–civil war environments require a delicate balancing act between all these and often additional factors. Bringing former warring parties together and then moving forward as one is what post–civil war settings are all about. In the last chapter, we are going to learn about building democratic armies after reunification and apartheid, settings not entirely dissimilar from the one we have just discussed.

TABLE 3.1

After Civil War: Bosnia-Herzegovina, El Salvador, and Lebanon

		Country Period	Bosnia 1995–2010	El Salvador 1992–2010	Lebanon 1990–2008
Peace treaties	peace treaty		Dayton	Chapúltepec	Ta'if
	positives		ended war, added new constitution	ended war, created basis for democratization, stamped out military's societal influence	ended war, removed militias, rearranged political institutional balance, defined new political system
	negatives		undermined state authority, produced new sources of insecurity	no stipulation of economic reforms, failed to specify numerous civil-military issues	legitimized Syria's presence, failed to address many questions of internal political reform
	attempts at evasion		yes, "hiding" soldiers and arms	yes, maintaining arms caches	yes, some uncooperative militias
State	main tasks		demobilization, disarmament, reintegration, demilitarization of politics	demobilization, disarmament, reintegration, demilitarization of politics	demobilization, disarmament, reintegration, demilitarization of politics
	civilian political leadership		sharply divided along ethnic lines	growing strength and institutionalization	frequent and serious political instability
	political institutions and trend		functional but divided	overcivilianization	full civilian (party) control
	executive control		strong but divided presidency	somewhat limited by military prerogatives	limited by Syria's clout and Hezbollah
	legislative oversight		firm	weak	medium
	ethnic quotas for public offices		yes	irrelevant	yes
	old armies purged		yes	yes	no

TABLE 3.1   *(continued)*

After Civil War: Bosnia-Herzegovina, El Salvador, and Lebanon

	Country *Period*	*Bosnia* *1995–2010*	*El Salvador* *1992–2010*	*Lebanon* *1990–2008*
	foreign influence	high: USA/NATO EU/UNHR	high: UN	high: Syria
Military	new army	integration of Serb, Bosnian, and Croat armies into one	integration of FMLN guerrillas into FAES	integration of militias into LAF
	behavior during transition	nonconfrontational	trying to safeguard perks and institutional autonomy	restrained
	interference in politics	none	low but growing	medium, Hezbollah also a key political factor
	domestic function	no	police work	police functions
	advisory function	low	high	high
	institutional attributes	from three armies to one	relatively high institutional autonomy	two legitimate forces: LAF and Hezbollah
	effectiveness	no evidence	no evidence	low
	commitment to democracy	probable	unclear	unclear
Society	independent civilian experts	few and lacking influence	few and lacking influence	few and lacking influence
	military's prestige	medium	medium	medium
	soldiers in society	growing integration	growing transparency	"army of the nation"
	conscription	no	no	no
Political system at the end of the period		parliamentary democracy (not consolidated)	parliamentary democracy (not consolidated)	parliamentary democracy (not consolidated)

BUILDING DEMOCRATIC ARMIES
AFTER REGIME CHANGE

CHAPTER 4

After Military Rule in Europe:
Spain, Portugal, and Greece
※ ※

This is the first of four chapters in which we are investigating the ways in which democratic armies were built in response to regime change, and the first of three chapters where, more specifically, we are concerned with building new armed forces after military or praetorian rule in three different continents.[1] Praetorianism is one of the most common versions of authoritarian government, and we will learn about additional cases in the last part of the book. Both Pakistan and Ghana went through periods of military rule though our primary interest in them is how they developed their armies as a result of state transformation, as postcolonial states. In this chapter our main cases, Spain and Portugal, are not "classic" examples of military rule. For most of their long authoritarian periods, generals and colonels did not run the state to the same extent as they did in some more typical, more explicitly *military* regimes even if both were born and sustained as a result of the armed forces' consistent support.

In both Iberian countries the military played a fundamental role. In Spain, following the Civil War (1936–39), "the center of gravity, the true support of the regime . . . was the army."[2] In Portugal, too, the armed forces were a critically important institutional pillar of the state. When Philippe Schmitter argued in 1973 that "Portugal is already a military dictatorship, only no one is aware of it yet," he meant that the military and colonial bureaucracies so tightly constrained Prime Minister Marcelo Caetano's space for political maneuver that "for all intents and purposes, they were already running the country."[3] The Portuguese Armed Forces were also most unusual insofar as they were directly responsible for bringing down the regime they once supported. After decades of authoritarianism, placing the Spanish military under civilian control proved to be a relatively straightforward and brief process. The transformation of Portuguese civil-military relations, on the other hand, was more contentious, took far longer, and did not succeed as completely as Spain's.

Greece, our secondary case in this chapter, had a much shorter but more intense experience with praetorianism; its return to democracy and democratic civil-military relations was quick albeit not without some shortcomings.[4] The Greek colonels' regime was more in line with the "full-fledged" military governments we will encounter in the next two chapters in Latin America and Asia. Samuel Huntington designated Portugal's transition as the start of the third wave of global democratization. He classified all three of our Southern European cases as "second-try democracies" in recognition of their earlier experiences with democratic governance.

This chapter begins with a brief background section to help us situate Spain and Portugal in a historical perspective. Four parts follow. In the first two, we examine military politics in the two Iberian states during the authoritarian era and the changes they went through during democratic transition and consolidation. In the third section, we look at the Greek experience with military rule. Finally, we assess the influence of international organizations, particularly NATO, on the democratization of the three states and their defense establishments.

BACKGROUND

The two Iberian states presented a distinct subset in much of twentieth-century Europe. The installation of authoritarian regimes as a consequence of independent military action in Spain (1939) and Portugal (1926) were anomalies in post–World War II Europe. While both General Francisco Franco (1892–1975) and António de Oliveira Salazar (1889–1970) did their best to lay to rest any identification with European fascism and fit their regimes into the family of conservative, right-wing authoritarian states, West European democratic leaders found cooperation with them difficult. The government of the United States—often given to viewing the world in exclusively Cold War terms—was less constrained in maintaining relations with them. Still, Washington tended to agree with France and Great Britain on the isolation of Spain and Portugal as a new Europe was being built through the Marshall Plan and the European Coal and Steel Community that, in time, evolved into the European Economic Community and finally, to the European Union. It ought to be noted, however, that the West viewed Salazar less negatively than Franco because the former was never seen as a German ally and had maintained Portugal's traditionally close ties to Great Britain.

Franco and Salazar followed different paths to power. Franco was the commanding officer who led Nationalist forces to a military victory over the Republicans in 1939 after a bloody civil war. Originally a university economics professor, Salazar was named Portugal's finance minister in 1928 and within two years managed to consolidate dictatorial powers in his hands. He became prime minister in 1932 and remained in that position until 1968, when he was incapacitated by a stroke. Franco and Salazar firmly established their regimes well in advance of the end of World War II. Both enjoyed long tenures at the pinnacle of power in large part owing to their success in building independent power bases that made them accountable to no one, either military or civilian. After World War II, Franco and Salazar suppressed the fascist components that supported them during the 1930s and 1940s and were still present in their movements. Both civilianized their regimes to better respond to the economic challenges of the 1950s and 1960s; in the Portuguese case this effort started even earlier.

Despite great differences in their economic policies and major changes in their economies, the final decade and a half of authoritarianism was characterized by political stasis in both countries. During these years Franco governed Spain more as a civilian regent than as a military officer. His control over the armed forces represented a departure for a country whose strong tradition of military interference in politics had rendered it unstable.[5] Salazar also took close personal control of the armed forces: he made all major promotion decisions based primarily on the candidates' ideological credentials and loyalty to the regime. As prime minister for thirty-six years, he established the primacy of that office at the expense of the presidency. When his protégé, Marcelo Caetano, succeeded him, Caetano did so as prime minister.

Both dictators managed to reshape executive institutions to serve their own needs and retained undisputed authority over national politics. They established centralized executive organizations and extended centralized control mechanisms that successfully compromised the military's institutional autonomy. Not only were the armed forces subordinated to the personal policy preferences of Franco—who dealt directly with his generals and did his best to appease them—and Salazar, but they were also brought under the oversight of government ministries. This prior institutional history had a profound impact on the Spanish and Portuguese transitions from authoritarian rule in the 1970s. Notwithstanding their divergent origins and guiding ideologies, the two Iberian regimes were similar to each other in three important ways: the longevity of their respective regimes to the point that there were no viable alternatives to them up until the eve of their collapse; the transformation of the economy and the polity they inherited from their predecessors into highly centralized command structures; and the subordination of military officers to the dictates of each "new" state.

Notwithstanding these parallels, civil-military relations in Spain and Portugal must be seen according to their relative isolation from each other since the 1940s. Political and military leaders in each country had pursued their foreign and defense policies independently and directly with the same set of regional and international actors and organizations, but rarely if ever in consultation with each other. Portugal was a founding member of NATO while Spain could not join until after the democratic transition.

CIVIL-MILITARY RELATIONS UNDER AUTHORITARIANISM

Spain

The 1936 revolt of the armed forces against the Spanish Republic plunged the nation into civil war, with enormous costs in lives and property. When the Civil War ended in 1939 with the victory of Nationalist forces, Spain was thoroughly devastated. Franco took power following a military victory in a country profoundly split between Nationalists and Republicans. His first government was a broad conservative coalition of military officers and civilians who supported the revolt against the Republic in 1936 and defeated the Republicans and communists in 1939. Together they ruled the country as a garrison state. From the beginning, however, Franco was in command and the Council of Ministers served at his behest. Furthermore, in all the cabinets appointed from 1938 through 1974, at no point did Franco give the military a majority. To be sure, there was consistent military representation in government through the years; but especially in the first cabinet, political appointments took precedence over military ones. Hence, of the twenty-five men serving in the "victory cabinet" of January 1938–May 1941, thirteen were political appointments, seven were military, and five were technical.[6]

What these divisions mask is the bitter division between the Falangists (members of a radical, right-wing, republican, and quasi-fascist organization) and monarchists who remained at odds with each other even after Franco brought most of them into a single political organization in 1937. When Catholic representation is added to this mix, it becomes apparent that these political rifts served Franco well. Playing off one side against the other and never giving one faction the upper hand, he managed to hold on to power until his death in November 1975.

The structuring of civil-military relations under authoritarianism followed the original prescription drawn up by Franco when he charged his first cabinet with the task of reorganizing the state after the civil war. Among the changes made in 1939 was the creation of a single ministry for internal security affairs, the *Gobernación* (a model Mexico would follow when it consolidated the modern state). The Gobernación replaced the republican ministries of interior and public order and provided the government with a single organization establishing control over the countryside. Its mandate included the supervision of the *Guardia Civil* (the paramilitary police force tasked with maintaining order and security at the subnational level) as well as local administration and communications. Importantly, whereas controls over civil society were centralized, military authority was divided. In place of the ministry of defense, the cabinet created three new ministries—a practice later followed in praetorian Brazil and Argentina—one for each branch of the armed forces. Their ministers reported separately to Franco without any civilian involvement.

In 1962 Franco reestablished the office of vice president, which had been abolished in 1939. With the exception of the last two years of his reign, this office was assigned to the military. General Agustín Muñoz Grandes served as vice president until July 1967; he was succeeded by Admiral Carrero Blanco until June 1973, when Franco nominated him as president of the government. During the final years of Franco's rule, as he prepared for a successor regime with King Juan Carlos on the throne and Carrero Blanco as head of government, it became clear that Franco conceived of the military as the guarantor of the status quo, which he sought to perpetuate.[7] These plans were disrupted with Carrero Blanco's assassination in December 1973, since Franco had no replacement in mind for him and it was too late to groom another person of confidence. With the regime in disarray, with Franco increasingly incapacitated by old age and poor health, and with Carlos Arias-Navarro in center place as the new prime minister, negotiations began in 1974 for a democratic opening that would lead the country in a very different direction from anything Franco had envisioned.

Between 1938 and 1969 twenty-four Spanish military officers served in ministerial positions. All shared combat experience in the Civil War; most actually fought with Franco in the Moroccan Wars (1919–26). Most of them headed the separate ministries for the branches of the armed forces, though five directed civilian ministries (three the Internal Security Ministry and two the Ministry of Foreign Affairs).[8] Even more influential was the regime's staffing strategy to reserve government jobs for Nationalist veterans, particularly for those held prisoner by the Republicans during the Civil War. This policy became the Law of August 25, 1939, stipulating that no less than 80 percent of government employees had to be Nationalist veterans or their family members, virtually guaranteeing the unswerving loyalty of the bureaucracy to Franco's regime. Additional laws in 1953 and 1958 extended civil employment specifically to military men wishing to exercise their professions in a civilian capacity generally and in a civilian ministry specifically. This institutional preference was gradually put into practice, and by 1975 "bureaucrats constituted 81.5% of active-duty officers in the army, 94% in the navy and 82.5% in the air force."[9]

Not surprisingly, there was a close relationship between the armed forces and the organs of internal security, a privileged connection that was to be replicated in Argentina, Brazil, and Chile as well. Throughout the Franco regime, militarization of the country's security forces was a constant pattern. Within the Armed Police, infantry and cavalry officers received special consideration and it was common practice in the Civil Guard to draw upon army cadres to meet staffing needs.[10] Thus, even if Franco had maintained a regime of "limited pluralism" in which all groups in the Nationalist coalition were represented in his cabinets, there was continuous interaction between the regime and the armed forces throughout his rule. At the same time, the gradual civilianization of the regime, even if less extensive than in Portugal, meant that the military officers' participation in political institutions, such as the *Cortes Generales* (parliament) and the Council of the Realm, had gradually become more restricted.[11]

Another, seldom appreciated facet of the Spanish polity was the great extent to which military values pervaded the regime's unofficial ideology and provided a solid base for building and sustaining the Francoist edifice. Rather than being at variance, traditional Catholic values were quite compatible with the professional military subculture that permeated Spain during these years. Throughout the history of the regime, Franco presented himself as the supreme *caudillo*. Moreover, the "application of the military principle of unified command reinforced the figure of the caudillo as a form of leadership by the victorious heroic soldier."[12] The close interaction among military officials, civilian bureaucrats, and political leaders promoted the cross-fertilization of perspectives in which the armed forces were politicized by a conservative, nationalist rhetoric, and politicians and civil servants were militarized in their adherence to a unified chain of command that emphasized the values of loyalty, sobriety, and compliance with orders.[13]

Portugal

Portugal's authoritarian state was born in 1926 when the republic was overthrown by a military coup with, in stark contrast to Spain, minimal damage or destruction. The Portuguese experience with authoritarianism differed from Spain's in three important ways. First, it was more institutionalized, as a function of its greater longevity and success in the consolidation and transfer of executive power. Second, it was more ideological, in the sense that the practice of corporatism permeated more fully the regime's political culture. Third, it was more "civilized," that is, armed forces personnel were kept apart from interaction with civilians incorporated into the regime and were subordinated to civilian rule.[14]

Given the absence of a clear-cut military victory and an identifiable enemy, the Portuguese transition to authoritarianism was more extended and amorphous than the Spanish. The parallels here are far greater with Brazil than they are with Spain. In both Portugal and Brazil, the failure of their civilian republics centered around leadership crises—in which civilian elites were unable to transcend factional differences to provide stability in government—and unresolved economic problems. Although one can clearly mark the collapse of these experiments with limited democracy (1926 in Portugal and 1930 in Brazil), it took years before successor regimes could be clearly defined. In Portugal the military officers who led the coup in 1926 proved incompetent when it came to economic policy. At the time, it was not at all clear that the appointment of António Salazar as finance minister and his success in creating the conditions for economic stability would result in his appointment as prime minister in 1932, and his accrual of dictatorial powers and creation of a "New State" (the *Estado Novo*) under a new constitution in 1933. Yet, from 1930 onward there was no doubt that an authoritarian regime was taking shape. That year marks the establishment of the National Union, an "anti-party" institution that served to pull together into a single organization the civilian forces supporting the new regime.[15]

Once consolidated, the New State regime proved to be more enduring than any other authoritarian regime in Western Europe. Uniquely, in Salazar's Portugal power became institutionalized in the Office of the Prime Minister and in the regime's capacity to devise a workable succession mechanism once the dictator was incapacitated. Ensconced in power as Salazar's successor, Marcelo Caetano gave every sign in the early 1970s of being able to continue the New State to which he had dedicated his life as an advocate and defender of its corporatist principles. When, after forty-eight years, authoritarian rule finally came to an abrupt end in 1974, the military coup that overthrew the regime caught everyone by surprise. Portugal's protracted colonial wars (1961–74) had gradually enfeebled the state and poisoned its relationship to the armed forces. When the regime collapsed in a matter of hours on April 25, 1974, the whole institutional order so carefully crafted by Salazar came unglued.

The second key difference from Spain was the successful implantation of a corporatist ideology that replaced the pluralist assumptions that underlie Western liberal democracy and changed Portuguese political culture extensively. Whereas Spain remained a divided society during the decades of Franco's regime, Portuguese elites developed a form of rule in which society was compartmentalized and restructured according to different sets of interests organized and regulated by the state. Under Salazar and Caetano's New State regime corporatist interest representation and corporatist organization of society were enduring characteristics of Portuguese political culture.[16] The restructuring of state and society was never clearly defined in line with the official precepts designed by Salazar in installing the regime. Popular participation in the state, society, and the economy was confined to official or government-sanctioned organizations. Regime opponents had two choices: emigration or resignation.

Third, though there was a system of internal security controls and government informers that effectively identified potential "trouble makers," even in its early years, the Portuguese authoritarian regime created nothing resembling the garrison state sustained by paramilitary organizations and the armed forces in post–Civil War Spain.

Under the Estado Novo, social control was exercised through the organization and regulation of interest groups and was closely linked to civil-military relations. Portuguese military officers had to be as careful as civilians in censuring their remarks and in monitoring their own behavior. They were taken seriously, kept at arm's length, and their directives were obeyed. The security forces—organized during Salazar's reign as the *Polícia Internacional e de Defesa do Estado* and reorganized as the *Direcção-Geral de Segurança* under Caetano, consisted essentially of plainclothesmen who could be found in all walks of life—identified with an autonomous organization directly accountable to the prime minister and administered through his office, the *Presidência do Conselho*. Complementing them were the Republican National Guard and the Security Police, under the control of the Interior Ministry. Their job was to maintain public order and control in the countryside and urban areas.

Institutionally, the armed forces were controlled and regulated through service ministries and state secretariats, staffed by officers from the respective services. During the "wartime" years, which for Salazar began with the Spanish Civil War in 1936 and extended to 1947, he added the Ministries of War and Foreign Relations to his responsibilities as finance minister and prime minister. In the immediate postwar era (1947–58) the growth of the military bureaucracy paralleled the expansion in state-controlled economic organizations. These developments resulted in the creation of a defense ministry to coordinate overall control of the armed forces as represented in distinct ministries for the army and the navy. The air force also acquired some institutional autonomy, first through the designation of an under-secretary of state and later through the creation of a State Secretariat for the Air Force.[17]

These patterns in military bureaucracy continued in force through the Caetano years. As a rule, except when Salazar assumed the portfolio for defense, the minister of defense was a senior army officer, held in close confidence by the prime minister. This reflected the fact that from 1961—when insurrections first broke out in the Portuguese colony of Angola—till the collapse of the regime in 1974, the army was the most important military institution. Still, the defense ministry remained a small organization made up of the minister, a small civilian office staff, and military aides. Their main responsibilities were to coordinate military policy and to broker relations with the government, as constituted through the primacy of the Prime Minister's Office and the Council of Ministers. The efforts of the new elites targeting democratic consolidation in the mid-1980s drew on this pattern of institutional arrangement.[18]

Civil-military relations in authoritarian Portugal were never as placid as the regime's stability suggested. At least nine garrison-type revolts occurred between 1927 and 1961, which left behind a residue of frustrated careers, clique networks, and fear of political volatility.[19] After 1958 the regime's recruitment policy, which created an influx of middle-class entrants and untried junior officers into the officer corps, only increased the uneasiness within the armed forces. The protracted colonial wars in Africa drove an even sharper wedge between the regime and its soldiers. Portuguese military officers were generally kept apart from civilian bureaucrats on the mainland with the significant exception of their stationing in the Interior, Communications, and Overseas Ministries from 1947 to 1961. Following the two crises of 1961, a nearly successful coup attempt by the military on the mainland and the outbreak of guerrilla warfare in Angola, the separation of soldiers from bureaucrats was reinforced. After 1961 the military's missions were expanded, shifting from the defense of the mainland to an all-inclusive concern with Portuguese overseas territories. Accordingly, there was a drop in the armed forces' representation on the Council of Ministers after 1960—and even earlier in the National Assembly and the Corporative Chamber—as well as a steady increase in civilian technocrats. From 1958 to 1968 there were a total of twenty-two technocrats serving in the cabinet, as opposed to eight military men and three politicians.[20] Under Caetano the practice of giving weight to civilian bureaucrats with technical and professional qualifications continued.

MILITARY POLITICS DURING
DEMOCRATIC TRANSITION AND CONSOLIDATION

The Spanish transition to democracy, nested in the Franco regime's legal framework and benefiting from its economic modernization drive, sharply differed from the Portuguese (and Greek) experiences. The pretransition Spanish armed forces did not suffer the humiliation that their Greek and Argentine counterparts did: they remained loyal to Franco and supported his chosen successor. It is noteworthy that Franco had the foresight to negotiate his military's withdrawal from the Sahara in 1975 while Salazar and Caetano presided over a seemingly interminable colonial war that turned the increasingly politicized and radicalized Portuguese Armed Forces against the state.

The evaluation of the military's role in the two Iberian states' transitions to democracy depends largely on what sociopolitical variables are privileged in the assessment. If the increasingly technocratic orientation of the two regimes is emphasized, then the transitions may be viewed as primarily the work of civilian elites.[21] In this context, the armed forces' efforts at shaping the transition process may even be seen as largely incidental. Military incursions into politics—more extended in Portugal and quite brief in Spain—thus appear aberrations, and following their return to the barracks, the activities of soldiers during the transition are no longer of much interest to the analyst.[22]

The alternative approach stresses the role played by the military elites and the security forces in sustaining a repressive apparatus of the ancien régime. This method focuses attention on the changes in the mentality of the armed forces and their break with the old order. In the Portuguese case, the spotlight is on the conditions that led to a military coup and radicalization of the military institution.[23] In the case of Spain, on the other hand, the focus is on the conditions that led the armed forces to abandon their powerful position in Franco's regime and to accept civilian supremacy in the new democratic order.[24]

Spain

To begin with, it is helpful to ponder two key points. First, by virtually any standard, the Spanish transition to democracy was of relatively short duration. The transition period coincided with the building of civilian elite consensus on democratic procedures, 1976–78. In order to appreciate the significance of the attempted military coup in February 1981 and why it was successfully isolated, it is more helpful to consider the transition process as lasting significantly longer. Looking at it this way, the process involved military and civilian personnel as well as society at large and extended up through 1982.[25] Moreover, our attention is also drawn to the national debate that preceded the 1982 legislative elections that brought to power Spain's first socialist government since the Republic.

Second, enormous changes took place within the military establishment during these years. Political elites were sensitive to societal moods that generally supported moderate policies. To be sure, fears of backlash from the armed forces—that were most resistant to the extensive modernization pressures of the late Francoist regime—restrained urges to table radical policy proposals.[26] Adolfo Suárez, Spain's first democratically elected prime minister (1976–81), moved prudently. He first sought and obtained the collaboration of influential military circles who were concerned primarily with the future of the armed forces. He approached the confirmed democrats in the officer corps who might have been objectionable to the former group only afterward.[27] Further reforms were also implemented with the coordination of the services and only after prior consultation with them. According to some observers, the "most prominent trait of the political transition from dictatorship to democracy in Spain is the peaceful manner in which the armed forces abdicated their powerful formal position in institutions and political life, accepting the normative establishment of civil supremacy."[28]

King Juan Carlos, who became head of state two days after Franco's death, was a significant factor in Spain's democratic transition. Franco designated him as Spain's next ruler in 1969 and he was widely perceived as the dictator's legitimate successor in the armed forces. The Political Reforms Act of 1976 and the Moncloa Palace Pacts of 1977 were central to the accords around which consensus was built on the desirability of adherence to democratic procedures. From these agreements followed a referendum that approved the new constitution in 1978 as well as legislative and municipal elections in 1979. These agreements signified movement away from a corporatist form of interest-group representation under an authoritarianism in which a limited set of groups and individuals were recognized and sanctioned by the state as legitimate participants. In place of the unitary, highly centralized Spanish state, a much more open society developed that recognized the legitimacy of a plurality of interests.[29] In place of the old emphasis on unitary government and controls, a highly decentralized state emerged with extensive provisions for regional autonomy and local self-government. The first two articles of the Constitution structure the state along the lines of a parliamentary monarchy complete with separation of powers and national sovereignty emanating from the people.

Changes within the military institution were indispensable to the success of the transition. In fact, the alteration in the military's outlook—the main source of which was intensifying contacts between Spanish and Western, particularly American, military personnel—was just as far-reaching and significant as any of the changes in civil society. As the senior military cadres with civil war experience aged and passed into retirement, younger officers moved up the ranks and were able, once the opportunity came, to open Spain to the outside world and to respond with new training initiatives, proposals for reorganization, and a willingness to work with civilian counterparts. They were to form the core of advocates within the military establishment for joining NATO and participating in U.N. peacekeeping operations.

The changes in Spanish civil-military relations occurred as quickly as in the social and political realms. The first round of reforms, in 1977–82, defined the new legal context under which the military would be subordinated to civilian authority. Under the 1978 Constitution these entailed the creation of the Ministry of Defense in July 1977 and the definition of the government's role as director and executor of defense policy, with the head of government as its coordinator. Article 8 of the Constitution defines the armed forces' functions as the defense of the state's sovereignty and territorial integrity. Law 85 (December 28, 1978) established the basic norms governing internal armed forces operations. The Organic Law of July 1, 1980, set out provisions for military organization and the determination of defense policy. The 1980 Defense Law determined the range of competence between political and military institutions that is at the heart of the central administration for defense. This law was the continuation of the institutionalization of new agencies in the management and running of defense and, in particular, the creation of a Ministry of Defense, which replaced the three existing ministries in July 1977.[30]

From 1982 through 1985 major modifications were introduced into the 1980 Organic Law through the organization of a defense ministry that could assume responsibility for defining and implementing foreign and defense policy. These changes included the redefinition of defense policy, in which the role of the defense minister was specified and increased through assigning him/her greater policy-making responsibilities. The structure of the defense ministry within which civilian and military bureaucrats were integrated was also modified. Moreover, major revisions were implemented in the procedures of military promotions and retirement, military justice, and procurement. Finally, the size of the armed forces was cut based on a ten-year reduction plan. A powerful central ministry capable of reinforcing and securing civilian oversight authority of the armed forces emerged, putting Spanish institutional controls on a par with those found among long-established European democracies. These changes were followed in 1986–89 by the development of a new national defense concept in which Spain joined the Western alliance system.[31]

The attempted military coup of February 23, 1981, and the strong public reaction to the terms negotiated by Leopoldo Calvo-Sotelo's short-lived (1981–82) government for European integration—linking economic and security policy together—led to renewed determination in the socialist government (in power from 1982 to 1996) to find a more effective way to secure democratic governance. The coup attempt led by Lt. Col. Antonio Tejero reflected the reluctance and/or opposition by a considerable part of the Spanish military to adapt to the democratic system especially as the government seemed unable to handle economic problems and the increasingly brazen terrorist acts of the Basque separatist group, ETA.

Tejero led a submachine-gun wielding Civil Guard unit of two hundred to the Congress of Deputies of the legislature and did not abide by the order of Acting Defense Minister General Manuel Gutiérrez Mellado to desist.[32] In the meantime, the head of the third military region, Captain General Jaime Milans del Bosch, ordered tanks onto the streets of Valencia and declared an emergency in support of the coup. The quick and decisive action of King Juan Carlos, however, had gone far in saving Spain's fragile democracy. He appeared in his Captain General of the Armed Forces (the highest military rank in Spain) uniform on national television to denounce the coup and uphold the Constitution. The government supported the court's stance that those involved in the attempted coup must be sanctioned firmly and directly. (Both Tejero and Milans del Bosch received thirty-year prison terms.)

Felipe González's enduring (1982–96) socialist government succeeded in defeating those in the armed forces who looked askance at a democratic polity. The old guard of the military leadership became demoralized once the center and the right in civilian politics collapsed, the socialist government was able to maintain a clear-cut majority in the Cortes throughout the 1980s, and ranks of officers whose service dated back to the Civil War were thinning out.

The biggest challenge during the long tenure of Narcís Serra as Spain's defense minister (1982–91) was the adoption of the January 1984 Defense Law that established better coordination among military commanders and reaffirmed the supremacy of civilian control over the direction of the armed forces. According to this law, the decision to use the armed forces and to exercise effective command belongs to the prime minister with the king restricted to a formal and honorific position while retaining the title of commander in chief of the armed forces. In effect, "the law designated the king as Supreme Commander even though the *real* head of the armed forces is the prime minister."[33] The 1984 law strengthened the defense minister's role and changed the relatively ineffective Chiefs of Staff Committee (established in 1977) by replacing its chairman with a Chief of the Defense Staff who was directly responsible to, closely collaborated with, and also acted as a military adviser to the minister.[34]

Unlike in many modern defense establishments, in the Spanish military the traditional differences between the branches have largely survived rendering each service unique. The air force has a reputation of laid-back and easy-going attitudes; the army is the most strictly institutionalized and operationally capable; and the navy is the most conservative, alertly guarding its relative autonomy and rich historical traditions. For instance, after the king and the Suárez government had the political wisdom and courage to legalize the Communist Party in April 1977, the ministers representing the three armed services resigned in protest. Appointing compliant replacements from the army and the air force was not difficult, but it was impossible to find an active-duty admiral from the navy who would dishonor a colleague by replacing him, so one had to be picked from the reserves.[35] (A few months later, as noted above, a single defense minister, General Gutiérrez Mellado, replaced the three at the head of a new Ministry of Defense.) According to Serra, perhaps the most credit for Spain's peaceful military transition is due to Gutiérrez Mellado who served not only as defense minister (1977–81) but also as deputy prime minister (1976–81) in Adolfo Suárez's cabinets.[36] Incidentally, the then nearly sixty-nine-year-old Gutiérrez Mellado was one of the three members of the Spanish Congress—the other two were Prime Minister Suárez and Communist Party leader Santiago Carillo—who physically confronted the Guardia Civil troops during the failed coup d'état (the other deputies ducked under their desks).

Portugal

The coup-makers who overthrew the Caetano government on April 25, 1974, hastening the collapse of the New State regime had few doubts about the significance of their actions. Their Armed Forces Movement (*Movimento das Forças Armadas*, MFA) had begun in 1973 with the limited goal of readjustment in salaries for middle-level officers and enlisted men.[37] Many founding members of the MFA were career officers who fought in the colonial war in Guinea-Bissau in West Africa. An important reason for the coup was that changes in the law allowed the *milicianos*, in effect, conscripts-turned-low-ranking-officers, to have some of the same retirement benefits that theretofore had been the monopoly of the professional officer corps.

More generally, many officers had come to realize in the course of their involvement in the New State's African wars that they were on the wrong side of history, fighting for a repressive colonial power against forces representing the wish of the African majority to be free. As the military's political radicalization was stoked by the Portuguese Communist Party and other rapidly forming leftist organizations, members of the MFA had gradually come to see their role as a wider, revolutionary one: liberation of the mainland and independence for the overseas territories.[38] In essence, military officers who identified with the MFA wanted to destroy what they had come to consider a quasi-fascist regime.

The civilians who responded to the MFA's initiative with street demonstrations and enthusiastic reception of the coup participants were equally assertive. In their minds the old order was not a neutral authoritarian regime with a restrictive concept of citizenship but a repressive regime identified with European fascism and white minority rule in Africa. The MFA unleashed a radical leftist movement. All across the country military officers and civilians organized groups—such as workers' committees, peasant cooperatives, and neighborhood commissions—seized control of factories, took over landed estates, and encouraged the homeless to occupy vacant residences.[39] Many conservatives, equally opposed to the Caetano government, moved quickly to expand their influence within the Junta of National Salvation and to constitute a new moderate government with the MFA. Overseas, MFA officers collaborated with the African liberation movements in Guinea Bissau, Angola, and Mozambique to accelerate the transition to independence as Portuguese colonists fled to safe havens in the Republic of South Africa or in mainland Portugal.

By the summer of 1975, Portugal found itself shorn of its overseas territories (except the island of Macau off the coast of China) and on the brink of civil war. While the cities of Lisbon and Setúbal and the rural population in the south were dominated by citizen groups allied the MFA, people in the north and on the Azores and Madeira islands organized themselves against the revolution and in defense of private property. A multitude of new political parties, representing various constituencies and covering the political spectrum from left to right, also took form, with their leaders competing for the control of the government. The proliferation of groups, approaches, and political ideologies finally led to what seemed for some time inevitable: the split within the armed forces.[40]

With military cadres associated with the old regime increasingly isolated or out of the picture, the MFA, afflicted with numerous divisions, found not only that it lacked any semblance of organizational coherence but also that large segments of the officer corps and enlisted men rejected its appeals. Out of the new center that emerged within the armed forces came a new movement of moderates. They mounted a counter coup on November 25, 1975, and displaced the radicals from the centers of power. Then, just as quickly as revolutionary social movements and leadership groups had emerged to take control of the government in 1974–75, countervailing moderate social and political forces came to the fore to establish a new, popularly based democratic regime. In early 1976, civilian elites representing new center-left and center-right parties reached an accord on holding legislative elections in April, presidential elections in June, and on the ratification of a new constitution by referendum later in the year. In sum, the speed with which a competitive democracy emerged during 1976 was as great as the events a year earlier that brought Portugal to the brink of a revolution.

Nevertheless, it took a decade for the commitment to competitive elections to produce stable governance. From 1976 to 1986 Portugal's new semipresidential parliamentary system was symbolized by a consistently divided government. Separate responsibilities and unresolved questions of jurisdiction between president and prime minister led to constant competition between the two in determining major policy issues. In addition, continually shifting parliamentary alliances in the Assembly of the Republic led to fluctuation in party dominance, with various Socialist governments in power initially followed by a series of technocratic governments, and, after 1980, a succession of center-right governments. Beginning in 1986 with the election of Mário Soares, the first civilian as president in well over half a century, and then with the election of the first government with a clear-cut majority under the leadership of Aníbal Cavaco Silva of the Social Democratic Party (PSD) in 1987, party alignments solidified into what has become a dominant two-party system.

In the midst of all these changes, the armed forces underwent major alterations. The Armed Forces Movement's pact with the political parties in February 1976 was significant insofar as it gave the latter primacy in determining the formation of governments through competitive elections, and in greatly restricting the military's political role. In 1982 constitutional revisions abolished the MFA's top body, the Council of the Revolution where the military had representation and veto authority over acts of parliament, a situation that violated if not the letter then certainly the spirit of the Constitution. These amendments strengthened the powers of the parliament, the Assembly of the Republic, and the prime minister, weakened those of the president, and placed the military under civilian control. An important part of these adjustments was the passing of a new Defense Law that same year. The law, which was appended to the Constitution, spelled out the military's mission and the nature of civil-military relations under a democratic republic in detail. The five-year (1982–87) conflict between the president and the prime minister, centered on who would exercise direct jurisdiction over the armed forces, nonetheless attested to the Defense Law's remaining ambiguities. This was eventually resolved by recognizing that within the cabinet the prime minister and the defense minister would have primary responsibility for defense, with the understanding that the government would only nominate senior military officers to positions within the General Staff and as heads of the individual services after consultation and concurrence with the president.

A major achievement in Spain's democratic transition and consolidation was the prompt organization of an effective and powerful defense ministry. In Portugal, however, creating a new defense ministry and staffing it with government employees overseeing the military services was a lengthy process. The implementation of the 1982 Defense Law's stipulations was slow and the chiefs of staff of the armed services maintained considerable leverage.[41] From 1987 through 1992, the defense ministry remained a small office, centered around the minister of defense and the secretary of state for defense. Much more important was the bureaucratic staff of the General Staff of the Armed Forces, in which military officers handled most questions of military policy. Effective civilian oversight authority was established only around 1989 through the use of the defense ministry's budgetary authority. The practice of naming the defense minister also as deputy prime minister served to reinforce civilian control over the armed forces. Only in 1992, with the staffing and expansion of the defense ministry and with the government's willingness to give that ministry more effective oversight authority, did Portuguese civil-military relations come to resemble the Spanish pattern.

Due to these delays with the staffing and organization of the defense ministry, one can date the consolidation of Portugal's democratic regime to the year 1989, that is, fifteen years after the revolution. By this time effective civilian oversight authority was in place as demonstrated by the reductions in the armed forces' manpower, the reallocation of priorities favoring a larger navy and air force and a smaller army, and the implementation of effective budgetary controls through the defense ministry. Moreover, the last obstacles in the constitution to a full-fledged market economy had also been removed by deleting the articles making the nationalizations during the revolution irreversible and committing the nation to the goal of establishing a socialist republic. Nonetheless, Portuguese generals managed to maintain a higher political profile than their Spanish colleagues.

Spain and Portugal consolidated their democracies in 1982 and 1989, respectively.[42] To be sure, even after these dates, significant issues divided political elites and parts of the population, but the breakdown of democratic government supported by a coup or mass movement was no longer a realistic possibility. As we have seen, the two countries took very different routes to democracy. The Portuguese experience demonstrates that democratic transitions can survive radical pressures from below; the Spanish transition was a great deal more peaceful even if extremist elements—kidnappings and political killings rose steadily through 1979 and 1980, respectively—were far from absent.[43]

As in any other armed forces, Spanish and Portuguese officers continued to debate defense- and security-policy priorities as well as issues related to mission, modernization, and budget. Despite financial limitations and reductions in manpower, Spain and Portugal have developed extremely professional military establishments partly as a result of their participation in NATO. In placing effective civilian oversight mechanisms over the military they created budgetary and personnel controls through their defense ministries to ensure that they, rather than military officers in the General Staff, determined the final resolution of such questions. Even in Portugal, by the early 1990s sufficient advances had been made in expanding civilian control over defense and security policy to effectively match developments in Spain and elsewhere in Western Europe.

The question of the military's professional prestige in the context of Iberian democracies is particularly interesting because of the differences between the two states. Both countries came into their transitions with officer corps that enjoyed high occupational prestige. Primarily owing to their leadership in overthrowing the old regime and their willingness to relinquish their role in politics to civilian leaders once democracy was secure, the Portuguese military emerged with their prestige intact. The armed forces topped the list—the government came in second—in a 1988 poll asking respondents which institutions had the greatest prestige.[44] In Spain, however, the status of the military occupation had plummeted for three distinct reasons. First, the armed forces did not play a role in the pacts that produced a democratic settlement. Second, a major proportion of the officer corps continued to identify with the Franco regime. Finally, although the failed coup attempt of February 1981 was only supported by a small minority of Spanish officers, it nonetheless perpetuated the public image of the military as a conservative institution.

GREECE: THE COLONELS' RULE AND ITS AFTERMATH

The Greek military dictatorship, often compared with the praetorian regimes of Argentina, Brazil, and Chile, was actually very different in many respects and does not fit their type of bureaucratic authoritarianism. Most importantly, perhaps, Greek military rule was not spurred by a serious capitalist crisis or a threat to the prevailing economic system.[45] Military interference in politics was pretty much the norm in twentieth-century Greece.[46] After the 1946–49 civil war between nationalist government forces and communist insurgents, backed by the United States and the Soviet Bloc, respectively, the Greek military had grown in size and influence. Aside from a short centrist interlude in 1964–65, the country was governed by conservative forces through the years leading up to the military coup of April 21, 1967.

When considering the Greek authoritarian regime—as well as its Portuguese and Spanish counterparts—it ought to be acknowledged that in the Cold War climate the United States and its NATO allies were more concerned with the strategic balance than "pulling struggling Western allies to the democratic flock."[47] The Greek armed forces had enjoyed Washington's consistent support, were dominated by conservative officers, and had been virtually independent of civilian control. They justified the coup mainly by referring to "the communist threat" that, they later admitted, was of "negligible danger."[48] Actually, more likely reasons were the coup makers' recognition that the advance of international détente reduced the military's domestic political influence and their growing dissatisfaction with their pay and perquisites.[49] The coup was sparked by a conflict between Prime Minister George Papandreou and King Constantine II that resulted in the gradual emancipation of some officers from political and royal tutelage.[50] The army's takeover was unusual in Greek politics because the colonels who led it took power instead of appointing politicians to govern. Another anomaly was that at the time of the coup, right-wing political forces headed by Prime Minister Panagiotis Kanellopoulos controlled the government and they were unambiguously opposed to the military takeover. In fact, Kanellopoulos was held under house arrest throughout the junta's rule, and many of his associates were jailed and tortured. The junta's persecution of conservative democratic politicians and their banning of all political parties and trade unions ensured that it would receive little civilian support and that in the eyes of all political actors its rule would be illegitimate.[51] The ill-fated countercoup attempt by the king in December 1967 created important vacancies in the political system filled by the new regime's allies and ultimately sealed the fate of monarchy in Greece.

The postcoup Revolutionary Council of twelve colonels was soon replaced by the personalized dictatorship of George Papadopoulos. It is important to note that the junta was the regime of *army colonels*; it was by no means the rule of the entire armed forces. In particular, the air force and especially the navy were notable for their less than enthusiastic backing of the regime; indeed, they played only a minor role in the government. (In

May 1973 naval officers were implicated in an unsuccessful countercoup attempt.) In 1967–72 the junta retired some three thousand officers and thereby seriously undermined the armed forces' effectiveness and morale as their performance in the 1974 Cyprus crisis all too clearly demonstrated. The junta was more interested in promoting its supporters than in maintaining professional standards: at the end of its rule the Greek officer corps consisted of 54 percent majors and colonels and only 43 percent lieutenants and captains.[52]

When the colonels came to power, they had no clear policies, ideology, let alone consistent views on fundamental political, economic issues. The junta did not possess the necessary skills and vision to promote economic development and had trouble recruiting capable civilian professionals. The colonels' most important policies were the purging of "decadent" Western influences and debt relief to the peasants that created a modicum of societal support for their regime. Nonetheless, the junta's economic record was by no means disastrous: despite increasing debt and inflation, the momentum of Greece's economic growth that began in the 1950 was not reversed partly because it remained a "paradise for [domestic and foreign] capital."[53] Still, this fairly good economic performance did not lead to regime legitimation primarily because the colonels possessed an "inexhaustible capacity for alienating even those party leaders who might otherwise have been expected to show sympathy for at least some of their aims."[54] Military rule was rooted in clientelistic networks and kinship connections. The junta excelled in enriching its members in a variety of ways. Within two years of seizing power, defense spending rose drastically with corresponding decreases in education and health care budgets.[55]

In 1973 Papadopoulos sought a way out of Greece's domestic and diplomatic isolation but his clumsy attempts to civilianize the military regime resulted in his overthrow by Brigadier Dimitrios Ioannides. The latter wanted to save the "revolution" and saw Papadopoulos's attempts to transfer some political power to civilians as a betrayal. In July 1974 the Cypriot National Guard, staffed by ethnic Greeks, and Greek officers stationed on Cyprus overthrew President Archbishop Makarios who had long been a critic of the colonels' regime. The Turkish invasion of the island—to protect Cyprus's large Turkish minority, which had been subjected to acute discrimination under Makarios and, Ankara feared with good reason, worse was to come under a new regime—caught the colonels in Athens unprepared. They miscalculated—just like their colleagues in Argentina seven years later as we shall see in the next chapter—expecting the United States to avert any Turkish reaction that might result in a war with Greece. By this time the junta was imploding and instead of achieving the rallying-around-the-flag effect it had hoped for, the overthrow of Makarios precipitated a warlike situation with Turkey and growing domestic instability.[56]

The Cyprus fiasco—Turkey eventually seized 40 percent of Cyprus's territory—stigmatized the army and left it humiliated and discredited in the eyes of the public: it was a critical juncture in the life of the regime and it sealed its fate.[57] In late July 1974 some 250 officers of the powerful 3rd Army Corps in Salonika signed a declaration demanding the "immediate formation of a Council of National Salvation" to consist of military and political leaders including former Prime Minister Constantine Karamanlis who returned from exile and was sworn into office on July 24. Unlike in Portugal and Spain, where authoritarian rule lasted for two generations, the brevity of the Greek colonels' regime allowed for a relatively quick return to parliamentary politics. The military disaster in Cyprus also bolstered the leverage of the junta's opponents, including that of the moderate elements in the officer corps who were to have a major role in the new, democratic Greek armed forces.

The Karamanlis government declared the colonels' 1968 Constitution null and void and resuscitated the 1952 basic law, which was amended to designate civilian authorities responsible for appointing key military commanders. High-ranking officers associated with the junta were dismissed but the purge of the military did not probe too deeply—Roehrig called it "a cautious prosecution"—in order to avoid a deep schism in politics: only torturers were tried and punished.[58] The new civilian Defense Minister, Evangelos Averoff, promised to judge officers' future performance not their past service, thereby securing smooth relations between the government and the military. More than 80 percent of the professional soldiers remained in the armed forces, and some officers who were cashiered by the junta returned and assumed a major role in rebuilding the army.[59] Karamanlis's conservative New Democracy government took steps to reassure the military and increased budgetary appropriations for defense in view of what most political forces agreed was a tangible Turkish threat to Greek security. In 1981 the military's apprehension regarding the defense policies of the newly elected Andreas Papandreou and his socialist party turned out to be misplaced. The new prime minister's nationalist rhetoric and the extension of U.S. base rights in Greece paved the way for smooth civil-military relations.[60]

When the military regime ended, right-wing army officers made a few isolated attempts at political intervention that badly backfired. The most important, in February 1975, the fourth after the colonels' fall, was a conspiracy by thirty-seven officers loyal to Ioannides who planned to restore the dictatorship. They were called *kadafiki* owing to the resemblance of their extremist views to those of Libya's Colonel Muammar Gaddafi.[61] Though some minor plots did take place in late 1970s and early 1980s, as one would expect and Huntington predicts, in countries where the armed forces had been embarrassed by defeat or politicized by personal dictators, the purge following hardliners' arrests marked the end of the transition period.[62]

Civilian control over the armed forces was swiftly established in post-junta Greece. New legislation (Act 660) nullified the colonels' legal measures and established a Supreme Council of National Defense—comprised of the prime minister, the minister of defense, the chief of the general staff, and the heads of the three branch services—with responsibility for defense and security issues.[63] According to the 1985 constitutional amendments the president of the Republic is the supreme commander of the armed forces but his powers are mostly symbolic as weighty decisions are made by the prime minister and his cabinet. The Government Council on Foreign Affairs and Defense prepares national security policy and appoints the chief of the Hellenic National Defense General Staff and the service chiefs of staff.[64] The Ministry of National Defense, in turn, prepares the annual defense budget in close consultation with the uniformed leadership. A 1995 law further centralized the authority of the defense ministry and its head vis-à-vis the chief of staff and the service chiefs and generally enhanced civilian control over the armed forces. This legislation also created positions for civilian experts to advise the minister of defense on military-strategic issues.

The legislature's weak role is the most important flaw in Greek civil-military relations. Parliamentary oversight of the armed forces is very limited partly because of the traditionally strong position of the executive branch in Greek politics and also because national defense may be the only major issue on which there has been a consensus between the opposition and the ruling parties. The conviction of political elites that Turkey has posed a constant threat to Greece resulted in an atmosphere in which disagreement on defense issues would be divisive and viewed by voters as "unpatriotic."[65] Thus, the legislature's Committee on Foreign Affairs and Defense has lacked any real authority, and other than holding mostly pro forma hearings and organizing briefings, its role has been largely symbolic.

During the 1970s and 1980s ruling political parties often interfered with promotion processes attempting to ensure the advancement of their favored officers, but by the 1990s this practice had abated. The political involvement of Greek military officers had gone from one extreme to another in a complete reversal of the past. The officer corps has been effectively depoliticized, and military personnel do their best not to be identified with any political position.[66] Active-duty soldiers cannot run for political office and they seldom do even after retirement; for instance, usually there is no former officer among parliamentary deputies. Military officers, even high-ranking ones, have become quite possibly too timid in expressing their views on professional matters allowing the intrusion of often unqualified politicians into these matters.[67] Civilian experts—working in the media, at universities, and at a growing number of think tanks and NGOs—have tried to fill this vacuum though their influence on policy, as in Iberia, has been underwhelming. In Portugal and Greece the role of civilian defense experts still needs to expand in order for society to benefit more fully from their input; Spain has been somewhat more successful in this regard.

The Greek military's reputation had plummeted after the fall of the junta and thus paralleled the Spanish experience. Officers, who had traditionally constituted an influential segment of Greek society, often deny their occupation and prefer not to wear their uniform in public. The government, in the meantime, not only attempted to modernize the defense establishment—an effort that included significant weapons procurements—but also tried to shore up military's esprit de corps and to shape a new social identity for the armed forces. The goal has been to encourage military professionals to think of themselves not as separate from but as an organic part of Greek society. The reform of the military education system targeted the closer integration of armed forces personnel into civilian society and included measures such as the standardization of entrance examinations to military and civilian colleges and the modernization of the military academies' curricula of military colleges.

Greece remains one of the few European democracies with mandatory military service that is rationalized by the ostensibly perennial Turkish security threat and Turkey's own compulsory conscription. A serious problem remaining in the Greek draft system is that while the option of alternative service is offered to conscientious objectors, at a duration of three and a half years it is punishingly long compared to the nine-month-long regular service, an issue that Athens has received some international criticism for. At the same time, steps were taken to protect the individual rights of soldiers and officers, "loyalty tests" were abolished, and the remuneration of all public servants (including armed forces personnel) was regulated according to the same principles. In short, this postjunta government has made a largely successful effort—at least partly explained by long-standing Greco-Turkish tensions—to rehabilitate the officer corps and democratize the military establishment.

THE EXTERNAL DIMENSION: THE IMPACT OF
NATO AND THE EEC

One of the important similarities among the three cases we studied in this chapter is that all three authoritarian regimes and their transitions to democracy were strongly influenced by external actors. Foremost among these foreign powers were the United States and two international organizations, NATO and the European Economic Community (EEC). The Cold War had a decisive impact on the three states' defense policies and, to a large extent, on their domestic politics.

In the 1940s and 1950s the United States—desperate to forestall the expansion of Soviet power in Southeastern Europe, and lacking allies with resources to spare—was a key influence in Greek politics. Washington generously supported the Greek military during the civil war and continued to strongly influence them throughout the 1950s and 1960s.[69] Under the U.S. Military Assistance Program between 1950 and 1969, 11,229 Greek military personnel received training in the United States.[70] Both the United States and NATO wanted to prevent a showdown between Greece and Turkey over the Cyprus issue in 1974, just as they had, successfully, in 1963. The two countries, members of the Atlantic Alliance since 1952, were of critical strategic importance in securing NATO's southern flank. In 1974, however, as Turkish generals well realized, conditions were different, given the shaking foundations of and little international sympathy for their colleagues' regime in Athens. After regaining the prime ministership, Constantine Karamanlis withdrew Greece from NATO's military structure, arguing that an alliance that could not prevent its members from waging war against one another was of little value to his country. (Greece rejoined in 1980.)

NATO officials did not publicly criticize the colonels' regime, though other international organizations—particularly the Council of Europe and the EEC—often did. This is important particularly because Greece had signed an association agreement with the EEC in 1961 and aspired toward full membership. This was unlikely to happen while the colonels ruled the country given the EEC's strict "democracies only" criterion. In essence, the prospect of EEC membership was a safety valve for the irreversibility of democratic practices. Karamanlis's government understood that there was a direct causal relationship between democratization and EEC membership. Thus, the subordination of the armed forces to civilian authorities was an essential task that had to be completed before Athens could join the EEC, an ambition realized in 1981.

For many reason, Portugal has traditionally been more outward looking and more comfortable in dealing with foreigners than its neighbor to the east. Portuguese society has been much more homogeneous than Spanish society, which still faces unresolved regional problems. (In fact, as recently as in 2006 a Spanish general, José Mena Aguado, was arrested for publicly suggesting that Catalan demands for authority raised serious concerns within the military regarding the unity of Spain.[71]) During the Cold War and afterward, Lisbon's relations with Washington were never as tense as Madrid's often became.[72] Aside from European democracies—particularly Germany and Norway—the United States, NATO, international financial institutions, such as the World Bank and the IMF, and a variety of foundations actively assisted the Portuguese transition to democracy. Anxious to prevent the pro-Moscow Portuguese Communist Party from radicalizing the political scene of an important strategic ally, the United States and its NATO allies developed a counterstrategy that supported noncommunist political forces and aimed to get the military officers out of politics and into more professional pursuits. The West possessed the institutional frameworks to channel Portugal's development and the capacity to offer Portuguese officers and political elites incentives—such as modern training and equipment and membership in the EEC, the club of prosperous and democratic Europe—to effectively counter Soviet entreaties to Lisbon. In fact, the Portuguese case was the first in which the West used these agents (international organizations and NGOs), strategies, and instruments to promote democratization.[73]

One of the main sources of the Spanish officers' professionalization beginning in the 1960s was their intensifying contacts with military counterparts, particularly U.S. armed forces personnel, engaged in Europe's defense.[74] In this respect, it is hard to overestimate the significance of the 1953 Bases Agreement with the United States. While Spain was excluded from the Atlantic Alliance, contact with U.S. military officers based in Spain gave younger officers the opportunity to compare their own position with that of others abroad. American air force and naval bases on Spanish territory also provided a vehicle through which Spain could be integrated indirectly into European defense, and its officers gained exposure to new concepts in military education, tactics, and strategy through military contact programs, base visits, and interaction with other officers.

After the consolidation of democracy, Spain joined NATO though with less than overwhelming popular support. As with many of their East-Central European counterparts a decade later, Spaniards were often more interested in the material benefits of EEC membership than in what they, especially those voting for the Socialist party, saw as the responsibilities attached to NATO membership. In 1982 Spain joined the Alliance but later that year, the newly elected socialist government withdrew from NATO's integrated military command. The socialists, eager to negotiate a public po-

sition in which major adjustments could be made in Spain's NATO commitment without abandoning its integration into the Western alliance system,
reversed their preelection position. In the end, Felipe González succeeded
in obtaining majority support in the March 1986 national referendum on
NATO in favor of continued participation.[75] (In the same year, both Spain
and Portugal became full members of the EEC.)

CONCLUSION

What patterns emerge, what generalizations can we make based on the three
southern European states' experiences following military rule? First of all,
after military rule the main political task of democratizers everywhere is to
get the armed forces out of politics and reduce the officer corps' autonomy,
privileges, and size. Second, as in virtually all postpraetorian settings, the
most important factor influencing politics and, more precisely, the difficulty
of removing the military from political affairs, is the amount of leverage the
military enjoys after leaving power. In this chapter we encountered three
elites with different degrees of such residual influence. The most atypical
was the situation in Portugal. There the usual task of getting the military out
of politics was complicated because army officers *were* the democratizers by
virtue of overthrowing the authoritarian regime. Therefore, at least until the
period of democratic consolidation, the Portuguese top brass possessed an
influential political position. The Spanish officer corps fell somewhere between the two other cases. The majority of military elites made a relatively
quick and clean break with the authoritarian regime that limited the damage
to the armed forces as an institution. Spain's transition was extraordinary
in the way civilian officials succeeded in asserting their prerogatives over
Spanish defense-security affairs and in establishing their supremacy over the
military realm.[76] More generally, Spain's democratic consolidation has been
often held up as a model for democracy promoters elsewhere, and Spanish
democracy activists were sought out for their advice by colleagues in Eastern Europe and Latin America in the 1980s and 1990s. Greek officers, like
other praetorian leaders whose rule ends with defeat in war, had very little
leverage as they left the political arena. Unlike the two long-enduring and
relatively civilianized authoritarian regimes in Iberia, the Greek colonels established a heavily militarized regime. They attempted to set some conditions as the price for their departure from politics but owing to internal
disunity, low prestige, poor overall performance, and their defeat in Cyprus,
they were in no position to succeed.[77]

Third, the prosecution of culpable military officers and purges of personnel that are ordinarily a common policy of postmilitary rule regimes were quite limited in the Southern Europe of the 1970s. Why? In Spain and Portugal there were hardly any prosecutions in the first decade after the fall of the regimes partly because the Franco and Salazar regimes had lasted so long that many of those suspected of crimes and abuses were no longer around and the guilt of individual military officers was difficult to establish. Moreover, the officer corps in both countries, with the obvious exception of those attempting to mount coups d'état and were duly punished, acquiesced to systemic political changes or actually promoted them.[78] In Greece the handful of generals and colonels at the apex of the regime were prosecuted and sentenced but fears of a Turkish attack and the desire for political stability prevented an extensive purge of the armed forces. As a result, some of those directly responsible for torturing thousands of regime opponents generally suffered little more than dismissal from the armed forces. This aspect of postauthoritarian regimes has attracted more attention in Latin America where, as we shall see in the next chapter, people who managed to dodge prosecution in the short-term were often held accountable decades later.

Fourth, international organizations, particularly NATO and the EEC, played an important and positive role in the democratic transition of all three polities as well as, more particularly, in the democratization of their civil-military relations. The chief reason is that in many ways Europe was at the center of the Cold War, during which international organizations could be powerful political actors. Such organizations had far less impact on the political transitions of the Asian and Latin American countries that we will learn about in the next couple of chapters.

Finally, the contention that democracy cannot be consolidated without the commitment of military elites to democratic rule is supported by all three cases in these chapters. In Spain it took several years until the bulk of the officer corps actively threw its support behind the new government in part because those who served for decades Franco's state and were its beneficiaries could not be easily converted; indeed, many of them left the military within the framework of the army's size reduction. In Portugal, given the military's political role in the regime change, this process took even longer and, as noted, was not fully completed until 1992. Finally, attaining the support of the Greek officer corps for democratic governance was easier—even if one allows for the minor incidents that were, importantly, backed by only a small fraction of military elites—because of the brevity and failure of the colonels' rule and because only a minority of officers benefited from it.

TABLE 4.1

After Military Rule in Europe: Spain, Portugal, and Greece

	Country *Period*	*Spain* *1975–1985*	*Portugal* *1975–1992*	*Greece* *1974–1990*
Background	end of military regime	death of leader, no military defeat	drawn out colonial war; military coup against the old regime	military defeat
	overall military regime performance	fair	fair to poor	poor
	leverage of military when leaving power	medium	initially high (military at first led democratization)	low
State	main tasks	get the military out of politics, the economy, and internal security; reduce its autonomy, privileges, and size; create new institutional frameworks for democratic civil-military relations	get the military out of politics, the economy, and internal security; reduce its autonomy, privileges, and size; create new institutional frameworks for democratic civil-military relations	get the military out of politics, the economy, and internal security; reduce its autonomy, privileges, and size; create new institutional frameworks for democratic civil-military relations
	civilian political leadership	careful sequencing of reforms, consultation with influential elements in the officer corps, relatively quick, successful process	lengthy process with some institutional ambiguities remaining	brief military regime allows quick return to parliamentary democracy
	political institutions and trend	strong and maturing	political stability did not emerge until 1987 when two-party system solidified	institutions in place—measures implemented by military rule quickly erased

TABLE 4.1 *(continued)*

After Military Rule in Europe: Spain, Portugal, and Greece

		Spain	*Portugal*	*Greece*
	Country *Period*	*1975–1985*	*1975–1992*	*1974–1990*
	civilian involvement in defense affairs	strong, decisive, but "considerate"	initially hesitant because of institutional turf questions	strong, decisive, highly invasive
	executive control	strong (especially MoD)	divided between prime minister and president; prime minister's power increases after 1982; MoD weak until 1989 when its fiscal authority established	good balance between prime ministers and president
	legislative oversight	strong	increasing after 1982 constitutional amendments	weak
	purge of the military	no (10-year force reduction plan)	no	yes (very limited)
	foreign influence	USA/NATO/EEC, positive influence on professionalization and democratization	USA/NATO/EEC, positive influence on professionalization and democratization	USA/NATO/EEC, positive influence on professionalization and democratization
Military	behavior during transition	peaceful, cooperative	split between military factions, contentious, assertive	mostly peaceful and subdued
	interference in politics	minimal other than 1981 coup attempt	strong voice in defense policy through 1980s	several inept coup attempts in late 1970s and 1980s
	domestic function	none (other than disaster relief)	none (other than disaster relief)	none (other than disaster relief)

TABLE 4.1 *(continued)*

After Military Rule in Europe: Spain, Portugal, and Greece

	Country	Spain	Portugal	Greece
	Period	*1975–1985*	*1975–1992*	*1974–1990*
	advisory function	advice offered when requested	advice offered when requested	military marginalized
	institutional attributes	enduring cultural differences between branch services	MFA's top body abolished in 1982, General Staff remains influential in defense debates	army's "first among equal" status broken, many military families
	effectiveness	no evidence (adequate performance in international PKOs)	no evidence (adequate performance in international PKOs)	no evidence (adequate performance in international PKOs)
	commitment to democracy	yes	yes	yes
Society	independent civilian experts	yes, some influence	yes, little influence	yes, little influence
	military's prestige	low	remains high	low
	soldiers in society	medium level of integration	medium level of integration	"organic part of society"
	conscription	no	no	yes
Political system at the end of the period		consolidated parliamentary democracy	consolidated parliamentary democracy	consolidated parliamentary democracy

CHAPTER 5

After Military Rule in Latin America:
Argentina, Chile, and Guatemala

⊣≣ ≣⊢

Walking the streets of Santiago and Buenos Aires, it is hard not to notice that an inordinately large share of public statues and monuments depict generals and admirals in their heavily ornamented uniforms, often on horseback. This is all the more curious because most generals there distinguished themselves not protecting their domain from foreign enemies or conquering faraway lands but fighting indigenous peoples, suppressing domestic "undesirables," and governing their countries. Praetorian politics has a long tradition in Latin America, and, unlike in many other contexts, military rule often did not go hand in hand with low levels of socioeconomic development. In fact, Argentina and Chile are two of the continent's most advanced societies. Nonetheless, both had experienced military rule in the twentieth century, albeit Argentina far more frequently (1930–32, 1943–45, 1955–58, 1966–73, 1976–83) than Chile (1924–32 and 1973–89).

In this chapter I describe, compare, and explain the politics following the two countries' last bout with authoritarianism. In spite of some important similarities between Argentina and Chile, military rule and the subsequent democratization process have been dissimilar. The main argument of this chapter is that the disparate performance of the Argentine and Chilean praetorian elites yielded for them different bargains with the opposition; consequently, the starting points for the two transition processes were also quite different. In the end, these different deals combined with the radically dissimilar policies followed in the two states led to vastly different outcomes, that is, profound disparities between military politics in contemporary Chile and Argentina. Second, I contend that in Chile democratizers have succeeded in gradually reducing the military's political autonomy to a level acceptable by democratic standards. Their Argentine colleagues, on the other hand, have gone too far in what has amounted to a virtual vendetta against the military as an institution and, in the process, seriously impaired its ability to protect and project Argentine national interests. This chapter's secondary case is Guatemala, a Central American state ruled for most of the Cold War by unusually brutal military dictators. The Guatemalan army soundly defeated an internal insurgency and was not compelled to make too many concessions once leaving power. After a protracted but incomplete democratization process, the armed forces there remain a key political institution, thus the Guatemalan example provides a different dimension on postpraetorian politics in Latin America.

I introduce this chapter by briefly outlining the precoup situation and then pointing out the differences between the types of military rule and the circumstances surrounding the generals' departure from Argentine and Chilean politics. I continue with an analysis of the military policies of Argentine and Chilean presidents with particular attention to the most controversial issue, the approach to past human rights abuses. In the rest of the chapter, I address a range of issues from rebellions against the state to defense budgets and how they have affected the position of the two armies in contemporary Argentine and Chilean society. In the final section I will explore how postmilitary rule in Guatemala differs from that in the two South American countries. The chronological span of this chapter begins with the transition to democracy and concludes in 2010, a year that marked the end of Michelle Bachelet's presidency in Chile and the demise of Néstor Kirchner in Argentina.

MILITARY RULE

Background

Historically, Latin American armies have been far more active in governing, repressing domestic groups, maintaining public order, and acting as a political power broker than in defending the national territory. In the nineteenth century the armies of Chile and Argentina played an important role in consolidating the state. They conducted expeditions to suppress and bring under control native peoples that allowed the incorporation of southern regions into the realm.[1] In Argentina—where the army fought in a number of early civil wars that, in the end, permitted the creation of a strong federal state—the military has been involved in politics since the origins of the country.[2] Chile's army supported the central government against feudal landowners and warlords thereby consolidating the state. South American states hosted foreign—Spanish, French, German—military missions by the early 1900s to build and train their armed forces. Many Argentine and Chilean officers were trained by Prussian military advisers, who may have imparted professional skills but not a democratic orientation. In fact, Chileans still like to say, "We have a British navy, an American air force, and a Prussian army."[3] In the early part of the twentieth century, the military in several more developed Latin American states—including Argentina, Brazil, and Chile—was an institution supportive of modernization and middle-class reform. During the 1940s the Bolivian, Guatemalan, and Honduran armies also adopted this mission. But, by the 1950s most of the region's armies had become more conservative as social mobilization gradually brought the lower classes, often with radical views, into politics.

Argentina's first coup, supported by middle-class groups, occurred in 1930 when General José F. Uriburu attempted to establish a praetorian regime in some ways akin to Benito Mussolini's fascist state. Following Uriburu's brief reign, the military was in and out of power—with truly civilian governments seldom enjoying more than a few consecutive years in office—until 1983. The army's political involvement was partially motivated by their aversion to Peronist influences in politics. Juan Perón, a former army colonel who took an important role in the 1943 coup and subsequently served as minister of labor, was thrice elected president (1946, 1952, and 1973) and became immensely popular among the lower classes. The armed forces detested Perón's left-wing populist policies and, backed by opposition parties and the Roman Catholic Church, toppled his regime in 1955. Following an eighteen-year exile, Perón returned to Buenos Aires and to power in 1973 only to be felled by heart attacks nine months later. His successor, his extraordinarily incompetent wife, Isabel, was unseated by the military three years later.

Owing to its professional stance and, especially, its commitment to the constitution, the Chilean military's political involvement has been less extensive. Following several months of political paralysis, in September 1924 officers staged a coup but stayed in power for merely six months. Generals again ventured into politics in 1927–32, first under the quasi-fascist rule of Carlos Ibáñez del Campo and then under military juntas, some of which were quite progressive.[4] The lesson Chilean officers learned from these experiences was that their institutional interests and professional capabilities were undermined by direct governance. In the four decades that followed, the army—socially marginalized and considered useless by progressive social groups—maintained its adherence to the constitution, received most of its personnel from military families, and developed an uncompromisingly anti-Marxist worldview. In contrast to Argentina and Uruguay, Chile's right-wing parties were historically quite successful, which partly explained the armed forces' absence from politics.

In both countries, as in much of Latin America, the military is considered a traditional, conservative, national institution. Unlike in some Latin American armies—the Peruvian, for instance, where a strong left-wing current was present in the officer corps during the Cold War—the Argentine and Chilean armed forces had maintained a conservative and virulently anticommunist stance.

Before the Coups d'État

Military takeovers in Argentina (1976) and Chile (1973) were quite different, but the political and socioeconomic turmoil that preceded them was similar. Although the increasingly radical policies of Salvador Allende's socialist government had generated opposition from a broad spectrum of societal groups from the beginning of his tenure in 1970, by 1973 socioeconomic conditions had become chaotic and support for a military takeover was mounting. In fact, a popular push for the coup began soon after Allende's inauguration. By 1971 people were throwing corn in front of parading military units to suggest that they were "chicken," that is, that the military would not interfere in politics even as the country was being devastated by the Allende regime's policies.[5] In time, calls for a military takeover came from many quarters, from Supreme Court justices to segments of the labor movement.[6] One year after the coup, the former reformist president, Eduardo Frei Montalva (1964–70), remarked that

> Allende had no scruples about destroying the country to install a Leninist program and annihilate the opposition. . . . The military has saved Chile. . . . The military was called on by the nation and complied with its legal duty, since the legislature and judiciary, the congress, and the supreme court had publicly denounced that Allende's presidency and his regime did not respect the Constitution nor the laws of the legislature. . . . Allende came to install communism through violence, not democratically. . . . [W]hen a people has been so weakened and harassed (*acosado*) that it cannot rebel . . . then the Army substitutes and does the work.[7]

The Chilean military takeover may be viewed as both a rollback coup—insofar as it aimed to reverse the political and socioeconomic policies of the reviled Allende regime—and a foundational coup to the extent that the new regime was quite different from the pre-Allende polity and espoused rather different long-term goals.

While armed resistance to the emerging military rule in Chile was insignificant, in Argentina violent opposition to the rule of Isabel Perón's rule—three years of social upheaval and economic crisis—and later to the military dictatorship was considerable. By early 1976 Argentina was in complete disorder with Peronist (the *Movimiento Peronista Montonero* or briefly, the

Montoneros) and Marxist (*Ejército Revolutionario del Pueblo*, ERP) guerilla groups fighting against the armed forces and paramilitary organizations. Societal support for the coup was, if anything, more extensive in Argentina than in Chile. The generals took power in March 1976, supported
by a multitude of social and political forces that even included the Communist Party of Argentina, when Isabel Perón conceded the presidency to
military forces led by General Jorge Videla.

Two Kinds of Military Rule

Chilean praetorianism was a thoroughly institutionalized regime at the center of which stood General Augusto Pinochet. Even though he was a last-
minute addition to the coup-plotters, he soon emerged as the undisputed
leader of the military government.[8] In 1974 he had himself designated as
president and remained in full control until 1989. He recognized the importance of retaining his command of the armed forces and did so until 1998,
long after he left the presidency. Pinochet had amassed enormous political authority relative to his peers elsewhere in the region primarily because
the junta insisted on one man holding the top executive position for the
duration of the regime—an arrangement very different from military rule
in Brazil, for instance, where fixed terms were envisioned for military presidents. Nonetheless, the highly institutionalized nature of Chilean military
rule imposed clear limits on Pinochet's power. A crucial internal regulation
required that all decisions by the four-member military junta (the legislative
authority) be reached by consensus. In fact, the junta successfully opposed
Pinochet on a number of key issues demonstrating that while he was certainly very powerful, he was hardly the omnipotent, patrimonial ruler some
scholars have portrayed him as being.[9] In other words, this was a military
regime not a personalized or patrimonial one.[10]

The junta abolished all political parties but permitted their return in the
mid-1980s. Eschewing the populist mobilization route of their colleagues
in Brazil and Paraguay, Chilean generals believed that a successful structural transformation of the economy would create, over time, solid and durable support for the regime. The junta's pragmatist orientation allowed
close interaction with policy-makers and business groups and resulted in
growth-friendly policies.[11] Between 1976 and 1980, and 1984 and 1989,
the economy was characterized by high growth, low inflation, virtually balanced budgets, and high rates of investment.[12] Active-duty officers served
in many areas of administration—though readily replaced by technocrats if
necessary—but for seldom longer than two or three years, after which they
returned to their units; only a tiny minority held political appointments for

longer periods. Unlike in Argentina, corruption had been historically low in Chile, and the junta maintained an overwhelmingly clean state. The financial improprieties of Pinochet and his family were revealed only after the military left government. Even opponents of the regime, like Edgardo Boeninger, Minister Secretary-General of the Presidency in the first democratic government after military rule, concede that the junta's economic legacy was "extremely positive."[13] In fact, civilian governments have retained the fundamental Pinochetista economic program and its principles ever since.[14]

Things could not have been more different in Argentina where in a few years the military government managed to alienate practically every segment of society. The polity ruled by Argentine generals was poorly institutionalized with authority dispersed between the five corps commanders in five regions of the country. The Argentine junta started the "process of national reorganization" (the *Proceso*) by closing the national and provincial legislatures, removing all elected officials, banning political parties, placing labor and some business organizations under military control, and enacting a number of other measures designed to expand the armed forces' authority over politics and society.[15] The junta's mismanagement of the economy led to increasing foreign debt and deteriorating external financial conditions. At the same time, restrictions on reducing military budgets and privatizing military-controlled state enterprises added to the economy's problems.

The Argentine generals' foreign policy record was also extraordinarily poor. A long-standing dispute between Argentina and Chile, regarding their territorial and maritime boundaries, was decided by an international Court of Arbitration in favor of Chile in 1977. In the following year Argentina repudiated the arbitration decision and, in late December, initiated military action against Chile. Only the swift intervention of the U.S. government and the mediation of the Vatican averted war just hours before a full-fledged naval battle was about to take place in the South Atlantic.[16] Although the war was avoided, the arbitration decision and the generals' impetuous behavior signaled a major defeat for the junta and Argentina's detachment from the international community.

In 1982 the generals provoked an ill-advised war with Great Britain that, in the end, lay bare their grave professional deficiencies. Like many wars, the Falklands/Malvinas War was initially popular and publicly supported even by many opposition figures like the later president Néstor Kirchner. And yet, it has become a textbook case of how *not* to fight a war owing to the Argentine generals' many avoidable mistakes in planning and execution as well as the inadequate coordination between the armed services. (While the army and the air force performed poorly, the navy executed its missions much more successfully.) Instances of direct insubordination and disregard for the chain of command exposed the top brass's inability to effectively control their forces. Their defeat surprised and embarrassed the generals because they were confident they had achieved an adequate level of force modernization and because of their assumption that their success in fighting leftist insurgents would translate into victory in a conventional war.[17] In short, few military regimes have been less successful than the Argentine one.

Perhaps the most important legacy of the two praetorian states consists of their extensive violations of human rights. The Chilean regime's campaign against its domestic enemies was less reliant on the judiciary, more radical, and far more repressive than the generals' rule in Brazil (1964–85) but more moderate than that of the Argentine junta. In the latter, the judicial system was basically ignored by the regime's repressive machinery except to serve as a cover for state terror.[18] The agencies of the military tortured and killed thousands of leftists and other opponents of the regime. The death toll in Chile is estimated at 3,000, while in Argentina estimates range anywhere from 11,372 to 30,000.[19] Argentine praetorianism was not only more repressive than Chilean but also far more diverse in its methods. The Argentine army—the army was much more responsible for human rights violations than the considerably smaller navy and air force in both countries[20]—hunted down, tortured, and killed thousands of leftist activists, guerillas, and other opponents of its regime. But soldiers also forced victims to sign over their property, looted what they could, and transferred what they did not need to the police. More than five hundred children were abducted from their "politically unreliable" families and placed with regime supporters—only 100 or so were subsequently reintegrated. Both in Chile and in Argentina the terror campaigns were quick and hard; the vast majority of state violence against the population occurred at the beginning of military rule.[21]

Foreign governments and NGOs relentlessly criticized the two states' brutal suppression of their political adversaries. Argentine generals, hopeful that a positive opinion would diminish their growing international isolation, actually invited the Inter-American Commission on Human Rights (IACHR) of the Organization of American States in 1979. Nevertheless, the resultant IACHR report sharply criticized their human rights record.[22] This sort of censure, and the fear of having to face Nuremberg-style trials, may have added to the military elites' resolve to stay in power.

Different Exits, Different Deals

The dissimilar political and socioeconomic legacies of the Argentine and Chilean regimes produced different transitions to democracy. Military regimes like Chile (and Brazil) that compile relatively successful socioeconomic records and retain a significant degree of societal support are able to *control* the transfer of power and convert their strength into political leverage in the transition and consolidation. Under these conditions democratizers possess what Harold Trinkunas called "narrow opportunity structures" and are compelled to appease generals, who, in turn, tend to carefully prepare their abdication of power and to preside over united and highly cohesive military establishments.[23] Moreover, democratic transitions following relatively successful praetorian regimes tend to be gradual and prolonged.

Ineffective praetorian rulers—like those in Argentina or, as described in the previous chapter, Greece—are in a weak bargaining position. They are usually afflicted with a fragmented military establishment and enjoy insufficient leverage to preserve a broad array of their privileges, even in the short run. In these situations democratizers have more opportunities to craft lasting civilian control and to transform civil-military relations more comprehensively. Put differently, their relative success enabled Chilean generals to *hand over* power to civilians on their own terms. Their Argentine colleagues did not have this luxury. Regardless of these differences, perhaps the most prominent trait of political transition in Latin America from dictatorship to democracy, was the overwhelmingly peaceful manner in which the armed forces—gradually in some cases, more rapidly in others—left politics and accepted the establishment of civilian supremacy.

Argentina

After the June 1982 surrender, the army leadership pressured President General Leopoldo Galtieri, who started the Falklands/Malvinas War, to resign. Within weeks, General Reynaldo Bignone became president and reluctantly allowed a gradual political opening. The armed forces hoped to negotiate the terms of democratization but the reemerging political parties refused to openly bargain with an unpopular regime that, in any event, was falling apart. Although the military government set fifteen conditions—including the "non-revisability" of the "dirty war against subversion" and of deeds of corruption, and preserving the continuity of the judicial system—the political parties dismissed them.[24] The transition to civilian rule was at first hampered by the culture of fear bred by the brutality of military rule, nonetheless, divisions within the armed forces and the opposition's response to the generals' calls for negotiation with mobilization sealed the regime's fate. In its waning days the military government issued decrees that amnestied itself for human rights violations. The generals also released, in April 1983, a "Final Document of Military Justice on the War against Subversion and Terrorism" in which they conceded "some regrettable excesses" and blamed Isabel Perón for giving them the freedom to crack down on leftist guerillas.

The particular type of military rule Argentine generals had maintained had several consequences. The fact that they were able to stay in power for eighteen months after Galtieri's resignation—so this was certainly not a "collapse" of praetorian rule as in Greece—meant that there would be no reformist policies during Bignone's interim government.[25] During this period the military's power had actually diminished owing to the deep cleavages between its various factions. The generals' last-ditch efforts to redeem themselves changed few civilian minds regarding the junta's record particularly as mass graves were being excavated and large popular demonstrations were calling for retroactive justice. National elections were held in October 1983 and won by Raúl Alfonsín of the Radical Civic Union (UCR) by a wide margin. His cabinet—that, unlike Patricio Aylwin's in Chile, represented a clean break with the past—quickly pronounced the army's face-saving decrees illegal.

Chile

What can successful military regimes obtain for their strong political leverage? The Chilean case offers an instructive example. In Chile consolidating democracy was difficult because from a legal-institutional standpoint the civilian government's elbow room was very limited: the military regime devised electoral systems that privileged the allies of the ancien régime and set requirements that impeded constitutional reform.[26] In the legislative domain, the long transition had begun in 1978 when the generals passed an amnesty law that proved to be a formidable obstacle to bringing those responsible to justice. The 1980 Constitution—approved at the height of the economic boom by 67 percent of the voters in a tightly controlled plebiscite (the opposition was not allowed to campaign, and proper electoral registration was lacking)—legalized the army's political involvement in areas that were reserved to the legislative and executive branches before the coup. The Constitution created nine non-elected senatorial seats to be designated by the junta at the eve of democratic restoration. This measure tilted the parliamentary power balance in favor of the right-wing opposition. In addition, former presidents were to become senators for life, which allowed Pinochet—whose larger-than-life personality loomed behind all these issues—to obtain a seat in the senate and with it, parliamentary immunity after his tenure as commander in chief expired in 1998. The new democratic regime had to respect the constitutional functions granted to the armed forces; could not replace service commanders; was to maintain the prestige of the military and protect it from political attacks; and had to refrain from meddling in defense policy, budgetary provisions, the armed forces' internal affairs; along with other restrictions.

The Constitution extended Pinochet's rule until 1989 but it also established a schedule for institutional changes. Most importantly, it arranged for a referendum on military rule to be held in 1988. The junta abided by this timetable and, to its genuine surprise, was defeated in the referendum as 56 percent of the voters said no to continued military rule. Although the generals kept their promises, their strong position allowed them to drive a hard bargain. They were not willing to compromise on issues such as the prosecution of past human rights abuses, the fate of General Pinochet, and the authoritarian enclaves in the legal and institutional framework that put Patricio Aylwin's incoming *Concertación*—a coalition of opposition parties—government (1990–94) at a severe disadvantage in case it wanted to establish democratic civil-military relations.[27]

In sum, Chilean democrats inherited a constitution and a large body of laws that explicitly intended to guarantee a tutelary role for the military in the country's political development.[28] Pinochet and his government were able to plan and control a slow transition that, in 1990—when Aylwin, a Christian Democrat, was sworn in as president—seemed to amount to "more a change of administrations than a change of systems."[29] Symbolism was important in Chile as the generals wanted everyone to know that they *voluntarily* transferred power to civilians. Nonetheless, it is important to recognize that turning over power was not voluntary for the military, as they were bound by their own constitution—which they had expected would allow Pinochet to stay in power. In the end, Pinochet was forced by other junta members to accept the results of the 1988 referendum, which he was intent on subverting, and this, too, shows he was less powerful than often assumed.[30]

DEMOCRATIZATION AND THE MILITARY

Since 1990 Chile has become a stable and prosperous democracy. Though democratic, Argentina has been more politically volatile and the victim of major fluctuations in its economy. Both countries have become consolidated democracies and have established democratic civil-military relations though in Chile, given the strong position enjoyed by the outgoing military elites, this process took considerably longer than in Argentina.

Presidents, the Military, and the Human Rights Issue

The Argentine and the Chilean polities are presidential systems where the executive enjoys considerably more authority than in the United States. One of the few restrictions on Argentine executive power is that the president cannot promote officers to the rank of general without the Senate's consent. Despite the broad military autonomy Chilean generals retained, civilian politicians did enjoy four prerogatives:[31] the president's veto power over the promotion of top officers; his/her right to approve military acquisitions and to refuse to sign the National Defense Plan; and some control over the defense budget (taking advantage of the fact that the military's 1989 law required its adjustment for inflation but not economic growth). All of Chile's postauthoritarian executives—whose term in office was changed from four to six years, after which a 2005 constitutional amendment restored it to four—have thus far completed their tenure; in Argentina this feat was accomplished only by Carlos Menem, Néstor Kirchner, and his wife, and Cristina Fernández de Kirchner (who was reelected for second term in 2011). Let us survey the most important military-related policies of the two countries' presidents before we proceed to look at more specific policy areas.

Argentina

RAÚL ALFONSÍN (1983–89)

The Alfonsín administration took advantage of the weak position of the armed forces and commenced a decades-long humiliation of the army as an institution by pushing through Latin America's most punishing antimilitary program. Alfonsín's key objective was to bring the armed forces under constitutionally sanctioned civilian control. Within a year of assuming office, he expelled all generals serving the dictatorship from the armed forces, drastically cut military spending, and reorganized the central defense structures.[32] Several paramilitary organizations theretofore under military control—coast guard, gendarmerie (police), federal police, airport and prison security units—were taken away from the armed forces and eventually transferred to the ministry of justice. New laws removed decision-making authority regarding national security affairs (including budget, arms production, defense policy) from the generals to the ministry of defense whose previously all-uniformed staff became dominated by civilians without the requisite knowledge of or professional experience in defense issues. Service commanders were downgraded to chiefs of staff with reduced powers. The military's prerogatives were also decreased in the legal field and in the sphere of intelligence, they were banished from politics, and their business interests were radically curtailed. The Alfonsín government established what Samuel Huntington called "subjective control" of the armed forces, as shown by the appointment of chiefs of staff Generals Héctor Ríos Ereñú and Dante Caridi that was based on ideological affinities rather than professional merit.[33]

The 1988 National Defense Law separated external defense from internal security for which police forces and border patrols now became primarily responsible. The law specified the military's mission solely as repelling foreign aggression, prohibited them even from preparing of plans for countering internal contingencies and from using military intelligence for domestic purposes, clarified the chain of command, and established joint commands. Equally important, the law denied the military a seat on the National Defense Council thereby allowing civilians to set defense priorities without any military interference. The National Defense Law—whose authors closely studied both the Spanish National Defense Law (1980) and the U.S. Goldwater-Nichols Act (1986)—was a vital contribution to cementing civilian supremacy over the armed forces.[34]

By bringing to trial the leaders of the Proceso, Alfonsín changed Argentine political culture and strengthened the foundations for democratic development. He assumed, incorrectly, as it turned out, that the sting had been taken out of the officer corps and that it would not resist. As the number of prosecuted officers increased, so did the size of military demonstrations. Facing growing opposition, the president backtracked and introduced a law halting legal action against officers if they were not indicted within sixty days. When this measure did not satisfy the army, Alfonsín went a step further by supporting a "due obedience law," which in essence said that officers under the rank of colonel could not be prosecuted because they acted following orders. Nevertheless, the proposed cut-off date (*punto final*) for the prosecutions evoked the anger both of the human rights community and, owing to the rush of new cases to court, that of the military as well. Most of the critics objected not to the law itself but to the inequitable and erratic ways in which it was implemented.

In the end, the Alfonsín government brought to justice all of the superior officers who ruled Argentina in 1976–82, while trying to (a) limit both the duration of the trials and the number of the accused; (b) differentiate between those who issued orders violating human rights and those who carried them out; and (c) reassure the armed forces that their legitimate role in the nation was not questioned.[35] In their violent campaigns against their opponents, Argentine military rulers circumvented the judiciary, which in turn allowed the post-transition regime to use the legal system in prosecuting the military. Alfonsín wanted to develop more judicial independence, though he could not weed out corruption in the legal system. He also insisted on a semblance of fairness and thus the prosecution of a few Montoneros who terrorized the population and were responsible for the deaths of 790 people in 1969–79.[36]

CARLOS MENEM (1989–99)

When Menem was elected he enjoyed a stronger position vis-à-vis the army than his predecessor but the situation was still far from stable. While Alfonsín's main objective was to reintroduce civilian rule into the vacuum created by the military dictatorship, Menem—himself a victim of the Proceso—was intent on reintegrating the armed forces into society and made several concessions to them. Most importantly, he stopped new prosecutions and—in October 1989 and again in December 1990—pardoned members of the junta and other military personnel incarcerated for human rights violations and those participating in anti-Alfonsín revolts. These measures satisfied most of the military and eased the expulsion of rebellious officers from the ranks.

At the same time, Menem undertook reforms that further decreased military autonomy. He eliminated obligatory conscription that generals long considered an indispensable cornerstone of the socialization of Argentine youths and implemented additional cuts in the military's budget, personnel, and business interests. In December 1990 disgruntled officers mutinied once again, but Menem's policy to promote more professional and less political officers made the quick suppression and harsh punishment of the rebels possible. Since then, there has been no overt military interference in politics. When in 2001 a court declared some of the laws passed under Alfonsín unconstitutional raising the possibility of new indictments of officers, the armed forces stridently criticized the decision but did not revolt.

Menem packed the Supreme Court with loyalists by increasing the number of justices from five to nine thereby reducing the chances of judicial opposition to his policies. It is a credit to his political instincts that the armed forces held him in high regard even though during his decade-long reign he did not raise military salaries. But Menem made numerous well-publicized visits to military bases, promoted peacekeeping activities as a worthwhile activity that all Argentines could be proud of, and maintained cordial relations with influential military officers.

FERNANDO DE LA RÚA (1999–2001)
AND EDUARDO DUHALDE (2002–2003)

Between the departure of Menem in December 1999 and the swearing in of Néstor Kirchner in May 2003, Argentina had five presidents, three of whom were in office for less than eight days. Fernando de la Rúa of the Radical Party, however, held the office for nearly two years that were mostly notable for cooperation between the state and the armed forces.

Still, the military gained little for its "good behavior" as its funds and capabilities continued to diminish to the point where its head, General Ricardo Brinzoni, declared that "If the budget of 2001 were maintained, in 2002 the organizational capacity of the Army will be truly minimal."[37] The promised restructuring of the defense sector did not materialize in part because de la Rúa's term was afflicted by an ongoing economic crisis, interminable squabbling between coalition parties and within the cabinet, and mass demonstrations and riots. Eduardo Duhalde's presidency had no major impact on civil-military relations. One noteworthy tension that had developed under de la Rúa and continued during Duhalde's term concerned the military's role in internal security. In 1994, while he was governor of the province of Buenos Aires, Duhalde actually declared that the armed forces needed to prepare to fight terrorism in response to extremist attacks on Jewish institutions in 1992 and 1994. Although the generals and some right-wing political forces supported this view, one of the keystones of the 1988 National Defense Law was the strict separation of external and internal security and the explicit prohibition of a military role in the latter.

Néstor Kirchner (2003–2007)
and Cristina Fernández de Kirchner (2007–)

The policies of the Peronist presidents Kirchner—Néstor (2003–2007) followed by his wife Cristina (2007–)—have further humiliated an army already devastated by low budgets, salaries, and social esteem. In public addresses to military audiences—such as at the Colegio Militar and Army Day ceremonies—the Kirchners incited tensions by provocative rhetoric, saying "I am not afraid of you!" and the like. Many of these speeches were delivered to cadets and junior officers born long after the end of the military dictatorship. In 2010, during Argentina's bicentennial celebrations, Cristina Fernández did not attend the military parade of five thousand troops in which delegations from numerous Latin American states participated, a gesture widely considered contemptuous of the Argentine armed forces twenty-seven years after the transition began.

The Kirchners—who were financial beneficiaries of the Proceso[38]—have acted as if they were pursuing a personal vendetta against the military, the *institution*, not individual culprits who in most cases have died or already been prosecuted. Upon entering office Néstor Kirchner drastically trimmed the upper echelons of military leadership, forcibly retiring forty-four officers. Kirchner, collaborating with the Congress and the courts, invalidated the "*punto final*" and "due obedience" in order to facilitate the renewed prosecution of military personnel. Ironically, quite a few of the judges and the congresspeople were the same individuals who passed these laws. A number of former officers who already completed prison sentences, alongside others who were not tried earlier, now found themselves on the prosecutors' lists once again.[39] The legality of these measures is seldom challenged because Argentine legal practices are fungible and there is a fair amount of executive interference in judicial affairs.[40] Those who committed human rights abuses on the political left are not only not prosecuted—even mentioning the subject is considered politically incorrect—but in many cases have received jobs in the administration: some cabinet members were Montoneros implicated in terrorist acts against the state in the 1970s and 1980s.

The obsessive focus on past human rights violations further divides the population and is used as a political smoke screen to divert attention from the electoral improprieties and widespread corruption of the Kirchners— Néstor died in 2010—and their administrations.[41] Nevertheless, aside from some radicalized ideological segments of the population, the majority of Argentines consider dealing with past human rights violations a legitimate issue that is fundamental to the construction of a new society. In the meantime, protests and riots have become a frequent occurrence that the government does not stand up to because, in part, what may be a normal law-enforcement issue elsewhere is a sensitive issue in Argentina given the legacy of the junta's brutal suppression of demonstrations and questions regarding the public's ability to handle a muscular police response.

The Kirchners have taken advantage of the military's institutional weakness and further damaged its prestige, conditions, effectiveness, and capabilities. The current state of Argentine military politics may be described as a toxic combination of politicians who care and know little about defense issues but are prejudiced against the armed forces that in turn have been debilitated by a quartercentury of state persecution and neglect. As one of the framers of the 1988 Defense Law, José Manuel Ugarte, told me in 2008, "the current government is confused about the military: they think that a vengeful human rights policy equals defense policy."[42]

Chile

PATRICIO AYLWIN (1990–94)

At first, Chile's democratic reformers were forced to trade off civilian control of the armed forces for short-term regime survival.[43] The ultimate goal of the Concertación governments was to destroy the foundations of the 1980 Constitution and erase the authoritarian political order.[44] The military was still popular and powerful, and all Aylwin and his government could do was try to consolidate and expand presidential and state power over the armed forces.

President Aylwin could not dismiss the chiefs of the armed forces or wish away the powerful National Security Council that was able to supervise government performance, given that its personnel makeup was predetermined by the military. While his elbow room was admittedly limited, there *were* a number of things he could do and he succeeded in doing them. Although those responsible for human rights violations were protected by law, in a stroke of political genius, Aylwin established the Commission on Truth and Reconciliation—the so-called Rettig Commission—to search for the truth, identify victims, and investigate accountability. The government's action amounted to moral reparation and monetary compensation, though the military, insisting that its 1973 intervention was a "patriotic mission," refused to apologize.

Aylwin also made a point of demonstrating his constitutional powers whenever possible and emphasizing the notion of civilian control over the armed forces. He used his authority to freeze the careers of officers involved in human rights violations even if he could not fire them. The government also refused to schedule regular meetings for the National Security Council—it was stacked with generals—and to consult with the top brass unless their professional expertise was required. At the same time, Aylwin was careful not to antagonize the military by meddling in its internal affairs, and abided by the laws that protected the army. Among the many accomplishments of his tenure, the settlement of over twenty pending border issues with Argentina stood out as it lifted remaining tensions with Chile's most important neighbor partner.

Critics of the Aylwin government have charged that it was excessively cautious about the junta's human rights violations. This is not a fair accusation. First, Aylwin's main goal was to begin a process of democratic consolidation that could only succeed if soldiers returned to their barracks and stayed there. This objective could only be realized if the military did not feel threatened. Second, the governing coalition had to be considered successful by the voters so it would be reelected, otherwise Pinochet and the junta might well have returned. For its economic and social programs to work, however, the government needed the cooperation of opposition parties that would have been withheld if confrontational issues—and the human rights issue was the most confrontational of them all—were pursued. Finally, the government simply did not have the votes in the legislature to abolish the remaining "authoritarian enclaves," such as the 1978 amnesty law.[45]

EDUARDO FREI (1994–2000)

The main policy thrusts of the Frei administration were infrastructural modernization, and health care and education reform, while the human rights issue received lesser emphasis. In contrast with his predecessor, Frei engaged the armed forces through defense policy issues intended to create a more cooperative relationship while strengthening the notion of civilian supremacy. Among the parliamentary parties, there were serious debates regarding the swearing-in of Pinochet as senator for life once his term as commander in chief ran out in 1998; in the end he was allowed to proceed. Frei's conciliatory gestures toward the armed forces included increasing their salaries and fostering good relations with military leaders, in particular with Pinochet's successor, General Ricardo Izurieta.

In 1998 Pinochet was detained in London by British authorities on various human rights charges brought by Spain, another European Union member state. The military expressed unqualified solidarity with Pinochet but supported the government's efforts—emphasizing diplomatic immunity and national sovereignty—to get the general released. Nonetheless, Pinochet's removal from Chilean politics was a major turning point: it fostered democratic consolidation, a steady improvement in civil-military relations, and, more specifically, the revisiting of human rights abuses during his regime. Frei intended to extract, as much as possible, the emotional quotient from this issue by insisting that it was a legal matter and pressuring the judges, some of whom were party to the repression, to prove their independence and impartiality.

RICARDO LAGOS (2000–2006)

Upon his return from London after a sixteen-month absence, Pinochet found a different Chile. The new president was a lifelong socialist—appointed by Allende in 1972 as Chile's ambassador to the Soviet Union (though Congress never confirmed him)—and one of the general's most fervent opponents. Lagos treated both past human rights abuses and Pinochet's immunity from prosecution as strictly legal issues and stressed the autonomy of the judiciary from the government, thereby indicating to both the political right and left that pressuring him was futile. In this spirit, he refused to bargain with military leaders who would have traded constitutional reforms for Pinochet's immunity. Although a Santiago court removed the general's immunity soon after his return, an appeals court found him mentally incompetent to stand trial in July 2001, and with this ruling, Pinochet's political role came to an end.

In 2000 the military members of the *Mesa de Diálogo*—a roundtable of politicians, civil society activists, and armed forces officers first convened by Frei to diffuse tensions and devise a solution to the human rights issue acceptable to all sides[46]—first conceded that abuses were committed under Pinochet's rule and promised to provide all the information they could pertaining to victims. They did so seven months later although some of their records—e.g., the location of victims' bodies—were inaccurate. In

2002 Lagos chose as his defense minister Michelle Bachelet, who previously served as minister of health and was the daughter of an air force general imprisoned and tortured by the Pinochet regime for his opposition to the 1973 coup. The appointment of Bachelet, the first female defense minister in Latin America, signaled the revitalization of the national reconciliation process.

Perhaps one of the most important achievements of the Lagos administration was the 2005 constitutional amendment that abolished the position of designated senators, permitted the president to remove the commander in chief of the armed forces provided that he or she gave advanced notice to the defense committees in both chambers of the legislation. The influence of the National Security Council, which used to be made up of four military commanders and four politicians, was also reduced to an advisory role within the larger framework of the armed forces' gradual move away from politics. The NSC is now composed of the chairmen of the Senate and the House of Representatives and the Supreme Court, the commanders in chief of the armed forces, the general director of the Carabineros (the uniformed national police and gendarmerie), and the general comptroller of the republic.

Michelle Bachelet (2006–2010)

A physician by profession, Bachelet received substantial academic training in military and strategic affairs in Chile (at the army's War Academy) and in the United States (at the Inter-American Defense College) in the 1990s. During her presidency Chilean civil-military relations became increasingly cooperative and consensual. In late 2006 Pinochet died with a much-diminished reputation even among his former supporters, many of whom felt "defrauded" by revelations of his financial misconduct.[47] In fact, the armed forces did not permit the burial of Pinochet's remains in any military grounds.[48]

Under Bachelet's watch the military justice system's space of authority was downgraded, and Congress, after some delays, promulgated a new defense law in February 2010. Among other things the comprehensive law restructured the defense ministry, created a Joint Chiefs of Staff as the advisory organ for the minister, and transferred the police (Carabineros) from the MoD to the ministry of interior. The gradual diminution of the military's role in the National Security Council as well as a number of less conspicuous but still important developments, such as the end of military representation on the National Television Council, indicated the subtle but steady shift in favor of civilians in Chilean military politics.[49]

It is somewhat ironic that it was Bachelet's government that, less than two weeks before its term expired, called in the armed forces to help restore order in the city of Concepción, following widespread looting in the wake of a devastating earthquake in February 2010. In fact Bachelet was even criticized for not sending out the troops sooner. Few saw this as a controversial measure: by this time the military as an institution had enjoyed strong societal support because it was widely perceived as efficient, professional, and obedient to civilian authority.[50]

Rebellions and Tensions

Argentina experienced several military revolts of progressively decreasing size, intensity, and internal support under Alfonsín and Menem that critically delayed democratic consolidation. These upheavals were not surprising given the "explosion of retribution" against the military in politics and in the media, the inability of the Alfonsín government to formulate a coherent defense policy, and the perception of many officers that they were hounded for what they considered justified acts carried out in the context of war against domestic terrorist groups, the Montoneros and the ERP.[51] The deep-seated multidimensional cleavages within the army were confirmed by the fact that no officers above the rank of colonel were involved in the revolts. The continuing division between the "official" army—which evinced no interest in retooling the military into an effective force—and the rebels (also called *carapintadas* [painted faces] for the camouflage makeup they wore), whose objectives were primarily professional even if their actions spilled into the political sphere, damaged both sides and, in the end, facilitated the rise of the most professional and apolitical segments of the officer corps.[52]

The ostensible purpose of the first rebellion, led by Colonel Aldo Rico in April 1987, was to protest the human rights trials. The rebels—who refused to comply with their superiors' call for surrender, gambling correctly that the government would not suppress their revolt—were met by Alfonsín, who agreed to transfer human rights cases to the military's jurisdiction. Subsequently Rico and his comrades were suspended, demoted, and placed in preventive detention, but they rose again, in January 1988, this time to protest a court decision to put them under a harsher kind of incarceration. Another rebellion in December 1988 was led by Colonel Mohamed Alí Seineldín who actually inspired Rico's first revolt. Alfonsín this time insisted that there would be no further modifications to the course of justice. The army quickly quashed the rebellion; Seineldín and his co-conspirators were tried and imprisoned.[53]

In October 1989 Menem pardoned not only eighteen officers charged with human rights transgressions but also the rebels. This action had two contradictory implications. On the one hand, it suggested that the government was granting reprieve under duress because officials held meetings with Seineldín. On the other hand, it vindicated the actions of renegade elements in the military, which actually diminished divisions in the armed forces.[54] The last military revolt, in December 1990, involved about five hundred junior officers and NCOs who supported Seineldín and objected to his marginalization and forced retirement as well as to further budget cuts. The rebels started the insurrection just two days before U.S. President George H. W. Bush's visit to Argentina, hoping that the timing would force Menem to negotiate quickly with them. But the revolt was opposed by much of the military leadership, and this enhanced Menem's ability to respond decisively in quelling it.[55]

Armed insurrections like those in Argentina did not occur in Chile. In fact, after leaving office Aylwin publicly expressed his appreciation of Pinochet's participation in the democratic transition process for having kept the armed forces unified and under his control, thereby preventing the possibility of uprisings along Argentine lines. But Chilean presidents, particularly Aylwin, did have to deal with a number of extremely sensitive situations. On two occasions the military engaged in pure intimidation—one may call it "show of force"—to pressure the government into reversing its actions. First, in 1990 a parliamentary commission investigated Pinochet's family for their suspicious financial transactions (the so-called *Pinocheques* case), and Aylwin asked the general for clarification. Given the timing—so early after the transfer of power—the military reacted vigorously and, along with the right-wing parties, claimed the investigation contravened the 1978 amnesty law. Pinochet decreed a state of "highest alert" for the armed forces across the country without previous consultation with the government, which was completely taken by surprise.[56] A second crisis, in May 1993, was occasioned by the legislature's renewed inquiry into the *Pinocheques* case. The top brass ordered all units to their barracks for five days and held ominous and well-publicized high-level meetings in full combat uniform while elite troops were deployed outside La Moneda, the presidential palace. In the end, notwithstanding some verbal sparring between the government and the military leadership, tensions were resolved via informal channels that functioned reasonably well in settling disputes.

Under Frei's administration three civil-military confrontations demonstrated that his more conciliatory approach did not pressure the armed forces into submission. Early in his term Frei asked a police general, Rodolfo Stange, to resign owing to his cover-up of police involvement in crimes during the military dictatorship. Stange refused, but after the government held up the police promotion list and continued to pressure him for months, he retired in late 1995. The second conflict involved the sentencing of General Manuel Contreras, head of the infamous Chilean intelligence service (DINA) during the dictatorship, and his deputy. After a protracted negotiation the government agreed to open a special prison for military personnel. Finally, the army also used this crisis to demand a decision on the *Pinocheques* case, which refused to go away. In the end Frei "resolved" it by asking the State Defense Council to suspend its investigation.[57] These were the most dramatic actions the Chilean military had taken to flex its muscles vis-à-vis the civilian government. By the second year of Lagos's term—with Pinochet out of the picture—civil-military relations calmed down and have become steadily calmer ever since.

DEFENSE MINISTRIES AND LEGISLATURES

The responsibility of the Argentine Defense Ministry is to direct, organize, and coordinate activities related to national defense not exclusively or directly controlled by the president or other official bodies, while its Chilean counterpart is "the highest body in assisting the President in its government and administration functions of national defense."[58] After the dictatorships, separate branch ministries were replaced by single ministries of defense led by civilian ministers in Argentina and Chile. Both countries have had female defense ministers: Nilda Garré in Argentina, Bachelet and Vivianne Blanlot in Chile—incidentally, women have recently held the defense portfolio in Colombia, Ecuador, and Uruguay as well.

Soon after assuming office, Alfonsín assigned the top five positions in the MoD to civilians. He drastically raised the ministry's influence, which was negligible under the dictatorship, and inserted it into the chain of command between himself and the armed forces. Alfonsín downgraded service commanders to chiefs of staff who are accountable to the Joint Staff—an advisory body that is outside of the chain command—when considering joint operations, but their ultimate responsibility is to the defense minister. These measures, along with the expansion of the defense ministry bureaucracy that placed additional layers of authority between the civilian officials and the armed forces, further diminished the military's clout.[59] The generals were also stripped of their control of public-sector defense-industry enterprises, most especially the *Dirección General de Fabricaciones Militares*, which under their rule had become a massive conglomerate of thirteen separate industrial complexes with fourteen thousand employees.[60]

In 2005 Néstor Kirchner appointed Nilda Garré, a former leftist militant—her husband was one of the founders and the intelligence chief of the Montoneros—to lead the defense ministry. During her ministership (2005–2010), she attempted to obtain additional resources for the ministry and tried, unsuccessfully, to get Chile and Brazil to invest in the Argentine defense industry in a misguided effort to make her country self-sufficient in weapons. She also planned to implement a number of necessary changes, such as a logistics reform and to streamline pilot training by integrating the three separate air forces (army air force, navy air corps, and the air force).[61] Such reforms depended on a coherent overall defense plan that the ministry did not have. Revamping pilot training may be necessary but is difficult without available airplanes or money for fuel and maintenance. Garré also presided over the abolition of the military justice system and conducted a vigorous campaign against corruption in the military, in one of South America's most corrupt states, which took the shape of a virtual witch-hunt.

From the perspective of the overall picture, however, it is far more important that Garré showed nothing but contempt and disdain toward the armed forces as an institution. She displayed leftist posters and mementos in her offices and was said to be allergic to uniforms, so active-duty officers did not dare wear them in her presence. Garré and the all-civilian ministry leadership did not ask for the generals' advice, and she seldom met with service chiefs. The ongoing tension between the ministry and the military benefited neither.

In Chile, given the sensitivity of issues related to the armed forces, an implicit agreement was reached between politicians that these matters would be conducted primarily by the president and the defense minister. Following the 2010 defense reform, there are now only three under-secretaries of defense—one each for the three services—as the head of the police was transferred to the interior ministry. Unlike in Argentina, there is no ministerial level strategic planning unit in the Chilean MoD. Aylwin's defense minister, Patricio Rojas, played an important role in the transition but, not surprisingly given the civil-military power balance and the government's objective to reduce military autonomy, was very unpopular in the armed forces. Frei's cabinet expanded the government's role in the formulation of defense policy and tried to alleviate civil-military conflict in the ministry. Toward this end, the newly appointed minister, Edmundo Pérez-Yoma, was not only close to Frei but also developed good relations with Pinochet. The government managed to increase the civilian component of the ministry—which, unlike in Argentina, is still predominantly staffed by uniformed officers—and to expand the role of civilian defense experts. Defense ministers have tried to develop a long-term civilian defense staff—the ministry has struggled to retain civilian officials for more than two or three years—in part to expand the civilians' clout and continuity in the ministry.

Concertación governments intended to reform intelligence but the military was not willing to give up its control over this issue without a fight. In fact, in the mid-1990s there were still some cases of military intelligence spying on civilian politicians.[62] Following the September 2001 terrorist attacks on the United States, the government created a new National Intelligence Agency (ANI) but did not challenge the autonomy of the military intelligence organizations. The Chilean intelligence establishment remains highly decentralized and the individual agencies of the armed services as well as the police and the Directorate of Public Security and Information have little formal connection to one another.[63]

Unlike Nilda Garré, Michelle Bachelet—who, if anyone, would have had every reason to conduct a personal vendetta against the military—established cordial relations with and was a popular defense minister among military personnel. She promoted the reconciliation between the military and victims of the dictatorship, oversaw a reform of the military pension system, increased the profile of women in the services, continued the modernization of the armed forces with purchases of new equipment, and supported armed forces participation in international peace operations. In her cabinet, too, the MoD was dominated by socialist politicians: former Defense Minister José Goñi was a member of the left-wing revolutionary movement while the under-secretary for the air force, Raúl Vergara, was a commander of the Sandinista air force in Nicaragua in the 1980s. Goñi's predecessor, Vivianne Blanlot, did not hesitate to strip Pinochet's grandson of his captaincy in December 2006 after he defended his grandfather's rule during his eulogy. In the meantime, the civilian component in the MoD's Advisory Committee was gradually increased.

Latin American parliaments, in contrast to presidents, are far less powerful than their counterpart in Washington. The Argentine and Chilean congresses cannot declare war or make peace but their authorization is necessary for the entry of foreign troops into or the deployment of national troops outside the country. While the approval of the Argentine Congress is needed to appoint senior armed forces officers, the Chilean legislature does not have this authority. Generally speaking, Latin American parliamentary deputies do not prioritize defense issues or stay long enough in their positions to accumulate expertise on military matters. Consequently, defense committees have not carved out detailed and unique agendas.[64] Owing to their relatively limited influence, legislatures rarely accomplish anything important, such as the aforementioned 1988 defense law that transformed the Argentine military establishment. In practice, Argentine deputies have little say over the defense budget given the overwhelming influence of the executive branch.[65] The heads of the defense committees are usually political hacks co-opted by the government and have neither the expertise nor the incentive to make probing inquiries about military expenditures.[66]

Deputies in Buenos Aires and Santiago enjoy limited access to itemized details of the defense budget. Parliamentary defense committees—that in Argentina have a permanent staff though not in Chile—are not empowered to open, examine, or rewrite the defense budget and their ability to actually *control* the budget is severely impaired. Interestingly, it is not via the legislature's defense dommittee but the finance ministry that budgetary oversight is exercised.[67] In Argentina, defense expenditures are controlled by an evaluation unit within the ministry of defense—there is no such body in Chile. Nonetheless, elected officials in Chile in the past two decades have gradually become more willing to contest the military and its financial affairs. For instance, civilian experts have thoroughly examined and trimmed down the air force's acquisition program while making sure that justifiable requests get funded when possible.

The development of independent civilian expertise on defense matters remains a thorny problem in most Latin American states where there is no tradition of education on military subjects for civilians because authoritarian regimes discouraged such education. Since then, defense education has opened up to civilians both in Argentina and in Chile. Santiago's War College, for instance started to enroll bureaucrats, journalists, and university students as early as 1993. There are two problems in this regard. First, an overwhelming majority of civilian defense experts tend to focus on civil-military relations and civilian control issues rather than the more practical aspects of defense and security policy. Furthermore, virtually all of the NGOs, universities, not to mention research institutes financed by political parties have a recognizable political orientation that calls into question the impartiality of the experts who work in them. In some cases—such as several civilian defense advisers under Fernando de la Rúa in Argentina— experts were in contractual relations with the armed forces and thus their objectivity was in doubt.[68]

THE NEW ARMIES

Military personnel in Chile and Argentina are not as well integrated into mainstream society as their North American counterparts. In Argentina the public has a fairly negative view of, and no support for, the military owing to the terrible legacy of military rule. During a military parade in Buenos Aires in 2000—the last prior to the aforementioned 2010 spectacle celebrating the bicentennial—hecklers yelled "genocide" and many booed those marching by.[69] Morale has been very low as has pride in the uniform: one rarely sees members of the armed forces wearing their uniform in public in the capital. Officers are still embarrassed about the military's performance in the Falklands/Malvinas War, the outcome of which, as recent studies show, could have easily been very different had it not been for the high command's easily avoidable mistakes.[70] They talk about it as if it had just happened last year.

A substantial portion of Chileans continue to believe not only that in 1973 the armed forces saved their country from an impending communist dictatorship but that the junta's record—aside from the human rights abuses, of course—was overwhelmingly positive. While the social esteem of the Chilean military remains relatively high, the army's sheen has lost some of its luster as a result of the financial scandals (which were limited to the Pinochet family and a few others) and the human rights issue. The armed forces' excellent performance in natural-disaster and rescue missions as well as in international peacekeeping activities is widely appreciated and contributes to its image as a professional and competent institution. While the share of defense expenditures in the overall budget has declined, military elites have no reason to complain, and do not.

Chile's "copper law"—which guarantees a minimum yield from copper sales (the state's largest single sources of export revenue) of CODELCO, the National Copper Corporation—actually dates from 1958, though it was modified in 1987. The amendment stabilized the floor of the defense budget and supplemented it with a fixed percentage of profits from copper sales. Aylwin, in turn, ensured that what the law prescribed as the minimum defense budget would be set as the maximum, thereby transforming what was originally considered a powerful tool of military autonomy into a political tool that would demonstrate some civilian control over the armed forces.[71] Lagos wanted to do away with the copper law but doing so would have been politically risky given the human rights trials that already threatened the relative tranquility of civil-military relations. The armed forces are resigned to the fact that their Copper Fund—which can be spent on acquisition and equipment but not on day-to-day operations (for which there is a separate budget)—may eventually be integrated into the budget.[72] Between 1998 and 2005 Chilean defense budgets had steadily increased from US$2.115 billion to US$3.401 billion.[73] Military salaries in Chile are comparable to those of civil servants of the same grade/rank.

The situation could hardly be more different in Argentina where military salaries have been losing ground compared to civil service salaries, causing many officers to get second jobs. The Argentine military has had to make do with drastically cut budgets under both Alfonsín and Carlos Saúl Menem (between 1982 and 1990 the military's share of public sector expenditures had plummeted from 32.3 to 18.4 percent).[74] Although trimming military outlays—and the size of the armed forces—was an important *political* objective, these governments were strongly affected by economic obstacles inherited from the junta that spent more on the armed forces than on health and education combined.[75] In recent years nearly the entire defense budget has gone to salary and benefits with only 0.36 percent and 0.75 percent of military outlays earmarked for acquisition in 2004 and 2006, respectively, although the share of investments did increase to 3.1 percent by 2008.[76] To make matters worse, recent weapons acquisitions were seemingly motivated not because they fit into some sound defense plan but because they were inexpensive.[77] In both countries the defense budget's share in the overall government expenditures had declined in 2006–2010, by 1.49 percent in Argentina and by 2.86 percent in Chile.[78]

Conscription was abolished in Argentina—technically, it was suspended as it is still on the books—in 1994 while in Chile military service is essentially voluntary, meaning that more young men want to be in the armed forces than there is a need for so no one is drafted against his will. As opposed to Argentina's still top-heavy officer corps, Chile has only thirty-eight generals for its 35,500-strong army proper. To advance in rank to general in Chile, all serving generals vote on the candidate whose promotion subsequently must be approved by the president. In 2007 a newly promoted general was forced to resign when it turned out that, as a lieutenant in 1973, he was involved in the transportation of the bodies of some murdered opposition activists. Overall, it is hardly surprisingly that the military occupation is far more popular in Chile than in Argentina though difficult economic times ensure that recruitment targets are easily met in both countries.

The political identity of both these armed forces has been radically altered since the end of the military dictatorships. In Argentina a coup d'état is no longer a viable alternative for the military but two problems, the lack of a coherent defense policy and confusion regarding what role the state assigns to the armed forces, remain.[79] The state's public disdain of the armed forces has actually diminished cleavages within the military, which currently is devoid of political power though experts claim it is still a "politically thinking" institution that challenges civilian power whenever it is given the chance and that it will jump at the opportunity to wrest a little more political influence and autonomy.[80] The Argentine experts and officers I talked with seemed to concur that, while members of the armed services generally agree with democratic principles, they believe they have been treated so poorly by civilian governments that they have a right to make some mischief—not to interfere in politics, certainly, but, perhaps, to improve their salaries and work conditions.

In Chile the situation is quite different starting with the fact that military rule was more of an aberration in its history. Many young officers consider the Pinochet era ancient history and support the prosecution of those who violated human rights if only because the issue has tarnished their professional image. In any case, it is worth noting that, as of 2008, Chile's most senior generals had graduated from military college in 1973 as second lieutenants, and soon they, too, will retire. According to Edgardo Boeninger—who, along with Carlos Cáceres, was chiefly responsible for the smooth transfer of power in 1990—there is "no civil-military relations problem in Chile."[81]

The Argentine army does not have any legal pretext for participating in politics while the only "political" responsibility the Chilean military has is that of ensuring public order during elections. Both armies' active-duty personnel enjoy the right to vote but not the right to run for political office, and neither is allowed to publicly voice their political opinions. Though by the lofty standards of Spanish or American civil-military relations the Chilean army might have too much institutional autonomy, the trend toward increasing civilianization and civilian control is ongoing and incontestable.

Idle militaries, especially armies with histories of praetorian intervention, are often tempted to interfere in domestic politics.[82] Unlike in the case of European states, in South America there is no major alliance like NATO in the activities of which states emerging from authoritarian rule can busy themselves, though the international community has been quite helpful in trying to divert the attention of Latin American armed forces from politics to something more constructive, particularly to international peacekeeping. As a result, both Argentine and Chilean armies have participated in numerous U.N.-sanctioned international peacekeeping operations (PKOs). Carlos Menem, especially, was a strong advocate of such activities believing they would readmit Argentina into the international community as a reliable partner and would also help create a much-needed new identity for the military. PKOs have been beneficial to the armed forces, as they give soldiers an important and useful function and also satisfy the thirst for adventure that attracted them to join the military in the first place.[83] Argentina has established a Joint Peacekeeping Training Center to prepare Argentine and foreign peacekeepers and has developed an integrated peacekeeping battalion with Chile. Argentine and Chilean forces have participated in peacekeeping activities in Cyprus, Haiti, Kosovo, Lebanon, and elsewhere.

During the Cold War, U.S. foreign policy toward Latin American countries was controversial given Washington's frequent interference in their domestic politics in support of conservative political forces and, often, right-wing dictatorships. In the post–Cold War era, U.S. focus has shifted to trade issues, democracy promotion, developmental programs, and in some countries narcotics eradication or control. In terms of civil-military relations, the West (and especially the United States) has been primarily interested in encouraging the armed forces' full withdrawal from politics with the new strategic objectives including not only strengthening democratic institutions but also "enhancing the role of the military in democratic society."[84] This objective centers on assisting South American armies to restructure and redefine their roles in support of developing democracies and to protect and promote the human rights of their citizens.

Of all Argentine presidents since military rule, Carlos Menem was most keenly interested in gaining Washington's approval because, as an internationalist, he believed that a positive international role for Argentina would yield many benefits. He sent Argentine warships to the first Gulf War and achieved major non-NATO ally status with the United States. At the time there were even speculations in the press that Argentina would become a NATO member.[85] After the presidency passed to the Kirchners and the leftist-nationalist wing of the Peronist party, Argentina became a steady and vocal critic of the United States. Western democracies have encouraged the passing of terror finance legislation and enhanced bank supervision in Latin America and elsewhere, but in Argentina there is the special concern about how a government that has been partly staffed by former members of a guerrilla or terrorist organization—according to many experts, the Montoneros was a bona fide terrorist group[86]—would define terrorism.

GUATEMALA: PROBLEMS OF A DIFFERENT MAGNITUDE

In 1954 a CIA-sponsored invasion of this small Central American country ended the decade-long and thus far only genuinely democratic experience its people have known. What followed was Latin America's longest and bloodiest military or quasi-military rule, which claimed the lives of 200,000 civilians.

For approximately thirty-six years, Guatemalan generals fought an insurgency that contemporary government and military elites describe as "war against communist guerillas" and those on the political left describe as "civil war." Polemics aside, for most of the Cold War, the army ran Guatemala as its fiefdom, dominating not only the government and the bureaucracy but also education and broad swaths of the civil sector. The military called the shots behind the scenes even during the short intervals (e.g., 1966–70) when civilians occupied the presidential palace. By the mid-1980s the armed forces gained a strategic victory over guerilla forces through a combination of terror, civic action, and the mobilization of the rural population into mandatory civil patrols.[87]

The long, drawn-out peace process started in 1985 with the election of Vinicio Cerezo as a civilian president who served out his term (1986–90), and during this time, the Cold War ended, depriving the armed forces of one of the main justifications of its repressive policies.[88] Societal reconciliation was actually spurred by and continued following President Jorge Serrano's attempted self coup, or *auto golpe*, through which he tried to resolve a number of profound socioeconomic problems the country was confronting. This was a major turning point in the peace process because the military chose not to support the "Serranazo," and Congress appointed an unlikely new president, Ramiro de León Carpio, who theretofore had served as the human rights ombudsman. Between 1994 and 1996 a number of peace accords were signed between the government (and the armed forces) on the one hand, and the opposition parties and the Guatemalan National Revolutionary Unity (URNG)—an organization of various guerilla groups founded in 1982—on the other, dealing with a variety of issues from human rights to the resettling of displaced people. The military's strong position earned it many concessions: for instance, while Truth Commissions were established, they were not allowed to reveal the names of human rights violators.

From our perspective, the most important event was the 1996 Agreement on the Strengthening of Civilian Power and the Role of the Armed Forces in a Democratic Society.[89] This accord mandated constitutional reforms to subordinate the army to civilian control, restricted the military's mission to external defense, eliminated counterinsurgency units, created a new civilian police force to handle all internal security matters, and stipulated a reduction in the army's size and budget by a third. In the decade and a half since the accord, some positive measures have taken place. The army's political influence over state administration has diminished, officers have been subject to the civilian justice system (some imprisoned on criminal charges),[90] some central institutions—most importantly the National Security System—have been created to strengthen civilian control over security and intelligence, and civil society has become better educated in security and defense matters and has gained some influence in public affairs.[91] The military police were disbanded, and the budget and size of the armed forces were severely cut (to 0.40 percent of the GDP and 2.62 percent of the state budget in 2010, and from a troop strength of 45,000 in 1996 to 14,906 in 2010, respectively).[92] The MoD has been reorganized and now includes departments for human rights and for strategic analysis. Forced military conscription has nearly disappeared along with most of the notorious civilian patrols. The courts were able to prosecute a few military officers responsible for human rights abuses even if the sentencing judges were often threatened or killed or escaped into exile.

The president appoints the commander in chief of the army, a general who is responsible to the defense minister, though he or she must have the approval of the defense minister who is by law a uniformed military officer. In 2003 civil-military relations were improved by the creation of a Defense Community comprised of civilian and military members that worked together in assessing defense sector requirements.[93] Other than this, the opportunities for civilians to influence defense-policy decisions continue to be severely constrained. Substantive defense reform has been very limited because the army decisively defeated the guerillas, remained cohesive, and retained a significant amount of popular support. Consequently, it did not need to make many costly concessions to the opposition.

While Guatemalan social and political institutions are weak—so much so that President Álvaro Colom was said to have inherited "a caricature of state structure" when taking office in 2008[94]—the army remains a strong and unified institution. The security forces vehemently opposed the findings of truth commissions that in several reports attributed to them the responsibility for the vast majority of killings during military rule. Bishop Juan Gerardi—who founded the Archbishop's Human Rights Office—was assassinated just two days after releasing one such report; his killing remains unsolved.[95] One of the key problems of the Peace Accords was that they made too many promises to too many constituencies—according to some analyses the number of commitments exceeded six hundred[96]—with a remarkable lack of clarity as to how they would be realized. As a result, most of the agreements have not been implemented.

A 1999 referendum on strengthening civilian supremacy over the military and limiting the army's functions was defeated, signifying a major setback to the democratization process. In the meantime, the armed forces have been the most corrupt institution in a corrupt state. Defense ministry employees—including the minister—and high-ranking officers are beneficiaries of a variety of bribes and extortion schemes; they apparently consider it a perfectly natural perk of reaching a higher rank.[97] Many who led the armed forces in the 1980s and 1990s hold responsible government jobs; former officers are prominent in all political parties save for the left-wing ones. The brutal former dictator, Efraín Ríos Montt was allowed to run for the presidency, and while he was defeated at the polls in 2003, he still did well enough to preside over Congress.

The military has not only been able to safeguard its influence in many-spheres but, in recent years, has actually become stronger. The proliferation of fearless street gangs and drug cartels—mostly working for drug barons across the border, in Mexico—has made Guatemala one of the most dangerous places in the Americas. Organized crime, internal violence, and institutional failure have become the hallmarks of Guatemalan politics. In 2008 six thousand murders took place in a population of thirteen million.[98] By early 2009 more than 362 settlements—comprising more than half of all Guatemalan villages and towns—have actually requested military presence for protection against crime the National Civil Police cannot curb.[99] The state has reacted by preparing thousands of soldiers to respond to requests and reopening military bases in the country's interior to recover areas where drug trafficking organizations have settled and, in December 2010, by declaring a state of siege in Alta Verapaz province to reclaim cities that had allegedly been taken over by drug gangs.[100] During the two-month siege the army was the ultimate authority in Alta Verapaz: it conducted searches without warrants, detained suspects, controlled the local media, and prohibited public gatherings.

President Colom defended the military's enhanced role by saying that the "drug traffickers have us cornered" and arguing that the "state of siege was beginning to accomplish its objective."[101] In fact, more and more Guatemalans have come to demand a strong military presence on their streets, and all three top contenders for the September 2011 presidential elections promised to satisfy them. The more than 60 percent of Guatemala's registered voters who are between eighteen and thirty years old have little knowledge and practically no memory of the the civil war—schools do not include lessons on the war—and tend to believe that the army would be far more effective in fighting the drug gangs than the thoroughly corrupted police.[102] Many of those clamoring for increased military involvement in policing seem unaware not only of the army's past tradition of brutally suppressing innocent civilians but also the of the fact that it has not been immune—along with the judicial, legislative, and executive branches of government—from infiltration by organized crime.[103]

Foreign influence helped bring about military rule in 1954 but it also helped end it four decades later. The United Nations played an important role mediating between the government and the opposition helped by the supportive role of the "Group of Friends" including Mexico, Norway, Spain, and the United States.[104] The U.N. mission, phased out in 2004, focused on issues like human rights, judicial autonomy, and achieving a modicum of civilian control over the military as did a number U.S. programs run by civilian experts.

The Guatemalan armed forces have ruled the country through most of its history. They have developed social networks, economic clout, and political influence that they can and do easily exercise even if they are not actually in power. This unique, age-old, historic relationship between the army and civilians "can only beg the question of whether civilian control over the military is possible"[105] The Guatemalan experience demonstrates that regular and more or less free and fair elections—since 1986!—are far from sufficient to guarantee a functioning democracy. In a twenty-country survey, Latin America experts considered only Haiti less democratic than Guatemala in 2002.[106] Things have changed but little in the past decade.

CONCLUSION

In most of the empirical chapters in this book it is quite easy to distinguish between the "good" case and "bad" case in terms of postauthoritarian military politics. But which is the good case here? Argentine politicians certainly fully subjugate their armed forces to civilian rule but they may have gone too far. The government's virulently antimilitary policies are both counterproductive and difficult to comprehend. More than three decades have passed since the human rights violations of the Proceso that, not coincidentally, the military justified by the terrorist activities of groups some of whose members are now in the government. But the most troubling aspect of this affair is that the witch-hunt is conducted not against guilty individuals, nearly all of whom are imprisoned or dead, but against an institution. The combination of on the one hand humiliating treatment from state and society, cripplingly low budgets and salaries, loss of professional effectiveness, and sagging morale, and on the other hand the military's hatred of its political masters "down to the last serviceman," as one of my interviewees told me, does not in any way benefit civil-military relations.[107] If anything, the political stance of Argentine officers may well be more unpredictable and their relations to civilians more fragile than those of their colleagues on the other side of the Andes even if the latter have retained more political clout.

Chile and Chilean civil-military relations have benefited from political continuity since the transfer of power. Unlike in Argentina where differences between individual governments—between say, those of Alfonsín and Menem or de la Rúa and the Kirchners—have been significant, making military politics quite unpredictable, the four Chilean Concertación administrations maintained a steady political orientation. In Buenos Aires the government's defense advisers were replaced as the government changed; the new experts often espoused ideas quite different from those of their predecessors. In Santiago, on the other hand, the civilian team working on military-security issues has had few changes in personnel that allow for consistency. Not surprisingly, then, defense reform and the democratization of civil-military relations have been choppy and volatile in Argentina while in Chile far more gradual and, in the past decade, more consensual. The counterintuitive bottom line is that even though Argentine politicians have cowed their army into submission, military politics have ultimately become more successful and confidence-inspiring in Chile.

Which of the generalizations we made in the post–military rule context in the Southern European settings hold true for our Latin American cases? The main task for democratizers, getting the military out of political affairs, is clearly the same for all postpraetorian cases. The second generalization, the direct correlation between a military regime's overall performance and the amount of leverage outgoing military elites enjoy is also supported by the three cases in this chapter.

Two other generalizations we made in chapter 4, however, are not valid for the Latin American cases. Whereas for a number of mostly unique, contextually determined reasons those who committed human rights abuses were not held accountable in any systematic fashion in Spain, Portugal, and Greece, the picture that emerges from our three cases studies in this chapter is quite different. Individuals violating human rights were quickly held accountable in Argentina—the country where the military held little leverage after leaving power. In Chile, however, those culpable escaped prosecution at the time of regime transition owing to the deals Pinochet could make, given the clout he enjoyed. Nevertheless, as the process of democratization continued and democratic consolidation came to be realized, the army began to gradually lose its political influence and, with it, its immunity from prosecution. In other words, in the end those guilty of human rights abuses had their day of reckoning in Chile as well. Guatemala, where few officers were held responsible for their crimes, is an outlier but it is not a consolidated democracy. What about the role of international organizations, so prominent in Southern Europe? In Latin America's democratic transition they played a negligible role, with the partial exception of Guatemala where the United Nations' mediation was instrumental in ending military rule but, of course, could not ensure sustained democratization.

Are military elites in Argentina and Chile committed to democratic rule? There can be little doubt that by 2010, the end of the period we studied, they were. Although Argentine soldiers have justly felt disrespected by the state and would certainly prefer a government less connected to the terrorist groups of the past, there is no indication that they would contemplate turning against their democratically elected civilian masters. On the other hand, it is rather difficult to be sanguine about the democratic leanings of officers and generals in Guatemala, an authoritarian state where political and military elites have learned to effectively accommodate each other's interests.

TABLE 5.1

After Military Rule in Latin America: Argentina, Chile, and Guatemala

	Country *Period*	*Argentina* *1989–2011*	*Chile* *1983–2010*	*Guatemala* *1996–2010*
Background	end of military regime	negotiated and controlled by the military	military defeat and eroding authority	negotiated and controlled by the military
	overall military regime performance	strong (especially economic policy), extensive human rights violations	poor, extensive human rights violations	poor, extensive human rights violations
	leverage of military when leaving power	high	low	high
State	main tasks	get the military out of politics, the economy, and internal security; reduce its autonomy, privileges, and size; create new institutional frameworks for democratic civil-military relations	get the military out of politics, the economy, and internal security; reduce its autonomy, privileges, and size; create new institutional frameworks for democratic civil-military relations	get the military out of politics, the economy, and internal security; reduce its autonomy, privileges, and size; create new institutional frameworks for democratic civil-military relations
	civilian political leadership	restrained	clean break with the past	restrained
	political institutions and trend	medium, getting stronger	strong	weak and beleaguered
	civilian involvement in defense affairs	gradually increasing	pervasive	weak and tentative
	executive control	gradually increasing	strong	quite weak though MoD reorganized
	legislative oversight	weak	weak	weak

TABLE 5.1 *(continued)*

After Military Rule in Latin America: Argentina, Chile, and Guatemala

		Argentina *1989–2011*	*Chile* *1983–2010*	*Guatemala* *1996–2010*
	Country *Period*			
	prosecution of human rights abuses	initially not, began a decade after the transition	yes, extensive	very few affected
	foreign influence	not an important factor	not an important factor	"group of friends" and UN mediating peace treaty
Military	behavior during transition	mostly calm except for several "shows of force"	several small rebellions (1987–1990)	domineering
	interference in politics	gradually diminishing	no	yes
	domestic function	ensuring public order during elections	none (not even counter-terrorism)	policing, internal security
	advisory function	yes	no	yes
	effectiveness	no evidence (adequate performance in international PKOs)	no evidence (adequate performance in international PKOs)	no evidence (adequate performance in international PKOs)
	commitment to democracy	yes	yes	unclear
Society	independent civilian experts	some: not influential and rarely impartial	some: not influential and rarely impartial	many: well prepared and relatively influential
	military's prestige	high	low	high
	soldiers in society	separation	sharp separation	separation
	conscription	if volunteers are insufficient	no (suspended in 1994)	yes
Political system at the end of the period		consolidated parliamentary democracy	consolidated parliamentary democracy	electoral authoritarianism

CHAPTER 6

After Military Rule in Asia:
South Korea, Thailand, and Indonesia

⇥ ⇤

While most authoritarian systems in South America during the Cold
War were of the praetorian variety, in East- and Southeast Asia military or quasi-military regimes (e.g., Burma, Indonesia, the Philippines, South Korea,* Taiwan, Thailand) were complemented by state-socialist polities (e.g., Cambodia, China, Laos, Vietnam). In this chapter we are concerned with the first group of states. Third-wave democratization for postmilitary regimes has resulted in sharply different outcomes in East- and Southeast Asia. In East Asian states such as South Korea and Taiwan, economic growth and the development of civil society spurred a political opening and, in time, produced a consolidated democracy. In Southeast Asia, however, the course toward democratization has been uneven and remains very much a work in progress in Thailand, Indonesia, and the Philippines. Here the military, a traditional bastion of antidemocratic power, has reinforced authoritarian currents and continues to be the single most important obstacle in the way of democratic consolidation.

In this chapter we will learn about three Asian states. Our "good" case, Korea, has been remarkably successful in consolidating democracy and carving out a proper place in the new institutional architecture for its armed forces. Our "bad" case is Thailand where, after a promising though difficult fifteen-year democratization process, the military overthrew the elected government in 2006. Finally, our "interesting" case is Indonesia, the world's most populous Muslim-majority state, where, against the expectations of most experts, the armed forces' political presence and influence have gradually diminished since 1998. My aim here is to explain why Korean officers

---

* Unless otherwise specified, in this chapter "Korea" stands for South Korea. Also, as in chapter 2 with respect to Japanese names, here, too, I use the Korean and Thai practice of putting last names first with the exception Syngman Rhee who Anglicized his name.

have become the servants of the state, why their Indonesian colleagues—seemingly against all odds—have more or less given up their intention to run their country, and why members of the Royal Thai Armed Forces (RTAF) have been far more reluctant to relinquish their political role.

Democratization processes started relatively recently in East Asia: in South Korea in 1987, in Thailand in 1992, and in Indonesia in 1998. The time frame for this chapter is from the beginning of democratization until the end of Kim Dae-jung's presidency (2003) in South Korea, until the end of President Yudhoyono's first term in office in Indonesia (2009), and until late 2009 in Thailand. This chapter is divided into four parts. In the first, I summarize military rule in the three countries while in subsequent parts I discuss separately the evolution of military politics in each state.

MILITARY RULE IN THREE ASIAN STATES

Historically, in all three countries the armed forces were the most powerful political institutions. According to military folklore, in Indonesia and Thailand, soldiers were not just a part of society but they effectively *created* the nation, and South Korean generals have considered themselves the guarantors of national survival.[1] As in the former military regimes of Southern Europe and Latin America, the main challenges in the three Asian states have also been the extraction of the armed forces from the political realm. Politicians in South Korea, Thailand, and Indonesia have approached these challenges differently given their disparate political and socioeconomic settings.

Korea

When South Korea became an independent state in 1948, the military was by far its best organized social force and remained so for about half a century. The armed forces were heavily influenced by Japan, whose colonial army left a deep impression on the Korean soldiers and officers, and by the United States—an American military government de facto ruled the country in 1945–48.[2] President Syngman Rhee's (1948–60) civilian but intensely authoritarian rule relied on the police and the armed forces. He took advantage of factional struggles within the military to consolidate his rule and to prevent the evolution of a unified power center in the army. During the social and political upheaval that followed the overthrow of Rhee's regime by a student revolution, the armed forces continued to restrain their political ambitions. The appointment of a civilian defense minister and his attempt to reduce military expenditures, the widespread corruption, and the civilian regime's alleged inability to defend the country from communist threats led to a bloodless military coup and ushered in the long rule of Park Chung-hee (1961–79).[3]

Park declared martial law, dissolved the National Assembly, abolished political parties, banned political activities, and established a classic military dictatorship. The all-military Supreme Revolutionary Council for National Reconstruction took over all executive, legislative, and judicial functions of government. In 1963, following strong U.S. and public pressure, political power was transferred to the civilian sphere, though the armed forces' political interference continued.[4] At this point, in a concession to the Constitution that stipulated civilian control over the armed forces and forbade the election or appointment of uniformed officers as presidents, Park and fellow officers who had entered the government retired from the armed forces. Nonetheless, during the remainder of his regime, though the army as an *institution* stayed out of politics, recruitment of its retired officers for political position continued unabated. In fact, the ratio of former military personnel in the cabinet and in the legislature had increased.[5] In 1964–79 ex-officers held 118 of the 314 ministerial portfolios and occupied between 16 and 22.4 percent of the seats in the National Assemly.[6] Park managed to politically control the generals by patronizing the influential Hanahoe faction and positioning its members in strategic posts within the military, by mobilizing intelligence agencies to detect and prevent moves by the armed forces, and by co-opting retired officers into the government and thereby alleviating their political grievances. The officer corps were staunch supporters of Park's regime, and retired generals constituted the backbone of the government. Notwithstanding its civilian façade, Park's regime was, in fact, a military regime.

In late 1979 General Chun Doo-hwan organized mutiny against the old-guard generals and engineered a coup in May 1980. The change at the top resulted in few substantive policy alterations. Constitutional changes increased executive power over the other branches of government. Like Park, Chun and his associates retired from the military, and they established a new political party (the Democratic Justice Party [DJP]) and successfully controlled the armed forces. At the same time, Chun limited the retired officers' participation in government and relied almost exclusively on the Hanahoe group as the talent pool for military and government elites throughout his reign.[7] For the eight years (1980–88) of his regime Chun suffered from a legitimacy deficit owing to his forcible seizure of power and, even more so, for having crushed the Kwangju Uprising in May 1980 that took the lives of over two hundred people and also created much anti-American sentiment among young South Koreans. Chun's entire tenure was accompanied by the unrelenting and gradually expanding and intensifying resistance of civil society, which eventually forced the introduction of limited measures of political and economic liberalization.

Thailand

In Bangkok, a group of civil servants and army officers staged a bloodless coup d'état in 1932 that ended the era of absolute kings and inaugurated that of constitutional monarchy and military rule. At that point, the Thai army entered politics, according to the generals who believed that the military was a democratic institution, in order to support democracy.[8] Far more likely, however, military elites overturned absolute monarchy so that they could become a dominant political force. Thai generals have maintained an exalted view of their own political importance to this day. According to their supreme commander

> In accordance with the Constitution, the Royal Thai Armed Forces has [sic] the responsibility of safeguarding the sovereignty, security, and national interest of the State, conducting armed conflict or war, acting as a deterrent in order to protect the Institution of the Monarchy, and suppressing and deterring rebellion and anarchy in order to maintain the security of the State and to develop a country.[9]

Few indicators drive home the point of the Royal Thai Armed Forces' enduring political power better than a walking tour of central Bangkok: the capital city is liberally dotted with military bases and installations of all sorts even though there is no strategic reason for their presence. The Thai military's ethos and prestige have served to justify the ostensible need for a strong, dictatorial state that can overcome external (communist insurgencies) and internal (the financially powerful Chinese minority, Muslim separatism, etc.) threats and challenges.[10] Through much of the Cold War, members of the RTAF shared important unifying experiences: combating external foes (communist insurgents from Vietnam, Laos, and Cambodia) and internal ones (home-grown communists and Muslim separatists in the south). Since 1946 the one constant in Thai politics has been the king, Bhumibol Adulyadej (Rama IX), the world's longest-ruling monarch (as of January 2012), who has reigned through fifteen military coups, sixteen constitutions, and twenty-eight changes of prime minister.[11] The widely respected king has maintained considerable political influence and has not shied away from vetoing legislation or supporting military coups.[12]

In 1973 a popular uprising signaled the emergence of civilians onto the political stage. During the three years of civilian rule the generals continued to call the shots from behind the scenes, but three important changes took place in civil-military relations: the RTAF lost some prominent leaders as several high-ranking officers were forced into exile; with civilians in charge of the government, the potential existed for the politicization of the military's promotion process; with the advent of parliamentary rule the struggle against communist insurgents became more open to scrutiny.[13]

In 1976 a large-scale massacre of "communist" students by the police and military forces at Thammasat University ended competitive politics and returned the army to power. In the 1980s Thailand experienced a slow and uneven process of political liberalization occasionally punctuated by military coups spawned by differences between RTAF factions over the pace of change. The number of seats military men held in the legislature had slowly diminished while civilian politicians, especially provincial entrepreneurs, gradually took over cabinet ministries that had earlier been held by retired officers.[14] At the same time, the number of generals rapidly expanded (to over one thousand) creating intense competition at the top. Fighting a political war had politicized the army and created new fissures and deepened old ones in the institution. In this environment, mid-ranking officers—those with direct control over men and firepower—acquired more influence because their backing was critical for feuding generals.[15]

The 1978 Constitution permitted the king to appoint senate members. Between 1989 and 1991, 161 (or 60.3 percent) of the Upper House's 267 members were active-duty military personnel, although the Lower House and the Office of the Prime Minister remained civilian domains. During the same period, eleven of the forty-six ministers were retired military officials.[16] The end of the Cold War fundamentally changed Thailand's security environment. At the same time, as in Korea a decade earlier, economic growth and political liberalization fostered the expansion of interest-group activity.[17] By the early 1980s, the army had found itself in a changed sociopolitical and economic situation. The country needed to accelerate industrialization but the generals in power lacked vision; for them economic progress mainly signified greater access to relatively cheap weapons. It was at this point that Thai business elites realized they could no longer entrust economic development to the armed forces.

Indonesia

Four years after declaring independence and fighting a costly guerilla war against the returning Dutch, Indonesia became a parliamentary democracy (1949–59) and then an authoritarian state portrayed by its leading elites as a uniquely Indonesian system of "Guided Democracy" (1959–65). Indonesia's increasingly autocratic dictator, Sukarno, had tried to maintain a delicate balance between the country's two most powerful institutions: the Indonesian Armed Forces (ABRI), which never restricted themselves to an exclusively military role, and the Indonesian Communist Party (PKI). In 1965 Sukarno's regime was unseated by generals anxiously viewing the PKI's growing power.[18] The PKI was destroyed, and the military became the most influential political institution under Sukarno's successor, Suharto, a former ABRI lieutenant general.

ABRI's enormous political power was legitimized by the "dual function" (*dwifungsi*) doctrine, which stipulated that in addition to strictly military tasks, the armed forces were entitled to a direct role in political life.[19] Both these functions were facilitated by the separatist threats the country faced in Aceh, East Timor, and Papua, and by ABRI's doctrine that prescribed close cooperation between military units and the civilian population. This strategy of "total people's defense" was in turn fostered by ABRI's territorial defense structure, which instituted a military presence throughout the country. Furthermore, ABRI justified its exercise of civilian functions—territorial warfare, civil defense, involvement in the economy—by taking a leadership role in the country's "functional groups" (workers, peasants, youth, and women).[20]

Under Suharto's "New Order" state (1965–98), the armed forces was guaranteed 20 percent of the seats in the legislative bodies at all levels of government, and by the mid-1990s, fourteen thousand ABRI officers were employed in various administrative and economic positions.[21] Nevertheless, during the last decade of his rule, Suharto gradually reduced his reliance on the generals by forming coalitions with Islamists and technocrats, and consulting his own palace clique (including his family members). In 1993 ABRI reacted against the downgrading of its position by forcing Suharto to accept one of its own, General Try Sutrisno, as vice president, but the president retaliated by decreasing the military's presence in his cabinet.[22] Moreover, Suharto deliberately created schisms along religious—and, for the first two decades of his rule, occasionally political and ethnic—lines within ABRI and periodically reshuffled large numbers of military officers in order to strengthen his authority and prevent the emergence of consensus and independent power centers within the military elites.[23]

Serious challenges to ABRI's power came from three sources: Suharto, who occasionally took positions directly at odds with the wishes of the top brass; tensions within military elites; and, particularly in the later years of Suharto's regime, opposition from the intelligence community and from the emerging civil society groups.[24] Importantly, none of these factors was able to challenge ABRI's deep penetration of society, particularly rural society.

Comparing Praetorian Rule

When contrasting the three military regimes, it is worth underscoring that political intervention in Korea was exercised by individual generals and not the armed forces as an institution, that the Thai military's influence was more expansive and less elite based, and that in Indonesia—given ABRI's territorial organization—the entire officer corps could be said to possess some political clout. In a like vein, in Korea the spoils of the coups d'état—and of military rule, more generally—were enjoyed by those who were personally involved in the 1961 and 1979 takeovers. Those who remained in the barracks not only did not benefit from but, in fact, were disadvantaged by military rule because public opinion did not differentiate between the two army groups. In Thailand and Indonesia, however, larger segments of the armed forces profited materially from the military's political position and were involved in corruption.

The personalized rather than institutionalized pattern of military intervention eased the Korean armed forces' exit from politics. The regimes there were not "pure" military governments but, rather, semicivilian regimes that enjoyed the army's extensive support. In Thailand the RTAF called the shots but as time went on the necessities of economic development demanded growing reliance on civilian expertise and involvement in structuring and administering business activities. At the other end of the scale was, again, Indonesia where economic growth was slower, and the generals, notwithstanding some constraints on their power, managed to maintain their dominant political position.

The praetorian rule of the three states cannot be viewed in isolation from the Cold War. The Korean military's claim that it held the key to national survival was justified in a very real sense, something the population was occasionally reminded of by the brazen operations of North Korean military and intelligence.[25] In Thailand and Indonesia, communist insurgents and/or separatist forces did not amount to an existential threat but certainly qualified as significant security challenges that had to be defeated. The Cold War context also raises the issue of the role of foreign political actors. All three of these states were firmly allied with the West though none more so than Korea whose defense was guaranteed by the presence of the U.S. Eighth Army on Korean soil. The Thai military regime also enjoyed American support though not always to the degree usually assumed.[26] Washington, of course, was delighted by the coup that unseated the increasingly communist-friendly Sukarno in 1965 and, along with Australia, was a steadfast backer of Suharto. There is a profound irony here: The United States had been a committed supporter of all three authoritarian regimes as long as it needed their cooperation in the anticommunist and anti-Soviet struggle. With the winding down of the Cold War, however, Washington emerged not just as a stern critic of the repressive actions of the same regimes but also as a dependable supporter of democratization efforts.[27]

Military rule must be viewed within the context of its time. In all three countries, the armed forces made major contributions to modernization and socioeconomic development. Especially in rural areas, they played an essential role in socializing and training the population as well as improving the physical infrastructure by building roads, bridges, canals, and so on. In Korea, nearly all young men received useful technical training in the armed forces owing to the compulsory draft. It was in large part this kind of training that enabled the country's successful pursuit of labor-intensive industrialization.[28] Thai soldiers, on the other hand, were de facto nation builders: as recently as the 1960s and 1970s people in border regions with Cambodia and Laos lacked an unambiguous national identity. RTAF activities in these areas were as important for their strategic and economic contributions as they were for nation-building. In Indonesia, the army's territorial organization fostered close ties between soldiers and the local population and facilitated ABRI's intensive economic participation.

In all three societies the public consideration of the military regimes remains polarized. Predictably, those on the left side of the political spectrum and those who actually suffered from military rule have little regard for it. Unlike many praetorian regimes in Africa, Asia, and Latin America, the three under consideration here compiled *mixed* records: alongside the column dominated by dictatorial behavior, occasional brutality, and corruption, there is also a column of achievements. When Park Chung-hee declared martial law in 1961, Korea's level of economic development was similar to Ghana's.[29] A crucial consequence of the Thai military's preoccupation with containing communist insurgents was the promotion of desperately needed rural development.[30] Many Indonesians have maintained high esteem for the military regime for creating stability, keeping the prices of basic necessities low, promoting infrastructural development, and establishing universal access to education.[31]

KOREA'S ROAD TO DEMOCRATIC CONSOLIDATION

Transition

In 1986 Chun Doo-hwan's government, having suffered from a persistent legitimacy crisis, introduced some semiparticipatory elements into the political system and agreed to a constitutional debate. The military had ample opportunity for political interference before democratic transition began but an influential group of moderate officers opposed getting involved.[32] Democratization in Korea was an anticlimactic affair. Following heated deliberations regarding a constitutional amendment prior to the upcoming presidential election, Chun's hard-liner government allowed only for an indirect presidential election through an electoral college, which infuriated opposition political parties and civil society that demanded a direct popular vote. In May–June 1987 demonstrations and public protests of an unprecedented scale took place. Chun realized that he overplayed his hand, reopened negotiations with the opposition parties over a new constitution and eventually agreed to an amendment for the direct popular presidential elections.[33] The December 1987 election was won by the ruling Democratic Justice Party's (DJP) candidate, Roh Tae-woo, a moderate general who was aided by a three-way split in the opposition bloc. The armed forces, convinced by Roh that their position and perks would not be threatened, stood by during the first peaceful transfer of power in forty years.

Though Roh was elected through a relatively free and fair electoral process, he was not the breath of fresh air many Koreans had hoped for given that he was a co-conspirator in the 1979–80 military coup and a key partner in Chun's regime. Nonetheless, Roh Tae-woo turned out to be precisely the kind of transitional figure who is indispensable for the continued democratization of some countries. A loyal member of the army's Hanahoe faction (most of them members of the Korean Military Academy's eleventh class of 1955), Roh promoted his erstwhile classmates into the top brass thereby consolidating his authority and checking potential military opposition. In any case, the army was not threatened by Roh's moderate policies, particularly because officers constituted nearly one-fifth of his cabinet and no major military reforms were introduced. Still, Roh allowed increasing legislative oversight of defense expenditures and ensured the generals' disengagement from politics during his five-year term.

Democratization progressed further when three opposition parties won enough seats in the 1988 National Assembly elections to deny the DJP a majority.[34] A "grand alliance" of conservative political forces provided Roh and his government with the necessary support and stability to serve out their terms. In the meantime, North Korea became increasingly isolated in the wake of the Cold War, allowing South Korean politicians and activists to focus on democratization. Prior to the 1992 presidential elections, Roh made two important decisions that demonstrated his commitment to a smooth transfer of power: during the campaign he announced his intention to resign as the DJP's president, and he introduced strict electoral laws, including a shorter campaign period and spending limits.[35] By doing so Roh increased political stability and helped to alleviate the already modest danger of what Huntington called the "praetorian problem" in democratic transitions.[36]

Kim Young-sam (1993–98)

A pro-democracy activist, Kim Young-sam was elected by a landslide in 1992 and became Korea's first truly civilian president in three decades. Although he left office five years later beleaguered by an economic crisis, charges of corruption in his cabinet, and low popularity ratings, he significantly moved forward Korea's democratization process.[37] Most importantly, Kim managed to greatly diminish the military's political influence by undertaking a major purge in the army, reforming the structure of defense administration, and replacing potentially problematic generals with those committed to democracy.

Kim started out with a broad agenda of political and economic reforms but his first target was the armed forces. He contacted top generals to discuss his reform proposals and, in the process, gained their support. He neutralized potential military opposition by relying on generals from his native Pusan and South Kyongsang region capitalizing on existing regional sentiments in the armed forces. One of Kim's main achievements was to destroy the army's traditional locus of political influence, the Hanahoe group, by removing more than one thousand high-ranking officers.[38] Kim reshuffled the fifty top generals and excluded all Hanahoe members from promotions and division commands.[39] In 1996 he succeeded in putting on trial and getting convictions for former presidents Chun and Roh along with thirteen generals—something that would have been unthinkable just a few years before—for large-scale corruption and their roles in the 1979 coup and the 1980 suppression of the Kwangju uprising.[40] At the same time, Kim reduced the authority of the General Staff and augmented that of the ministry of defense. The cumulative result of these measures was the dismantling of the military regime's long-established power base and the institutionalization of civilian control over the armed forces.

During Kim's presidency the legal and organizational foundations of the defense-security establishment were thoroughly reformed. The legislature revised laws on intelligence agencies to ensure full governmental authority to formulate and implement policy. The Korean Central Intelligence Agency—renamed the Agency for National Security Planning, with a civilian director—and the Military Security Command were brought under parliamentary oversight, their chain of command altered to enhance actual government control; and they were prohibited from conducting surveillance of public and private entities and individuals and were forced to return to their original missions.[41] The reduction in military autonomy went hand in hand with an expanded governmental role in the formulation of defense and security policy.

Kim's success in reforming Korean civil-military relations was facilitated by several factors. First, he enjoyed strong and wide public support. Second, moderate civil society groups that focused on institutional reform bolstered Kim's reform drive and deterred military resistance to reform. Third, a more cohesive and professional armed forces readily accepted the broadening of civilian oversight. Fourth, the low-level external security threats provided Korea with a structural condition that favored democratic reforms and military withdrawal from politics.[42] Finally, Kim's reform took place during a period of strong economic growth, which allowed him to authorize high procurement budgets that appeased a large segment of the military establishment.

Kim Dae-jung (1998–2003)

The election of Kim Dae-jung in 1998 marked the consolidation of democracy. He was not just the first minority-party candidate to get elected but also the country's "most famous dissident and inveterate prodemocracy fighter."[43] The fact that Kim's election provoked no opposition from the armed forces despite public concerns, demonstrated just how far democratization had progressed in a decade.

Unlike his predecessor, Kim Dae-jung did not implement radical military reforms. His most important innovation in security affairs was the introduction of the so-called sunshine policy that placed relations with North Korea on a new foundation. This initiative explicitly dropped the notion of unification through absorption as the stated goal of the Republic of Korea and recognized that the route to self-security required reducing the insecurity of the North.[44] Given their utmost concern with South Korea's security, the generals were understandably nervous about the implications of the "sunshine policy" but remained silent even though conservative parties vociferously opposed such a drastic shift in foreign policy. The top brass also abided by Kim Dae-jung's orders to offer only restrained responses to violations of South Korean waters by North Korean naval vessels.

Kim Dae-jung was intent to mollify the armed forces. Just four days after being elected, he decided to release the former military leaders prosecuted and jailed under his predecessor in a gesture aiming at national reconciliation.[45] He did not discriminate against members of the Hana-hoe faction, he based assignments and promotion decisions on professional qualifications, and he eschewed regional favoritism. Under Kim the legislature expanded its involvement in national security issues, and NGOs became somewhat more influential in public discussions of defense matters. Kim furthered the cause of civilian control in 2001 by establishing the National Security Council (NSC) as a presidential advisory body to deliberate a broad range of national security issues—its members were the president; the ministers of unification, foreign affairs and trade, defense; the director of the National Intelligence Service; and the senior presidential secretary for national security and foreign affairs.[46] During Roh Moohyun's presidency (2003–2008), the NSC ultimately became the primary defense decision-making agency and the military's role was diminished to bystander status.[47]

It is important to recognize that Kim Dae-jung's achievements in the field of security policy, and his moderate policies toward the armed forces, were made possible by Kim Young-sam, who was *the* pivotal Korean leader in terms of the process of establishing democratic civil-military relations. It was Kim Young-sam's substantive reforms and courageous stance vis-à-vis the armed forces that enabled his successor to make magnanimous gestures toward that institution.

Military in State and Society

The Korean president has the right both to command and to administer the armed forces. In practice, these executive privileges devolve to the defense minister and his ministry. As in most advanced democracies, the MoD is responsible for general policy, management, organizational matters, and public diplomacy regarding defense-security issues. All uniformed personnel are subordinate to the minister. The Joint Chiefs of Staff deals with military practice and the implementation of policy. In case of natural disasters, local or national administrators can ask the military for assistance. In national emergencies the president and the parliament must agree before the former can declare a national emergency and ask the defense minister to mobilize the armed forces.

Most defense ministers have been retired generals. Although the number of retired officers in government positions has declined, the security sector continues to serve as a major source for the recruitment of personnel for senior political and bureaucratic positions. Given their top-notch education and training, the unique skill set erstwhile officers bring to the job market, and the crucial importance of security in Korean politics, this issue should be seen as a pragmatic use of human resources not as a heritage of authoritarianism. Importantly, Korean law prohibits the employment of former officers by defense industries for five years after retirement.

Since the late 1980s Korea's legislative branch has come a long way as an independent and influential political institution. The National Assembly is active in military-security affairs, both in terms of monitoring the armed forces and in terms of influencing national security policy formulation and implementation. The number of parliamentary deputies with military backgrounds has been decreasing. In 2009 there were two retired four-star generals on the legislature's Defense Committee, which participates in the budget process—committee members examine and, if necessary, alter the budget proposal—that culminates in a parliamentary vote.[48]

Although there may be some corruption inside the military—procurement issues are often hard to scrutinize for politicians or the National Assembly—there has been no evidence of any serious misappropriation of funds much less a hint of systematic fraud. The MoD has an experienced auditing department, and the services maintain their own prosecutorial offices. The rare occurrence of corruption is partly explained by the prohibition on the army to operate enterprises or own business assets. Another explanation is that Korean military professionals are reasonably well paid, allowing them to maintain middle-class lifestyles.[49] Lifetime pension benefits and job security make the military an attractive career choice, especially during difficult economic times.

Civil society played a critical role in Korea's democratic transition, and since then, NGOs and mass media organizations have become even more engaged in national security affairs, especially regarding unification policy and the defense budget.[50] Still, public discourse on security issues could benefit from more and higher-quality debate. There are few independent institutions for defense and foreign policy. Recently universities began offering courses on military-security affairs but relatively few students have signed up for them.

The Military as a Security Provider

From its inception, the Republic of Korea has faced real and acute security threats. In 1993, when the development of nuclear weapons by North Korea became a real danger, the fundamental existential threat to South Korea was reinforced. Deadly naval clashes took place in 1999 and 2002 but smaller skirmishes occur frequently—North Korea's navy violated South Korean–held water more than twenty times in 2009 alone.[51] Surprisingly, most South Koreans are not particularly interested in security issues even though they live in close proximity to one of the world most unpredictable and dangerous dictatorships. One reason is the sense among many Koreans that their country depended for five hundred years on Chinese protection and, since the 1950s, on American security guarantees, so there is no reason for them to worry too much about defending their own country. Another reason is the unpopular mandatory two-year military service for males. Most conscripts consider the time spent in the army wasted; former President Roh Moo-hyun recently publicly agreed with that assessment.[52] According to the prominent political scientist, Choi Jang-jip, Koreans are not worried about security but they are deeply nationalist and the younger generation is highly patriotic.[53] In view of their aversion to military service, one wonders how substantive their patriotism really is.

The consolidation of democracy included the establishment of firm civilian control and uniformed officers no longer making security policy. Nonetheless, by the elevated standards of ideal civil-military relations, retired officers remain quite influential in national-security management. The constant military threats emanating from North Korea, the relative lack of societal concern about them, and the fact that few politicians possess the requisite interest in and knowledge of military-security issues put the problem in a different light.

Korean security is closely intertwined with the United States and the U.S. Eighth Army stationed in the country, which has enjoyed a reputation as one of the most effective and successful facilitators of peace and stability on the Korean peninsula. After the Korean War the U.S. military government in South Korea in effect created the South Korean armed forces; its role was far more extensive than in the founding of the Bundeswehr or Japan's Self-Defense Forces. Although the presence of the U.S. Forces in Korea (USFK) has become less conspicuous in Korean population centers, among them, Seoul, the influence of American forces on Korea's military would be hard to exaggerate. The Korean government, despite some popular protest, sent the third largest force to participate in the Iraq War and it has supported Washington's plans for the relocation of USFK units in its own country.[54] Through the last five decades, thousands of Korean officers have trained and received some sort of advanced military education in the United States.

For decades, the key American concern has been stability on the peninsula and, more specifically, social stability in South Korea. During the transition process, both the U.S. administration and, through informal channels, USFK generals left no ambiguity about their strong support for democratization. In fact, Korea is an important model for America's democracy promotion efforts in Asia. Within a remarkably short time it consolidated democracy in the maximalist sense as it has come to acquire "widespread, robust legitimacy among the mass public."[55]

THAILAND'S RESILIENT GENERALS

The 1992 Transition

Thailand's democratization process began following the Royal Thai Armed Forces' vicious assault on civilians, resulting in hundreds of casualties, to suppress a popular uprising in May 1992. The roots of this brutal clampdown reach back to the February 1991 coup d'état when the top brass decided that another military takeover was necessary to purge the country of its corrupt politicians.[56] In the March 1992 general elections the military-backed party won and General Suchinda Kraprayoon—the leader of the army's National Peacekeeping Council, which conducted the 1991 coup—necame prime minister. The generals canceled legal proceedings against former ministers suspected of fraud, and several politicians the military earlier accused of corruption were named to the new cabinet. Thus, the junta metamorphosed from the scourge of money politics into its patron.[57]

As it became clear that the armed forces were planning to stay in politics, the urban middle class joined by protesters from rural areas began to stage mass demonstrations. The junta's claim that that the revolt was "an attack on nation, religion, and king" was absurd; this was a bona fide middle-class revolution. In the end, the monarch ordered the leader of the protest, Bangkok Governor Chamlong Srimuang—himself a former army general—and Suchinda to stop the violence. Following what has become known as the Black May Massacre (May 17–20, 1992), the military as an institution lost much of its social esteem—pictures of the army's brutality were transmitted worldwide—and political capital. For a short time, men in military uniform were abused in the streets and were refused treatment at hospitals.[58] The RTAF-supported government was forced to resign, and a general election was scheduled for September 1992.

Politics and the Military during Democratization (1992–2001)

The May 1992 uprising signified a major political defeat for the Royal Thai Armed Forces, whose place in Thai politics and society could now be altered. One of the new legislature's first actions was to pass a constitutional amendment that restricted the prime ministership to elected members of parliament thus preventing generals from entering politics directly. Further changes limited the power of appointed senators to initiate debates against the government and to vote on no-confidence motions to prevent military elites from gaining control of the legislature.[59] Major laws that granted the armed forces extraconstitutional powers in crises were repealed or modified—for instance, the use of the military to control riots now required government authorization—and the Capital Peacekeeping Command, key to controlling security in Bangkok since 1976, was dissolved.[60]

In the months following the uprising, Anand Panyarachun's civilian caretaker government achieved what few thought was possible and became deeply involved in military appointments for the first time. Anand removed high-ranking officers implicated in the 1992 massacre and transferred others, including the army's commander in chief, to positions of lesser power and access to politics. The many vacant positions at the top of the RTAF hierarchy were filled with competent but politically passive generals, a move that spurred the Thai military toward more professionalism for the first time in modern Thai history.[61]

The two civilian governments of Chuan Leekpai (1992–95, 1997–2001) managed to significantly reorder Thai civil-military relations by reducing the armed forces' influence on elite recruitment and public policy-making, decreasing their prerogatives in foreign policy issues, and halting the practice of active-duty officers serving in the cabinet and in the Senate. At the same time, the representation of retired military personnel was also reduced from 152 (out of 260) appointed senators in 1992 to only 48 in 1996. Following the 2000 Senate elections, former RTAF officers only held eighteen of the two hundred seats.[62] The 1997 financial crisis paved the way for Chuan to return for a second stint as prime minister. He once again added the defense portfolio to his prime ministerial responsibilities and pushed the military toward various reforms. (The defense portfolio has always been held by prime ministers or retired generals; the most powerful defense official, however, is the chief of the army, an active-duty general.)

Despite these successes, the military remained an essential political force in large part because it was never depoliticized but was merely "willing to pretend to accept limit and controls, on condition that it remained unreformed."[63] The civilian government did not shut out the army from politics and was not in a position to demand major concessions from the RTAF: for instance, the excessive military presence in Bangkok, which can only be explained by political reasons, was never contested. The RTAF managed to retain its dominant position in formulating national security policy partly because the legislature did not have effective defense-security committees and partly because both the National Assembly and the government lacked individuals with solid defense-related expertise. Moreover, both of Chuan's governments and Thai civil society failed to incorporate information and analysis of military-security affairs into their political discourse and activism.[64] These shortcomings, in turn, compelled civilians to depend on the

RTAF for advice. In sum, the government still needed to court the army and have its support.

The armed forces' internal reform failed because no one forced them to implement it. More specifically, the RTAF effectively fended off the governmental schemes it found unacceptable, such as initiatives aimed at raising efficiency and reforming promotion regulations as well as cutting the number of generals without actual responsibilities. At the same time, the military enthusiastically implemented other reforms pushed by the government that happened to match the RTAF's own plans—such as force reduction—thereby creating the impression of a compliant institution. While Army Commander General Surayud Chulanont—whose troops were seen shooting at demonstrators in May 1992[65]—insisted that the top brass must leave the conduct of foreign policy to the ministry of foreign affairs, he soon recognized that it was impossible to force his colleagues out of one of the RTAF's traditional policy domains.

Thaksin and the Royal Thai Armed Forces (2001–2006)

In 1998 Thaksin Shinawatra, an ex–police colonel and one of Thailand's most successful entrepreneurs, founded a new political party, *Thai Rak Thai* (or TRT, meaning, "Thais Love Thais," a protectionist response to the financial crisis). Thaksin led TRT to a massive win in the January 2001 elections.

With Thaksin's accession to the prime ministership, the gradual process of reducing the military's political clout was reversed. Upon taking office, Thaksin commenced transforming the armed forces into his own power base by granting them a number of new privileges and restoring several old ones. Most importantly, he not only increased the military's budget, which was considerably lowered by Chuan's governments, but he hastily approved the RTAF's procurement list for 2005–2013. Moreover, Thaksin consented to the renewal of the army's powerful position in foreign policy formulation. Although the RTAF's representation in the legislature was diminished, Thaksin compensated the top brass by appointing fifty-five army generals to the exalted position of Adviser to the Prime Minister and later increased their number by thirty.[66]

Thaksin's courting of the armed forces did not conceal his underlying ambition to control them, however. Thanks to the legislative and policy decisions of the 1990s, the military as an institution possessed no veto power over the formation and dissolution of governments, and active-duty army personnel were prohibited from holding public office. During Thaksin's first term in office, his landslide victory, vast popularity among the masses, and the implementation of the 1997 Constitution with its strict limitations on military prerogatives resulted in probably the highest level of civilian control over the military in Thai history.[67]

That the prime minister's leverage over the armed forces turned out to be ephemeral was his own fault. Notwithstanding his many conciliatory gestures toward the RTAF—which included, in his first couple of years in power, steering his cabinet away from meddling in the army's internal affairs—Thaksin also enraged the top brass by repeatedly interfering in the army's promotion procedures in order to solidify his support base. Not discerning or choosing to ignore signals of the deep-seated displeasure his actions provoked among the generals, he continued to appoint supporters and even family members to top RTAF posts. These dangerous measures ultimately sacrificed not only Thaksin's own regime, but more broadly, civilian rule in Thailand.

In 2005 Thaksin became the first Thai prime minister to serve out his term in office and win reelection. He won, again, by a large margin, and began to exploit his popularity by increasing his already dominant political influence over all three branches of government. For example, his administration passed a decree that allowed the prime minister to authorize a three-month state of emergency to respond to domestic and foreign threats, while, using his network of personal contacts, he centralized his authority over the Royal Thai Police.[68] Nonetheless, Thaksin was a polarizing political figure whose policies set off the lower classes and much of the rural population against the urban middle class. The media harshly criticized his government for widespread corruption and abuses of power.

Demonstrations against Thaksin had begun in the fall of 2005, and they only intensified in early 2006, after he sold his business for a tax exempt US$1.9 billion. Following several more months of public protests, instability, and political maneuvering, the military staged a bloodless coup in September 2006 when Thaksin was out of the country. The coup enjoyed the backing of the business community, intellectuals, social activists, and the media; people actually put flowers in the turrets of the tanks on the streets of Bangkok.[69] To justify their actions, the putschists shrewdly used Thaksin's allegedly disrespectful behavior toward the institution of the monarchy, the sacred cow of Thai politics (at least during the current king's reign); graft and corruption in the government and the government's attempts to silence the media.[70] The underlying reason for the coup, however, was Thaksin's persistent meddling with promotions and attempts to restructure the military leadership.

The Military Government and the Return to "Normalcy" (2006–2008)

The September 2006 military takeover was a "royalist coup" insofar as it was supposed to reassert a perception of the monarchy as above-criticism, and because it did enjoy at least the king's tacit backing.[71] Royal support for the coup is hardly surprising because the king's principal commitment has always been to social stability, and, after nearly a year of political and social chaos, he was ready to see order restored. The coup-makers professed unwavering loyalty to the monarch and successfully mobilized royalist sentiments to oust a government perceived by various societal groups as a direct threat to the monarchy.[72] Demonstrations had become increasingly emotional displays of support for the king with people chanting, "We defend the King," and calling on him to dismiss the disrespectful, greedy, and corrupt Thaksin.

To some extent the coup was facilitated by democracy activists who thought that the military was no longer the Thai polity's chief underlying problem and, in effect, took their eyes off the ball. There were few independent civilian defense experts, most of them journalists or academics, but they were no more favorably disposed toward Thaksin and the TRT than the army. As far as the coup-makers were concerned, their putsch was a last-ditch defense against the consolidation of Thaksin's personalized regime, which would have, in the end, neutralized the military as an autonomous political force.[73] Once back in power, the generals regained their erstwhile position in policy formulation and implementation, monopolized public policy areas of paramount concern to them—national security, foreign policy—and imposed limitations on media freedoms. The junta banned political parties and demonstrations until July 2007, and a new National Legislative Assembly—76 (or 31.4 percent) of its members had backgrounds in the military or the police—drew up yet another constitution endorsed by the top brass.[74]

In 2006–2008 the military ruled directly, appointed cabinet members and the prime minister—none other than the aforementioned Surayud Chulanont, now a retired general—and possessed veto power over the formation and dissolution of cabinets. Unlike the army leaders of old, many of whom were seasoned bureaucrats and expert political operators, the group of generals at the helm in 2006–2008 had little political experience—after all, they *had been* out of power since 1992. The popularity of the RTAF's fifteen-month rule was short-lived. The junta appointed mostly dull old bureaucrats who did little to solve the multitude of quickly surfacing socioeconomic and political problems. All in all, it was a profoundly dormant government whose efforts at effective governance were halfhearted at best.[75] The junta allowed elections to be held in December 2007; they were won by the People's Power Party—the successor to Thaksin's TRT party, which was outlawed in 2006—led by Samak Sundaravej, a veteran politician.

In the Thai context, return to civilian rule is a relative concept. Outwardly civilians may be in government, to be sure, but the generals continue to enjoy a privileged political position. If, from the perspective of democratizing civil-military relations, the 1992–2001 era was two steps forward, then Thaksin's five years in government and the military rule that followed were two steps backward. Although the generals are no longer in the cabinet, they cast a long shadow over the polity. While the Lower House of the legislature remains entirely elected, in accord with the stipulations of the 2007 Constitution, of the 150 senators only 76 are directly elected, the rest appointed. In 2008, 23 senators were ex-soldiers, 14 of these appointees.[76] Although the RTAF no longer enjoys veto power over cabinet appointments, the top brass have repeatedly tried to influence political processes and to interfere with the composition of cabinets. The Privy Council, a powerful group of advisors to the king that considers legislation and civil service appointments, has long been the locus of military clout because its members are selected by the monarch, who, in any case, has maintained close relations with the RTAF for decades.

Even after they withdrew to the barracks in 2008, Thai soldiers have been perfectly capable of indirectly dominating civilian governments if it suits their purposes, just as they have done in one way or another since 1932.[77] In late 2009, a *Bangkok Post* article on the Thai political leadership noted that the prime minister, Abhisit Vejjajiva, phoned the deputy army chief General Prayuth Chan-ocha several times a day to check on updates of events, to pass on messages to Defense Minister, General Prawit Wongsuwon, and RTAF Commander in Chief, General Anupong Paochinda, as well as to solicit advice on relevant matters as if this were a routine practice in democracies at peace.[78] There is no reason to suppose they will be stripped of this capacity in the foreseeable future. On April 10 and May 13–19, 2010, the army once again brutally cracked down on demonstrators in Central Bangkok who called for the government to dissolve parliament and hold elections. The RTAF's actions resulted in more than eighty civilian deaths and over two thousand injured. Thai media dubbed the assaults, which ended with the surrender of protest leaders and numerous arrests, "Cruel April" and "Savage May."[79]

Security and Personnel Issues

In Thailand all defense-security-related political bodies—the most important are the Defense Council, the Council of Armed Forces Commanders, and the National Security Council—are directly or indirectly dominated by the RTAF. Some of these organizations include civilians, and during periods of democratization, there might be some jockeying for control between them and their uniformed colleagues. When matters the generals deem important are decided, however, they virtually always carry the day. Their authority to make and implement defense policy had somewhat diminished during 1992–2006 but since then they have regained much of their lost clout. For example, the Defense Policy White Paper, issued in 2008 and approved by the prime minister, was essentially the work of military officers with only perfunctory civilian participation.

Notwithstanding its powerful political position, the RTAF is a professional and mission-oriented organization. Thai elites responded to regional instabilities by building up the country's military capabilities; the improvements achieved in the Royal Thai Navy are especially impressive.[80] The RTAF has been engaged in countering several security threats in recent years. The armed forces' internal security function has been its paramount concern given that Thailand has faced domestic challenges that no other organization is equipped to deal with. Since 2004, Muslim insurgents in the south of the country have conducted a campaign of separatist violence that until late 2009 had claimed the lives of nearly four thousand Thais. The area is populated by mostly ethnic Malay Muslims but Bangkok has ruled out granting them autonomy. The RTAF has run the counterinsurgency operations without civilian intervention and has benefited from the US$3 billion the government has poured into the area.[81] Thailand has also been contending with serious border-security issues—mostly in the form of refugees, drug-trafficking, and smuggling—on its borders with Myanmar, Cambodia, and Laos. Neither the RTAF's antiseparatist campaign in the south nor its handling of the refugee situation in the north has been particularly effective.

A controversial issue regarding the competence of RTAF personnel is that time-in-service rather than qualification has been the basis for advancement. The upshot is that promotion has been viewed as an entitlement and so there are far more generals than there are actual positions for them. In 1998, for instance, there were 1,859 generals but 616 had no concrete responsibilities.[82] Moreover, officers from the class entering the military academy in 1985 will not reach mandatory retirement age (sixty) until about 2025 so, given that almost no one leaves the services voluntarily, plans to reduce troop strengths are unlikely to pan out.

The military is a ruling caste of Thailand. Once selected for the prestigious Armed Forces Academy Preparatory School—a two-year institution for students aspiring to work in the police or the armed forces—cadets become members of an elite group. Ties to and within the AFAPS are extremely important, even more so than connections to higher-level educational/training institutions. For instance, young Thai men who get their initial military education abroad are at a disadvantage because they were not members of an AFAPS class that would endow them with valuable connections lasting their entire careers.

The first AFAPS class (Class 1) graduated in 1960; former Prime Minister Thaksin graduated in Class 10. Although the Thai military has been highly prone to factionalism, it has occasionally become united for the sake of a larger purpose, such as trumping civilian authority to gain political or economic concessions.[83] As in many other armies and large professional organizations, there are different groups and loyalties within the RTAF, based on career choices, shared service, regions of origin, and so on. When officers are promoted, it is customary for them to take loyal colleagues with them and, once they are retired, to give one another lucrative consultancies. This is not the result of some nefarious scheme but the standard nepotism that is inherent in the system.

The RTAF's Budget, Economic Role, and Social Status

The military's funds primarily come from the state budget and from military-controlled state enterprises. In addition, the RTAF has been involved in a number of profitable illegal or semilegal activities. Although under Prime Minister Chuan these endeavors were subject to government crackdowns, little headway was made owing to the economic crisis in the late 1990s and the absence of effective government sanctions. During the democratic transition, the legislature's ability to scrutinize the defense budget and to monitor its disbursement increased. Nonetheless, military coups generated massive increases in state allocations for defense—for instance, defense spending rose by 60 percent in fiscal year 2007 and by 18 percent the following year.[84] Since the return of civilian rule, the army has still been able to pretty much get what it wants. The problem is not that there are no legal mechanisms to avoid financial misdeeds and corruption but that the problems lie in details civilians cannot oversee much less control.[85]

After 1992 the Thai business community was increasingly critical of the military's economic involvement, especially their presence on state enterprise boards, particularly because most officers were not competent businessmen. During 2006–2008 the junta put some of its own personnel in charge of running public companies but they left after the return of the civilian government. The RTAF has long been extensively in-volved in rural development that has greatly benefited Thai society. In fact, the military's role in development has been enshrined in the constitution.[86]

Since the beginning of the Cold War, the armed forces have owned and operated numerous broadcast media outlets—including two of the country's six noncable television channels. This position has made it easy for the military to manage and shape their own image, and they have been expert propagandists. During their 2006–2008 stint in power, the generals put into effect a Broadcasting Act that granted additional concessions to the RTAF's media interests. Military-owned radio and television stations downplay or deny reports of the widespread corruption in weapons procurement and craft the image of an army that works for and with the people.[87] Partly as a result, the military continues to be a very popular institution. People generally trust the armed forces, soldiering is considered a prestigious and honorable profession, and, notwithstanding the expanding employment opportunities produced by a quickly growing economy, the RTAF still gets some of the brightest young Thais to join. Military personnel are well remunerated and enjoy access to inexpensive housing and their own hospitals. And, if active-duty officers should find themselves serving in the government or the legislature, they will be able to draw salaries from both of their employees.

A PLEASANT SURPRISE: INDONESIA

In 1997 when the Asian economic crisis began, Suharto was seventy-six, isolated from everyday politics, and mostly interested in taking care of his inner circle. The widespread corruption of his government unleashed massive anti-Suharto demonstrations in February 1998 that turned into violent riots claiming over one thousand lives in Jakarta alone and causing much property damage. Following protracted, mostly back-room negotiations with politicians and military leaders, Suharto resigned in May 1998 and was succeeded by his protégé and vice president B. J. Habibie. Indonesia held its first free elections after more than forty years in June 1999, and in October 1999, the new legislature—the People's Consultative Assembly—elected a civilian president, Abdurrahman Wahid.

The military was an important participant in the negotiations that led to the transitions from Suharto to Habibie and then from Habibie to Wahid.[88] The intense power struggle within the army that preceded Suharto's resignation was won by General Wiranto, who managed to obtain the backing of the country's largest Muslim organization.[89] Wiranto's victory was sealed when he garnered the support of incoming President Habibie, both for his leadership of the armed forces and for his sacking of Lieutenant-General Prabowo Subianto, Suharto's son-in-law and, as head of the Army Strategic Reserve command, Wiranto's chief rival.[90]

The evolution of post-Suharto military politics can be easily traced through the tenures of Indonesia's four post-Suharto presidents. They heavily depended on their personal relationships with leading generals and left the task of reforming the armed forces to them. Some observers condemn Indonesia's military reform for the minimal civilian participation in it.[91] One can also argue, however, that staying out of the nitty-gritty of defense reform was a wise decision: by not forcing reforms on the military but letting its leaders formulate and implement them, the armed forces automatically acquired "ownership" of these reforms and was more likely to respect them. Even so, the process of military reform, as Marcus Mietzner argued, has been anything but a linear development, as it has reflected the fluctuations of the political reform process at large.[92]

Habibie (1998–99) and the ABRI/TNI

Although Habibie's government struggled with the economy, the independence movement in Indonesia's province of East Timor, and numerous other social and political problems, during its seventeen-month term Indonesian civil-military relations had changed considerably. Commander in Chief Wiranto, who also served as Minister of Defense and Security, quickly set to reform the armed forces. Habibie's close relationship with Wiranto and other military leaders—who decided to depoliticize the military and to redefine its role—eased ABRI's acceptance of the reforms.

Perhaps most importantly, the *dwifungsi* doctrine was jettisoned in favor of the "New Paradigm" that signified the separation of the armed forces and the police, stopped the practice of promoting active-duty military officers to nonmilitary jobs, and generally reduced ABRI's influence in politics. The number of parliamentary seats assigned to the armed forces was cut from seventy-five to thirty-eight, the generals apologized for past human rights abuses, and quite a few of the most notorious officers were dismissed. The military leadership declared ABRI's political neutrality as well as its withdrawal from *Golkar*, the Party of Functional Groups—formed in 1964 with the backing of army generals to counter the increasing influence of the communists—the de facto ruling party under Suharto and Habibie. Another important measure was the separation of the National Police from the armed forces. The change of the military's name to TNI (Armed Forces of

Indonesia) in April 1999 was a symbolic expression of the reforms it was undergoing.

When he entered office, Habibie declared that sovereignty for East Timor was out of the question, though he did not take expanded autonomy off the table. Nonetheless, in January 1999 he detonated a political bomb by agreeing to a referendum to decide between autonomy and independence to be held in East Timor. Not surprisingly, this decision made Habibie very un-popular in the military, which was heavily invested in the province. Four out of five of the 98 percent East Timorese who participated in the referendum favored independence, and, after a great deal of bloodshed and brutality, TNI units and paramilitary troops withdrew from the province.[93]

Civil-Military Relations under Wahid (1999–2001)

Abdurrahman Wahid's twenty-month term was marked by an erratic style of governance, a growing perception of incompetence, corruption scandals, and controversies. He was removed from office by a Special Session of the People's Consultative Assembly in July 2001 after months of demonstra-tions and political instability. The fundamental reason for Wahid's downfall, however, was that he alienated those who brought him to power, among them the army leadership.

As in other policy areas, Wahid's approach to the military was unpredict-able and impulsive. Soon after entering office he made several decisions that appeared to further weaken TNI's political position. He selected a civilian defense minister and appointed generals known for their reformist think-ing to senior military posts. Moreover, Wahid enthusiastically supported the prosecution of TNI officers for their alleged human rights violations. In Oc-tober 1999 Wahid appointed Wiranto as Coordinating Minister for Security and Political Security Affairs, an important position that nonetheless re-moved him from TNI's chain of command. A few months later Wahid sacked Wiranto from his ministership and transferred him along with seventy-four other commanders and staff officers. Wahid justified these actions as part of the ongoing investigations of the army's human rights abuses in East Timor, but, more likely, he wanted to "break the myth of army power" by destabi-lizing the top brass.[94]

The measure that proved to be most damaging for Wahid's political longevity—and that also contributed to Thaksin's undoing—was the one armies everywhere find most objectionable: repeated interference with their promotion processes. To be sure, Wahid's meddling in the TNI's internal affairs mostly focused on advancing the careers of "reformist" generals but the end result was the same: he lost the top brass's support. At the end of the day, no substantial progress was made in the armed forces' democratization under Wahid. In fact, civil-military relations took a step backward during his term because his thoughtless policies created an opportunity for TNI to reclaim its political influence.[95]

Megawati Sukarnoputri (2001–2004) and Her Generals

Megawati, Sukarno's daughter, was brought to power as an antidote to Wahid's mercurial rule and enjoyed solid TNI backing. She was heavily indebted to the armed forces, and in return, she became their reliable friend in the Presidential Palace. Several retired officers—many of them reform skeptics—received key positions in Megawati's administration. Arguably the most important appointment Megawati made, however, was of Susilo Bambang Yudhoyono, a retired lieutenant general from TNI's reformist wing who served as Coordinating Minister for Security and Political Affairs and was responsible for ensuring domestic stability and civilian control over the military.

"SBY," as he is widely known in Indonesia, oversaw the search for and arrest of the perpetrators of the October 2002 Bali bombing and earned a reputation at home and abroad as one of the few Indonesian politicians serious about fighting international terrorism. Nonetheless, SBY was measured in his approach to the separatist movement in Aceh and was one of the few cabinet members who cautioned against a full-blown war there. SBY also succeeded in convincing Megawati to declare martial law there in 2003. Overall, his term as coordinating minister was relatively uneventful but it allowed him to burnish his public image as a calm, polite, and charismatic figure. Yudhoyono's growing popularity and his alienation from conservative generals had resulted in his increasing marginalization within the cabinet by Megawati, who, for good reasons, began to see in him an emerging rival.

Megawati reduced the authority of the ministry of defense as the executive's primary institutional link to the military and depended more on personal connections to top generals. The result of this practice, in combination with other political and institutional concessions to TNI, was sharply diminishing state oversight of the armed forces.[96] In sum, Megawati's years in power were synonymous with rising military autonomy. At the same time, it is important to note that the two major defense-related laws (Law No. 3 of 2002 on state defense, and Law No. 34 of 2004 on the Indonesian defense forces) were approved by the legislature under her tenure.

Susilo Bambang Yudhoyono (2004–)

Long before Suharto's exit from the political scene, General Yudhoyono, who graduated first in his class of the military academy in 1973, had advocated a diminishing political role for the armed forces. Though a former general, his election in no way signified a return to praetorianism, because SBY was always considered an outsider in ABRI; he was never seen as a great field commander, and he was an intellectual and an accomplished musician. SBY married the daughter of Sarwo Edhie Wibowo, a general who, as the commander of the army's special forces, was instrumental in the destruction of the PKI.[97] Not being liked by the top brass was probably an electoral asset for the new president but, once he entered office, his outsider status turned into a liability in his dealings with the army. Some of the generals SBY put in place were his academy classmates and from his circle of confidants, but several were selected owing to their high professionalism and reformist outlook. Nevertheless, partly because of his weak position in the military, no serious reforms have been implemented during his tenure and both the MoD and the TNI have been largely left to reform themselves.

Under Yudhoyono the legislature has become more assertive, though its all-civilian Armed Forces Committee—known as "Commission One," it also covers foreign policy and communications—does not have full oversight of the budget. Then again, even the minister of defense and the TNI commander lack complete information about budget implementation not to mention TNI's many business interests. A number of nongovernmental organizations—such as the Centre for Strategic and International Studies and KontraS—and government think tanks (e.g., Lemhannas) have emerged that have generated public discussion of defense-security affairs and have kept a critical eye on the defense establishment. Nonetheless, the legislature does not, as a general rule, take advantage of the considerable defense expertise located in these institutions by consulting their staff.

SBY astutely picked Juwono Sudarsono as his defense minister. A political scientist who held the defense portfolio—the first civilian in fifty years to do so—in Wahid's cabinet in 1999–2000, Sudarsono's service as defense minister spanned SBY's first term (2004–2009). By this time, civilian control over the TNI had solidified, and the army's privileges had been reduced: unelected military officers could no longer hold parliamentary seats, ambassadorships were closed to active armed forces personnel, and military courts were subordinated to the Supreme Court. During Sudarsono's term, TNI as an institution became a supporter of democratization and market reform, particularly on the village, local, district, and provincial levels. According to Sudarsono, his most important achievement as defense minister

was successfully convincing young officers from all service branches to prepare themselves for civilian life by acquiring skills in management, finance,
law, and so forth.[98]

SBY succeeded in improving soldiers' conditions, procuring some big-
ticket weapons, and reducing factionalism within the top brass (by, among
other things, not meddling in high-level promotions). Moreover, military
affairs, shrouded in much secrecy under Megawati's rule, have become far
more transparent under SBY's presidency.[99] He was reelected by over 60
percent of the popular vote in 2009. In his second term his priority has been
to develop an indigenous defense industry and thereby lower procurement
costs in the long term.

Remaining Shortcomings

Although much has been achieved in democratizing Indonesian civil-military
relations, several problem areas remain. The head of the TNI reports directly to the president not to the minister of defense. The MoD is still primarily staffed by officers (especially army officers) and the top brass retains
a dominant role in the formulation of national security policy. Furthermore,
members of the armed forces have not been held accountable for their past
human rights abuses.

Perhaps the biggest problem is the continued involvement of TNI in
the national economy; partly as a result, its political influence in villages,
towns, and districts endures. Early in his fist term SBY promised to eliminate or at least drastically scale down the armed forces' economic involvement, and in October 2004 a law passed by the legislature required TNI
businesses to cease operations by 2009. In fact, only modest progress was
made. Faced with the impending deadline, in October 2009 a presidential
decree followed by a ministry of defense directive required only a partial
restructuring of military cooperatives and foundations that have held most
of the armed forces' investments.[100] These basic facts, however, hide a more
complex truth.

In 2004–2009 Indonesia's defense budget averaged between US$3.5–4.2
billion (0.68 percent of the GDP and 4.5 percent of the annual budget),
notwithstanding its ongoing security challenges from separatist movements.
For the sake of comparison: Indonesia is the world's largest archipelagic
state whose landmass of over 740,000 square miles includes nearly fourteen thousand islands. In the past several years Singapore, a 274-square-mile
city-state with a population of four million, spent nearly twice as much on
defense as Indonesia.[101] For five years Sudarsono lobbied for substantially
increased defense expenditures, but in the end he realized that the TNI had

to yield to social programs, poverty alleviation, education (that took 75 percent of the state budget), and infrastructural development.[102]

Instability—political, economic, and social—was the most important attribute of the context in which Indonesia began its post-Suharto transition. It must be acknowledged, then, that in order to ensure that the process of transition would not be reversed, concessions had to be made to the armed forces, traditionally the country's most important political actor. Keeping TNI's budget extremely low *and* halting their economic activities would have been tantamount to taking away the soldiers' livelihood. TNI has already agreed to a significantly reduced political role and the erosion of many of its privileges. Its generals would have been hard pressed to tolerate the cessation of their business interests without some sort of protest or uprising that Indonesia's fragile democracy may not have survived. The military appears to be satisfied with the current political situation but the peace between civilians and soldiers is predicated on the latter's continued rent-seeking activity, albeit on a much smaller scale.[103] The appropriate time to force the armed forces out of the economy will come when the defense budget is able to maintain TNI without outside revenue sources.

All in all, for most expert observers, Indonesia's post-Suharto development has been a pleasant surprise.[104] The country has not disintegrated despite secessionist challenges; inter-ethnic relations—particularly the occasionally tense nexus of the Indonesian majority with the small but financially powerful ethnic Chinese minority—are under control; and the Muslim majority, by and large, has not been radicalized. Furthermore, even though their political role has diminished beyond most expectations, the armed forces have attempted no coup, and, according to one of the top observers of Indonesian affairs, the possibility of a military takeover in the foreseeable future approaches zero as long as the current civilian polity remains stable.[105]

CONCLUSION

South Korea, Thailand, and Indonesia have undergone very different democratization processes. Unlike the praetorian states and their successors in Southern Europe and Latin America we learned about in the preceding two chapters, the three military regimes discussed here have had to contend with serious security challenges that affected their militaries' position, social esteem, and the conditions of their withdrawal from politics. The important distinction between the external threats Korea has had to contend with and the internal threats secessionist movements pose to Thailand and Indonesia supports Michael Desch's argument that settings in which internal threats are combined with the absence of external ones undermine civilian control of the armed forces.[106]

Given the existential threat posed to it, the Korean state had to build an economy in order to defend itself. Economic development, in time, fostered the formation of a vibrant civil society that, in turn, demanded democratization. Importantly, economics or, more precisely, the 1997 financial crisis, had a major political impact in all three states but especially in Thailand, where it brought down an incompetent government, and in Indonesia, where it was the spark that ignited the democratization process. The three cases here lend support to the contention of modernization theory that the higher the level of socioeconomic development the better the chances of successful democratization.[107]

Although the democratization processes of both Korea and Thailand originated in brutal state action—the Kwangju Uprising from which Chun never truly recovered and the Black May Massacre that impelled defense reform—it would be hard to find two more different cases in East Asia. The slower pace of economic transformation combined with a cultural factor, the excessive reverence for authority—rooted in the godlike status enjoyed by the king—delayed the evolution of an activist civil society in Thailand. The monarchy itself has also inhibited democratization in Thai politics. The king's often unqualified backing of the armed forces and his support for the 2006 coup puts him in sharp contrast with the actions of Spain's Juan Carlos following the attempted putsch there a quarter century earlier.

Korea enjoyed a relatively neat and straight path to democratic consolidation without major setbacks and upheavals. In contrast, the process in both Thailand and Indonesia proceeded in fits and starts, though only Thailand had experienced the dramatic reversal of a full-blown military coup. This point is well illustrated by looking at the records of individual leaders and, in turn, underscores my more general argument about the decisive role individual leaders often play in the destiny of their countries. The pivotal leaders discussed in this chapter, those whose occasionally courageous actions really turned the tide, are Kim Young-sam, Anand Panyarachun, Chuan Leekpai in his first term, and B. J. Habibie. They were the first leaders after democratization began and were able to exploit the opportunity that opened as the military was losing ground. The examples of Anand and Habibie, in particular, demonstrate that caretaker executives can be extremely effective transitional leaders. The major achievement of Chuan in his second turn as prime minister, and of Yudhoyono, was that they returned their countries to the track of diminishing military influence after the setbacks suffered under their predecessors.

The two main generalizations we stated regarding the postpraetorian context pertaining to the six case studies of the previous two chapters are borne out by the experiences of the three states in Asia as well. The central task of democratizers was to get the armed forces out of politics—even if they succeeded only partially in Indonesia and, in Thailand's case, at times not at all. And the kind of leverage the top brass enjoyed as they returned to the barracks was an important predictor of the way they were treated by the incoming civilian government. The Korean transition to democracy is similar to the Chilean experience in regard to the generals' gradual loss of privileges and the relatively smooth transfer of power. At the same time, Korean generals had less leverage, owing to the Chun government's loss of legitimacy than their Chilean colleagues. It seems that Thai military elites retained little political influence when they left power in 1992. Nonetheless, due to their traditionally prevalent position in the Thai political landscape and to the civilians' inability to thoroughly depoliticize the RTAF, they continued to preserve much of their political strength. The political position of Indonesian soldiers was more akin to the Korean model: as *participants* in the negotiations leading to the transition, they enjoyed relatively high leverage and then gradually lost some of their political power—but not nearly as much as their counterparts in Korea.

Based on the experiences of the Southern European transitions we could generalize that no systematic prosecution of those guilty of human rights violations took place, a statement that does not stand up with respect to our Latin American cases. The three Asian experiences are similar to the Southern European cases insofar as there has been no systematic prosecution of military personnel guilty of human rights abuses. The reasons here, however, are different than they were in Southern Europe. In Indonesia and Thailand, civilian governments have not been in a strong enough position vis-à-vis the military to contemplate a thorough purge of the armed forces. In Korea, on the other hand, the prosecution of generals was limited because of the interest in societal reconciliation. The chapter titles of Terence Roehrig's book on the prosecution of former military leaders tellingly refer to "extensive," "cautious," and "reluctant" prosecution in Argentina, Greece, and Korea, respectively.[108] The Asian post–military rule cases are more similar to our Latin American ones in terms of the relatively minor role played by international actors, with the exception of the involvement of the United States and its army in Korea.

Are the generals of South Korea, Indonesia, and Thailand committed to democratic rule? Only in the Korean case can one answer with a confident affirmative; one would have to be extremely skeptical about the democratic leanings of Thai generals, and though, while in all likelihood Indonesian officers have gradually become more respectful of democratic values in the past decade, at this point the strength of their commitment is certainly debatable. The case studies in this chapter also support one of the main arguments of this book that the support by military elites of democratic rule is a necessary, if insufficient, ingredient for democratic consolidation. The political allegiances of the Korean, Thai, and Indonesian officer corps aptly correspond to the status of democratic consolidation in their countries.

This chapter also illustrates the importance of carefully sequencing military reforms. Specific contexts determine what measures are feasible in the initial transition process without provoking the ire of military elites and when is it more advisable to hold off until more stability is achieved. In settings where the government is flush with money, such as in Korea under Kim Young-sam, the chance to in effect purchase the armed forces' acquiescence by allowing them to procure new weapons and equipment—"Give them toys," is how Huntington referred to this tactic[109]—should be utilized. Interfering with the promotion practices of a yet-unreformed military establishment, as Thaksin had done, is usually asking for trouble. At the same time, excessive appeasement of the generals for their political support can be counterproductive and, as Megawati's term nicely illustrates, can easily halt the process of the military's democratization.

TABLE 6.1

After Military Rule in Asia: South Korea, Thailand, and Indonesia

	Country Period	South Korea 1987–2003	Thailand 1992–2009	Indonesia 1998–2008
Background	end of military regime	peaceful, gradual	societal uprising	negotiated and controlled by the military
	overall military regime performance	strong (economic policy), extensive human rights violations	mixed, advances in economic development and nation-building, extensive human rights violations	mixed, advances in economic development and nation-building, extensive human rights violations
	leverage of military when leaving power	high	medium (in 1992)	high
State	main tasks	get the military out of politics, the economy, and internal security; reduce its autonomy, privileges, and size; create new institutional frameworks for democratic civil-military relations	get the military out of politics, the economy, and internal security; reduce its autonomy, privileges, and size; create new institutional frameworks for democratic civil-military relations	get the military out of politics, the economy, and internal security; reduce its autonomy, privileges, and size; create new institutional frameworks for democratic civil-military relations
	civilian political leadership	thoughtful, restrained, effective	bold but short-lived	varying quality
	political institutions and trend	strong and improving	some good reforms but many reversed	strengthening
	civilian involvement in defense affairs	gradually increasing, strong, balanced civilian control	bold but over-reaching	tentative, government lets military reform itself
	executive control	gradually increasing to great strength	strong until reversal	varying strengths depending on leader
	legislative oversight	growing active in budget issues	weak, ineffective	weak

TABLE 6.1   *(continued)*

After Military Rule in Asia: South Korea, Thailand, and Indonesia

	Country Period	*South Korea* *1987–2003*	*Thailand* *1992–2009*	*Indonesia* *1998–2008*
	prosecution of human rights abuses	yes, in the mid- 1990s but very limited	no	no
	foreign influence	high (USA)	not an important factor	not an important factor
Military	behavior during transition	nonconfronta- tional	trying to safe- guard perks and institutional autonomy	surprisingly restrained
	interference in politics	minimal, some in defense policy	intensive, military never depoliticized	drastically reduced
	domestic function	no	defeat separat- ist insurgencies, wide policing functions	defeat separat- ist insurgencies, wide policing functions
	advisory function	yes	yes, military usually domi- nates foreign and defense policy	yes
	effectiveness	high	medium	medium
	commitment to democracy	yes	no	probable
Society	independent civilian experts	yes, slowly growing influence	yes, problems with impartiality	yes, little influence
	military's prestige	medium	high	medium to high
	soldiers in society	efforts to reduce separation	a separate social caste	some integration
	conscription	yes	no	yes
Political system at the end of the period		consolidated parliamentary democracy	parliamentary democracy not consolidated	parliamentary democracy not consolidated

CHAPTER 7

After State-Socialism in Europe:
Slovenia, Russia, and Romania

⚔ ⚔

Having learned about building democratic armies following military regimes in three continents, in this chapter we turn our attention to how
this objective has been approached in regimes following another type of
authoritarianism. Although "state-socialist" or "communist" regimes have
taken root in a number of regions, they originated in and were most prominent in the eastern part of Europe after the Bolshevik revolution of 1917.[1]
Most East European communist states shared many similarities in terms of
their political institutional framework, economic system, and social relations owing to the Soviet Union's control of much of the region and adherence to Marxist-Leninist ideology. With the passage of time, however,
particularly after Joseph Stalin's death in 1953, and as the limited slacken-
ing of Moscow's domination allowed domestic factors an expanding role,
the substantial differences that existed across the region's countries prior to
state-socialism began to reemerge. These differences, in turn, became expo-
nentially magnified after the fall of communism in 1989–91.

State-socialism ended differently in different places in the region and,
in the past two decades the East European states have become as different from one another as they were before the Cold War, even allowing
for the forty-plus years of by-and-large similar communist development.
Their approaches to reforming their military establishments have also been
very different. In this chapter we are going to learn about three states that
could hardly be more unalike: Slovenia, a small country that has enjoyed a
smooth transition to democracy and market economy; Russia, the world's
largest state, which has failed to establish democratic rule; and Romania,
our secondary case, a medium-sized Balkan country that, following some
early stumbling, found its way into NATO and the European Union. In this
chapter we will follow Slovenia and Romania from the fall of communism
to 2002, the year they received NATO's invitation to membership, and Rus-

sia from the breakup of the Soviet Union to the end of Vladimir V. Putin's presidency (2008). We begin with a brief primer on communist civil-military relations and continue with an introduction to the three case-study states. The bulk of the chapter is devoted to key aspects of military politics from the three armies' roles in the collapse of communism through issues of institutional design and the influence of foreign organizations on democratizing their armed forces.

CIVIL-MILITARY RELATIONS IN COMMUNIST STATES

The most glaring differences between democratic and communist political systems was that, in the latter, the ruling communist party controlled or attempted to control all political actors and actions in the polity. To be sure, the party's control was somewhat relaxed in some states and in some periods but its ultimate authority over the policy-making process changed little until the end game, the late 1980s, in Eastern Europe and the Soviet Union. In essence, the communist party's self-perceived vanguard role created a political system in which the party was sovereign, and in practice its hegemony depended on its success in controlling other political institutions.[2] State-socialist systems tended to be more militaristic than democratic ones, partly because their political culture was dominated by a combative Marxist-Leninist ideology. They tended to maintain large armies, and their militarism was independent of both their level of economic development and the security threat they might have faced.[3] Hegemonic communist states—like the Soviet Union and China—were by their very nature externally oriented and in domestic contexts displayed the characteristics of Herbert Spencer's "military societies" and "garrison states."[4] All communist armed forces were based on conscription, which, aside from providing them with a large pool of draftees, served as an effective vehicle for political socialization.

In communist states neither civilian nor military elites subscribed to the norm that the military ought to be apolitical. Marxist-Leninist ruling parties maintained symbiotic relations with their armies whose support was indispensable for their regimes' survival. In many cases such as Yugoslavia, Albania, Cuba, and China, the revolutionary army at first *was* the party. Moving away from such a close relationship was gradual and in some cases (e.g., Cuba, Angola) incomplete. The crucial point about the military's political role is that it was *in support of* the communist party and not independent of it.[5]

Civil-military relations in communist systems may be perceived as tightly controlled interdependent alliances in which the party was in the dominant position. On the one hand, such systems needed armed forces that were loyal to the party and could reliably discharge their missions, including the defense of the regime from its external *and* internal foes. On the other hand, the army needed the party for a stable political environment and the preservation and improvement of its material status and social prestige. The communist party's control of the military did not preclude instances of occasional conflict, ordinarily generated by the party leadership's fear of the potential "Bonapartism" of popular military leaders. The Soviet regime confronted this fear with strategies ranging from large-scale violence (e.g., the decimation of the armed forces command in the 1930s) to appeasement (e.g., Marshal Georgy Zhukov's appointment to the Presidium of the Communist Party of the Soviet Union in 1957).

The most important way of deterring real or imagined military threat, however, was the party's penetration of the armed forces by means of a variety of political control mechanisms. From their creation, communist armed forces were watched over by a large organization of political officers—the Main Political Administration—whose main function was the maintenance of ideological purity within the military. The hierarchy of political officers extended from the highest echelons of the military leadership down to the battalion or even company levels. Other tools of party control were the secret police, military intelligence agencies, the granting of privileges to the officer corps, as well as the co-optation of high-ranking military officers into various levels of party and state bureaucracies.

Among communist polities we may distinguish between independent regimes and those that were ruled by another state. Most European communist states—with the exception of Albania, Yugoslavia, and, from the mid-1960s, the partial exception of Romania—were controlled by the Soviet Union. Although the main characteristics of communist civil-military relations were similar everywhere, the USSR's domination produced a fundamental difference, namely, that an external actor, the Soviet Army (representing the Soviet political elites), supervised the armed forces of these states. There were several mechanisms at Moscow's disposal to control these armies, but the most useful were its military occupation of the East European communist states[6] and their compulsory membership in the Soviet-led Warsaw Pact (1955–91). The East European states' satellite status detracted from their domestic political legitimacy and diminished their authority vis-à-vis their armed forces.

The East European military establishments' record in political crises (e.g., Hungary 1956; Czechoslovakia 1968; Poland 1970, 1976, 1980–81) suggests that—notwithstanding the regimes' intensive indoctrination efforts—major segments of their military elites were reluctant or unwilling to repress internal challenges to the communist regime.[7] The disparities in the civil-military relations in the region were demonstrated by the dissimilar roles these armed forces played in the revolutions of 1989 when their performance ranged from non-involvement (Hungary, Poland), to limited involvement (Czechoslovakia), to a determinant role (Bulgaria and Romania). What explains such profound differences in their behavior? The most important reasons are the basic nature of these late-communist regimes and the kind of relations they maintained with their armed forces. That is, reform-oriented regimes (Hungary, Poland) attempted to appease their militaries by relaxing political indoctrination, improving service conditions, and raising the level of professionalism. Their orthodox counterparts (Bulgaria, Czechoslovakia, Romania), in contrast, strove to increase control over their armies by expanding political and neglecting professional training. As in other contexts, the extent of the armed forces' political interference during the revolutions correlated negatively with the speed of the transfer of power: gradual and prepared transfers of political power, in contrast with sudden ones, drew little military involvement.[8]

Democratization theorists tend to agree that civil-military relations is one area in which the postcommunist past is beneficial rather than detrimental for democratizing states.[9] In the ancien régime, the reasoning goes, the armed forces were under firm civilian (i.e., communist party) oversight and kept in check by the internal security forces and other control mechanisms. In short, there were no major problems that endangered civilian oversight, and this fact, as conventional wisdom would have it, must bode well for the democratic era. Although this argument makes sense, it is subject to three important limitations.

The first relates directly to what Thomas Nichols has called the "constitutional complication," the notion that although legal regulations governing civil-military relations in communist states existed, they meant little owing to the predominant position of the communist party over state institutions, including the judiciary.[10] This proviso is significant because, given that constitutional and legal norms were more or less inconsequential, the shifting power dynamics in the late 1980s allowed different interpretations of loyalty. Put more concretely, a very real dilemma was bound to arise: should officers be loyal to the party tenets they had been indoctrinated with or, in the Soviet case, should they try to follow the unpredictable political signals emanating from Mikhail Gorbachev's Kremlin?

The second qualification has to do with the fundamental changes that took place in civil-military relations at the end of the Soviet era. Gorbachev encouraged internal debate not only in the communist party but also in the ranks of the military by actually *inviting* serving officers to voice their views and otherwise participate in politics. Officers turned out to be most responsive: they soon began to publicly criticize Gorbachev and his policies and stood for election to the Supreme Soviet (the legislature). In sum, the USSR's last president expunged the positive influence communist-era civil-military relations might have had in the post-Soviet era by reversing the solid control of civilians over the armed forces. Finally, while communist states closely monitored their armed forces, this type of civilian oversight was not balanced between branches of government but was exercised by one political actor, the party, and, as such, it is hardly an example to be emulated by newly democratizing states.

BACKGROUND: THREE POSTCOMMUNIST STATES

Slovenia

Despite a common misconception, contemporary Slovenia is not a Balkan state, a designation it fits neither geographically nor politically, neither historically nor culturally. Apart from its unambiguous geographical position, it was ruled for nearly eight hundred years prior to 1918 by the Austrian Habsburgs, and, in terms of its economic and cultural orientation, Slovenia is by far the most "Western" country of Eastern Europe. It "became" a part of the Balkans after World War I when it was incorporated into what was to become Yugoslavia.

On June 25, 1991, the Slovene legislature passed a Declaration of Independence signaling Slovenia's separation from Yugoslavia. This act was the logical culmination of a five-year liberalization process. It began in 1986, when reform-minded cadres led by Milan Kučan became the dominant force in the League of Communists of Slovenia. Thus, Slovenia may have been the first East European country—albeit not yet an independent one—to set out on a path toward democratization.[11] In the first post–World War II multiparty elections held in April 1990, Slovenes elected the former communist leader, Kučan, who represented the new Social Democratic Party, as their president. One of the region's few erstwhile communists who had made a genuine transition to becoming a social democrat, Kučan held the presidency until the end of 2002, having been consistently reelected by large margins.[12]

Slovene independence is rooted in a December 1990 plebiscite in which 88 percent of the voters chose sovereignty. Although the European Economic Community, the United States, and the federal Yugoslav government all stressed their opposition to Slovene independence, politicians in Ljubljana forged ahead.[13] Following a week of clashes between units of the federal Yugoslav army and the Slovene territorial defense forces, in early

July international mediators met with federal and Slovene emissaries who agreed to a cease-fire and to the gradual withdrawal of Yugoslav troops from Slovenia. In late October the last Yugoslav soldier left Slovene territory and President Kučan jubilantly announced: "Citizens of Slovenia, the Republic of Slovenia is free."[14]

Since 1992 Slovenia has been a pure parliamentary system, dominated by the ninety-member National Assembly. Slovenia's president enjoys limited powers, and its party system has been relatively stable, especially in comparison to other East European states like Romania. The first freely elected Slovene prime minister, Christian Democrat Lojze Peterle, held the office for two years (1990–92). His center-right government successfully guided the country from a constituent republic in a federal state to a sovereign democracy. But it could not achieve consensus on a number of major issues ranging from foreign policy to privatization and was unable to avert a governmental crisis in early 1992. In May 1992 the Slovene National Assembly elected as prime minister the leader of the leftist Liberal Democrats, Janez Drnovšek, who, apart from a six-month hiatus had headed Slovenia's coalition governments for a decade, after which he succeeded Kučan as president (2002–2007).[15] The governing coalitions at times were born after difficult negotiations following long delays that in 1998 and 2000 resulted in problems for Slovenia's ability to deal with both its NATO and EU accession processes.[16]

The Liberal Democrats' chief political rival has been the right-wing and thus misnamed Social Democrat Party (SDS), led by the most controversial Slovene politician, Janez Janša. In his early life, Janša was a leader of the communist youth organization but by the late 1980s he adjusted his sails to the changing political winds and began his ideological journey "from radical Marxist left to the extreme anti-communist and nationalist-xenophobic right."[17] Much of what was objectionable in Slovene politics from the perspective of democratic consolidation in the 1990s was, in some way, connected to Janša. In the first multiparty government he became a defense minister, a portfolio he retained until 1994. His stance on national defense evolved from pacifism to neutrality to ardent support of Slovene NATO membership.

Although Slovene politics has lacked the frequent political dramas of many postcommunist states, some controversies in public affairs have occurred. Janša, a veteran of four parties, founded the SDS and used it as a pool for political appointees in the Slovene Ministry of Defense.[18] While he was defense minister and following his dismissal in 1994 (decided by a National Assembly vote), Janša repeatedly sought to embarrass President Kučan, castigating him for his communist past even as he overlooked his own. During the mid-1990s, the prime minister and cabinet members acquired more power in practice than constitutional provisions would have allowed and ministers—particularly in the case of Janša—could get away with using their ministries as their personal fiefdoms.[19]

These problems were trivial, however, compared to the trials and tribulations of other postcommunist states. In fact, Slovenia has been *the* postcommunist success story: it is easily one of the most democratic states with the cleanest government and it is certainly the most prosperous one. The EU's 2000 report on Slovenia's progress toward accession recognized that Ljubljana essentially met all political criteria. In 2004 it received full NATO and EU membership, and in 2007 Slovenia became the first former communist state to introduce the Euro as its official currency.

Russia

The coup attempt of August 1991, a few months prior to the collapse of the USSR, was conceived and supported by a group of politicians opposed to democratization and committed to the preservation of the Soviet Union. The plotters—whose ranks included a number of top politicians including Soviet Defense Minister Dmitry Yazov—were unable to impose their will on the commanders of Moscow-area military detachments who carried the day by convincing their subordinates of the coup's folly. The army's decision not to support the overthrow of Russian President Boris Yeltsin effectively prevented a successful coup.

Even if the first couple of years of the new Russia under Yeltsin were tumultuous and occasionally chaotic, democratization continued to progress, parliamentary opposition was robust, broadcast and print media were free, and civic organizations continued to proliferate. The turning point in the democratization process was Yeltsin's face-off with the legislature in the fall of 1993. In late September of that year, to put an end to the prolonged conflict between the Kremlin and the Supreme Soviet, Yeltsin disbanded the legislature, called for new elections, and scheduled a constitutional referendum.[20] The hard-line members of parliament responded by deposing and impeaching him and installing an acting president—Vice President Aleksandr Rutskoi—and a new "government." The crisis was resolved when army units came to Yeltsin's rescue to storm the White House in Moscow where renegade lawmakers took refuge.[21] At this point the period of advancing democratization ended, and, with the promulgation of the December 1993 Constitution, a new type of authoritarian polity was beginning to take shape. To be sure, all remnants of democratization had not disappeared in one fell swoop in late 1993, but since then the arrow signaling the direction

of Russia's political trajectory has pointed not toward further democratization but toward an increasingly authoritarian model.[22]

In spite of his extensive and growing powers, Yeltsin repeatedly broke
the law and trespassed on parliamentary prerogatives. For instance, the
Constitution was clear in denying the president the right to dissolve the
legislature, yet this is precisely what he did in September 1993. The 1993
Constitution—one of the practical results of the president's victory over the
Supreme Soviet—reflected the new power configuration but Yeltsin still violated its Articles 8 and 88 by not informing the parliament prior to deploying the armed forces in Chechnya. To make matters worse, in August 1995
the Constitutional Court created a troubling precedent by refusing to rule
against the president. The political and economic turmoil in 1998 presented
yet another profound challenge to Russian democratization and economic
transition processes.

For much of the first post-Soviet decade, Russian politics was marked
by an ongoing power struggle between the president and the legislature,
and the outcome of this confrontation was the evolution of dramatically
increased executive powers, in effect, a form of "superpresidentialism." The
concept of superpresidentialism denotes a kind of semidemocratic regime
that differs from autocracy to the extent that regular and partly free elections are held. In this type of regime the strong president—supported by a
massive executive apparatus—enjoys significant influence over the legislature and the judiciary and has no incentive to develop institutions that could
potentially challenge him later.[23] To safeguard his own personal power, Yeltsin subordinated to himself a number of security organizations to offset
the influence of the armed forces and encouraged the rivalry between the
ministry of defense and the "power bloc." Nonetheless, when he handed the
reins of Russia over to Vladimir Putin in late 1999, some hope could still be
mustered that Russia's democratization project might survive.

Such optimism was dashed in Putin's first full presidential term (2000–
2004), and his second term was synonymous with the burial of the democratization experiment and the forming of a type of polity that may be called
superpresidential authoritarianism. This profile was underscored by several
major issue areas. Russia's human rights record remained abysmal, and fundamental human rights were not guaranteed in the country. Speech, assembly, and other universal rights were only allowed—as had been the case in
the Soviet Union—if they did not alarm the state. Individuals could be and
were sentenced to long prison sentences for speaking with foreigners about
sensitive subjects even though they might have possessed no access to classified materials. As the human rights activist Sergei Kovalev summed up,

"The authorities only talk about human rights with the media or foreign colleagues. Citizens are seen as instruments of the state."[24]

At the end of Putin's presidency the broadcast media was under state control, and few sparks of independent life were left in the press. Domestic calamities provided the Kremlin with justification to further strengthen its hold on the country. For example, after the Kursk submarine accident (2000), media freedoms notably diminished, while the tragedy at the Beslan school (2004) impelled Moscow to take its political dominance to a new level by revoking the voters' right to elect their regional governors directly.[25] In fact, by then, the autonomy of regions had already been slashed because upon taking office one of Putin's first "reforms" was to establish seven supraregional districts and appoint his own supporters, mostly former KGB and army generals, as their leaders. These "viceroys," in turn, did their best to undermine the authority of regional officials and subordinate them to the Kremlin.

The most important area of politics that clearly displays Russia's slide toward autocracy has been the systematic undermining of all political institutions independent of the presidency. Following the 2003 parliamentary elections, the legislature could no longer be regarded as an independent source of political power. Registration procedures for new parties became more restrictive, in case a political force emerged to challenge the Kremlin. As in Soviet times, the judiciary could apply the law selectively: those who failed to meet with the authorities' approval were seldom spared. The December 2005 law that drastically reduced the independence of nongovernmental organizations operating in Russia was merely a step along the way in the Kremlin's decade-long harassment of one of the last vestiges of institutional autonomy. Under Putin even the government was relegated to play a secondary political role; instead, the most influential actor on the stage of Russian politics was the presidential administration dominated by the *siloviki*, a group of individuals with professional backgrounds in the state security apparatus.[26]

Putin did not succeed in raising the efficiency of the state, which remained extraordinarily corrupt. The 2005 study by Transparency International—a respected international think-tank specializing on corruption—found that Russia had dropped to 126th place in the world between Niger and Sierra Leone.[27] At the same time, the report of the democracy watchdog Freedom House concluded that Russia had experienced the largest decline in democratic standards among all former communist states, and downgraded it from the "partly free" to the "not free" classification. There was little doubt that even after Putin transferred the presidency to his protégé, Dmitry Medvedev—through the sham presidential elections of 2008—he would continue to be a major influence on Russian politics, in his new role as prime minister.

Romania

Romania provides an interesting and important lesson about postcommunist democratization for several reasons. First, it is the only former Warsaw Pact member-state where large-scale violence accompanied the fall of communism. Second, partly due to the brutality of Nicolae Ceauşescu's regime and absent the tradition of intellectual opposition, there was no prodemocracy movement or dissident group in Romania; in fact it was the only authoritarian state in Europe or South America where not a single full-blown *samizdat* (underground) publication appeared.[28] This lack of organized opposition to communist rule, in turn, ensured that the new regime was going to be dominated, at least in the short term, by the "reform communists" of the ancien régime. Third, the Romanian experience also shows that a postcommunist polity with even a most inauspicious start can turn its fortunes around given some favorable circumstances, in this case the lure of EU and NATO membership.

The defining moment of the fall of Romania's communist regime was the execution of the dictator and his wife on December 25, 1989, as the culmination of a swift, farcical, and closed-door trial that foreshadowed the difficulties Romania was to face with democratic transition. Still, if one uses only regularly recurring elections and a pluralist political system as the key hallmarks of democracy, then Romania became one relatively quickly. Nevertheless, the Romanian case demonstrates the problems with such a minimalist definition. For the first dozen or so years after the fall of communism, Romanian politics was characterized by populist, authoritarian, and illiberal features and the absence of a decisive break with the centralized, bureaucratic, and statist traditions inherited from the past. The lack of real bargaining, compromise, and power-sharing was a nagging reminder that the transition to polyarchy was severely hampered.[29]

Romania's has been one of the least stable party systems in Eastern Europe. According to a 2000 EU report, its legislature was "dogged by bureaucracy and lacks an organized and efficient consultation process" (in 1999 only 59 of the 453 draft laws submitted to parliament were adopted).[30] Unlike Slovenia, Romania's is a presidential-parliamentary polity with broad presidential powers. Between 1989 and 2004 Romania had two presidents. Under the former communist-turned-populist Ion Iliescu (1990–96, 2000–2004), political elites squandered nearly seven years' worth of opportunities to consolidate a liberal democracy and plundered national resources instead of implementing substantive economic reform. Emil Constantinescu's presidency (1996–2000) was as disappointing as Iliescu's and no less corrupt. Perhaps more than anything, four years of relatively liberal rule demonstrated that progressive forces were fragmented, inefficient, incompetent, and scarcely superior to their political foes. In the June 2000 elections, the electorate drew its conclusions from the Democratic Convention's lackluster performance and reelected Iliescu. Four more years under Iliescu brought much of the same, although some economic reforms—demanded by the IMF and EU agencies—were starting to be implemented. Iliescu and his governing elites were unable to turn their backs to their reform-communist roots and their support of state ownership of major enterprises. Owing to the economy's lack of competitiveness and the absence of structural changes, poverty became so widespread that, according to Prime Minister Adrian Nastase, only Albania, Russia, and Moldova had a higher proportion of impoverished people in Europe in 2001.

Though Romania continued to face an uphill battle to expand democratization—effective anticorruption measures and judicial reform were just two of the many serious problems—and to introduce economic reforms, it succeeded in many respects (such as public administration, police reform, policies toward ethnic minorities) in gradually improving its record. The most important goal of Romanian governments after 1989 was to join NATO and the European Union. The many positive changes in Romania underscored the direct influence of these international organizations to bring about positive policy outcomes. Romania also conducted a convincing campaign to join NATO after it was turned down at the 1997 Madrid Summit because of its poor record of political and economic reforms. Following the September 2001 terrorist attacks in New York and Washington, the United States renewed its support for a second round of NATO expansion, and Romania was one of the beneficiaries, eventually joining the alliance in 2004. Since then, it has been one of the NATO's most reliable and enthusiastic members.

Building Democratic Armies

As in the other contexts in which democratic armies are being built, the post-communist scenario, too, requires addressing some issues unique to it. Perhaps the most distinctive feature of communist armed forces was that they were heavily politicized and indoctrinated with Marxist-Leninist dogma. Therefore, after state-socialism, the crucial task was the *depoliticiziation of the military*—this in sharp contrast to postpraetorian regimes where the main focus of democratizers had to be on the *demilitarization of politics*, as the preceding chapters explained. Another important objective was endowing the legislature with the substantive role of oversight because, in communist states, parliaments rarely have more than a merely rubber-stamp function.

The Role of the Armies in the Fall of Communism

Unlike in Russia, in Slovenia and Romania the military played an important role in ending communist rule. In 1990 the Yugoslav National Army (JNA), the military of federal Yugoslavia, appointed a non-Slovene general to head Slovenia's Territorial Defense (TD) even though that position had always been held by an ethnic Slovene. This measure contributed to the already tense relations between Slovenia and Yugoslavia in general, and between the Slovene military establishment and the JNA in particular. On June 25, 1991, the Slovene legislature passed a Declaration of Independence and, thereby, its secession from Yugoslavia. In the seven-day war that followed, the spirited TD, bolstered by good intelligence, triumphed over and humiliated the small and unenthusiastic JNA contingent dispatched from Belgrade to reestablish order.[31] The clashes between the two sides resulted in fifty-four dead, over three hundred wounded, and considerable property damage, but the hostilities were not accompanied by intercommunal violence. Belgrade's willingness to leave Slovenia undoubtedly had much to do with its concern about neighboring Croatia's substantial Serbian minority, given that Croatia had also declared its independence on June 25, 1991.

The fact that no military coup took place in December 1991, as the Soviet Union fell apart, surprised many experts. Three reasons help explain why. First, following the collapsed coup attempt four months earlier, the most hard-line politicians (including Yazov) were apprehended and no longer at liberty to hatch new schemes. Second, the failure of the August coup attempt itself served as a warning regarding the poor chances of another similar action. Third, though it may be surprising given Russia's tumultuous history, generals there have not staged a successful coup d'état for over two centuries. Organizational culture theory—with its focus on "the unique experiences in the life of an organization as an explanation for subsequent behavior"—may offer the most persuasive explanation to this puzzle because it emphasizes the officer corps' view that armed intervention against the country's civilian leaders was fundamentally wrong.[32] In the end, the powers of the commander in chief were transferred from Soviet President Mikhail Gorbachev to Russia's new president, Boris Yeltsin, on December 25, 1991, and the Soviet-Russian armed forces did not interfere.

In Romania, the army's role in the fall of communism was much more dramatic and decisive. Communist-party control over the military was more extensive and intensive than elsewhere in Eastern Europe and the military had an institutional rival, the security police (*Securitate*), which enjoyed priority treatment from the state. Moreover, the army was

increasingly used as a captive labor force for Ceauşescu's pharaonic construction projects as well as many agricultural and industrial work sites.[33]
In all of Eastern Europe, the fall of the ancien régime was most sudden in
Romania where the armed forces actually decided the fate of the revolution. Between December 17 and 21, 1989, the army obeyed its generals'
controversial orders to fire on demonstrators in the Transylvanian city
of Timişoara and elsewhere. After December, 21, following a few days of
vacillation among the top brass, the military sided with the population—
"The Army is with us!" (*Armata e cu noi!*) was among the most memo-
rable exultations of the demonstrators—and fought successfully against
pro-Ceauşescu forces until the end of the year. Altogether 1,104 people
were killed during the revolution, more than 20 percent of whom were
soldiers.[34]

Specific Issues in the Postcommunist Context

Depoliticization

The single most important task before postcommunist democratizers was
to depoliticize the armed forces. This meant that the Main Political Administration had to be abolished, the party organizations in the armed forces
had to be disbanded, and the political officers had to be either expelled or
retrained. Although this process was not accomplished in all postcommunist
states quickly or without problems, all East European militaries have been
convincingly depoliticized. In Russia, however, three presidential decisions
signified "formative moments" that demarcated the military's undemocratic
path and underscored its continuing politicization. First, in the late-1980s
Mikhail Gorbachev invited armed forces to air their own political concerns,
which led to the unprecedented politicization of the Russian officer corps.
Second, Yeltsin not only failed to block the military's political participation but permitted the development of a polity in which army officers could
play a legitimate *independent* political role (running in elections, acquiring consequential political positions, etc.). Third, though Putin appointed
senior officers to political posts and allowed the military establishment to
continue its opposition to defense reform, he nevertheless brought an end
to the generals' political independence and demanded their active support.[35]
Postcommunist depoliticization, the banishing of the communist party from
the armed forces, of course did not make the military apolitical in a one fell
swoop but it removed an institutional anomaly that permitted the establishing of balanced civilian control.

Loyalty

Eastern Europe's democratizing polities encountered the "red or expert" problem, forcing them to make difficult choices about retaining competent officers who remained loyal to the ancien régime. In several states communist-era officers were required to sign loyalty oaths to the democratic state or be dismissed. Although most of the hard-core communists left of their own volition, there were numerous exceptions. In 2001, for instance, it was discovered that fifteen employees of the Slovak MoD were agents of the former communist counterintelligence agency. In fact, NATO's Office for Security expressed its apprehension about the approximately five thousand Slovak officials with access to classified information who were exempted from security background checks.[36] Another problem was breaking the bonds between senior East European military officers and their colleagues in Russia. This was a particular concern in Bulgaria where the army was more closely integrated with Soviet forces and had been more effectively socialized by them than any other state in the region.

The Breakup of Federal States

The fall of communism allowed the self-determination of many nations stuck in unpopular federal states. All three federations of the region— Czechoslovakia, the Soviet Union, and Yugoslavia—broke up during the 1990s eventually creating twenty-four new entities. Obviously this phenomenon had a major impact on the armed forces that the erstwhile federal states had maintained. Two of our case studies in this chapter were affected although, to be sure, in quite different ways. Russia was able to retain much of the Soviet arsenal because it was the predominant part of the federal state in terms of population and size as well as political and economic power. Following the breakup of the USSR, the division of military assets was completed with remarkably little difficulty. This is not to say that there were no disagreements or that careful negotiations were not necessary, particularly between Russia and Ukraine regarding the Black Sea Fleet and its facilities, to reach compromises. Still, considering the magnitude of the endeavor the outcome was reached without major animosity. At the same time, the repatriation of hundreds of thousands of military personnel and their dependents from the internal and external Soviet empire who needed jobs, housing, and socioeconomic infrastructure signified a tremendous burden on Russia.

Slovenia, on the other hand, found itself having to create a new military establishment. It was at much more of a disadvantage than Slovakia, given that the Czechoslovak "velvet divorce" had been followed by an amicable and proportionate division of assets. Slovenia, however, faced a belligerent Serbia that, furthermore, dominated the JNA infinitely more than the Czechs held sway over the Czechoslovak army. Ethnic Slovenes accounted for only 2.8 percent of JNA officers and NCOs even though Slovenia's share in Yugoslavia's population was 8.2 percent.[37] After the withdrawal of the JNA the only military force in Slovenia was the Territorial Defense Force, which was later renamed the "Slovene Army" (*Slovenska Vojska*). Slovene defense experts like to point out that their military was not "reformed" after 1991; it was started pretty much from scratch. Romania was one of only five countries in the postcommunist world—along with Albania, Bulgaria, Hungary, and Poland—whose territory, and thus, control over its armed forces did not change.

Concerns Unique to the Case Studies

Following Yugoslavia's breakup the question of Slovenia's need for conventional armed forces was widely discussed in policy circles; similar debates took place in the Czech Republic as well. After all, Slovenia was bordered by states—Austria, Croatia, Hungary and Italy—that posed no conceivable threat to the country as its defense minister and much of its population readily recognized.[38] Slovene political elites had two reasons for maintaining a military. First, to possess a force capable of reacting to or deterring cross-border incursions; and second, to be able to utilize the armed forces as a part of a broader security policy for Slovenia while also demonstrating that it was a responsible member of the international community.[39] Another distinctively Slovene issue was that due to its lack of a tradition of statehood and military doctrine and because of the frequent changes of personnel at the top of the ministries of defense and foreign affairs, its elites needed a great deal of time to define key national interests in the security and foreign policy field. Finally, the notion that Slovenia had to build its armed forces anew rather than transforming an extant organization presented it with a number of challenges. At the same time, this might also have been a blessing, given that reforming an organization disinclined to change is often more difficult than building one from scratch.

Post–Soviet Russia faced numerous civil-military-relations dilemmas; I briefly mention three. Up to the mid-1980s the military occupation's social prestige and the living standards of professional soldiers were second to none in the Soviet Union. Within a decade, however, owing to the end of the Cold War, economic troubles, and a policy of willful neglect, the armed forces were demoralized, humiliated, and impoverished. By the mid-1990s, "military officer" was one of the least desired career paths among young

Russians, and recruiters were unable to attract the kind of officer candidates they needed. The second issue lay in the abysmal conditions for conscripted soldiers. Pervasive hazing and physical abuse led many to desertion or suicide every year, and this further diminished societal support for the draft. At the time of this writing (early 2012), however, a satisfactory solution has yet to be found. A third, uniquely Russian concern has been the large-scale and mostly unpunished looting of the military's resources by senior officers throughout the 1990s. Although in the past several years, the magnitude of corruption is said to have declined, the nearly two-decades-long practice of what Putin himself called "unbridled thievishness" in the armed forces has exacerbated already poor conditions and further lowered morale.[40]

Two issues stand out when considering specifically Romanian dilemmas of postcommunist military politics. The first was coming to terms with the role of military elites in the 1989 Revolution. This was important because, unlike in Hungary or Czechoslovakia, the military had been a respected organization during Romania's communist period—it was not considered the defender of Soviet interests—and enjoyed some public sympathy for its hardships in contrast to the widely maligned Securitate. The prosecution of the generals implicated in the shooting of civilians was guided by party politics, however: during the left-leaning presidencies of Iliescu they were not bothered, but under Constantinescu—who repeatedly declared that the army carried no "collective guilt"—they were vigorously pursued. In the end, their prison sentences were suspended by the returning Iliescu regime, and the controversy eventually ran out of steam. The second issue was Romania's long-standing problem with its Hungarian ethnic minority, which had embittered relations between Bucharest and Budapest for decades. The quest for NATO (and later EU) membership, however, persuaded the two sides to improve relations, and by the late 1990s, only cross-border smuggling of strategic materials, illegal trade of conventional weapons, drug trafficking, and illegal immigration were seen as major security challenges.[41]

Domestic Use of the Military

This important issue of civil-military relations was not a concern in the Slovenian context but it was a major problem in Russia. During the September–October 1993 crisis, both sides demanded the army's support. Rutskoi, a bona fide hero of the Afghan War, urged his fellow officers to take a stand against the president—in essence, inviting a mutiny—while Ruslan Khasbulatov, the Supreme Soviet's Chairman declared, "We must have military units here today . . . not just men in military greatcoats, but military units."[42] Finally army units came to Yeltsin's rescue but only after he agreed to give in writing his unconstitutional order instructing Defense Minister Pavel Grachev to storm the White House where renegade lawmakers took refuge.[43]

Another example is the armed forces' deployment in the Chechen Wars of 1994–96 and 1999–2009. Yeltsin's order to use the troops in 1994 was not sanctioned by the constitution; furthermore, he launched the war without adequate prior consultation with military commanders, many of whom spoke out strongly against it. The military's renewed attack on Chechen rebels in 1999 was less controversial because of overwhelming popular support. While the official justification for the first war was to "restore constitutional order" to a region wrecked by civil war and political turmoil, the second war was rationalized as a defense of Russia's population from the attacks of "international terrorist gangs" and irredentist attacks aiming to separate the North Caucasian republics from the Russian Federation.[44] Armed force was also used against Russian citizens frequently—breaking up demonstrations, operations against "terrorists"—but owing to the numerous paramilitary formations at the state's disposal, the army itself did not need to be activated.

In the early 1990s the Romanian military was also utilized on several occasions in domestic scenarios albeit never violently. Essentially, political elites sought "to include defense of the social order and the political leadership against domestic challengers" as one of the army's legitimate tasks.[45] With the decreasing power of the security apparatus after 1989, politicians realized that the state's coercive authority had declined. To counter this situation, the president repeatedly relied on the military by asking it to defend not the constitutional order but the regime deploying army units alongside the police in, for instance, the Transylvanian city of Targu Mureş when violence broke out between ethnic Romanians and Hungarians 1990 or in the following year during two days of rioting in front of government headquarters in central Bucharest.[46] These incidents called attention to the lack of clear legislation pertaining to the military's permissible domestic functions; the appropriate laws were passed by the parliament in 1999.[47]

Civilian Oversight

Executive and Legislative Authority

In most of postcommunist Europe, executive-legislative relations were sorted out early on. Given the different amount of power vested in the presidency (ranging from largely ceremonial head of state in Slovakia to strong executive authority in Poland), one cannot generalize about its influence on defense issues. The Slovene president is the titular commander in chief of the armed forces but has no specific powers with regard to the military. The bicameral legislature defines the basic directives for defense organization and implementation. The notion that several committees in the legislature are specialized for security affairs (e.g., Defense; Budget and Public Finance Control; National Security Resolution) has received some criticism because some MPs sit on more than one defense-related committee. Nevertheless, given the small number of MPs (altogether 130 in the two chambers) in general, and the very small number of MPs with interest in security issues in particular, this may be difficult to avoid. The government organizes preparations for defense and leads its implementation; and, since military personnel are considered public servants, it also oversees the armed forces' personnel policy. Established in 1998, the National Security Council is a consultative and advisory body comprised of "strategic" ministers (defense, interior, foreign affairs, etc.).

At the other end of the spectrum, the successive constitutional decisions political elites took in the late Soviet period and at the birth of the new Russia—such as ambiguously differentiated roles between the legislative and executive branches—in effect led to the 1993 crisis that hastened the executive's acquisition of superpresidential powers. Civilian control there has become tantamount to presidential control since the legislature's independent authority has shrunk to pre–Gorbachev Soviet levels.

The power of the Duma—the Russian legislature's lower house—to oversee military affairs has gradually diminished since the 1993 Constitution removed its controls over the armed forces. Although until 2003 there was still a vigorous opposition in the Duma, the parliamentary elections that year eliminated the sources of genuine disagreement with the presidency in legislative politics. Since then, new laws and regulations have been the outcome of executive branch initiatives not of independent parliamentary deliberations. In short, under Putin the Duma became a pliant presidential tool described by one expert as "little more than a Kremlin-controlled puppet show."[48]

In other postcommunist states the legislature has become a more meaningful locus of civilian oversight as parliamentary defense committees have begun to exercise their authority to oversee military affairs. Nonetheless, the scope of their activities is often narrower than would be ideal. One reason for this lies in institutional arrangements hammered out at the beginning of the postcommunist transition that favored the executive branch. Romania's president, for instance, is not only the commander in chief but, according the July 1994 Law on National Defense, also the guarantor of the country's territorial integrity; he chairs the Supreme Council of National Defense and, in exceptional cases, can mobilize the military and not seek parliamentary approval for five days. Romanian MPs serving on defense committees—especially if they sat on the wrong side of the aisle—at times did not even have access to pertinent legislation prior to submission for vote until recently. As democratic consolidation has progressed, these issues have been gradually worked out, but it has often proved difficult—in Romania as well as in other postcommunist states—to change laws and old practices.

The Ministry of Defense and the General Staff

In Slovenia, as in most East-Central European states, civilian defense ministers replaced active-duty military officers at the beginning of the transition to democracy. Elsewhere, generals continued to head the ministries—in Romania, for instance, until 1994—in order to "avoid political debates and due to views that a civilian defense minister would be incompetent and arrogant."[49] Such arguments were not without merit considering the lack of prior expertise or even demonstrated interest in military affairs of some postcommunist defense ministers. One example is democratic Hungary's first defense minister, Lajos Für (1990–94), a scholar of nineteenth-century agricultural history whose curiosity regarding military affairs was largely satisfied by studying historical uniforms. The need—indeed, the Western expectation—to switch to civilian defense ministers in accord with accepted democratic standards was nonetheless clear to all East European states and eventually they replaced active-duty generals everywhere.

In contrast, the Russian top brass publicly opposed the idea of a civilian defense minister throughout the 1990s. Technically, General Igor Rodionov became Russia's first civilian defense minister in 1996 when Boris Yeltsin transferred him to the reserves in order to "reflect the progress of Russian democracy." The emptiness of this gesture was demonstrated by the fact that the defense ministry had continued to be staffed entirely by military men and by the active-duty status of Rodionov's successor, Igor Sergeev. Russians finally did get a civilian defense minister of sorts in 2001 when Putin appointed his close associate Sergei Ivanov, a retired KGB general, to the post. Ivanov, in turn, was followed in 2007 by Anatoliy Serdyukov, a bona fide civilian whose military background was limited to an eighteen-month conscript service. Serdyukov, a former top official of Russia's Federal Tax Service, was charged with fighting corruption and inefficiency in the armed forces.

All executive responsibility related to Slovenia's security is invested in the ministry of defense, which prepares changes for the defense law, elaborates strategic documents (to be debated by parliament), and devises and implements development and modernization programs. Since 1991 the MoD has been thoroughly civilianized and its managerial style has come to stress interdepartmental participation. The majority of positions in the ministry are filled by civilians. Some critics of the MoD have noted that the civilianization process may have gone too far, given that specialized military expertise is at times lacking.[50] The counterargument justifies this "overcivilianization"—particularly in the early years following independence—in the face of the widespread rejection of the previous Yugoslav model of civil-military relations, the paucity of Slovene military traditions, the underdeveloped corporate identity and professionalism of officers, and the military elites' low political profile.[51]

The excessive civilianization of the Slovene Defense Ministry is exceptional in the postcommunist world. In the early 1990s there were few civilians available to be employed in ministries of defense, because during the communist-era, security-defense training was the monopoly of the armed forces. Given domestic and foreign pressures—in particular from NATO and the European Union—to hire more civilians at East European defense ministries, in some cases the authorities resorted to "token civilianization": they retired military officers or transferred them to the reserves and then rehired them as civilian employees.[52] Genuine civilianization began in several states once security specialists could be trained. For instance, following the mid-1990s, Romania's defense establishment underwent a substantial civilianization process. In the main military institutions, including the MoD, a growing number of civilian experts were put in charge of making defense policy. At the same time, by the late 1990s, more than half the graduates of Bucharest's Higher Military Academy were civilians, part of governmental efforts to create a pool of civilian defense experts.[53]

Russia has been immune to these developments. Both political and military elites there discouraged the rise of civilian specialists on defense-security issues because they had nothing to gain and much to lose from independent scrutiny of the military establishment.

The Slovene General Staff (GS) is integrated into and housed in the same building complex as the MoD. The Chief of the General Staff (CGS) answers to the minister of defense who, in turn, is accountable to the prime minister. The GS is responsible for military readiness and executes tasks concerning the organization, training, and performance of the armed forces. The Romanian MoD was restructured in 1993 (separate general staffs for the various services were established) and reorganized in 1997.[54] At that time, in order to strengthen the civilian role in controlling defense policy, the Head of the Defense Policy and International Relations Department with the rank of state secretary was created and the CGS's responsibilities were limited to purely military tasks.

Nevertheless, for a nearly a decade, the Russian General Staff had engaged in open opposition to official defense policy The GS publicly disagreed with the MoD over spending priorities and, more broadly, over Russia's defense doctrine and future military stature. The MoD wanted to concentrate defense outlays on the Strategic Nuclear Forces (not incidentally, Defense Minister Sergeev's own branch of service), while CGS Anatoly Kvashnin advocated boosting investment in conventional weapons. Eventually—a move that further undermined the chances of democratic civil-military relations—Putin came down on Kvashnin's side in what was often a public feud. In 2000 Putin fired six senior commanders, all ardent Sergeev supporters, and—a few months later—replaced their patron himself.[55]

By naming Sergei Ivanov as the new defense minister in March 2001, Putin signaled the elevation of the ministry over the General Staff. Nonetheless, his new appointment did not suggest a move toward more robust civilian control of the armed forces, and nor did it portend a radical transformation of the military—mainly because Ivanov was unable to gain the generals' confidence and he received no mandate from the president beyond overseeing the implementation of the defense budget and increasing the MoD's foreign contacts and international exposure.[56]

Establishing straightforward chains of command over and inside the military has at times been difficult for a number of other reasons, such as legislative lacunae or ambiguities, individual misconduct, or lack of understanding regarding democratic procedures. In Slovenia, numerous troublesome incidents occurred in the mid-1990s, when Defense Minister Janša exploited a legal void created by the new constitution—which was not accompanied in time by new corresponding legislation—as he effectively made himself the commander in chief by depriving President Kučan of relevant information and issuing major orders without proper authorization.[57] Romania's CGS is unambiguously subordinated to the defense minister, and no violations of the constitutionally prescribed chain of command occurred.

In this respect, too, Russia has been quite different from the East European cases. The decade-long rift between defense ministers Sergeev and Ivanov and CGS Kvashnin was also manifested in Kvashnin's repeated violation of the chain of command. He left the minister out of key decisions, resisted the implementation of defense reforms, and fueled the tensions between the MoD and the GS. In June 1999 he masterminded the surprise action of Russian paratroopers who left their bases in Bosnia and raced to Kosovo's capital, Prishtina, to seize control of its airport without any coordination with NATO forces. This incident was important from a civil-military-relations perspective because President Yeltsin permitted Kvashnin to leave the government—including Sergeev—in the dark about it.[58]

In essence, Yeltsin consented to Kvashnin's disregard of the chain of command within the MoD and the government. This incident also compounded the ambiguities created by the 1996 Defense Law that signaled the elevation of the General Staff to or above the level of the ministry. In the summer of 2000, Kvashnin once again bypassed Sergeev and sent his own defense reform proposal to Putin. This was another contravention of the chain of command—Kvashnin acted as if he had only one direct superior, the president—and, to make matters worse, the incident quickly became public knowledge. Instead of immediately firing Kvashnin for this gross breach of conduct, Putin and his advisors treated the issue as an intellectual discussion between military specialists and pretended that nothing was amiss.[59]

Even after Ivanov's appointment, disputes between the MoD and the GS remained although they became more polite for several reasons. First, Kvashnin and the GS recognized the close relationship between Putin and Ivanov and were mindful of the risks of antagonizing the latter. Second, the new defense minister had come around to support many of the GS's views regarding doctrine and military reform. Finally, unlike Sergeev, Ivanov did not play favorites among the branches perhaps because he did not have professional ties to them, having never served in the military. In the end, Putin had apparently had enough of Kvashnin's persistent defiance. The June 2004 insurgent attack in Ingushetia that resulted in nearly one hundred dead soldiers and civilians, along with Kvashnin's sharp public criticisms of the 2005 preliminary defense budgets, served as convenient reasons for Putin to fire him.[60]

In the same month, in response to the protracted conflict between the two institutions, the Duma modified the Defense Law and formally established the defense minister and the ministry's superiority over the General Staff and its chief. The amended law entrusted the MoD with the administrative and operational command and control of the armed forces. This was potentially the most important defense-related legislation of the decade and it codified the GS's worst-case scenario. "Potentially," because laws passed by a mostly rubber-stamp legislature often mean very little in Russia: they can be open for varying interpretations or rewritten as changing circumstances demand. In any case, it was difficult to envision the GS's loss of command and control functions at the stroke of a pen before an alternative structure was put in place.[61] Still, the fact that until this time the GS and its chief were not formally subordinated to the minister and his ministry was a major shortcoming in the legislation that made possible the long and destructive feud between the two institutions and their leaders.

Budget Control

The Slovene defense budget is established and implemented much like that of other consolidated democracies. The process itself is open to media scrutiny. The defense minister, together with his top civilian and military colleagues (especially the CGS), prepares a budget proposal including the MoD's needs and, after consultation with the ministry of finance, sends it to the government. The latter might modify and prioritize the budget and then present the aggregate budget to the legislature. After close scrutiny and consultation with the government, which may result in further modification, the legislature adopts the budget. Parliament also controls the implementation of the budget for which the defense minister is accountable.[62]

In Romania, too, the civilians' oversight of the defense budget has not been a major concern especially since the mid-1990s. The most important problem in this regard through much of the 1990s was Romania's precarious economic situation, which kept the military relatively poor. Not surprisingly, the MoD argued for larger defense allocations using every conceivable argument. In 1991, for instance, Defense Minister Victor Stanculescu managed to convince the legislature to increase the MoD's budget in part to counter the ostensible military threat from Hungary.[63] Four parliamentary committees—one Defense, Public Order, and National Security Committee in each of the two chambers, and separate joint committees for NATO and internal affairs—are actively involved in the budget process.[64] The defense budget is first drafted by the Directorate for Integrated Defense Planning, submitted to the Secretary of State for Defense Planning, who turns it over to the minister of defense. The defense minister may modify the budget in consultation with the finance minister, and then present it to the government. The final arbiter of the defense budget is the legislature. The defense minister is accountable to the government for all of the MoD's activities—including how allocated funds are spent—and, as a member of the government, he also reports to parliament.[65]

In contrast, the Russian legislature's power to oversee the military's budget and how the money is spent had gradually eroded from the late 1990s to the point where, by 2008, it was negligible. The government, and especially the MoD, routinely refused to share pertinent information with the legislature or supplied opaque data. Few details of the defense budget were accessible even to Duma deputies whose budgetary oversight was limited owing to their inability to independently analyse the budget or defense policy. At the same time, the government viewed the legislature's attempts at scrutinizing the armed forces' finances as hostile acts. This lack of transparency violated the 1998 Law on Budget Classification.[66] Much of the defense budget is still shrouded in secrecy. Even Duma Defense Committee members—to say nothing of the press and the general population—are furnished with virtually no detail about how the MoD actually spends the funds once they are allocated.

Political Role of the Military

The Slovene and Romanian armed forces were thoroughly depoliticized. Active-duty military personnel may not join political parties, run for or hold political office, but they are allowed to vote. The process went smoothly in Slovenia though in Romania a number of incidents suggested that the political neutralization of the military was not entirely accomplished in the first postcommunist decade.[67] In November 1999, for instance, President Constantinescu's office circulated letters with official letterhead among professional soldiers encouraging them to take an anti-opposition stance on various issues. A month later the MoD's spokesman issued a press communiqué condemning the opposition for allegedly showing contempt for the military. And in April 2000, the Chief of the General Staff, Mircea Chelaru, publicly—and without success—advocated the political involvement of the military through the establishment of ten senatorial seats for military officers and the abolition of the constitutionally mandated Supreme Council of National Defense.[68]

Whatever problems Romania had were trivial when compared to the Russian case. The election of forty-four military officers as People's Deputies of the Russian Republic in 1990—the last republic-level election in the USSR—was a pivotal event in Soviet civil-military relations because these officers obtained their seats as a result of the increasing political activism in the armed forces fostered by Gorbachev's reforms.[69] By October 1992 these officer-politicians had become well integrated into the Russian legislature; three of them had even chaired parliamentary commissions. The distinction that is important to recognize is that while the political influence of the armed forces as an institutional player had diminished in the Gorbachev era, the political activism of individual officers—virtually unthinkable in the Soviet period—now could begin unhampered by legal regulations. Yeltsin and the new Russian polity agreed to new institutional rules codified in the 1992 Defense Law that legitimized the norms dating from the Gorbachev period, such as officers serving as independent parliamentary deputies. To make matters worse, the law also permitted military personnel to hold positions in the government while serving in the armed forces, a regulation that further weakened the prospects of accountability and created a conflict of interest.[70]

The type of constitutional control over the armed forces that was emerging in Russia did not require the exclusion of the military from politics and was a direct source of the officer corps' further politicization. Several prominent generals—such as Aleksandr Rutskoi, Aleksandr Lebed, Lev Rokhlin—managed to convert their popularity into creditable political careers. In the Yeltsin era they were all "independents" who built their political careers often in spite of—rather than because of—their commander in chief.[71] The political influence the military may have acquired in the 1990s quickly diminished under Putin who *reinforced* the course of military politics by (a) appointing high-ranking officers to important political posts, especially in his first term; (b) co-opting generals he rightly dismissed for their inappropriate behavior by giving them responsibilities in the state bureaucracy; and most importantly, (c) permitting the top brass to resist radical defense reforms that he himself advocate at the beginning of his term.

There are noteworthy differences in the generals' political role in the 1990s and afterward. In the increasingly authoritarian environment created by Putin, the political participation of the top brass was invariably dependent on presidential goodwill. In other words, they were no longer "independents"; they were "appointees" and thus could not get away with the defiant conduct characteristic of Lebed or Rodionov. If under Yeltsin only the generals' own ambitions limited their political prospects, in the Putin era their roles were strictly confined to their appointed positions and limited by the loyalty they owed their patron. Especially in his first term, Putin actually urged trusted generals to enter politics, selected numerous military cadres to head the country's federal districts as presidential envoys, and actively supported the candidacy of high-ranking officers for elected office. In his second presidential term, however, Putin's enthusiasm for appointing generals to top administrative positions diminished while the role of the *siloviki* expanded.

Independent Defense-Security Expertise

The relative dearth of independent civilian defense-related expertise is an important reason for the limited legislative oversight of defense establishments in the postcommunist context although in this respect, too, there are great disparities. The fact that Slovenia has had no shortage of civilians with the requisite knowledge to advise politicians on defense matters is the legacy of the Yugoslav government's policy to establish defense-studies departments in all republic capitals (except for Montenegro) starting as early as the mid-1970s.[72] In Romania and Poland military academies started to accept civilians into their programs in a conscious attempt to increase the pool of civilian defense experts, already in the late 1990s.

Russia is an outlier in this regard as well, given that its political elites have forcefully discouraged the rise of civilian specialists on military-security issues because they have nothing to gain and much to lose from the independent scrutiny of the defense establishment. The small but influential group of civilian defense experts that emerged in the Gorbachev era was excluded from the policy mainstream under Yeltsin and, especially, Putin. There are few autonomous organizations that focus on military matters, and they tend to be supportive of state policy. Another factor thwarting the emergence of civilian defense specialists is the continued obsessive secrecy in Russia— virtually everything having to do with security and defense is considered a "state secret"—which has deterred individuals from trying to acquire expertise on these matters.

Foreign Influence

In the postcommunist states the West (meaning established democracies) had an important leverage with which to influence democratization processes. I am referring not to the economic aid conditionally offered by international organizations or to the role of the European Union but to the essential and overwhelmingly positive role NATO played in the democratization of postcommunist military affairs.[73] Given that all East European members of the former Warsaw Pact identified NATO membership as one of their crucial foreign policy objectives, the Atlantic Alliance possessed powerful bargaining chips and used them well.

NATO's various programs—such as the Partnership for Peace, launched in 1994, and the Membership Action Plan—specified the goals individual states needed to satisfy, provided ongoing advice and evaluation, and offered tangible assistance in a variety of ways such as multilevel officer training, surplus equipment, and grant programs. The United States played an important and enormously positive role in setting up offices of defense cooperation in U.S. embassies where security assistance officers evaluated and supported, and the United States financed programs that fostered the establishment of democratic civil-military relations and professional competence (a big-ticket item was English-language training).[74] In July 1994 President Bill Clinton announced America's commitment to provide U.S. assistance to new democracies for the purpose of advancing Partnership for Peace objectives. The resulting Warsaw Initiative, financed by the Congress, disbursed $570 million between 1994 and 2000 to twenty-two partner states to support equipment grants, training, and information technology.[75]

Several states requested teams of defense experts from NATO member states, which assisted their preparations for membership. In Romania, for instance, a small delegation of officers and civilian experts from the British

Ministry of Defence provided a resident advisory role to their colleagues in the Romanian Defense Ministry.[76] Another example of success is the George C. Marshall European Center for Security Studies in Garmisch-Partenkirchen, Germany, that has since 1993 enlightened hundreds of high-ranking officers and public servants from postcommunist states about the proper place of the armed forces in a democracy. At the same time, U.S. defense consultants offered help to a number of states in the region regarding issues ranging from defense legislation to procurement imperatives.[77]

Russia did not need to live up to any NATO or EU standards because it was not a candidate for entry into either of these organizations. Consequently, the democratic West had no leverage over how Russia transformed its defense establishment or civil-military relations. The aid Moscow received from Washington and its allies was generally intended to facilitate the scrapping, elimination, and/or clean-up of nuclear, biological, chemical, as well as conventional weapons. The criticisms of Western democracies and NGOs (such as Freedom House or Transparency International) over Russia's gradual slide toward autocracy have mostly fallen on deaf ears, particularly under Putin's reign.

CONCLUSION

The three postcommunist states suggest very different experiences of building democratic armies. The shift went as well as possible in Slovenia in relation to the two other states and also within the larger postcommunist context. The most remarkable aspect of the Slovene transformation of military politics may be the civilian domination of military affairs, which is to some extent similar to the Indian experience, as we will see in the next chapter. No postcommunist country had fewer major problems in establishing democratic civil-military relations than Slovenia, even though it had to create a new army on the rather flimsy foundations of the Territorial Defense Force. Slovenia is small, prosperous, its population strongly supports democratic governance, and yet, even in Slovenia, things could and did go wrong. Many of the difficulties, to be sure, were connected to one mercurial individual, but still, the transition from postcommunism to democracy and the transition from a republic of a federal state to a unitary state created legal vacuums, identified problems for which no preparations could be made, and produced temptations that people anywhere would be hard put to resist.

Romania's postcommunist record of building civil-military relations falls between the two others in terms of democratic performance, though it is much closer to Slovenia than to Russia. In fairness, it ought to be pointed out that Romania's starting point compared to Slovenia's was much less favorable—one of the region's most repressive dictatorships versus a very liberal and reform-minded regime—which puts Bucharest's achievements in a more flattering light. The unduly strong executive authority accompanied by a relatively weak legislative side that was at the root of many problems was—as in several other postcommunist states—the legacy of the state-socialist framework that Bucharest had a difficult time casting off. Perhaps the most revealing aspect of the Romanian case is that it points to the tremendous practical impact an external actor—in this case, the Atlantic Alliance—can have on building democratic armies.

Generally speaking, the more difficult a regime's situation is—in terms of political stability, economic performance, and societal support—the more enthusiastic it is to join international organizations that offer the advantages of membership. For the former East European Warsaw Pact states—most of which had no external security threats to contend with once the Cold War ended—joining NATO was primarily a seal of approval by the West, an invitation to the club that conferred legitimacy both abroad and, more importantly, at home. Not surprisingly, for countries doing well, say for the Czech Republic and Slovenia, NATO membership promised little practical benefit so they were less enthusiastic about joining. Nevertheless, the laggards of transition—Bulgaria and Romania, come to mind—were keen to ingratiate themselves with NATO and, consequently, were willing to make the major policy adjustments the Alliance required, because they had much to gain.

Institutionally balanced civilian control of the armed forces is at the heart of democratic civil-military relations, which, in turn, is an indispensable component of a democracy. The Russian military, however, became a de facto presidential institution, a status cultivated by the top brass because it inherently denied any legislative interference into its affairs. Given the minimal role of parliament, the civilian control of the military—just like most other policy areas in contemporary Russia—is heavily dependent on one person, the president. The absence of democratic civil-military relations, on the one hand, poses a serious obstacle to the realization of democratic transition because it is a major component of that process. The specific shortcomings of Russian military politics, on the other hand, well reflect the power relations that have doomed Russia's democratization prospects. At the same time, it is worth reiterating that the armed forces do not display any interest in overthrowing the government, and the vast majority of the officer corps is firmly opposed to the army's political intervention. In any event, the numerous deep-seated cleavages in the officer corps—interservice rivalries, rank, age, assignment, and so forth—effectively preclude concerted action.

The reform of the armed forces is closely connected, through the broader issue of civil-military relations, to the general state of Russian democratization. The politics of defense reform is at the core of Russia's domestic politics given the crucial role the military establishment has played throughout Russian history, including in the more than seven decades of communist rule. Because the civilian control of the armed forces is a matter directly relevant to the executive and legislative spheres, the interactions of these branches of government with the military impacted all these institutions.

At the end of our period of analysis, both Slovenia and Romania fully satisfied the basic criteria of democratic civil-military relations outlined in chapter 1. They are consolidated democracies, and their military personnel are committed to democratic rule. It is easy to pinpoint the areas of major shortcomings in Russian civil-military relations. Most importantly, in post–Soviet Russia the armed forces' political influence has dramatically increased, certainly in the period under study. The defense ministry's refusal to provide the legislature with information that would allow actual oversight of military expenditures, and the absence of civilian participation in the defense-security sphere, are particularly troublesome. Having said this, the political clout of the Russian armed forces is a good deal less than militaries hold in praetorian dictatorships, but a lot more than they possess in democracies.

What additional generalizations can we make to help us understand civil-military relations in the postcommunist context? First of all, the main task of democratizers in these environments is not to take the military out of politics—as in the post–military rule settings—but quite the opposite: to take the politics out of the military, that is, to depoliticize the armed forces. In practical terms, this means the abolition of the communist party's ideological influence over the army and ensuring that the officers are loyal to the constitution.

Some of the issues so critical in countries after postpraetorian regime change, such as the leverage of the armed forces or the prosecution of those who violated human rights, have not really been germane to postcommunist cases, at least not the three in this chapter. Why? The military was the tool of and thoroughly controlled by the party-state and enjoyed no political leverage on its own. Therefore, once the communist regime crumbled, the army's institutional position became weak, and integrating it into the newly democratizing state was a relatively easy task. Moreover, although in communist states, human rights were routinely violated, the military was seldom involved in these activities as the state assigned other institutions, primarily the secret police, to the task of societal repression.

TABLE 7.1

After State-Socialism: Slovenia, Russia, and Romania

	Country Period	Slovenia 1990–2002	Russia 1991–2008	Romania 1989–2002
Background	end of the old regime	brief war of independence	peaceful	brief war between army and secret police
State	main tasks	depoliticizing and professionalizing the military, establish civilian control balanced between legislature and executive branch	depoliticizing and professionalizing the military, establish civilian control balanced between legislature and executive branch	depoliticizing and professionalizing the military, establish civilian control balanced between legislature and executive branch
	civilian political leadership	generally competent and effective	increasingly heavy-handed	of varying quality
	political institutions and trend	strong	ever more authoritarian	strengthening and improving
	executive control	restrained, appropriate	very strong	strong
	legislative oversight	strong	weak	increasingly substantive
	foreign influence	medium: NATO/EU	low	high: NATO/EU
Military	behavior during transition	nonconfrontational	trying to safeguard perks and institutional interests	restrained
	interference in politics	minimal, some in defense policy	intensive, military not completely depoliticized	drastically reduced to minimal
	domestic function	no	unconstitutional deployments against domestic enemies	in the early 1990s some police work

TABLE 7.1   *(continued)*

After State-Socialism: Slovenia, Russia, and Romania

		Country	*Slovenia*	*Russia*	*Romania*
		Period	*1990–2002*	*1991–2008*	*1989–2002*
		advisory function	yes, appropriate	yes, highly influential	yes, appropriate
		institutional attributes	small but increasingly professional	General Staff often at odds with MoD	benefiting from multifaceted NATO training
		effectiveness	no evidence	low	medium to high (in NATO operations)
		commitment to democracy	yes	no	yes
	Society	independent civilian experts	yes, influential	very few, few are impartial	yes, some influence
		military's prestige	low	low	low
		soldiers in society	efforts to reduce already low separation	a separate social caste	some integration
		conscription	no	yes	no
	Political system at the end of the period		consolidated parliamentary democracy	electoral authoritarianism	consolidated parliamentary democracy

BUILDING DEMOCRATIC ARMIES
AFTER STATE TRANSFORMATION

CHAPTER 8

After Colonial Rule in Asia:
India, Pakistan, and Bangladesh

B uilding a military establishment that is loyal to the constitution and supports the democratically elected government poses special challenges in
postcolonial environments. In this chapter and the next, I am going to examine how this objective has been approached in countries that have some
similarities but are also set apart by important differences. The focus here
is on the two pivotal states of South Asia: India and Pakistan; Bangladesh,
the secondary case, is connected to the two others by many organic ties.
The entire region that now encompasses the three states—and some others
besides—was colonized by the British.

India and Pakistan gained their independence in 1947, Bangladesh—a
part of Pakistan for nearly a quarter century—in 1971. As in the other chapters, my goal here is to cover a time span sufficient to recognize the basic
trends that shaped military politics in these countries. India succeeded in
placing its armed forces under firm and virtually unchallenged state control
right from the beginning of independence. My coverage will stop in 1975
when the handling of the "Emergency" confirmed, yet again, the Indian generals' lack of political ambition. Civil-military relations in Pakistan, however, have been far more "eventful." In this case, I will look at the period
starting with independence and ending with 1988, the end of General Zia-
ul-Haq's dictatorship, which heralded the arrival of a civilian government
once again.

This chapter makes three arguments. First and most important, by the
end of the first postcolonial decade, the patterns for the drastically different military politics of India and Pakistan were already set. Second, of the
numerous reasons for the evolution of different civil-military relations in the
two countries, several lie in the circumstances of the 1947 Partition and in
the immediate post-Partition period. Third, the British colonial period left
behind profound legacies, most of which have positively influenced military
affairs in the Subcontinent. After a short examination of the British legacy, I

look at the impact of Partition on Indo-Pakistani military affairs. I continue with some comparative commentary on the two armies followed by an exploration of the main themes of Indian and Pakistani civil-military relations. Finally, I briefly address Bangladesh—from its independence in 1971 to the military take-over in 2007—and what sets its military politics apart from Pakistan's.

THE BRITISH LEGACY

Few imperial powers succeeded in leaving behind such durable impact on their subject peoples as the British did in India and, to a lesser extent, Pakistan. The British were more successful colonizers than their European rivals, or—and there is an important lesson here—the more recent vintage of American and other Western "democracy promoters" for several reasons.[1] They may not have been less exploitative or racist than others, but they were more effective because they worked hard at understanding the people they were governing, recruited individuals who were prepared to spend their careers in the provinces of a single alien nation, and then invested in teaching them the local language and culture. Moreover, the British established effective bureaucracies and integrated local elites into governing structures on every level. In some cases Indians occupied high positions in the bureaucracy so that at the time of independence a fairly large percentage of the elite Indian Civil Service consisted of Indians. In short: the British thought about and planned for the long term. That bureaucracies and large organizations are resistant to change is a truism, but it is interesting that after more than six decades of independence, no other Indian or Pakistani institution retains as much of its British origins as the armed forces.

The British India Army (BIA) originated in the armed force created by the British East India Company for the protection of its personnel and property. When the conquest of India began in earnest in the late eighteenth century, the British faced native troops that had a reputation for individual bravery, and some of them were equipped with cannons and muskets. The advantage of the British vis-à-vis other colonial or native military formations lay primarily in organization, training, and drill, which paid dividends in battlefield discipline. For its personnel, BIA benefits were characterized by a welcome predictability: regular pay, regular orders, and a regular system.[2] British commanders realized not only that a few of their troops could prevail over large but disorganized Indian forces but also, later on, that the Indians themselves were amenable to discipline.[3]

The British India Army served the empire with distinction. Even if most *sepoys* (native Indian soldiers) were highly disciplined and unswervingly obedient to the British, mutinies did occur, and two of them are noteworthy. About seventy thousand sepoys joined the Mutiny of 1857, thirty thousand remained loyal to the British, and another thirty thousand were disarmed or deserted. This was a significant turning point in Indian history: had all the sepoys mutinied at the same time, British rule in India quite conceivably could have ended.[4] After 1857 the colonizers changed their personnel policies and paid more attention to the "divide-and-rule" principle.[5] The second significant mutiny broke out in February 1946—following World War II, morale in the BIA eroded—and seven thousand sailors joined it, a quarter of the navy. The rebels hoisted the flags of the two native political forces, the Congress Party and the Muslim League, on their vessels, which encouraged the rioting onshore. The mutiny—which clearly suggested the slipping away of imperial authority—stunned both the government in Delhi and the Congress Party.[6]

During World War II, the Indian National Army (INA) posed an even more important challenge to the BIA. Established in 1942 principally by Subhas Chandra Bose in collaboration with the Japanese occupying force in Southeast Asia, the INA—its recruiting message was "what's the use of fighting with/for your colonial masters when you can fight for your freedom?"—wanted to overthrow the British Raj with Japanese assistance. The INA's first members were BIA prisoners of war captured by the Japanese. They were joined by expatriate Indians from Burma and Malaysia and, in time, also by some BIA personnel. According to British military intelligence in 1944, twenty thousand Indian (BIA) troops had gone over to the Japanese, two out of every seven captured. In 1945 they identified a hard core of 7,600 INA fighters who were devoted to their charismatic leader, Bose, and had actively assisted the Japanese and in some cases committed "horrendous war crimes."[7] The INA's potential to cause front-line soldiers to surrender was taken seriously by the government, though, in the end, it did not make a major impact on the war.

The INA's size was dwarfed by the BIA—1,789,000 Indians were fighting with the British in World War II in Africa, Asia, Europe, and the Middle East.[8] India was also a major source of industrial materiel in support of the war effort. The BIA also played an important role in handling the sporadic rioting, civil unrest, noncooperation, and resistance from Gandhi and the Congress Party during the war; its Indian officers and NCOs did not participate in the struggle for their country's independence, which put them in a curious position once it was achieved.

Four distinct legacies of the British India Army made a lasting stamp on its successor forces. Three of these—professionalism, ethnocentric recruitment, and the army's aid to civil authorities—have had a similar effect on the armies of both successor states. The fourth—the British insistence on clear separation between the political and military domains—had a strong impact on India but eluded Pakistan.[9] Let us take a closer look at these legacies.

Professionalism

The British provided rigorous and modern training and an attractive career option to qualified native Indians. The cream of the crop received officer education at Sandhurst in England, and training was ongoing in the garrisons and bases throughout British India, not just at the BIA's three regional headquarters in Madras, Bombay, and Calcutta. After the opening of the Indian Military Academy at Dehra Dun in 1932, all Indian officers were trained there. Until 1939 the officer corps was relatively small and tight-knit, but the need for a much larger force in World War II required its quick expansion and the abandonment of some recruiting principles. During the war the ratio of British to Indian officers changed from 10:1 to 4.1:1.[10] Most importantly, the British instilled a military ethos that put high value on professional competence; the officer corps of both independent Pakistan and India has kept these traditions alive.

Ethnic Preference in Recruitment

One of the pillars of the BIA's success was the careful recruitment of soldiers and prospective NCOs and officers. After 1857 recruiters generally avoided enlisting Bengalis and drew from regions in the west, for example, Punjab, which had largely remained loyal to the British at the time of the mutiny. In any event, the British firmly believed in "martial races," that people originating from the northwest corner (Punjab) of India, Sikhs, the Gurkhas of Nepal, and members of the ksatriya (warrior) castes were better suited for military service than others (such as Bengalis or Sindhis).[11] Most of the soldiers were middle-class peasants, promotion was based solely on ability and merit, and the BIA developed a distinctive and powerful esprit de corps.[12] The obedience of the vast majority of rank-and-file soldiers was the result of attracting politically reliable and pliable individuals.[13] Perhaps the greatest achievement of the British in the military realm was the creation of a personnel system based on competition and excellence rather than religious identity. That religion was not a central issue in the BIA was the consequence of careful British policy in this regard. To avoid tensions, most units were organized by religion, and soldiers took a religious (Hindu, Sikh, or Muslim) oath administered by regimental priests. Because the British were particularly concerned with Muslim recruits after the Mutiny of 1857 there were no all-Muslim regiments. Nonetheless, Muslims were well represented among the ranks of the prestigious King's Commissioned Officers and Viceroy's Commissioned Officers; in fact, they held slightly more than their proportionate share (roughly one-third) of positions.[14]

Aid to the Civil Power

The British developed a system—called "aid to the civil power"—for contingencies when local disturbances could not be contained by law enforcement personnel. In such cases authority was passed from the civil administrator to the local military commander for the duration of the conflict. Though British officials feared that these maneuvers against the civilian population would try the loyalty of sepoys and Indian officers, they caused few cases of insubordination or desertion. In any event, there were conscious efforts to use troops from other regions (thus, south Indians might be used to put down riots in Bombay).

Separating the Army from Politics

Although in the early years some of the proconsuls who governed British India were military officers, the BIA soon settled into a position that remained outside and above politics. The principle of the army's political subordination was unambiguous, and the division between the civil and military spheres was unassailable: the army was responsible for recruitment, training, discipline, and strategic advice. Beyond that, civilians made the decisions, including when and in the service of what objective the army should be deployed.

Notwithstanding the many adverse effects of British reign, it established a number of institutions indispensable to democratic governance: an independent judiciary, an effective and relatively upright civil service, political parties, and police and armed forces that were above politics. Some regions of Pakistan—especially in the west and northwest—were colonized by the British only in the late nineteenth century whereas much of what became

India proper had been under British rule since the 1770s. Regions with shorter exposure to these institutions were at a disadvantage when independence came.

THE PARTITION AND ITS IMPACT

The partition of British India into an independent India and Pakistan in 1947 remains *the* formative moment in the political path of the Subcontinent that explains many of the profound differences between the two states and their armed forces. More specifically, it helps one understand not so much why India became a democracy—with civil-military relations befitting a democracy—but, far more so, why Pakistan did not.

The Muslim movement in British India was distrustful of democracy due to its conviction that in an independent India the large Hindu majority would marginalize Muslims. The main Muslim political organization, the All-India Muslim League, announced its support for a separate state to be named Pakistan in 1940. It has been argued that the League's longtime leader, Mohammed Ali Jinnah, did not really want an independent Muslim state but overplayed his hand by making such excessive demands—e.g., a separate Muslim electorate, guaranteed seats in parliament—that Hindus could not accept it.[15] In a thoughtful recent book, Jaswant Singh, a leader of the Bharatiya Janata Party, India's Hindu nationalist opposition party, argued that the blame for the partition of British India should actually be placed at the doorstep of Jawaharlal Nehru, India's first prime minister, and his Congress Party.[16] (For this "sacrilege" Singh was expelled from his party and the book was initially banned.) In any event, by the mid-1940s Pakistan had become a virtual inevitability. Although Jinnah wanted a homeland for Muslims, but not an Islamic state, in its final stages the campaign for Pakistan became a religious movement.[17]

The most ardent support for an independent Pakistan originated principally from the minority Muslim provinces—in fact, most of Pakistan's leaders came from there. In the provinces where Muslims were in a majority, they expected to retain political control and, therefore, did not see the need for a Muslim state. On Independence Day, Jinnah (originally from Bombay) became governor-general, and his close associate, Liaquat Ali Khan (who spent most of his life in north India), became prime minister. Resentment built quickly against these "foreigners," called Muhajirs, in the new state because they monopolized leadership positions and designated their mother tongue, Urdu, as the country's official language even though Urdu language and tradition was alien to much of Pakistan—and certainly to all of Bengali-speaking

East Pakistan, where the majority of the population lived.[18] Many Muslims still felt their interests lay with India or were simply unable to emigrate and stayed there: they now comprise the world's largest religious minority.

The British ruling on the boundaries of the two states, the Radcliffe Award, was presented in August 1947. It was based in part on the result of the 1945–46 elections for the Constituent Assembly and various other legislative bodies and named after its author, Cyril Radcliffe, who had never set foot in India and worked from outdated maps and census information. Pakistan was carved out of five provinces of British India, including two partitioned provinces, Punjab and Bengal, and some princely states. The arrangement required the relocation of as many as ten million people—some six million Muslims from India to Pakistan and four million Hindus and Sikhs to India—and its announcement was followed by extensive riots in several regions, particularly in the Punjab. The ethno-religious bloodletting that took place there and elsewhere after independence—a series of massacres and countermassacres, looting and arson—claimed the lives of at least half a million people.[19]

The hasty British retreat from the Subcontinent led to what the leading Indian essayist, Pankaj Mishra, recently called "one of the twentieth century's greatest fiascoes."[20] The fact that the British did not make the necessary preparations to help accommodate the population exchange exacerbated the difficulties. The matter of the princely states' accession on the eve of independence heightened the animosity between Muslims and Hindus and brought the armed forces into the conflict. Although parts of the army became embroiled in the violence and could not be relied upon to reestablish order, most of the military units in the area—British, Indian, and Pakistani—tried to contain the killing and prevent even more destruction.[21]

The eastern part of Bengal—what became East Pakistan and, after the 1971 Civil War, the independent state of Bangladesh—was slightly more populous than the western part and about 85 percent Muslim with a 15 percent Hindu minority. All in all, the population of Pakistan was about one-fourth that of India. There were many disagreements that can be traced back to the hastily prepared Partition and the pro-India sympathies of Lord Mountbatten—the last viceroy of the British Empire and independent India's first governor-general (1947–48). The feud regarding the state of Jammu and Kashmir could not be resolved and eventually led to war in October 1947, ending with a United Nations–brokered cease-fire in December 1948. This issue has not been settled and has been the source of numerous serious conflicts, some armed, between the two states.[22]

Muslim suspicions about Hindu intentions were reinforced by India's handling of the division of British India's assets. Delhi refused to release large amounts of funds that were Pakistan's due, and cut off the flow of water of the Indus River despite a water-sharing agreement because it did not want to aid Pakistan while they were embroiled in an armed conflict in Kashmir. In protest of Indian policies, Mahatma Gandhi started a well-publicized fast in January 1948, which he declined to break until the government adopted an "honorable" course regarding the release of Pakistan's property.[23] India's unfair treatment of Pakistan extended to the BIA's military equipment, which was to be divided between the two successor states. The Delhi government failed to honor its pledge to deliver Pakistan its share: for instance, only 3 percent of the Pakistani portion of 165,000 tons of ordnance stores was delivered by April 1948, and none of its allocation of 249 tanks was ever transferred.[24]

The Pakistani share of institutions and infrastructure amounted to important naval bases in Karachi and Chittagong, the Staff College at Quetta, the Royal Indian Service Corps School at Kakul, and some other facilities such as regimental training centers.[25] In terms of personnel, Pakistan's inheritance was a paper army of roughly 150,000 officers and men in 508 units—40 percent of them still on Indian soil on Independence Day (August 14, 1947). In fact, the staff of the new Pakistani General Headquarters arrived only in October 1947 in Rawalpindi—but without many key documents, because Indian officials refused to release them.[26]

The officers of the BIA were told to choose between the Indian and the Pakistani armed forces. For Muslim officers who lived in India—and for the far fewer Hindu and Sikh officers living in Pakistan—Partition meant having to leave their homes, uproot their families, and lose their property. After Partition nearly all Muslim officers went to Pakistan and virtually all Hindu officers moved to or remained in India proper. The departure of Muslim officers to Pakistan after Partition was not unexpected given their background and the opportunities that opened up in a new and understaffed army. A few Muslim officers stayed in the new Indian Army, and some actually managed to rise high in the hierarchy.[27] During the politically tense years leading up to Partition, a remarkable amity prevailed among most Hindu, Muslim, and Sikh officers. Field Marshal Mohammed Ayub Khan, the Pakistani leader of the 1950s and 1960s, recalled in his memoirs that in 1947 the senior Indian officer of the BIA, General K. M. Cariappa asked him to support efforts to keep the army undivided, which of course Ayub could not do, as "the army was the instrument of sovereignty and the shield of the people."[28]

In spite of their dissimilar postindependence development, at the time of Partition, the two armies were not so different from each other. They came from the same body, shared a single ethos and institutional culture, and played no role in the political movement that led to independence. Owing to the shortage of high-ranking officers, both the Pakistani and the Indian armed forces employed British officers for more than a decade after independence. Pakistan's 150,000-man army should have had 4,000 officers but there were only 2,500; to fill this deficiency, the government retained 500 British officers and accelerated the promotion of native officers to fill higher ranks.[29] The first Indian Chief of the Naval Staff, Vice Admiral Ram Dass Katari, assumed office only in April 1958—nearly eleven years after independence—with the retirement of his predecessor, Vice Admiral Stephen Hope Carlill.[30] The real difference lay in the political culture in which the two armies were to function. The very nature of the creation of Pakistan goes far in explaining their different evolution.

Six Reasons for Pakistani Praetorianism

By the mid-1950s, most of the important moves had been made on the Pakistani chessboard that would determine what kind of state it would become. A number of interrelated factors of varying importance help to explain why Pakistan—as opposed to India—failed to sustain democratic governance and why its armed forces assumed a dominant political role. Some of these are rooted in British India, others in the Partition, still others in the early postindependence years.

The Geographic and Social Separation between East and West Pakistan

The geographic disconnection between East and West Pakistan was produced by the Partition, and it facilitated the isolation of the politically less influential but numerically greater Bengali population. The Pakistani political establishment was itself responsible for shortsighted and divisive policies—e.g., Bengali, the mother tongue of the majority of Pakistanis, did not become an official language; Bengal's economic development was impeded by pro-West Pakistan (and especially Punjab-centric) economic policies—that all but ensured losing the eastern part of the country. During the twenty-four-year union of East and West Pakistan (1947–71), tensions between the two were constant over the patronizing, inequitable, and heavy-handed policies of Islamabad toward its citizens in the east.

The Social Consequences of Partition

The Partition had two major long-lasting effects on Pakistani society. First, the movement of millions of migrants to the new state—by 1951 migrants from India constituted about 10 percent of all Pakistanis—created instability and social upheaval. Second, the superimposition of the Urdu-speaking political and intellectual elite that was alien to the extant population of Pakistan (comprised of numerous distinct ethnic groups) generated widespread and long-term resentment and mistrust and made governance more difficult.

Low-Level Social Development, Incompetent and Corrupt Civilians

The state structures the British developed stayed in India. In terms of political and administrative infrastructure, Pakistan started with little more than nothing. It is worth looking at the photographs of a 1948 issue of *Life* magazine depicting the seat of the new Pakistani government as a row of tents.[31] Contrasting this image with the palatial government buildings of India housing a small army of experienced and capable administrators makes the quandary of the young Pakistani state easier to appreciate.[32] In 1947 Pakistan was essentially a feudal country with land concentrated in the hands of a few families, virtually no middle class, a minuscule intelligentsia, and an enormous poverty-ridden underclass whose extremely low level of literacy limited the evolution of public opinion.

Pakistan started out with extremely weak political institutions; its bureaucracy was small, disorganized, and incompetent. In fact, the armed forces was the only functioning state institution Pakistan inherited. Therefore, the inability of civilians to control the educated, disciplined, and ambitious officer corps is hardly surprising. The disparity with India, with its relatively cohesive institutions and a strong political leadership bent on subduing the military, could hardly be sharper.

Bad Luck with Founding Fathers

Sheer misfortune also contributed to Pakistan's woes. Within a year of independence its founder, Mohammed Ali Jinnah, died of tuberculosis and the country's first prime minister, Liaquat Khan, was assassinated at a political rally in 1951—one of the first in a long line of Pakistani politicians to be murdered. This is not to suggest that they were necessarily wise politicians— Liaquat, for instance, in more than four years as prime minister made no serious attempt to write a constitution—but the contrast with India, again, is striking. While India benefited from brilliant and practiced leaders like Jawaharlal Nehru and others who represented stability and continuity in the country's formative years, Pakistan became rudderless soon after independence, at a time when political direction, constancy, and steadfastness were most needed. This pattern has continued to play out since then: India has been led by legitimate, and by and large effective civilian leaders without whom there would have been no democratic civil-military relations. Pakistan has not been so fortunate.

The Insecurity Syndrome

From the beginning, Pakistani elites believed that India was an adversary, out to harm their country, and therefore turning Pakistan into a fortress against India was essential. Pakistan's obsession with security was bolstered by and partly rooted in India's failure to adhere to the terms of Partition, viewed by Islamabad as an act of supreme betrayal.[33] Being the smaller, less populous state, with what has been viewed an untrustworthy larger neighbor, has continually reinforced Pakistan's need to maintain a strong military machine. Most importantly, Pakistan's security deficit justified that the disproportionate share of the state budget be devoted to defense, thus increasing the armed forces' influence and diverting scarce resources from social and economic projects.[34] The Pakistani army, then, came to have a vested interest in continued hostility—thus rationalizing its claim on public resources. In fact, the Kashmir conflict was a ready-made cauldron that the army had a stake in keeping at a boil.

The Military as a State Builder

In traditional societies the armed forces often fulfill three functions: maintain the established order, provide a channel for upward mobility, and spearhead modernization.[35] Over time, the Pakistani army fulfilled all three of these missions. They were more disciplined, deeply patriotic, and especially early on, better educated than civilians. The primary motivation in the Pakistani generals' drive for political power was not self-enrichment but guarding the national interest. Although Pakistani officers were not responsible for achieving Pakistani independence, they did play a crucial role in keeping the country together.[36] Circumstances practically forced them to abandon the "military-stays-out-of-politics" dictum of the BIA and to become the essential state-building institution. A few months after Pakistan's founding, its army was deployed against its former brothers-in-arms in the October 1947 Kashmir War. The military acquitted itself well, despite its restrained all-British high command, and made an important contribution to the stabilization of the post-Partition situation. Given the yawning political vacuum and the feebleness of public institutions, it was only a matter of time until the army would take charge of Pakistan's political administration. From the perspective of democratic development, this was a most ominous position for a military establishment. In stark contrast, the Indian military's political masters succeeded in ensuring its continued apolitical stance.

As Husain Haqqani observed, "The dominance of the military in Pakistan's internal affairs is a direct outcome of the circumstances during the early years of statehood."[37] The earliest experiences of Pakistan forced its leaders to recognize the need for strong state institutions to protect the country's basic interests. But who were the individuals who comprised the state, the people who worked in state institutions? Young, mostly inexperienced bureaucrats on the one hand and army officers with superior discipline, education, and a record of personal sacrifice on the other. The early political role of the Pakistani generals was, in spite of repeatedly revised constitutions and quasi-democratic interludes, a prologue to four coups d'état and several decades of military rule. To be sure, as coup-makers in many other settings, the top brass usually enjoyed significant support from a population fed up with dishonest and inept politicians and were quick to justify their political interventions on the basis of the inability and dishonesty of civilian rulers.

TWO DIFFERENT ARMIES

In both the Indian and Pakistani armies, recruitment along the lines of the British "martial races" principles continued for decades after independence. In India, officers and NCOs from the Punjab were over-represented while regions like Madras, Kerala, and West Bengal produced far less than their fair share of recruits. The Indian government had decided to abolish caste identity as the organizing principle of military units decades earlier. The components of the two relatively young services, the air force and the navy, have been for a long time completely integrated. The abolition of all units based on ethnic, religious, or caste identity has not been completed in India though it has been the subject of an ongoing public debate. Opponents have argued that people from similar backgrounds fight better together and sacrifice more readily for one another than in mixed units. In any case, only a few single-group regiments remain in the army; these units go back a long way—some trace their histories to the eighteenth century. Conversations with military officers indicate that pure regiments are the repositories of tradition and history and are often characterized by extraordinarily high morale and pride in service.[38]

Three types of infantry battalions emerged: pure (single caste or ethnic group), partially mixed (regiments segregated by company), and totally mixed (open for anyone eligible for military service). Although concerted efforts were made to make the army more representative, in 1974 Punjabis still comprised over 15 percent of the army, several times more than their number in the population.[39] In 1978–82, 57 percent of the cadets attending the Indian Military Academy came from the northwest suggesting that the overrepresentation of this region in the Indian armed forces has declined hardly at all since colonial times.[40]

Their numerical strengths in the officer corps notwithstanding, Sikhs, particularly, have been concerned about the lack of their constituency in the high command. Moreover, on at least three occasions, Sikh generals in line for the position of chief of Army Staff were passed over by less senior Hindu officers. The 1984 government assault on the Golden Temple in Punjab to remove Sikh militants precipitated a Sikh mutiny in the army that included about two thousand personnel. It showed that the armed forces—often viewed as a symbol of national unity hardened in battles against the Chinese and the Pakistanis—can also be an example of ethno-religious rift.[41] These chasms have been bridged, however, and, according to one of the country's top military experts, "With its multi-religious, multi-lingual, and multi-cultural composition, the army is a shining example of the national goal of achieving 'unity in diversity'."[42]

As in armed forces everywhere, the appeal of the military profession is negatively correlated with the fortunes of the national economy. Under the British and in the first couple of decades of independence, the military—along with the elite administrative services—was the occupational bailiwick of the upper middle class. Since then there has been a gradual shift toward the lower middle class, given the profession's fading luster, owing to faraway deployments, considerably lower salaries, and fewer advancement opportunities than for comparable civil service personnel. By one calculation the total benefits of company and battalion commanders fell between 60 and 70 percent in real terms during 1947–82.[43] This trend has served to eradicate the elitist aura surrounding the officer corps and to diminish its social status.

The occupational prestige of soldiering is far higher in Pakistan for several reasons: national defense is a higher priority, the Pakistani economy offers fewer promising employment opportunities, and the military's dominant sociopolitical rule practically ensures its personnel will be better provided for. Pakistani society has a genuine connection to the armed forces; as in Turkey and Indonesia, there is a profound social connection rooted in history and traditions, which is missing in India.[44] Moreover, the Pakistani military is heavily involved in the national economy. A tenth of civil service appointments must go to officers, and the armed forces possess a US $20 billion business empire and are probably the country's largest land developer, as officers' loyalty is secured with land grants.[45] According to two Indian experts, the Pakistan Army has been "a parasite feeding on the body politic extracting 'rent' in the form of land, bureaucratic appointments, and other spoils of office" in return for supposedly keeping the country safe.[46]

The Indian Armed Forces is the largest volunteer military establishment in the world. Until 1977 soldiers enlisted for seven years with an additional eight years in the reserves; since then they have enlisted for seventeen years. The threshold of entry for enlisted men has been relatively low: little more than a successful physical exam and literacy.[47] Although a generation or two ago many officers' sons followed their fathers into the armed forces, this is no longer the case: new cadets tend to be the sons of NCOs and to come from small towns.[48] Unlike in the rest of Indian society, corruption is not a major problem in the armed forces partly because its disciplining structure remains excellent.[49]

Since independence both the Indian and the Pakistani militaries have become highly professional forces with rigorous training and educational requirements. One of the basic tenets of Indian military training is that armed forces and politics do not mix; for decades junior officers were literally taught to be political illiterates.[50] Although the Indian Army may no longer get the best and the brightest young people, entry into the profession remains competitive. The new National Defence Academy (NDA) opened its doors in 1955—the ceremony was witnessed by the Shah of Iran and Soviet leader Nikita Khrushchev and his defense minister, Marshal Georgy Zhukov. Its success persuaded the Ethiopian government to request the NDA's help in setting up a similar institution, the Haile Selassie Military Academy.[51]

One of the key differences between the Indian and Pakistani armies is that in Pakistan, the shared Muslim identity of military personnel is supposed to prevail over historical and cultural differences. Because officially all Muslims are equally eligible to bear arms and serve in the armed forces the ethnic imbalances in the Pakistani army are all the more noticeable. Bengalis, long considered unsuited for military life, have suffered harsh discrimination under this system and constituted only a small percentage of military personnel. Even though they were Pakistan's majority population, in the 1960s they made up only 7 percent of the Pakistani Armed Forces—their proportion in the bureaucracy was 24 percent[52] Not surprisingly, Bengali grievances fueled their drive for independence. For many years, Pakistani officers were actually taught that the country's "core area" was Punjab and that the other regions were merely "invasion routes," something that could not but increase the defiance of Baluchi, Bengali, Sindhi, and other non-Punjabi citizens.[53] With the loss of East Pakistan in 1971, the discrimination against those of Baluchistani and Sindh backgrounds became even greater.

Nevertheless, the British regard for the martial virtues of Punjabis and, to a lesser extent, Pashtuns, continued; some experts even talked about the "Punjabization" of the Pakistani Armed Forces. Political activists from Baluchistan and the Sindh have called the Pakistani Armed Forces the instrument of the Punjabi-Pashtun ruling elite, not of the federation of Pakistan.[54] In the 1980s 75 percent of soldiers came from three districts of Punjab and two districts of the Northwest Frontier Provinces, which contained only 9 percent of Pakistan's male population.[55] Nevertheless, Punjabis and Pashtuns (who share ethnic identity with roughly 50 percent of Afghans) are divided on a number of issues, especially their views regarding the Taliban in Afghanistan and in the northwest frontier. Most Pashtun pilots, for instance, refuse to shoot at or bomb the Taliban.[56]

Another major difference between the two armies is that while the Indian Army's personnel are relatively isolated from mainstream society, Pakistani officers and NCOs are much more integrated into it. Pakistani soldiers spend as many as two hundred days a year away from their units—annual or casual leave, vacation, holidays, weekends—and during this time they return to civilian life.[57] Perhaps this close social proximity makes the military more acceptable and its appearance in other—including political—roles, more palatable. Upon retirement, Pakistani officers, particularly those who achieve higher ranks, are often rewarded with lucrative jobs in the country's large defense-related civilian sector as bureaucrats, advisors, and experts. This has not been a widespread practice in India—particularly given its far larger military establishment and proportionately smaller defense sector—though in recent years some retired officers, appalled by the politicians' shabby treatment of armed forces personnel, have entered the political arena.[58]

INDIA: COMPREHENSIVE STATE CONTROL OVER THE MILITARY

On Independence Day, August 15, 1947, the government of India adopted the collaborationist army—that is, the Indian component of the British India Army—as its national military force and with it accepted the attendant problems of legitimacy and trust.[59] In part because the British kept the BIA distinct from Indian society, its native-born officers and soldiers proved generally reliable quelling riots and fighting nationalists. Still, Nehru and the rest of the political leadership agreed early on that India needed stability and an effective and disciplined military force, and there was no alternative to the army in place. In any case, virtually all Indian officers serving in the BIA at that time were young and posed no political threat.

The retention of the native component of the colonial army is an unusual occurrence in postcolonial states. Independence movements ordinarily had their own liberation armies that, once independence was achieved, served as the nucleus of the new military. In national liberation armies, however, officers tended to have highly developed political views and were used to voicing them. Perhaps if Nehru and the new Indian leadership had been interested in recruiting the remnants of Subhas Chandra Bose's INA—they were not, though some INA fighters did receive pensions—the new Indian Army would have been less apolitical. Nevertheless, most Indian political elites viewed the BIA as a repressive feudal institution, wanted to hold the new army separate from society, and to drastically reduce its internal policing role, so prevalent under the British.

Nehru had little interest in defense matters, was indifferent to the armed forces, and had no strategic vision. He famosly said, "India doesn't need an army, it needs a police force. We have no enemies."[60] A contemporary army officer likened the government's attitude toward the military to that of "a teetotaler who had inherited a brewery."[61] The Nehru administration did its utmost to prevent military interference in political matters—efforts were redoubled after the 1958 coup in Pakistan owing to worries about India's own army—through a number of mutually reinforcing regulations, arrangements, and practices. The position of commander in chief (CiC), theretofore the chief of the army and the main source of military advice for the government, was abolished on Independence Day in concert with Nehru's and others' view that in a democracy the head of state should be the supreme commander.

The heads of the three services—the army, navy, and the air force—were placed on the same level and rank, signifying a tremendous blow to the prestige and influence of the army, by far the largest and oldest service. The three service chiefs were now reporting to the civilian defense minister, who took over the previous role of the CiC. In this new system the CiC designation made no sense; in 1955 the heads of the services were renamed the chiefs of the Army/Navy/Air Force Staff. For decades, the military has lobbied in vain for the appointment of a fourth chief—the Chief of the Defence Staff (CDS)—something similar to the chairman of the Joint Chiefs of Staff in the United States, but one has yet to be appointed. From the government's perspective, the introduction of a CDS would go against the grain of earlier regulations as it would almost certainly increase the influence of the army, given that the two other services would have little hope of having one of their own selected.

The Indian Constitution of 1950 vests the supreme command of the armed forces in the president but de facto control over the government is the prime minister's responsibility. Through the years no president has attempted to independently command the military.[62] The government's top forum dealing with defense issues has changed with the passage of time from the Defence Committee of the Cabinet to the Cabinet Committee on Political Affairs to the current Cabinet Committee on Security (CCS) whose members include the prime minister and the ministers of defense, finance, home (interior). This body—assisted by a large civilian bureaucracy—makes the most important decisions regarding defense and security matters. The one constant feature of this institutional evolution has been the continually shrinking influence of generals and admirals. The Parliamentary Standing Committee on Defence conducts several reviews annually of different areas of the armed forces. The actual reviews are carried out by civil servants; most committee members, in any case, have modest knowledge or background in military affairs. Only about 5 percent of their recommendations are eventually adopted and they play only a minor role in military politics.[63]

The Ministry of Defence became dominated by civilians. MoD bureaucrats received a great deal of decision-making authority that expanded with the passage of time and allowed them to further reduce the access of uniformed personnel to politicians. There is no formal interaction between military leaders and members of parliament except in cases when a legislative committee asks generals to testify.[64] MoD bureaucrats intervene even in relatively minor military matters: their approval is necessary for all promotions above the rank of major. In the meantime the finance ministry's power to make adjustments to the defense budget and to expand its control on how funds were spent has increased.

The relative standing of military officers vis-à-vis civilian bureaucrats has gradually diminished.[65] The military goes through a pay review every ten years, a process that—except in 1984 when salaries were substantially increased—has been synonymous with the steady devaluation of military salaries compared to civil service wages.[66] After the politicians' interference in the conduct of the 1962 war against China, the generals received unprecedented operational freedom although at the price of the growing civilian mistrust and monitoring of the army.[67]

Indian officers have never contemplated a political intervention. To be sure, there were and are jokes among military officers about politics, and there is privately voiced criticism of the incompetence or corruption of this or that politician—just like among any other occupational groups. Armed forces personnel enjoy the right to vote but their electoral participation is lower than the rest of the population. This is partly explained by the process: the Electoral Commission has to announce new elections a minimum of thirty days in advance. There are postal ballots for soldiers on duty in remote areas but often there is not enough time to mail in their ballots, or when they return to their camps and bases, voting may not be their first priority.[68]

In private, Indian officers are critical of the inefficiencies of the political process and resent politicians' lack of interest in strategic issues and their reluctance to involve military leaders in defense policy discussions.[69] Their attitude points out the most important shortcoming of Indian civil-military relations: in their concerted efforts to ensure the political submissiveness of its armed forces, politicians do not take advantage of the tremendous store of strategic and doctrinal knowledge the military possesses and Indian society has paid for.

Challenges to Indian Civil-Military Relations

Over more than six decades Indian military politics have been devoid of serious crises and have weathered—without major upheavals—defeat and victory in war, the government's increasingly frequent requests to the army to stop civil conflicts, and the armed forces' diminishing socioeconomic status. Some stresses did develop in the 1947–75 period, however; I will briefly mention four. The theme common to all of them is that civilians—mostly political leaders—not the military, initiated them.

The War with China (1962)

India's leaders early on decided that defense did not deserve a high priority and limited their focus on Pakistan as the country's likely enemy. Defense spending was kept to a minimum in keeping with the government's view that it was detrimental to both economic growth and civilian dominance.[70] This view was to have dire consequences in 1962 when China—responding to Nehru's provocative Himalayan border policy—attacked a largely unprepared India. The Indian army's reluctance to enter into war was rooted in its concerns about tactical challenges and the continued supply of war materiel from the Soviet Union. Most importantly, however, the generals were keenly aware of the political constraints imposed upon their conduct of the war.[71] They were not incorrect. To begin with, the communist-leaning Defense Minister, Krishna Menon—a friend and long-time associate of Prime Minister Nehru—refused to believe that China would attack India. Although they advocated the strict separation of politics from military affairs, Menon and Nehru—neither had any military experience—supervised the placement of army units from individual brigades to platoons, with disastrous results. When Indian troops were overrun by superior Chinese forces, Menon resigned, and perhaps the best general in independent India's history, General Sam Manekshaw, was rushed to the front to rally the retreating Indian forces until a cease-fire was declared.[72]

The War with Pakistan (1971)

Nehru's naïveté about strategic issues, aversion to things military, and especially his reluctance to utilize the armed forces as a source of strategic advice changed drastically once his daughter, Indira Gandhi, became prime minister in 1966. She was quite willing to link military force with political power and remains India's most militaristic prime minister.[73] At the height of the "Bangladesh crisis," in December 1971, after an eight-month-long buildup, the Indian army soundly defeated Pakistani forces—taking advantage of the increased operational freedom and expanded autonomy it had gained in 1962 to fight using its own strategies. The slight civil-military tension in this case was caused by the trigger-happy Mrs. Gandhi, who, displaying a "complete lack of awareness . . . about India's ill-preparedness for war," wanted her forces to attack Pakistan in as early as the spring of 1971.[74] General Manekshaw resisted her demands insisting that the campaign be put off until the monsoon season ended and the military was better equipped and trained. Just before the campaign began in December, she asked him, "General, are you ready for the war?" He replied, "I'm always ready, sweetie" and within three weeks, delivered. The ever-quotable Manekshaw said that he could not bring himself to call Mrs. Gandhi "Madame" because it reminded him of a bawdy house.[75]

The Emergency (1975)

In June 1975 Prime Minister Indira Gandhi declared a state of emergency and suspended democracy in response to widespread demonstrations, strikes, and rioting that, in her judgment, threatened social order and the economy. The disturbances also had national security implications given that a war with Pakistan had just recently been concluded. (The protests originated in a court decision convicting Gandhi on minor election-related charges and declaring her election to parliament null and void.) After eighteen months of ruling by decree, constructing an economic program, and defeating the civil disobedience campaign (140,000 people were arrested,

40,000 of them Sikh), elections were held in 1977 in which the Congress Party's dominance was reduced and Mrs. Gandhi lost her parliamentary seat. The main concern for us, of course, is the military's behavior. Even in this heavily charged atmosphere the ever-obedient military was willing to follow the government's lead. Naturally, there was anxiety in the armed forces regarding the drift into disorder. In particular, commanders were concerned about the effect of the chaotic economic and social conditions on military personnel on home leave.[76] Still, when Mrs. Gandhi questioned Field Marshal Manekshaw about rumors that he was plotting to depose her, he asked if she wanted his resignation on grounds of mental instability.[77]

Aid to the Civil Authority

Unlike the singular events described above, the Indian army's involvement in containing civilian—mostly ethno-religious—conflicts originated in the colonial era, was ongoing in the 1947–75 period, and since then has become more frequent and pervasive. (In 1951–70 the army was called out 476 times; in 1982–89 721 times.)[78] It constitutes the most troubling aspect of Indian civil-military relations, so much so that, according to Stephen Cohen, "India is not a democracy in many of its districts where the army and the paramilitary forces supplanted the judiciary, the civil administration, and the ballot box as the ultimate arbiter."[79] (The army's "aid to the civil" is concentrated in Kashmir and the tribally unstable northeast and, during the 1980s, in the Punjab.)

The fundamental problem with the state's increased reliance on the military for internal security duties is exacerbated by several factors. First, the army is rarely free to deal with the situation as it sees fit, particularly because many internal operations involve paramilitary forces and the police. Second, this law and order function harms morale and the integrity of the forces. Third, professional socialization and experience have ingrained in the Indian military that the suppression of civil disturbances is one of their important and legitimate functions, in other words that they are the only effective force standing between chaos and order.[80] Indian military experts seem more bothered with political incompetence that necessitates the army's involvement than the fact of the army's deployment against civilians.[81]

Few endeavors could be more antithetical to democratic civil-military relations than the army's participation in domestic law and order issues. Such participation poses a challenge to the political neutrality of the armed forces as has been clearly demonstrated in many contexts in Africa, Latin America, and elsewhere. Thus, it is all the more remarkable that in India the state's control of the military has remained virtually unshaken.

PAKISTAN: THE EVOLUTION OF A PRAETORIAN STATE

Above I identified six reasons for the development of authoritarianism and military rule in Pakistan that were rooted in the Partition and set Pakistan so clearly apart from India. The disparities between the two states also help clarify why, given the circumstances, the political intervention of Pakistani generals was not only not surprising but almost inevitable. How did this happen?

Instead of the general elections that followed independence in India, in Pakistan only indirect elections were held through provincial assemblies. Elections, starting with those held in the Punjab and the Northwest Frontier Province in 1951, soon began to be tainted by allegations of foul play. (In fact, with the sole exception of the 1970 elections, there were no Pakistani elections between 1947 and 1988 that were not affected by varying levels of corruption and cheating.) After the assassination of Prime Minister Liaquat Khan in 1951, the swiftly deteriorating conditions of Pakistani domestic politics were revealed by the rapid turnover of prime ministers and other top officeholders. Two important clues about the erosion of democratic practices were offered by Governor-General Ghulam Muhammad: in 1953 he dissolved Prime Minister Khwaja Nazimuddin's cabinet, and a year later, he disbanded the legislature when it attempted to place checks on executive authority. One consequence of the protracted squabbles between political actors was their difficulty in approving budgets that directly threatened the flow of funds for defense.

The traumatic experience of Partition, the Kashmir War, and a number of subsequent war scares increased the Pakistani officer corps' distress about military weaknesses and soon taught them that the exigencies of state-building overrode the old British insistence on the separation of politics and the armed forces. The army's conviction of civilian incompetence was reinforced from early on by the frequent "aid-to-civil" missions when the civil administration called out the troops to quell sectarian riots.[82] In 1951, army officers in Rawalpindi, dissatisfied with the government's moral and material support of the military in Kashmir, conspired to assassinate General Douglas Gracey, the army's British commander in chief and some top officials. The plot was easily suppressed but it hinted at a future military involvement in politics.[83]

From the beginning, the Pakistani state gave its armed forces priority treatment. Already in 1948 Liaquat Khan announced that "the defence of the state is our foremost consideration; it dominates all other governmental activities."[84] In January 1951 he appointed active-duty General Mohammad Ayub Khan as defense minister, an action that was tantamount to relinquishing civilian supremacy over the military establishment. If the competition with social and economic institutions for resources brought the military into politics, pressures on the defense establishment provided the earliest impetus for expanding their role.[85] Responding to the protracted political instability, in October 1958 President Iskander Mirza—himself a Sandhurst-educated former general—abrogated the Constitution, abolished political parties, removed the civilian government, and appointed Ayub Khan as chief martial law administrator. Three weeks later Ayub—who had publicly contended a few years earlier that the army did not belong in politics[86]—replaced Mirza in what was Pakistan's first coup d'état and started the country's long subsequent history of military rule (1958–71, 1977–88, 1999–2008).

For the first four years, Ayub ruled via a moderate martial law regime in which the military's chain of command was preserved and major decisions were reached at General Headquarters in Rawalpindi. He launched the "Basic Democracies" initiative with the stated objective of strengthening democracy at the grassroots level, but the real purpose was to increase rural support for his regime.[87] The system—relying on elected and non-elected representatives with a local administration "acting as the eyes, ears, and stick for the central government"—was a form of guided democracy not unlike President Sukarno's experiment in Indonesia after 1957.[88] In order to stabilize the political situation, Ayub created an equal relationship between the military—that lacked the administrative experience—and the civilian bureaucracy that resulted in his running the country more efficiently than his civilian predecessors. Through the coercion of some politicians and the co-optation of others, the military succeeded in creating a reasonably successful and legitimate political regime that accommodated their own corporate interests.[89]

In 1960 Ayub, having retired from the army, became a civilian president and began to involve influential civilian politicians in governance. In 1962 he introduced a new constitution that promised a return to democracy and he started the gradual civilianization of his administration. By the time of his 1965 electoral victory, Ayub was primarily relying on civilian political allies for their networks in securing his victory.[90] He not only did not disturb the position of Pakistan's ruling economic elites, but his economic policies actually widened the large disparities between East and West Pakistan and the inequities between rural and urban areas. In 1968, twenty years after the country's birth, twenty-two families owned 68 percent of Pakistani industries and 87 percent of its banking and insurance assets.[91]

In 1969 the ill and politically isolated Ayub Khan handed power over to General Yahya Khan, the Chief of the Army Staff, who declared a new martial law regime. This second bloodless coup was exceptional because the new leader had no plans to reform the state or to "straighten out" Pakistan's political order.[92] The transition was also unconstitutional since in a case of presidential resignation, power should have been transferred to the speaker of the National Assembly. Even though Ayub strengthened civilian institutions in the second half of his reign, the top brass were reluctant to give up power. The transition from Ayub to Yahya merely underscored the armed forces' supraconstitutional authority.

During his short-lived regime (1969–71) Yahya Khan extended the military's role as the guardian of the country's "ideological frontier," a reality that has prevailed ever since.[93] His rule is most remembered by the December 1970 general elections—the country's first—and the war that followed and resulted in Pakistan's dismemberment. The Awami League won 160 of the 162 seats reserved for East Pakistan in the 300-seat National Assembly; the runner-up Pakistan People's Party (PPP) won only 81 of the 138 seats reserved for West Pakistan. The two parties' support came exclusively from the eastern and the western parts of the country, respectively. Postelection talks between the two sides—regarding the division of power between the central government and the provinces and the formation of a national government to be headed by the Awami League—went nowhere because West Pakistanis were unwilling to be ruled by the despised eastern part of the country they viewed and treated as a colony. Yahya Khan indefinitely postponed the pending National Assembly session, precipitating massive civil disobedience in East Pakistan. In March 1971, despite a military crackdown by the Pakistan Army, the Awami League leader, Sheikh Mujibur Rahman, proclaimed East Pakistan's independence and renamed it Bangladesh. As fighting escalated between the Pakistan Army and the Bengali Mukti Bahini ("freedom fighters"), about ten million Bengalis, mainly Hindus, sought refuge in India. In early December India intervened on the Bangladeshis' side, and within two weeks, the outmatched Pakistani forces surrendered. Yahya Khan handed political power to Zulfikar Ali Bhutto, the head of the PPP, who emerged as the new, smaller Pakistan's undisputed leader.

Bhutto reinforced the concept of civilian control over the armed forces and took political, administrative, and legal steps to disengage the military from politics. A new constitution was drafted in 1973 that endorsed a parliamentary form of democracy, vested executive power in the prime minister, and turned the president into a figurehead. Still, some of Bhutto's closest advisers were generals, he shared the military's hawkish views on national security matters, and he embarked on an ambitious weapons acquisition and modernization program. In order to further appease the armed forces, Bhutto granted generals a role in his administration. Nonetheless, when he asked military leaders to curb political unrest in major cities, they refused to shoot at people.[94]

In March 1976 Bhutto appointed General Muhammad Zia-ul-Haq as the new Chief of the Army Staff. Zia was not known for his brilliance, and he was junior to six other generals in line for the position, but his sycophancy earned him the job. When Zia changed the army's credo to *Iman, Taqwa, Jihad fi Sabil Allah* (Faith, piety, and jihad for the sake of God) soon after taking office, Bhutto did not object.[95] In fact, the army's Islamization had begun much earlier. Although Jinnah favored a secular state, Muslim officers already in 1947–48 had used the Islamic notion of jihad to mobilize the tribesmen they recruited for the fight for Kashmir.[96]

Zia's coup in 1977, the third in Pakistan's brief history, was a case of reactive militarism. The army—once again assuming a self-appointed role as the final arbiter of politics—responded to widespread allegations that Bhutto rigged the 1977 elections and declared that he was no longer capable of running the country. Upon taking power Zia needed to build a strong support base and succeeded in co-opting the civil bureaucracy as a junior partner in the martial law government. More significantly, he started the practice of involving military officers directly in politics—who now, for the first time, received the opportunity to advance their careers and seek lucrative jobs in the civil sector—and of appointing reliable retired officers into high-ranking civilian posts.[97] Zia accelerated the nuclear program started by Bhutto and worked hard to restore the army's flagging morale and prestige following the 1971 war.

Zia managed to stay in power for more than a decade. Realizing the importance of constitutional protection against unchecked powers, he strengthened the role of the president in a constitutional amendment that served as the legal basis for his dismissal of national and provincial assemblies (and later the firing of civilian governments). Just as important, Zia maintained his control over the military. Even as president, he remained the Chief of the Army Staff—just like Augusto Pinochet in Chile—thereby virtually guaranteeing his job security as head of state.[98] He ruled with a firm hand and further enhanced the role of the armed forces as *the* quintessential *political* institution of the state.

Zia died in a plane crash in August 1988. His demise was followed by a military-controlled transition to civilian rule and a decade-long experimentation with democracy featuring four elections and four civilian governments (two each headed by Benazir Bhutto, Zulfikar Ali Bhutto's daughter, and Nawaz Sharif), none of which completed their scheduled tenure. Even during this brief quasi-democratic interlude there was merely an appearance of civilian supremacy over the armed forces. In Pakistan, only a thin line separates military and political power, and once generals decide that their institutional and corporate interests are no longer sufficiently safeguarded by the government, they take over the reins of power, as did, in October 1999, General Pervez Musharraf, who stayed in power for nine years before very reluctantly allowing the return of a civilian administration.

BANGLADESH

Bangladesh may be looked at as another postcolonial case. Not as a former colony of Britain but of Pakistan, whose political and military leaders for a quarter century treated this vast region as if it were a less developed dependency and not the home of their country's majority population. East Pakistani officers particularly resented the discrimination they suffered at the hands of West Pakistanis and that the East was left virtually defenseless—with four regiments only—in case of an Indian attack.[99] In 1972, after a war for independence that claimed three million lives, Bangladesh (the "Country of Bengal") became a parliamentary democracy, adopted a constitution, and signed a friendship treaty with India. Military rule arrived already in 1975 in the shape of a coup d'état that killed the country's founding father, Mujibur Rahman. Two years and two further coups later the army's chief of staff, General Ziaur Rahman, declared himself president only to be assassinated in 1981 by a group of army officers.[100] In the following year General Hussain Muhammad Ershad, also a former army chief of staff, mounted a successful coup against the incompetent civilian government and stayed in power until 1991.

Between 1991 and 2007, civilian rule returned with the daughter of Sheikh Mujibur Rahman, Sheikh Hasina Wajed, and the widow of General Ziaur Rahman, Khaleda Zia, at the helm of their respective political parties, the Awami League (AL) and the Bangladesh Nationalist Party (BNP). For sixteen years the two rivals rotated in and out of power, their rule marked by ever-increasing corruption, astonishing ineptitude, autocratic habits, and mutual loathing. In January 2007 the United Nations actually nudged the armed forces to intervene into politics—another take-over heralding a nearly two-year-long state of emergency—in order to prevent what was widely anticipated to be a murderous election.

As in Pakistan, the Bangladeshi Armed Forces remained a major political force even under the weak but functional democratic rule of the BNP and the AL. Despite the civilian governments' efforts to control the military, they also tried to keep the military satisfied: they committed to a defense modernization program, kept defense expenditures high, and employed a large number of retired officers in their administrations.[101] Both Pakistani and, even more so, Bangladeshi Armed Forces have been heavily involved in United Nations peacekeeping operations, In the Bangladeshi case these activities have constituted a major source of prestige and resources.[102]

There are many similarities this brief sketch of Bangladesh reveals between it and Pakistan—the rapid advent and recurring nature of post-independence military rule, the incompetent and corrupt political elites, the weak political institutions—but there are at least three noteworthy differences between the two armed forces:[103]

First, the Bangladeshi army's officer corps is not rooted in the BIA, given the tiny number of Bengali officers in the Pakistan Army of 1947–71.[104] Therefore, the traditional professionalism and noblesse-oblige socialized into Pakistani officers by the British is entirely missing from the Bangladeshi Armed Forces.

Second, the Bangladeshi officer corps is more heterogeneous than the Pakistani. Many of its officers were former freedom fighters of the Mukti Bahini, which received priority treatment after independence as the new elite of the armed forces—and, of the bureaucracy and economic life—in contrast to those who served in the Pakistan Army. The privileges they enjoyed in promotions, assignments, and perquisites created deep-seated cleavages within the officer corps that prevailed until the early 1980s and is reflected in the coups and countercoups that followed from 1975. Zia reorganized the army to try to end the factional conflict between former freedom fighters and repatriated officers from the Pakistan Army.

Third, Bangladeshi generals have not become as adept at manipulating politicians as their Pakistani colleagues. They were far less educated—at independence no more than one hundred had any genuine academic training[105]—and sophisticated. At the same time, when in power, the generals ruled no more incompetently and certainly were less corrupt than their civilian counterparts.

CONCLUSION

Notwithstanding the many commonalities in their heritage, the polities and the armed forces of India and Pakistan have experienced starkly contrasting developmental trajectories. In terms of the institutional arrangements governing civil-military relations, the two states could not be more different. The executive branch possesses great power over the Indian armed forces, power that is—in this parliamentary democracy—both formally and substantively complemented by legislative authority. In Pakistan both branches of government are much weaker in their position vis-à-vis the military. The political position of the defense minister—who is a bona fide civilian—is powerful while that of the service chiefs (there is still no first-among-equals chief) is almost negligible and is limited to an advisory function in India. In Pakistan, however, the defense minister is a retired military officer who enjoys limited influence; real political power is vested in the Chief of the Army Staff. The Indian legislature receives the complete and detailed information necessary to produce the defense budget, and it is assisted by various institutional channels to ensure that monies are disbursed appropriately. In Pakistan, however, legislators can obtain little specific information about—and, in practice, have modest influence over—military expenditures.

Active-duty military personnel in both states enjoy the right to vote. In Pakistan, at least from a legal perspective, soldiers and officers *should* stay out of politics, but "extraordinary circumstances" have caused them to enter into the political realm. Pakistani generals have tended to be concerned about the legality of their political interventions and sought to legitimate their actions, at least retrospectively, through legislation. In India there is a network of sophisticated and independent defense experts employed by newspapers, NGOs, and universities, while under the conditions of Pakistani authoritarianism, a pool of truly independent defense experts could not develop. In both states the armed forces maintain a number of highly professionalized research institutes.

The most important foreign influence on Indian and Pakistani civil-military relations has been, of course, the legacy of the British Empire. Although with the passing of time the shadow of the Empire has gradually faded, no institution has remained more "British" in either country than the military. Pakistan, both during the Cold War and since, has been strongly affected by its alliance with the United States, which has allowed its armed forces access to weapons, technology, and high-level training.[106] This alliance, it is important to note, was conceived to offset Pakistan's disadvantages in resources and at no point meant to indicate that Islamabad was "pro-American." In a similar vein, India developed close relations with the USSR, but it did not mean—as many in the West assumed—that Delhi was enamored with Moscow or Soviet-style communism.

India has baffled democracy experts because against many odds—widespread poverty, illiteracy, social, and ethnic divisions—it has maintained fiercely democratic institutions save for the eighteen months of the Emergency.[107] The Indian military played—and continues to play—a negligible role in defense and security policies, which is a disservice to the people of India particularly given the traditional (and enduring) lack of military expertise among India's government leaders.[108] Perhaps no democracy—

other than Argentina's under the two presidents Kirchner—has so tightly constrained its officer corps as India. In Pakistan, notwithstanding the many similarities between the two societies, a political system evolved in which real power is held by the military. Whatever authority they grant to the politicians, and for how long, is entirely up to the generals.

There are a number of ways to explain the profound disparities between India and Pakistan and their civil-military relations. Different experiences under colonialism, external security threats (constant and high for Pakistan, far less pressing for India), feeble versus robust public institutions, and weak as opposed to strong legitimacy of civilian political elites provide important clues to the puzzle.[109] Rebecca Schiff's concordance theory points us in another direction as she focuses on the different political roles of the Indian and Pakistani armies by arguing that four factors—the social composition of the officer corps, the political decision-making process, the method of recruitment, and military style—are illuminating in making sense of the disparities between the military politics of the two countries.[110] Historical circumstances—namely, the colonial heritage in general, the Partition and its aftermath, and the first decade or so of independence—have also played a major role in the different development of civil-military relations on the Subcontinent. In the next chapter, we will see whether British colonialism left behind a similarly deep footprint in Africa.

Clearly, the postcolonial context signifies different tasks for democratizers than the ones we have studied thus far. The main objective here is to establish armed forces independent of the colonial power. A chief component of this endeavor, as we have seen in both Pakistan and India, is to educate and train a new corps of native-born officers, something that could not or could only partially take place under the colonial power. Getting rid of the remnants of the old colonial officer contingent that had to be employed until a sufficient number of indigenous officers could be trained was a good incentive to prioritize the training of the new officer corps. Among the three cases in this chapter, only the Indian military elites can be said to have a firm commitment to democratic governance; not surprisingly, India is the only state with a consolidated democracy. Pakistan has been governed or dominated by generals throughout its history, while the specter of military rule seems perennially to hang by a thread over Bangladesh's feeble parliamentary democracy.

TABLE 8.1

After Colonialism in South Asia: India, Pakistan, and Bangladesh

		Country Period	India 1947–1975	Pakistan 1947–1988	Bangladesh 1971–2009
Background	native military force under the British		British India Army—highly professional, increasing role for locals, martial races concept	British India Army—professional, increasing role for locals, martial races concept	marginalized role in the Pakistan Army
	colonial influence on new military		strong	strong to moderate	strong
State	main tasks		establish independent armed forces, train new officer corps, get colonial officers out, prepare for war	establish independent armed forces, train new officer corps, get colonial officers out, prepare for war	establish independent armed forces, train new officer corps, prepare for war
	civilian political leadership		competent and strong	absent or inept, corrupt	mostly inept and corrupt
	political institutions and trend		strong and growing stronger	weak, little maturation	weak but growing stronger
	civilian involvement in defense affairs		pervasive	minimal	minimal
	executive control		strong	weak	weak
	legislative oversight		weak to moderate	weak	weak
	ethno-religious and regional policies		uniting	divisive	uniting
	purges of the military		no	no	no
	foreign influence		USSR: moderate	USA: moderate PRC: small	India: high PRC: small
Military	interference in politics		none	extremely high	high

TABLE 8.1   *(continued)*

After Colonialism in South Asia: India, Pakistan, and Bangladesh

	Country Period	India 1947–1975	Pakistan 1947–1988	Bangladesh 1971–2009
	domestic function	aid-to-the-civil (growing)	aid-to-the-civil, protect regime (especially under military rule)	aid-to-the-civil, protect regime (especially under military rule)
	advisory function	minimal	very high (under civilian rule)	very high (under civilian rule)
	institutional attributes	highly professional	professional, "institutional swagger"	personnel from guerrilla forces and Pakistan Army
	effectiveness	compromised by overly intrusive civilians	varies, leadership prone to miscalculation	high, largest UN PKO contributor
	commitment to democracy	yes	no	no
Society	independent civilian experts	yes, some influence	yes, little influence	yes, some influence
	military's prestige	low to medium	high	high
	soldiers in society	relatively isolated	active engagement in economy and society	well integrated
	conscription	no	no	no
Political system at the end of the period		consolidated parliamentary democracy	electoral authoritarianism with intermittent military rule	parliamentary democracy with intermittent military rule

CHAPTER 9

After Colonial Rule in Africa:
Ghana, Tanzania, and Botswana

In the previous chapter we saw the different trajectories of military politics in India and Pakistan. In this chapter our attention shifts to Africa but we will stay with the postcolonial context as we get acquainted with three other countries that experienced British rule prior to independence. The primary cases here are Ghana in West Africa and Tanzania in East Africa, the erstwhile Gold Coast and Tanganyika, respectively. In 1957 Ghana was the first Sub-Saharan European colony to gain independence; Tanganyika became a sovereign state in 1961. Our secondary case is Botswana, a former British protectorate in southern Africa that became independent in 1966.

The people in these three British colonial holdings did not have to declare war to become masters of their fate, though particularly in Ghana and Tanzania, there was a purposeful effort—or *Uhuru* ([freedom] struggle) in Swahili, the main language of Tanzania. Another important parallel between them is that they all benefited from the guidance of charismatic leaders who spearheaded the road to independence. These and other similarities notwithstanding, there are also major disparities between them regarding their natural endowments and the effects of colonial rule. In terms of carving out a proper institutional place for the armed forces in their emerging postcolonial states, they could hardly be more different: Tanzania has never known military rule and Botswana has not even had a coup attempt, whereas Ghanaian soldiers executed four coups d'état and ruled their country for more than two decades until democratization began in 1992.

The time frame for our analysis of the two primary cases in this chapter is from independence till 1979, a year that was an important milestone for both countries. In Ghana, 1979 was the year of a countercoup and the end of a second stretch of military rule that gave way, albeit briefly, to a third attempt at civilian governance. The same year marked the end of Tanzania's victorious war against neighboring Uganda. For the short discussion of Botswana, the coverage will stop in 1998 when the commander who transformed its military resigned. We begin by looking at the British colonial legacy in Ghana and Tanzania and then proceed with an assessment of the political role of the two countries' founding leaders. Following an analysis of Tanzanian military politics under one-party rule, we will consider the reasons for and the record of recurrent military dictatorship in Ghana. Finally I will explain why Botswana has been so unusual in African politics and military affairs.

THE BRITISH LEGACY

As in India, the British presence in Western Africa was dictated by commercial interest. In the Gold Coast, the Empire's formal relationship began with the Bond of 1844 granting trading rights.[1] Thereafter London assumed control of a territory that it would rule for the next century and a quarter, when colonial devolution spread from Asia to Africa where it often resulted in a remarkably nonviolent transfers of power. The Gold Coast was a lucrative source of "exploitables" for the Empire and thus, worthy of investment. At independence, Ghana inherited a reasonably well-developed physical infrastructure—particularly in the coastal areas—a superior body of indigenous civil servants, and a small segment of well-educated natives.[2]

Tanzania was colonized in the late nineteenth century by Germans (as *Deutsch Ostafrika*) but at the beginning of the 1905–1907 Maji-Maji War, a rebellion launched by indigenous communities, the Africans nearly defeated the colonists.[3] Reinforcements from the *Vaterland* saved the day for the Germans who ended up slaughtering the spear-carrying warriors with machine guns and via forced starvation.[4] The November 1914 British amphibious assault on German fortifications in East Africa was the first major battle of World War I on the continent. Following the war, the region changed masters, as the British, with the blessing of the League of Nations, took over the territory in 1920 and renamed it Tanganyika, after the lake. Tanganyika became the largest of the United Nations' Trust Territories after World War II and remained under London's administration till independence in 1961. Unlike Ghana, the resource-poor though strategically valuable Tanganyika was not slated for colonial development. Missionaries were primarily responsible for building schools and hospitals, and administering social welfare programs. The British ruled Tanganyika for forty-three years but at independence it had only two trained engineers, twelve doctors, and an adult illiteracy rate of 85 percent.[5]

Colonial Armies in the Gold Coast
and Tanganyika

The armed forces of British-ruled West Africa trace their origins to the 1897 amalgamation of troops from the Gold Coast, Nigeria, Sierra Leone, and Gambia to form the Royal West African Frontier Force (RWAFF). In 1901 the Gold Coast Regiment was constituted in which all officers and most senior NCOs continued to be British. The RWAFF's main function was dealing with internal disturbances, but during World War I they saw action in both West and East Africa where their performance was so impressive that the Imperial War Office sought the recruitment of an African army to be deployed in Europe.[6] The beginnings of the King's African Rifles (KAR) in East Africa go back to the days of chartered companies, the earliest days of the British conquest. The KAR, according to a contemporary author, was "a normal instrument of the civilized authority, never intended to take part in anything but localized operations against a savage or at most a semi-savage."[7] In any event, it was charged with maintaining internal security, which chiefly meant reining in local labor movements and curbing political activities. Between the two world wars the colonial armies in Africa were little more than a reasonably well-organized and military-based gendarmerie.[8]

Just like in India, the British—consistent with their belief that people from some regions were more suitable for military duty than from others—recruited from areas where prospective soldiers were unlikely to harbor radical or nationalist views. Unlike in India, where social class came into play at recruitment, it mattered little in African societies, which were far less hierarchical. Instead, recruiters tended to avoid towns and focused on appealing to the sons of peasants or low-ranking bureaucrats in remote regions. In the Gold Coast, native-born officer candidates were drawn primarily from the more educated and socially mobile ethnic groups: the Ga, Ewe, and Fante tribes produced 73 percent of all officers. In contrast, the large, prosperous, and cohesive Ashanti, who were not considered a "martial race" by the colonists, made up no more than 7 percent of the native officer corps.[9] Army recruits in Tanganyika were also drawn from the tribes—especially the Hehe, Kuria/Watende, and Yao—whom the British considered the "martial races." Though, the King's African Rifles were ethnically imbalanced, in Tanganyika ethnicity was never the critical political factor that it was in many African states, including Ghana, and its significance diminished further after independence.

Nearly half a million Africans fought in World War II. Of the 63,038 men from the Gold Coast, 41,888 served overseas.[10] They, along with the thousands who fought in the KAR, performed their duties courageously and effectively first in East Africa (particularly against the Italians in Abyssinia) and then against the Japanese in India and Burma. Even today, Ghana's largest defense installation, just outside of Accra, is called the Burma Camp, commemorating that campaign. The highlight of the war for the KAR was the Battle of Colito where the First KAR Infantry Battalion captured 489 Italian and 31 African prisoners of war along with a great deal of war materiel.[11] For many Africans the war presented the opportunity to learn how to speak, read, and write English; master new skills and travel; experience other countries; and generally broaden their horizons. World War II also boosted the education and socialization of a small but important segment of Africans who often became leaders of the independence struggle and, in due course, of the postcolonial governments of their countries.

Soon after World War II, the drawdown of colonial armies began. What to do with the potentially disruptive force of ex-servicemen represented a serious concern for colonial administrators. Veterans organizations were formed in several British (and French) colonies and turned into hotbeds of nationalist agitation. The West Africa Command closed in 1956 and its organizational remnant, the Army Advisory Council for West Africa, was finally dissolved two years later, following Prime Minister Kwame Nkrumah's decision to withdraw Ghana from the organization. Some native RWAFF officers enjoyed illustrious careers in the Ghanaian military and civil service. None more so than the Sandhurst-educated Major Seth Anthony, who became a prominent diplomat. In 2008, a few months before his death at ninety-three, the British finally overcame their reluctance to extend recognition to their colonial soldiers and decorated Anthony with the Burma Star Badge.[12]

The British felt that Africans possessed lower officer potential than Indians, and British unwillingness to train all but a few locals kept educational standards low and retarded the development of armies in their African colonies.[13] At independence in 1957, Ghana's military was headed by British Major-General A. G. Paley, who commanded 237 officers of whom 29 were Ghanaians.[14] Tanganyika was even worse off. Its highest-ranking soldiers were NCOs and warrant officers whose distinctions were loyalty, reliability, subordination, and experience, qualities that temporarily replaced education and technological qualifications due to the exigencies of the times.[15]

The British policy of slow Africanization of the officer corps—justified with the poor academic preparation of the recruits and their own opposition to lowering training standards—served their interests well. At the same time, while the Indian Congress Party pressured the colonists as early as the 1920s to increase the number of Indians in the British India Army, the

nationalist politicians of the Gold Coast and Tanganyika took little interest in the composition of the colonial forces until independence. Just as
in India and Pakistan, in both Ghana and Tanzania, British generals and
officers continued to lead and serve in the armed forces for years after the
end of colonial rule owing to the dearth of qualified locals. The last British
active-duty officers left the Ghanaian army only in September 1961, when
President Kwame Nkrumah ordered them—Chief of Defence Staff General
Henry Alexander, 80 officers, and a 120 NCOs—out of the country just
before the visit of Queen Elizabeth II, presumably to impress upon her the
sovereignty of her former colony.[16] Their colleagues in the renamed Tanganyika Rifles left in 1964.

NKRUMAH, NYERERE, AND THEIR POLITICS

In political environments with low levels of institutionalization and societal development, individual politicians often become larger than life and
amass great authority. Julius Nyerere in Tanzania and Kwame Nkrumah in
Ghana, as well as Seretse Khama in Botswana, were the point men for their
countries' struggles for sovereignty and became their foremost leaders after
independence.

Fathers of the Nation

Both in the Gold Coast and in Tanganyika the creation of political par-
ties signaled the beginning of independence struggles. In Tanganyika, Julius
Nyerere (1922–99), a teacher armed with degrees from Makerere University
in Uganda and the University of Edinburgh, founded the Tanganyika African
National Union (TANU) in 1954, for the purpose of achieving sovereignty.
The British were initially unsympathetic, but with the appointment of Sir
Richard Turnbull as governor in 1958, the process of colonial devolution
accelerated. In the first free elections, in September 1958, TANU-supported
candidates won all fifteen seats in the Legislative Council, and Nyerere became the leader of the opposition. Six months later, TANU members received four portfolios in the newly created Council of Ministers. In the August 1960 elections, TANU won all but one of the seventy-one seats and
Nyerere became the first Internal Self-Government Administration's Chief
Minister. He was the obvious choice to be Tanganyika's prime minister in
December 1961, and when it became a republic the following year, to be its
first president. With the union of Tanganyika and the Indian Ocean island
state of Zanzibar in 1964, Nyerere became the president of the United Re-

public of Tanzania, a position he held until his resignation in 1985. Nyerere detested corruption in all forms and did nothing to enrich himself or his family. He is one of the few African leaders who left office voluntarily and whose memory is surrounded by genuine respect and affection.

Kwame Nkrumah (1909–72), the leader of the Gold Coast and later of Ghana, shared some attributes with Nyerere. After earning two degrees each from Lincoln University and the University of Pennsylvania in the United States, he returned to his homeland to found a political organization, the Convention People's Party (CPP), in order to achieve sovereignty. He was soon acknowledged both by the British and his countrymen as the colony's preeminent native politician. In 1951 Nkrumah was appointed "Leader of Government Business," served as prime minister from 1952 until independence in 1957, and retained that office until 1960, when Ghana, too, became a republic.

The 1960 Constitution created a strong presidential state and endowed the president, Nkrumah, with sweeping executive powers. Unlike Nyerere, Nkrumah became increasingly dictatorial as time went on. Already in 1958, his regime introduced the Preventive Detention Act that allowed arrest without charge, and imprisonment without trial. Potential sources of opposition—the media, trade unions, the judiciary and universities—were brought under rigid government control. By 1960 a full-blown cult of personality had developed around him: he became "untouchable," any criticism directed at him or his policies bound to draw severe sanctions. In 1964 Nkrumah declared a single-party state and installed himself as "President for Life." The CPP, the government, and Nkrumah personally engaged in massive corruption, which only increased the broad-based popular support for the overthrow of his regime in 1966.[17] Nkrumah was out of the country at the time and was not allowed to set foot in Ghana for the rest of his life.

African Socialism: Two Variants

Nyerere wanted to build a socialist society based on community and brotherhood. He believed that communist China's developmental model was most suitable for Tanzania's conditions. At first the state merely encouraged cooperative farming but with the 1967 Arusha Declaration, the pursuit of state-socialism became official policy, and the collectivization of agriculture the national mission. Nyerere used the single-party system to govern society more or less benevolently, running an authoritarian state in which political opposition had no place. The concept of *ujamaa* (Swahili for familyhood) served to justify the forcible relocation of millions of peasants to "ujamaa villages," and to make them pay high taxes even though they produced little owing to low morale and the loss of personal property.[18] Actually, the idea behind ujamaa was deeply flawed: Nyerere extrapolated from his own tribal experience—his Zanaki tribe was well known for its egalitarian spirit—which was in stark contrast to that of most other tribes, in which communal ownership did not exist. The party-state owned and managed the country's major assets and imposed severe restrictions on income and private property, thereby effectively robbing people of the incentive to work. The results were disastrous: a steep economic decline began in the mid-1970s replete with food shortages and growing dependence on international donors. In 1977 TANU merged with the Afro-Shirazi Party—the ruling party on the island of Zanzibar—to form the CCM (*Chama cha Mapinduzi*) (Swahili for Party of the Revolution) and has dominated politics even after the reintroduction of the multiparty system in 1992.

When Nyerere stepped down as president in November 1985 he openly conceded, "I failed. Let's admit it," alluding to his inability to create a sound economy.[19] Still, his achievements may well have outweighed his shortcomings. He substantially improved Tanzanian health care, education, and public services and strove to reverse inequality, uproot extreme poverty, and attack discrimination of any sort. In an ethnically volatile region Nyerere managed to prevent violent ethnic conflicts and to build a nation out of a diverse population of some 126 tribes. By insisting that Swahili, not English, had to be the primary language, he did a lot to create a real sense of national pride and unity, which is lacking in most other African countries. Tanzanians traditionally value peace and stability above all, and Nyerere's success in delivering these must not be underestimated. Under his rule conspicuous consumption was socially unacceptable and elites were restrained, taking their cues from a popular and ascetic president. Virtually all Tanzanians agree that he was a great man who was interested in nothing more than serving his people the best way he knew how.[20] He is customarily referred to as *Mwalimu* (Swahili for teacher) or as *Baba wa Taifa* (the father of the nation).

Perhaps no other African country started independence with more promise than Ghana but within a decade its economy was wrecked and its international reputation in tatters, mostly due to Nkrumah's ill-advised and irresponsible policies. Nkrumah's conception of socialism, particularly his notion of social mobilization and economic development, was also strongly influenced by Maoist China.[21] Unlike in Tanzania, in Ghana the emphasis in economic development was placed on "total industrialization" with a corresponding neglect of agricultural production. Nkrumah's asinine policies effectively destroyed the vibrant cocoa industry, Ghana's main source of export income. Moreover, the plummeting world-market price of cocoa and the lack of raw materials meant that the country was unable to feed itself and ensured the failure of quick industrial development. By 1966 Ghana was bankrupt and most Ghanaians were far worse off than they had been even a few years earlier.[22]

While Nyerere was sensitive to ethnic issues, Nkrumah neglected or antagonized tribal leaders who continued to enjoy an exceedingly important position in Ghanaian society. Like Nyerere, Nkrumah drew the wrong conclusions from his own background. His roots in one of the tiniest groups, the Nzima of southwest Ghana, predisposed him to advocate intensive political centralization with sharply negative consequences for the larger ethnic groups, particularly the influential Ashanti of Central Ghana, who strongly opposed his regime.[23]

Pan-Africanism

Both Nkrumah and Nyerere were committed pan-Africanists. Nkrumah sought the creation of a pan-African state founded on the "African personality" that would eliminate the artificial boundaries between Africans created by colonial powers. He envisioned a common all-African market and currency area, and the development of a continent-wide transportation and communication systems within the framework of an African superstate with himself as its all-powerful leader.[24] Along with the gradual widening of African unity, Nkrumah also pursued the idea of a pan-African army and an African Military Command but neither his generals, nor those of other African states, were the least bit interested.[25]

Two weeks after installing himself as Ghana's president, Nkrumah deployed his army to help nationalists in the newly independent Democratic Republic of the Congo in a move that worsened his already precarious relations with the military.[26] When in June 1960 Belgian paratroops descended on the Congo, Prime Minister Patrice Lumumba asked for Nkrumah's help until the arrival of the United Nations troops. Within a week, 1,193 Ghanaian soldiers were in Léopoldville, and by late August 1960, their number had grown to nearly 2,400. In the same month, a secret Ghana-Congo union agreement was signed that Nkrumah envisaged as the first result of his grand strategy for Africa—but it was never implemented. The Ghanaian military contingent remained for three of the four years of the U.N. operations, contributing a total of more than 39,000 man-months (only Nigeria and Ethiopia sent more soldiers).[27] Though Ghana has participated extensively in international peacekeeping operations, it has not fought a war since independence.[28]

Nyerere was a founder of the Organization of African Unity and a proponent of an East African Federation of Kenya, Tanzania, and Uganda. During his long tenure, Tanzania played an important role as a "frontline state" in the international response to white supremacist regimes in southern Africa. Tanzania supported African liberation movements and antiracist and anti-apartheid forces far and wide with arms, men, training facilities, and by providing a safe haven for foreign insurgents. During the Cold War, Tanzania managed to remain an autonomous actor in African politics because it had no imperial patron; though the country received substantial aid through the years from Beijing, it never became a "client state" of China.[29]

The Ghanaian Military under Nkrumah (1957–66)

After independence the control of the Ghanaian Armed Forces was primarily exercised by the defense ministry, which, under the leadership of a minister and his deputy, was divided into a civil wing, headed by a Chief Director, and a military wing, administered by the Chief of Defence Staff (CDS). For coordination and cost-reduction purposes joint headquarters for the three services were established in 1962. The National Security Committee assessed security requirements and decided, as early as 1958, to expand the military and increase defense spending as the state began to consider the armed forces a potential tool of foreign policy. Nkrumah wanted to build a large army to put military muscle behind his ideas of African liberation. The armed forces were gradually expanded, and by 1966—with fourteen thousand officers and men—were the largest in West Africa.[30] The government insisted quality was more important than quantity in officer training but standards suffered due to the imperative to quicken the pace of the officer corps' Africanization. As in Pakistan, once the British trainers left, the message to keep the army out of politics no longer had a forceful advocate in Ghana.

From the beginning, Nkrumah had a contentious relationship with his soldiers. Like many intellectuals in former colonies—recall Nehru and Menon—Nkrumah and the Ghanaian political elite were disdainful of military officers, ignorant about security issues, and their policies harmed both the army and Ghana. In contrast to Tanzania, where Nyerere eliminated ethnic identity as a relevant attribute of army personnel, after 1961 Nkrumah manipulated the armed forces to ensure that tribes whose support he enjoyed would improve their position in the military.[31] After Nkrumah deepened his alliance with communist states, he began to send some officers to be educated in the communist bloc (primarily in the Soviet Union) while others continued to receive their training at Western military academies (in Britain and Canada, primarily). The top brass was worried that this policy would create a divided officer corps in which one part received top-notch professional training while the other acquired heavy doses of Marxist-Leninist indoctrination. As one prominent general saw it, "The saying that 'East is East and West is West and never the twain shall meet' came to acquire a new and more vivid meaning for me when Nkrumah took his leftward turn and tried to drag the country and the Army with him."[32]

Not surprisingly, the army as an institution disliked Nkrumah's policies and despised the concentration of power in his hands, the widespread corruption, and the "capricious exercise of power" by a president who ran the country "as if it were his own personal property."[33] The decision to intervene in the Congo was especially unpopular among the officers because it focused attention on two of their major concerns: their own professional integrity and the international reputation of their government.[34] Few expressed the view of the high command more succinctly than the coup participant and future president Akwasi Afrifa, who wondered, "Could it be that we had been sent to the Congo to foster the ambition of Kwame Nkrumah?"[35]

During the first few post-independence years, the government trusted the military's autonomous professionalism and based civil-military relations on the Huntingtonian concept of objective control. As Nkrumah's regime became increasingly dictatorial, and socioeconomic conditions continued to deteriorate, he realized that the support of the armed forces could not be taken for granted. Therefore, as in other state-socialist polities, the regime gradually extended its control over the military, devising several mechanisms to assure its quiescence and loyalty. The Armed Forces Bill of 1961 aimed at reining in the troops, while the Security Service Act of 1963 consolidated what some observers called a "counter-military system."[36] A 1962 defense ministry directive introduced mandatory party education into the army through an Armed Forces Bureau and sent officers to take extended courses at the Kwame Nkrumah Institute of Ideological Studies.[37] Membership in the Convention People's Party and identification with the party-state became the basic criteria for hiring and promotion; the political indoctrination of armed forces personnel with tenets of scientific socialism was given greater emphasis in training and education; and all influential military officers were held under surveillance by the security apparatus. In addition, the army was increasingly tribalized as members of Nkrumah's own Nzima tribe and of supportive northern tribes were appointed to all sensitive posts in the defense-security establishment. The regime also introduced the practice of simultaneously appointing two or more persons of different ethnic backgrounds to positions of overlapping responsibility in order to encourage rivalries and mistrust between people.[38]

Moreover, the state created additional security and intelligence formations to spy on, compete with, and counterbalance the regular armed forces. These included the quasi-military Workers' Brigade (conceived as an armed reserve of the CPP), the National Security Service, and, most importantly, the Presidential Guards. Established in 1960 as a company-sized unit, the Presidential Guards were gradually expanded and by 1966 had grown to 1,150 men and 50 officers and was renamed the President's Own Guard Regiment.[39] The Guards—like other special armies of the executive branch from Romania to Iraq—were better paid and equipped than the regular forces; their commander even received special training in Moscow. The existence of a privileged parallel force created a direct threat to the regular army's professional autonomy and self-image and intensified the officer corps' already deep-seated resentment of Nkrumah's regime.

THE EVOLUTION OF TANZANIAN MILITARY POLITICS

The Tanganyika Rifles (1961–64)

Civil-military relations during the first three years of independence were remarkably uneventful, and aside from its name, the army Tanganyika inherited from its colonial masters had changed little. The command structure—with the exception of one company based at the Colito base in Dar es Salaam—continued to be dominated by the British. Command positions that were inherited from the KAR were held by thirty-five British officers and twenty-five British NCOs.[40] In other words, native soldiers could wonder with good reason whether they were serving in the army of their own sovereign state. Military personnel, especially NCOs, were paid poorly compared to other government employees, earning the Tanganyika Rifles (TR) the nickname "a refuge for up-country illiterates."[41] Unlike in Ghana, where Nkrumah's government was in daily contact with the army's British leadership until their dismissal in 1961, Nyerere had no regular interaction with Brigadier Patrick Douglas, and the TANU party elite left the army's management entirely to the British. This is significant because until 1966 there were no separate ministries to conduct defense or foreign affairs; both of these state functions were under the direct control of the prime minister (i.e., Nyerere). Several leading Tanganyikan politicians argued that since the country had no enemy, national defense should not enjoy priority status on their agenda.

Matters changed in 1963, in response to the crystallization of an activist foreign policy that put a premium on aiding liberation movements.[42] That year saw the creation of independent defense and foreign ministries and a protracted budget debate in the National Assembly that culminated in an agreement to beef up and improve conditions in the armed forces. At this point, the issues of genuine national control of the military and of the officer corps' Africanization also received attention and support.

Both Tanzania and Ghana experienced one crucial event that changed the course of their civil-military relations for the long term although their effects could not have been more dissimilar. The mutiny in Tanganyika, as Nyerere liked to remark afterward, "enabled us to build an army almost from scratch. Many institutions we have inherited, but the army is something we built ourselves."[43] The first military coup in Ghana in 1966, on the other hand, heralded a quarter-century of intermittent military rule.

Critical Juncture I: The Mutiny of 1964

Nyerere's confidence in the armed forces was shattered in January 1964 when two battalions of the Tanganyika Rifles mutinied. The uprising was essentially a soldiers' strike for more pay and for accelerated replacement of British officers by Tanzanians; some participants referred to the events as "an industrial paystrike."[44] Its objective was *not* to overthrow the regime: the only political action of the mutineers was their two trips to the State House in Dar es Salaam for the purpose of seeking an audience with the president to air their grievances. Therefore, their action should not be labeled a "coup attempt."

In view of the armed insurgencies and political turbulence earlier or roughly at the same time in other African states (Congo, Togo, Kenya, Uganda), it may be understandable that Nyerere overreacted and went into hiding (some say, "unceremoniously disappeared") during the mutiny.[45] In his absence, the foreign and defense minister, Oscar Kambona, stepped into the political vacuum and helped diffuse the situation. The political leadership realized the disturbances had to be stopped quickly and for want of an alternative called upon the British to intervene by disarming the Tanganyika Rifles. Sixty British marine commandos quickly and effectively did what they were asked to do. The mutiny was a humiliating lesson for Tanganyika's ruling elites, as it revealed their continued dependence on their colonial masters. In February 1964 Nyerere convened a meeting of the Organization of African Unity in Dar es Salaam to explain why he had asked the British to intervene—one African scholar called this "a cleansing ceremony"—and he publicly expressed his thanks to them (unlike his Kenyan and Ugandan colleagues whose regimes were saved by British soldiers in similar fashion).[46]

Although different experts have offered varying interpretations of the mutiny, internal factors explain the events most conclusively. A few years after gaining independence, these states were politically fragile and poorly institutionalized making them particularly vulnerable to military rebellions. In many cases, internal order and public-safety issues had not yet been sorted out, or, as in the case of Tanganyika, the state had not yet assumed full control of its military establishment. In such environments, even mild and merely "existential" demands from the armed forces could and did generate public disorder easily.[47] For Tanganyika, the mutiny was an alarm bell indicating that the army was strong enough to create havoc and needed to be brought under civilian control as quickly as possible.[48] Moreover, the mutiny revealed the lack of TANU's capacity to mobilize the mass support that might have contained the mutiny.[49] This shortcoming, too, had to soon be remedied.

The Military under One-Party Rule

As indicated earlier, in April 1964 the United Republic of Tanzania was formed with the unification of Tanganyika and Zanzibar. Shortly before, the island had experienced its own coup d'état, which ended the Sultanate and prepared the ground for the union—which, incidentally, is the only instance in which two independent African states have given up their sovereignty to unite.[50] The 1967 Arusha Declaration committed Tanzania to a socialist development, and an essential component of the state-building and institutionalization program was the transformation of the armed forces.

The institutional design of Tanzanian civil-military relations was very similar to that of other socialist states. The party's authority trumped that of the government—the two had a symbiotic relationship—and the legislature enjoyed no autonomous decision-making power. One of the main missions of the renamed Tanzanian People's Defence Force (TPDF) was to ensure domestic political stability; it was, after all, the army of the party-state. It could be called to action for crowd control and to give assistance to the civil power, as we have seen in the cases of other former British colonies. The defense ministry became an independent bureaucracy only in 1966, and the minister was at times civilian with an officer as deputy, at other times the other way around; the state also tried to balance mainland and Zanzibari politicians in leadership positions. The ministry of defense—unlike in many other authoritarian and socialist states—always had a large contingent of civilian employees. The armed forces' leader in peacetime was the Chief of the Defence Force—in wartime his title was changed to Chief of the Defence Forces because then his responsibilities included overseeing a number of additional services, including the police, the prison system, and the militia. The TPDF included (and its successor still includes) the three conventional branches and the National Service, a semimilitarized societal organization. There were no nongovernmental organizations to employ independent military experts. Military spending was relatively high—partly owing to the overall militarization of society and in view of recurring security threats, particularly from neighboring Uganda in the late 1970s. In general, militarization tended to be the most intense among the poorest African societies—Mozambique, Somalia, Ethiopia, and Chad—and Tanzania was no exception.[51]

After the 1964 Mutiny the rapid Africanization of the officer corps began. The ringleaders of the mutiny were prosecuted but most participants were simply released with a note on their records decreeing that they could not serve in the future armed forces. The government even provided train fare for soldiers far from home.[52] Loyal officers benefited from fast-tracked promotions: for instance, Captain M. Sarakikya, who emerged as a lieutenant colonel after the mutiny, was elevated to major general in three weeks; he became commander of the new army.[53] Upon Nyerere's instructions the new army was built around the TANU Youth League (similar to the Soviet *Komsomol*), and political indoctrination became as important a component of training as conventional military education. In concert with the regime's egalitarian policies, women were first recruited in 1964–65, but they were all released by 1966 owing to the lack of an infrastructure to accommodate them. These problems were remedied by 1972, when the TPDF reinstated women's recruitment.[54]

Tanzania was an exceptional case in Africa in that at a time when most African leaders grew wary of their armed forces, Nyerere developed a politically active military in order to co-opt potential opposition to one-party rule. Thus, overt politicization of the army became official policy, and the notion of politically neutral troops was explicitly discarded. Nyerere wanted every member of the armed forces to be active and engaged supporters of the state. Membership in TANU and, after 1977, in the CCM, became a mandatory entrance requirement—not quasi-obligatory, as in most European socialist states—and remained so till 1992. As in other socialist armies, every unit had its own party branch and political commissar responsible for the ideological vigor of the troops.[55] The military academy was merged with the party cadre school in 1977 underscoring the party's influence on military life.

After 1972, armed forces personnel could contest parliamentary seats and receive unpaid leave from the military during their service as legislators.

The politicization of the military went hand in hand with the militarization of governance. Not only did the party enter the army as politicians served as political commissars, but army officers routinely received appointments in the party or government bureaucracies. During the early 1970s, for example, at times more than one third of Nyerere's cabinet was composed of military officers.[56] Many officers received jobs in state or party organizations and enterprises upon retirement from the military. The relationship between the military and the party-state, in other words, was a two-way street and has been described as "the party in the army and the army in the party."[57]

Nyerere intended to create a positive image for the army as an integral part of society. He told officers, "You are just as much citizens of the country as are farmers and fishermen. There is no reason, therefore, of refusing any citizen of the country to have a say in the politics of the country."[58] His understanding of citizen-soldiers shared some attributes with the West German concept of *Staatsbürger in Uniform*. Following the 1964 Mutiny, the regime began to search for an appropriate model of social mobilization in order to bring together young people from all geographical, economic, ethnic, and religious backgrounds so as to build a sense of national identity. Nyerere and his colleagues were particularly impressed by the Israeli kibbutz system as well as the broad social basis of the Israeli Defense Forces, and adopted some of their components. By the mid-1960s some Tanzanian soldiers received training in Israel, and IDF officers went to Tanzania to train military personnel and set up what became National Service Camps. The diversification of sources for officer training abroad (in Britain, Canada, Nigeria, the Soviet Union, the United States, etc.) became official policy in Tanzania, enabling it to maintain its neutrality in international politics and professional balance in the officer corps.

The National Service was officially created in 1965 and became one of the key pillars of Tanzanian social development, occupying an important place between the civilian and military realms. Soon after 1966, when university students demonstrated against their National Service obligations, the Service was subordinated to the TPDF. From this point on, joining the National Service was mandatory for high school and university graduates, who—despite their protest—had to serve for two years as a way of reimbursing the state for the cost of their education.[59] There was no standard conscription in Tanzania but the National Service also functioned as a recruitment pool for the TPDF. In fact, many youths with lesser education, particularly from economically underprivileged areas, joined the National Service with the hope of being absorbed into the armed forces. After 1976 the National Service assumed an additional role as the production unit of the TPDF, producing boots and uniforms and performing various agricultural and business activities.[60] Even today, the ministry is called "Ministry of Defence and National Service."

When necessary, the military intervened in domestic politics as the servant of the government; in the late 1960s, for instance, the army broke the occasionally violent resistance of farmers to resettlement in ujamaa villages.[61] The army as an institution was also a reliable adversary of post-1964 coup plotters. Minor coup attempts occurred in 1969, 1972, and 1982, but they were nonviolent, poorly planned, and enjoyed virtually no public support. The rotation of officers in and out of politics and of politicians in and out of the TPDF gravely complicated matters for would-be coup plotters. To enhance its control over the armed forces, the state created paramilitary organizations, most importantly the People's Militia, which was a reservoir of people with military training; its access to weapons lessened the likelihood of the army's political intrusion. Founded in 1963 and established as one of the components of the TPDF in the 1966 National Defence Act, the Militia provided valuable assistance to civil authorities in maintaining law and order and in combat operations during the 1978–79 war with Uganda.[62]

The final watershed event of the period under consideration was the Uganda-Tanzania War that, like so many other wars, stemmed from gross miscalculation. Ugandan dictator Idi Amin, who was losing control of his army to more bellicose subordinates, falsely claimed that Tanzanian troops entered Uganda and leveled dozens of settlements near the border. Amin, in an attempt to demonstrate his authority, ordered Ugandan forces to take up arms against northern Tanzania where they killed many villagers and looted everything of value. In the end, the TPDF—buoyed by extensive social support, a relatively full treasury, and more volunteers than could be enlisted—convincingly routed Ugandan government forces thereby hastening the demise of Amin's regime.[63]

GHANA: RECURRENT MILITARY RULE

The first clear indication that some segments of the military were ready for political intervention occurred already in 1958 when a Ghanaian officer, Captain Benjamin Awhaitey, was arrested and subsequently imprisoned for conspiring to assassinate Nkrumah.[64] The first military coup—aptly described as "lightning action at the top, in which violence is the ultimate determinant, even if it is not used"[65]—that unseated Nkrumah and his regime took place eight years later and was followed by several more coups and twenty-two years of intermittent military rule.

Critical Juncture II: The 1966 Coup d'État

Brigadier M. M. Hassan, the Director of Military Intelligence, frequently warned Nkrumah of the potential threat posed by the armed forces. When in late February the president and several regime loyalists in the military leadership were abroad, a 500-strong contingent from the army—with the strong support of the police, who were equally dissatisfied with Nkrumah's dictatorship—seized the opportunity and took power. Armed resistance to the insurgents was not substantial; fighting was limited to skirmishes between the Presidential Guard and regular army units.

The conditions preceding the Ghanaian coup comprise a textbook case of military takeovers. By early 1966 the military was fed up with Nkrumah's dictatorial rule and ruinous economic policies. The army and its leadership were hurt by the president's divisive schemes, particularly his favoritism of politically loyal officers with promotions and assignments, retirement of competent generals who refused to flatter him, cutbacks in amenities and services for the regular armed forces, and threats and rumors regarding deployments in support of risky foreign adventures.[66] The coup's objectives included the rehabilitation of several prominent officers, among them Generals Joseph Ankrah and Stephen Otu, whom Nkrumah shunted aside, indicating that esprit de corps issues were also important coup motivators.[67] Most importantly, the conspirators truly believed that they were ridding Ghana of an authoritarian leader. By any measure, the coup was remarkably popular, as most social groups supported the replacement of Nkrumah's dictatorship with a pluralist political system, just what the coup-makers had promised.

Military Rule, 1966–69

Ruth First rightly observed that "the coup as a method of change that changes little has become endemic to Africa's politics."[68] Still, the 1966 Ghanaian coup is something of an exception. Robert Pinkney argued that the most obvious contribution an African army could make to democracy was to remove authoritarian governments that cannot be removed by other means and then to permit free elections, which was more or less the pattern in Ghana in 1966–69.[69] Still, it must be stressed that the army's returning power to freely elected civilians was rare in Africa, and elsewhere, and that in Ghana, the coup created a precedent that helped make future military takeovers seem acceptable.

The Ghanaian military leadership along with their many political allies—the bureaucratic, professional, business, and traditional elites—was committed to reestablishing what they saw as a Westminster model of democracy.[70]

The new National Liberation Council (NLC)—composed of four military and four police officers—suspended the 1960 Constitution, disbanded the CPP, and dissolved the legislature composed overwhelmingly of Nkrumah's sycophants. In practice, military rule meant a military-administrative system in which a few generals, most of all Ankrah and Emmanuel Kotoka, oversaw a civilian bureaucracy.[71] The total number of armed forces officers who were employed in extra–military roles seldom exceeded twelve.[72] The NLC liberalized the media and permitted the articulation of different political approaches. Already in 1966 the NLC appointed the members of the Constitutional Commission and the Political Committee, and ten of the seventeen, and thirteen of the twenty-three members, respectively, represented opposition groups.[73]

Compared to other experiences of military rule, the 1966–69 Ghanaian regime was progressive and enlightened but it was primarily in the political arena that it left a positive legacy by restoring a pluralistic political landscape. The NLC frequently reminded the population that their aim was to liberate Ghana from an arbitrary dictatorship—not to change the structure of society—and to hand over power to a representative civilian government as soon as possible. It embarked on a campaign to visit seven hundred towns and villages to explain the reason for the coup, and created a network of advisory committees through which the population via various pressure groups could convey their demands.[74] Furthermore, the NLC established a number of advisory commissions and committees to hold inquiries regarding the injustices committed under Nkrumah's regime and to address a variety of societal grievances.

The military government also repealed some harmful legislation, such as the 1962 Rents (Stabilization) Act to "restore the customary rules of land tenure," and to respond to the tribal chiefs' demand for greater judicial power.[75] Because the NLC had no particular ideological allegiance, it could pursue pragmatic policies and respond to social pressures. The economy benefited from sharp increases in world cocoa and diamond prices but the NLC's economic policy was most of all one of non-interference in the private sector. The government's heavy reliance on the West for economic development and managerial skills served to perpetuate Ghana's economic dependence.[76]

The generals were not above repeatedly promoting themselves, doling out patronage appointments, and ensuring that their corporate grievances were quickly rectified. Although they introduced some austerity policies to pull the country out of the economic morass Nkrumah left behind, army allocations went up by an annual 22 percent.[77] Another round of promotions by the top brass to celebrate the first anniversary of their coup provoked, in April 1967, an unsuccessful countercoup attempt by junior officers who killed General Kotoka. In its aftermath, hundreds of civilian and military opponents of the regime were imprisoned. With Kotoka's assassination the original circle of conspirators began to disintegrate, and for the military, governance fatigue—a useful concept Samuel Finer called attention to[78]—set in. In April 1969 General Afrifa replaced Ankrah as head of state owing to the latter's involvement in a bribery scandal. In the following month the NLC lifted its ban on political parties, laid the foundations for national elections, and returned to the barracks in September.

The Armed Forces under the Democratic Interlude, 1969–72

The Progress Party of Oxford-educated professor Kofi Busia won the August 1969 elections by a landslide. Busia, a political opponent of Nkrumah's, returned to Ghana only in 1966 and received various important positions during the military regime, including the chairmanship of the NLC's National Advisory Committee. Once in power, Busia made no gesture of reconciliation toward Nkrumah's supporters and rejected the broader African nationalism that many educated Ghanaians endorsed. During his term in office nearly half-a-million Nigerian citizens were deported from Ghana and the country's currency, the cedi, was devalued by 44 percent.[79] Both of these policies were met with strong popular disapproval. Busia's regime was also hammered by the sharp drop in world cocoa prices, which ruined farmers and severely constricted the government's economic policies. As the overall economic situation deteriorated and living standards plummeted, Busia made other political choices that antagonized more and more segments of Ghanaian society and eroded his support base.

At the outset, the military was a strong backer of Busia and his conservative policies and fared well owing to the aftereffects of its own compensatory three-year rule. The top brass believed that Busia, their erstwhile protégé, was beholden to them and would accord them priority treatment. But Busia did not take advantage of the generals' goodwill even though their support could have taken him through some hard times.[80] He made several serious mistakes that the generals considered unforgivable. First, because he believed that Ghana faced no credible security threats, he imposed deep cuts in the defense budget and implemented severe restrictions on training and exercises, activities any peacetime military thrives on. Second, Busia exacerbated the rising tide of ethnic antagonisms within the armed forces as he deliberately replaced Ewe officers with Akans in important command positions.[81] Third, the real incomes of officers sharply declined in part owing to Busia's policies. For instance, they had to make mandatory contributions to economic development projects and their prized vehicle allowance was abolished (though it was later reinstated). Finally, several senior officers retired to take jobs in the private sector leaving the army's leadership in young and unsteady hands. Some of these younger officers recognized the need to rally the people behind more popular and less divisive policies.[82] These and other factors led to the military coup that unseated Busia's democratically elected but underperforming government in early 1972.

Coup, Military Rule, and Countercoups, 1972–79

Following a bloodless and popular coup on January 13, 1972, Col. I. K. Acheampong set up a new military regime. The coup-makers of 1966 stressed that exceptional circumstances were responsible for their intervention and did their best to return power to civilians. Six years later, Acheampong and his colleagues saw nothing wrong with overthrowing a functioning democracy in order to redress their grievances. By this time military intervention was no longer seen as exceptional, short term, or requiring elaborate moral justification.[83]

The newly created National Redemption Council (NRC) was different from the NLC insofar as it appointed many more military officers to head ministries, government agencies, and state corporations. The NRC— renamed the Supreme Military Council in 1975—itself was composed of ten high-ranking officers. In terms of economic performance, Acheampong's record was as good as that of any African military regime. In the first couple of years of its tenure, the government managed to preserve an image as honest patriots. Like leaders of the previous military regime, Acheampong and his colleagues were also devoid of ideological constraints, which allowed them to act pragmatically and to respond to popular expectations. The NRC refused to make payments on Ghana's debt to the IMF saying that the people did not benefit from those loans: both the slogan ("We Won't Pay!") and the policy were wildly popular. The government also managed to energize the population, encouraging more self-reliance— "Operation Feed Yourself" urged people to use every available plot to produce fruits and vegetables—and to implement local development projects designed to win the hearts and minds of the electorate.[84] Ethnic problems in the military were also alleviated as tribal groups gained more balanced representation in the armed forces.

The generals were unchallenged masters of politics. Corruption was widespread in the later years of the regime but the ministry of finance retained some control over the defense budget in keeping with the fiscal prudence of the generals (as long as it did not impact their own wallets).[85] Despite the introduction of large-scale agricultural-development programs, by 1977 the economic situation had deteriorated, prompting the leadership to return power to the civilians. Before they could have done so, a countercoup in July 1978 forced Acheampong's government out. The coup-makers—led by Acheampong's deputy, Chief of Defence Staff and member of the Supreme Military Council, General Fred Akuffo—justified their action, citing the government's corruption and extreme centralization of power. In reality, the coup was driven by an intramilitary quarrel rooted in the unrealized promotion hopes of a group of disgruntled officers. Akuffo promised to hand over power to a civilian administration in the following year.

But Akuffo did not get the chance to deliver on his pledge because in June 1979, less than eleven months later, he himself was overthrown by junior officers led by Flight Lieutenant Jerry Rawlings. The purpose of this coup was to "clean the military's house" and to punish those suspected of widespread corruption so civilian politicians would not take over and allow the culprits to keep their ill-gotten gains. Within a few weeks, Rawlings and his men proceeded to execute eight military leaders—including Afrifa, Akuffo, and Acheampong—following kangaroo court proceedings. Rawlings abided by his pledge to let elections go ahead in September 1979, and the following month, a civilian government began a tenure that, perhaps not surprisingly, was shorter than anticipated.

Epilogue

In December 1981 Rawlings once again took over the reins of power in a coup—"in order to restore a worthy government"—and held on until 2001. Owing to economic troubles and growing criticism of his rule, he legalized political parties and held elections in 1992. Those elections—resulting in a landslide Rawlings win—were neither fair nor free but four years later he was elected president once again, and this time there was no doubt about the authenticity of the outcome. He proved to be a popular and upright president with many socioeconomic achievements to his credit.[86] After two terms in office Rawlings was constitutionally barred from seeking reelection and he stepped down. Unlike Tanzania, which has remained a de facto one-party state even after the reinstatement of the multiparty system in 1992, Ghana has gradually become a functioning democracy where governing parties have actually lost power and been replaced peacefully by political rivals.[87]

EXCEPTIONAL BOTSWANA

Known as the British protectorate of Bechuanaland from 1885, when it gained independence in 1966, Botswana was one of the poorest countries in the world with no known natural resources, with nearly three-fourths of its mostly flat land covered by the Kalahari Desert, and with five miles of tarred road, twenty-two university graduates, and a per capita income of US $60.[88] Nonetheless during its forty-five years of sovereignty, it has been one of the most stable, prosperous, and democratic states in Africa and has known no war or major social upheaval.

This most unlikely outcome is actually easy to explain. First, since independence Botswana has had a multiparty democracy, a generally free press, and no systematic abuses of human or political rights. Botswana's critics have called it a "paternalistic democracy" and a "soft autocracy" mainly because the same party, the Botswana Democratic Party, has ruled the country since independence.[89] Nonetheless, the BDP has not seriously hindered the political activities of its rivals, and Freedom House and other reputable organizations have recognized its elections as regular, free, and fair.[90] Second, the discovery of large diamond deposits in 1967 allowed Botswana to become the world's top producer of gem-quality diamonds, which helped finance the world's fastest per capita income growth rate.[91] Third, Botswana has benefited from relatively honest leaders who understood the country's limitations and planned for the long term. For instance, by the late 2000s, the government set aside a US $7 billion-plus "rainy-day fund" in anticipation of diminishing future international demand for diamonds. Finally, Botswana has had no serious ethnic conflicts in good measure because of its relatively small (1.8 million people in a Texas-sized country) and a fairly homogeneous population. Its nine principal tribes all speak dialects of the same language and have long had an effective mechanism for conflict resolution. This is the *kgotla*, regular meetings of chiefs and adult males (women, children, and even non–community members are allowed to attend) functioning as a traditional court.[92]

What makes Botswana particularly interesting from our perspective is another one of its exceptional attributes, namely that for eleven years after independence it chose not to maintain a military. Most postcolonial states cannot or will not withstand the temptation to outfit a standing army. Botswana went the other way, equipping a small Police Mobile Unit rooted in the colonial period and foregoing the prestige of having its own army. How to explain this decision?

To begin with, as Botswana's first president, Seretse Khama (1966–80), clearly realized, the new country faced no real security threat. When the opposition politician, P. G. Matante, kept insisting that Botswana needed its own military, Khama ridiculed him by asking, "And who are we going to fight?"[93] Just as important, for several years following independence Botswana was so poor that the United Kingdom actually subsidized a fair proportion of its national budget. The government had to make hard choices and establish priorities: having an army was not one of them. In any case, outfitting even a modest force would have been far beyond the realm of its financial possibilities. And political elites did not take lightly the potential of a prospective army to overthrow the government; they openly worried that the "greedy and self-seeking leaders" of a would-be military force might kill Botswana's democracy with a coup.[94] In sum, the absence of security threats, the shortage of financial resources, and the political elites' good sense allowed the young sovereign state to develop its democracy and avoid the pitfalls that had befallen so many newly independent countries.

Botswana's options were fundamentally transformed and expanded with the discovery of diamonds.[95] In the mid-1970s, raids by armed commandos from Rhodesia and South Africa—pursuing radicals and anti-apartheid activists seeking safe haven in Botswana—along with some unresolved border issues posed threats to the country's sovereignty. Poachers also became more active, menacing Botswana's nature reserves and budding tourism industry. The state responded by forming an armed force, via a parliamentary act (Botswana Defence Force Act, No. 13 of 1977), after eleven years of independence.

The Botswana Defence Forces and the State

The Gaborone government committed itself to creating one of the most professional and capable fighting forces in Africa, and by the early 1990s, it had achieved this goal. The BDF's development sped up in 1989–98 when it was commanded by Seretse Khama Ian Khama, the son of the first president and, since 2008, the sitting president. His determination to transform the BDF into a lean and mean fighting force was likely partly motivated by its poor performance against South African commandos in June 1985. Ian Khama was a strict disciplinarian and a puritanical man to boot with a hands-on leadership style and seemingly boundless energy to transform the BDF. To be sure, changes in the international security environment—particularly the establishment of majority rule in South Africa in 1994—favored Botswana though plenty of challenges remained: a nagging poaching problem, the influx of refugees from neighboring states (especially Zimbabwe), and an ongoing row with Namibia regarding the shared border.

Under Ian Khama military education and training were updated and intensified and nearly every officer above the rank of captain was sent for advanced training abroad—particularly to Britain and the United States. By the late 1990s Botswana possessed a 10,000-strong, well-equipped military force with a number of modern facilities, including a new air base at Molepole. Defense expenditures were high—4.1 percent of the GDP in the 1990s—exceeding spending on education or health care.[96] Ian Khama stressed high ethical standards, accountability, and pride in service. Decent pay reduced the incentive for graft and ensured that the armed forces attracted the best and brightest of Botswanan men and women (the latter first entered the service in 2008).[97] The BDF performed well in its antipoaching operations, which emerged as one of its main missions.[98] The army's greatest challenge has been responding to the needs of its HIV-positive personnel who make up as much as 35 percent of its manpower.[99] During its thirty-plus-year history, the BDF has shown no sign of restiveness; the likelihood of a coup or mutiny has been virtually nil.[100] Soldiers have the right to vote but are not allowed to participate in political activities.

Although since 1998 the institutional underpinnings of Botswanan civil-military relations have become more intricate, in the first two decades of the BDF, they were quite uncomplicated. Botswana's political system is heavily dominated by the president, and executive control of the armed forces—again, particularly until 1998—has been nearly complete. The president is the BDF's commander in chief, appoints all the BDF's superior officers (lieutenant colonel and above) though in this task he or she is aided by a Promotion Advisory Board. Although the Botswana Defence Force Act established a Defence Council, it is entirely under the direction of the president, who determines its membership.[101] Most importantly, however, the Council has rarely been convened, at times idling for years. Defense was merely a department in the Office of the President employing, for the most part, very capable retired generals. (It is currently an Office of the President for Justice, Defence, and Security.) The minister of state in the President's Office is, on paper, responsible for the day-to-day running of the BDF. In practice, however, the hierarchy of civilian control is ambiguous, as is the precise relationship between the president and the minister of state.[102]

The legislature has played a limited role in military affairs, serving pretty much as a rubber-stamp body. Parliamentarians receive very limited information on military-security issues and habitually sign defense budgets without seriously questioning them.[103] The government is deeply concerned with secrecy; the National Security Act of 1986 has shielded the armed forces from publications of all but the most harmless information.[104] Politicians have seldom sought out the few independent defense experts working at universities and NGOs who, in turn, have had to be cautious about airing their views in public.

CONCLUSION

In the previous chapter it was easy to discern the "good" and the "bad" cases. In this chapter, however, our answer cannot be so unequivocal. The difficulty arises not with postcolonial Ghana and its recurring military rule. But what about Tanzania? The country was a one-party state although the amount and quality of internal political debates within the TANU far exceeded those in Soviet-controlled socialist polities.[105] After the army was tamed in 1964, Tanzanian civil-military relations were similar to those of other socialist countries with the virtual fusion of party and state that exercised multifaceted subjective control over the military through various institutional mechanisms. Nonetheless, Tanzania was also quite distinctive in the communist world because of the *extent* and *regularity* of personnel exchange between party and military positions. In other words, unlike Ghana, Tanzania was successful in establishing civilian control over the armed forces. Civilian control must not be confused with democratic control, however. In Tanzania, civilian control was unitary, the party-state's domination of the armed forces hardly surprising considering there was no independent legislature, judiciary, or any other political organization free of TANU/CCM control. Tanzania's example demonstrates that civilian control can be successful while incorporating the armed forces into the general political arena. Botswana's situation is similar to Tanzania's insofar as one party has ruled the country since independence, but with the major difference that in Botswana during the same time period free elections have been held at regular intervals. Still, given the dominant position of the executive in the Botswanan polity, its civil-military relations are also far from ideal.

Several scholars have argued that, all things being equal, the longer the duration of British—as opposed to other European—colonial rule, the higher the likelihood of democratic survival.[106] This argument was supported by our South Asian cases but not by the experience of the three African states in this chapter. After all, the British were longer and more intensively involved in Ghana than in Tanzania or Botswana, yet only Ghana had to endure first Nkrumah's repressive dictatorship and then several bouts of military rule.

Another factor that assumes special significance in many postcolonial contexts is the treatment of ethnic groups in the armed forces. This has been a virtual non-issue in Botswana because its society is marked by relative homogeneity and a long tradition of intertribal amity. Tanzania's leadership—which really meant Nyerere personally, given his practically limitless political power—must be recognized for pretty much eliminating the "ethnic factor" from the armed forces as well as from politics at large in a complex and diverse tribal environment. The magnitude of this achievement may be best appreciated by considering the many other societies in Africa and elsewhere ravaged by ethnic conflict. In contrast to Tanzania, tribal relations in Ghana occasionally became fraught with tension. Interestingly, it was not the military rulers who mishandled this issue but the civilian governments of especially Nkrumah and to a lesser extent Busia who, for their political ends, manipulated and exploited tribal communities.

As in the postcolonial settings of the previous chapter, in both Ghana and Tanzania the task of state-builders was to build new, indigenous armies independent of the colonists and to send home the remaining British officers as soon as their native successors could be trained. Botswana is an outlier here because the British had stationed no colonial army in Bechuanaland, and a new army could be built after 1977. Foreign influence was important in these states in part owing to the lingering impact of the colonial period but also due to the influence of the contending powers of the Cold War: China, the Soviet Union, the United Kingdom, and the United States.

During the periods under study here, Ghana experienced intermittent military rule while Tanzania was a socialist state; their armed forces were not committed to democracy and, in Ghana's case, not even to civilian rule. Botswana was a very different case in many respects, and its officer corps appeared to develop a strong allegiance to democracy. Nonetheless, the small size of the country's armed forces and of the state apparatus in Gaborone, the relatively undeveloped political and institutional arrangements of the defense establishment, not to mention the more general nature of Batswana[107] exceptionalism do not allow using the country as the basis for useful generalizations about postcolonial Africa.

One commonality in all postcolonial settings we studied regardless of whether they were democratic or authoritarian is the weakness of the legislature's oversight authority vis-à-vis the executive branch. Even in this respect, however, some caveats must be stated: the Indian legislature is somewhat stronger than the others, while in Pakistan and Bangladesh the (civilian) executive branch's control over the armed forces lacks potency. The generalization we *can* make is that it is extremely difficult to make useful generalizations from the six postcolonial experiences we learned about in this and the previous chapters.

TABLE 9.1

After Colonialism in Sub-Saharan Africa: Ghana, Tanzania, and Botswana

	Country Period	Ghana 1957–1979	Tanzania 1961–1979	Botswana 1977–1998
Background	native military force under the British	Gold Coast Regiment: limited responsibilities for locals, tribal preferences	King's African Rifles: very few responsibilities for locals	no British military force or local involvement in defense
	colonial influence on new military	moderate	weak to moderate	virtually none
State	main tasks	establish independent armed forces, train new officer corps, get colonial officers out, project power abroad	establish independent armed forces, train new officer corps, get colonial officers out	establish armed forces for border security and antipoaching operations
	civilian political leadership	inept, corrupt (Nkrumah)	popular, honest, inspiring	strong, progressive, responsible
	political institutions and trend	weak, improving little	weak but growing stronger	quickly strengthening
	civilian involvement in defense affairs	strong (Nkrumah) then weaker	pervasive	strong
	executive control	strong	strong	strong
	legislative oversight	weak	weak	weak
	ethno-religious and regional policies	divisive under civilian rule, uniting under military rule	uniting	uniting (not a major issue)
	purges of the military	yes, recurrent	after 1964 mutiny	no
	foreign influence	PRC, USSR, then USA: moderate	PRC: moderate	UK, USA, South Africa: moderate

TABLE 9.1 (*continued*)

After Colonialism in Sub-Saharan Africa: Ghana, Tanzania, and Botswana

	Country Period	Ghana 1957–1979	Tanzania 1961–1979	Botswana 1977–1998
Military	interference in politics	high	active, military co-opted, a key political institution, minor nonviolent coup attempts	moderate (under Ian Khama as defense minister), then much less
	domestic function	occasional power broker	regime protection, breaking up protests	none
	advisory function	very high (under civilian rule)	minimal	small
	institutional attributes	under Nkrumah formations to balance army	symbiotic relationship with party-state	highly trained and professional
	effectiveness	unclear	medium	high
	commitment to democracy	no	no	yes
Society	independent civilian experts	no	no	few, seldom consulted
	military's prestige	high	medium	high
	soldiers in society	separation	"citizen soldiers"	a separate entity
	conscription	no	no	yes
Political system at the end of the period		authoritarianism with intermittent military rule	state socialism	parliamentary democracy

CHAPTER 10

After (Re)Unification and Apartheid:
Germany, South Africa, and Yemen

-茸 茸-

In chapter 3, I explained how armies may be built after civil war. The topic of this chapter is similar to the extent that here, too, we are interested in cases where two entities are brought together and, in some cases, brought together *again*. We are going to look at three different but equally intriguing cases. In that of Germany, the armed forces of the newly reunified state reflected the outcome of the Cold War: very little remained that could remind one of the erstwhile army of East Germany. In Yemen, the secondary case, North and South Yemen, two Cold War adversaries, fought against each other in brief wars before they became unified. South Africa is a unique case because its borders did not change though a large segment of the population previously excluded from official politics and the armed forces was not only made a part of them but became the *dominant* part. The similarity in all three cases is the combining of two separate and dissimilar components in a new, single political entity. Furthermore, in all three, the two parts brought together had been enemies who fought against each other or were trained to do so. We will consider how to reconcile the past, how to bring these parts together, and the principles that drive these processes.

Although Germany, South Africa, and Yemen may seem exceptional, they are not. There are, in fact, quite a few similar examples in modern history. We may think of the Italian military after the Risorgimento movement achieved unification in 1861, the post–Civil War reorganization of the U.S. armed forces, or again, the U.S. Army after its desegregation in the 1950s. These and other experiences may be useful for future reference, because there are a number of potential new cases: for instance, the two Koreas as well as mainland China and Taiwan may decide to unify and field integrated armies in the not-too-distant future.

In all three of the present cases, 1990 is a critical year, as it marks the reunification of Germany, the unification of Yemen, and the beginning of the end for South Africa's apartheid regime. We will follow events from that starting point for approximately a decade and then briefly consider more recent developments.

POST–COLD WAR GERMANY

The Cold War ended with a rapidity that few could have imagined just a few months earlier. Once Soviet President Gorbachev announced that Moscow would not interfere in the domestic affairs of East European states, communist regimes there started to fall like so many dominoes. The German Democratic Republic—GDR, whose name supports the assertion that any state with the word "democratic" in its name is not a democracy—crumbled within a few weeks, defying the regime's carefully managed reputation as an enduring bastion of Marxism-Leninism. From our perspective the most interesting aspect of this phenomenon is the role of the East German army— the *Nationale Volksarmee* or NVA—in the collapse of the regime and what happened to it after reunification. This section is divided into three parts: in the first I will describe the NVA and its relationship to the GDR and the Soviet Union; in the second why the NVA was abolished in the particular way it was; and in the third, we will consider military politics in post–Cold War Germany.

The Nationale Volksarmee

Because of its strategic position on the very frontline of the Cold War, the NVA—officially organized in 1956, a few months after the creation of the Bundeswehr across the border—was by far the most important Warsaw Pact army aside from the Soviet armed forces. Soviet control over the NVA was more intensive and extensive than over other Warsaw Pact forces. In fact, the East German army was compelled to develop within the larger framework of the Soviet military establishment rather than as an independent national army.[1] The GDR's communist party, the SED (*Sozialistische Einheitspartei Deutschlands*—Socialist Unity Party of Germany), was heavily dependent on Soviet political, ideological, and military support. The bulk of the NVA's troops were stationed near the border of West Germany, a free and increasingly prosperous state, whose army was staffed, in some cases literally, by their cousins. For this reason, the GDR regime's control over the NVA *had to be* uncompromising and strict.

East Germany was devoid of a *national* tradition, and an alternative to ideology as a basis for military loyalties had to be found. The SED was heavily invested in trying, in effect, to *create* a nation that would seduce the population into believing in a myth of its own distinct cultural heritage and traditional value system. The NVA was recognized by the Soviets and the SED leadership as an instrument for changing and rebuilding political consciousness, and it was to become a robust support base for Marxist-Leninist policies and ideological goals for the entire GDR society.[2] These goals were buttressed by the GDR's status as a showpiece of socialism: even though by Western—especially West German—standards East German living conditions were inferior, they were better when compared to other Warsaw Pact states.

In order to control the NVA, the SED politicized virtually all aspects of military life. The NVA's telephone network, for instance, was linked with regional party headquarters. The SED routinely disregarded military procedures in order to ensure political reliability. The NVA's political import was such that all of its ministers until November 1989 were members of the SED's ruling Politburo and/or Central Committee. Party membership in the NVA (96 percent of officers, 94 percent of warrant officers)[3] was the highest among all of the East European armed forces. In addition, many NVA officers belonged to or worked with the secret police, the Stasi. Political reliability easily trumped professional competence: anyone judged less than completely reliable was dismissed.[4] Within the army, the Politapparat, the large hierarchy of political officers, was a second chain of command. Its responsibility was to train and indoctrinate soldiers, particularly conscripts, and to turn them into communist activists.[5] Chiefs of the NVA's Main Political Administration essentially ran the NVA and even could become ministers of defense, as Heinz Keßler did in 1985. A key difference between the GDR and Soviet military political structures was that NVA political officers did not enjoy the power to countersign orders to authenticate them as their Soviet colleagues did in certain periods. The reason for this was that NVA officers were the de facto subordinates of Soviet officers assigned to NVA units as so-called *Verbindungsoffiziere* (liaison officers). Their job was to make certain that NVA units functioned according to Soviet expectations.[6]

The NVA, ever eager to prove itself as the army most loyal to the USSR, sent many soldiers to serve as Moscow's proxies in North Africa and the Middle East: in 1985–86, 2,370 were deployed there.[7] The quality of the NVA as a fighting force was decidedly mediocre. As elsewhere in the communist world, officers were discouraged from showing initiative, their motivations were all too often purely of the careerist variety, they did not receive up-to-date training, and the quality of their weapons was generally inferior to those of their adversaries. The NCO corps was ineffective compared to their Western equivalents; junior officers frequently found themselves having to do the NCOs' jobs.[8] With the deterioration of the GDR's economy, a growing number of conscripts were assigned to perform agricultural or industrial work for a substantial part of their mandatory military service. By the late 1980s the general malaise in the GDR, and its population's clear recognition that the NVA was a servant of the party-state, reduced the already low occupational prestige of soldiering.

The NVA could not have been more different from the Bundeswehr. The former operated according to highly directed and specific principles (*Befehlstaktik*), whereas the Bundeswehr was based on *Auftragstaktik*, goal-oriented principles, in which specific objectives and general guidance were given by officers, and all else was left to their subordinates.[9] The NVA's professional personnel were isolated from civilian society and constituted an elite charged with external defense and with protecting the communist regime from its internal foes. The West German army, on the other hand, was designed to keep its soldiers as close to the rest of society as feasible. While East Germans were entirely shut out from the life of the NVA, West Germans were encouraged to use the Bundeswehr's sporting and recreation facilities, participate in its celebrations, and enter its educational institutions. The Bundeswehr's "citizen in uniform" principle underscored the participatory aspect of a democratic society and that soldiers were an integral part in that society even while in the armed forces.[10] The vigilant protection of the Bundeswehr soldiers' human rights stood in sharp contrast to the heavy-handed treatment of NVA conscripts. In short, the Bundeswehr was a non-ideological defensive army that served the constitution of a democratic state. The NVA, on the other hand, was a heavily indoctrinated agent of supranational interests and the servant of the communist regime.

From State Collapse to Reunification

Mikhail Gorbachev's October 1989 visit to East Berlin for the GDR's fortieth-anniversary celebrations ironically precipitated the country's demise. Although two months later he "declare[d] with all decisiveness that we will not leave the GDR in the lurch," this is exactly what the USSR did once West Germany expressed its willingness to compensate Moscow for the costs of withdrawing its occupation troops from East Germany.[11] By late 1989 the Kremlin signaled that it would not interfere with German reunification. Gorbachev's insistence that a united Germany's membership in NATO was unacceptable to the USSR also soon changed. Only Soviet Defense Minister Dmitry Yazov remained resolutely opposed to the idea. In July 1990, West German Chancellor Helmut Kohl agreed with Gorbachev that the unified German armed forces would have a troop strength of no more than 370,000. (During much of the Cold War the Bundeswehr had 500,000 soldiers and the NVA 175,000.) In the view of the much of the GDR's political and military elites, Moscow sold out the GDR by making a deal at its expense.[12]

In the meantime, the movement toward reunification sped out of control and could not be contained by the state. The billboards of East German demonstrators proclaimed both that "*Wir sind ein Volk*" (We are *one* people) and "*Wir sind das Volk*" (We are *the* people), demanding reunification and democratic governance. Another often displayed placard carried a thinly veiled threat—"*Kommt die D-Mark, bleiben wir, kommt sie nicht, geh'n wir zu ihr!*" (If the Deutsche Mark comes, we will stay, if it doesn't, we'll come to it!)—demanding the rapid introduction of the much respected West German currency in place of the nonconvertible East German one.

The NVA did not impede the collapse of communism. With the exception of some crowd-control operations and minor incidents in Dresden, the NVA remained perfectly restrained during the large-scale demonstrations that marked the rapid collapse of Erich Honecker's dictatorial regime. On November 7, 1989, the government resigned. Defense Minister Heinz Keßler was persuaded to do the same at a meeting of SED activists and was replaced by Admiral Theodor Hoffmann four days later. In January 1990 all career NVA personnel were ordered to renounce their party membership. Political officers became "reeducation" officers though this reflected little substantive change. A strike of soldiers in the garrison in Beelitz demanding the shortening of military service and the improvement of conditions signaled that the NVA had reached the end of the line.[13]

In March 1990 the GDR held its first and only free general election, resulting in a massive win for the CDU—the Christian Democratic Party—that was, auspiciously, West Germany's party in government. Rainer Eppelmann, a former peace activist with little knowledge of military affairs, became the head of the newly named Ministry of Disarmament and Defense (*Ministerium für Abrüstung und Verteidigung*) in Lothar de Maizière's cabinet that took the GDR to reunification on October 3, 1990. This six-month period was most eventful for the GDR and its armed forces.

In retrospect, it is surprising that Eppelmann and the Chief of the NVA (another newly created position), Admiral Theodor Hoffmann, continued to believe there would be two separate German armies, one a member of NATO and the other of the Warsaw Pact. Eppelmann saw no important difference between the two alliances—apparently unaware that membership in NATO, unlike in the Warsaw Pact, was voluntary—while Hoffmann insisted the NVA could contribute its experience of cooperation with the Soviet Union and Eastern European states to the Bundeswehr.[14] In the waning months of the GDR, they introduced several "too little too late" reforms into the NVA, such as a five-day workweek and respect for the rights of conscripts. They commissioned a new oath for NVA soldiers and even had new uniforms designed. Senior NVA personnel over the age of fifty-five were sacked. In the meantime, the army was slowly melting away as over sixty thousand of its soldiers, taking advantage of the newly opened borders to West Germany, simply deserted.[15] Fundamentally, Eppelmann and Hoffmann wasted a lot of time and effort on their quixotic dream to keep the NVA alive. The NVA could not be reformed and the GDR government had basically no leverage in the new Germany.

The Takeover of the NVA

In October 1990—at the time of German reunification—West German Defense Minister Gerhard Stoltenberg appointed Bundeswehr General Jörg Schönbohm to head Kommando-Ost, the organization made up of six hundred officers and NCOs, and two hundred civilians tasked with dismantling the NVA.[16] Stoltenberg wanted to do as little as possible with the NVA's professional personnel. He and the vast majority of (West) German policy and military elites generally agreed on two key points. First, the NVA was a tool in the hands of the Soviet Union, trained not only to destroy the West but also to control and subjugate the GDR's population by suppressing internal dissent. Second, and perhaps more important: no one in the GDR was forced against his or her will to become a professional soldier and thus, a member of a repressive, hard-line-communist organization. In other words, former NVA officers were not victims; they were the victimizers of the recent past. Therefore, they concurred, the NVA had to be dismantled, not integrated or absorbed.

Kommando-Ost, based in the former NVA headquarters in Strausberg, just outside of Berlin, finished its work on July 1, 1991. During the preceding nine months, the NVA was effectively terminated. Schönbohm, by all accounts a brilliant officer whose patience and diplomatic skills made him perfect for the assignment, received little political guidance other than some key objectives.[17] First, the NVA was to be terminated on October 15, 1990, its members temporarily joining the Bundeswehr. Second, all NVA units were to be gradually disbanded. Third, given the necessary reduction in the overall strength of the new Bundeswehr, up to thirty thousand career and short-service personnel of the NVA could be taken on for two years. The military's total strength in Eastern Germany would be fifty thousand: twenty thousand former NVA members as career or short-service personnel; five thousand Bundeswehr career and short-service personnel, and twenty-five thousand conscripts and volunteers. Fourth, the training of conscripts from the GDR would be changed to accord with the Bundeswehr's training program. Finally, during the transition period, the armed forces in the eastern states (the former GDR) would be under the authority of Kommando-Ost, a body directly subordinate to the federal ministry of defense. In short, after a brief transition the NVA had to be taken over (*Übernahme*) not integrated.

In place of the old NVA units, new units had to be organized in view of the new, smaller post–Cold War Bundeswehr's force structure. Dissolving the NVA while simultaneously activating new units required much organizational finesse and coordination.[18] General Schönbohm never tired of visiting old and new units, talking to former NVA officers and soldiers, and trying to ensure that everyone was treated fairly. The takeover process turned out to be successful in that it caused no glitches in the overall functioning of the Bundeswehr. Since the former NVA and the SED were defeated organizations in every sense of the word, Schönbohm did not have to contend with any overt resistance to the process. Still, looking back over two decades later, Schönbohm readily admits that he underestimated the effects of fourty years of communist indoctrination—which, he says, basically amounted to little more than "hate education"—on the NVA's officers and NCOs. Moreover, he did not quite appreciate just how lacking in initiative the NVA's personnel were, a trait that ultimately might have made his job easier as once former NVA cadres received clear and detailed directives they were ready to get to work without asking questions.[19]

An important problem Schönbohm needed to tackle was the dismantling, destruction, or sale of the NVA's weapons, equipment, and ammunition. The massive reduction in the new Germany's arsenal was also necessitated by the 1990 Treaty on Conventional Forces in Europe. Large caches of NVA weapons were transferred to former Warsaw Pact nations. The Bundeswehr decided to put very few of the NVA's mostly obsolete weapons into its inventory. One of the exceptions was a squadron (twenty-four) of sophisticated Soviet-made MiG-29 jet fighter aircraft that "came with" experienced pilots and technicians. Retaining some of the NVA's field equipment turned out to have one unforeseen advantage. As an offensive army, the NVA was kitted out for foreign deployments but the Bundeswehr—equipped to fight a defensive war on its own territory—was not. When German forces were deployed to eastern Turkey and the eastern Mediterranean during the first Gulf War in 1991, some of the NVA's gear and materials came in handy.[20]

The Bundeswehr also inherited hundreds of barracks and warehouses all over the former GDR whose safeguarding occupied thousands of soldiers. Most of these facilities were in disastrous condition. Many of them would be sold while others were refurbished: by the end of 1994 3.5 billion Deutschmarks were spent on their renovation.[21] Schönbohm developed good relations with the leadership of the Soviet occupation forces—over 350,000 troops and the dependents of tens of thousands of officers—which began to vacate the almost one thousand sites they occupied in order to satisfy the deadline (December 1994) for their complete withdrawal.[22]

The most challenging issue of the NVA's takeover was the reduction of personnel: from a combined troop strength of 585,000 troops at the time of unification in October 1990, the Bundeswehr had to slim down to a force of 370,000 within four years.[23] When the NVA was dissolved in the fall of 1990, it had 88,797 soldiers and 22, 676 officers in its employ. The conscripts served out their terms but what happened to the NVA's still-active officers and NCOs? First of all, most of them did not want to put on the uniform of the Bundeswehr, the army they had been trained to hate for decades. Second, the vast majority of NVA officers were not eligible even to apply to be taken into the Bundeswehr because they were over age fifty-five, had achieved the rank of lieutenant colonel, were hard-line communists, and/or had worked for the Stasi. All these people lost their privileged position overnight and became the pariahs of German society, scorned by their compatriots east and west. They were prohibited from using the military ranks they had earned in the NVA even with the "retired" designation, which many of them found unfair since West German law permitted the World War II veterans of the Wehrmacht to use their ranks.

Many former NVA members received free education and training from the Vocational Assistance Service, which enabled them to transition into civilian life.[24] Nevertheless, a large number of erstwhile NVA officers could not find employment—unemployment rates in the east were much higher than in the west—other than as night watchmen, security guards, or truck drivers. Their socioeconomic marginalization extended to the area of pension benefits. Only after some sixteen years of petitions, complaints, and lobbying by the *Deutscher Bundeswehrverband*—the German Army Association that NVA veterans could enter if they were not former Stasi members—was the issue of their pensions resolved.

The government promised not to dismiss Bundeswehr personnel as a way of satisfying troop reduction quotas; it just did not replace retiring officers and NCOs. The Bundeswehr initially accepted twenty thousand NVA officers and soldiers, the vast majority of whom were released after two years. Ultimately 2,507 NVA officers and about 7,600 enlisted personnel—all of them were vetted by the "Independent Committee for Suitability Screening"— were allowed to stay in the Bundeswehr past their two-year trial period as career officers and NCOs.[25] When considering the relatively small number of NVA members who ended up serving in the united Germany's army, it is also important to remember that the NVA was a top-heavy force where officers were promoted much more quickly—many thirty-nine-year-olds were full colonels—than in the Bundeswehr. There were 2,110 colonels (1.2 percent) in the 175,000-strong NVA while only 1,800 colonels (0.36 percent) among the Bundeswehr's 495,000 uniformed personnel.[26] The ratio of NCOs to enlisted personnel was 1:1 in the NVA but 1:3 in the Bundeswehr.[27] Moreover, West German officers had received more education and training and shouldered more responsibility than East German officers of the same rank. Therefore, most NVA officers who were taken over by the Bundeswehr were demoted, usually by one but occasionally by two grades in rank, following an assessment of their skills and former service. In 2006, sixteen years after reunification, there were eight hundred Bundeswehr officers who had begun their careers in the NVA; most of them adjusted to their new environment with few difficulties.[28]

"Just Don't Say 'War'!"

Reunification and the takeover of the NVA have not changed the Bundeswehr and German civil-military relations significantly: there is now a larger country to protect, an army officers' training academy moved from Hannover in northern Germany to Dresden in the east, a small number of NVA troops have been integrated into the armed forces, and the military's recruitment pool has expanded and changed. The one major effect of reunification on the Bundeswehr was the drastic albeit short-lived deterioration of the Bundeswehr's operational readiness as it threw almost all its energy into the absorption of the NVA.[29] Owing to the high unemployment rate in the eastern German states (*Länder*), the Bundeswehr currently recruits 40 to 45 percent of its officers and NCOs there, even though the region is home to less than one quarter of the population.[30]

Conscription continued though fewer and fewer young men actually served and for shorter and shorter periods of time because of the limited number of draftees needed and the many types of exemption (for students, married men, apprentices, etc.). The vast majority of those who served, 90,000 in 2010, chose civilian service (*Zivildienst*). Because of Germany's history, the "citizen in uniform" concept, and the much-needed and appreciated contribution of those who serve their Zivildienst in hospitals, retirement homes, and facilities for the handicapped, phasing out the draft entirely for many years seemed unlikely. Nonetheless, this is precisely what happened. In November 2010, after a protracted public debate, the popular and charismatic Defense Minister, Karl-Theodor zu Guttenberg, announced that conscription would be suspended in July 2011. Nevertheless the draft would be retained in the federal constitution—the names of military age Germans would continue to be collected—and could be reactivated with a simple parliamentary majority.[31]

The institutional principles of (West) German civil-military relations have remained more or less unchanged since they were originally laid out in the 1950s. The powerful parliamentary defense commissioner still oversees the forces and reports annually to the legislature and the public. The Commissioner—whose office is a part of the legislature and who has constant access to all defense installations and military documents—to all intents and purposes supervises the defense minister who is, of course, a member of the executive branch. The legislature's Defense Committee prepares all major acts of parliament that affect the Bundeswehr and monitors the government's activities in the defense-security area.[32] The highest-ranking uniformed officer, the Chief of the Defense Staff (*Generalinspekteur*), is the top military adviser to the MoD and to the federal government, but, as in the 1950s, he is still not in the chain of command between the defense minister and the armed forces. Few states have gone this far to ensure the accountability of their military establishments. The constitutional provisions and the institutional setup put in place in the late 1940s and 1950s has effectively left the Bundeswehr in a virtual straitjacket when it comes to even the slightest proposal for change. The military is run by the legislature, and even minor issues pertaining to it occasion seemingly interminable and seldom conclusive parliamentary debates.

The main reason the Bundeswehr has changed in the past twenty years is *not* the result of reunification but of the end of the Cold War. During the Cold War, an actual war was inconceivable for most Germans because they believed that, in all likelihood, it would have meant a nuclear war. Generations of Bundeswehr personnel served out their careers without ever having been in combat. Officers and NCOs moved around Germany to their assignments but never abroad (except while on training or education assignments). Since 1990, however, things have changed. Bundeswehr units have participated in UN-, EU-, and NATO-led peacekeeping and peace-enforcement operations from Somalia, Bosnia, and Lebanon, to Kosovo, Macedonia, and Afghanistan. The military's participation in these out-of-country operations has changed it far more than reunification. For instance, there are now many junior officers but very few senior ones with combat experience in the Bundeswehr.

Several of Germany's EU allies (France, Great Britain, and the Netherlands) have responded to their drastically altered security environment with far-reaching military reforms.[33] Nevertheless, the reforms passed by two succeeding German defense ministers, Volker Rühe (1992–98) and Rudolf Scharping (1998–2002), did not transform their army or allow it to participate more effectively in crisis-management operations.[34] In 2008 the Christian Democrats' proposal to create a U.S.-style National Security Council and to lift some of the constitutional limits on foreign deployments of the armed forces in order to face new threats like international terrorism caused a predictable political furor.[35] German politicians and society have been very slow in realizing that being a dominant European power in the post–Cold War world goes along with some unpleasant obligations.

Three examples should suffice. As I noted in chapter 2, the German Constitution does not allow the use of the military for domestic functions with the exception of assisting the state police and the border guards under extremely strictly regulated conditions. In the aftermath of the September 11, 2001, terrorist attacks on the United States, a major public debate took place on the issue of whether the Bundeswehr was allowed to shoot down a terrorist plane and came to the conclusion that it was not.[36] A short while later the Bundeswehr had trouble mustering and equipping 7,000 soldiers for peacekeeping duty in Afghanistan despite having 285,000 soldiers and an annual budget of €25 billion.[37] Once in Afghanistan, German soldiers were reluctant to fight or even place themselves in danger and meticulously observed such regulations—intended for peacetime activities in Germany— as the environmental restrictions on military vehicles and how much rest soldiers were supposed to have before driving.[38] In what *The Economist* called a "new low" for German policy, Berlin refused to back United Nations Security Council Resolution 1973 that authorized the protection of civilians in civil war-torn Libya in the spring of 2011. Even though its European NATO allies, France and Britain—other participants included with Belgium, Denmark, Italy, Norway, as well as Canada, the United States, and a number of non–NATO members—were determined leaders of the operation, Germany withdrew all practical support for the NATO mission, even jeopardizing the early phase of the campaign by pulling its crews out of the alliance's airborne warning and control aircraft.[39] The influential former foreign minister, Joschka Fischer, described his country's conduct as "perhaps the biggest foreign policy debacle since the founding of the Federal Republic of Germany."[40]

Sixty-five years after the end of World War II, the military is still a remarkably unpopular institution in Germany. Most people do not want to hear about the military and if so only in the most innocuous and idealized context. The media expect German soldiers to be part of reconstruction projects, to build bridges and schools but not to fight. Although the

Bundeswehr has been deployed in Afghanistan since 2002 and of its 4,400 soldiers more than 35 have died in combat, the word "war" cannot be used in public without repercussions in Germany. Even then–Defense Minister Guttenberg shied away from calling it a "war" in his 2010 Good Friday speech and, instead, declared that the Bundeswehr was facing a "warlike situation" (*"kriegsähnliche Zustände"*) in southern Afghanistan.[41] In late May, in yet another display of German political correctness run amok, Horst Köhler became the first German president in forty years to resign. For days the German media hounded the president and conducted a hate-filled campaign against him for daring to say during a visit to Bundeswehr troops in Afghanistan that they were deployed there to protect German interests, including economic ones.[42]

In November 2010, several defense reforms were announced along with the suspension of the draft. These drastically cut the military posts in the MoD, relocated the service chiefs' offices from the ministry, broadened the role of the Chief of the Defense Staff, and reorganized the MoD's procurement process. The overall size of the Bundeswehr's uniformed personnel will be decreased from about 240,000 to approximately 180,000, with the suspension of conscription contributing significantly to this reduction. At the same time, the number of deployable personnel will increase from 7,500 to 10,000—far lower than the goal of 14,000 set in a 2006 White Paper.[43] These changes are intended to streamline the command structures, to anticipate future operational requirements, and, perhaps most importantly, to save a great deal of money. These reforms will be implemented by a new defense minister because Guttenberg quit in March 2011 after revelations that he plagiarized parts of his 2006 doctoral thesis. His successor is the erstwhile interior minister, Thomas de Maizière, who is, incidentally, the cousin of the aforementioned Lothar de Maizière and the son of General Ulrich de Maizière, discussed in chapter 2.

In sum, then, the Bundeswehr's takeover of the NVA was a successful operation that created an army for all Germans. The NVA had little to offer the Bundeswehr and West Germany, and they had basically no leverage to affect political outcomes. The best that can be said about the former NVA is that it did not try to protect Honecker's dictatorship from the popular movement that was bent on its destruction and that it did not resist its own abolition.

SOUTH AFRICA AFTER APARTHEID

The transformation of the South African armed forces is unusual because it remedied a division that was based on racial discrimination and not on the breakup of a state. To the extent that it integrated previously antagonistic military entities, South Africa's experience is similar to the German and Yemeni cases.

The system of apartheid—the institutionalized separation of people classified into four racial groups (white, colored, Indian, and black) with specific rights and restrictions attached to each—was introduced by the National Party when it was elected to power in 1948. The apartheid regime systematized and intensified existing segregationist laws that privileged the white minority vis-à-vis the vastly larger black majority. The white population controlled the country's substantial and growing wealth, which had been generated by rapid industrialization in the post–World War II era. For whites, South Africa became one of the world's most prosperous countries. For blacks, however, apartheid signified severe discrimination. In 1961, South Africa became a republic and left the British Commonwealth, whose members had grown increasingly critical of Pretoria. By the 1980s, worldwide opposition to apartheid had gradually intensified, manifested in international sanctions and divestment. Within South Africa, the anti-apartheid movements and organizations—most importantly the African National Congress (ANC)—had organized strikes, sabotage, protests, and armed resistance including bombings and terror attacks against an increasingly besieged state.

With the passage of time apartheid became an ever more difficult system to sustain particularly for a white society that was unwilling to sacrifice what a South African political scientist has called a "Masada mentality."[44] A growing number of whites believed that maintaining the apartheid regime— with its numerous internal and external economic, social, and political contradictions—was not in their long-term interest. P. W. Botha, South Africa's prime minister (1978–84) and, after the introduction of a new Constitution, president (1984–89) abolished more than seventy pieces of apartheid legislation and put several important processes—such as the desegregation of the army to include the commissioning of colored officers—in motion. He has not received credit for, as Nelson Mandela said, "the steps he took to pave the way towards the eventual peacefully negotiated settlement in our country."[45] Botha will be likely remembered more for *not* taking the opportunity to dismantle apartheid in an August 1985 speech in which he was widely anticipated to outline how South Africa would begin to democratize. Against all expectations, Botha did not cross the Rubicon: he said nothing new because he refused to antagonize his National Party.[46]

The international condemnation of South Africa deepened, as did South Africa's isolation, following what became known as Botha's "Rubicon Speech." The strategy of the ANC, the most important black opposition organization, was based on four pillars: encouraging South Africa's international isolation; fueling civil disobedience; an "armed onslaught" executed by its military wing *Umkontho we Sizwe* (Spear of the Nation), abbreviated as MK; and steady economic pressure realized through the staging of boycotts, sabotage, and strikes. It was Botha's successor, the last apartheid-era president, F. W. de Klerk, who responded to these pressures by dismantling apartheid. He went further than domestic and international observers anticipated when, in February 1990, he announced the unbanning and legalization of the African National Congress and other anti-apartheid parties, lifting the restrictions on opposition groups such as the internal wing of the struggle, the United Democratic Front, and the unconditional release of Nelson Mandela and other political prisoners. At the same time, the state relaxed its control over the media's coverage of opposition politics.[47]

Following de Klerk's February 1990 speech, events gained momentum encouraged by a 1992 referendum in which over two-thirds of the white population supported major reforms. In a very real sense the Cold War kept apartheid alive, and its end had a profound impact on South African politics. For the first time in two hundred years no outside power was meddling in the region and South Africans could be masters of their own fate. The fall of the Berlin Wall reduced the stake of white elites in apartheid and loosened the ties of black leaders to their now-bankrupt backers in the international communist movement, removing obstacles for serious negotiations to commence between the two sides regarding the shape of a new South Africa.

The SADF and Black Opposition Forces

Our main interest in South Africa's transition from apartheid to democracy is the creation of a new democratic multiracial military force—the South African National Defence Force (SANDF)—from the erstwhile tool of the apartheid state, the South African Defence Force (SADF) and the military forces of the Liberation Armies and the four Homeland States. (Ten tribally based homelands were set up in 1958. Four of these—Transkei, Ciskei, Bophuthatswana, and Venda—became nominally independent states that had their own armed forces.)[48] Let us take a look at the SADF, the MK, and the other, much smaller armies maintained by other black organizations that were to be integrated into the new SANDF.

By the late 1980s the South African Defence Force had become, man for man, one of the best armies in the world. Its personnel were well prepared—the training of privates, NCOs, and officers alike received serious attention—and highly disciplined, they had access to top-notch equipment, and frequent deployments ensured their combat readiness. The SADF was an able tool in the service of the regime's foreign policy goals: it fought in Angola, Namibia, and Mozambique compiling a record of consistently superb performances in frontier operations and bush warfare.[49] Military service was compulsory and white men ordinarily spent four years in the army: two years of uninterrupted service followed by two years in the reserves (sixty to ninety days per year, up to the age of fifty-five).

While the SADF's conventional force went off to fight in service of the regime's policies of regional destabilization and illegal occupation in Angola, Mozambique, and Namibia,[50] its internal forces—organized under ten regional headquarters—responded to domestic security challenges. The SADF's direct internal involvement against the ANC and its military force was limited, but it did participate in "aid to civil power" operations mainly to stabilize crime-infested areas.[51] In addition, the SADF was heavily involved in border-control activities. In the last few years of apartheid, the SADF was deployed in black townships—it first played a backup role to the police, then worked in conjunction with them, and, after largely succeeding by early 1987, it began to play a less prominent role—to separate the armed forces of two black groups intent on annihilating each other, the ANC and the Zulu nationalist Inkatha Freedom Party.[52]

The SADF's officer corps generally despised party politics and had little interest in direct political interference even if the government was increasingly relying on military power both for its foreign policy goals and to maintain domestic calm.[53] (A number of senior SADF officers were members of the *Broederbond*—an influential secret society of white Protestant men dedicated to advancing Afrikaner causes—that was intensely involved in politics.) In the late 1980s SADF officers were divided in their views of apartheid's sustainability, suggesting—along with a number of other factors—the need to reach a political solution. Importantly also, by 1990, as a result of numerous internal reforms, only about 60 percent of the regular forces were white, as Indians (particularly in the navy) and "coloreds" (people of mixed ancestry, mostly in the army) were able to join the SADF in large numbers.

Apartheid-era South Africa had both a diverse and centralized security establishment that maintained a number of separate agencies and organizations, including police forces, intelligence agencies, and the SADF. Nonetheless, the state's long-standing monopoly over the means of modern violence was broken in the early 1980s when automatic rifles, explosives, and even rockets became available to its political opponents, particularly the ANC. Common criminals, too, took advantage of this new situation and began stealing and trafficking in arms, which led to more violent crimes and the diminishing ability of the police to solve them.[54] By the late 1980s the only organization capable of maintaining order was the SADF, which was merely buying time for the politicians to find a solution to an increasingly untenable situation. In fact, much of the high command was pleased when they did.[55]

On the other side of the ledger were the armed forces of the black majority. These included, first and foremost, the ANC's MK; the Azanian People's Liberation Army (APLA), the military wing of the Pan Africanist Congress; the KwaZulu Self-Protection force of the Inkatha Freedom Party; and the four homeland armies. The MK was a relatively large force—perhaps as many as twenty-five thousand individuals with varying levels of membership—though few of its personnel had anything resembling proper military training. Most of MK's actions involved throwing petrol grenades and committing low-tech terrorist acts—in other words, the tactics open to activists opposed to apartheid—although they executed some more sophisticated acts of sabotage as well. Few MK leaders had an understanding of conventional armies, how large formations were managed, or what strategic goals could be achieved with a complex military force. The MK never got beyond the planning and execution of terrorist acts.

Virtually all the formal training MK cadres received was provided by the Soviet Union and its East European allies. The ANC sent selected individuals to the Soviet Bloc for two years of coursework and practical training. The education they acquired in the theories of warfare was of nebulous value, because after all, the MK's true mission was sabotage, armed attacks on vulnerable rural communities, and the physical elimination of popular blacks who disagreed with ANC policies. Training offered by the KGB or other intelligence organizations that related to insurgency tactics, explosives, and small arms was far more useful. Most MK students already closely identified with communist tenets but they—like everyone else studying in communist states—were subjected to massive doses of Marxist-Leninist indoctrination. The ANC was heavily infiltrated by the South African Communist Party and the MK's training and conduct was consistent with that ideological tradition.

Many considered the APLA's much smaller military force superior to the MK in large part because it received the bulk of its training from the Chinese, who imparted solid and practical military education and went light on Maoist indoctrination.[56] Owing to the ANC's privileged situation and the MK's size advantage, APLA cadres received relatively few choice positions in the new South African National Defence Force. The KwaZulu Self-Protection Force of the Inkatha Freedom Party also joined the program that led to the creation of the integrated SANDF along with the armies of the four "independent" homelands that represented no serious military strength.

Negotiations and Planning for the Transition

The transition from apartheid culminated, in 1994, in a new South African electoral democracy and a new military, the South African National Defence Force. Secret talks between the state—with the knowledge of President Botha but not of his cabinet—and the ANC had begun in November 1985. Initially these were negotiations about negotiations (or "talks about the talks") with the aim of generating a series of understandings about the contours of the future polity. In December 1991 the Convention for a Democratic South Africa (CODESA) commenced with the participation of all major political groups and parties, although, to be sure, proceedings were dominated by the National Party government and the ANC. The participants were motivated by a shared desire to inherit a peaceful social environment and a functioning economy. Though the process was not without complications and controversies, it concluded with the ratification of an Interim Constitution in November 1993 that prepared the legal-institutional ground for the upcoming elections. In May 1994 the ANC garnered 62 percent of the ballots, and Nelson Mandela became the president of the Government of National Unity, also joined by the National Party that was supported by 20 percent of the voters.

The first official meeting between SADF and MK leaders took place only in March 1993. Things progressed quickly, however, and by the end of the following month, sufficient consensus was reached to allow the formation of a staff-level group—the Transitional Executive Council's Subcouncil on Defence—which started work on specific plans. The negotiations featured a remarkable mismatch. The MK's representatives were politically sophisticated but possessed little substantive knowledge of military affairs. On the other side of the table, the SADF officers were often politically naïve and lacked negotiating skills, which were far more important at this stage than their obvious mastery of military issues. The MK cadres seemed not to understand that the phrase "civil-military" referred to two distinct and separate spheres, because in the Soviet Union, their main reference point, the military, was the tool of the Communist Party. In the SADF, however, soldiers grew up with the distinction of separate civil-military spheres but the generals were seldom equipped to explain to the ANC/MK representatives the finer points of civilian control balanced between democratic institutions.

The official transition agreement provided for a shotgun marriage: former members of the underground would be integrated into the new force at all levels. This process began with the assessment of the fighters' skills and experience for the purpose of determining their rank. This was no easy task. ANC officials handed a list of names and desired ranks—such as, "XY should be a colonel, YZ should be a major general"—but those who took a professional army seriously obviously needed more than this. To ensure a balanced evaluation of the former guerilla combatants for the purposes of establishing their rank in the new SANDF it was decided to bring in outside assessors. After some debate, ANC and SADF representatives agreed to ask Britain for assistance. The role of the British Military Advisory and Training Team (BMATT) and the British Peace Support Team (BPST) was to evaluate prospective soldiers and to design and implement military training programs partly to bring the ex-combatants' skills up to a certain rank level.[57] In practice, a group composed of MK, SADF, and BMATT personnel appraised what courses and training an individual needed to take to qualify for a certain rank. The courses were conducted by the SADF with BMATT personnel acting as observers. If disputes among the three parties could not be resolved, then the issue was transferred to the legislature's defense subcommittee on integration. Actually, though the BMATT was fairly balanced in its judgments, if former MK members did not satisfy standards or were unable to master the courses, the British trainers occasionally pushed them through anyway "because they did not need the political flak."[58] They were also mindful of the admonition of T. E. Lawrence (of Arabia)—often cited during the recent reconstruction of Iraq—that it was "better that they do it imperfectly than you do it perfectly, for it is their country."[59]

Not surprisingly, as the transition process advanced, the SADF's leverage gradually diminished while that of the ANC/MK correspondingly increased. Perhaps the best illustration of the shifting power relations during the transition phase and the first years of ANC rule is the career trajectory of Johannes "Joe" Modise. A founder of the MK in 1960, Modise played a central role in the negotiations leading to the creation of the SANDF three decades later. Trained in the Soviet Union, Czechoslovakia, and Vietnam in the 1960s and 1970s, he became well known for his brutal suppression of dissenters within the ANC ranks. Many considered Modise a common thug whose human rights abuses during exile were specifically cited in an internal ANC inquiry in 1993.[60] Nonetheless, Modise became South Africa's first post-apartheid defense minister, a position in which he distinguished himself by cozying up to the white military elite and by the amount of public funds—earmarked for arms purchases—he was able to embezzle.[61] Modise also managed to get an appointment for his wife—Jackie Sedibe the MK's former head of communications—as a *major-general* in the SANDF.

The SADF's officer corps—with the exception of a handful of senior generals and those, like the trainers of "makeup" courses for erstwhile MK personnel, who directly engaged in the army's transformation—were pretty much kept in the dark regarding the nitty-gritty of the transition. Several former SADF leaders—including former SADF Chief General Constand Viljoen and Defense Minister Magnus Malan—testified before the Truth and Reconciliation Commission in 1997. While they admitted actions like approving cross-border raids against enemy targets in southern Africa, they viewed them as normal functions of the state. They categorically denied authorizing the assassination of anti-apartheid activists or, more generally, that the SADF was "guilty of gross violations of human rights on a substantial scale."[62]

What went well and what went poorly in the process of the SANDF's creation from its constituent parts? Perhaps most noteworthy was the willingness of all sides to cooperate and the high level of professionalism the SADF displayed throughout the transition period. Whatever qualms Mandela's government may have had about the military's loyalty to the new regime—in the early years, it was still very much the SADF that was trained to crush the ANC—evaporated as the armed forces proved their professionalism. The MK's activities, on the other hand, were driven by its leaders' ambitions for position and power and their ability to exploit the SADF's political inexperience.[63]

The biggest mistake of the transition was the appointment of people who were unsuitable for their new positions to begin with and then fast-tracking them for accelerated advancement. In any army worthy of the name, those who attain the rank of lieutenant-colonel must first serve as lieutenants, captains, and majors and compile at least a fifteen-or-so-year service record. One should not become a senior officer of a major professional army based on stone throwing or even guerilla experience, but many in the SANDF did because the ANC/MK negotiators trivialized the importance of and even derided "professionalism" and "experience." Little wonder, then, that many of the most competent white officers and NCOs who found their careers stalled and their promotion prospects diminished left the armed forces.

The Result: The Democratic SANDF

The Interim Constitution of 1993 featured a chapter on defense, stated the functions of the South African National Defence Forces, and laid out the institutional framework of civil-military relations and civilian control. Although the SADF was subject to civilian oversight, it was not under *parliamentary* control in any real sense.[64] The new, 1996 Constitution (Chapter 11, Article 198d) asserts that "national security is subject to the authority of

Parliament and the national executive." The Constitution (Article 199 [8]) also states that "multi-party parliamentary committees must have oversight of all security services in a manner determined by national legislation or the rules and orders of Parliament."[65] Furthermore, the president—as the head of the national executive, the commander in chief of the defense force—must inform the legislature when the defense force is employed and must provide the required information to the appropriate parliamentary oversight committees. The new Constitution drastically improved the legal basis for civilian control by creating a substantive role for the legislature. While it gives the SANDF's active-duty personnel the right to vote, they may not belong to a political party or run for elected office.

The president appoints not only the defense minister—the political head of the ministry of defense (called the Department of Defence)—but, unusually, also the Chief of the National Defence Force (CSANDF), the top uniformed officer of the land. The Department of Defence is headed by a minister (DM) and his/her deputy who have very limited staff. The DM is the political head of defense and is supposed to provide political guidance and make policy. The 1999 Public Finance Management Act also designated the minister as the "executive authority" for the military budget.[66] The defense budget is the product of a democratic process that involves the ministry, the cabinet, and the legislature. The budget and military expenditures are audited by the Auditor General who is designated by the Constitution as an independent institution to uphold democratic principles, including transparency.

The Department of Defence is divided into two main bodies, the SANDF, headed by the CSANDF and the Defence Secretariat, led by a Secretary for Defence. The SANDF embraces four branches (army, navy, air force, and military health services). The CSANDF executes military policy, directs the work of the Defence Headquarters, and manages the overall functioning and operations of the SANDF. The Defence Secretariat is responsible for the financial management of the entire ministry. The CSANDF and the Secretary for Defence are the principal advisers to the DM on military operations and defense policy, respectively. The highest policy-making body is the Council on Defence—comprised of the defense minister and his or her deputy, the Secretary for Defence, and the CSANDF—which is supposed to hold weekly meetings. Through its various committees, the bicameral South African legislature plays an important and substantive role in defense matters. Parliamentary oversight of the budget is extensive and exercised by the reasonably capable and well-informed members of the Portfolio Committee on Defence.

The year 1996 saw an important defense-related milestone, the parliamentary approval of the White Paper on National Defence.[67] The demand for the White Paper was created by Parliament when, already in 1994, its defense committee charged Modise with the formulation of a defense policy suitable for the new South Africa. The White Paper, a policy-guiding instrument, was to a large extent prepared by scholar-activist Laurie Nathan, a former defense expert for the MK whose 1994 book, *The Changing of the Guard*, served as its basis.[68] Nathan closely collaborated with Deputy Defence Minister Ronnie Kasrils, a former member of the ANC's Executive Committee, and the soldier-scholar Major General Len le Roux, then Director of Strategy for the SANDF. The White Paper is a comprehensive document that lays out the democratic principles of civil-military relations, strategic environment, personnel and budgetary issues, and matters pertaining to nuclear weapons, the defense industry, and even environmental protection with a keen awareness of South Africa's particularities and political transition. The result of a genuinely consultative process that occasionally included sharp debates, the White Paper has gone a long way in shaping the SANDF into what it is today.[69]

According to some critics, the White Paper's failure to present a realistic and accurate threat assessment permitted the continued maintenance of unnecessarily bulky armed forces. In the absence of conventional security threats, they claim, South Africa simply does not need a large military, but having to run one has encouraged extensive corruption in the defense realm as often superfluous and inappropriate weapons are purchased.[70] Le Roux disagrees and points out that the White Paper had to lay the foundations and framework of military politics—civilian control issues, the rules of how the military is governed, affirmative action and gender issues—in the new democratic state. Only once this task had been completed could substantive details for defense posture, doctrine, force design, and the like be addressed as they were in the 1998 South African Defence Review.[71] Opposition experts were also extensively consulted for the Defence Review, in large part the work of Rocky Williams, a former ANC fighter, SANDF colonel, and highly regarded defense expert.

In South Africa there is a strong community of highly professional civilian defense experts. Indeed, a number of them were instrumental in the conceptualization of what national defense might look like in a post-apartheid South Africa. Some of these individuals—like le Roux and Jackie Cilliers—were former SADF officers. Others helped bring apartheid down in different ways: Nathan was a leader of the anticonscription campaign in the waning years of apartheid and led the ANC's Military Research Group, while Williams (a Caucasian like Nathan) was an active MK combatant. South Africa's example, then, also demonstrates how former anti-apartheid activists and military officers can work together to democratize civil-military relations. Though the preparation of the main documents was largely accomplished by a small elite of defense experts, security-focused NGOs cropped up and publicly debated defense-security issues.[72] Cilliers and others founded the Institute for Security Studies (originally named the Institute for Defence Policy—IDP) in 1991 to study South African and Sub-Saharan defense-security issues, which played a significant role in the transformation of South African defense and security and has become a world-class research organization.

The Problems: Corruption and Incompetence

South Africa has succeeded in establishing a democratic military establishment in which all races have been fully integrated. Nonetheless, the transformation of the SADF has been very costly in terms of integrity of the armed forces' leadership and quality of its personnel. The SANDF has suffered from corrupt and inept leadership.

Joe Modise—post-apartheid South Africa's first defense minister under President Nelson Mandela—was an able man notwithstanding the liberties he is widely alleged to have taken with public funds. Just as importantly, his deputy, Ronnie Kasrils, and three succeeding CSANDFs—Generals Kat Liebenberg, Georg Meiring, and Sipihwe Nyanda—were rational, pragmatic, and effective leaders. Things in South Africa went downhill in many ways after Mandela left office, and defense is no exception. President Thabo Mbeki prioritized playing the role of an international statesman, even if it meant conducting a see-no-evil foreign policy, rather than tending to some of his country's many pressing problems, including an AIDS epidemic and escalating rates of violent crime.[73]

The political climate Mbeki created made possible the unabashed neglect of his defense minister, Mosiuoa Lekota, to meet his responsibilities. Lekota was also the National Chairperson of the ANC, and fighting the ANC's internal battles commanded virtually all his attention at the expense of overseeing the armed forces. In sum, just when it needed one most, the SANDF had no advocate in the cabinet, notwithstanding its severe resource pressures. Lekota actually harmed the military by publicly contradicting in the legislature the Chief of the SANDF, who explained the army's financial strains in the face of expanding responsibilities in Burundi, the Democratic Republic of the Congo, Sudan, and elsewhere. Under Lekota, the Defence Secretariat—run by amateurish political appointees who spent their time ingratiating themselves with politicians—was unable to take to its responsibilities and became a lame duck institution. The DoD became a top-heavy department resembling an upside-down hierarchical pyramid.

One of the most important attributes of the post-apartheid defense establishment has been the scale of corruption, which eclipses even the fraud and theft commonplace in other areas of South African public affairs. Why were people like Modise not sanctioned by Mandela and other top ANC leaders? The massive corruption of the ANC is easy to explain. Liberation movements are not meritocracies but are characterized by a deep sense of the collective. Their fundamental principle is that one's allegiance is first and foremost to one's comrades, and no matter how badly they behave, one does not "sell them out." The ANC is very much a collectivist organization. The dominant thinking of its elites continues to be that if its members want to "compensate" themselves for decades of torture, humiliation, and suffering, then so be it. This notion hints at why Mandela had not restrained Modise and others who looted the South African state. The purchase of a variety of major weapons systems and equipment created the opportunity for large-scale corruption stemming from the selection of the supplier and the price to be paid, a temptation that the new South African elites could seldom withstand.[74]

The quality of the SANDF as a fighting force is inferior to that of the SADF for a simple reason: the overall professionalism of SANDF personnel and the quantity and especially the quality of the training its members receive has diminished in the past decade and a half. The ANC 1997 National Conference identified two main priorities: speedy transformation and cadre deployment.[75] In other words, the armed forces and other institutions should, as soon as possible, reflect the demographic composition of the country, and loyal ANC supporters should be placed in influential positions even if they lack the necessary qualifications. The impact of this policy on the SANDF's quality as a military force has been predictably disastrous.

The level of training declined as many former SADF officers left the service—both through retirement and resignation—and a large proportion of former MK and other black opposition force fighters entered who were not ready for the rigors of a disciplined professional army. The academic preparedness of many black entrants to the SANDF was inadequate, in part owing to the ANC's long-standing "liberation before education" campaign that turned out a generation of unemployable, ignorant, and functionally illiterate people in the townships.[76] Because of the imperative to employ ANC/MK supporters, the part of the defense budget devoted to personnel has significantly increased at the expense of funds earmarked for training. Owing to the massive rank inflation, many incompetent people became senior officers: the SANDF is now home to numerous active-duty colonels who cannot read or write.[77]

During the negotiations that led to the establishment of the SANDF, some MK leaders insisted that some of their apartheid-era fighters be transferred to the police because they were, even in their leaders' judgment, undisciplined thugs not suited for the armed forces.[78] (This measure may be partly responsible for the drastically diminished public safety standards in post-apartheid South Africa.) Many former MK combatants had no identification documents, had assumed names, or were actually not MK members but were friends or family members of ANC or MK personnel who were in need of employment.

In the negotiation phase, MK and other opposition representatives insisted in the face of SADF's disagreement that their comrades entering the SANDF should not be disqualified for medical reasons. As it happened, a considerable proportion of these new entrants were HIV positive and, as such, they have not been able to fully participate in field training, nor can they be deployed outside their barracks. According to some estimates, about 20 to 25 percent of the army's personnel are HIV positive and 30 percent of the SANDF are not deployable for medical reasons.[79] This issue is a serious liability for the military and its budget. Notwithstanding these difficulties, the SANDF's record in international peacekeeping operations remains respectable and it has maintained the ability to provide security on relatively short notice in faraway places such as during the 2001 disturbances in Burundi and the 2006 Comoros elections.

Another major mistake has been the abolition of the country's commando system. The commandos were paramilitary units supporting the work of and supervised by the SADF. They were responsible for the protection of a specific urban or rural community, which included community participation, and also for other tasks such as border security. Although they played a critical role in public safety, owing to their compromised apartheid-era role they were disbanded in a classic "throwing the baby out with the bathwater" decree. The large vacuum the measure created has not been filled and has clearly contributed to the skyrocketing criminality in the country.[80] Owing to various "reforms," the SADF's world-class reserve force has also deteriorated in quality and has been much reduced in number (now perhaps 40,000-strong), but occasionally it is still deployed in the absence of available and properly trained active-duty units.[81]

When comparing the SADF and its successor, it is important to consider changes in South Africa's sociopolitical and economic environment that had a tremendous impact on its defense establishment. Until 1993, there was mandatory military service in South Africa, and the SADF oversaw a pool of about 100,000 well-educated and more-or-less socially homogeneous conscripts. In most years the SADF had about 4.8 percent of the country's GDP at its disposal and benefited also from its exploitation of the black labor force. After the integration of the SANDF, the quality of soldiers—in terms of education, physical fitness, health, and discipline—plummeted. So did the budget of the military, which was reduced to about 1.8 percent of the GDP.[82]

THE YEMENI ENIGMA

Of the twenty-seven countries in this book, Yemen proved to be the most challenging to learn about. A number of Western military officers I tracked down confessed that they acquired little solid information while serving in their countries' embassies in Sana'a. When, in February 2009, I arrived at a prearranged interview with Yemen's Defense Attaché in his embassy in Washington, D.C., he failed to show up. I was directed to the Deputy Chief of Mission who offered evasive answers, directly contradicted himself several times, or provided demonstrably false information during our ninety-minute interview. In her recent book Sarah Phillips, one of the few Western academics who can claim to be an authority on Yemen, hints at the difficulty of writing about Yemeni military affairs. In the span of a couple of pages she qualifies her assertions with: "a point of great contention," "shrouded in secrecy," "Yemen's notoriously inaccurate self-reported statistics," "extremely vague," "an unknown quantity," "casting further doubt on the reliability of any figures presented," and "accurate figures are still impossible to obtain."[83] In sum, as Robert Kaplan said, "in a place like Yemen the truth emerges by accident."[84]

The Road to Unification

In 1962 Yemeni officers seized the reins of power after the last imam's natural death. In 1967 the British colonists left Aden, in south Yemen after 128 years. Both parts of the country were gripped by a vicious cycle of revolutions and war through much of the 1960s.[85] In the north, Egypt supported the republican side while Saudi Arabia backed the royalists in a bloody civil war. After years of fighting, in 1970 a compromise was reached with royalists receiving some seats in a republican-dominated government in Sana'a. Although traditional social organizations continued to play an important role, a modern constitution was ratified by the new legislature and the Yemen Arab Republic (YAR) began to make considerable economic progress.

South of the border originally set by the Ottomans and the British, the Federation of South Arabia, an organization of small states under British protection, had experienced growing instability and animosity between the colonists and Arab nationalists. The Federation was abolished, and from it, the Protectorate of South Arabia and the People's Republic of South Yemen emerged in 1967. In 1970 the latter became the first Arab Marxist state and called itself the People's Democratic Republic of Yemen (PDRY). The regime was backed by the Soviet Union and its East European allies as well as China and Cuba. The Yemeni Socialist Party (YSP) became the country's all-controlling political force and emphasized social transformation and increasing educational standards while restraining independent initiative in the economic sphere. By the late 1970s Aden's brand of Marxism had transformed the PDRY into an economic backwater with little prospect for advancement.[86] The PDRY, with the assistance of some sympathizers north of the border, started three border wars in an attempt to bring North Yemen under Marxist rule, but the North eventually prevailed.

In Sana'a an ambitious military officer, Ali Abdullah Saleh, ascended to the presidency following a successful coup in 1978. Both of Saleh's immediate predecessors were assassinated, and few predicted a long career for him either, but he has remained at the helm after more than three decades, even in the face of growing opposition by a movement in the south and the Huthi Rebellion in the northwest.[87] Saleh gradually established an extreme form of personalized rule by placing his sons, brothers, nephews, male in-laws, and tribesmen into some of the most sensitive military positions.[88] In a country where politics was dominated by the tense but fluid relationships between the central government and influential tribal leaders, Saleh worked hard and quite successfully to reach compromises with the sheikhs.

Aside from initiating a number of economic programs, Saleh modernized and strengthened YAR's armed forces.[89] He introduced conscription (which was later abolished but recently reinstated) coupled with professional training for the officer corps, and initiated three separate re-equipment programs in the first decade of his rule. These advances were partly compromised by the extension of new privileges to high-ranking officers in general and, in particular, to officers from Saleh's own tribe. After rebuilding the armed forces, Saleh turned his attention to further safeguarding his rule and extending his personal monopoly of the state's mobilizational capacity. The president established a 50,000-strong Republican Guard, many of whose personnel were recruited from his own tribe, equipped with sophisticated weapons, and endowed with special perquisites. He also modernized the Political Security Organization and established a new force, the Central Security Organization, a part of the ministry of interior. All of these organizations were controlled by Saleh's relatives.

Unification and Civil War

Unlike East and West Germany and North and South Korea, the two Yemens remained on relatively friendly terms notwithstanding frequent tensions. Therefore, the unification of the two Yemens was not just a popular objective on both sides of the border; unity was "a deeply shared cultural priority."[90] Nonetheless, when unification did take place, on May 22, 1990, it was a rushed and, with hindsight, badly handled affair. Yemen became a unified state, but a federal arrangement might have been preferable, because in the previous quarter century, the two societies had become very different. The South Yemenis succeeded in establishing and upholding the principle that having ceded the head of state position to Saleh and the majority of the Presidential Council to the North Yemenis, half of the ministerial portfolios—including defense—and other leadership positions in the new government should go to them even though they represented only 20 percent of the country's population of thirteen million.[91]

The new Republic of Yemen was governed by a five-member Presidential Council headed by President Saleh and Vice President Ali Salim al-Beidh, the leader of the erstwhile PDRY and the YSP's secretary-general. The legislative body, the 301-seat Council of Representatives, was made up of 159 members of the YAR's presidentially appointed advisory council, 111 members of the PDRY's Supreme People's Council, and 31 new appointees. Relatively prosperous Sana'a was flooded with South Yemenis because most of the PDRY's civil servants were also absorbed into the political administration of the unified state.

Aware of the inferiority of their forces and their expected vulnerability in the unified state, PDRY military commanders were hardly enthusiastic about unification but had gone along with it for the time being. The two defense ministries and the general staff were merged into integrated bodies. In order to appease the South, the North allowed the YSP to control just under half of Yemen's ground forces, all coastal patrol forces, the bulk of the country's SCUD missiles, and the majority of the air force.[92] Integration on the rank-and-file level, however, was left to take place over a protracted period of time in order not to sacrifice military efficiency.[93] Troops were withdrawn from the old common border and a number of regiments from the North and South, together with their commanders, in effect, changed places. Some northern commanders treated their comrades from the South condescendingly. The low salaries paid to southern officials were not raised quickly enough, causing resentment among them. It is important to note that, in this first period of unification, the PDRY's political and military structures were not *taken over* by the North, as happened in the case of West vis-à-vis East Germany, but a more or less genuine attempt was made at real *integration*.

The YSP's leaders, headed by Vice President al-Beidh, had hoped that they would have an equal partnership with the new regime in Sana'a. They were soon disappointed, however, as the North was able to carve out a dominant political position in the new Yemen, for several reasons. First, the North represented four-fifths of the electorate and its leaders were able to obtain, for the time being, the support of the powerful tribal chiefs, many of them devout Muslims who despised the secular infidels in the South and who probably saw which way the wind was blowing and made a political calculation. Second, unlike politicians in the South, Saleh was able to point at the economic successes of the North and offer an attractive developmental alternative. Third, the North received the overwhelming support of two classes of returnees to Yemen: the nearly one million Yemeni guest workers who were expelled from Arab countries in 1991 in response to Sana'a's support of Saddam Hussein in the first Gulf War and an influential group of Yemeni mujahideen who returned from Afghanistan after fighting the Soviets. Finally, Saleh's control over state resources, especially the revenue produced by the southern oil fields, increased his influence and room for maneuver.[94]

In the new multiparty system the YSP's clout was dwarfed by Saleh's General People's Congress (GPC)—essentially a broad movement rather than a conventional party—and the newly established Yemeni Reform Rally, which was associated with the GPC. The YSP did not change its radical Marxist policies, which were losing in popularity even in the South and never made much of an impression in the North. The results of the April 1993 elections—generally free and fair, though not without very significant irregularities that included a string of assassinations against YSP officials—confirmed the power relations and left the YSP in a very junior role. The elections were supposed to be a major step in the implementation of the new, pluralist constitutional order but ended up exacerbating tensions between Saleh's GPC and al-Beidh's YSP.

In August 1993 al-Beidh withdrew to Aden and readied his forces—the YSP preserved control over some of the old PDRY military units that had not been effectively brought into the northern army. In the meantime, the GPC resolved to eliminate the YSP once and for all and conducted an assassination campaign of southern officials: according to al-Beidh over 150 YSP members were killed by late 1993.[95] The deepening crisis culminated in al-Beidh's declaration of the South's independence in May 1994, and the nine-week civil war that followed. The president's forces slowly wore down the YSP's troops, who proved thin on the ground in many regions. Northern clerics issued fatwas prohibiting reconciliation with southern secessionists and sanctioning their killing.[96] Some YSP units were not willing to fight; many southern soldiers were bought off. Most of the fighting was done by northern conscripts.[97] In the end, the war cost over seven thousand lives and resulted in the utter defeat of the southern secessionist forces and the exile of most YSP leaders.

Military Politics in Contemporary Yemen

The civil war reinforced the northern regime's dominance. Yahya Alshawkani, the Deputy Chief of Mission at Yemen's Washington, D.C., Embassy insists that Yemen is democratic "because the people get what they want,"[98] while some U.N. officials consider it the most democratic state in Arabia.[99] The bar, admittedly, is very low, and whatever positive impression may have existed has shifted markedly downward in recent years: in fact, post–civil war Yemen has become an authoritarian state headed by a strong-man basking in a personality cult. According to an official biography, Saleh "loved his homeland so much. This love made him elected president to the country in a [sic] first time in which Yemen has elected president."[100] In the 1999 presidential elections, he received 96 percent of the vote, reminiscent of the numbers regularly racked up by the likes of Brezhnev, Castro, and Ceausescu. In 2006, when he was elected to another seven-year term with "only" 77 percent of the ballots, Saleh faced a more credible challenger, encouraging some hope regarding the quality of elections and representation in Yemen. Contemporary Yemen reminds some experts of the "peripheral, less developed Arab military dictatorships more typical of the Middle East of the 1950s–70s."[101]

The various military and security organizations and the Supreme National Defense Council (SNDC—its name is occasionally translated as National Security Council)are thoroughly controlled by Saleh's kin and tribal associates. The defense ministry is little more than an administrative appendage of the armed forces that disburses salaries and manages pensions.[102] The armed forces' Chief of Staff is subordinated to the defense minister and to the SNDC. The Republican Guard and other military and security units—some created since 2001—are separate, but their heads, all Saleh's people, are said to report to the minister of defense.[103] The "military" in Yemen has actually become a group of fragmented apparatuses and organizations rather than a single, cohesive institution.[104]

The legislature has little influence over defense-security matters other than, in theory, overseeing the budget. There is no tradition of ever posing more than pro forma questions about defense expenditures, however, and legislators who tried would likely find themselves in trouble. In Yemen, as in other Arab parliaments with the exception of Kuwait, deputies usually treat defense and security matters as taboo.[105] There are no independent civilian defense experts to speak of. Precise numbers are hard to obtain but there is no doubt that the Yemeni government devotes an inordinately large proportion of its meager resources to defense. According to a 2005 United Nations Development Program report, in that year 7 percent of Yemen's GDP ($885.5 million or 20 percent of the state budget) was spent on defense while the health care sector received 1.3 percent of the GDP.[106] These numbers largely correspond to more recent independent estimates.[107]

A major vehicle Saleh has utilized for regime consolidation is the Military Economic Corporation (MECO), which emerged in the mid-1980s. At its inception, this entity integrated foreign trade and agricultural corporations but later focused its activities on import-export businesses and currency transactions. The tax-exempt and essentially unregulated MECO has become an increasingly prosperous conglomerate largely overseen by military officers and has turned into the main source of revenue for the president. After unification, MECO's profile diminished under pressure from the YSP. After the YSP's defeat in 1994, however, MECO's bustling activities were restored and expanded to include the South.[108] In 1999, MECO was renamed the Yemeni Economic Corporation but the new name signified no substantive change.[109]

After the civil war, there were no longer any efforts to integrate the two armies. Northern forces completely dominated the South, whose officers and NCOs were increasingly sidelined. Conscription was discontinued in 2001, in part to make sure that the composition of personnel of the various forces could be controlled by the regime. The president has used the military and security services as a baseline guarantee against a serious challenge to his power. The officer corps is closely watched by military security, officers are not allowed to participate in unsanctioned group meetings, and some who were suspected of organizing politically have disappeared.[110] Professional personnel have the right to vote, but, again, in *theory*, must resign their commissions before taking on public office.

The government's deployment of military and paramilitary units has usually been a response to an overt challenge to the regime's authority.[111] The key function of the Yemeni military is in the domestic sphere: to control the population through actual or threatened coercive action. Yemen has faced several pressing security challenges: a tribal insurgency in the North (since 2004), a secessionist movement in the South (since 2007), and an ever bolder terrorist group affiliated with al-Qaeda, whose core leadership is made up of former mujahideen fighters in Afghanistan.[112] Porous land and sea borders, growing incidents of piracy, the largest number of firearms per capita in the world (over eighty million in a population of twenty-three million), along with growing water shortages, a 35 percent unemployment rate, looming economic collapse (oil reserves are expected to be depleted within a decade), and the fact that the government does not control large chunks of the country's territory explain why recent articles on Yemen bear the titles "A Nation on the Brink," "Is Yemen the Next Afghanistan?," and "The World's Next Failed State."[113]

The Yemeni armed forces have not been able to master these challenges. Their officers lack initiative, are often poorly trained and motivated, and are easily bribable. Most of the equipment of the Huthi insurgents in the North is captured booty; most were bought from corrupt officers. Army units are often hollow—tribal sheikhs favored by the regime are granted the ability to draw an income for soldiers they *claim* to have sent to the army—and it is not unusual for soldiers to desert or switch sides.[114] In the meantime, the United States and its allies are desperately trying to achieve a modicum of success in training Yemeni soldiers and counterterrorism units. Understandably, Washington is reluctant to alienate one of its few supporters in the Middle East even if that support may be fleeting and based entirely on money.

Saleh's regime did not escape the wave of uprisings that spread through North Africa and the Middle East in early 2011.[115] Soon after protests began, Saleh cut taxes, hiked food subsidies, and promised not to extend his rule beyond 2013 and not to permit his son Ahmed—the commander of the elite Republican Guard—to succeed him. The crowds, initially dominated by students, were not satisfied with these concessions and demanded that Saleh immediately resign. The ensuing violence, and particularly the killing of fifty-two protesters by security forces on March 18, 2011, galvanized the opposition and divided the armed forces.

The biggest loss for the regime was the defection of General Ali Mohsen al-Ahmar, Saleh's tribesman and longtime ally, who had distinguished himself during the past decade by fighting Huthi separatists in the north. A dozen generals joined Ahmar. Although the defense minister insisted the military was still faithful to Saleh, many ordinary soldiers either went over to General Ahmar and the opposition or simply deserted. To keep his hold on power, Saleh relied on the better-equipped and -trained Republican Guard, Central Security Forces, and elite army units, whose loyalty he retained. By mid-2011, Yemen was in a state of civil war, notwithstanding the mediation efforts of the Gulf Cooperation Council, with its army split and the outcome of the fighting uncertain. In June, Saleh was flown to Saudi Arabia to receive medical treatment after a rocket attack during clashes between his troops and tribal fighters severely injured him. In his absence, the combat between government and opposition forces has continued unabated. Saleh returned to Sana'a in September and promised to step down to ease the transition to a more stable regime in November 2011. Two months later, he was still very much a key factor in Yemeni politics having successfully manipulated the country's multiplying security problems for his own benefit.[116] Consequently, at the time of this writing (January 2012) an end to the hostilities seems remote.

CONCLUSION

In this chapter we saw how three armies were brought together in three very different post–Cold War contexts. The Cold War as background is extremely important in the two unification cases—it was the indirect reason Germany and Yemen were divided and stayed divided. To be sure, the division between North and South Yemen was not nearly as ironclad as that between the two Germanys, and Aden and Sana'a continued to pay at least lip service to their desire for unification throughout most of their separation. That the Bundeswehr and the NVA never actually fought each other, while the forces of YAR and PDRY were involved in several small-scale conflicts, may be in part explained by the very different stakes involved; after all, an inter-German confrontation almost certainly would have involved the two superpowers and possibly their allies. The Cold War also had a significant impact on South Africa albeit in different ways. The ANC was a long-term beneficiary of the Soviet Bloc's support, while the apartheid regime enjoyed the backing of the West, though as time went on, its policies became less and less palatable for an increasing number of liberal democracies.

The intention to create democratic armies was present in all three of these cases but in very different ways. Although one may consider the West German treatment of the GDR in some respects heavy-handed, politicians and military leaders in Bonn saw the GDR and the NVA precisely for what they were: a ruthless dictatorship and its tool for internal repression. The West German government's policies of reunification were conducted fairly, transparently, and effectively. Criticism leveled at Germany's cumbersome political procedures regarding force deployment, the daunting difficulties of changing legislation regarding anything connected to the armed forces, and the plethora of impractical regulations that damage the Bundeswehr's effectiveness are on the mark, but the purely democratic nature of German military politics is unassailable.

Germany's case raises an important issue. Even though some may consider Germany a standard-bearer with respect to the institutional arrangements of its civil-military relations, these very same arrangements—particularly the virtually unchecked powers of the legislature over the executive branch in terms of the military's civilian oversight—essentially render the armed forces ineffective. One might wonder what purpose the German army serves if it is not allowed to shoot down a terrorist plane or to participate in a U.N.-sanctioned operation to protect civilians. What emerges in Germany's case is that, in fact, German civil-military relations may be just as institutionally unbalanced as Russian military politics; except in Germany the legislature has a predominant role whereas in Russia the executive branch does.

In South Africa, too, the aim was to build a democratic army upon the ashes of the apartheid regime. Nearly two decades later it is easy to be blasé about what happened there, but one must appreciate just how amazing a feat it has been to bring together erstwhile enemies in one organization in a process marked with so little vindictiveness and overt acrimony. The very real problems that accompanied the creation of the SANDF should not be trivialized. These problems had little to do with the institutional framework of civil-military relations, as in Germany; rather, they were mostly rooted in personnel management. Nonetheless, the end result here, too, was the diminished effectiveness of the new military. All in all, it ought to be underscored that South Africa's difficulties in the realm of building a new, democratic army are dwarfed by the monumental achievement of a peaceful transition.

Yemen's unification was very different from German reunification. To begin with, the Yemeni process unfolded in two easily separable stages. At first, it was clear that the YAR, the side that held the stronger cards, was equally or even more interested in unification than the PDRY for three reasons.[117] First, Saleh wanted to reap the political benefits of being the architect of unification, most Yemenis' long-sought goal. Second, in 1989–90 Saleh badly needed political and economic successes after a number of domestic and foreign policy fiascos. Finally, he needed to consolidate the government's position vis-à-vis the northern tribes. The second stage of the unification process had begun by early 1993 when it became clear that the animosity between the GPC and the YSP was unlikely to disappear. Another major difference between Germany and Yemen is that although Yemeni political elites may consider their country democratic, it is actually far from anything approximating a democratic system. After the 1994 civil war, however, there were no serious attempts to build even a façade of a balanced process: the North simply overtook the South.

Are there factors that could help us make generalizations about the outcomes in the three different settings of this chapter? Considering issues like the "level of democracy" and the "level of development" helps explain the smoothness of the transitions in Germany and South Africa. After all, both countries enjoyed decades-long traditions of competitive elections, democratic governance, and strong political institutions—though, of course, in apartheid-era South African only a minority of citizens benefited from it—and high levels of socioeconomic development. Yemenis, on the other hand, have been far less fortunate in both respects. The most important outcome predictor of the three different processes in this chapter, however, is the answer to the question: "Which side had the leverage?" The only leverage the NVA had vis-à-vis the Bundeswehr was to disrupt the process of its abolition. Realistically, however, this was hardly going to happen as long as a significant number of NVA officers wanted to join the Bundeswehr. The leverage of the SADF rapidly diminished once the ANC was legalized. Throughout the negotiations, the SADF was in a weak and vulnerable position and had no serious alternative to cooperating with the ANC. In Yemen the YSP's great trump card was their knowledge that the GPC seriously desired unification. After al-Beidh squandered the PDRY's position by making outlandish demands and more or less provoking a military showdown that his forces could well expect to lose, South Yemen lost whatever leverage it might have enjoyed earlier.

Another smaller but important point is that in situations where two or more military entities are merged, determining the rank of personnel will be a sensitive issue that needs to be handled carefully. As we have seen, the issue of purging the armed forces and holding to account those responsible for human rights abuses is also likely to become relevant in these kinds of settings. Foreign influence was important in all of our cases, though to different degrees. The end of the Cold War was clearly a necessary condition for German reunification, while it was a factor that indirectly encouraged the end of apartheid and Yemeni unification. Finally, one can confidently note that in this chapter, too, the two consolidated democracies have established democratic civil-military relations with armed forces personnel committed to democratic governance, while the opposite is true for Yemen, an authoritarian state that lacks substantive democratic attributes.

TABLE 10.1

After (Re)Unification and Apartheid: Germany, South Africa, and Yemen

	Country Period	Germany 1990–2000	South Africa 1994–2000	Yemen 1990–2000
Background	armies and the end of the old regime	NVA restrained throughout	SADF restrained and cooperative	two armies calm in 1990
State	main tasks	absorb small part of the NVA into the Bundeswehr	integration of MK and APLA and SADF to create SANDF, establish democratic civil-military relations	integrate the armies of North and South; after 1994: North to absorb army of the South
	civilian political leadership	purposeful (WG), collaborative (GDR)	collaborative	contentious
	political institutions and trend	mature	mature	weak
	executive control	strong but less so than parliament	strong	strong
	legislative oversight	intensive, the true master of the military	active, appropriate	negligible
	quotas for integrated troops?	yes	yes	no
	integration or absorption?	absorption, dismantlement of the NVA	integration	first integration, then (after 1994) absorption
	army purged?	yes (NVA)	no	yes (after 1994)
	foreign influence	to allow reunification, otherwise minimal	minor	minor (Saudi Arabia)
Military	military behavior during the transition	NVA/East German elites cooperative	SADF active participant in the transition	transition contested, civil war ensued
	interference in politics	no	no	yes
	domestic function	none	none	yes, fighting separatists

TABLE 10.1   *(continued)*

After (Re)Unification and Apartheid: Germany, South Africa, and Yemen

	Country *Period*	*Germany* *1990–2000*	*South Africa* *1994–2000*	*Yemen* *1990–2000*
	advisory function	minor	minor	yes
	institutional attributes	extreme reluctance to execute defense functions and alliance obligations	major rank inflation for former guerrillas, many white personnel leave SANDF	Republican Guard is Saleh's private force, army has strong economic interests
	effectiveness	low because of constitutional constraints	declining	unclear
	commitment to democracy	yes	yes	no
Society	independent civilian experts	yes, quite influential	yes, numerous and influential	few with little clout
	military's prestige	low, population is wary of anything "military"	medium	medium
	soldiers in society	"citizen in uniform"	somewhat growing integration	little integration
	conscription	suspended in 2011	no, abolished in 1994	discontinued in 2001
Political system at the end of the period		consolidated parliamentary democracy	consolidated parliamentary democracy	electoral authoritarianism

Conclusion

⫤ ⫥

What wisdom can we distill from the trajectory of military politics following our exploration of the three contexts in six settings and twenty-seven cases? In this concluding section I will assess the arguments and then attempt to answer the general questions posed at the beginning of the book in light of the evidence presented in the case-study chapters. In the second half of the conclusion I will outline the policies and conditions that advance or inhibit the development of armies supportive of democratic rule. I will discuss these issues and formulate some policy recommendations to assist democracy activists and policy-makers in their efforts to build democratic armies.

THE THREE ARGUMENTS

Democratic Consolidation and Military Elites

The fundamental contention of this book is that consolidated democracies cannot exist without military elites committed to democratic governance, that their support is a necessary if insufficient condition of democratization. As we have seen, when the armed forces do not support democratic rule, they pose a threat—even if it may be a dormant threat—to the survival of the democratizing state. In such environments if officers believe that state policies jeopardize their corporate, material, strategic, or other interests, they may well decide to mount an armed challenge to civilian rule.

The generals do not have to *like* one government or another but they must support the principle of democratic governance and be obedient to the freely elected leaders of the state. In all of the twenty-seven countries in our case-study pool where democracy has been consolidated (e.g., Slovenia, South Korea, and Spain), the armed forces are steadfast supporters of a democratic polity and compliant servants of the state. Truly democratic armies continue to endorse democratic ideals even if the state treats them poorly (Argentina), even if they are marginalized in defense policy-making (India and Japan), and even if they lack societal esteem and professional prestige (Germany).

It was easy to discern that the armed forces were not committed to democratic values in the authoritarian states we examined. Nonetheless, the generals' lack of democratic credentials in such cases did not necessarily mean they were not kept under firm civilian control. Think of the military elites in post–World War II Hungary, postcolonial Tanzania, or postcommunist Russia. In yet other countries, of course, the absence of the military's devotion to democratic ideals actually did coincide with the absence of effective civilian oversight, as in Pakistan and Thailand.

Still, it is important to reiterate that the presence of a military establishment devoted to democratic rule is, in itself, hardly enough to consolidate democracy. Regularly held competitive elections, peaceful transfers of political power between contending parties, democratic political institutions, and a host of other requirements must also be present. But, again, a democratic army is an indispensable prerequisite: democratizers must ensure that the army is loyal to them before they can attend to the many tasks they need to accomplish in order to consolidate democratic rule.

Different Contexts, Different Challenges

In the introduction, I argued that the six settings present different challenges to would-be democratizers intent on crafting democratic armies and civil-military relations. What patterns emerge regarding the main tasks to be carried out, and how did these tasks differ in the various settings?

After devastating defeat in a major war—I occasionally used the shorthand term "post–World War II" for this category—the key tasks were to demobilize, disarm, and purge the armed forces of their compromised elements, and then to recruit new soldiers untainted by the past, rearm them, and begin the process of indoctrinating them with democratic values. The armies had to be built from the ground up, with the massive assistance of foreign powers, often in the face of vocal political opposition from emerging domestic democratic elites who, not unexpectedly, wanted nothing to do with soldiers and weapons so short a time after an annihilating defeat. In their efforts to create iron-clad guarantees against the political interference of their new armies, both Japan and, to a lesser extent, Germany placed them in a constitutional strait-jacket that to some extent sacrificed their effectiveness on the altar of democracy. As the case of Hungary illustrated, in countries where the postwar political direction pointed toward communist dictatorship, many of the tasks were actually quite similar. The old army had to be disarmed and its personnel extensively purged before it could be transformed, and the ideological commitment of the new cadres to communist tenets was nonnegotiable and outweighed the importance of their professional standing.

Some of the main challenges *after civil war* also included demobilization, disarmament, and removal of those guilty of human rights violations. The availability of an influential external intermediary was critical in most cases—we saw this especially in El Salvador and Bosnia-Herzegovina—both to guide the warring parties to the peace treaty and then to help keep things on track in the period of reconciliation and rebuilding. An additional task in the post–civil war context was the integration of former combatants fighting on opposite sides into the new democratic army. In countries where the civil war is caused by ethnic, regional, or religious grievances, the careful balancing of the new army's personnel among the various groups is an essential task. A key issue in all post–civil war contexts is the deep gap in trust between erstwhile enemies, which even in the best of circumstances can only be bridged gradually, one step at a time.

What about the two settings following regime change? The key challenges *after military rule* and *after state-socialist regimes* are essentially reversed. Once the army leaves power, the chief concern of democratizers is to take the military out of politics, that is, to terminate the generals' interference in political life. If the military had a role in overseeing the economy or participated in business activities, they need to be removed from this sector as well. In both of these settings, training independent civilian defense experts is an important task. Given the communist party's comprehensive control of the armed forces in socialist states, in postcommunist systems, the main job is exactly the opposite: to take the politics out of the military, in other words, to banish the communist party and its agents (political officers, party organizations, etc.) from the barracks. An additional question to be concerned about in these settings is one of professionalism: after all, under communist rule the dominant (and often only) factor in promotions and advancement is not merit but fealty to the regime. After military rule a whole new institutional framework must be erected for the democratic functioning of civil-military relations, with special attention to establishing civilian control balanced between the executive and legislative branches. In postcommunist states where the army was under close civilian (i.e., communist party) control, the more specific job is to bolster the legislative oversight of the armed forces because in state-socialist regimes parliaments were little more than façade institutions.

The tasks in the two settings following state transformation were quite different. In *postcolonial* environments, the first order of business was to establish independent armies and to educate and train a new native officer corps so the residual contingent of colonialist officers could be sent home. Even within this category, however, there were major differences between individual cases. From its very birth, the Pakistani military had to prepare for war against India. In the African examples the additional tasks early on included protecting the new regimes from their internal enemies in Ghana and Tanzania, projecting power abroad in Ghana, and establishing secure borders and fighting poachers in Botswana.

Integration was the primary purpose of army builders in countries *after (re)unification and apartheid.* Nonetheless, integration implies bringing together more or less equal sides, which was certainly not the case in Germany, South Africa, and Yemen. In the German context, the East German side had virtually no leverage and West German elites had no reason to accommodate their recent adversaries. The process, then, is more aptly described as the absorption of the former East German army by the West German military. In South Africa, once democratization began the political leverage of the white nationalist government had quickly diminished. Consequently, the integration of the guerrilla forces on the one hand and the armed forces of the state on the other proceeded pretty much on the former's terms. Following unification in Yemen the merger of the two states' armies initially evinced some genuinely integrative features, but after the brief civil war, the armed forces of the South were more or less incorporated into the army of the North. Another sensitive task for democratizers in this setting is determining the rank of officers and NCOs in the new integrated armed forces.

No General Theory (but Numerous Useful Generalizations)

The foregoing makes it abundantly clear that, as I argued at the beginning of this book, *it is virtually impossible to come up with a general theory that provides substantive and useful explanations for civil-military relations in such diverse political and socioeconomic environments.* One can certainly make generalizations that fit individual settings, as I have done above, but generalizations that accommodate *most* of these settings *and* are insightful beyond the level of triviality are not possible to formulate. My contention that military elites' preferences determine whether democratic consolidation is possible is amply supported by the case studies, but I certainly would not wish to stake a claim that it constitutes a "grand theory."

In my field research for this book I interviewed many politicians, military officers, scholars, journalists, and NGO staff around the globe. The point of this exercise, of course, was to see things for myself and learn from the experts about their countries. One oft-repeated anecdote I heard from Romania to Ghana and from Argentina to Thailand was about the visit of this or that (usually American) academic star of general comparative politics who came not so much to listen to local experts but to tell them what "really" was going on in their countries and how those experiences figured in the "big picture." They often arrived armed with unsupported assumptions and preconceived notions, eager to force ill-fitting empirical pieces into their theoretical pigeonholes. The contradictory evidence they frequently found appeared not to temper their enthusiasm for grand theory. For instance, when one of the central figures of the democratization literature arrived in Jakarta, he "told" those who devoted their careers to studying Indonesian civil-military relations that the Indonesian generals agreed to the 2005 Aceh Peace Accord because their forces were exhausted. In fact, as his puzzled sources told him, nothing could have been further from the truth—the generals signed because of political pressure and the tsunami disaster that forced both sides to reevaluate their positions. But the great man only stopped insisting when several local researchers who had just interviewed the generals in question refused to back down to accommodate his theory.

What generalizations can we make—*in addition to* those concerning the various tasks facing democratizers outlined above—that, though possibly not standing up to scrutiny in every political environment, will help us think theoretically about civil-military relations and democratization in different settings?

After devastating defeat in war:

1. Foreign actors are likely to be extensively involved in postwar state-building, including the building of the armed forces.
2. The magnitude of the old regime's and the old army's defeat usually advances the building of the new regime because it increases the victors' leverage and, in democratizing states, society's openness to a new political system and a new military.
3. The traditions of the old, defeated army are likely to be rejected by the emerging postwar political elites and social groups that may overcompensate by passing regulations and laws that would restrain the normal functions (e.g., national defense, alliance participation) of the new military.

Following civil war:

1. Foreign actors, especially international organizations, ordinarily play a major role in post–civil war army-building.
2. Peace agreements ending civil wars that leave key issues ambiguous, whether related to the armed forces (e.g., demobilization, weapons collection) or not, are likely to be contested, possibly with arms.

3. Army-building may be expected to take a longer time in post–civil war settings than in other situations, owing to sensitive and time-intensive undertakings like building trust between former adversaries.

After military rule:

1. The military government's record will go far in determining the outgoing military elites' leverage in their dealings with the civilian successor regime.
2. The most important concessions the former praetorian rulers want from their civilian successors are a continued voice in politics (particularly in foreign affairs and defense), immunity from prosecution (for the violation of human rights and other rights while in power), large defense budgets and the authority to control their allocation, and the autonomy to conduct military affairs as they see fit.
3. During the transition period, prudent democratizers prepare for the possibility of coup attempts and acts of political interference by and/or mutinies in the armed forces.
4. International organizations enjoy an influential position in regime transitions (both in postpraetorian rule and postcommunist settings) only if they have something substantial to offer (e.g., the prestige of membership, significant economic aid) to the democratizing state.

After state-socialism:

1. In newly independent post–socialist states the societal prestige of the military occupation will rise because officers are the defenders of national not, as in the past, supranational (i.e., Soviet) interests.
2. The more difficulties a transitioning regime encounters, the more keenly it pursues membership in military alliances.

Following colonial rule:

As I noted at the end of chapter 9, finding patterns common to all six postcolonial experiences in our case pool was exceedingly difficult because these countries, even though they are all former British colonies (with the partial exception of Bangladesh), have had very dissimilar political trajectories. Still, here are four generalizations that would hold water in at least five of the six cases.

1. In postcolonial environments of especially less developed countries the importance of competent political leadership is hard to overstate.

2. Ethnic/tribal/religious identity is one of the most sensitive issues in the building of political institutions, including the armed forces.
3. Postcolonial leaders are often prejudiced against the armed forces—they remain suspicious of the officers' intentions and motivations—a bias that inevitably affects their approach to military-security issues. (This is hardly surprising: for native activists the military was the embodiment of the most oppressive feature of colonial power.)
4. The flip side of the robust executive control of the military in most postcolonial environments is the legislature's weakness in this regard.

After unification/integration:

1. The Cold War is an important background in all of these cases and its end promoted the (re-)unification of Germany and Yemen and the fall of the apartheid regime in South Africa.
2. The comparative leverage or strength of the sides that are being united largely determines the shape of the post–unification/integration regime, including the kind of armed forces it will maintain.

Notwithstanding my skepticism regarding grand theories, we can certainly identify a number of patterns that should be useful for policy-makers and democracy promoters, no matter what setting they find themselves in or are interested in studying. In the last part of this conclusion, I will summarize what they should do and what they should avoid doing to become successful builders of democratic armies.

RESPONDING TO THE GENERAL QUESTIONS

Let us now turn to two of the three general questions I posed in the introduction. We shall respond to the third question—that sought answers to what policies and conditions promoted and inhibited the building of democratic armies—in the balance of the conclusion.

Which pre-democratic settings are more conducive to the successful democratization of military politics and why?

I organized the nine empirical chapters under three different contexts—war, regime change, and state transformation—that prompted democratization and the building of democratic armies. There are, as we have seen, profound disparities not just between these contexts and the six ettings they encompass, but also within the individual regional settings themselves. Furthermore, though I included "good" and "bad" cases in the empirical chapters in order to present a range of experiences and outcomes, one might conceivably argue that there were more bad cases in, say, the postcommunist setting—just think of all the authoritarian states spawned by the breakup of the Soviet Union—than one might think having read chapter 7. This may or may not be correct, depending on the setting, but here I am concerned primarily with the *range* of outcomes and consider the individual cases representatives of their respective settings.

The settings that hold out the most promise of successful democratization are those following a devastating defeat in a major war, those following military rule in Europe, and those following a communist regime. Let us look at them one by one. Four things become immediately clear about the success of democracy-building in Germany and Japan. First, their democratization process had enduring, and committed support from powerful democratic states. Second, both enjoyed high levels of social and economic development that aided postwar reconstruction. Third, because of the overwhelming political defeat of the ancien régime, institution builders could start pretty much with a clean slate and did not need to excessively concern themselves with appeasing the old ruling class. Finally, these societies' memories of the excesses of militarism and the devastation visited on them by a horrible, self-inflicted war are likely to have motivated the extraordinary dedication of political and societal elites to create a democratic future and democratic civil-military relations. My "interesting" case in this context, Hungary after World War II, was decisively influenced by a well-nigh omnipotent external power, the Soviet Union, that turned the country into a communist dictatorship.

As we have seen, another setting favorable to democratization was Southern Europe after military rule. Although the shining example in this regard is clearly Spain, Portugal has also succeeded in developing democratic military politics even if it has taken longer. Greece is somewhat of an outlier primarily because of the weakness of its parliament in defense-security affairs. The important commonality in all three cases is the lure of membership in international organizations, particularly the European Economic Community (the precursor of the European Union), which hold out the promise of prosperity and international respectability for the sake of which political compromises are worth making.

Postcommunist states, particularly European postcommunist states, have also been quite adept at transforming their civil-military relations. Slovenia was perhaps the most successful among them but several others—Poland, the Czech Republic, and Hungary—had compiled strong records as well. The prospect of NATO and European Union membership were strong incentives for postcommunist states, especially those, like Bulgaria, Romania, and Slovakia, whose progress toward democratic consolidation was more halting in the 1990s. In other words, just as in Southern Europe, in Eastern Europe, too, international organizations were able to push domestic policies in a more democratic direction. Another reason for the relative success in building democratic armies in the postcommunist context is that this setting posed comparatively few difficult challenges for transforming civil-military relations. Most importantly, communist armies were firmly under civilian control even if that control was exercised by the communist party. Once party organizations were banished from the barracks, the hardest project was to infuse legislative oversight with substance.

Nonetheless, the evidence from our case studies suggests that the kind of context we are considering has no decisive correlation with the successful democratization of military affairs. The after-military-rule setting spawned positive examples in the Southern European context, but experiences in Latin America and Asia were more mixed. And as I noted above, it would have been easy to select three cases of failed democratization from the postcommunist world—say Azerbaijan, Kyrgyzstan, and Turkmenistan—had I not been concerned with studying a range of experiences.

In the other settings we considered, there were few cases of democratizing civil-military relations that did not have some serious drawbacks. The exception may be South Korea, which succeeded for a number of reasons that included solid political leadership, relative economic prosperity, robust civil society, and the absence of the divisive issue of ethno-religious identity, the last particularly important in postcolonial and post–civil war settings. Botswana could be another such outlier were it not for the domineering role of the executive branch in its civil-military relations.

Are there ever good reasons to dismantle the old army before building the new one?

I began this book by invoking the Iraqi Army's dismissal by American officials, which many considered a major policy error. Has there ever been a solid justification for taking such a step?

After World War II the German and Japanese armed forces were demobilized, however not so much because they were defeated but because they represented genocidal regimes, and, therefore, new armies had to be built on democratic foundations. (Even if one considers Saddam Hussein's regime similarly diabolical, the virtually inevitable and immediate practical consequences of dismissing his army should have counseled against that decision.) In any event, as we saw, some of the members of both the German and the Japanese wartime armies were allowed to join the Bundeswehr and the Self-Defense Forces after a thorough cleansing of personnel because their skills were urgently needed.

American policy-makers in Iraq should have followed a three-step process. First, they should have taken the Iraqi Army as it was at the end of the war and carefully purged from it elements whose past human rights abuses, manifest incompetence, and active political loyalties (i.e., more than pro forma Ba'ath party membership) made them unsuitable to serve in the new army even in the short term. Second, while retaining the acceptable officers, NCOs, and soldiers from the old armed forces, the United States should have built, trained, and educated a new army based on democratic principles. Third, once the objective of building a new army was accomplished, it should have removed the remaining personnel from the old army if such was so desired.

Policy-makers the world over have adopted this approach in a variety of contexts. The Bolsheviks did not dismiss the czarist army, because they needed it, at least temporarily. In early 1979 Ayatollah Khomeini also recognized the imperative to maintain domestic order and to thwart foreign military threats and, therefore, the necessity to reconstitute the Shah's armed forces prudently.[1] In postcolonial India, Pakistan, Ghana, and Tanzania, not only did the extant armies remain—recall that Nehru preferred to retain the personnel of the British India Army instead of adopting the Indian National Army that had been active in the anticolonial struggle—but so did some of their British leadership while circumstances required. Of all our cases, Tanzania's Julius Nyerere probably came closest to discharging the army following the 1964 Mutiny, but a substantial portion of the personnel, including the majority of officers, stayed in the new Tanzanian People's Defence Force, which was extensively reformed and rebuilt but certainly not "from scratch," as Nyerere occasionally claimed. Postcommunist armies also found a new lease on life after democratization began and undesirable officers were removed and/or retired. In fact, after surveying the six different settings and twenty-seven military establishments with all their disparities, we encountered no armed forces, other than the Wehrmacht and the Imperial Japanese Army, that were dismissed following the fall of the old regime. Quite simply, it is a choice that is awfully difficult to justify.

POLICY RECOMMENDATIONS:
WHAT TO DO, WHAT TO AVOID

The third general question I asked in the introduction regarded the main conditions and policies that fostered the development of democratic civil-military relations. What attributes are shared by the states and societies that have succeeded in building democratic armies and military politics? What should democracy activists and politicians do in the defense-security domain to hasten democratic consolidation? What should they avoid doing? What advice can we offer to those who formulate and implement policy?

Good Leaders

The availability of inspired and inspiring leadership is obviously not a "policy recommendation" but a factor that can be and has often been exceedingly important in successful democratization. Generally speaking, the more sophisticated the network of political institutions and the more highly developed the political system, the less impact individual leaders can have. In contrast, where political institutions are embryonic and basic political relationships are yet to be defined—such as, for instance, after colonial rule—good leaders can be hugely influential. Put differently, a long-standing consolidated democracy can successfully weather a mediocre and even an incompetent leader, while for a fragile state in the process of regime transition, a bad leader could be ruinous. Charismatic postcolonial leaders like Jawaharlal Nehru, Kwame Nkrumah, and Julius Nyerere are often instrumental in establishing their countries' first effective political parties.[2]

From our study, Nyerere and Seretse Khama emerge as great postcolonial leaders who astutely conceived the proper role of the armed forces in their states. Following the 1964 Mutiny, Nyerere understood that Tanzania's political stability required close collaboration between the party-state and the military. Seretse Khama, however, wisely refused to establish a standing army until security threats made it necessary, more than a decade after independence. It is easy to appreciate the stature of these politicians when they are contrasted with someone like Nkrumah, who, while no less charismatic a person, was far more concerned with burnishing his own myth while needlessly antagonizing the army and running his country into the ground. Nehru is an unusual example of an otherwise great leader who was utterly ignorant of military affairs but, nonetheless, got deeply involved in them. He marginalized and humbled India's highly professional armed forces and involved the country in an unnecessary war it could not win.

Strong and enlightened political leadership is especially beneficial during regime change. Several states we studied were fortunate to have excellent, even visionary leaders like Konrad Adenauer and Yoshida Shigeru in times of epochal transformations. A number of them were instrumental in democratizing or attempting to democratize civil-military relations: Kim Youngsam in South Korea, Chuan Leekpai in Thailand, Raúl Alfonsín in Argentina, Patricio Aylwin and Ricardo Lagos in Chile, and Alfredo Cristiani in El Salvador. As in other contexts, some leaders rise to the challenge in difficult times while others do not. Michelle Bachelet, a victim of Pinochet's rule, became an outstanding politician and an able and judicious steward of the Chilean armed forces as defense minister and later, as president. But Néstor and Cristina Kirchner needlessly antagonized and humiliated the Argentine military as an institution decades after the fall of the praetorian regime. Monarchs, unelected as they are, are no exception. Spain was lucky to have King Juan Carlos during the heady days of the 1981 coup attempt; Thailand's widely idolized King Bhumibol Adulyadej, however, has continued to support coup-makers and military rule and has remained deeply apprehensive about real, substantive, democracy.

Clarity: Unambiguous and Transparent Institutional Framework

Providing the armed forces with a transparent political environment ought to be a key objective of democratizers. Constitutions should be clear about the chain of command in peacetime, wartime, and in cases of national emergency. Just how important it is to clarify what signifies a "national emergency" was demonstrated by the Salvadoran example. What is an acceptable political endeavor by active-duty, reserve, and retired armed forces personnel—should they be able to vote? join parties? appear in uniform in political rallies? run for office?—must be explained and regulated, and the consequences of noncompliance unambiguously and consistently applied.

In its dealings with the armed forces leadership, the government should strive for transparency. If at all possible, political leaders should explain to the top brass, for instance, the political, social, economic justifications for the defense budget, why the promotion of General X is vetoed by the prime minister, or the reasons for party debates regarding the abolition of universal conscription. Such transparency reduces insecurity, builds trust, and helps eliminate rumor mongering and scheming.

Gradualism and Compromise

In many democratic transitions following military rule, swift and drastic changes are inadvisable, because they might unnecessarily provoke the ire of those for whom regime change means the loss of their power and privileges. Following a gradualist approach that favors coalition-building and a willingness to make acceptable compromises is usually a prudent way to proceed. For instance, Adolfo Suárez, Spain's first democratically elected prime minister, was smart to collaborate with reformist groups within the army and implement changes after consulting with them. In South Korea, too, Kim Young-sam was wise to discuss his reform initiatives with influential generals. They, in turn, became supporters of his reform program and used their clout to neutralize budding opposition to it in the high command.

In countries where the armed forces retain some political clout and public esteem after withdrawing from power, it is especially important not to needlessly antagonize them by overly rapid reform programs designed to reduce their autonomy and perquisites. The inability of politicians to compromise when necessary or to cut some slack to the generals on issues of minor importance might easily serve to alienate people who would be otherwise willing to subordinate themselves to civilian control. In other words, strategic compromises can enhance the prospects of successful democratic consolidation and civilian control over the armed forces. For example, Patricio Aylwin was wise not to start prosecuting generals for human rights abuses, because he understood that the timing was not right and that insistence on expediency could have resulted in a military coup. Nevertheless, by establishing the Rettig Commission, he signaled to Chileans that neither Pinochet's victims nor his henchmen would be forgotten. In due course, once the army's political influence had faded and Pinochet was no longer a lightning rod for the officers' political activism, those guilty of human rights violations began to be held accountable. In a like vein, Indonesian President Yudhoyono acted judiciously by not insisting on terminating the armed forces' business activities in late 2009. He understood that budgetary restrictions did not permit the drastic expansion of defense outlays that would have been imperative to cover the revenue—revenue which, in part, was used for operational expenses—the military would lose if they were banished from the economic realm. This concession ensured the generals' quiescence while allowing the state to gradually improve finances and create the fiscal conditions for the army's complete withdrawal from money-making ventures.

Strengthen Legislative Involvement

One of the important conclusions of this book is that there is a direct correlation between vigorous parliamentary participation in defense-security affairs and democratic civil-military relations. Consequently, enhancing the legislature's clout—by increasing the authority of its defense committee(s) and encouraging or even requiring its substantive contribution to procedures and deliberations pertaining to the armed forces—should be a priority for democracy activists. In fact, the legislature's robust involvement in defense issues is usually a reliable predictor of democratic civil-military relations.

In consolidated democracies members of parliament are (or, at any rate, should be) genuine representatives of their constituents. Nevertheless, in many democracies legislators do not play an independent role in overseeing the armed forces owing to limitations in their ability to act, insufficient access to objective data and information imposed by a more influential executive branch, or lack of expertise or interest in defense matters. Inadequate legislative involvement in the defense-security domain is a shortcoming in numerous states—such as Botswana, Greece, and Japan—that otherwise have overwhelmingly positive civil-military relations.

In only a few polities does the legislature play the kind of role necessary for properly balanced civilian control of the military. This role comprises not just the debating and passing of defense-related bills but, crucially important, taking an active part in three aspects of the armed forces' fiscal affairs: determining the process of how defense budgets are devised and by what institutions; participating in the formulation of the actual defense budget; and overseeing the disbursement and implementation of defense outlays. In our case pool the countries with a long-term—say, twenty-year—record of active and vigorous parliamentary oversight were Germany and Spain; we can add to this group Bosnia and Herzegovina, Slovenia and South Africa if we relax the condition requiring sustained performance.

Giving the legislature too much power over the armed forces, however, can result in an unbalanced institutional arrangement. This is admittedly a rare occurrence, its emblematic case is post–Cold War Germany, but it is nonetheless associated with serious problems. More specifically, a dominant role over the army by the legislature hampers expeditious political decision-making and compromises the armed forces' fundamental functions in a democracy, namely as able and ready defenders of the state and/or as active and useful participants in military alliances.

It is worth noting that the effectiveness of both Germany and Spain as NATO members is diminished, but not because their armies lack professionalism. Rather, politicians in Berlin and Madrid are loath to send their armed forces to participate in NATO operations, and when they do, German and Spanish units operate under restrictions that limit their utility. There seems to be a positive correlation between legislative authority and a lack of enthusiasm for military deployments abroad. One might argue that parliamentarians enjoy a closer link with society, which ultimately spawns soldiers, than members of the executive branch, the policy-makers who are more directly involved in decisions regarding military deployments.

Promote Civilian/Societal Participation in Security Affairs

Independent civilian defense experts, nongovernmental organizations, and journalists focusing on security issues can play a beneficial role in advising elected officials and the public about military affairs. Their involvement encourages transparency and promotes confidence between society, the state, and the armed forces. Introducing defense-related courses at universities, allowing civilians—journalists, bureaucrats, politicians, etc.—to enroll in appropriate programs at military academies, and providing public funding on a competitive basis to NGOs studying defense issues would contribute to the overall improvement of democratic civil-military relations. In general, guaranteed media freedoms are not just a requisite of democratic civil-military relations; without them democracy cannot be consolidated. Democratizing elites must accept that supervising the media is not the state's function; rather, it is the media's responsibility to keep an eye on the state.

Civic Education and Military Training: The Proper Role of the Military

Both in the school system and in military colleges and academies, students, trainees, and cadets should be taught about the appropriate role of the armed forces in a democratic state and society. The state must make an effort to teach its citizens from early on in their formal education that the army's role is limited to protecting them from foreign threats, providing assistance following natural disasters, and, if possible, assisting international peacekeeping operations. Similarly, professional military instruction from the basic training of conscripts or enlisted soldiers to the staff academy courses catering to senior officers must feature educational components at the appropriate level on democratic political systems, civic engagement in security affairs, and the professional socialization of military personnel, underscoring again and again that, other than casting their votes, people in the military have no political role to play.

Military Reforms: Sequencing and Interference

As we have seen, different settings require different types of defense reforms. The main tasks for democracy-builders range from building new independent armies on the shaky or absent foundations left behind by imperial powers all the way to drastically reducing the autonomy, privileges, and size of the armed forces in postpraetorian environments. The thoughtful sequencing of defense reforms can be exceedingly important in ensuring the military's compliance and cooperation. Consulting with democratic-minded senior officers regarding the details and order of reform usually signals the state's willingness to consider the perspectives of the armed forces and can be expected to foster an agreeable interinstitutional climate. Such discussions do not mean, of course, that the government is obligated to take its generals' advice, but, as the Spanish case suggests, they are helpful in learning the top brass's preferences and usually benefit both sides. Military elites who are closely consulted by the state about prospective defense reforms are more likely to take ownership of the reforms, even if they do not agree with every single measure, than those who are cut out of the loop.

There are numerous other steps the state should take, such as, following Samuel Huntington's advice and decreasing the military's presence in the capital city and other political centers and developing political organizations capable of mobilizing throngs of supporters to help avert potential coup attempts.[3] Another eminently sensible Huntingtonian advice to civilian rulers is to identify themselves with the armed forces, attend their ceremonies, award medals, and praise the soldiers as exemplifying the most noble virtues of the nation.[4] To illustrate the good sense of this point, we need look no further than postpraetorian Argentina. As I noted in chapter 5, President Carlos Menem significantly reduced the military's political autonomy and budget and yet was held in high regard by the officer corps due to his positive gestures signaling his appreciation of the armed forces. In contrast, the Kirchners created an unpleasant atmosphere between the executive branch and the army that has been damaging to civil-military relations.

Ideally, the army's involvement in the economy should be terminated. At the same time, sequencing is critical: practical issues must be considered before hastily outlawing the military's commercial pursuits. For instance, if the resources the military gains from its business activities are used for vital operational expenses, where will the funds to cover those costs come from? If there is no satisfactory answer to this dilemma, a timetable should be set for the military's gradual withdrawal from the economy during which the state must find the resources to compensate for the lost revenue. Rigidly abiding by the timetable, however, is not advisable and compromises might have to be made—as in Indonesia—for the sake of the larger public good, democratic consolidation.

The state should have the ability to oversee the promotion of the most senior members of the armed forces. (In small- and medium-sized armies promotions over the rank of colonel should be approved by appropriate civilian officials; in a large army, perhaps such approval should be extended to those to be advanced beyond the two-star-general level.) At the same time, if politicians veto promotions, they must make sure their reasoning is based on solid evidence regarding the objectionable candidate's professional incompetence, or political attitudes incompatible with democratic civil-military relations. Politicians should not interfere with the routine promotions of those in the lower ranks nor should they get in the way of military education, training, and professional concerns unless these are in conflict with fundamental democratic values.

Identifying New Missions

In numerous countries experiencing democratic transitions, the obvious question of "what do we need armed forces for" has been the subject of public debate. Why maintain an expensive army, people in the Czech Republic and Slovenia asked in the absence of any real security threats or troublesome neighbors? In Argentina and Chile, too, journalists and pundits frequently question the utility of the armed forces. Nonetheless, there are very real uses for the military even in the post–Cold War world. A state ought to have the capacity to protect itself from potential threats to its security and to fulfill its alliance obligations. Armed forces are also needed, for instance, to defend a country's air space from unauthorized air traffic and to repel illegal fishing vessels from its coastal waters. Conventional armed forces ordinarily are unique in possessing the capacity to provide help in natural disasters.

Huntington wrote that policy-makers should equip their armies with "new and fancy tanks, planes, armored cars, artillery, and sophisticated electronic equipment," in other words, "give them toys" to keep them happy and occupied.[5] But most states do not enjoy the resources necessary to take this advice; what should they do? One important part of the solution is to search for new missions for the military. For instance, the government could sign up the armed forces to participate in international peacekeeping operations. These activities will make soldiers feel useful, enhance their own prestige as well as the international regard for their countries, and, might even be a significant source of income for military personnel in poor states. In addition, the special skills and training that peacekeepers require creates the need for international peacekeeping centers, conflict prevention, management, and resolution programs that boost international cooperation and improve the army's public image at home.[6]

Alternatively, the armed forces can also be trained to provide humanitarian assistance and disaster relief abroad. Such a strategy generally requires enhancing the military's airlift and transportation capabilities though such services may be provided by a more prosperous partner nation. Another worthwhile objective is preparing specialized military units for counterterrorism operations. The military should participate in these sorts of missions abroad, however, within the framework of international operations. Domestic counterterrorist activities that might involve the generals in politics should be avoided and left to the police, intelligence, and/or paramilitary organizations. In general, a sensible government would seek to design and build an increasingly outward-looking military establishment.

Maintaining a military establishment is an expensive proposition, and, especially for states undergoing the democratization process, it can often be politically risky. Therefore, if no productive endeavors can be found for active-duty armed forces personnel, if there is no societal support for keeping the army at its current size, *and* if the political risks of reducing the military establishment are manageable, then it should be pared down to the level politicians, experts, and societal groups believe is indispensable for national security.

Use the Military's Expertise

States and societies make considerable sacrifices to educate, train, equip, and otherwise maintain their armed forces. Marginalizing military officers by not asking their advice in the process of devising defense and/or foreign policy, let alone military strategy—as in Argentina and India, for instance—is irresponsible public policy and wasteful of public resources. In other words, officers acquire their specialized knowledge at a significant cost to taxpayers who should get some return on their investment.

Limiting the Public Engagement of Retired Generals

In many countries, including some liberal democracies such as the United States, high-ranking officers accept lucrative jobs as lobbyists, consultants, and military advisers as soon as they retire. Former generals who are hired by defense contractors turn into acquisition consultants whose influence is used to serve the interests of their employers and contravene those of the public. This practice is unethical and harmful to civil-military relations.[7] South Korean law prohibits the employment of officers by defense firms for five years after their retirement. This is an excellent example of an important lesson that the United States and other long-consolidated democracies could learn from relative newcomers to their ranks.

The Bottom Line

Finally, I want to reiterate that these recommendations depend largely on local conditions. While allowing the South Korean armed forces to continue their business activities would have been a serious mistake it was an acceptable compromise in Indonesia. Organizing army units by ethnic group or religion generally impedes societal integration, but doing so in post–civil war settings for a limited time may be the price to pay for stability and democratic consolidation. Many other examples could be cited from our case-study pool. The point is that what makes sense in one place may not in another. Good leadership helps as do good laws, sensible defense reforms, active parliamentary involvement, societal participation, and so on. And, as always, sheer luck plays a significant role. At the end of the day, we must recognize that, as disappointing as it is, there is no sure-fire road map to democratization.

There is no perfect democracy, and there are no perfect civil-military relations. True democracies are perennially engaged in the process of democratization. It is a continuous undertaking; as times change, new circumstances develop producing new challenges that require constant rethinking, adjustment, and improvement. The most important objective, as I stated at the beginning of this book, is to continue advancing toward that elusive ideal, the perfect democracy. If politicians manage to do this, they will ultimately succeed in improving their democracies and building truly democratic armies.

NOTES

⊰⊱

INTRODUCTION

1. Ali Allawi, *The Occupation of Iraq: Winning the War, Losing the Peace* (New Haven, CT: Yale University Press, 2007), 157.

2. David L. Phillips, *Losing Iraq: Inside the Postwar Reconstruction Fiasco* (New York: Basic Books, 2005), 153.

3. *Democracy and the Market* (New York: Cambridge University Press, 1991), 29.

4. *Democracy and Its Critics* (New Haven: Yale University Press, 1989), 245.

5. Bermeo, "Surprise, Surprise: Lessons from 1989 and 1991," in Bermeo, ed., *Liberalization and Democratization: Change in the Soviet Union and Eastern Europe* (Baltimore, MD: Johns Hopkins University Press, 1992), 198; and Stepan, *Rethinking Military Politics* (Princeton, NJ: Princeton University Press, 1988), ix.

6. Cambridge, MA: Belknap Press of Harvard University Press, 1957.

7. New Haven, CT: Yale University Press, 1968.

8. Norman: University of Oklahoma Press, 1991.

9. Alain Rouquié, *The Military and the State in Latin America* (Berkeley: University of California Press, 1989), 2.

10. Paul Pierson, "When Effect Becomes Cause: Policy Feedback and Political Change," *World Politics*, 45:4 (July 1993): 602. See also Kathleen Thelen, "Historical Institutionalism in Comparative Politics," *Annual Review of Political Science*, 2 (June 1999): 369–404.

11. The large majority of explanatory variables—organized by their primary relevance to state, military, and society—appear in *every* table and thus facilitate comparisons. Tables for chapters discussing the same settings (following military rule and after colonialism) for multiple regions present virtually identical sets of variables.

12. See David Collier and James Mahoney, "Insights and Pitfalls: Selection Bias in Qualitative Research." *World Politics*, 49:1 (1996): 56–91; and John Gerring, "Is There a (Viable) Crucial-Case Method?" *Comparative Political Studies*, 40:3 (March 2007): 231–53.

13. Gary King, Robert O. Keohane, and Sidney Verba, *Designing Social Inquiry: Scientific Interference in Qualitative Research* (Princeton, NJ: Princeton University Press, 1994), 209–12.

14. Serra, *The Military Transition: Democratic Reform of the Armed Forces*. Translated by Peter Bush (Cambridge, UK: Cambridge University Press, 2010), 39.

Chapter 1

1. Niccolò Machiavelli, *The Prince*. Edited and translated by David Wootton (Indianapolis/Cambridge: Hackett Publishing Company, Inc., 1995), 38. I thank Nancy Bermeo for bringing this quote to my attention.

2. Max Weber, *The Theory of Social and Economic Organization* (New York: Free Press, 1964), 154.

3. E-mail communication from Adam Przeworski (2 March 2011).

4. Randall Collins, *Weberian Sociological Theory* (New York: Cambridge University Press, 1986), 31–322.

5. Plato, *The Republic*. Translated by G.M.A. Grube (Indianapolis: Hackett, 1974), 43.

6. Juvenal, *Sixteen Satires*. Translated by Peter Green (New York: Penguin, 1999), 45.

7. Peter D. Feaver, "The Civil-Military Problematique: Huntington, Janowitz, and the Question of Civilian Control," *Armed Forces & Society*, 23:2 (Winter 1996): 150.

8. Samuel P. Huntington, *The Soldier and the State* (Cambridge, MA: Belknap Press of Harvard University Press, 1957), 2.

9. Douglas L. Bland, "Patterns in Liberal Democratic Civil-Military Relations," *Armed Forces & Society*, 27:4 (Summer 2001): 529.

10. Thucydides, *History of the Peloponnesian War*. Translated by Richard Crawley (London: Dent, 1993), 67–71.

11. See Sandra J. Bingham, "The Praetorian Guard in the Political and Social Life of Julio-Claudian Rome" (Ph.D. diss., University of British Columbia, August 1997); and Jonathan P. Roth, *Roman Warfare* (New York: Cambridge University Press, 2009), 151–90. I am grateful to Dr. Bingham for her comments (e-mail communication, 25–26 August 2010).

12. See, for instance, Sara Elise Phang, *Roman Military Service* (New York: Cambridge University Press, 2008).

13. Plato, *The Republic*, 44.

14. Ibid., 43.

15. Sun Tzu, *The Art of War*. Translated by Samuel B. Griffin (Oxford: Oxford University Press, 1963), 35–36.

16. Sun Tzu II, *The Lost Art of War*. Translated by Thomas Cleary (New York: HarperCollins, 1996), 73.

17. Ibid., 111–13.

18. Sun Tzu, *The Art of War*, 64.

19. Machiavelli, *The Prince*, 45–46.

20. Niccolò Machiavelli, *The Art of War*. Translated by Neal Wood (Cambridge, MA: Da Capo Press, 1964), xiii, 22. The eminent 19th–20th century Italian political

``scientist, Gaetano Mosca, thought that "once regularly organized mercenaries have become the preponderant force in a country, they have normally tried to force their rule upon the rest of society." See *The Ruling Class*. Translated by Hannah D. Kahn (New York: McGraw-Hill, 1939), 226.

21. Harvey C. Mansfield, *Machiavelli's Virtue* (Chicago, IL: University of Chicago Press, 1996), 198, 201.

22. Machiavelli, *The Art of War*, 33–34.

23. Collins, *Weberian Sociological Theory*, 92.

24. See for instance, Ian Gentles, *The New Model Army—In England, Ireland and Scotland 1645–53* (Oxford: Blackwell, 1994).

25. Carl von Clausewitz, *On War*. Translated by Michael Howard and Peter Paret (Princeton, NJ: Princeton University Press, 1989), 592.

26. Huntington, *The Soldier and the State*, 37.

27. Ibid., 73.

28. Douglass C. North, John Joseph Wallis, and Barry R. Weingast, *Violence and Social Orders: A Conceptual Framework for Interpreting Recorded Human History* (New York: Cambridge University Press, 2009), 153, 176.

29. Thomas N. Winter, "Cincinnatus and the Disbanding of Washington's Army," *Classical Bulletin*, 51:6 (April 1975): 81–86.

30. Richard K. Betts, "Are Civil-Military Relations Still a Problem?" in Suzanne C. Nielsen, and Don M. Sneider, eds., *American Civil-Military Relations: The Soldier and the State in a New Era* (Baltimore, MD: Johns Hopkins University Press, 2009), 41. See also, Russell F. Weigley, "The American Military and the Principle of Civilian Control from McClellan to Powell," *Journal of Military History*, 57:5 (October 1993): 27–58.

31. See Alexander Harrison, *Challenging De Gaulle: The OAS and the Counterrevolution in Algeria, 1954–1962* (New York: Praeger, 1989); and Alistair Horne, *A Savage War of Peace: Algeria 1954–1962* (New York: New York Review of Books, 2006).

32. Morris Janowitz, *The Professional Soldier: A Social and Political Portrait* (Glencoe, IL: Free Press, 1960).

33. Ibid., 225.

34. See, for instance, James Burk, "Theories of Democratic Civil-Military Relations," *Armed Forces & Society*, 29:1 (Fall 2002): 14.

35. See, for instance, Bland, "Patterns," 527; and John P. Lovell and David E. Albright, "Merging Theory and Practice," in Lovell and Albright, eds., *To Sheathe the Sword: Civil-Military Relations in the Quest for Democracy* (Westport, CT: Greenwood Press, 1997), 1.

36. See Peter D. Feaver and Erika Seeler, "Before and After Huntington: The Methodological Maturing of Civil-Military Studies," in Nielsen and Snider, eds., 72–90.

37. See, for instance, John J. Johnson, ed., *The Role of the Military in Underdeveloped Countries* (Princeton, NJ: Princeton University Press, 1962); Edward Luttwak, *Coup d'État: A Practical Handbook* (Cambridge, MA: Harvard University Press, 1968); and Donald L. Horowitz, *Coup Theories and Officers' Motives* (Princeton, NJ: Princeton University Press, 1980).

38. Finer, *The Man on Horseback: The Role of the Military in Politics* (London: Pall Mall, 1962), 140–63.

39. Stepan, *Rethinking Military Politics: Brazil and the Southern Cone* (Princeton, NJ: Princeton University Press, 1988), 92–97.

40. Serra, *The Military Transition: Democratic Reform of the Armed Forces.* Translated by Peter Bush (Cambridge, UK: Cambridge University Press, 2010), 43–49.

41. Risa A. Brooks, "Militaries and Political Activity in Democracies," in Nielsen and Snider, eds., 213–38.

42. One of the major theories is the principal-agent approach, furthest advanced by Peter D. Feaver in his *Armed Servants: Agency, Oversight, and Civil-Military Relations* (Cambridge, MA: Harvard University Press, 2005). This, however, is an America-centric approach that does not "travel" well and thus has limited relevance to my study.

43. Michael C. Desch, *Civilian Control of the Military: The Changing Security Environment* (Baltimore, MD: Johns Hopkins University Press, 2001), 11.

44. Jongseok Woo, *Security Challenges and Military Politics in East Asia: From State-Building to Post-Democratization* (New York: Continuum, 2011), 10.

45. Andrew Cottey, Timothy Edmunds, and Anthony Forster, "The Second Generation Problematic: Rethinking Democracy and Civil-Military Relations," *Armed Forces & Society*, 29:1 (Fall 2002): 31–56.

46. Serra, 39–89.

47. "Building Trust: Civil-Military Behavior for Effective National Security," in Nielsen and Snider, eds., 287.

48. Huntington, *The Soldier and the State*, 18.

49. Feaver, "The Civil-Military Problematique," 153–54.

50. Betts, 26.

51. Desch, *Civilian Control of the Military*, 4.

52. Richard H. Kohn, "How Democracies Control the Military," *Journal of Democracy*, 8:4 (October 1997): 142.

53. Samuel P. Huntington, "Civilian Control and the Constitution," *American Political Science Review*, 50:3 (September 1956): 678.

54. Huntington, *The Soldier and the State*, 83.

55. Claude E. Welch, Jr. "Civilian Control of the Military: Myth and Reality," in Welch, ed., *Civilian Control of the Military: Theory and Cases from Developing Countries* (Albany: State University of New York Press, 1976), 2.

56. Desch, *Civilian Control of the Military*; and Feaver, *Armed Servants*.

57. Kohn, "How Democracies Control the Military," 14.

58. Robin Luckham, "Democratic Strategies for Security in Transition and Conflict," Gavin Cawthra and Robin Luckham, eds., *Governing Insecurity: Democratic Control of Military and Security Establishments in Transitional Democracies* (London: Zed Books, 2003), 15. See also, Andreas Schedler, ed., *Electoral Authoritarianism: The Dynamics of Unfree Competition* (Boulder, CO: Lynne Rienner, 2006).

59. Robert A. Dahl, *Democracy and Its Critics* (New Haven, CT: Yale University Press, 1989), 245.

60. Jean Kinney Giraldo, "Legislatures and National Defense: Global Comparisons," in Thomas C. Bruneau and Scott Tollefson, eds., *Who Guards the Guardians and How* (Austin: University of Texas Press, 2006), 43.

61. A few democracies, most prominently the United Kingdom, do not have written constitutions but they do have clearly established rules governing institutions and institutional interactions.

62. Kohn, "How Democracies Control the Military," 148–49.

63. Larry Diamond, *Developing Democracy: Toward Consolidation* (Baltimore, MD: Johns Hopkins University Press, 1999), 113.

64. Juan J. Linz, *The Breakdown of Democratic Regimes: Crisis* (Baltimore, MD: Johns Hopkins University Press, 1978), 30.

65. Thomas C. Bruneau and Richard P. Goetze, Jr., "Ministries of Defense and Democratic Control," in Bruneau and Tollefson, eds., 78–81.

66. I use the qualification of "modern" because, for instance, in foregone eras, the armed forces of North and South American states played a major role in their country's geographical expansion.

67. Christopher Dunn, "Democracy in the 21st Century: Canada Needs a War Powers Act," *Canadian Parliamentary Review*, 30:3 (Autumn 2007): 2–3.

68. Anthony Lang, ed., *Political Theory and International Affairs: Hans J. Morgenthau on Aristotle's The Politics* (Westport, CT: Praeger, 2004), 76.

69. Peter D. Feaver, "Civil-Military Relations," *Annual Review of Political Science*, 2 (June 1999): 226.

70. Thomas-Durrell Young, "Military Professionalism in a Democracy," in Bruneau and Tollefson, eds., 22.

71. Paul Shemella, "The Spectrum of Roles and Missions of the Armed Forces," in Bruneau and Tollefson, eds., 124.

72. Whitehead, "International Aspects of Democratization," in Guillermo O'Donnell, Philippe Schmitter, and Laurence Whitehead, eds. *Transitions from Authoritarian Rule: Comparative Perspectives* (Baltimore: Johns Hopkins University Press, 1986), 20.

73. See, for instance, Zoltan Barany, "NATO's Peaceful Advance," *Journal of Democracy*, 15:1 (January 2004): 63–76.

74. See Thomas Bruneau and Harold Trinkunas. "Democratization as a Global Phenomenon and Its Impact on Civil-Military Relations," *Democratization*, 13:5 (December 2006): 776–90.

75. See Deborah Avant, "War, Recruitment Systems, and Democracy," in Elizabeth Kier and Ronald Krebs, eds., *In War's Wake: International Conflict and the Fate of Liberal Democracy* (New York: Cambridge University Press, 2010), 235–52.

76. Cited in Lang, ed., *Political Theory and International Affairs*, 76.

77. Young, "Military Professionalism in a Democracy," in Bruneau and Tollefson, eds., 28.

78. The most complete representation of this view is in Peter D. Feaver and Richard H. Kohn, eds., *Soldiers and Civilians: The Civil-Military Gap and American National Security* (Cambridge, MA: MIT Press, 2001). See also Beth Bailey, *Amer-*

ica's Army: Making the All-Volunteer Force (Cambridge, MA: Harvard University Press, 2009).

79. See, for instance, Henry Dietz, Jerrold Elkin, and Maurice Roumani, eds., *Ethnicity, Integration, and the Military* (Boulder, CO: Westview, 1991).

80. The desegregation of the armed services did not officially end until Secretary of Defense Charles Erwin Wilson announced on 30 September 1954 that the last all-black unit had been abolished.

81. For very different views on these subjects, see for instance, Stephanie Gutmann, *The Kinder, Gentler Military: Can America's Gender-Neutral Fighting Force Still Win Wars?* (New York: Scribner, 2000); Martin van Creveld, *Men, Women & War: Do Women Belong in the Front Line?* (London: Cassell & Co., 2001); and Marion Andersen-Boers and Jan Van der Meulen, "Homosexuality and the Armed Forces in the Netherlands," in Wilbur J. Scott and Sandra Carson Stanley, eds., *Gays and Lesbians in the Military* (Hawthorne, NY: Aldine de Gruyter, 1994), 205–18.

82. See Charles C. Moskos and John Sibley Butler, *All That We Can Be: Black Leadership and Racial Integration the Army Way* (New York: Basic Books, 1996); and James Burk, "The Military's Presence in American Society, 1950–2000," in Feaver and Kohn, eds., *Soldiers and Civilians*, 247–74.

83. Young, "Military Professionalism," 29.

84. See, for instance, William V. Kennedy, *The Military and the Media: Why the Press Cannot Be Trusted to Cover a War* (Westport, CT: Praeger, 1993); and Laura Roselle, *Media and the Politics of Failure: Great Powers, Communication Strategies, and Military Defeats* (New York: Palgrave Macmillan, 2006).

85. See Przeworski, "Capitalism, Democracy, and Science," in Gerardo L. Munck and Richard Snyder, eds., *Passion, Craft, and Method in Comparative Politics* (Baltimore, MD: Johns Hopkins University Press, 2006), 495.

86. Gaetano Mosca, *The Ruling Class*. Translated by Hannah D. Kahn (New York: McGraw-Hill, 1939), 229.

87. Finer, *The Man on Horseback: The Role of the Military in Politics* (London: Pall Mall, 1962), 5. Italics in the original.

88. Joseph S. Nye, "Epilogue: The Liberal Tradition," in Larry Diamond and Marc F. Plattner, eds., *Civil-Military Relations and Democracy* (Baltimore, MD: Johns Hopkins University Press, 1996), 151–56.

89. Jason K. Dempsey, *Our Army: Soldiers, Politics, and American Civil-Military Relations* (Princeton, NJ: Princeton University Press, 2010), 194–95.

90. See Giuseppe Di Palma, *To Craft Democracies* (Berkeley: University of California Press, 1990), 39.

91. David Pion-Berlin, "Political Management of the Military in Latin America," *Military Review*, January–February 2005, 31.

92. David R. Mares, "Conclusion," in Mares ed., *Civil-Military Relations* (Boulder, CO: Westview, 1998), 246.

93. See Nye, 152–53.

Chapter 2

1. Amos Perlmutter, *The Military and Politics in Modern Times* (New Haven, CT: Yale University Press, 1977), 45.

2. Donald Abenheim, *Reforging the Iron Cross: The Search for Tradition in the West German Armed Forces* (Princeton, NJ: Princeton University Press, 1988), 35.

3. Edward A. Shils and Morris Janowitz, "Cohesion and Disintegration in the Wehrmacht in World War II," *Public Opinion Quarterly*, 12:2 (Summer 1948): 280–315.

4. See, for instance, Omer Bartov, "Soldiers, Nazis, and War in the Third Reich," *Journal of Modern History*, 63:1 (March 1991): 44–60.

5. Samuel P. Huntington, *The Soldier and the State* (Cambridge: Belknap Press of Harvard University Press, 1957), 134–35.

6. See Roger F. Hackett, *Yamagata Aritomo and the Rise of Modern Japan, 1838–1922* (Cambridge, MA: Harvard University Press, 1971.)

7. Harold D. Lasswell, "The Garrison State," *American Journal of Sociology*, 46:4 (January 1941): 455–68.

8. Robert Guillain, "The Reemergence of Military Elements in Japan," *Pacific Affairs*, 25:3 (1952): 213.

9. Yale Candee Maxon, *Control of Japanese Foreign Policy: A Study of Civil-Military Rivalry, 1930–1945* (Berkeley: University of California Press, 1957), 196.

10. Wilfried Freiherr von Bredow, "Central Organization of Defense in the Federal Republic of Germany," in Martin Edmonds, ed., *Central Organizations of Defense* (Boulder, CO: Westview, 1985), 67.

11. Britain, Australia, and New Zealand played a much smaller role. New Zealand, for instance, provided a 12,000-strong force for the occupation between February 1946 and August 1948. For its fascinating history, see Laurie Brocklebank, *Jayforce: New Zealand and the Military Occupation of Japan, 1945–48* (Auckland: Oxford University Press, 1997).

12. "Missing," *Time Magazine*, 7 July 1952; and "Homecoming," *Time Magazine*, 12 October 1953.

13. See Gunter Bischof and Stephen E. Ambrose, eds., *Eisenhower and the German POWs: Facts Against Falsehood* (Baton Rouge: Louisiana State University Press, 1992); and Niall Ferguson, "Prisoner Taking and Prisoner Killing in the Age of Total War: Towards a Political Economy of Military Defeat," *War in History*, 11:2 (April 2004): 148–92.

14. Tetsuya Kataoka and Ramon H. Myers, *Defending an Economic Superpower: Reassessing the U.S.-Japan Security Alliance* (Boulder, CO: Westview, 1989), 10–11.

15. See I. I. Morris, *Nationalism and the Right Wing in Japan: A Study of Post-War Trends* (London: Oxford University Press, 1960).

16. Robert McGeehan, *The German Rearmament Question: American Diplomacy and European Defense after World War II* (Urbana: University of Illinois Press, 1971), 6–7, 12.

17. A. J. Birtle, *Rearming the Phoenix: U.S. Military Assistance to the Federal Republic of Germany, 1950–1960* (New York: Garland, 1991), 12.

18. See Clayton Will's article in *Freedom & Union*, June 1949, 9–10. Papers of Clayton Will, Hoover Institution Archives (Stanford, CA).

19. Dean Acheson, *Present at the Creation: My Years in the State Department* (New York: Norton, 1969), 436.

20. Jean Monnet, *Memoirs*. Translated by Richard Mayne (London: Collins, 1978), 337.

21. Thomas A. Schwartz, "Europe as the Solution: John J. McCloy and the Rearmament of Germany, 1949–1952" (Harvard University, 28 April 1986), unpublished paper, 19 pp.—this cite: 16 (Hoover Institution Archives.). See also, Alaric Searle, *Wehrmacht Generals, West German Society, and the Debate on Rearmament, 1949–1959* (Westport, CT: Praeger, 2003).

22. Hans-Erich Volkmann, "Die innenpolitische Dimension Adenauerscher Sicherheitspolitik in der EVG-Phase," in *Die EVG-Phase: Anfänge westdeutsche Sicherheitspolitik 1945 bis 1956*. Vol II. (Munich: Oldenbourg, 1990), 478.

23. See George R. Packard, *Protest in Tokyo: The Security Treaty Crisis of 1960* (Princeton, NJ: Princeton University Press, 1966); and Hanji Kinoshita, "Echoes of Militarism in Japan," *Pacific Affairs*, 26:3 (September 1953): 244–51.

24. Abenheim, 42. See also David Clay Large, *Germans to the Front: West German Rearmament in the Adenauer Era* (Chapel Hill: University of North Carolina Press, 1996).

25. Konrad Adenauer, *Memoirs, 1945–53*. Translated by Beate Ruhm von Oppen (Chicago, IL: Henry Regnery, 1966), 300.

26. Ralph Giordano, *Die Traditionslüge: Vom Kriegerkult in der Bundeswehr* (Cologne: Kiepenheuer & Witsch, 2000), 40–41.

27. "General Kielmansegg, a NATO Leader, Dies at 99," *New York Times*, 4 June 2006.

28. Jean Monnet's comment on the EDC's failure was that "forces of the past and those of the future tore the country apart." See Monnet, *Memoirs*, 397.

29. Birtle, 288.

30. Freiherr von Bredow, 77–78.

31. Birtle, 322.

32. See Ekkehard Lippert, Paul Schneider, and Ralf Zoll, "The Influence of Military Service on Political and Social Attitudes," *Armed Forces & Society*, 4:2 (February 1978): 265–82.

33. See Richard W. Kedzior, *Evolution and Endurance: The U.S. Army Division in the Twentieth Century* (Santa Monica, CA: RAND, 2000), 23–29.

34. Birtle, 327.

35. Abenheim, 234–35.

36. See John Dower, *Empire and Aftermath: Yoshida Shigeru and the Japanese Experience, 1878–1954* (Cambridge, MA: Harvard East Asia Center, 1988).

37. Kataoka and Myers, 4.

38. James Dobbins et al., *America's Role in Nation-Building: From Germany to*

Iraq (Santa Monica, CA: Rand, 2003), 41. See also, Harold S. Quigley, "The Great Purge in Japan," *Pacific Affairs*, 20:3 (September 1947): 299–308.

39. Masashi Nishihara, "The Japanese Central Organization of Defense," in Martin Edmonds, ed., *Central Organizations of Defense*, 134.

40. Richard J. Samuels, *Securing Japan: Tokyo's Grand Strategy and the Future of East Asia* (Ithaca, NY: Cornell University Press, 2007), 33.

41. Ron Matthews, "Japan's Security into the 1990s," in Ron Matthews and Keisuke Matsuyama, eds., *Japan's Military Renaissance?* (Basingstoke: Macmillan, 1993), 4.

42. Interview with Sabine Frühstück (Santa Barbara, CA, 19 May 2008). In a 1981 poll 82 percent of the Japanese regarded the SDF as constitutional; only 8 percent opposed it. See Nishihara, 135.

43. Yoshida Shigeru, *Yoshida Shigeru: The Last Meiji Man*. Edited by Hiroshi Nara, translated by Yoshida Ken'ichi and Hiroshi Nara (Lahham, MD: Rowman & Littlefield, 2007 [1961]), 157.

44. Richard J. Samuels, *Machiavelli's Children: Leaders and Their Legacies in Italy and Japan* (Ithaca, NY: Cornell University Press, 2003), 210.

45. Michael J. Green, *Arming Japan: Defense Production, Alliance Politics, and the Postwar Search for Autonomy* (New York: Columbia University Press, 1995), 10.

46. Morris, *Nationalism and the Right Wing in Japan*, 212.

47. Yoshida, 154.

48. Tetsuo Maeda, *The Hidden Army: The Untold Story of Japan's Military Forces*. Translated by Steven Karpa (Chicago: edition q, inc., 1995 [1990]), 73.

49. Maeda, 94–95.

50. Count Wolf von Baudissin, "The New German Army," *Foreign Affairs*, 34:1 (October 1955): 3. For a more comprehensive exposition, see his *Soldat für Frieden: Entwürfe für eine Zeitgemässe Bundeswehr* (Munich: S. Piper, 1969). For a recent history of *Innere Führung*, see Frank Nägler, *Der gewollte Soldat und sein Wandel* (Munich: Oldenbourg, 2009).

51. Cited in Freiherr von Bredow, 71–72.

52. See Rudolf J. Schlaffer, *Der Wehrbeauftragte 1951 bis 1985: Aus Sorge um den Soldaten* (Munich: Oldenbourg, 2006), particularly the first two parts that deal with the immediate post–World War II setting and the 1951–59 period (and how German policy-makers modified the Swedish model), respectively.

53. Abenheim, 217.

54. I thank Dale R. Herspring for clarification.

55. Samuels, *Machiavelli's Children*, 359.

56. Peter J. Katzenstein and Nobuo Okawara, *Japan's National Security: Structures, Norms and Policy Responses in a Changing World* (Ithaca, NY: Cornell University Press, 1993), 49–50.

57. Morris, 260.

58. Akio Watanabe, "Japan's Postwar Constitution and Its Implications for Defense Policy," in Matthews and Matsuyama, eds. *Japan's Military Renaissance?* 36.

59. See Richard J. Samuels, "Politics, Security Policy, and Japan's Cabinet Legislation Bureau: Who Elected These Guys, Anyway?" Japan Policy Research Institute PRI Working Paper No. 99 (March 2004).

60. Gaston J. Sigur, "Power, Politics, and Defense," in James H. Buck, ed., *The Modern Japanese Military System* (Beverly Hills, CA: Sage, 1975), 189.

61. Maeda, 136.

62. E-mail communication from Richard Samuels (May 2010).

63. Ian Gow, "Civilian Control of the Military in Postwar Japan," in Matthews and Matsuyama, eds. *Japan's Military Renaissance?* 59.

64. Abenheim, 90–91.

65. Freiherr von Bredow, 71. See also Manfred Dormann, *Democratische Militärpolitik* (Freiburg: Rembach, 1970).

66. Mark N. Gose, "The Role of the Military in Building Political Community: The Case of the Two German States" (Ph.D. diss., University of Colorado, 1995), 155.

67. Cited in Birtle, 221. See also Dieter Rossmeisl, *Demokratie von Aussen: Amerikanische Militärregierung in Nürnberg, 1945–1949* (Munich: Deutscher Taschenbuch Verlag, 1992), 156–57.

68. See Rüdiger Wenzke, *Staatsfeinde in Uniform?* (Berlin: Ch. Links Verlag, 2005), 7–10.

69. Birtle, 284.

70. I am grateful to Donald Abenheim for this point.

71. On these issues see Birtle, 259–64.

72. Ibid., 333.

73. Abenheim, 172–73.

74. Yoshida, 155–56.

75. See, for instance, Sabine Frühstück, *Uneasy Warriors: Gender, Memory, and Popular Culture in the Japanese Army* (Berkeley: University of California Press, 2008).

76. Maeda, 16–17.

77. Ibid., 101.

78. Thomas M. Brendle, "Recruitment and Training in the SDF," in James H. Buck, ed., *The Modern Japanese Military System* (Beverly Hills, CA: Sage, 1975), 67–96; here 71.

79. Cited in Maeda, 55.

80. Ibid., 57.

81. See, for instance, Krisztián Ungváry, *The Siege of Budapest: One Hundred Days in World War II* (New Haven, CT: Yale University Press, 2005).

82. See Peter Kenez, *Hungary from the Nazis to the Soviets: The Establishment of the Communist Regime in Hungary, 1944–1948* (New York: Cambridge University Press, 2006).

83. Bennett Kovrig, *Communism in Hungary from Kun to Kadar* (Stanford, CA: Hoover Institution Press, 1979), 154–210.

84. See, Stephen Kertész, *The Last European Peace Conference* (Lanham, MD: University Press of America, 1985).

85. Zoltan Barany, *Soldiers and Politics in Eastern Europe, 1945–90* (London: Macmillan, 1993), 41–42.

86. See Mark von Hagen, *Soldiers in the Proletarian Dictatorship: The Red Army and the Soviet Socialist State, 1917–1930* (Ithaca, NY: Cornell University Press, 1990).

87. F. Rubin, "The Hungarian People's Army," *RUSI Journal*, 121:3 (September 1976): 59.

88. János Kecskés, *"Vezéráldozatok"' vagyis mit tesznek a kiskirályok pánikban* (Budapest: Tornado Damenija, 1990), 8.

89. Béla Király, *Honvédségből Néphadsereg* (Budapest: Co-Nexus, 1989), 121.

90. Sándor Mucs, *Politika és hadsereg Magyarországon, 1944–1948* (Budapest: Zrínyi-Kossuth, 1985), 114–15.

91. See Barany, *Soldiers and Politics*, 47–49.

92. Ibid., 39.

93. Ibid., 43.

94. Ernő Zágoni, *Hadsereg, honvédelem* (Budapest: Zrínyi, 1968), 151.

95. Zoltan Barany, "Soviet Control of the Hungarian Military under Stalin," *Journal of Strategic Studies*, 14:2 (June 1991): 153.

96. Birtle, 167.

97. E-mail communication with Richard Samuels (May 2010).

98. On this issue, see Ian Buruma, *The Wages of Guilt: Memories of War in Germany and Japan* (London: Jonathan Cape, 1991).

99. Gow, 51.

100. See, for instance, B. H. Liddell Hart, *The Other Side of the Hill* (London: Cassell, 1948).

101. Birtle, 281–85.

102. Ibid., 285.

CHAPTER 3

1. Stathis N. Kalyvas, *The Logic of Violence in Civil War* (New York: Cambridge University Press, 2006), 17. For definitional issues, see Nicholas Sambanis, "What Is a Civil War? Conceptual and Empirical Complexities of an Operational Definition." *Journal of Conflict Resolution* 48:6 (December 2004): 814–58.

2. Lise Morjé Howard, *UN Peacekeeping in Civil Wars* (New York: Cambridge University Press, 2008), 88–89.

3. Ibid., 108. See also Margaret Popkin, "The Salvadoran Truth Commission and the Search for Justice," *Criminal Law Forum*, 15:1-2 (March 2004): 105–24.

4. Jack Snyder, *From Voting to Violence: Democratization and Nationalist Conflict* (New York: Norton, 2000), 204.

5. Stuart J. Kaufman, *Modern Hatreds: The Symbolic Politics of Ethnic War* (Ithaca, NY: Cornell University Press, 2001), 196.

6. Susan L. Woodward, "Bosnia and Herzegovina: How Not to End Civil War," in Barbara F. Walter and Jack Snyder, eds., *Civil Wars, Insecurity, and Intervention* (New York: Columbia University Press, 1999), 82.

7. Lara J. Nettlefield, *Courting Democracy in Bosnia and Herzegovina* (New York: Cambridge University Press, 2010), 217.

8. Cited in Tricia Juhn, *Negotiating Peace in El Salvador* (New York: St. Martin's Press, 1998), 10.

9. Ibid., 47–48.

10. Roland Paris, *At War's End: Building Peace after Civil Conflict* (New York: Cambridge University Press, 2004), 98.

11. Philip J. Williams and Knut Walter, *Militarization and Demilitarization in El Salvador's Transition to Democracy* (Pittsburgh, PA: University of Pittsburgh Press, 1997), 151.

12. For analyses of Washington's role during the civil war, see Michael J. Hennelly, "US Policy in El Salvador: Creating Beauty or the Beast?" *Parameters*, Spring 1993, 59–69; and Robert D. Ramsey, *Advising Indigenous Forces: American Advisors in Korea, Vietnam, and El Salvador* (Ft. Leavenworth, KS: Combat Studies Institute Press, 2006).

13. Howard, 92.

14. Ibid., 88.

15. Terry Lynn Karl, "El Salvador's Negotiated Revolution," *Foreign Affairs*, 71:2 (Spring 1992): 154.

16. Interviews in Sarajevo (April 2010).

17. Robert D. Kaplan, "Man versus Afghanistan," *Atlantic Monthly*, April 2010, 62.

18. For the full text of the agreement, see http://www.elsalvador.com/noticias/especiales/acuerdosdepaz2002/index.html.

19. See Andrew P. Miller, *Military Disengagement and Democratic Consolidation in Post-Military Regimes* (Lewiston, NY: Edwin Mellen, 2006), 69.

20. Juhn, 4.

21. Interview with Carlos Dada, editor of the San Salvador daily *El Faro* (Austin, TX, 18 November 2010).

22. Douglas A. Kincaid, "Demilitarization and Security in El Salvador and Guatemala," *Journal of Interamerican Studies and World Affairs*, 42:4 (Winter 2000): 44.

23. Woodward, 87.

24. See http://www.ohr.int/dpa/default.asp?content_id=380.

25. Mary Kaldor, "Security Structures in Bosnia and Herzegovina," in Gavin Cawthra and Robin Luckham, eds., *Governing Insecurity: Democratic Control of Military and Security Establishments in Transitional Democracies* (London: Zed Books, 2003), 220.

26. Woodward, 103.

27. Patrice C. McMahon and John Western, "The Death of Dayton," *Foreign Affairs*, 88:5 (September–October 2009): 70.

28. This paragraph draws on Holbrooke's *To End a War* (New York: Random House, 1998), 363–64.

29. Woodward, 104.

30. Lord Robertson, "The Work Ahead in Bosnia," *New York Times*, 25 November 2000.

31. Howard, 125.

32. See, for instance, Oliver Jütersonke, Robert Muggah, and Dennis Rodgers, "Gangs, Urban Violence, and Security Interventions in Central America," *Security Dialogue*, 40:4–5 (August–October 2009): 373–97; and Sonja Wolf, "*Maras transnacionales*: Origins and Transformations of Central American Street Gangs," *Latin American Research Review*, 45:1(2010): 256–65.

33. Paris, 114.

34. Holbrook, 344.

35. On the 2010 election, see Dan Bilefsky, "Bosnians Doubt Vote, and Future, Too," *New York Times*, 4 October 2010; and Joanna Kakissis, "In Bosnia One Step Closer to Unity—or Collapse?" *Time*, 4 October 2010. For a more general assessment, see Christopher S. Chivvis, "The Dayton Dilemma," *Survival*, 52:5 (October–November 2010): 47–74.

36. "Only Stable Bosnia Can Ensure Balkan Peace," *New York Times*, 2 September 2010.

37. Interview with NATO's Maxwell Rohan (Sarajevo, 14 April 2010).

38. Patrice C. McMahon, "Rebuilding Bosnia: A Model to Emulate or to Avoid?" *Political Science Quarterly*, 119:4 (Winter 2004–2005): 587.

39. Interview with Deputy High Representative Dr. Raffi Gregorian (Sarajevo, 14 April 2010).

40. Graeme P. Herd and Tom Tracy, "Democratic Civil-Military Relations in Bosnia and Herzegovina," *Armed Forces & Society*, 32:4 (July 2006): 558; and Sultan Barakat and Steven A. Zyck, "State Building and Post-Conflict Demilitarization: Military Downsizing in Bosnia and Herzegovina," *Contemporary Security Policy*, 30:3 (December 2009): 548–72.

41. See Michael Dobbs, "Muslim-Croat Federation Agrees To Form Joint Defense Ministry," *Washington Post*, 15 May 1996.

42. Interviews with army colonels, Senad Kljačić and Robert Susać, at the U.S. Naval Postgraduate School (Monterey, CA, 10 June 2008) and with Zeljko Grubešić of the legislature's Joint Defense and Security Committee (Sarajevo, 12 April 2010).

43. Kaldor, 215.

44. See Defence Reform Commission, *The Path to Partnership for Peace* (Sarajevo: Defence Reform Commission of Bosnia and Herzegovina, September 2003).

45. Interviews with Zeljko Grubešić and Leila Dizdarević of NATO (Sarajevo, 13 April 2010).

46. Interviews with Ahmet Hadziomerović, Assistant Minister of Defense for Policy and Planning (Sarajevo, 14 April 2010), and Maxwell Rohan.

47. Ambiguities originate in changing property relations from the Yugoslav National Army, to entity-level structures, and, finally, to the state of Bosnia and Herzegovina.

48. Howard, 114–15.

49. Miller, 72–73.

50. Kincaid, 44.

51. Howard, 115–16.

52. Tommie Sue Montgomery, *Revolution in El Salvador: From Civil Strife to Civil Peace* (Boulder, CO: Westview, 1995), 253.

53. See, for instance, Juhn, 168.

54. Interview with Dada.

55. Red de Seguridad y Defensa de América Latina, *A Comparative Atlas of Defence in Latin America* (Buenos Aires: Ser en el 2000, 2008), 199.

56. For a comparative perspective, see Mark Ensalaco, "Truth Commissions for Chile and El Salvador: A Report and Assessment," *Human Rights Quarterly*, 16:4 (November 1994): 656–75.

57. Williams and Walter, 169–70.

58. Ibid., 170.

59. For a more general perspective on this issue, see Charles Call, "War Transitions and the New Civilian Security in Latin America," *Comparative Politics*, 35:1 (October 2002): 1–20.

60. Ricardo Córdova Macías, *El Salvador: Reforma Militar y Relaciones Cívico-Militares* (San Salvador: Fundación Dr. Guillermo Manuel Ungo, 1999), 7.

61. See Alfredo Gonzales, "Civil-Military Relations in El Salvador: Change, Continuity, or Transformation?" paper presented at the Annual Meeting of the Western Political Science Association (Portland, OR, 6 April 2004).

62. Alexander Brockwehl and Juan Pablo Pitarque, "Concessions of a Leftist Party: The FMLN's Dilemma in the Face of Funes' Centrist Policies," *Council on Hemispheric Affairs Research Report*, 28 June 2010.

63. Tracy Chamoun, *Au nom du père* (Paris: J.-C. Lattès, 1992), 10 and 23, cited in Kalyvas, 59.

64. See Joseph A. Kéchichian, "The Lebanese Army: Capabilities and Challenges in the 1980s," *Conflict Quarterly*, 5:1 (Winter 1985): 15–39.

65. This paragraph draws on Oren Barak, *The Lebanese Army: A National Institution in a Divided Society* (Albany, NY: SUNY Press, 2009), 153–59.

66. Barak, 162.

67. See Hassan Krayem, "The Lebanese Civil War and the Taif Agreement," in Paul Salem, ed., *Conflict Resolution in the Arab World: Selected Essays* (Beirut: American University of Beirut Press, 1997), 422.

68. Krayem, 423. See also Imad Harb, "Lebanon's Confessionalism: Problems and Prospects," Peace Brief (United States Insitute of Peace, March 2006), http.usip .org/publications/lebanons-confessionalism-problems-and-prospects.

69. Barak, 180–81.

70. Karen Abi-Ezzi, "Lebanon: Confessionalism, Institution Building, and the Challenges of Securing Peace," in Vanessa E. Shields and Nicholas D. J. Baldwin, eds., *Beyond Settlement: Making Peace Last after Civil Conflict* (Teaneck, NJ: Fairleigh Dickinson University Press, 2008), 163–64.

71. Joseph A. Kéchichian, "A Strong Army for a Stable Lebanon," *The Middle East Institute Policy Brief*, #19 (September 2008), 5.

72. Fouad Makhzoumi, "Lebanon's Crisis of Sovereignty," *Survival*, 52:2 (April–May 2010): 7.

73. See for instance Farid el-Khazen, "Lebanon—Independent No More," *Middle East Quarterly*, 8:1 (2001): 43–50, and others cited by Barak, 171–72.

74. Adam Nerguizian and Anthony H. Cordesman, *The Lebanese Armed Forces: Challenges and Opportunities in Post-Syria Lebanon* (Washington, DC: Center for Strategic and International Studies, 2009), 21–22.

75. Barak, 179.

76. Ibid., 188–89.

77. Nerguizian and Cordesman, 22.

78. This paragraph draws on Barak, 164.

79. Ibid., 177.

80. Ibid., 173. See also Kari Karamé, "Reintegration and the Relevance of Social Relations: The Case of Lebanon," *Conflict, Security, and Development*, 9:4 (December 2009): 495–514.

81. Nerguizian and Cordesman, 9.

82. *The Military Balance, 2008* (London: International Institute for Strategic Studies, 2008), 251. See also http://www.lebarmy.gov.lb/English/FlagService.asp.

83. Interview with Rayan Ghazal of the Hoover Institution (Stanford, CA, 27 May 2008).

84. Nerguizian and Cordesman, 10.

85. Yezid Sayigh, "'Fixing Broken Windows': Security Sector Reform in Palestine, Lebanon, and Yemen," *Carnegie Papers* #17 (Washington, DC: Carnegie Endowment for International Peace, October 2009), 8.

86. Nerguizian and Cordesman, 10.

87. Kéchichian, "A Strong Army," 2.

88. Nerguizian and Cordesman, 17.

89. See Robert Fisk, "Hizbollah Rules West Beirut in Iran's Proxy War with U.S., *Independent*, 10 May 2008; and Makhzoumi, 6.

90. For Hezbollah's 2006 war against Israel, see Thanassis Cambanis, *A Privilege to Die: Inside Hezbollah's Legions and Their Endless War Against Israel* (New York: Free Press, 2010), 39–54 and 63–97.

91. Stephen John Stedman, *Implementing Peace Agreements in Civil Wars* (New York: International Peace Academy, 2001), 10.

CHAPTER 4

1. Parts of this chapter draw on Zoltan Barany and Lawrence S. Graham, *Democratic Transitions and Civil-Military Relations: Comparing Eastern and Southern Europe* (NATO Research Grant Report, 1994).

2. Cited in José Antonio Olmeda Gómez, "The Armed Forces in the Francoist Political System," Rafael Bañón Martínez and Thomas M. Barker, eds., *Armed Forces and Society in Spain: Past and Present* (New York: Columbia University Press, 1988), 249.

3. Philippe C. Schmitter, "Liberation by *Golpe*: Retrospective Thoughts on the Demise of Authoritarian Rule in Portugal," *Armed Forces & Society*, 2:1 (November 1975): 6.

4. The Greek military played a key role in other periods of modern history as well, including in 1949–67 (between the end of the civil war and the coup).

5. José-Maria Comas, "The Central Organization of Defense in Spain," in Martin Edmonds, ed., *Central Organizations of Defense* (Boulder, CO: Westview, 1985), 178.

6. Paul H. Lewis, "The Spanish Ministerial Elite, 1938-1969," *Journal of Politics,* 5:1 (October 1972): 96, 99.

7. See Cristina Palomares, *The Quest for Survival after Franco: Moderate Franco-ism and the Slow Journey to the Polls, 1964–1977* (Portland, OR: Sussex Academic Press).

8. Lewis, "The Spanish Ministerial Elite," 97–98.

9. Rafael Bañón Martínez, "The Spanish Armed Forces During the Period of Political Transition, 1975–1985," in Bañón Martínez and Barker, 346.

10. Olmeda Gómez, 255.

11. Felipe Agüero, "Democratic Consolidation and the Military in Southern Europe and South America," in Richard Gunther, P. Nikiforos Diamanduros, and Hans-Jürgen Puhle, eds., *The Politics of Democratic Consolidation: Southern Europe in Comparative Perspective* (Baltimore, MD: Johns Hopkins University Press, 1995), 140.

12. Olmeda Gómez, 257.

13. Ibid., 256–61.

14. See the comparative table on military participation in the two Iberian legislatures in Felipe Agüero, *Soldiers, Civilians, and Democracy: Post-Franco Spain in Comparative Perspective* (Baltimore, MD: Johns Hopkins University Press, 1995), 49.

15. António Costa Pinto, "The Salazar 'New State' and European Fascism," *EUI Working Paper* HEC No. 91/12 (Badia Fiesolana, San Domenico, Italy: European University Institute, 1991), 67.

16. See Howard Wiarda, "The Corporatist Tradition and the Corporative System in Portugal: Structured, Evolving, Transcended, Persistent," in Lawrence S. Graham and Harry M. Makler, eds., *Contemporary Portugal: The Revolution and Its Antecedents* (Austin: University of Texas Press, 1979), 89–122.

17. Paul H. Lewis, "Salazar's Ministerial Elite, 1932–1968," *Journal of Politics,* 40:3 (August 1978): 631–33.

18. See the discussion of partial settlements as a vehicle for promoting elite consensus and the interaction between military and civilian authorities in Lawrence S. Graham, "Redefining the Portuguese Transition to Democracy," in John Higley and Richard Gunther, eds., *Elites and Democratic Consolidation in Latin America and Southern Europe* (New York: Cambridge University Press, 1992), 287–95.

19. See Schmitter, "Liberation by *Golpe,*" 23.

20. Lewis, "Salazar's Ministerial Elite," 640.

21. The category of authoritarian regime which applies to these cases is "bureaucratic-authoritarian"; this line of thinking follows the model developed by Guillermo O'Donnell in his essay, *Modernization and Bureaucratic-Authoritarianism: Studies in South American Politics* (Berkeley: Institute of International Studies, University of California, 1973). For Iberian case studies, see Charles W. Anderson, *The*

Political Economy of Modern Spain: Policy-Making in an Authoritarian System (Madison: University of Wisconsin Press, 1970); and Lawrence S. Graham, *Portugal: The Decline and Collapse of an Authoritarian Order* (Beverly Hills, CA: Comparative Politics Series No. 01-053, 1975).

22. See especially Thomas C. Bruneau and Alex Macleod, eds., *Politics in Contemporary Portugal: Parties and the Consolidation of Democracy* (Boulder, CO: Lynne Rienner Publishers, 1986); and Raymond Carr and Juan Pablo Fusi, *Spain: Dictatorship to Democracy* (London: George Allen & Unwin, 2nd edition, 1981).

23. See Kenneth Maxwell, "The Hidden Revolution in Portugal" and "Portugal under Pressure," *New York Review of Books*, 17 April 1975, 29–35, and 29 May 1975, 20–30, respectively; and Maxwell, "Regime Overthrow and the Prospects for Democratic Transition in Portugal," in Guillermo O'Donnell, Philippe C. Schmitter, and Laurence Whitehead, eds., *Transitions from Authoritarian Rule: Southern Europe* (Baltimore, MD: Johns Hopkins University Press, 1986), 109–37.

24. See Julio Busquets, "Prólogo, La Transición: Conveniencia de su Estudio," 7–12; Narcís Serra, "La Política Española de Defensa," 173–86; and Agustin Rodríguez Sahagún, "La Reforma Militar de los Gobiernos de Suárez," 189–94; all in the special issue of the *Revista Española de Investigaciones Sociológicas*, No. 36 (October–December 1986).

25. An example of the former perspective is Richard Gunther, "Spain: The Very Model of the Modern Elite Settlement," in Higley and Gunther, eds., 38–80. Identified with the latter perspective are Antonio Marquina, "Spanish Foreign and Defense Policy since Democratization," in Kenneth Maxwell, ed., *Spanish Foreign and Defense Policy* (Boulder, CO: Westview, 1991), 19–62.

26. Agüero, *Soldiers, Civilians, and Democracy*, 9–10.

27. Fernando Rodrigo, "A Democratic Strategy toward the Military: Spain, 1975–1979," in Constantine Danopoulos, ed., *From Military to Civilian Rule* (London: Routledge, 1991), 2.

28. Bañón Martínez, 311. See also Constantine Danopoulos, "Democratizing the Military: Lessons from Mediterranean Europe," *West European Politics*, 14:4 (October 1991): 25–41.

29. See Giuseppe Di Palma, *To Craft Democracies* (Berkeley: University of California Press, 1990), 86–101.

30. Comas, 179.

31. Two major Spanish Defense Ministry publications detail these changes: *Memoria Legislatura 1982–86* (Madrid: Ministerio de Defensa, 1986) and *Memoria Legislatura 1986–89* (Madrid: Ministerio de Defensa, 1989).

32. For a fascinating interpretation of the coup and its aftermath, see Javier Cercas, *The Anatomy of a Moment: Thirty-Five Minutes in History and Imagination* (New York: Bloomsbury, 2011).

33. Interview with former Defense Minister Narcís Serra (Barcelona, 3 September 2009).

34. Comas, 194.

35. Interview with Serra.

36. Ibid.

37. See Kenneth Maxwell, *The Making of Portuguese Democracy* (New York: Cambridge University Press, 1995); and Rona M. Fields, *The Portuguese Revolution and the Armed Forces Movement* (New York: Praeger, 1976).

38. Thomas C. Bruneau and Harold Trinkunas, "Democratization as a Global Phenomenon and Its Impact on Civil-Military Relations," *Democratization*, 13:5 (December 2006): 779.

39. See Nancy Bermeo, *The Revolution within the Revolution: Workers' Control in Rural Portugal* (Princeton, NJ: Princeton University Press, 1986).

40. Lawrence S. Graham, *The Portuguese Military and the State* (Boulder, CO: Westview, 1993), 25–30.

41. Agüero, "Democratic Consolidation and the Military," 131–32.

42. These dates are based on the analysis of the Spanish and Portuguese transitions in Gunther, "Spain," and Graham, "Redefining," in Higley and Gunther, eds., 38–80 and 282–99, respectively.

43. Nancy Bermeo, "Myths of Moderation: Confrontation and Conflict during Democratic Transitions," *Comparative Politics*, 29:3 (April 1997): 309, 311.

44. Thomas C. Bruneau, "Defense Modernization and the Armed Forces in Portugal," *Portuguese Studies Review*, 1:2 (Fall–Winter 1991–93), 37.

45. See, for instance, Nancy Bermeo, "Classification and Consolidation: Some Lessons from the Greek Dictatorship," *Political Science Quarterly*, 110:3 (Autumn 1995): 435–52.

46. Theodore A. Couloumbis, "The Greek Junta Phenomenon," *Polity*, 6:3 (Spring 1974): 345.

47. Agüero, *Soldiers, Civilians, and Democracy*, 4. See also, Jon V. Kofas, *Under the Eagle's Claw: Exceptionalism in Postwar U.S.-Greek Relations* (Westport, CT: Praeger, 2003).

48. Richard Clogg, "The Ideology of the 'Revolution of 21 April 1967,' " in Richard Clogg and George Yannopoulos, eds., *Greece under Military Rule* (New York: Basic Books, 1972), 38–39.

49. See George A. Kourvetaris, "The Contemporary Army Officer Corps in Greece" (Ph.D. diss., Northwestern University, 1969), especially 32, 62–63.

50. Thanos Veremis, *The Military in Greek Politics: From Independence to Democracy* (Montréal: Black Rose Books, 1997), 154.

51. See Bermeo, "Classification and Consolidation," 441–44.

52. Veremis, 154.

53. Bermeo, "Classification and Consolidation," 448–50. For a less sanguine view, see Constantine P. Danopoulos, "From Military to Civilian Rule in Contemporary Greece," *Armed Forces & Society*, 10:2 (Winter 1984): 237–38.

54. Veremis, 160.

55. See John Pesmazoglu, "The Greek Economy since 1967," in Clogg and Yannopoulos, 75–108, here cited 90–91. See also, Andreas Papandreou, *Democracy at Gunpoint: The Greek Front* (Garden City, NY: Doubleday, 1970).

56. Danopoulos, "From Military to Civilian Rule," 239.

57. Duman Özkan and Dimitris Tsarouhas. " 'Civilianization' in Greece versus 'Demilitarization' in Turkey," *Armed Forces & Society*, 32:3 (April 2006): 413.

58. Harry J. Psomiades, "Preface," to Theodore A. Couloumbis, *The Greek Junta Phenomenon: A Professor's Notes* (New York: Pella, 2004), 14; and Terence Roehrig, *The Prosecution of Former Military Leaders in Newly Democratic Nations* (Jefferson, NC: McFarland & Co., 2002), 112–36.

59. Interview with Prof. Thanos Veremis (Athens, 13 March 2007).

60. Özkan and Tsarouhas, 414.

61. Veremis, 172.

62. Huntington, *The Third Wave*, 233.

63. Danopoulos, "Democratizing the Military," 34–35.

64. Thanos Dokos, "The Evolution of Civil-Military Relations and Progress in Greek Security Sector Reform," in Dokos, ed., *Security Sector Transformation in Southeastern Europe and the Middle East* (Amsterdam: IOS Press, 2007), 43.

65. Interviews with Veremis and Thanos Dokos at Eliamep: Hellenic Foundation for European & Foreign Policy (Athens, 13 March 2007).

66. Interview with Veremis.

67. Interview with Dokos.

68. Ibid.

69. Veremis, 155.

70. Couloumbis, *The Greek Junta Phenomenon*, 41.

71. "Spain Arrests General after Remarks," *New York Times*, 8 January 2006.

72. Eusebio Mujal-Leon, "Democracy Comes to the Iberian Peninsula," in Binnendijk, Hans, with Peggy Nalle and Diane Bendahmane, eds., *Authoritarian Regimes in Transition* (Washington, DC: Foreign Service Institute of the U.S. Department of State, 1987), 173–221 here cited: 174.

73. Bruneau and Trinkunas, 780–81.

74. Interview with General Francisco Laguna (Madrid, 11 March 1993).

75. Anthony Gooch, "A Surrealistic Referendum: Spain and NATO," *Government and Opposition* 21:3 (Summer 1986): 300–16. See also, Agüero, *Soldiers, Civilians, and Democracy*, 203–6.

76. Agüero, *Soldiers, Civilians, and Democracy*, 12.

77. Juan J. Linz and Alfred Stepan, *Problems of Democratic Transition and Consolidation* (Baltimore, MD: Johns Hopkins University Press, 1996), 191.

78. Alfred Stepan, *Rethinking Military Politics: Brazil and the Southern Cone* (Princeton: Princeton University Press, 1988), 69.

CHAPTER 5

1. See Miguel Centeno, *Blood and Debt: War and Nation-State in Latin America* (State College: Pennsylvania State University Press, 2003); and idem, *Warfare in Latin America*, Volumes I & II (Aldershot, UK: Ashgate, 2007).

2. Francisco Fernando de Santibañes, "The Effectiveness of Military Governments During War: The Case of Argentina in the Malvinas," *Armed Forces & Society*, 33:4 (July 2007): 612–37.

3. Paul Sigmund, "Approaches to the Study of the Military in Latin America," *Comparative Politics*, 26:1 (October 1993): 114. See also, Frederick Nunn, *Yesterday's Soldiers: European Military Professionalism in South America, 1890–1940* (Lincoln: University of Nebraska Press, 1983).

4. Eduardo Silva, "Chile," in Harry E. Vanden and Gary Prevost, ed., *Politics of Latin America* (New York: Oxford University Press, 2006), 438.

5. Interview with Cristián Labbé, Mayor of Providencia (Santiago, 23 June 2008).

6. Interview with Pinochet's Finance Minister, Carlos Cáceres (Santiago, 23 June 2008). See also Brian Loveman, "Antipolitics in Chile, 1973–94," in Brian Loveman and Thomas M. Davies, eds., *The Politics of Antipolitics: The Military in Latin America* (Wilmington, DE: Scholarly Resources, 1997), 273.

7. Cited in Brian Loveman, *For la Patria: Politics and the Armed Forces in Latin America* (Wilmington, DE: Scholarly Resources, 1999), 188.

8. Eduardo Silva, "Chile Past, Present and Future: The Long Road to National Reconciliation," *Journal of Interamerican Studies and World Affairs*, 33:4 (Winter 1991): 133–46.

9. See, for instance, Karen L. Remmer, "Neopatrimonialism: The Politics of Military Rule in Chile, 1973–1987," *Comparative Politics*, 21:2 (January 1989): 156.

10. See Robert Barros, *Constitutionalism and Dictatorship: Pinochet, the Junta, and the 1980 Constitution* (New York: Cambridge University Press, 2002); and Carlos Huneeus, *The Pinochet Regime* (Boulder, CO: Lynne Rienner, 2006).

11. Eduardo Silva, "From Dictatorship to Democracy: The Business-State Nexus in Chile's Economic Transformation, 1975–1994," *Comparative Politics*, 28:3 (April 1996): 299.

12. Pion-Berlin, David. "Military Autonomy and Emerging Democracies in South America," *Comparative Politics*, 25:1 (October 1992): 91.

13. Interview with Edgardo Boeninger at CIEPLAN: Corporación de Estudios para Latinoamérica (Santiago, 27 June 2008).

14. Interview with Boeninger.

15. Aldo C. Vacs, "Argentina," in Vanden and Prevost, ed., *Politics of Latin America*, 406.

16. Andrea Wagner, *Der argentinisch-chilenische Konflikt um den Beagle-Kanal: Ein Beitrag zu den Methoden friedlicher Streiterledigung* (Frankfurt: Peter Lang, 1992).

17. David Pion-Berlin, *Through Corridors of Power: Institutions and Civil-Military Relations in Argentina* (State College: Pennsylvania State University Press, 1997), 142. See also Silvio Waisbord, "Politics and Identity in the Argentine Army: Cleavages and the Generational Factor," *Latin American Research Review*, 26:2 (1991): 166–68; and Jack Levy and Lily Vakili, "Diversionary action by authoritarian regimes: Argentina in the Falklands/Malvinas case," in Manus Midlarsky, ed., *The Internationalization of Communal Strife* (New York: Routledge, 1992), 118–46.

18. Anthony W. Pereira, *Political (In)Justice: Authoritarianism and the Rule of Law in Brazil, Chile, and Argentina* (Pittsburgh, PA: University of Pittsburgh Press, 2005), 172–92.

19. Deborah Norden, *Military Rebellion in Argentina* (Lincoln: University of Nebraska Press, 1996), 59. As of August 2011, the Chilean government recognized 40,018 official victims of the military dictatorship (the total number of people killed, tortured, or imprisoned for political reasons). See Eva Vergara, "Chile Recognizes 9,800 More Pinochet Victims," AP (Santiago), 18 August 2011.

20. Interview with General (ret.) Patricio Chacón (Santiago, 25 June 2008).

21. Interview with Alejandro Avenburg and Facundo Salles Kobilanski (Buenos Aires, 26 September 2008).

22. The report is available at http://www.cidh.oas.org/countryrep/Argentina80eng/toc.htm.

23. Harold A. Trinkunas, *Crafting Civilian Control of the Military in Venezuela: A Comparative Perspective* (Chapel Hill: University of North Carolina Press, 2005). See also Felipe Agüero, "The Military and the Limits of Democratization," in Scott Mainwaring, Guillermo O'Donnell, and J. Samuel Valenzuela, eds. *Issues in Democratic Consolidation: The New South American Democracies in Comparative Perspective* (Notre Dame, IN: University of Notre Dame Press, 1992), 153–98.

24. Carlos Santiago Nino, *Radical Evil on Trial* (New Haven: Yale University Press, 1996), 61.

25. Juan J. Linz and Alfred Stepan, *Problems of Democratic Transition and Consolidation* (Baltimore, MD: Johns Hopkins University Press, 1996), 192.

26. Felipe Agüero, "A Political Army in Chile: Historical Assessment and Prospects for the New Democracy," in Koonings and Kruijt, eds., *Political Armies*, 123–24.

27. Patricio Silva, "Searching for Civilian Supremacy: The Concertación Governments and the Military in Chile," *Bulletin of Latin American Research*, 21:3 (July 2002): 375.

28. Patricio Silva, "Between Autonomy and Subordination Government-Military Relations in Post-Authoritarian Chile," in Cawthra and Luckham, eds., 102.

29. Craig L. Arceneaux, *Bounded Missions: Military Regimes and Democratization in the Southern Cone and Brazil* (State College: Pennsylvania State University Press, 2001), 106.

30. I am grateful to Felipe Agüero for this point.

31. Claudio Fuentes, "After Pinochet: Civilian Policies Toward the Military in the 1990s Chilean Democracy," *Journal of Interamerican Studies and World Affairs*, 42:3 (Autumn 2000): 117–19.

32. David Pion-Berlin, "Military Autonomy and Emerging Democracies in South America," *Comparative Politics*, 25:1 (October 1992): 97.

33. Ernesto López, "Latin America: Objective and Subjective Control Revisited," in David Pion-Berlin, ed. *Civil-Military Relations in Latin America: New Analytical Perspectives* (Chapel Hill: University of North Carolina Press, 2001), 103.

34. Interview with José Manuel Ugarte, Buenos Aires (18 September 2008). See also Wendy Hunter, "Continuity or Change? Civil-Military Relations in Democratic Argentina, Chile, and Peru," *Political Science Quarterly*, 112:3 (Autumn 1997): 463–64.

35. Raúl Alfonsín, "The Transition toward Democracy in a Developing Country: The Case of Argentina," in Daniel N. Nelson, ed., *After Authoritariansm* (Westport, CT: Praeger, 1995), 23–24.

36. Norden, *Military Rebellion in Argentina*, 59.

37. Cited in Rut Diamint, "Crisis, Democracy, and the Military in Argentina," in Edward Epstein and David Pion-Berlin, eds., *Broken Promises? The Argentine Crisis and Argentine Democracy* (Lanham, MD: Lexington Books, 2006), 172.

38. The Kirchners purchased twenty auctioned-off pieces of real estate—they had insider information regarding the time of the auctions—sold by the desperate victims of the *Proceso*. Interview with Avenburg and Kobilanski. See also Ramiro Duran, "Los negocios de Kirchner durante la dictadura," *AR-News Buenos Aires*, 29 September 2006; http://arnews.wordpress.com/2006/09/29/los-negocios-de-kirchner-durante-la-dictadura/; accessed on 4 February 2011.

39. Interview with Sebastián Vigliero (Buenos Aires, 17 September 2008). See also, "Argentine Dirty War Officers Punished," *New York Times*, 29 January 2008; and "Argentine Ex-Army Chief Gets Life Sentence in 'Dirty War' Crimes," *New York Times*, 25 July 2008.

40. Interview with Prof. Rut Diamint (Buenos Aires, 19 September 2008).

41. Interviews with Juan Recce and Hernán Lapieza Spota (Buenos Aires, 19 September 2008).

42. Interview with Ugarte.

43. Trinkunas, *Crafting Civilian Control*, 4.

44. Brian Loveman, "¿*Misión Cumplida?* Civil-Military Relations and the Chilean Political Transition," *Journal of Interamerican Studies and World Affairs*, 33:3 (Fall 1991): 35–74.

45. Interviews in Santiago with Claudio Fuentes (FLACSO) and Felipe Agüero (Ford Foundation) (25 June 2008); and with Boeninger. See also Silva, "Searching for Civilian Supremacy," 378.

46. Thomas C. Wright, *State Terrorism in Latin America* (Lanham, MD: Rowman & Littlefield, 2007), 208.

47. "Defrauded" is the word several high-ranking officers used in our interviews in Santiago (June 2008). Also, interview with Guillermo Pattillo and Juan-Miguel Izquierdo at the Instituto Libertad (Santiago, 23 June 2008).

48. "Pedregoso camino para que cenizas de Pinochet llegaran a Los Boldos," *La Nación*, 26 December 2006.

49. See Marcos Robledo, "Democratic Consolidation in Chilean Civil-Military Relations: 1990–2005," in Thomas Bruneau and Harold Trinkunas, eds., *Global Politics of Defense Reform* (New York: Palgrave-Macmillan, 2008), 95–127.

50. Larry Rohter, "After the Earthquake, a Military Chile Can Love Again," *New York Times*, 12 March 2010.

51. Norden, *Military Rebellion in Argentina*, 3. See also Waisbord, "Politics and Identity," 157–70.

52. David Pion-Berlin and Ernesto López, "A House Divided: Crisis, Cleavage, and Conflict in the Argentine Army," in Edward C. Epstein, ed., *The New Argentine Democracy* (Westport, CT: Praeger, 1992), 65.

53. Nino, *Radical Evil on Trial*, 103.

54. Pion-Berlin and López, "A House Divided," 84. See also Marcelo Fabián Saín, *Los levantamientos carapintada, 1987–1991* (Buenos Aires: Centro Editor de América Latina, 1994).

55. Patrice McSherry, *Incomplete Transition: Military Power and Democracy in Argentina* (New York: St. Martin's Press, 1997), 240–42.

56. Patricio Silva, "Between Autonomy and Subordination," 110.

57. Silva, "Between Autonomy and Subordination," 113.

58. Red de Seguridad y Defensa de América Latina, *A Comparative Atlas of Defence in Latin America and Caribbean* (Buenos Aires: RESDAL, 2010), 43.

59. David Pion-Berlin, "Civil-Military Circumvention: How Argentine State Institutions Compensate for a Weakened Chain of Command," in Pion-Berlin, ed., *Civil-Military Relations*, 141–42.

60. Pion-Berlin and López, "A House Divided," 66.

61. Interview with Prof. Thomas Scheetz (Buenos Aires, 22 September 2008). Garré's reforms are also described—in unrealistically positive terms—on the Defense Ministry's website; see www.mindef.gov.ar.

62. Gregory Weeks, "A Preference for Deference: Reforming the Military's Intelligence Role in Argentina, Chile, and Peru," *Third World Quarterly*, 29:1 (February 2008): 50–51.

63. Weeks, "A Preference for Deference," 46.

64. See David Pion-Berlin and Harold Trinkunas, "Attention Deficits: Why Politicians Ignore Defense Policy in Latin America," *Latin American Research Review*, 42:3 (October 2007): 76–100.

65. Interview with Diamint.

66. Interview with Luis Tibiletti (Buenos Aires, 24 September 2008).

67. Pion-Berlin and Trinkunas, "Attention Deficits," 92.

68. Diamint, "Crisis, Democracy, and the Military in Argentina," 171.

69. Interview with Vigliero.

70. See, for instance, de Santibañes, "The Effectiveness of Military Governments During War."

71. Fuentes, "After Pinochet," 125.

72. Interviews with Boeninger and with Chilean generals (Santiago, June 2008).

73. See *Report on the Security Sector in Latin America and the Caribbean* (Santiago: FLACSO-Chile, 2007), 27.

74. Wendy Hunter, *Eroding Military Influence in Brazil: Politicians against Soldiers* (Chapel Hill: University of North Carolina Press, 1997), 162.

75. Thomas Scheetz. "The Evolution of Public Sector Expenditures: Changing Political Priorities in Argentina, Chile, Paraguay, and Peru," *Journal of Peace Research*, 29:2 (1992): 179.

76. Interview with Scheetz. In 2011 Argentina put military modernization—particularly increased defense acquisitions—on the government's long-term agenda to refurbish the country's obsolete weapons arsenals. See "Argentina Mulls Higher Defense Spending," UPI (Buenos Aires), 19 August 2011.

77. Interviews with Diamint, Recce, and de Santibañes.

78. *A Comparative Atlas*, 54.

79. Diamint, "Crisis, Democracy, and the Military," 164

80. Interviews with Diamint and Ugarte.

81. Interview with Boeninger.

82. Stanislaw Andrzejewski has discussed this issue extensively in *Military Organization and Society* (London: Routledge Kegan Paul 1954).

83. Katherine J. Worboys, "The Traumatic Journey from Dictatorship to Democracy: Peacekeeping Operations and Civil-Military Relations in Argentina, 1989–1999," *Armed Forces & Society*, 33:2 (January 2007): 160–62.

84. A. J. Ramos, R. C. Oates, and T. L. McMahon, "The U.S. Southern Command: A Strategy for the Future," *Military Review*, 72:11 (November 1992): 34.

85. Interview with Avenburg and Salles. See also Alberto Miguez, "Argentina's Budding Relations with NATO," *NATO Review*, 41:3 (June 1993): 28–31.

86. See, for instance, Frank Kurz, "Ein 'tragisch-groteskes' Missverständnis: Das Scheitern der argentinischen *Montoneros*," in Alexander Straßner, *Sozialrevolutionärer Terrorismus* (Wiesbaden: VS Verlag für Sozialwissenschaften, 2008), 387–410; and the website of the National Consortium for the Study of Terrorism and Responses to Terrorism, a center of the U.S. Department of Homeland Security based at the University of Maryland: http://www.start.umd.edu/start/data_collections/tops/terrorist_organization_profile.asp?id=236.

87. Kees Koonings, "Political Armies, Security Forces, and Democratic Consolidation in Latin America," in Cawthra and Luckham, eds., *Governing Insecurity*, 141.

88. See Mitchell Seligson, "Democracy on Ice: The Multiple Challenges of Guatemala's Peace Process," in Frances Hagopian and Scott Mainwaring, eds., *The Third Wave of Democratization in Latin America* (New York: Cambridge University Press, 2005), 204–207.

89. The document is available at http.c-r.org/our-work/accord/guatemala/civilian-power-armed-forces.php.

90. In June 2011 General Héctor Mario López, a former military chief of staff became the highest-ranking former official to be arrested for the massacres of in the 1980s. See "Guatemala: Former Military Chief Is Charged with Genocide," *New York Times*, 17 June 2011.

91. Gabriel Aguilera Peralta, "Guatemala's Armed Forces: 15 Years After Peace," in *A Comparative Atlas*, 230–31.

92. *A Comparative Atlas*, 222, 227, respectively. The maximum size of the budget is set at 0.66 percent of the GDP by law.

93. *Report on the Security Sector*, 17–18.

94. "Guatemala Coming Full Circle," *Guatemala Times*, 17 December 2008.

95. Susanne Jonas, "Guatemala," in Vanden and Prevost, *Politics of Latin America*, 288.

96. Seligson, "Democracy on Ice," 208, fn. 5.

97. Jennifer Schirmer, "The Guatemalan Politico-Military Project," in Koonings and Kruijt, *Political Armies*, 77–78.

98. Sarah Grainger, "Mexican Drug Gang Menace Spreads in Guatemala," *Reuters* (Guatemala City), 18 February 2009.

99. "Remilitarization of Guatemala Already a Fact," *Guatemala Times*, 16 February 2009.

100. "Guatemalan Military Seizer Drug-Plagued Province," *New York Times*, 19 December 2010. See also Hal Brands, *Crime, Violence, and the Crisis in Guatemala* (Carlisle, PA: Strategic Studies Institute, 2010) and Thomas C. Bruneau, Lucía Dammert, and Elizabeth Skinner, eds., *Maras: Gang Violence and Security in Central America* (Austin: University of Texas Press, 2011).

101. Megan McAdams, "Bloodshed in Guatemala as Cartels and Street Gangs Wage War," Council on Hemispheric Affairs Report (www.coha.org), 7 March 2011.

102. Damien Cave, "Desperate Guatemalans Embrace an 'Iron Fist,'" *New York Times*, 10 September 2011.

103. Julie López, *Guatemala's Crossroads: Democratization of Violence and Second Chances* (Washington D.C.: Woodrow Wilson Center Latin American Studies Program, December 2010), 24–29.

104. Jonas, "Guatemala," 284.

105. Schirmer, "The Guatemalan Politico-Military Project," 85.

106. See Phil Kelley, "Democracy in Latin America," *LASA Forum*, 33:1 (Spring 2002).

107. Interview with an Argentine military analyst (Buenos Aires, 20 September 2008).

CHAPTER 6

1. Aurel Croissant and David Kuehn, "Patterns of Civilian Control of the Military in East Asia's New Democracies," *Journal of East Asian Studies*, 9:2 (May–August 2009): 191.

2. Jinsok Jun, "South Korea: Consolidating Democratic Civilian Control," in Muthiah Alagappa, ed., *Coercion and Governance: The Declining Political Role of the Military in Asia* (Stanford, CA: Stanford University Press, 2001), 123.

3. For a definitive assessment of Park's rule, see Byung-Kook Kim and Ezra F. Vogel, eds., *The Park Chung Hee Era: The Transformation of South Korea* (Cambridge, MA: Harvard University Press, 2011) and particularly Joo-Hong Kim's chapter, "The Armed Forces," 168–99.

4. Jun, 128.

5. Ibid., 129.

6. Cited in Jongseok Woo, *Security Challenges and Military Politics in East Asia: From State-Building to Post-Democratization* (New York: Continuum, 2011), 71.

7. Jun, 129.

8. James Ockey, "Thailand: The Struggle to Redefine Civil-Military Relations," in Alagappa, ed., *Coercion and Governance*, 191–92.

9. Cited in Panitan Wattanayagorn, "Thailand: The Elite's Shifting Conceptions of Security," in Muthiah Alagappa, ed., *Asian Security Practice: Material and Ideational Influences* (Stanford, CA: Stanford University Press, 1998), 423–24.

10. See David A. Wilson, "The Military in Thai Politics," in John J. Johnson, ed., *The Role of the Military in Underdeveloped Countries* (Princeton, NJ: Princeton University Press, 1962), 253–76.

11. Ben Doherty, "Fears for Thai Monarch Set Stockmarket Tumbling for Second Day," *The Guardian* (London), 15 October 2009.

12. Paul M. Handley, *The King Never Smiles: A Biography of Thailand's Bhumibol Adulyadej* (New Haven, CT: Yale University Press, 2006), 126, 233.

13. Ockey, 195.

14. Ibid., 198.

15. Chris Baker and Pasuk Phongpaichit, *A History of Thailand* (Cambridge: Cambridge University Press, 2005), 232.

16. Paul Chambers, "U-Turn to the Past? The Resurgence of the Military in Contemporary Thai Politics." Paper presented at the public forum on "The Military in Thai Politics: What's Next?" Bangkok: Institute of Security and International Studies, Chulalongkorn University, 1 September 2009; 14.

17. Surachart Bamrungsuk, "Changing Patterns of Civil-Military Relations and Thaliand's Regional Outlook," in David R. Mares, ed., *Civil-Military Relations: Building Democracy and Regional Security in Latin America, Southern Asia, and Central Europe* (Boulder, CO: Westview, 1998), 191.

18. See John Roosa, *Pretext for Mass Murder: The September 30th Movement and Suharto's Coup d'État in Indonesia* (Madison: University of Wisconsin Press, 2006).

19. Geoffrey Robinson, "Indonesia: On a New Course?" in Alagappa, ed., *Coercion and Governance*, 227.

20. Herbert Feith, "Indonesia's Political Symbols and their Wielders," *World Politics*, 16:1 (October 1963): 79–97.

21. Harold Crouch, *The Army and Politics in Indonesia* (Ithaca, NY: Cornell University Press, 1988 [Rev. ed.]), 273–303; and Woo, 131.

22. Angel Rabasa and John Haseman, *The Military and Democracy in Indonesia: Challenges, Politics, and Power.* (Santa Monica, CA: RAND, 2002), 37.

23. Woo, 134.

24. Robinson, 228.

25. Joseph S. Bermudez, Jr., *The Armed Forces of North Korea* (London: I. B. Tauris, 2001), 13–16.

26. See, for instance, Maynard Parker, "Subversion in Thailand," *Survival*, 8:10 (October 1966): 310–12.

27. See, for instance, James Lilley with Jeffrey Lilley, *China Hands: Nine Decades of Adventure, Espionage, and Diplomacy in Asia* (New York: Public Affairs, 2005), 264–96.

28. Jun, 139.

29. Herbert H. Werlin, "Ghana and South Korea: Explaining Developmental Disparities," *Journal of Asian and African Studies*, 29 (April 1994): 205–25.

30. Mark Beeson, Alex J. Bellamy, and Bryn Hughes, "Taming the Tigers? Reforming the Security Sector in Southeast Asia," *Pacific Review*, 19:4 (December 2006): 460.

31. Interviews with Indria Samego and Ikrar Nusa Bhakti, Indonesian Institute of Sciences (Jakarta, 16 and 17 December 2009).

32. Oren Barak and Gabriel Sheffer, "Continuous Existential Threats, Civil-Security Relations, and Democracy," in Sheffer and Barak, eds., *Existential Threats and Civil Security Relations* (Lanham, MD: Lexington Books, 2009), 131.

33. Jongryn Mo and Barry R. Weingast, *The Political Economy of Korea's Transition, 1961–2008* (September 2009 draft), 115.

34. See Hong-nack Kim, "The 1988 Parliamentary Election in South Korea," *Asian Survey*, 29:5 (May 1989): 480–95.

35. Woo, 111.

36. Samuel P. Huntington, *The Third Wave: Democratization in the Late Twentieth Century* (Norman, OK: University of Oklahoma Press, 1991), 231–51.

37. Victor Cha, "Security and Democracy in South Korean Development," in Samuel S. Kim, ed., *Korea's Democratization* (New York: Cambridge University Press, 2003), 207.

38. Croissant and Kuehn, 193.

39. Woo, 112.

40. See Terence Roehrig, *Prosecution of Former Military Leaders in Newly Democratic Nations* (Jefferson, NC: McFarland & Co., 2002), 160–85.

41. Larry Diamond and Doh Chull Shin, "Introduction: Institutional Reforms and Democratic Consolidation in Korea," in Diamond and Shin, eds. *Institutional Reform and Democratic Consolidation in Korea* (Stanford, CA: Hoover Institution Press, 2000), 10.

42. Woo, 113–14.

43. Chaibong Hahm, "South Korea's Miraculous Democracy," *Journal of Democracy*, 19:3 (July 2008): 136.

44. Cha, 214.

45. Kim Dae-jung was elected on 18 December 1997 and the generals were released on 22 December 1997. Kim's official presidential term did not begin until 25 February 1998 but the decision, likely to have been influenced by the ongoing financial crisis, was his and not the sitting president's. I am grateful to Jongseok Woo for this point.

46. Jun, 134.

47. Croissant and Kuehn, 193.

48. Interview with Kim Min-seok, Senior Expert Writer for the *Joong Ang Ilbo* newspaper (Seoul, 4 December 2009).

49. Interview with Kim Choong-nam, Visiting Fellow, Sejong Institute (Seoul, 4 December 2009).

50. See Sunhyuk Kim, "Civic Mobilization for Democratic Reform," In Diamond and Shin, eds. *Institutional Reform and Democratic Consolidation in Korea*, 279–304.

51. Chie Sang-hun, "Korean Navies Trade Fire in First Incident in Seven Years," *New York Times*, 11 November 2009.

52. Interview with Kim Choong-nam.

53. Interview with Choi Jang-jip (Seoul, 5 December 2009).

54. Chang-hee Nam, "Realigning the U.S. Forces and South Korea's Defense Reform 2020," *Korean Journal of Defense Analysis*, 19:1 (Spring 2007): 176–78.

55. Diamond and Shin, 5.

56. Ockey, 187–88.

57. Baker and Pasuk, 244.

58. Ibid., 246.

59. Panitan Wattanayagorn, "Thailand: The Elite's Shifting Conceptions of Security," in Muthiah Alagappa, ed., *Asian Security Practice: Material and Ideational Influences* (Stanford, CA: Stanford University Press, 1998), 429.

60. Surachart in Mares, ed.,193.

61. Panitan, 430.

62. Croissan and Kuehn, 197.

63. Duncan McCargo and Ukrist Pathmanand, *The Thaksinization of Thailand* (Copenhagen: Nordic Institute of Asian Studies Press, 2005), 129.

64. Surachart, 201.

65. Thomas Fuller, "Thai Junta Shores Up Role in Politics," *International Herald Tribune*, 1 October 2006.

66. Chambers, "U-Turn to the Past?," 21.

67. Ibid., 22.

68. Ibid., 24.

69. Interview with Ukrist Pathmanand of Chulalongkorn University (Bangkok, 12 December 2009).

70. Ukrist Pathmanand, "A Different *Coup d'État*?," *Journal of Contemporary Asia*, 38:1 (February 2008): 130–32.

71. Kate McGeown, "Thai King Remains Centre Stage," BBC, 21 September 2006. For a balanced assessment of the monarchy, see "As Father Fades, His Children Fight," *Economist*, 20 March 2010, 26–28.

72. Ukrist, "A Different *Coup d'État*?," 125.

73. Croissant and Kuehn, 197.

74. Chambers, "U-Turn to the Past?," 22–23.

75. Interviews with Prof. Surachart Bamrungsuk of Chulalongkorn University and Chris Baker (Bangkok, 12 and 13 December 2009).

76. Chambers, "U-Turn to the Past?," 24.

77. Surachart Bamrungsuk, *Military Trilogy, Coup, and Thai Politics* (in Thai) (Bangkok: The Predi Institute, 2008), 58–59.

78. Wassana Nanuam, "PM Abhisit, Gen Prayuth and Their Common Future," *Bangkok Post*, 10 December 2009.

79. See, for instance, two articles by Thomas Fuller, "Violence Spreads in Thailand after Crackdown," and "Bangkok Is Tense as Order Returns," *New York Times*, 19 and 20 May 2010, respectively.

80. Panitan, 440–42.

81. "The Trouble In Between," *Economist*, 12 December 2009, 48.

82. Ockey, 202.

83. Suchit, Bunbongkarn. *The Military in Thai Politics, 1981–86* (Singapore: Institute of Southeast Asian Studies, 1987), 9–34.

84. Chambers, "U-Turn to the Past?" 71.

85. Interview with Surachart.

86. Ockey, 204.

87. Interview with Baker.

88. See Jun Honna, *Military Politics and Democratization in Indonesia* (New York: RoutledgeCurzon, 2003), 38–52.

89. Terence Lee, "The Armed Forces and Transitions from Authoritarian Rule: Explaining the Role of the Military in 1986 Philippines and 1998 Indonesia," *Comparative Political Studies*, 42:5 (May 2009): 654–60.

90. See Ronald D. Palmer, "From Repression to Reform? Indonesian Politics and the Military, 1997–1999," in *American Diplomacy*, Winter 2000, available at http://www.unc.edu/depts/diplomat/AD_Issues/amdipl_15/palmer_reform1.html.

91. Croissant and Kuehn, 194.

92. Marcus Mietzner, *Military Politics, Islam, and the State in Indonesia* (Singapore: Institute of Southeast Asian Studies, 2009), 2.

93. Geoffrey Robinson, *"If You Leave Us Here, We Will Die": How Genocide Was Stopped in East Timor* (Princeton, NJ: Princeton University Press, 2009), 139–61.

94. Rabasa and Haseman, 41–42.

95. See Mietzner, *Military Politics*, 211–25.

96. Ibid., 227.

97. Interview with Marcus Mietzner (Jakarta, 15 December 2009) and e-mail communication from Evan Laksmana (16 October 2006).

98. E-mail message from Juwono Sudarsono (28 March 2010).

99. Interview with Frans Limahelu of Airlangga University (Austin, 18 October 2010).

100. See Lisa Misol, *Unkept Promise: Failure To End Military Business Activity in Indonesia* (New York: Human Rights Watch, 2010); and Harold Crouch, *Political Reform in Indonesia after Soeharto* (Singapore: Institute of Southeast Asian Studies, 2010), 161–69.

101. See the 2009 and 2010 issues of *The Military Balance 2009* (London: International Institute for Strategic Studies), 388 and 407; and 405 and 424, respectively.

102. E-mail message from Juwono Sudarsono (28 March 2010).

103. Interview with Prof. Jun Honna (Jakarta, 19 December 2009).

104. Interviews with Indria Samego, Kevin O'Rourke, Jun Honna, Marcus Mietzner, and Ikrar Nusa Bhakti (Jakarta, 15–19 December 2009). See also Susilo Bambang Yudhoyono, "The Democratic Instinct in the 21st Century," *Journal of Democracy*, 21:3 (July 2010): 5–10; and more generally, Crouch, *Political Reform*.

105. Interview with Mietzner.

106. Michael C. Desch, *Civilian Control of the Military: The Changing Security Environment* (Baltimore, MD: Johns Hopkins University Press, 1999), 111–12.

107. See, for instance, Adam Przeworski, et al., *Democracy and Development* (New York: Cambridge University Press, 2000), especially 78–141.

108. Roehrig, ix.

109. Huntington, *The Third Wave*, 252.

Chapter 7

1. For stylistic reasons I use the terms "state-socialism" and "communism" interchangeably, though I do prefer the former because communism was never realized in any "communist" state. I also prefer "state-socialism" to "one-party state," because, technically speaking, in some communist states, such as East Germany and Poland, there was more than one official political party even if yet another moniker, the "party-state," faithfully reflected that the communist party controlled the state. Moreover, not all one-party states were communist—other types of authoritarian regimes also abolished rival parties.

2. Amos Perlmutter and William M. LeoGrande, "The Party in Uniform: Toward a Theory of Civil-Military Relations in Communist Political Systems," *American Political Science Review*, 76:4 (December 1982): 779.

3. Thomas R. Dye and Harmon Ziegler, "Socialism and Militarism," *PS: Political Science and Politics*, 22:4 (December 1990): 810–13. The authors used several approaches to determine the "relative militarism" of democratic and communist polities. These included contrasting defense expenditure with GNP, military personnel per 1,000 population, and comparing these variables before and after revolutions.

4. Herbert Spencer, "Militancy and Industrialism," in J.D.Y. Peel, ed., *Herbert Spencer on Social Evolution: Selected Writings* (Chicago: University of Chicago Press., 1972), 149–66, especially 149–50. See also Andrew C. Janos, "Social Science, Communism, and the Dynamics of Political Change," *World Politics*, 44:1 (October 1991): 93–95.

5. Zoltan Barany, *Soldiers and Politics in Eastern Europe, 1945–90* (London: Macmillan, 1993), 9.

6. No Soviet troops were stationed in Bulgaria, Moscow's most loyal ally. They were withdrawn from Romania in 1958—one of Nikita S. Khrushchev's strategic blunders that allowed Romania's limited independence from the Soviet Union afterward—and occupied Czechoslovakia only after the Prague Spring of 1968.

7. This point is discussed in more detail in Barany, *Soldiers and Politics*, 113–75.

8. Zoltan Barany, "Democratic Consolidation and the Military," *Comparative Politics*, 30:1 (October 1997): 22–26.

9. See, for instance, Samuel P. Huntington, *The Third Wave: Democratization in the Late Twentieth Century* (Norman: University of Oklahoma Press, 1991), 232; and Valerie Bunce, "Rethinking Recent Democratization: Lessons from the Postcommunist Experience," *World Politics*, 55:2 (January 2003): 175.

10. Thomas M. Nichols, *The Sacred Cause: Civil-Military Conflict over Soviet National Security, 1917–1992* (Ithaca, NY: Cornell University Press, 1993), 11–12.

11. Sabrina Ramet, "Democratization in Slovenia—the Second Stage," in Karen Dawisha and Bruce Parrott, eds., *Politics, Power, and the Struggle for Democracy in South-East Europe* (New York: Cambridge University Press, 1997), 191.

12. Interview with Damjan Perlovšek, Slovenia's Ambassador to the Czech Republic (Prague, 25 August 1999).

13. Bojko Bučar, "The International Recognition of Slovenia," in Danica Fink-Hafner and John R. Robbins, eds., *Making a New Nation: The Formation of Slovenia* (Brookfield, VT: Dartmouth, 1997), 31–45.

14. *Večerno delo* (Ljubljana), 27 October 1991.

15. James Gow and Cathie Carmichael, *Slovenia and the Slovenes: A Small State and the New Europe* (Bloomington: Indiana University Press, 2000). See also "Janez Drnovsek, Slovenia's Dogged Guardian," *The Economist*, 22 April 2000.

16. See Gow and Carmichael, *Slovenia and the Slovenes*, 170, 173; "Bridging Europe," *Economist*, 11 January 1997, 49.

17. Anton Bebler, "Civil-Military Relations in Slovenia," in Constantine P. Danopoulos and Daniel Zirker, eds., *Civil-Military Relations in the Soviet and Yugoslav Successor States* (Boulder, CO: Westview, 1996), 207.

18. Bebler, "Civil-Military Relations in Slovenia," 208; Sabrina Ramet, *Balkan Babel* (Boulder, CO: Westview, 1993), 181.

19. Gow and Carmichael, *Slovenia and the Slovenes*, 142.

20. A fine account of these events is in Thomas M. Nichols, *The Russian Presidency* (London: Macmillan, 1999), 77–82.

21. For Yeltsin's own version of this incident, see Boris Yeltsin, *The View from the Kremlin* (London: HarperCollins, 1994), 271–83, and especially 278–79.

22. See Igor Kliamkin and Lilia Shevtsova, *Rezhim Borisa Vtoroga: Osobennosti postkommunicheskoi vlasti v Rossii* (Moscow: Carnegie Center, 1999), and Michael McFaul, *Russia's Unfinished Revolution: Political Change from Gorbachev to Putin* (Ithaca, NY: Cornell University Press, 2001), 207–209.

23. M. Steven Fish, "The Executive Deception: Superpresidentialism and the Degradation of Russian Politics," in Valerie Sperling, ed., *Building the Russian State: Institutional Crisis and the Quest for Democratic Governance* (Boulder, CO: Westview Press, 2000), 177–92, especially 178–79.

24. Cited in Andrew Jack, *Inside Putin's Russia: Can There Be Reform Without Democracy?* (New York: Oxford University Press, 2006), 26–27.

25. See, for instance, Uwe Klussmann, "Fuß auf dem Zünder: Moskau's Schlussforderungen aus dem Geiseldrama von Beslau," *Der Spiegel*, 4 July 2005, 94–95.

26. See Brian D. Taylor, *State-Building in Putin's Russia: Policing and Coercion after Communism* (New York: Cambridge University Press, 2011).

27. Yelena Panfilova, "Russia's Corruption Rating 'Critical,'" *Izvestia*, 19 October 2005.

28. Juan J. Linz and Alfred Stepan, *Problems of Democratic Transition and Consolidation* (Baltimore: Johns Hopkins University Press, 1996), 352–53.

29. Helga Welsh, "Political Transition Processes in Central and Eastern Europe," *Comparative Politics*, 26:4 (July 1994): 385.

30. Catherine Lovatt, "EC 2000 Progress Report on Romania," *Central Europe Review*, 2:39 (13 November 2000).

31. On this subject, see James Gow, *Legitimacy and the Military: The Yugoslav Crisis* (New York: St. Martin's, 1992); Janez Janša, *Premiki: Nastajanje in Obramba Slovenske Države, 1988–1992* (Ljubljana: Založba Mladinska Knjiga, 1992); and Janez J. Švajncer, *Obranili Domovino: Teritorialna Obramba Republike Slovenije v Vojni za Svobodno in Samostojno Slovenijo, 1991* (Ljubljana: Viharnik, 1993).

32. Brian D. Taylor, *Politics and the Russian Army: Civil-Military Relations, 1689–2000* (New York: Cambridge University Press, 2003), 17.

33. See, for instance, William Crowther, "'Ceausescuism' and Civil-Military Relations in Romania," *Armed Forces & Society*, 15:2 (Winter 1989): 207–25.

34. See Peter Siani-Davies, *The Romanian Revolution of December 1989* (Ithaca, NY: Cornell University Press, 2005).

35. Zoltan Barany, *Democratic Breakdown and the Decline of the Russian Military* (Princeton, NJ: Princeton University Press, 2007), 19–20.

36. Zoltan Barany, *The Future of NATO Expansion* (New York: Cambridge University Press, 2003), 69.

37. Anton Bebler, "The Yugoslav People's Army and the Fragmentation of a Nation," *Military Review*, August 1993, 38–51.

38. Anton Grizold, "The National Security of Slovenia: The View of Public Opinion," *Balkan Forum*, 3:3 (September 1995): 184.

39. Gow and Carmichael, *Slovenia and the Slovenes*, 187.

40. Viktor Myasnikov, "Putin Attacks Chronic Commercialization of Russian Armed Forces," *Nezavisimaia Gazeta*, 11 November 2005.

41. Interview with Ioan Mircea Pascu, Chairman of the Chamber of Deputies' Committee on Defense, Public Order, and National Security Committee (Bucharest, 3 November 1999).

42. "Dom Sovietov: s'ezd nachal rabotu," *Pravda*, 24 September 1993; and "Seeks Support of Military Units," Foreign Broadcast Information Service—Soviet Union, 27 September 1993, 27; both cited in Nichols, *The Russian Presidency*, 77.

43. See also Yeltsin, *The View from the Kremlin*, 278–79.

44. Robert Bruce Ware, "Will Southern Russian Studies Go the Way of Sovietology?" *Journal of Slavic Military Studies*, 16:4 (December 2003): 163–65. See also N. Grodnenskii, *Neokonchennaia voina: Istoria vooruzhennogo konflikta v Chechne* (Moscow: Charvest, 2004).

45. Larry L. Watts, "The Romanian Army in the December Revolution and Beyond," in Daniel N. Nelson, ed., *Romania After Tyranny* (Boulder, CO: Westview, 1992), 108.

46. See for instance, John Kifner, "Upheaval in the East; Fighting Abates in Transylvania but Not the Anger," *New York Times*, 27 March 1990; and "Miners' Rally in Romania Stirs Riots," Reuters (Bucharest), 25 September 1991.

47. Interviews with Larry Watts (Bucharest, 2 November 1999), Pascu (Bucharest, 3 November 1999), and Senator Nicolae Alexandru, chairman Defense, Public Order, and National Security Committee of the Senate (Bucharest, 4 November 1999)

48. Robin Shepherd, "Russia's Misplaced Pride Holds Back Its Democracy," *Financial Times*, 25 November 2005.

49. Interview with Larry L. Watts (Bucharest, 31 May 1993).

50. Interview with Arnejčič (Ljubljana, 3 December 1999).

51. Anton Bebler, "Civil-military Relations and Democratic Control of the Armed Forces in Slovenia," in Hans Born, Karl Haltiner, and Marjan Malešič, *Renaissance of Democratic Control of Armed Forces in Contemporary Societies* (Baden-Baden: Nomos, 2004), 129.

52. Zoltan Barany, "Hungary: Appraising a New NATO Member," *Clausewitz-Studien*, 14:4 (Winter 1999): 19–20.

53. Interview with Col. Anghel Filip (ret.), NATO/WEU Integration Directorate/ MOD (Bucharest, 1 November 1999), and Pascu (Bucharest, 3 November 1999).

54. *Two Years of Governance* (Bucharest: The Government of Romania, 1994), 28; Victor Babiuc, and interviews with Gheorghe-Vlad Niculescu, Monica-Mirela Malcoci (Bucharest, 4 November 1999) and Col. Alexandru Grumaz (Bucharest, 8 November 1999).

55. Simon Saradzhyan, "Putin Sacks 6 of Sergeev's Generals," *Moscow Times*, 1 August 2000.

56. See Jennifer G. Mathers, "Outside Politics? Civil-Military Relations during a Period of Reform," in Anne C. Aldis and Roger N. McDermott, eds., *Russian Military Reform*, 25; and Pavel Baev, "Reforming the Russian Military," in Yuri Fedorov and Bertil Nygren, eds., *Russian Military Reform and Russia's New Security Environment* (Stockholm: Swedish National Defence College, 2003), 45.

57. Bebler, "Civil-Military Relations in Slovenia," 208.

58. For different interpretations of the "Prishtina Dash," see Yu. Morozov, V. Glushkov, and A. Sharavin, *Balkany segodnia i zavtra: Voenno-politicheskie aspekty mirotvorchestva* (Moscow: Center of Military-Strategic Studies of the General Staff, 2001), 250–56; Strobe Talbott, *The Russia Hand* (New York: Random House, 2002), 332–349; and Lilia Shevtsova, *Putin's Russia* (Washington, DC: Carnegie Endowment for International Peace, 2003)—who contends that Yeltsin himself might well have been left out of the loop—endnote 11, 285.

59. Shevtsova, *Putin's Russia*, 130, and Vitaly V. Shlykov, "Does Russia Need a General Staff?," *European Security*, 10:4 (Winter 2001): 46–47, 64.

60. Pavel Felgenhauer, "Kvashnin Won't Be Missed," *Moscow Times*, 20 July 2004; and "Heads Roll at Long Last," *Economist*, 24 July 2004, 48–49.

61. See Pavel Felgenhauer, "General Staff in Command?" *Moscow Times*, 15 June 2004.

62. See Bogomil Ferfila and Paul Phillips, *Slovenia: On the Edge of the European Union* (Lanham, MD: University Press of America, 2000), 31–61, and especially 34; and Beno Arnejčič, "Some Aspects of the Accountability of the Slovenian Minister of Defense and Head of the General Staff of the Slovenian Defense Forces," paper presented at the "Democratic Civil-Military Relations Conference" (Ottawa, 26 March 1999), 79.

63. Dale R. Herspring, "The Process of Change and Democratization in Eastern Europe: The Case of the Military," in John R. Lampe and Daniel N. Nelson, eds.,

East European Security Reconsidered (Washington, DC: Woodrow Wilson Center Press, 1993), 66.

64. Interviews with Pascu and Alexandru. (Bucharest, 4 November 1999), chairmen of the Defense, Public Order, and National Security Committee of the Chamber of Deputies, and the Senate, respectively.

65. "Law on Ministry of National Defense," *Viitorul* (Bucharest), 19 January 1991, 3; translated in *Foreign Broadcast Information Service—Eastern Europe*, 1 February 1991.

66. See the interview with Lyobov Kudelina, "Increased Defense Spending Won't Benefit the Army," *Izvestia*, 27 September 2000; in Johnson's Russia List #4545 of the next day.

67. Larry Watts, "Reform and Crisis in Romanian Civil-Military Relations, 1989–1999," *Armed Forces & Society*, 27:4 (Summer 2001): 602.

68. Barany, *The Future of NATO Expansion*, 154.

69. Gregory J. Embree, "RSFSR Election Results and Roll-Call Votes," *Soviet Studies*, 43:6 (November 1991): 1065–84; and Alexander Sobyanin and Vladislav Sukhovolsky, "V korolevtsve krivykh zerkal," *Segodnia,* 10 March 1994.

70. Robert V. Barylski, *The Soldier in Russian Politics* (New Brunswick, NJ: Transaction, 1998), 231.

71. Viktor Baranets, *Yel'tsin i ego generali: Zapiski polkovnika genshtaba* (Moscow, Sovershenno Sekretno, 1998); and Aleksandr Golts, *Armiya Rossii: 11 poteriannikh let* (Moscow, Zakharov, 2004).

72. Interview with Professor Marjan Malešič of the Department of Defense Studies (Ljubljana, 2 December 1999).

73. Zoltan Barany, "NATO's Peaceful Advance," *Journal of Democracy*, 15:1 (January 2004): 63–76.

74. Interview with Lt. Col. Deborah Hanagan, a former SAO in Slovenia (Palo Alto, CA, 15 May 2008).

75. *U.S. Assistance to the Partnership for Peace*—Report to Congressional Committees GAO 01-734 (Washington, DC: U.S. Government Accounting Office, July 2001), 22.

76. See *Review of Parliamentary Oversight of the Romanian Ministry of National Defence and the Democratic Control of Its Armed Forces* (London: Ministry of Defence, February 1997).

77. Charles M. Perry and Dimitris Keridis, *Defense Reform, Modernization, & Military Cooperation in Southeastern Europe* (Dulles, VA: Brassey's, 2004), 129.

CHAPTER 8

1. Rory Stewart, *The Places in Between*. New York: Harvest/Harcourt, 2006, 247–48.

2. See Philip Mason, *A Matter of Honour: An Account of the Indian Army, Its Officers and Men* (London: Holt, Rinehart, and Winston, 1974).

3. Stephen P. Cohen, *The Indian Army: Its Contribution to the Development of a Nation* (New Delhi: Oxford University Press, 2001), 7.

4. John French, *Armies of the 19th Century: The British in India, 1825 to 1859* (Nottingham, UK: Foundry Books, 2006), 89–170; see also Cohen, *The Indian Army*, 35.

5. Interview with P.R. Chari, Institute of Peace and Conflict Studies (Delhi, 8 December 8, 2008).

6. Lawrence James, *The Rise and Fall of the British Empire* (New York: St. Martin's Press, 1994), 549.

7. Ibid., 502–503.

8. Ibid., 507.

9. This section draws on Zoltan Barany, "Authoritarianism in Pakistan," *Policy Review*, No. 156 (August–September 2009): 42–45.

10. Cohen, *The Indian Army*, 145.

11. Ibid., 45–47.

12. Ibid., 54.

13. Welch, Claude E., Jr., 1976a. "Civilian Control of the Military: Myth and Reality," in Welch, ed., *Civilian Control of the Military*, 29.

14. Interview with P. R. Chari.

15. Ayesha Jalal, *The Sole Spokesman: Jinnah, the Muslim League, and the Demand for Pakistan* (Cambridge, U.K.: Cambridge University Press, 1985).

16. Jaswant Singh, *Jinnah: India, Partition, Independence* (New York: Oxford University Press, 2010). See also Lydia Polgreen, "Politicians in India Turn Against One Another," *New York Times*, 7 October 2009; and "India Court Lifts Jinnah Book Ban," BBC News, 4 September 2009.

17. Husain Haqqani, *Pakistan: Between Mosque and Military* (Washington, DC: Carnegie Endowment for International Peace, 2005), 10.

18. Interview with Robert L. Hardgrave (Austin, 7 February 2008).

19. James, *The Rise and Fall*, 553–54.

20. Pankaj Mishra, "The Inner Voice: Gandhi's Legacy," *New Yorker*, 2 May 2011, 80.

21. Partap Narain, *Subedar to Field Marshal* (New Delhi: Manas, 1999), 230.

22. See, for instance, Sumit Ganguly, *The Crisis in Kashmir: Portents of War, Hopes of Peace* (New York: Cambridge University Press, 1997).

23. H. V. Hodson, *The Great Divide: Britain, India, Pakistan* (London: Hutchinson, 1969), 504–507.

24. Pervaiz Iqbal Cheema, *The Armed Forces of Pakistan* (New York: New York University Press, 2001), 18.

25. Stephen P. Cohen, *The Pakistan Army* (New Delhi: Himalayan Books, 1984), 7.

26. Shuja Nawaz, *Crossed Swords: Pakistan: Its Army and the Wars Within* (Oxford: Oxford University Press, 2008), 32–33.

27. N. Kunju, *Indian Army: A Grassroots Review* (New Delhi: Reliance, 1991), 17–18.

28. Mohammad Ayub Khan, *Friends Not Masters: A Political Autobiography* (New York: Oxford University Press, 1967), 19.

29. Pervaiz Iqbal Cheema, *Pakistan's Defense Policy, 1947–1958* (London: Macmillan 1990), 80.

30. Narain, *Subedar to Field Marshal*, 261.

31. See "Pakistan Struggles for Survival," *Life*, 15 January 1948, 16–20.

32. Interview with Brigadier (ret.) Faroz Khan (Monterey, CA, 10 June 2008).

33. Stephen P. Cohen, *The Idea of Pakistan* (Washington, DC: Brookings Institution Press, 2004), 47.

34. See Ayesha Jalal, *The State of Martial Rule: The Origins of Pakistan's Political Economy of Defence* (Cambridge, UK: Cambridge University Press, 1990).

35. A.F.K. Organski, *The Stages of Political Development* (New York: Alfred A. Knopf, 1965), 49–51.

36. Interview with Stephen P. Cohen (Austin, TX, 7 September 2007).

37. Haqqani, *Pakistan*, 313.

38. Interviews with Brigadier (ret.) Arun Sahgal and Brigadier (ret.) Gurmeet Kanwal (Delhi, 8 and 10 December 2008, respectively).

39. Cohen, *The Indian Army*, 210.

40. Stephen Peter Rosen, *Societies and Military Power: India and Its Armies* (Ithaca, NY: Cornell University Press, 1996), 221.

41. Raju G. Thomas, *Democracy, Security, and Development in India* (New York: St. Martin's Press, 1996), 101. See also Pradeep P. Barua, "Ethnic Conflict in the Military of Developing Nations: A Comparative Analysis of India and Nigeria," *Armed Forces & Society*, 19:1 (Fall 1992): 123–37.

42. Gurmeet Kanwal, *Indian Army: Vision 2020* (New Delhi: HarperCollins, 2008), 12.

43. Sunil Dasgupta, "India: The New Militaries," in Muthiah Alagappa, ed., *Coercion and Governance: The Declining Political Role of the Military in Asia* (Stanford, CA: Stanford University Press, 2001), 108.

44. Interview with Kanwal. See also Nawaz, *Crossed Swords*, xxxvi.

45. "Land of the Impure," *Economist*, 19 June 2010. For a book-length exposition of this issue, see Ayesha Siddiqa, *Military Inc.: Inside Pakistan's Military Economy* (London: Pluto Press, 2007).

46. Rajesh M. Basrur and Sumit Ganguly, "Pakistan's Self-Defeating Army," *Newsweek*, 4 May 2009.

47. Rosen, *Societies and Military Power*, 209.

48. Interview with Kanwal.

49. Interview with Manu Pubby, defense correspondent of the *Indian Express* (Delhi, 11 December 2008).

50. Cohen, *The Indian Army*, 184.

51. A group of nine Indian officers designed the parade ground and its building; the team stayed in Ethiopia for three and a half years (1956–60) till the academy was established. Narain, *Subedar to Field Marshal*, 262.

52. Haqqani, 61.

53. Cohen, *The Pakistan Army*, 45.

54. Babar Sattar, "Pakistan: Return to Praetorianism," in Alagappa, ed., *Coercion and Governance*, 394.

55. Rosen, *Societies and Military Power*, 217.

56. Public lecture by Stephen P. Cohen, University of Texas (Austin, 7 September 2007).

57. Rosen, *Societies and Military Power*, 217.

58. Interview with Pubby.

59. Dasgupta, "India," 94.

60. Interview with Kanwal.

61. Cited in Apurba Kundu, *Militarism in India: The Army and Civil Society in Consensus* (New York: St. Martin's Press, 1998), 82.

62. Stephen P. Cohen, "The Military and Indian Democracy," in Atul Kohli, ed., *India's Democracy: An Analysis of Changing State-Society Relations* (Princeton, NJ: Princeton University Press, 1988), 115.

63. Interview with Pubby.

64. Dasgupta, "India," 106.

65. Cohen, *The Indian Army*, 172–73.

66. Interview with Pubby.

67. Dasgupta, "India," 95.

68. Interview with Kanwal.

69. Interviews with active-duty and retired Indian officers (Delhi, December 2008).

70. Cohen, *The Indian Army*, 128.

71. Julian Schofield, *Militarization and War* (New York: Palgrave Macmillan, 2007), 60.

72. H. M. Patel, "The Situation of India," *Survival*, 4:6 (November 1962): 255–59.

73. Stephen P. Cohen, *India: Emerging Power* (Washington, DC: Brookings Institution Press, 2001), 135.

74. Schofield, *Militarization and War*, 53.

75. "Sam Manekshaw" (Obituary), *The Economist*, 5 July 2008. See also, Depinder Singh, *Field Marshal Sam Manekshaw: Soldiering with Dignity* (Delhi: Natraj, 2003).

76. P. R. Chari, "Civil-Military Relations in India," *Armed Forces & Society*, 4:1 (November 1977): 24.

77. "Sam Manekshaw" (Obituary), *The Economist*, 5 July 2008.

78. And twelve of the armed forces' seventeen major campaigns in 1947–95 were internal. See Dasgupta, 95–96.

79. Cohen, *The Indian Army*, xv.

80. Sumit Ganguly, "From the Defense of the Nation to Aid to the Civil: The Army in Contemporary India," *Journal of Asian and African Studies*, 26:1–2 (1991): 11–26.

81. Interviews in Delhi, December 2008.

82. Aqil Shah, "Praetorianism and Terrorism," *Journal of Democracy*, 19:4 (October 2008): 18.

83. See Ayub Khan, *Friends Not Masters*, 36–39.

84. Cited in Hasan-Askari Rizvi, *The Military & Politics in Pakistan, 1947–1997* (Lahore: Sang-e-Meel Publications, 2000), 42.

85. Schofield, *Militarization and War*, 36.

86. Brian Cloughley, *A History of the Pakistan Army: Wars and Insurrections* (Karachi: Oxford University Press, 1999), 33.

87. Ayesha Jalal, *Democracy and Authoritarianism in South Asia* (Cambridge: Cambridge University Press, 1995), 56–60.

88. Siddiqa, *Military Inc.*, 74.

89. Ibid., 73.

90. Schofield, *Militarization and War*, 40.

91. Saeed Shafqat, *Civil-Military Relations in Pakistan: From Zulfikar Ali Bhutto to Benazir Bhutto* (Boulder, CO: Westview, 1997), 57.

92. Cohen, *The Idea of Pakistan*, 125.

93. Haqqani, *Pakistan*, 51.

94. Cohen, *The Idea of Pakistan*, 81.

95. Haqqani, *Pakistan*, 111–12.

96. Ibid., 29.

97. Sattar, "Pakistan," 391.

98. See, for instance, Brian Cloughley, "Pakistan's Army and National Stability," Pakistan Security Research Unit, University of Bradford, U.K., Brief #47 (22 April 2009), 3–4.

99. Jérémie Codron, "Putting Factions 'Back in' the Civil-Military Relations Equation: Genesis, Maturation and Distortion of the Bangladeshi Army," *South Asia Multidisciplinary Academic Journal*, 2007 http://samaj.revues.org/document230.html, paragraph 7.

100. For an analysis of the Zia's rule, see Ashish Kumar Roy, *Praetorian Politics in Bangladesh, 1975–1981* (Kolkata: Progressive Publishers, 2002).

101. Amena Mohsin, "Bangladesh: An Uneasy Accommodation," in Alagappa, ed., *Coercion and Governance*, 221.

102. See Haqqani, Pakistan, 83–85; and Kabilan Krishnasamy, "Bangladesh and UN Peacekeeping: The Participation of a 'Small' State," *Commonwealth & Comparative Politics*, 41:1 (March 2003): 24–47.

103. For a good overview, see Bhulan Monoar Kabir, *Politics of Military Rule and the Dilemmas of Democratization in Bangladesh* (New Delhi: South Asian Publishers, 1999).

104. See Nazrul Islam, "Bengali Representation in Pakistan Defense Forces," *BIISS Journal*, 23:4 (2002): 363–69.

105. Sakhawat Hussain, "State of Law and Order in Military Involvement and Its Consequences," talk at the Institute of Regional Studies (Islamabad, January 2003), cited in Codron, paragraph 36.

106. Mohammad Asghar Khan, *Generals in Politics: Pakistan, 1958–1982* (New Delhi: Vikas, 1983), 200–203.

107. See Ashutosh Varshney, "Why Democracy Survives," *Journal of Democracy*, 9:3 (1998): 36–50.

108. For an excellent recent study that explores the implications of this point, see Stephen P. Cohen and Sunil Dasgupta, *Arming Without Aiming: India's Military Modernization* (Washington, D.C.: Brookings Institution Press, 2010).

109. See Zoltan Barany, "Why India, Why Not Pakistan? Reflections on South Asian Military Politics," Manekshaw (Occasional) Paper No. 11 (Delhi: Centre for Land Warfare Studies, 2009); and Philip Oldenburg, *India, Pakistan, and Democracy: Solving the Puzzle of Different Paths* (New York: Routledge, 2010).

110. See Rebecca Schiff, "Concordance Theory: The Cases of India and Pakistan," in David Mares, ed., *Civil-Military Relations* (Boulder, CO: Westview, 1998), 27–44.

CHAPTER 9

1. A. B. Assensoh and Yvette M. Alex-Assensoh, *African Military History and Politics* (New York: Palgrave, 2001), 2.

2. Edward Shils, "The Military in the Political Development of the New States," in John J. Johnson, ed., *The Role of the Military in Underdeveloped Countries* (Princeton, NJ: Princeton University Press, 1962), 38.

3. Robert B. Edgerton, *Africa's Armies: From Honor to Infamy* (Boulder, CO: Westview, 2002), 66–67.

4. See Ali A. Mazrui, ed., *The Warrior Tradition in Modern Africa* (Leiden: Brill, 1977); and Michelle Moyd, "'We Don't Want to Die for Nothing': *Askari* at war in German East Africa, 1914–1918," in Santanu Das, ed., *Race, Empire, and First World War Writing* (Cambridge, UK: Cambridge University Press, 2011), 90–107.

5. Interview with Julius Nyerere in the *Sunday Times* (London), 3 October 1999; cited in John Ndembwike, *Tanzania: The Land and Its People* (Pretoria: New Africa Press, 2008), 121.

6. Simon Baynham, *The Military and Politics in Nkrumah's Ghana* (Boulder, CO: Westview Press, 1988), 24.

7. William Lloyd-Jones, *K.A.R; Being an Unofficial Account of the Origins and Activities of the King's African Rifles* (London: Arrowsmith, 1926), 42.

8. Nestor N. Luanda and E. Mwanjabala, "King's African Rifles to Tanganyika Rifles: A Colonial Sliceup," in Tanzania People's Defence Forces, *Tanganyika Rifles Mutiny, January 1964* (Dar es Salaam: Dar es Salaam University Press, 1993), 11.

9. J. Bayo Andekson, "Army in a Multi-Ethnic Society: The Case of Nkrumah's Ghana, 1957–1966," *Armed Forces & Society*, 2:2 (February 1976): 253.

10. Baynham, 27.

11. Lt. Col. Hubert Moyse-Bartlett, *The King's African Rifles: A Study in the Military History of East and Central Africa, 1890–1945* (Aldershot: Gale & Polden, 1956), 478–574. See also, Timothy H. Parsons, *The African Rank-and-File: Social Implications of Colonial Military Service in the King's African Rifles, 1902-1964* (Portsmouth, NH: Heinemann, 1999) and John Nunneley, *Tales from the King's African Rifles* (London: Cassell, 2001).

12. Cameron Duodu, "Obituary: Major Seth Anthony," *The Guardian*, 13 January 2009.

13. W. F. Gutteridge, *Military Regimes in Africa* (London: Methuen, 1975), 30.

14. Baynham, 32.

15. Nestor N. Luanda, "Introduction," in *Tanganyika Rifles Mutiny*, ix.

16. Baynham, 109.

17. John Mukum Mbaku, *Institutions and Development in Africa* (Lawrenceville, NJ: Africa World Press, 2004), 131–34; and Edgerton, 149.

18. See Godfrey Mwakikagile, *Economic Development in Africa* (Huntington, NY: Nova Science Publishers, 1999), 58–62. See also, Goran Hyden, *Beyond Ujamaa in Tanzania: Underdevelopment and an Uncaptured Peasantry* (Berkeley: University of California Press, 1980).

19. Cited in Ndembwike, 107.

20. Interviews with Goran Hyden, Mwesiga Baregu, and Walter Bgoya (Dar es Salaam, on 7, 8, 9 April 2009, respectively). See also Godfrey Mwakikagile, *Nyerere and Africa: End of an Era* (Pretoria: New Africa Press, 2006).

21. Interviews with E. Gyimah-Boadi and Kojo Asante (Accra, 14 April 2009).

22. Edgerton, 149.

23. Andekson, 254; Shils, 31; and interview with Ben Kunbour (Accra, 14 April 2009).

24. Kenneth W. Grundy, "Nkrumah's Theory of Underdevelopment: An Analysis of Recurrent Themes," *World Politics*, 15:3 (April 1963): 450–51.

25. Interview with Amos Anyimadu (Accra, 14 April 2009).

26. Baynham, 128.

27. James S. Coleman and Belmont Brice, Jr., "The Role of the Military in Sub-Saharan Africa," in Johnson, ed., *The Role of the Military in Underdeveloped Countries*, 392; and Baynham, 93.

28. Eboe Hutchful, "Ghana," in Wuyi Omitoogun and Eboe Hutchful, eds., *Budgeting for the Military Sector in Africa: The Processes and Mechanisms of Control* (Oxford: SIPRI/Oxford University Press, 2006), 73.

29. Eboe Hutchful and Abdoulaye Bathily, "Introduction," in Hutchful and Bathily, eds., The *Military and Militarism in Africa* (Dakar, Senegal: CODESRIA, 1998), ix.

30. Hutchful, "Ghana," 72–73.

31. Interview with Samuel Atuobi (Accra, 15 April 2009).

32. Albert Orcan, *A Myth Is Broken: An Account of the Ghana Coup d'État* (London: Longmans, 1968), 15.

33. Cited in Robert Pinkney, *Ghana Under Military Rule, 1966–1969* (London: Methuen, 1972), 1.

34. Gutteridge, 64–65.

35. A. A. Afrifa, *The Ghana Coup, 24th February 1966* (London: Cass, 1967), 66.

36. Interview with Major-General (ret.) Carl Coleman (Accra, 15 April 2009).

37. Simon Baynham, "Civil-Military Relations in Post-Independent Africa," *South African Defence Review*, No. 3 (1992); accessed on 18 December 2010 at http://www.iss.co.za/Pubs/ASR/SADR3/Baynham.html.

38. Andekson, 264.

39. Baynham, *The Military and Politics*, 138; and interview with Kwame Boafo-Arthur (Accra, 15 April 2009).

40. Nestor Luanda, "A Changing Conception of Defence: A Historical Perspective of the Military in Tanzania," in Martin Rupiya, ed., *Evolutions and Revolutions: A Contemporary History of Militaries in Southern Africa* (Pretoria: Institute for Security Studies, 2005), 299.

41. N. N. Luanda and E. Mwanjabala, "King's African Rifles to Tanganyika Rifles: A Colonial Sliceup," in *Tanganyika Rifles Mutiny*, 27.

42. M. L. Baregu, "Perception of Threat and Conception of Defence Before the Mutiny," in *Tanganyika Rifles Mutiny*, 50.

43. Cited in William Edgett Smith, *Nyerere of Tanzania* (London: Gollancz, 1973), 121.

44. N. N. Luanda, "The Playout of the Mutiny, 19 to 21 January 1964," in *Tanganyika Rifles Mutiny*, 105–6.

45. Interview with Abillah Omari (Dar es Salaam, 9 April 2009).

46. See Ali Mazrui, *On Heroes and Uhuru Worship: Essays on Independent Africa* (London: Longmans, 1967), 92–94; and Gutteridge, 17.

47. See Ruth First, *The Barrel of a Gun: Political Power in Africa and the Coup d'État* (London: Allen Lane, 1970), especially 411–65; and Henry Bienen, *Armies and Parties in Africa* (New York: Holmes & Meier, 1978), 140–42.

48. Robert Pinkney, *Democracy and Dictatorship in Ghana and Tanzania* (London: Macmillan 1997), 121. See also Ali Mazrui, "The Soldier and the State in East Africa: Some Theoretical Conclusions on the Army Mutinies of 1964" *Western Political Quarterly*, 20:1 (March 1967): 82–96.

49. Cranford Pratt, *The Critical Phase in Tanzania, 1945–1968: Nyerere and the Emergence of Socialist Strategy* (New York: Cambridge University Press, 1976), 179.

50. A. B. Assensoh, *African Political Leadership* (Malabar, FL: Krieger, 1998), 131–33; and Martin Bailey, *The Union of Tanganyika and Zanzibar: A Study in Political Integration* (Syracuse, NY: East African Studies IX, Syracuse University, 1973), 1.

51. Hutchful and Bathily, "Introduction," ii.

52. I am grateful to Charles Thomas, a doctoral student in history at the University of Texas, for these points.

53. Luanda, "The Aftermath," 155.

54. Interviews with Brigadier Lilian Kinghazi and Major General (ret.) Herman Lupogo (Dar es Salaam, 6 and 11 April 2009).

55. Interview with Prof. Mwesiga Baregu (Dar es Salaam, 8 April 2009).

56. Interview with General Lupogo.

57. See, for instance, Abillah H. Omari, "Civil-Military Relations in Tanzania," in Williams, Cawthra, and Abrahams, eds., *Ourselves To Know*, 89–106.

58. Cited in Ali Mazrui, *Violence and Social Thought: Essays on Social Tensions in Africa* (London: Longmans, 1969), 33.

59. Herman Lupogo, "Tanzania: Civil-Military Relations and Political Stability," *African Security Review*, 10:1 (January 2001). Accessed on 18 December 2010 at http://www.issafrica.org/pubs/ASR/10No1/Lupogo.html.

60. Casta Tungaraza, "The Transformation of Civil-Military Relations in Tanzania," in Hutchful and Bathily, eds. The *Military and Militarism in Africa*, 299–301.

61. Pinkney, *Democracy and Dictatorship*, 121.

62. See Lilian Kinghazi, "Enhancing Human Resource Capability in the TPDF" (M.A. thesis, Naval Postgraduate School, June 2006), 28–30.

63. Andrew Mambo and Julian Schofield, "Military Diversion in the 1978 Uganda-Tanzania War," *Journal of Political and Military Sociology*, 35:2 (Winter 2007): 306; and interview with General Lupogo.

64. Baynham, *The Military and Politics*, 87–91.

65. First, 18.

66. Samuel Decalo, *Coups and Army Rule in Africa* (New Haven: Yale University Press, 1976), 19.

67. See Staffan Wiking, *Military Coups in Sub-Saharan Africa* (Uppsala: Scandinavian Institute of African Studies, 1983), 87.

68. First, 22.

69. Pinkney, *Democracy and Dictatorship*, 70.

70. Ibid., 160.

71. Edward Feit, "The Rule of the 'Iron Surgeons': Military Government in Spain and Ghana," *Comparative Politics*, 1:4 (July 1969): 487.

72. Gutteridge, 77.

73. Pinkney, *Ghana Under Military Rule*, 38.

74. Ibid., 20.

75. Ibid., 28.

76. See Robert M. Price, "A Theoretic Approach to Military Rule in New States," *World Politics*, 23:3 (April 1971): 399–430.

77. Decalo, 31.

78. Samuel E. Finer, *The Man on Horseback* (London: Pall Mall, 1962), 190–97.

79. Interview with Kwame Boafo-Arthur (Accra, 15 April 2009).

80. Interview with General Coleman.

81. Baynham, *The Military and Politics*, 262.

82. Gutteridge, 83.

83. Pinkney, *Democracy and Dictatorship*, 71.

84. Interview with Kwesi Aning (Accra, 17 April 2009).

85. Interview with Amos Anyimadu (Accra, 14 April 2009).

86. Interviews with Ben Kunbour and Kwame Boafo-Arthur (Accra, 14 and 15 April 2009). See also Jeffrey Herbst, *The Politics of Reform in Ghana, 1982–1991* (Berkeley: University of California Press, 1993).

87. See Alexander Boniface Makulilo, *Tanzania: A De Facto One Party State?* (Saarbrücken: VDM Verlag, 2008); and E. Gyimah-Boadi, "Another Step Forward for Ghana," *Journal of Democracy*, 20:2 (April 2009): 138–52.

88. Paul Sharp and Louis Fisher. "Inside the 'Crystal Ball': Understanding the Evolution of the Military in Botswana and the Challenges Ahead," in Rupiya, ed., *Evolutions and Revolutions*, 45.

89. See John Holm, "Botswana: A Paternalist Democracy," in Larry Diamond, et al., eds., *Democracy in Developing Countries*, Vol. 2. (Boulder, CO: Lynne Rienner,

1988), 214; and Kenneth Good, "Authoritarian Liberalism: a defining characteristic of Botswana," *Journal of Contemporary African Studies*, 14:1 (1996): 29–48.

90. See "Freedom in the World—Botswana (2008)," Freedom House, 2009 (http. freedomhouse.org); "The Good Example," and "Diamonds Are Not for Ever," *Economist*, 24 October 2009; 20 and 58–59.

91. See Abdi Ismail Samatar, *An African Miracle* (Portsmouth, NH: Heinemann, 1999); Joe Nocera, "Diamonds Are Forever in Botswana," *New York Times*, 8 August 2008; and especially, J. Clark Leith, *Why Botswana Prospered* (Montreal: McGill-Queen's University Press, 2005).

92. Isaac Schapera, *The Tswana* (London: Kegan Paul, 1953), 46–48.

93. Interview with Professor Mpho Molomo (Gaborone, 19 May 2009).

94. Ernest Chilisa, "MPs Give Blessing for Army Bill," *Daily News* (Gaborone), 31 March 1977, 1, 2.

95. Dan Henk, "The Botswana Defence Force: Evolution of a Professional African Military," *African Security Review*, 13:4 (2004): 86.

96. Kenneth Good, *Diamonds, Dispossession, and Democracy in Botswana* (Johannesburg: Jacana Media, 2008), 82–83.

97. Interview with Ross Sanoto (Gaborone, 18 May 2009).

98. See Dan Henk, *The Botswana Defense Force in the Struggle for an African Environment* (New York: Palgrave Macmillan, 2007).

99. Interview with Augustine N. Makgonatsotlhe (Gaborone, 14 May 2009). See also Raymond Molatole and Steven Laki Thaga, "Interventions against HIV/AIDS in the Botswana Defence Force," in Martin Rupiya, ed., *The Enemy Within: Southern African Militaries' Quarter-Century Battle with HIV and AIDS* (Pretoria: Institute for Security Studies, 2006), 19–64; and Unity Dow and Max Essex, *Saturdays Are for Funerals* (Cambridge, MA: Harvard University Press, 2009).

100. Richard Sklar, "On Democracy and Development in Botswana," in John Holm and Patrick Molutsi, eds., *Democracy in Botswana* (Athens, OH: Botswana Society and University Press, 1990), 277.

101. Government of Botswana, *Botswana Defence Force Act* (Gaborone: Government Printer, 1977), 12.

102. Sharp and Fisher, 53.

103. See Tendekani Malebeswa, "Civil Control of the Military in Botswana," in Williams, Cawthra, and Abrahams, eds., *Ourselves to Know*, 70–71, 77.

104. James Zaffiro, "The Press and Political Opposition in an African Democracy: The Case of Botswana," *Journal of Commonwealth and Comparative Politics*, 27:1 (1989): 66. See also, Good, *Diamonds, Dispossession, and Democracy in Botswana*, 60.

105. I am indebted for this point to General Lupogo who served for years at party headquarters. Personal e-mail exchange, 11–13 July 2009.

106. See, for instance, Myron Weiner, "Empirical Democratic Theory" in Myron Weiner and Ergun Özbudun, eds., *Competitive Elections in Developing Countries* (Washington, DC: American Enterprise Institute, 1987), 3–34; and Michael Bernhard, Christopher Reenock, and Timothy Nordstrom,"The Legacy of Western Overseas Colonialism on Democratic Survival," *International Studies Quarterly*, 48:1

(March 2004): 225–50. For a dissenting view see Kwasi Kwarteng, *Ghosts of Empire: Britain's Legacy in the Modern World* (London: Bloomsbury, 2011).

107. The adjective formed from the noun, "Bostwana" is "Batswana" or "Tswana."

CHAPTER 10

1. Douglas A. Macgregor, *The Soviet-East German Military Alliance* (Cambridge: Cambridge University Press, 1989), 106. See also Volker Koop, *Besetzt: Sowjetische Besatzungspolitik in Deutschland* (Berlin: bebra Verlag, 2008).

2. Mark N. Gose, "The Role of the Military in Building Political Community: The Case of the Two German States" (Ph.D. diss., University of Colorado, 1995), 105 and 111; and Ilko-Sascha Kowalczuk and Stefan Wolle, *Roter Stern über Deutschland* (Berlin: Ch-Links Verlag, 2001).

3. Theodor Hoffmann, *Das Letzte Kommando* (Berlin: Mittler & Son, 1993), 70.

4. Dale R. Herspring, *East German Civil-Military Relations* (New York: Praeger, 1973), 186.

5. Thomas M. Forster, *The East German Army* (London: Allen & Unwin, 1980), 171.

6. Dale R. Herspring, *Requiem for an Army* (Lanham, MD: Rowman & Littlefield, 1998), 25.

7. Gose, *"The Role of the Military,"* 119.

8. Jörg Schönbohm, *Two Armies and One Fatherland: The End of the Nationale Volksarmee*. Translated by Peter and Elfi Johnson (Providence, RI: Berghahn Books, 1996), 103; and Hans-Joachim Gießmann, *Das unliebsame Erbe: Die Auflösung der Militärstruktur der DDR* (Baden-Baden: Nomos, 1992), 33–35.

9. Frederick Zilian, Jr., *From Confrontation to Cooperation* (Westport, CT: Praeger, 1999), 73.

10. Mark N. Gose, "Political Socialization in the *Bundeswehr*: The Role of the Military in Integrating the East," unpublished paper, 1998, 16.

11. "Gorbatschow auf ZK-Plenum der KPdSU: Die Sowjetunion wird die DDR nicht im Stich lassen," *Neues Deutschland*, 11 December 1989; and "Wohin mit den Russen? 363,000 Sowjetsoldaten in der DDR," *Der Spiegel*, 16 July 1990, 26–36.

12. See, for instance, Egon Krenz, *Wenn Mauern fallen: Die friedliche Revolution* (Vienna: Neff, 1990).

13. See Hersrpring, *Requiem*, 89–95.

14. Schönbohm, *Two Armies*, 18–19. See also Hans Ehlert, *Armee ohne Zukunft: Das Ende der NVA und die deutsche Einheit* (Berlin: Ch. Links Verlag, 2002).

15. Tom Dyson, *The Politics of German Defence and Security* (Oxford: Berghahn Books, 2007), 36.

16. Hans Raidel, *Die Bundeswehr: Grundlagen, Rollen, Aufgaben* (Munich: Hanns-Seidel-Stiftung, 1998), 69.

17. In 1991 he was promoted to the post of Inspector of the Army, one of the highest-ranking officers in the Bundeswehr. After retirement from the military in

1992, he became a successful politician and served as the Minister of Interior for the state of Brandenburg in 1999–2009. See his fascinating memoirs, *Wilde Schermut: Erinnerungen einer Unpolitischen* (Berlin: Landt-Verlag, 2010).

18. Zilian, 5.

19. Interview with Lt. Gen. (ret.) Jörg Schönbohm (Kleinmachnow, 13 December 2011).

20. Interviews with Col. Dr. Winfried Heinemann (Potsdam, 7 April 2010) and Lt. Gen. (ret) Werner von Scheven (Geltow-Schwielowsee, 14 December 2011).

21. Schönbohm, *Two Armies*, 207.

22. See Matvei P. Burlakow, *Wir verabschieden uns als Freunde* (Bonn: InnoVatio Verlag, 1994); Bernhard Mroß, *Sie gingen als Freunde: Der Abzug der Westgruppe der sowjetisch-russischen Truppen, 1990–1994* (Harrislee: Bernhard Mroß im Eigenverlag, 2004); and, more generally, Celeste Wallander, *Mortal Friends, Best Enemies: German-Russian Cooperation after the Cold War* (Ithaca, NY: Cornell University Press, 1999).

23. *Armee der Einheit: 1990–2000* (Bonn: Bundesministerium der Verteidigung, Presse- und Informationsstab, 2000), 11.

24. Schönbohm, *Two Armies*, 206.

25. Gose, "Political Socialization," 29; and Zilian, 96.

26. Schönbohm, *Two Armies*, 62.

27. Herspring, *Requiem*, 163.

28. Andrew Bickford, "Soldiers, Citizens, and the State: East German Army Officers in Post-Unification Germany," *Comparative Studies in Society and History*, 51:2 (April 2009): 261.

29. Zilian, 7.

30. Interview with Col. Heinemann.

31. "Conscription in Germany to End Next Summer," *Spiegel Online*, 23 November 2010.

32. Jürgen Kuhlmann and Jean Callaghan, "About the Primacy of Politics over Military Matters," in Hans Born, Karl Haltiner, and Marjan Malešič, eds., *Renaissance of Democratic Control of Armed Forces in Contemporary Societies* (Baden-Baden: Nomos, 2004), 81–82.

33. See Tom Dyson, *Neoclassical Realism and Defence Reform in Post–Cold War Europe* (New York: Palgrave Macmillan, 2010).

34. Dyson, *Politics of German Defence*, 1. See also Mary Elise Sarotte, *German Military Reform and European Security* (Adelphi Paper #340; London: IISS, 2001).

35. See, for instance, Rainer Baumann and Günther Hellmann, "Germany and the Use of Military Force: 'Total War,' the 'Culture of Restraint,' and the Quest for Normalcy," *German Politics*, 10:1 (April 2001): 61–82.

36. Interview with Jörg Muth (Salt Lake City, 29 April 2008).

37. "Reforming Reticence," *Economist*, 17 June 2004. See also Klaus Naumann, *Einsatz ohne Ziel? Die Politikbedürftigkeit des Militärischen* (Hamburg: Hamburger Edition HIS Verlag, 2008).

38. Roger Cohen, "Time for the Bundesmacht," *New York Times*, 25 October 2007; Rudolf Schlaffer and John Zimmermann, *Wo bitte geht's zur Schlacht? Ku-*

rioses aus dem deutschen Militär von A-Z (Berlin: be.bra, 2009), 8; and interview with Dr. Martin Rink (Potsdam, 8 April 2010).

39. "A Troubling Victory: NATO after Libya," *Economist*, 3 September 2011, 58.

40. See the interview with Fischer, "Berlin Has 'Lost Touch with Reality,'" *Der Spiegel*, 29 August 2011, available at www.spiegel.de/international/germany/0,1518,783043,00.html.

41. Interview with Rink.

42. See Tim Collard, "German President Resigns: When Will His Countrymen Grow Up?," *Daily Telegraph*, 2 June 2010; Judy Dempsey, "German President Quits over Remarks on Military," *New York Times*, 31 May, 2010; and Denis MacShane, "Horst Köhler's Resignation Is Bad for Germany, for Europe and for Politics: Those Who Grasp Thorny Issues Should Be Lauded, Not Hounded," *Guardian*, 1 June 2010.

43. "German Armed Forces Face Big Changes," *IISS Strategic Comments*, 16:46 (December 2010).

44. Interview with Annette Seegers (Cape Town, 7 May 2009).

45. John Chiahemen, "Mandela Leads Tributes to S. Africa's Botha," Reuters (Johannesburg), 1 November 2006.

46. Patti Waldmeir, *Anatomy of a Miracle: The End of Apartheid and the Birth of the New South Africa* (New Brunswick, NJ: Rutgers University Press, 1998), 54–55.

47. David B. Ottaway, "S. Africa Lifts Ban on ANC, Other Groups," *Washington Post*, 3 February 1990.

48. See Jeffrey Butler, Robert Rotberg, and John Adams, *The Black Homelands of South Africa* (Berkeley: University of California Press, 1978).

49. See, for instance, Willem Steenkamp, *South Africa's Border War, 1966–1989* (Oxford, UK: African Books Collective, 1992); and David Williams, *On the Border, 1965–1990: The White South African Military Experience* (Cape Town: Tafelberg, 2010).

50. See, for instance, Gavin Cawthra, *Brutal Force: The Apartheid War Machine* (London: International Defence and Aid Fund for Southern Africa, 1986), especially 138–215.

51. Interview with Willem Steenkamp (Cape Town, 8 May 2009).

52. See, for instance, Laurie Nathan, "Troops in the Townships, 1984–1987," in Jacklyn Cock and Laurie Nathan, eds., *Society at War: The Militarization of South Africa* (New York: St. Martin's, 1989), 67–78; Heribert Adam and Kogila Moodley, "Political Violence, 'Tribalism', and Inkatha," *Journal of Modern African Studies*, 30/3 (1992): 485–510; and Franz Ansprenger, *Inkatha Freedom Party: Eine Kraft im demokratischen Südafrika* (Bonn: Bouvier, 1999).

53. Interview with Helmoed Heitman, a correspondent of *Jane's Defence Weekly* (Cape Town, 7 May 2009) and retired SADF officer.

54. Annette Seegers, *The Military in the Making of Modern South Africa* (London: I. B. Tauris, 1996), 311.

55. Interview with Major General (ret.) Len le Roux (Centurion, South Africa, 13 May 2009).

56. Interviews with Henri Boshoff of the Institute for Security Studies (Pretoria, 11 May 2009); le Roux, and Steenkamp.

57. Gordon Hughes, "Defence Transformation—A Project Still in Progress," *Cranfield CSSM Case Study Series* (Shrivenham, UK: Cranfield University, November 2007), 4.

58. Interviews with James Selfe, Member of Parliament (Cape Town, 8 May 2009) and Steenkamp.

59. Cited in Edward P. Joseph, "Ownership Is Overrated," *SAIS Review*, 27:2 (Summer–Fall 2007): 111. See also Philip Frankel, *Soldiers in a Storm* (Boulder, CO: Westview, 2000), 62–64.

60. Paul Trewhela, "Joe Modise" (Obituary), *Independent*, 30 November 2001. See also Stephen Ellis, "The ANC in Exile," *African Affairs*, 90: (1991): 439–47.

61. See for instance, ibid.; interview with Selfe; Joe Roeber, "Parallel Markets: Corruption in the International Arms Trade," Goodwin Paper #3 (London: Campaign Against Arms Trade, June 2005), available at http://www.controlbae.org/background/parallel_markets.pdf; and Robert J. Griffiths, "Parliamentary Oversight of Defense in South Africa," in Mitchell O'Brien, Rick Stapenhurst, and Niall Johnson, eds., *Parliaments and Peacebuilders in Conflict-Affected Areas* (Washington, DC: World Bank, 2008), 93–103, esp. 98–100.

62. Lyn S. Graybill, *Truth and Reconciliation in South Africa* (Boulder, CO: Lynne Rienner, 2002), 90; and Douglas Martin, "Magnus Malan, Apartheid Defender, Dies at 81," *New York Times*, 18 July 2011. See also, Robert I. Rotberg and Dennis Thompson, eds., *Truth vs. Justice* (Princeton, NJ: Princeton University Press, 2000). See also, Hilton Hamann, *Days of the Generals* (Cape Town: Zebra Press, 2001), 107–9, 217–21.

63. Interview with Len le Roux.

64. See Philip Frankel, *Pretoria's Praetorians* (New York: Cambridge University Press, 1984).

65. See chapter 11 ("Security Services") of *The Constitution of the Republic of South Africa*, 107. Available at http://www.justice.gov.za/legislation/constitution/SA%20Constitution_2011edition_eng.pdf. See also James Ngculu, "Parliament and Defence Oversight: The South African Experience," *African Security Review*, 10:1 (2001), available at http://www.iss.co.za/pubs/asr/10no1/Ngculu.html.

66. Len le Roux, "South Africa," in Wuyi Omitoogun and Eboe Hutchful, eds. *Budgeting for the Military Sector in Africa: The Processes and Mechanisms of Control* (Oxford: SIPRI/OUP, 2006), 198.

67. See the document at http://www.info.gov.za/whitepapers/1996/defencwp.htm.

68. *The Changing of the Guard: Armed Forces and Defence Policy in a Democratic South Africa* (Pretoria: Human Sciences Research Council, 1994).

69. On its preparation, see Kai Michael Kenkel, "Civil Society Participation in Defence Policy Formulation: Academic Experts and South Africa's Post-Apartheid Defence White Paper," *Journal of Security Sector Management*, 4:1 (January 2006): 1–26; and interview with Seegers.

70. Interview with Selfe.

71. Interview with le Roux. The document is available at http://www.dod.mil.za/documents/defencereview/defence%20review1998.pdf.

72. Gavin Cawthra, "From 'Total Strategy' to 'Human Security': The Making of South Africa's Defence Policy, 1990–1999," *Journal of Peace, Conflict, and Mil Studies*, 1:1 (Mar 2000), available at http://www.uz.ac.zw/units/cds/journals/volume1/number1/article4.html.

73. For interesting insights into Mbeki and his presidency, see Mark Gevisser, *A Legacy of Liberation: Thabo Mbeki and the Future of the South African Dream* (New York: Palgrave Macmillan, 2008).

74. See, for instance, Andrew Feinstein, *After the Party: Corruption, the ANC, and South Africa's Uncertain Future* (London: Verso, 2009); and Alec Russell, *Bring Me My Machine Gun: The Battle for the Soul of South Africa from Mandela to Zuma* (New York: Public Affairs, 2009).

75. http://www.anc.org.za/ancdocs/history/conf/conference50/

76. See, for instance, Isaac M. Ntshoe, "The Impact of Political Violence on Education in South Africa," *Current Issues in Comparative Education* (Teachers' College of Columbia University), 2:1 (2002): 62–69.

77. Interviews with former and current SANDF personnel (Cape Town, Johannesburg, and Pretoria, May 2009); and e-mail communication from Professor Annette Seegers (5 November 2010).

78. Interview with Selfe.

79. See Martin Rupiya, "Southern African Militaries' Battle against HIV/AIDS," in Rupiya, ed., *The Enemy Within: Southern African Militaries' Quarter-Century Battle with HIV and AIDS* (Pretoria: Institute for Security Studies, 2006), 7–18.

80. "South Africa's Shame," *Wall Street Journal*, May 28, 2008.

81. Interview with Steenkamp.

82. Interview with le Roux.

83. Sarah Phillips, *Yemen's Democracy Experiment in Regional Perspective* (New York: Palgrave-Macmillan, 2008), 69–71.

84. Robert D. Kaplan, *Imperial Grunts: The American Military on the Ground* (New York: Random House, 2005), 24.

85. Sheila Carapico, *Civil Society in Yemen* (New York: Cambridge University Press, 1998), 33, 36.

86. Charles Dunbar, "The Unification of Yemen: Process, Politics, and Prospects," *Middle East Journal*, 46:3 (Summer 1992): 460.

87. See Victoria Clark, *Yemen: Dancing on the Heads of Snakes* (New Haven, CT: Yale University Press, 2010), 246–52.

88. For a "user-friendly" conceptionalization of Saleh's inner circle, see Sarah Phillips, *Yemen and the Politics of Permanent Crisis* (New York: Routledge, 2011), 87–97.

89. This section draws on Ahmed Abdel-Karim Saif, "The Politics of Survival and the Structure of Control in Unified Yemen, 1990–1997" (M.A. thesis, University of Exeter, September 1997).

90. Michael C. Hudson, "After the Gulf War: Prospects for Democratization in the Arab World," *Middle East Journal*, 45:3 (Summer 1991): 423.

91. Dunbar, 466.

92. Youssef Aboul-Enein, "Islamist Militancy and Yemen's Internal Struggles," *Infantry*, 97:1 (January–February 2008): 46–47.

93. Dunbar, 462.

94. Saif, 13.

95. Gerd Nonneman, "The Yemen Republic: From Unification and Liberalisation to Civil War and Beyond," in Haifaa A. Jawad (ed.), *The Middle East in the New World Order* (London: Macmillan, 1997), 79.

96. Youssef, 47.

97. Paul Dresch, *A History of Modern Yemen* (New York: Cambridge University Press, 2000), 195–97.

98. Interview with Yahya Alshawkani (Washington, D.C., 27 February 2009).

99. U.N. security official Robert K. Adolph cited by Kaplan, 18. Far more instructive is Larry Diamond's article, "Why Are There No Arab Democracies?" *Journal of Democracy*, 21:1 (January 2010): 93–104.

100. "President Saleh Biography," *Yemen News Agency*, 13 July 2009 www.sabanews.net/en/news189750.htm, accessed 26 April 2010.

101. Barry Rubin, "The Military in Contemporary Middle Eastern Politics," *Middle East Review of International Affairs*, 5:1 (March 2001): 48.

102. Yezid Sayigh, "Security Sector Reform in the Arab Region," http.arab-reform.net, accessed 14 December 2007, 17–18.

103. Interview with Alshawkani.

104. See Ludmila du Bouchet, "State-building and the Military in Yemen in the Context of the 'Global War on Terror,'" paper presented at the annual meeting of the International Studies Association (San Francisco, March 2008).

105. Sayigh, 18. See also Arnold Luethold, "Security Sector Reform in the Arab Middle East," in Alan Bryden and Heiner Hänggi, eds., *Reform and Reconstruction of the Security Sector* (Münster: LIT Verlag, 2005), 93–118.

106. Phillips, 70

107. See, for instance, *The Military Balance, 2010* (London: IISS, 2010), 276–77.

108. Saif, 19.

109. Dresch, 208. See also Clark, 122–23.

110. Phillips, 68.

111. Lisa Wedeen, *Peripheral Visions: Publics, Power, and Performance in Yemen* (Chicago: University of Chicago Press, 2008), 76.

112. See Jonathan Schanzer, "Yemen's War on Terror," *Orbis*, 48:3 (Summer 2004): 517–31.

113. *Atlantic Monthly*, April 2010, 52–53; *New York Times Magazine*, 6 July 2010; and *Economist*, 12 September 2009, respectively.

114. Phillips, 70; Carapico, 78; and *Economist*, 12 September 2009.

115. This account draws on my article "Comparing the Arab Revolts: The Role of the Military," *Journal of Democracy*, 22:4 (October 2011): 27–39.

116. Jeffrey Fleishman and Zaid al-Alayaa, "Yemen President Capitalizes on His Political Wits," *Los Angeles Times*, 4 January 2012.

117. Dunbar, 469–70.

Conclusion

1. Gregory F. Rose, "The Post-Revolutionary Purge of Iran's Armed Forces," *Iranian Studies*, 17:2–3 (Spring/Summer 1984): 158.

2. See, for instance, Nancy Bermeo, "What the Democratization Literature Says—or Doesn't Say—About Postwar Democratization," *Global Governance*, 9:2 (April–June 2003): 167.

3. Samuel P. Huntington, *The Third Wave* (Norman, OK: University of Oklahoma Press, 1991), 252–53.

4. Ibid., 253.

5. Ibid., 252.

6. Interviews at the Kofi Annan International Peacekeeping Training Centre with Samuel Atuobi and Kwesi Aning (Accra, Ghana, 15 and 17 April 2009).

7. See, for instance, "Old Soldiers Never Cash Out," *New York Times*, 23 November 2009; and Matthew Moten, "Out of Order: Strengthening the Political-Military Relationship," *Foreign Affairs*, 89:5 (September-October 2010): 2–8, especially 7–8.

BIBLIOGRAPHY

This bibliography excludes newspaper articles. All references are in the endnotes.

Abenheim, Donald. *Reforging the Iron Cross: The Search for Tradition in the West German Armed Forces* (Princeton, NJ: Princeton University Press, 1988).

Abi-Ezzi, Karen. "Lebanon: Confessionalism, Institution Building, and the Challenges of Securing Peace," in Shields and Baldwin, eds., 159–72.

Aboul-Enein, Youssef. "Islamist Militancy and Yemen's Internal Struggles," *Infantry*, 97:1 (January–February 2008): 41–49.

Acheson, Dean. *Present at the Creation: My Years in the State Department* (New York: Norton, 1969).

Adam, Heribert, and Kogila Moodley. "Political Violence, 'Tribalism,' and Inkatha," *Journal of Modern African Studies*, 30:3 (1992): 485–510.

Adenauer, Konrad. *Memoirs, 1945–53.* Translated by Beate Ruhm von Oppen (Chicago, IL: Henry Regnery, 1966).

Afrifa, A. A. *The Ghana Coup, 24th February 1966* (London: Cass, 1967).

Agüero, Felipe. "The Military and the Limits of Democratization," in Scott Mainwaring, Guillermo O'Donnell, and J. Samuel Valenzuela, eds. *Issues in Democratic Consolidation: The New South American Democracies in Comparative Perspective* (Notre Dame, IN: University of Notre Dame Press, 1992), 153–98.

———. *Soldiers, Civilians, and Democracy: Post-Franco Spain in Comparative Perspective* (Baltimore, MD: Johns Hopkins University Press, 1995).

———. "Democratic Consolidation and the Military in Southern Europe and South America," in Richard Gunther, P. Nikiforos Diamandouros, and Hans-Jürgen Puhle, eds., *The Politics of Democratic Consolidation: Southern Europe in Comparative Perspective* (Baltimore, MD: Johns Hopkins University Press, 1995), 124–65.

———. "A Political Army in Chile: Historical Assessment and Prospects for the New Democracy," in Koonings and Kruijt, eds., 111–34.

Alagappa, Muthiah, ed. *Asian Security Practice: Material and Ideational Influences* (Stanford, CA: Stanford University Press, 1998).

———, ed. *Coercion and Governance: The Declining Political Role of the Military in Asia* (Stanford, CA: Stanford University Press, 2001).

Alfonsín, Raúl. "The Transition toward Democracy in a Developing Country: The Case of Argentina," in Daniel Nelson, ed., *After Authoritarianism* (Westport, CT: Praeger, 1995), 17–30.

Allawi, Ali A. *The Occupation of Iraq: Winning the War, Losing the Peace* (New Haven: Yale University Press, 2007).

Andekson, J. Bayo. "Army in a Multi-Ethnic Society: The Case of Nkrumah's Ghana, 1957–1966," *Armed Forces & Society*, 2:2 (February 1976): 251–72.

Andersen-Boers, Marion, and Jan Van der Meulen. "Homosexuality and the Armed Forces in the Netherlands," in Wilbur J. Scott and Sandra Carson Stanley, eds., *Gays and Lesbians in the Military* (Hawthorne, NY: Aldine de Gruyter, 1994), 205–18.

Anderson, Charles W. *The Political Economy of Modern Spain: Policy-Making in an Authoritarian System* (Madison: University of Wisconsin Press, 1970).

Andrzejewski, Stanislaw. *Military Organization and Society* (London: Routledge Kegan Paul 1954).

Ansprenger, Franz. *Inkatha Freedom Party: Eine Kraft im demokratischen Südafrika* (Bonn: Bouvier, 1999).

Arceneaux, Craig L. *Bounded Missions: Military Regimes and Democratization in the Southern Cone and Brazil* (University Park: Pennsylvania State University Press, 2001).

Arnejčič, Beno. "Some Aspects of the Accountability of the Slovenian Minister of Defense and Head of the General Staff of the Slovenian Defense Forces," paper presented at the "Democratic Civil-Military Relations Conference" (Ottawa, March 26, 1999).

Asghar Khan, Mohammad. *Generals in Politics: Pakistan, 1958-1982* (New Delhi: Vikas, 1983).

Assensoh, A. B. *African Political Leadership* (Malabar, FL: Krieger, 1998).

Assensoh, A. B., and Yvette M. Alex-Assensoh. *African Military History and Politics* (New York: Palgrave, 2001).

Avant, Deborah. "War, Recruitment Systems, and Democracy," in Elizabeth Kier and Ronald Krebs, eds., *In War's Wake: International Conflict and the Fate of Liberal Democracy* (New York: Cambridge University Press, 2010), 235–52.

Ayub Khan, Mohammad. *Friends Not Masters: A Political Autobiography* (New York: Oxford University Press, 1967).

Baev, Pavel K. "Reforming the Russian Military: History and Trajectory," in Yuri Fedorov and Bertil Nygren, eds., *Russian Military Reform and Russia's New Security Environment* (Stockholm: Swedish National Defence College, 2003), 37–55.

Bailey, Beth. *America's Army: Making the All-Volunteer Force* (Cambridge, MA: Harvard University Press, 2009).

Bailey, Martin. *The Union of Tanganyika and Zanzibar* (Syracuse, NY: East African Studies IX, Syracuse University, 1973).

Baker, Chris, and Pasuk Phongpaichit. *A History of Thailand* (Cambridge: Cambridge University Press, 2005).

Bañón Martínez, Rafael. "The Spanish Armed Forces During the Period of Political Transition, 1975–1985," in Bañón Martínez and Barker, eds., 311–53.

Bañón Martínez, Rafael, and Thomas M. Barker, eds. *Armed Forces and Society in Spain: Past and Present* (Boulder, CO: Social Science Monographs, 1988).

Barak, Oren. *The Lebanese Army: A National Institution in a Divided Society* (Albany, NY: SUNY Press, 2009).

Barak, Oren, and Gabriel Sheffer. "Continuous Existential Threats, Civil-Security Relations, and Democracy: A Comparative Exploration of Five Small States," Sheffer, Gabriel and Oren Barak, eds., *Existential Threats and Civil Security Relations* (Lanham, MD: Lexington Books, 2009), 119–51.

Barakat, Sultan, and Steven A. Zyck. "State Building and Post-Conflict Demilitarization: Military Downsizing in Bosnia and Herzegovina," *Contemporary Security Policy*, 30:3 (December 2009): 548–72.

Baranets, Viktor. *Yel'tsin i ego generali: Zapiski polkovnika genshtaba* (Moscow, Sovershenno Sekretno, 1998).

Barany, Zoltan. "Soviet Control of the Hungarian Military under Stalin," *Journal of Strategic Studies*, 14:2 (June 1991): 148–64.

———. *Soldiers and Politics in Eastern Europe, 1945–90* (London: Macmillan, 1993).

———. "The Military and Security Legacies of Communism," in Zoltan Barany and Iván Völgyes, eds., *The Legacies of Communism in Eastern Europe* (Johns Hopkins University Press, 1995), 101–17.

———. "Democratic Consolidation and the Military," *Comparative Politics*, 30:1 (October 1997): 21–44.

———. "Hungary: Appraising a New NATO Member," *Clausewitz-Studien*, 14:4 (Winter 1999), 1–31.

———. "Politics and the Russian Armed Forces," in Zoltan Barany and Robert G. Moser, eds., *Russian Politics: Challenges of Democratization* (New York: Cambridge University Press, 2001), 174–214.

———. *The Future of NATO Expansion* (New York: Cambridge University Press, 2003).

———. "NATO's Peaceful Advance," *Journal of Democracy*, 15:1 (January 2004): 63–76.

———. *Democratic Breakdown and the Decline of the Russian Military* (Princeton, NJ: Princeton University Press, 2007).

———. "Building Democratic Armies," in Zoltan Barany and Robert G. Moser, eds., *Is Democracy Exportable?* (New York: Cambridge University Press, 2009), 178–204.

———. "Authoritarianism in Pakistan," *Policy Review*, No. 156 (August–September 2009): 41–53.

———. "Why India, Why Not Pakistan? Reflections on South Asian Military Politics," Manekshaw (Occasional) Paper No. 11 (Delhi: Centre for Land Warfare Studies, 2009).

———. "Comparing the Arab Revolts: The Role of the Military," *Journal of Democracy*, 22:4 (October 2011): 27–39.

Barany, Zoltan, and Lawrence S. Graham. *Democratic Transitions and Civil-Military Relations: Comparing Eastern and Southern Europe* (Grant report prepared for NATO, 1994), 175 pp.

Baregu, Mwesiga L. "Perception of Threat and Conception of Defence Before the Mutiny," in *Tanzania People's Defense Forces*, 35–74.

Barros, Robert. *Constitutionalism and Dictatorship: Pinochet, the Junta, and the 1980 Constitution* (New York: Cambridge University Press, 2002).

Bartov, Omer. "Soldiers, Nazis, and War in the Third Reich," *Journal of Modern History*, 63:1 (March 1991): 44–60.

Barua, Pradeep P. "Ethnic Conflict in the Military of Developing Nations: A Comparative Analysis of India and Nigeria," *Armed Forces & Society*, 19:1 (Fall 1992): 123–37.

Barylski, Robert V. *The Soldier in Russian Politics* (New Brunswick, NJ: Transaction, 1998).

Baudissin, Count Wolf von. "The New German Army," *Foreign Affairs*, 34:1 (October 1955): 1–13.

———. *Soldat für Frieden: Entwürfe für eine Zeitgemässe Bundeswehr* (Munich: S. Piper, 1969).

Baumann, Rainer, and Günther Hellmann. "Germany and the Use of Military Force: 'Total War,' the 'Culture of Restraint,' and the Quest for Normalcy," *German Politics*, 10:1 (April 2001): 61–82.

Baynham, Simon. *The Military and Politics in Nkrumah's Ghana* (Boulder, CO: Westview Press, 1988).

———. "Civil-Military Relations in Post-Independent Africa," *South African Defence Review*, No. 3 (1992); accessed on December 18, 2010, at www.iss.co.za/Pubs/ASR/SADR3/Baynham.html.

Bebler, Anton. "The Yugoslav People's Army and the Fragmentation of a Nation," *Military Review*, August 1993, 38–51.

———. "Civil-Military Relations in Slovenia," in Constantine P. Danopoulos and Daniel Zirker, eds., *Civil-Military Relations in the Soviet and Yugoslav Successor States* (Boulder, CO: Westview Press, 1996), 195–212.

———. "Civil-military Relations and Democratic Control of the Armed Forces in Slovenia," in Born, Haltiner, and Malešič, eds., 121–32.

Beeson, Mark. "Civil-Military Relations in Indonesia and the Philippines: Will the Thai Coup Prove Contagious?" *Armed Forces & Society*, 34:3 (April 2008): 474–90.

Beeson, Mark, Alex J. Bellamy, and Bryn Hughes. "Taming the Tigers? Reforming the Security Sector in Southeast Asia," *Pacific Review*, 19:4 (December 2006): 449–72.

Bermeo, Nancy. *The Revolution within the Revolution: Workers' Control in Rural Portugal* (Princeton, NJ: Princeton University Press, 1986).

———. "Surprise, Surprise: Lessons from 1989 and 1991," in Nancy Bermeo, ed., *Liberalization and Democratization* (Baltimore, MD: Johns Hopkins University Press, 1992), 178–201.

———. "Classification and Consolidation: Some Lessons from the Greek Dictatorship," *Political Science Quarterly*, 110:3 (Autumn 1995): 435–52.

———. "Myths of Moderation: Confrontation and Conflict during Democratic Transitions," *Comparative Politics*, 29:3 (April 1997): 305–22.

———. "What the Democratization Literature Says—or Doesn't Say—About Postwar Democratization," *Global Governance*, 9:2 (April–June 2003): 159–77.

Bermudez, Joseph S. *The Armed Forces of North Korea* (London: I. B. Tauris, 2001).

Bernhard, Michael, Christopher Reenock, and Timothy Nordstrom. "The Legacy of Western Overseas Colonialism on Democratic Survival," *International Studies Quarterly*, 48:1 (March 2004): 225–50.

Betts, Richard K. "Are Civil-Military Relations Still a Problem?" in Nielsen and Snider, eds., 10–41.

Bickford, Andrew. "Soldiers, Citizens, and the State: East German Army Officers in Post-Unification Germany," *Comparative Studies in Society and History*, 51:2 (April 2009): 260–87.

Bienen, Henry. *Armies and Parties in Africa* (New York: Holmes & Meier, 1978).

Bingham, Sandra J. "The Praetorian Guard in the Political and Social Life of Julio-Claudian Rome" (Ph.D. diss., University of British Columbia, August 1997).

Birtle, A. J. *Rearming the Phoenix: U.S. Military Assistance to the Federal Republic of Germany, 1950–1960* (New York: Garland, 1991).

Bischof, Gunter, and Stephen E. Ambrose, eds. *Eisenhower and the German POWs* (Baton Rouge: Louisiana State University Press, 1992).

Bland, Douglas L. "Patterns in Liberal Democratic Civil-Military Relations," *Armed Forces & Society*, 27:4 (Summer 2001): 525–40.

Born, Hans, Karl Haltiner, and Marjan Malešič, eds. *Renaissance of Democratic Control of Armed Forces in Contemporary Societies* (Baden-Baden: Nomos, 2004).

Boucek, Christopher. "Yemen: Avoiding a Downward Spiral," Carnegie Papers No. 102 (Washington, DC: Carnegie Endowment—Middle East Program, September 2009).

Brands, Hal. *Crime, Violence, and the Crisis in Guatemala* (Carlisle, PA: U.S. Army War College Strategic Studies Institute, 2010).

Brendle, Thomas M. "Recruitment and Training in the SDF," in Buck, ed., 67–96.

Brocklebank, Laurie. *Jayforce: New Zealand and the Military Occupation of Japan, 1945–48* (Auckland: Oxford University Press, 1997).

Brockwehl, Alexander, and Juan Pablo Pitarque. "Concessions of a Leftist Party: The FMLN's Dilemma in the Face of Funes' Centrist Policies," *Council on Hemispheric Affairs Research Report*, June 28, 2010.

Brooker, Paul. *Non-Democratic Regimes: Theory, Government, & Politics* (London: Macmillan, 2000).

Brooks, Risa A. "Militaries and Political Activity in Democracies," in Nielsen and Snider, eds., 213–38.

Bruneau, Thomas C. "Introduction," in Bruneau and Tollefson, eds., 1–14.

———. "Defense Modernization and the Armed Forces in Portugal," *Portuguese Studies Review*, 1:2 (Fall–Winter 1991–93): 28–43.

Bruneau, Thomas C., Lucía Dammert, and Elizabeth Skinner, eds. *Maras: Gang Violence and Security in Central America* (Austin: University of Texas Press, 2011).

Bruneau, Thomas C. and Richard P. Goetze, Jr. "Ministries of Defense and Democratic Control," in Bruneau and Tollefson, eds., 71–98.

Bruneau, Thomas C., and Alex Macleod, eds. *Politics in Contemporary Portugal: Parties and the Consolidation of Democracy* (Boulder, CO: Lynne Rienner, 1986).

Bruneau, Thomas C., and Scott D. Tollefson, eds. *Who Guards the Guardians and How: Democratic Civil-Military Relations* (Austin: University of Texas Press, 2006).

Bruneau, Thomas C., and Harold Trinkunas. "Democratization as a Global Phenomenon and Its Impact on Civil-Military Relations," *Democratization* 13:5 (December 2006): 776–90.

Bučar, Bojko. "The International Recognition of Slovenia," in Danica Fink-Hafner and John R. Robbins, eds., *Making a New Nation: The Formation of Slovenia* (Brookfield, VT: Dartmouth, 1997), 31–45.

Buck, James H., ed. *The Modern Japanese Military System* (Beverly Hills, CA: Sage, 1975).

Bunce, Valerie. "Rethinking Recent Democratization: Lessons from the Postcommunist Experience," *World Politics*, 55:2 (January 2003): 167–92.

Bundesministerium der Verteidigung. *Armee der Einheit: 1990–2000* (Bonn: Bundesministerium der Verteidigung, Presse- und Informationsstab, 2000).

Burk, James. "Theories of Democratic Civil-Military Relations," *Armed Forces & Society*, 29:1 (Fall 2002): 7–29.

———. "The Military's Presence in American Society, 1950–2000," in Feaver and Kohn, eds., 247–74.

Burlakow, Matvei P. *Wir verabschieden uns als Freunde* (Bonn: InnoVatio Verlag, 1994).

Burrowes, Robert D. "Prelude to Unification: The Yemen Arab Republic, 1962–1990," *Journal of Middle East Studies*, 23:4 (November 1991): 483–506.

Buruma, Ian. *The Wages of Guilt: Memories of War in Germany and Japan* (London: Jonathan Cape, 1991).

Busquets, Julio. "Prólogo, La Transición: Conveniencia de su Estudio," *Revista Española de Investigaciones Sociológicas*, No. 36 (October–December 1986): 7–12.

Butler, Jeffrey, Robert Rotberg, and John Adams. *The Black Homelands of South Africa* (Berkeley: University of California Press, 1978).

Call, Charles. "War Transitions and the New Civilian Security in Latin America," *Comparative Politics*, 35:1 (October 2002): 1–20.

Cambanis, Thanassis. *A Privilege to Die: Inside Hezbollah's Legions and Their Endless War Against Israel* (New York: Free Press, 2010).

Carapico, Sheila. *Civil Society in Yemen* (New York: Cambridge University Press, 1998).

Carr, Raymond, and Juan Pablo Fusi. *Spain: Dictatorship to Democracy* (London: George Allen & Unwin, 2nd edition, 1981).

Cawthra, Gavin. *Brutal Force: The Apartheid War Machine* (London: International Defence and Aid Fund for Southern Africa, 1986).

———. "From 'Total Strategy' to 'Human Security': The Making of South Africa's Defence Policy, 1990–1999," *Journal of Peace, Conflict, and Military Studies*, 1:1 (March 2000): 51–67.

Cawthra, Gavin, and Robin Luckham, eds. *Governing Insecurity: Democratic Control of Military and Security Establishments in Transitional Democracies* (London: Zed Books, 2003).

Centeno, Miguel. *Blood and Debt: War and Nation-State in Latin America* (State College: Pennsylvania State University Press, 2003).

———. *Warfare in Latin America, Volumes I & II* (Aldershot, UK: Ashgate, 2007).

Cercas, Javier. *The Anatomy of a Moment: Thirty-Five Minutes in History and Imagination* (New York: Bloomsbury, 2011).

Cha, Victor. "Security and Democracy in South Korean Development," in Kim, ed., 201–19.

Chambers, Paul. "U-Turn to the Past? The Resurgence of the Military in Contemporary Thai Politics." Conference paper for the "The Military in Thai Politics: What's Next?" (Bangkok: Institute of Security and International Studies, Chulalongkorn University, September 2009).

Chamoun, Tracy. *Au nom du père* (Paris: J.-C. Lattès, 1992).

Chari, P. R. "Civil-Military Relations in India," *Armed Forces & Society*, 4:1 (November 1977): 3–28.

Cheema, Pervaiz Iqbal. *Pakistan's Defense Policy, 1947–1958* (London: Macmillan 1990).

———. *The Armed Forces of Pakistan* (New York: New York University Press, 2003).

Chivvis, Christopher S. "The Dayton Dilemma," *Survival*, 52:5 (October–November 2010): 47–74.

Clark, Victoria. *Yemen: Dancing on the Heads of Snakes* (New Haven, CT: Yale University Press, 2010).

Clausewitz, Carl von. *On War*. Translated by Michael Howard and Peter Paret (Princeton, NJ: Princeton University Press, 1989).

Clogg, Richard. "The Ideology of the 'Revolution of 21 April 1967,' " in Clogg and Yannopoulos, eds., 36–58.

Clogg, Richard, and George Yannopoulos, eds. *Greece under Military Rule* (New York: Basic Books, 1972).

Cloud, David, and Greg Jaffe. *The Fourth Star: Four Generals and the Epic Struggle for the Future of the United States Army* (New York: Crown, 2009).

Cloughley, Brian. *A History of the Pakistan Army: Wars and Insurrections* (Karachi: Oxford University Press, 1999).

———. "Pakistan's Army and National Stability," Pakistan Security Research Unit, University of Bradford, U.K., Brief No. 47 (April 22, 2009).

Codron, Jérémie. "Putting Factions 'Back in' the Civil-Military Relations Equation: Genesis, Maturation and Distortion of the Bangladeshi Army," *South Asia Multidisciplinary Academic Journal*, 2007. http://samaj.revues.org/document230.html

Cohen, Stephen P. *The Pakistan Army* (New Delhi: Himalayan Books, 1984).

———. "The Military and Indian Democracy," in Atul Kohli, ed., *India's Democracy: An Analysis of Changing State-Society Relations* (Princeton, NJ: Princeton University Press, 1988), 99–143.

Cohen, Stephen P. *The Indian Army: Its Contribution to the Development of a Nation* (New Delhi: Oxford University Press, 2001)

———. *India: Emerging Power* (Washington, DC: Brookings Institution Press, 2001).

———. *The Idea of Pakistan* (Washington, DC: Brookings Institution Press, 2004).

Cohen, Stephen P., and Sunil Dasgupta. *Arming Without Aiming: India's Military Modernization* (Washington, D.C.: Brookings Institution Press, 2010).

Coleman, James S., and Belmont Brice, Jr. "The Role of the Military in Sub-Saharan Africa," in Johnson, ed., 359–405.

Collier, David, and James Mahoney. "Insights and Pitfalls: Selection Bias in Qualitative Research." *World Politics*, 49:1 (1996): 56–91.

Collins, Randall. *Weberian Sociological Theory* (New York: Cambridge University Press, 1986).

Comas, José-Maria. "The Central Organization of Defense in Spain," in Edmonds, ed., 178–99

Costa Pinto, António. "The Salazar 'New State' and European Fascism," *EUI Working Paper*, HEC No. 91/12 (Florence: European University Institute, 1991).

Cottey, Andrew, Timothy Edmunds, and Anthony Forster. "The Second Generation Problematic: Rethinking Democracy and Civil-Military Relations," *Armed Forces & Society*, 29:1 (Fall 2002): 31–56.

Couloumbis, Theodore A. "The Greek Junta Phenomenon," *Polity*, 6:3 (Spring 1974): 345–74.

Creveld, Martin van. *Men, Women & War: Do Women Belong in the Front Line?* (London: Cassell & Co., 2001).

Croissant, Aurel, and David Kuehn, "Patterns of Civilian Control of the Military in East Asia's New Democracies," *Journal of East Asian Studies*, 9:2 (May–August 2009): 187–217.

Crouch, Harold. *The Army and Politics in Indonesia* (Ithaca, NY: Cornell University Press, 1988 [Rev. ed.]).

———. *Political Reform in Indonesia after Soeharto* (Singapore: Institute of Southeast Asian Studies, 2010).

Crowther, William. "'Ceausescuism' and Civil-Military Relations in Romania," *Armed Forces & Society*, 15:2 (Winter 1989): 207–25.

Dahl, Robert A. *Democracy and Its Critics* (New Haven: Yale University Press, 1989).

Danopoulos, Constantine P. "From Military to Civilian Rule in Contemporary Greece," *Armed Forces & Society*, 10:2 (Winter 1984): 229–59.

———. "Democratizing the Military: Lessons from Mediterranean Europe," *West European Politics*, 14:4 (October 1991): 25–41.

Dasgupta, Sunil. "India: The New Militaries," in Alagappa, ed., *Coercion and Governance*, 92–120.

Decalo, Samuel. *Coups and Army Rule in Africa* (New Haven: Yale University Press, 1976).

Defence Reform Commission. *The Path to Partnership for Peace* (Sarajevo: Defence Reform Commission of Bosnia and Herzegovina, September 2003).

Dempsey, Jason K. *Our Army: Soldiers, Politics, and American Civil-Military Relations* (Princeton, NJ: Princeton University Press, 2010).

Desch, Michael C. *Civilian Control of the Military: The Changing Security Environment* (Baltimore, MD: Johns Hopkins University Press, 2001).

Di Palma, Giuseppe. *To Craft Democracies* (Berkeley: University of California Press, 1990).

Diamint, Rut. "Crisis, Democracy, and the Military in Argentina," in Edward Epstein and David Pion-Berlin, eds., *Broken Promises? The Argentine Crisis and Argentine Democracy* (Lanham, MD: Lexington Books, 2006), 163–79.

Diamond, Larry. *Developing Democracy: Toward Consolidation* (Baltimore, MD: Johns Hopkins University Press, 1999).

———. "Why Are There No Arab Democracies?" *Journal of Democracy*, 21:1 (January 2010): 93–104.

Diamond, Larry, and Doh Chull Shin, eds. *Institutional Reform and Democratic Consolidation in Korea* (Stanford, CA: Hoover Institution Press, 2000).

———. "Introduction: Institutional Reforms and Democratic Consolidation in Korea," in Diamond and Shin, eds., 1–42.

Dietz, Henry, Jerrold Elkin, and Maurice Roumani, eds. *Ethnicity, Integration, and the Military* (Boulder, CO: Westview, 1991).

Dobbins, James, et al. *America's Role in Nation-Building: From Germany to Iraq* (Santa Monica, CA: Rand, 2003).

Dokos, Thanos. "The Evolution of Civil-Military Relations and Progress in Greek Security Sector Reform," in Dokos, ed., *Security Sector Transformation in Southeastern Europe and the Middle East* (Amsterdam: IOS Press, 2007), 39–49.

Dormann, Manfred. *Democratische Militärpolitik* (Freiburg: Rembach, 1970).

Dow, Unity, and Max Essex. *Saturdays Are for Funerals* (Cambridge, MA: Harvard University Press, 2009).

Dower, John. *Empire and Aftermath: Yoshida Shigeru and the Japanese Experience, 1878-1954* (Cambridge, MA: Harvard East Asia Center, 1988).

Dresch, Paul. *A History of Modern Yemen* (New York: Cambridge University Press, 2000).

du Bouchet, Ludmila. "State-building and the Military in Yemen in the Context of the 'Global War on Terror,' " Paper presented at the annual meeting of the International Studies Association (San Francisco, March 2008).

Dunbar, Charles. "The Unification of Yemen: Process, Politics, and Prospects," *Middle East Journal*, 46:3 (Summer 1992): 456–76.

Dunn, Christopher. "Democracy in the 21st Century: Canada Needs a War Powers Act," *Canadian Parliamentary Review*, 30:3 (Autumn 2007): 2–3.

Dye, Thomas R., and Harmon Ziegler, "Socialism and Militarism," *PS: Political Science and Politics*, 22:4 (December 1990): 810–13.

Dyson, Tom. *The Politics of German Defence and Security* (Oxford: Berghahn Books, 2007).

———. *Neoclassical Realism and Defence Reform in Post-Cold War Europe* (New York: Palgrave Macmillan, 2010).

Edgerton, Robert B. *Africa's Armies: From Honor to Infamy* (Boulder, CO: Westview, 2002).

Edmonds, Martin, ed. *Central Organizations of Defense* (Boulder, CO: Westview Press, 1985).

Ehlert, Hans. *Armee ohne Zukunft: Das Ende der NVA und die deutsche Einheit* (Berlin: Ch. Links Verlag, 2002).

el-Khazen, Farid. "Lebanon—Independent No More," *Middle East Quarterly*, 8:1 (2001): 43–50.

Ellis, Stephen. "The ANC in Exile," *African Affairs*, 90: (1991): 439–47.

Embree, Gregory J. "RSFSR Election Results and Roll-Call Votes," *Soviet Studies*, 43:6 (November 1991): 1065–84.

Ensalaco, Mark. "Truth Commissions for Chile and El Salvador: A Report and Assessment," *Human Rights Quarterly*, 16:4 (November 1994): 656–75.

Feaver, Peter D. "The Civil-Military Problematique: Huntington, Janowitz, and the Question of Civilian Control." *Armed Forces & Society*, 23:2 (Winter 1996): 149–78.

———. "Civil-Military Relations," *Annual Review of Political Science*, 2 (June 1999): 211–41.

———. *Armed Servants: Agency, Oversight, and Civil-Military Relations* (Cambridge, MA: Harvard University Press, 2003).

Feaver, Peter D., and Richard H. Kohn, eds. *Soldiers and Civilians: The Civil-Military Gap and American National Security* (Cambridge, MA: MIT Press, 2001).

Feaver, Peter D., and Erika Seeler. "Before and After Huntington: The Methodological Maturing of Civil-Military Studies," in Nielsen and Snider, eds., 72–90.

Feinstein, Andrew. *After the Party: Corruption, the ANC, and South Africa's Uncertain Future* (London: Verso, 2009).

Feit, Edward. "The Rule of the 'Iron Surgeons': Military Government in Spain and Ghana," *Comparative Politics*, 1:4 (July 1969): 485–97.

Feith, Herbert. "Indonesia's Political Symbols and Their Wielders," *World Politics*, 16:1 (October 1963): 79–97.

Ferfila, Bogomil, and Paul Phillips. *Slovenia: On the Edge of the European Union* (Lanham, MD: University Press of America, 2000).

Ferguson, Niall. "Prisoner Taking and Prisoner Killing in the Age of Total War: Towards a Political Economy of Military Defeat," *War in History*, 11:2 (April 2004): 148–92.

Fields, Rona M. *The Portuguese Revolution and the Armed Forces Movement* (New York: Praeger, 1976).

Finer, Samuel E. *The Man on Horseback: The Role of the Military in Politics* (London: Pall Mall, 1962).

First, Ruth. *The Barrel of a Gun: Political Power in Africa and the Coup d'État* (London: Allen Lane, 1970).

Fish, M. Steven. "The Executive Deception: Superpresidentialism and the Degradation of Russian Politics," in Valerie Sperling, ed., *Building the Russian State: Institutional Crisis and the Quest for Democratic Governance* (Boulder, CO: Westview Press, 2000), 177–92.

FLACSO. *Report on the Security Sector in Latin America and the Caribbean* (Santiago: FLACSO-Chile, 2007).

Forster, Thomas M. *The East German Army* (London: Allen & Unwin, 1980).

Frankel, Philip. *Pretoria's Praetorians* (New York: Cambridge University Press, 1984).

———. *Soldiers in a Storm* (Boulder, CO: Westview, 2000).

Freiherr von Bredow, Wilfried. "Central Organization of Defense in the Federal Republic of Germany," in Edmonds, ed., 65–84.

French, John. *Armies of the 19th Century: The British in India, 1825 to 1859* (Nottingham, UK: Foundry Books, 2006).

Frühstück, Sabine. *Uneasy Warriors: Gender, Memory, and Popular Culture in the Japanese Army* (Berkeley: University of California Press, 2008).

Fuentes, Claudio A. "After Pinochet: Civilian Policies Toward the Military in the 1990s Chilean Democracy," *Journal of Interamerican Studies and World Affairs,* 42:3 (Autumn 2000): 111–42.

Ganguly, Sumit. "From the Defense of the Nation to Aid to the Civil: The Army in Contemporary India," *Journal of Asian and African Studies,* 26:1–2 (1991): 11–26.

———. *The Crisis in Kashmir: Portents of War, Hopes of Peace* (New York: Cambridge University Press, 1997).

Gentles, Ian. *The New Model Army—In England, Ireland and Scotland 1645–53* (Oxford: Blackwell, 1994).

Gerring, John. "Is There a (Viable) Crucial-Case Method?" *Comparative Political Studies,* 40:3 (March 2007): 231–53.

Gevisser, Mark. *A Legacy of Liberation: Thabo Mbeki and the Future of the South African Dream* (New York: Palgrave Macmillan, 2008).

Gießmann, Hans-Joachim. *Das unliebsame Erbe: Die Auflösung der Militärstruktur der DDR* (Baden-Baden: Nomos, 1992).

Giordano, Ralph. *Die Traditionslüge: Vom Kriegerkult in der Bundeswehr* (Cologne: Kiepenheuer & Witsch, 2000).

Giraldo, Jean Kinney. "Legislatures and National Defense: Global Comparisons," in Bruneau and Tollefson, eds., 34–70.

Golts, Aleksandr. *Armiya Rossii: 11 poteriannikh let* (Moscow, Zakharov, 2004).

———. "The Social and Political Condition of the Russian Military," in Steven E. Miller and Dmitry V. Trenin, eds., *The Russian Military: Power and Policy* (Cambrdige, MA: MIT Press, 2004), 73–94.

Gonzales, Alfonso. "Civil-Military Relations in El Salvador: Change, Continuity, or Transformation?" paper presented at the Annual Meeting of the Western Political Science Association (Portland, OR, April 6, 2004).

Gooch, Anthony. "A Surrealistic Referendum: Spain and NATO," *Government and Opposition,* 21:3 (Summer 1986): 300–316.

Good, Kenneth. "Authoritarian Liberalism: a defining characteristic of Botswana," *Journal of Contemporary African Studies*, 14:1 (1996): 29–48.

———. *Diamonds, Dispossession, and Democracy in Botswana* (Johannesburg: Jacana Media, 2008).

Gose, Mark N. "The Role of the Military in Building Political Community: The Case of the Two German States" (Ph.D. diss., University of Colorado, 1995).

———. "Political Socialization in the Bundeswehr: The Role of the Military in Integrating the East," unpublished paper, 1998.

Government of Botswana. *Botswana Defence Force Act* (Gaborone: Government Printer, 1977).

Gow, Ian. "Civilian Control of the Military in Postwar Japan," in Matthews and Matsuyama, eds., 50–69.

Gow, James. *Legitimacy and the Military: The Yugoslav Crisis* (New York: St. Martin's, 1992).

Gow, James, and Cathie Carmichael. *Slovenia and the Slovenes: A Small State and the New Europe* (Bloomington: Indiana University Press, 2000).

Graham, Lawrence S. *Portugal: The Decline and Collapse of an Authoritarian Order* (Beverly Hills, CA: Comparative Politics Series No. 01-053, 1975).

———. "Redefining the Portuguese Transition to Democracy," in Higley and Gunther, eds., 282–99.

———. *The Portuguese Military and the State* (Boulder, CO: Westview, 1993).

Graybill, Lyn S. *Truth and Reconciliation in South Africa* (Boulder, CO: Lynne Rienner, 2002).

Green, Michael J. *Arming Japan: Defense Production, Alliance Politics, and the Postwar Search for Autonomy* (New York: Columbia University Press, 1995).

Griffiths, Robert J. "Parliamentary Oversight of Defense in South Africa," in Mitchell O'Brien, Rick Stapenhurst, and Niall Johnson, eds., *Parliaments and Peacebuilders in Conflict-Affected Areas* (Washington, DC: World Bank, 2008), 93–103.

Grizold, Anton. "The National Security of Slovenia: The View of Public Opinion," *Balkan Forum* 3:3 (September 1995): 173–206.

Grodnenskii, N. *Neokonchennaia voina: Istoria vooruzhennogo konflikta v Chechne* (Moscow: Charvest, 2004).

Grundy, Kenneth W. "Nkrumah's Theory of Underdevelopment: An Analysis of Recurrent Themes," *World Politics*, 15:3 (April 1963): 438–54.

Guillain, Robert. "The Reemergence of Military Elements in Japan," *Pacific Affairs*, 25:3 (1952): 221–25.

Gunther, Richard. "Spain: The Very Model of the Modern Elite Settlement," in Higley and Gunther, eds., 38–80.

Gutmann, Stephanie. *The Kinder, Gentler Military: Can America's Gender-Neutral Fighting Force Still Win Wars?* (New York: Scribner, 2000).

Gutteridge, W. F. *Military Regimes in Africa* (London: Methuen, 1975).

Gyimah-Boadi, E. "Another Step Forward for Ghana," *Journal of Democracy*, 20:2 (April 2009): 138–52.

Hackett, Roger F. *Yamagata Aritomo and the Rise of Modern Japan, 1838–1922* (Cambridge, MA: Harvard University Press, 1971.)

Hagen, Mark von. *Soldiers in the Proletarian Dictatorship: The Red Army and the Soviet Socialist State, 1917–1930* (Ithaca, NY: Cornell University Press, 1990).

Hahm, Chaibong. "South Korea's Miraculous Democracy," *Journal of Democracy*, 19:3 (July 2008): 128–42.

Hamann, Hilton. *Days of the Generals* (Cape Town: Zebra Press, 2001).

Handley, Paul M. *The King Never Smiles: A Biography of Thailand's Bhumibol Adulyadej* (New Haven, CT: Yale University Press, 2006).

Haqqani, Husain. *Pakistan: Between Mosque and Military* (Washington, DC: Carnegie Endowment for International Peace, 2005).

Harb, Imad. "Lebanon's Confessionalism: Problems and Prospects," *Peace Brief* (United States Insitute of Peace, March 2006), http.usip.org/publications/lebanons-confessionalism-problems-and-prospects.

Harrison, Alexander. *Challenging De Gaulle: The OAS and the Counterrevolution in Algeria, 1954–1962* (New York: Praeger, 1989).

Henk, Dan. "The Botswana Defence Force: Evolution of a Professional African Military," *African Security Review*, 13:4 (2004): 85–99.

Hennelly, Michael J. "US Policy in El Salvador: Creating Beauty or the Beast?" *Parameters*, 23:1 (Spring 1993): 59–69.

Herbst, Jeffrey. *The Politics of Reform in Ghana, 1982–1991* (Berkeley: University of California Press, 1993).

Herd, Graeme P., and Tom Tracy. "Democratic Civil-Military Relations in Bosnia and Herzegovina," *Armed Forces & Society*, 32:4 (July 2006): 549–65.

Herspring, Dale R. *East German Civil-Military Relations* (New York: Praeger, 1973).

———. "The Process of Change and Democratization in Eastern Europe: The Case of the Military," in John R. Lampe and Daniel N. Nelson, eds., *East European Security Reconsidered* (Washington, DC: Woodrow Wilson Center Press, 1993), 55–74.

———. *Requiem for an Army* (Lanham, MD: Rowman & Littlefield, 1998).

Higley, John, and Richard Gunther, eds. *Elites and Democratic Consolidation in Latin America and Southern Europe* (New York: Cambridge University Press, 1992).

Hodson, H.V. *The Great Divide: Britain, India, Pakistan* (London: Hutchinson, 1969).

Hoffmann, Theodor. *Das Letzte Kommando* (Berlin: Mittler & Son, 1993).

Holm, John. "Botswana: A Paternalistic Democracy," in Larry Diamond et al., eds., *Democracy in Developing Countries, Vol. 2.* (Boulder, CO: Lynne Rienner, 1988), 179–215.

Honna, Jun. *Military Politics and Democratization in Indonesia* (New York: RoutledgeCurzon, 2003).

Horne, Alistair. *A Savage War of Peace: Algeria 1954–1962* (New York: New York Review of Books, 2006).

Horowitz, Donald L. *Coup Theories and Officers' Motives* (Princeton, NJ: Princeton University Press, 1980).

Howard, Lise Morjé. *UN Peacekeeping in Civil Wars* (New York: Cambridge University Press, 2008).

Hudson, Michael C. "After the Gulf War: Prospects for Democratization in the Arab World," *Middle East Journal*, 45:3 (Summer 1991): 407–26.

Hughes, Gordon. "Defence Transformation—A Project Still in Progress," Cranfield CSSM Case Study Series (Shrivenham, UK: Cranfield University, November 2007).

Huneeus, Carlos. *The Pinochet Regime* (Boulder, CO: Lynne Rienner, 2006).

Hunter, Wendy. *Eroding Military Influence in Brazil: Politicians against Soldiers* (Chapel Hill: University of North Carolina Press, 1997).

———. "Continuity or Change? Civil-Military Relations in Democratic Argentina, Chile, and Peru," *Political Science Quarterly*, 112:3 (Autumn 1997): 453– 75.

Huntington, Samuel P. "Civilian Control and the Constitution," *American Political Science Review*, 50:3 (September 1956): 676–99.

———. *The Soldier and the State* (Cambridge, MA: Belknap Press of Harvard University Press, 1957).

———. *Political Order in Changing Societies* (New Haven, CT: Yale University Press, 1968).

———. *The Third Wave: Democratization in the Late Twentieth Century* (Norman: University of Oklahoma Press, 1991).

Hutchful, Eboe. "Ghana," in Omitoogun and Eboe Hutchful, eds., 72–100.

Hutchful, Eboe, and Abdoulaye Bathily, eds. *The Military and Militarism in Africa* (Dakar, Senegal: CODESRIA, 1998).

———. "Introduction," in Hutchful and Bathily, eds., i–xiii.

Hyden, Goran. *Beyond Ujamaa in Tanzania: Underdevelopment and an Uncaptured Peasantry* (Berkeley: University of California Press, 1980).

International Institute for Strategic Studies. *The Military Balance* (London: IISS, various years).

Islam, Nazrul. "Bengali Representation in Pakistan Defense Forces," *BIISS Journal*, 23:4 (2002): 360–81.

Jack, Andrew. *Inside Putin's Russia: Can There Be Reform Without Democracy?* (New York: Oxford University Press, 2006).

Jalal, Ayesha. *The Sole Spokesman: Jinnah, the Muslim League, and the Demand for Pakistan* (Cambridge: Cambridge University Press, 1985).

———. *The State of Martial Rule: The Origins of Pakistan's Political Economy of Defence* (Cambridge, UK: Cambridge University Press, 1990).

———. *Democracy and Authoritarianism in South Asia* (Cambridge: Cambridge University Press, 1995).

James, Lawrence. *The Rise and Fall of the British Empire* (New York: St. Martin's Press, 1994).

Janos, Andrew C. "Social Science, Communism, and the Dynamics of Political Change," *World Politics*, 44:1 (October 1991): 81–112.

Janowitz, Morris. *The Professional Soldier: A Social and Political Portrait* (Glencoe, IL: Free Press, 1960).

———. *Military Institutions and Coercion in the Developing Nations* (Chicago: University of Chicago Press, 1977).

Janša, Janez. *Premiki: Nastajanje in Obramba Slovenske Države, 1988–1992* (Ljubljana: Založba Mladinska Knjiga, 1992).

Johnson, John J., ed. *The Role of the Military in Underdeveloped Countries* (Princeton, NJ: Princeton University Press, 1962).

Jonas, Susanne. "Guatemala," in Vanden and Prevost, eds., 264–96.

Joseph, Edward P. "Ownership Is Overrated," *SAIS Review*, 27:2 (Summer–Fall 2007): 109–23.

Juhn, Tricia. *Negotiating Peace in El Salvador* (New York: St. Martin's Press, 1998).

Jun, Jinsok. "South Korea: Consolidating Democratic Civilian Control," in Alagappa, ed., *Coercion and Governance*, 121–43.

Jütersonke, Oliver, Robert Muggah, and Dennis Rodgers. "Gangs, Urban Violence, and Security Interventions in Central America," *Security Dialogue*, 40:4–5 (August–October 2009): 373–97.

Juvenal. *Sixteen Satires*. Translated by Peter Green (New York: Penguin, 1999).

Kabir, Bhulan Monoar. *Politics of Military Rule and the Dilemmas of Democratization in Bangladesh* (New Delhi: South Asian Publishers, 1999).

Kaldor, Mary. "Security Structures in Bosnia and Herzegovina," in Cawthra and Luckham, eds., 205–31.

Kalyvas, Stathis N. *The Logic of Violence in Civil War* (New York: Cambridge University Press, 2006).

Kanwal, Gurmeet. *Indian Army: Vision 2020* (New Delhi: HarperCollins, 2008).

Kaplan, Robert D. *Imperial Grunts: The American Military on the Ground* (New York: Random House, 2005).

———. "Man versus Afghanistan," *Atlantic Monthly*, April 2010, 60–71.

Karamé, Kari. "Reintegration and the Relevance of Social Relations: The Case of Lebanon," *Conflict, Security, and Development*, 9:4 (December 2009): 495–514.

Karl, Terry Lynn. "El Salvador's Negotiated Revolution," *Foreign Affairs*, 71:2 (Spring 1992): 147–64.

Kataoka, Tetsuya, and Ramon H. Myers. *Defending an Economic Superpower: Reassessing the U.S.-Japan Security Alliance* (Boulder, CO: Westview, 1989).

Katzenstein, Peter J., and Nobuo Okawara. *Japan's National Security: Structures, Norms and Policy Responses in a Changing World* (Ithaca, NY: Cornell University Press, 1993).

Kéchichian, Joseph A. "The Lebanese Army: Capabilities and Challenges in the 1980s," *Conflict Quarterly*, 5:1 (Winter 1985): 15–39.

———. "A Strong Army for a Stable Lebanon," *The Middle East Institute Policy Brief*, No. 19 (September 2008), 8 pp.

Kecskés, János. *"Vezéráldozatok," vagyis mit tesznek a kiskirályok pánikban* (Budapest: Tornado Damenija, 1990).

Kedzior, Richard W. *Evolution and Endurance: The U.S. Army Division in the Twentieth Century* (Santa Monica, CA: RAND, 2000).

Kelley, Phil. "Democracy in Latin America," LASA Forum, 33:1 (Spring 2002). http://www2.kenyon.edu/Depts/PSci/Fac/klesner/fitzgibbon/Kelly_LASA_Forum_2002.pdf

Kelsall, Tim. "Governance, Democracy, and Recent Political Struggle in Mainland Tanzania," *Commonwealth & Comparative Politics*, 41:2 (July 2003): 55–82.

Kenez, Peter. *Hungary from the Nazis to the Soviets: The Establishment of the Communist Regime in Hungary, 1944–1948* (New York: Cambridge University Press, 2006).

Kenkel, Kai Michael. "Civil Society Participation in Defence Policy Formulation: Academic Experts and South Africa's Post-Apartheid Defence White Paper," *Journal of Security Sector Management*, 4:1 (January 2006): 1–26.

Kennedy, William V. *The Military and the Media: Why the Press Cannot Be Trusted to Cover a War* (Westport, CT: Praeger, 1993).

Kertész, Stephen. *The Last European Peace Conference* (Lanham, MD: University Press of America, 1985).

Kim, Byung-Kook, and Ezra F. Vogel, eds. *The Park Chung Hee Era: The Transformation of South Korea* (Cambridge, MA: Harvard University Press, 2011).

Kim, Hong-nack. "The 1988 Parliamentary Election in South Korea," *Asian Survey*, 29:5 (May 1989): 480–95.

Kim, Joo-Hong. "The Armed Forces," in Kim and Vogel, eds., 168–99.

Kim, Samuel S., ed. *Korea's Democratization* (New York: Cambridge University Press, 2003).

Kim, Sunhyuk, "Civil Society in Democratizing Korea," in Kim, ed., 81–106.

Kincaid, A. Douglas. "Demilitarization and Security in El Salvador and Guatemala," *Journal of Interamerican Studies and World Affairs*, 42:4 (Winter 2000): 39-58

King, Gary, Robert O. Keohane, and Sidney Verba. *Designing Social Inquiry: Scientific Interference in Qualitative Research* (Princeton, NJ: Princeton University Press, 1994).

Kinghazi, Lilian. "Enhancing Human Resource Capability in the TPDF" (M.A. thesis, Naval Postgraduate School, June 2006).

Kinoshita, Hanji. "Echoes of Militarism in Japan," *Pacific Affairs*, 26:3 (September 1953): 244–51.

Király, Béla. *Honvédségből Néphadsereg* (Budapest: Co-Nexus, 1989).

Kliamkin, Igor, and Lilia Shevtsova. *Rezhim Borisa Vtoroga: Osobennosti postkommunicheskoi vlasti v Rossii* (Moscow: Carnegie Center, 1999).

Klussmann, Uwe. "Fuß auf dem Zünder: Moskau's Schlussforderungen aus dem Geiseldrama von Beslau," *Der Spiegel*, No. 27, July 4, 2005, 94–96.

Kofas, Jon V. *Under the Eagle's Claw: Exceptionalism in Postwar U.S.-Greek Relations* (Westport, CT: Praeger, 2003).

Kohn, Richard H. "How Democracies Control the Military," *Journal of Democracy*, 8:4 (October 1997): 140–53.

———. "Building Trust: Civil-Military Behavior for Effective National Security," in Nielsen and Snider, eds., 264–89.

Koonings, Kees. "Political Armies, Security Forces, and Democratic Consolidation in Latin America," in Cawthra and Luckham, eds., 124–51.

Koonings, Kees, and Dirk Kruijt, eds. *Political Armies: The Military and Nation Building in the Age of Democracy* (London: Zed Books, 2002).

Koop, Volker. *Besetzt: Sowjetische Besatzungspolitik in Deutschland* (Berlin: bebra Verlag, 2008).

Kourvetaris, George A. "The Contemporary Army Officer Corps in Greece" (Ph.D. diss., Northwestern University, 1969).

Kovrig, Bennett. *Communism in Hungary from Kun to Kadar* (Stanford, CA: Hoover Institution Press, 1979).

Kowalczuk, Ilko-Sascha, and Stefan Wolle. *Roter Stern über Deutschland* (Berlin: Ch-Links Verlag, 2001).

Krayem, Hassan. "The Lebanese Civil War and the Taif Agreement," in Paul Salem, ed., *Conflict Resolution in the Arab World* (Beirut: American University of Beirut Press, 1997), 411–35.

Krenz, Egon. *Wenn Mauern fallen: Die friedliche Revolution* (Vienna: Neff, 1990).

Krishnasamy, Kabilan. "Bangladesh and UN Peacekeeping: The Participation of a 'Small' State," *Commonwealth & Comparative Politics*, 41:1 (March 2003): 24–47.

Kuhlmann, Jürgen, and Jean Callaghan. "About the Primacy of Politics over Military Matters," in Born, Haltiner, and Malešič, eds, 77–102.

Kundu, Apurba. *Militarism in India: The Army and Civil Society in Consensus* (New York: St. Martin's Press, 1998).

Kunju, N. *Indian Army: A Grassroots Review* (New Delhi: Reliance, 1991).

Kurz, Frank. "Ein 'tragisch-groteskes' Missverständnis: Das Scheitern der argentinischen Montoneros," in Alexander Straßner, *Sozialrevolutionärer Terrorismus* (Wiesbaden: VS Verlag für Sozialwissenschaften, 2008), 387–410.

Kwarteng, Kwasi. *Ghosts of Empire: Britain's Legacy in the Modern World* (London: Bloomsbury, 2011).

Lang, Anthony, ed. *Political Theory and International Affairs: Hans J. Morgenthau on Aristotle's* The Politics (Westport, CT: Praeger, 2004).

Large, David Clay. *Germans to the Front: West German Rearmament in the Adenauer Era* (Chapel Hill: University of North Carolina Press, 1996).

Lasswell, Harold D. "The Garrison State," *American Journal of Sociology*, 46:4 (January 1941): 455–68.

Le Roux, Len. "South Africa," in Omitoogun and Hutchful, eds., 197–224.

Lee, Terence. "The Military's Corporate Interests: The Main Reason for Intervention in Indonesia and the Philippines?" *Armed Forces & Society*, 34:3 (April 2008): 491–502.

Leith, J. Clark. *Why Botswana Prospered* (Montreal: McGill-Queen's University Press, 2005).

Levy, Jack, and Lily Vakili. "Diversionary action by authoritarian regimes: Argentina in the Falklands/Malvinas case," in Manus Midlarsky, ed., *The Internationalization of Communal Strife* (New York: Routledge, 1992), 118–46.

Lewis, Paul H. "The Spanish Ministerial Elite, 1938–1969," *Journal of Politics*, 5:1 (October 1972): 83–106.

———. "Salazar's Ministerial Elite, 1932–1968," *Journal of Politics*, 40:3 (August 1978): 622–47.

Liddell Hart, B. H. *The Other Side of the Hill* (London: Cassell, 1948).

Lilley, James, with Jeffrey Lilley. *China Hands: Nine Decades of Adventure, Espionage, and Diplomacy in Asia* (New York: Public Affairs, 2005).

Linz, Juan J. *The Breakdown of Democratic Regimes: Crisis, Breakdown, and Reequilibrium* (Baltimore, MD: Johns Hopkins University Press, 1978).

Linz, Juan J., and Alfred Stepan. *Problems of Democratic Transition and Consolidation* (Baltimore, MD: Johns Hopkins University Press, 1996).

Lippert, Ekkehard, Paul Schneider, and Ralf Zoll. "The Influence of Military Service on Political and Social Attitudes," *Armed Forces & Society*, 4:2 (February 1978): 265–82.

Lloyd-Jones, William. *K.A.R: Being an Unofficial Account of the Origins and Activities of the King's African Rifles* (London: Arrowsmith, 1926).

López, Ernesto. "Latin America: Objective and Subjective Control Revisited," in Pion-Berlin, ed., 88–107.

López, Julie. *Guatemala's Crossroads: Democratization of Violence and Second Chances* (Washington D.C.: Woodrow Wilson Center Latin American Studies Program, December 2010), 59 pp.

Lovatt, Catherine. "EC 2000 Progress Report on Romania," *Central Europe Review*, 2:39 (13 November 2000).

Lovell, John P., and David E. Albright. "Merging Theory and Practice," in Lovell and Albright, eds., 1–11.

———, eds. *To Sheathe the Sword: Civil-Military Relations in the Quest for Democracy* (Westport, CT: Greenwood Press, 1997).

Loveman, Brian. "¿Misión Cumplida? Civil-Military Relations and the Chilean Political Transition," *Journal of Interamerican Studies and World Affairs*, 33:3 (Fall 1991): 35–74.

———. "Antipolitics in Chile, 1973–94," in Brian Loveman and Thomas M. Davies, eds., *The Politics of Antipolitics: The Military in Latin America* (Wilmington, DE: Scholarly Resources, 1997), 268–99.

———. *For la Patria: Politics and the Armed Forces in Latin America* (Wilmington, DE: Scholarly Resources, 1999).

Luanda, Nestor N. "Introduction," in *Tanzania People's Defence Forces*, i–x.

———. "The Playout of the Mutiny, 19 to 21 January 1964," in *Tanzania People's Defence Forces*, 75–115.

———. "A Changing Conception of Defence: A Historical Perspective of the Military in Tanzania," in Rupiya, ed., *Evolutions and Revolutions*, 295–310.

Luanda, Nestor N., and E. Mwanjabala. "King's African Rifles to Tanganyika Rifles: A Colonial Sliceup," in *Tanzania People's Defence Forces*, 1–34.

Luckham, Robin. "Democratic Strategies for Security in Transition and Conflict," in Cawthra and Luckham, eds., 3–28.

Luethold, Arnold. "Security Sector Reform in the Arab Middle East," in Alan Bryden and Heiner Hänggi, eds. *Reform and Reconstruction of the Security Sector* (Münster: LIT Verlag, 2005), 93–118.

Lupogo, Herman. "Tanzania: Civil-Military Relations and Political Stability," *African Security Review*, 10:1 (January 2001). Accessed on December 18, 2010 at http://www.issafrica.org/pubs/ASR/10No1/Lupogo.html.

Luttwak, Edward. *Coup d'État: A Practical Handbook* (Cambridge, MA: Harvard University Press, 1968).

Macgregor, Douglas A. *The Soviet-East German Military Alliance* (Cambridge: Cambridge University Press, 1989).

Machiavelli, Niccolò. *The Prince*. Edited and translated by David Wootton (Indianapolis/Cambridge: Hackett Publishing Company, Inc., 1995).

———. *The Art of War*. Translated by Neal Wood (Cambridge, MA: Da Capo Press, 1964).

Macías, Ricardo Córdova. *El Salvador: Reforma Militar y Relaciones Civico-Militares* (San Salvador: Fundación Dr. Guillermo Manuel Ungo, 1999).

Maeda, Tetsuo. *The Hidden Army: The Untold Story of Japan's Military Forces*. Translated by Steven Karpa (Chicago: edition q, inc., 1995[1990]).

Makhzoumi, Fouad. "Lebanon's Crisis of Sovereignty," *Survival*, 52:2 (April–May 2010): 5–12.

Makulilo, Alexander Boniface. *Tanzania: A De Facto One Party State?* (Saarbrücken: VDM Verlag, 2008).

Malebeswa, Tendekani. "Civil Control of the Military in Botswana," in Williams, Cawthra, and Abrahams, eds., *Ourselves to Know*, 67–80.

Mambo, Andrew, and Julian Schofield. "Military Diversion in the 1978 Uganda-Tanzania War," *Journal of Political and Military Sociology*, 35:2 (Winter 2007): 299–321.

Manning, Carrie. "Political Elites and Democratic State-Building Efforts in Bosnia and Iraq," *Democratization*, 13:5 (December 2006): 724–38.

Mansfield, Harvey C. *Machiavelli's Virtue* (Chicago, IL: University of Chicago Press, 1996).

Mares, David R., ed. *Civil-Military Relations: Building Democracy and Regional Security in Latin America, Southern Asia, and Central Europe* (Boulder, CO: Westview Press, 1998).

———. "Conclusion," in Mares, ed., 238–61.

Marquina, Antonio. "Spanish Foreign and Defense Policy since Democratization," in Kenneth Maxwell, ed., *Spanish Foreign and Defense Policy* (Boulder, CO: Westview, 1991), 19–62.

Mason, Philip. *A Matter of Honour: An Account of the Indian Army, Its Officers and Men* (London: Holt, Rinehart, and Winston, 1974).

Mathers, Jennifer G. "Outside Politics? Civil-Military Relations during a Period of Reform," in Anne C. Aldis and Roger N. McDermott, eds., *Russian Military Reform, 1992–2002* (London: Frank Cass, 2003), 22–40.

Matthews, Ron. "Japan's Security into the 1990s," in Matthews and Matsuyama, eds., 1–34.

Matthews, Ron, and Keisuke Matsuyama, eds. *Japan's Military Renaissance?* (Basingstoke: Macmillan, 1993).

Maxon, Yale Candee. *Control of Japanese Foreign Policy: A Study of Civil-Military Rivalry, 1930–1945* (Berkeley: University of California Press, 1957).

Maxwell, Kenneth. "The Hidden Revolution in Portugal" and "Portugal under Pressure," *New York Review of Books*, April 17, 1975, 29–35, and May 29, 1975, 20–30.

———. "Regime Overthrow and the Prospects for Democratic Transition in Portugal," in Guillermo O'Donnell, Philippe C. Schmitter, and Laurence Whitehead, eds., *Transitions from Authoritarian Rule: Southern Europe* (Baltimore, MD: Johns Hopkins University Press, 1986), 109–37.

———. *The Making of Portuguese Democracy* (New York: Cambridge University Press, 1995).

Mazrui, Ali A. *On Heroes and Uhuru Worship: Essays on Independent Africa* (London: Longmans, 1967).

———. "The Soldier and the State in East Africa: Some Theoretical Conclusions on the Army Mutinies of 1964," *Western Political Quarterly*, 20:1 (March 1967): 82–96.

———. *Violence and Social Thought: Essays on Social Tensions in Africa* (London: Longmans, 1969).

———, ed. *The Warrior Tradition in Modern Africa* (Leiden: Brill, 1977).

Mbaku, John Mukum. *Institutions and Development in Africa* (Lawrenceville, NJ: Africa World Press, 2004).

McCargo, Duncan, and Ukrist Pathamand. *The Thaksinization of Thailand* (Copenhagen: Nordic Institute of Asian Studies Press, 2005).

McFaul, Michael. *Russia's Unfinished Revolution: Political Change from Gorbachev to Putin* (Ithaca, NY: Cornell University Press, 2001).

McGeehan, Robert. *The German Rearmament Question* (Urbana: University of Illinois Press, 1971).

McMahon, Patrice C. "Rebuilding Bosnia: A Model to Emulate or to Avoid?" *Political Science Quarterly*, 119:4 (Winter 2004–2005): 569–93.

McMahon, Patrice C., and John Western. "The Death of Dayton," *Foreign Affairs*, 88:5 (September–October 2009): 69–83.

McSherry, Patrice. *Incomplete Transition: Military Power and Democracy in Argentina* (New York: St. Martin's Press, 1997).

Mietzner, Marcus. *Military Politics, Islam, and the State in Indonesia* (Singapore: Institute of Southeast Asian Studies, 2009).

Miguez, Alberto. "Argentina's Budding Relations with NATO," *NATO Review*, 41:3 (June 1993): 28–31.

Miller, Andrew P. *Military Disengagement and Democratic Consolidation in Post-Military Regimes* (Lewiston, NY: Edwin Mellen, 2006).

Ministerio de Defensa. *Memoria Legislatura 1982–86* (Madrid: Ministerio de Defensa, 1986).

———. *Memoria Legislatura 1986–89* (Madrid: Ministerio de Defensa, 1989).

Mishra, Pankaj. "The Inner Voice: Gandhi's Legacy," *New Yorker*, May 2, 2011, 80–83.

Misol, Lisa. *Unkept Promise: Failure to End Military Business Activity in Indonesia* (New York: Human Rights Watch, 2010).

Mo, Jongryn, and Barry R. Weingast. *The Political Economy of Korea's Transition, 1961–2008* (September 2009 draft).

Mohsin, Amena. "Bangladesh: An Uneasy Accommodation," in Alagappa, ed., *Coercion and Governance*, 209–25.

Molatole, Raymond, and Steven Laki Thaga. "Interventions against HIV/AIDS in the Botswana Defence Force," in Rupiya, ed., *The Enemy Within*, 19–64.

Monnet, Jean. *Memoirs*. Translated by Richard Mayne (London: Collins, 1978).

Montgomery, Tommie Sue. *Revolution in El Salvador: From Civil Strife to Civil Peace* (Boulder, CO: Westview, 1995).

Morozov, Yu., V. Glushkov, and A. Sharavin. *Balkany segodnia i zavtra: Voenno-politicheskie aspekty mirotvorchestva* (Moscow: Center of Military-Strategic Studies of the General Staff, 2001).

Morris, I. I. *Nationalism and the Right Wing in Japan: A Study of Post-War Trends* (London: Oxford University Press, 1960).

Mosca, Gaetano. *The Ruling Class.* Translated by Hannah D. Kahn (New York: McGraw-Hill, 1939).

Moskos, Charles C., and John Sibley Butler. *All That We Can Be: Black Leadership and Racial Integration the Army Way* (New York: Basic Books, 1996).

Moten, Matthew. "Out of Order: Strengthening the Political-Military Relationship," *Foreign Affairs*, 89:5 (September–October 2010): 2–8.

Moyd, Michelle. "'We Don't Want to Die for Nothing': Askari at war in German East Africa, 1914–1918," in Santanu Das, ed., *Race, Empire, and First World War Writing* (Cambridge: Cambridge University Press, 2011), 90–107.

Moyse-Bartlett, Lt. Col. Hubert. *The King's African Rifles* (Aldershot: Gale & Polden, 1956).

Mroß, Bernhard. *Sie gingen als Freunde: Der Abzug der Westgruppe der sowjetisch-russischen Truppen, 1990–1994* (Harrislee: Bernhard Mroß im Eigenverlag, 2004).

Mucs, Sándor. *Politika és hadsereg Magyarországon, 1944–1948* (Budapest: Zrínyi-Kossuth, 1985).

Mujal-Leon, Eusebio. "Democracy Comes to the Iberian Peninsula," in Hans Binnendijk, with Peggy Nalle and Diane Bendahmane, eds., *Authoritarian Regimes in Transition* (Washington, DC: Foreign Service Institute of the U.S. Department of State, 1987), 173–221.

Mwakikagile, Godfrey. *Economic Development in Africa* (Huntington, NY: Nova Science Publishers, 1999).

———. *Nyerere and Africa: End of an Era* (Pretoria: New Africa Press, 2006).

Nägler, Frank. *Der gewollte Soldat und sein Wandel* (Munich: Oldenbourg, 2009).

Nam, Chang-hee. "Realigning the U.S. Forces and South Korea's Defense Reform 2020," *Korean Journal of Defense Analysis*, 19:1 (Spring 2007): 165–89.

Narain, Partap. *Subedar to Field Marshal* (New Delhi: Manas, 1999).

Nathan, Laurie. "Troops in the Townships, 1984–1987," in Jacklyn Cock and Laurie Nathan, eds., *Society at War: The Militarization of South Africa* (New York: St. Martin's, 1989), 67–78.

———. *The Changing of the Guard: Armed Forces and Defence Policy in a Democratic South Africa* (Pretoria: Human Sciences Research Council, 1994).

Naumann, Klaus. *Einsatz ohne Ziel? Die Politikbedürftigkeit des Militärischen* (Hamburg: Hamburger Edition HIS Verlag, 2008)

Nawaz, Shuja. *Crossed Swords: Pakistan: Its Army and the Wars Within* (Oxford: Oxford University Press, 2008).

Ndembwike, John. *Tanzania: The Land and Its People* (Pretoria: New Africa Press, 2008).

Nerguizian, Adam, and Anthony H. Cordesman. *The Lebanese Armed Forces: Challenges and Opportunities in Post-Syria Lebanon* (Washington, DC: Center for Strategic and International Studies, 2009).

Nettlefield, Lara J. *Courting Democracy in Bosnia and Herzegovina* (New York: Cambridge University Press, 2010).

Ngculu, James. "Parliament and Defence Oversight: The South African Experience," *African Security Review*, 10:1 (2001), available at http://www.iss.co.za/pubs/asr/10no1/Ngculu.html.

Nichols, Thomas M. *The Sacred Cause: Civil-Military Conflict over Soviet National Security, 1917–1992* (Ithaca, NY: Cornell University Press, 1993).

———. *The Russian Presidency* (London: Macmillan, 1999).

Nielsen, Suzanne C., and Don M. Snider, eds. *American Civil-Military Relations: The Soldier and the State in a New Era* (Baltimore, MD: Johns Hopkins University Press, 2009).

Nino, Carlos Santiago. *Radical Evil on Trial* (New Haven: Yale University Press, 1996).

Nishihara, Masashi. "The Japanese Central Organization of Defense," in Edmonds, ed., 132–44.

Nonneman, Gerd. "'The Yemen Republic': From Unification and Liberalisation to Civil War and Beyond," in Haifaa A. Jawad, ed., *The Middle East in the New World Order* (London: Macmillan, 1997), 61–96.

Norden, Deborah. *Military Rebellion in Argentina* (Lincoln: University of Nebraska Press, 1996).

North, Douglass C., John Joseph Wallis, and Barry R. Weingast. *Violence and Social Orders: A Conceptual Framework for Interpreting Recorded Human History* (New York: Cambridge University Press, 2009).

Ntshoe, Isaac M. "The Impact of Political Violence on Education in South Africa," *Current Issues in Comparative Education*, 2:1 (2002): 62–69.

Nunn, Frederick. *Yesterday's Soldiers: European Military Professionalism in South America, 1890–1940* (Lincoln: University of Nebraska Press, 1983).

Nunneley, John. *Tales from the King's African Rifles* (London: Cassell, 2001).

Nye, Joseph S. "Epilogue: The Liberal Tradition," in Larry Diamond and Marc F. Plattner, eds., *Civil-Military Relations and Democracy* (Baltimore, MD: Johns Hopkins University Press, 1996), 151–56.

Ockey, James. "Thailand: The Struggle to Redefine Civil-Military Relations," in Alagappa, ed., *Coercion and Governance*, 187–208.

O'Donnell, Guillermo. *Modernization and Bureaucratic-Authoritarianism: Studies in South American Politics* (Berkeley: Institute of International Studies, University of California, 1973).

Oldenburg, Philip. *India, Pakistan, and Democracy: Solving the Puzzle of Different Paths* (New York: Routledge, 2010).

Olmeda Gómez, José Antonio. "The Armed Forces in the Francoist Political System," in Bañón Martínez and Barker, eds., 249–309.

Omari, Abillah H. "Civil-Military Relations in Tanzania," in Williams, Cawthra, and Abrahams, eds., 89–106.

Omitoogun, Wuyi, and Eboe Hutchful, eds. *Budgeting for the Military Sector in Africa: The Processes and Mechanisms of Control* (Oxford: SIPRI/Oxford University Press, 2006).

Orcan, Albert. *A Myth Is Broken: An Account of the Ghana Coup d'État* (London: Longmans, 1968).

Organski, A.F.K. *The Stages of Political Development* (New York: Alfred A. Knopf, 1965).

Özkan, Duman, and Dimitris Tsarouhas. "'Civilianization' in Greece versus 'Demilitarization' in Turkey," *Armed Forces & Society*, 32:3 (April 2006): 405–23.

Packard, George R. *Protest in Tokyo: The Security Treaty Crisis of 1960* (Princeton, NJ: Princeton University Press, 1966).

Palmer, Robert D. "From Repression to Reform? Indonesian Politics and the Military, 1997–1999," in *American Diplomacy*, Winter 2000, available at www.unc.edu/depts/diplomat/AD_Issues/amdipl_15/palmer_reform1.html.

Palomares, Cristina. *The Quest for Survival after Franco: Moderate Francoism and the Slow Journey to the Polls, 1964–1977* (Portland, OR: Sussex Academic Press).

Panitan, Wattanayagorn. "Thailand: The Elite's Shifting Conceptions of Security," in Alagappa, ed., *Asian Security Practice*, 417–44.

Papandreou, Andreas. *Democracy at Gunpoint: The Greek Front* (Garden City, NY: Doubleday, 1970).

Paris, Roland. *At War's End: Building Peace after Civil Conflict* (New York: Cambridge University Press, 2004)

Parker, Maynard. "Subversion in Thailand," *Survival*, 8:10 (October 1966): 310–12.

Parsons, Timothy H. *The African Rank-and-File: Social Implications of Colonial Military Service in the King's African Rifles, 1902–1964* (Portsmouth, NH: Heinemann, 1999).

Patel, H. M. "The Situation of India," *Survival*, 4:6 (November 1962): 255–.

Peralta, Gabriel Aguilera. "Guatemala's Armed Forces: Fifteen Years After Peace," in *Red de Seguridad y Defensa de América Latina, A Comparative Atlas*, 230–31.

Pereira, Anthony W. *Political (In)Justice: Authoritarianism and the Rule of Law in Brazil, Chile, and Argentina* (Pittsburgh, PA: University of Pittsburgh Press, 2005).

Perlmutter, Amos. *The Military and Politics in Modern Times* (New Haven, CT: Yale University Press, 1977).

Perlmutter, Amos, and William M. LeoGrande. "The Party in Uniform: Toward a Theory of Civil-Military Relations in Communist Political Systems," *American Political Science Review*, 76:4 (December 1982): 778–90.

Perry, Charles M., and Dimitris Keridis. *Defense Reform, Modernization, and Military Cooperation in Southeastern Europe* (Dulles, VA: Brassey's, 2004).

Pesmazoglu, John. "The Greek Economy since 1967," in Clogg and Yannopoulos, eds., 75–108.

Phang, Sara Elise. *Roman Military Service* (New York: Cambridge University Press, 2008).

Phillips, David L. *Losing Iraq: Inside the Postwar Reconstruction Fiasco* (New York: Basic Books. 2005).

Phillips, Sarah. *Yemen's Democracy Experiment in Regional Perspective* (New York: Palgrave-Macmillan, 2008).

———. *Yemen and the Politics of Permanent Crisis* (New York: Routledge, 2011).

Pierson, Paul. "When Effect Becomes Cause: Policy Feedback and Political Change," *World Politics*, 45:4 (July 1993): 595–628.

Pinkney, Robert. *Ghana under Military Rule, 1966–1969* (London: Methuen, 1972).

———. *Democracy and Dictatorship in Ghana and Tanzania* (London: Macmillan 1997).

Pion-Berlin, David. "Military Autonomy and Emerging Democracies in South America," *Comparative Politics*, 25:1 (October 1992): 83–102.

———. *Through Corridors of Power: Institutions and Civil-Military Relations in Argentina* (State College: Pennsylvania State University Press, 1997).

———. "Civil-Military Circumvention: How Argentine State Institutions Compensate for a Weakened Chain of Command," in Pion-Berlin, ed., 135–60.

———, ed. *Civil-Military Relations in Latin America: New Analytical Perspectives*. (Chapel Hill: University of North Carolina Press, 2001).

———. "Political Management of the Military in Latin America," *Military Review*, January-February 2005: 19–31.

Pion-Berlin, David, and Ernesto López. "A House Divided: Crisis, Cleavage, and Conflict in the Argentine Army," in Edward C. Epstein, ed., *The New Argentine Democracy* (Westport, CT: Praeger, 1992), 63–97.

Pion-Berlin, David, and Harold Trinkunas. "Attention Deficits: Why Politicians Ignore Defense Policy in Latin America," *Latin American Research Review*, 42:3 (October 2007): 76–100.

Plato. *The Republic*. Translated by G.M.A. Grube (Indianapolis: Hackett, 1974).

Popkin, Margaret. "The Salvadoran Truth Commission and the Search for Justice," *Criminal Law Forum*, 15:1–2 (March 2004): 105–24.

Pratt, Cranford. *The Critical Phase in Tanzania, 1945–1968: Nyerere and the Emergence of Socialist Strategy* (New York: Cambridge University Press, 1976).

Price, Robert M. "A Theoretic Approach to Military Rule in New States," *World Politics*, 23:3 (April 1971): 399–430.

Przeworski, Adam. *Democracy and the Market: Political and Economic Reforms in Eastern Europe and Latin America* (New York: Cambridge University Press, 1991).

———. "Capitalism, Democracy, and Science," in Gerardo L. Munck and Richard Snyder, eds., *Passion, Craft, and Method in Comparative Politics* (Baltimore, MD: Johns Hopkins University Press, 2007), 456–503.

Przeworski, Adam, Michael E. Alvarez, Jose Antonio Cheibub, and Fernando Limongi. *Democracy and Development* (New York: Cambridge University Press, 2000).

Psomiades, Harry J. "Preface," to Theodore A. Couloumbis, *The Greek Junta Phenomenon: A Professor's Notes* (New York: Pella, 2004), 9–14.

Quigley, Harold S. "The Great Purge in Japan," *Pacific Affairs*, 20:3 (September 1947): 299–308.

Rabasa, Angel, and John Haseman. *The Military and Democracy in Indonesia: Challenges, Politics, and Power* (Santa Monica, CA: RAND, 2002).

Raidel, Hans. *Die Bundeswehr: Grundlagen, Rollen, Aufgaben* (Munich: Hanns-Seidel-Stiftung, 1998).

Ramet, Sabrina P. *Balkan Babel: The Disintegration of Yugoslavia from the Death of Tito to the War for Kosovo* (Boulder, CO: Westview Press, 1999; 3rd ed.).

———. "Democratization in Slovenia—the Second Stage," in Karen Dawisha and Bruce Parrott, eds., *Politics, Power, and the Struggle for Democracy in South-East Europe* (New York: Cambridge University Press, 1997), 189–225.

Ramos, A. J., R. C. Oates, and T. L. McMahon. "The U.S. Southern Command: A Strategy for the Future," *Military Review*, 72:11 (November 1992): 32–39.

Ramsey, Robert D., III. *Advising Indigenous Forces: American Advisors in Korea, Vietnam, and El Salvador* (Ft. Leavenworth, KS: Combat Studies Institute Press, 2006).

Red de Seguridad y Defensa de América Latina. *A Comparative Atlas of Defence in Latin America* (Buenos Aires: Ser en el 2000, 2008).

———. *A Comparative Atlas of Defence in Latin America and the Caribbean* (Buenos Aires: RESDAL, 2010).

Remmer, Karen L. "Neopatrimonialism: The Politics of Military Rule in Chile, 1973–1987," *Comparative Politics*, 21:2 (January 1989): 149–70.

Rizvi, Hasan-Askari. *The Military and Politics in Pakistan, 1947–1997* (Lahore: Sang-e-Meel Publications, 2000).

Robinson, Geoffrey. "Indonesia: On a New Course?" in Alagappa, ed., *Coercion and Governance*, 226–58.

———. *"If You Leave Us Here, We will Die": How Genocide Was Stopped in East Timor* (Princeton, NJ: Princeton University Press, 2009).

Robledo, Marcos. "Democratic Consolidation in Chilean Civil-Military Relations: 1990–2005," in Thomas Bruneau and Harold Trinkunas, eds., *Global Politics of Defense Reform* (New York: Palgrave-Macmillan, 2008), 95–127.

Rodrigo, Fernando. "A Democratic Strategy toward the Military: Spain, 1975–1979," in Constantine Danopoulos, ed., *From Military to Civilian Rule* (London: Routledge, 1991), 63–77.

Roeber, Joe. "Parallel Markets: Corruption in the International Arms Trade," *Goodwin Paper No. 3* (London: Campaign Against Arms Trade, June 2005).

Roehrig, Terence. *The Prosecution of Former Military Leaders in Newly Democratic Nations* (Jefferson, NC: McFarland & Co., 2002).

Romania, Government of. *Two Years of Governance* (Bucharest: The Government of Romania, 1994).

Roosa, John. *Pretext for Mass Murder: The September 30th Movement and Suharto's Coup d'Etat in Indonesia* (Madison: University of Wisconsin Press, 2006).

Rose, Gregory F. "The Post-Revolutionary Purge of Iran's Armed Forces," *Iranian Studies*, 17:2–3 (Spring/Summer 1984): 153–94.

Roselle, Laura. *Media and the Politics of Failure: Great Powers, Communication Strategies, and Military Defeats* (New York: Palgrave Macmillan, 2006).

Rosen, Stephen Peter. *Societies and Military Power: India and Its Armies* (Ithaca, NY: Cornell University Press, 1996).

Rossmeisl, Dieter. *Demokratie von Aussen: Amerikanische Militärregierung in Nürnberg, 1945–1949* (Munich: Deutscher Taschenbuch Verlag, 1992).

Rotberg, Robert I., and Dennis Thompson, eds. *Truth vs. Justice* (Princeton, NJ: Princeton University Press, 2000).

Roth, Jonathan P. *Roman Warfare* (New York: Cambridge University Press, 2009).

Rouquié, Alain. *The Military and the State in Latin America* (Berkeley: University of California Press, 1989).

Roy, Ashish Kumar. *Praetorian Politics in Bangladesh, 1975–1981* (Kolkata: Progressive Publishers, 2002).

Rubin, Barry. "The Military in Contemporary Middle Eastern Politics," *Middle East Review of International Affairs*, 5:1 (March 2001): 47–63.

Rubin, F. "The Hungarian People's Army," *RUSI Journal*, 121:3 (September 1976): 59–66.

Rupiya, Martin, ed. *Evolutions and Revolutions: A Contemporary History of Militaries in Southern Africa* (Pretoria: Institute for Security Studies, 2005).

———. *The Enemy Within: Southern African Militaries' Quarter-Century Battle with HIV and AIDS* (Pretoria: Institute for Security Studies, 2006).

———. "Southern African Militaries' Battle against HIV/AIDS," in Rupiya, ed., *The Enemy Within*, 7–18.

Russell, Alec. *Bring Me My Machine Gun: The Battle for the Soul of South Africa from Mandela to Zuma* (New York: Public Affairs, 2009).

Sahagún, Agustin Rodríguez. "La Reforma Militar de los Gobiernos de Suárez," *Revista Española de Investigaciones Sociológicas*, No. 36 (October–December 1986): 189–94.

Saif, Ahmed Abdel-Karim. "The Politics of Survival and the Structure of Control in Unified Yemen, 1990–1997" (M.A. thesis, University of Exeter, September 1997).

Saín, Marcelo Fabián. *Los levantamientos carapintada, 1987–1991* (Buenos Aires: Centro Editor de América Latina, 1994).

Samatar, Abdi Ismail. *An African Miracle* (Portsmouth, NH: Heinemann, 1999).

Sambanis, Nicholas. "What Is A Civil War? Conceptual and Empirical Complexities of an Operational Definition." *Journal of Conflict Resolution*, 48:6 (December 2004): 814–58.

Samuels, Richard J. *"Rich Nation, Strong Army": National Security and the Technological Transformation of Japan* (Ithaca, NY: Cornell University Press, 1994).

———. *Machiavelli's Children: Leaders and Their Legacies in Italy and Japan* (Ithaca, NY: Cornell University Press, 2003).

———. "Politics, Security Policy, and Japan's Cabinet Legislation Bureau: Who Elected These Guys, Anyway?" *Japan Policy Research Institute PRI Working Paper No. 99* (March 2004).

———. *Securing Japan: Tokyo's Grand Strategy and the Future of East Asia* (Ithaca, NY: Cornell University Press, 2007).

Santibañes, Francisco Fernando de. "The Effectiveness of Military Governments During War: The Case of Argentina in the Malvinas," *Armed Forces & Society*, 33:4 (July 2007): 612–37.

Sarotte, Mary Elise. *German Military Reform and European Security* (Adelphi Paper No. 340; London: IISS, 2001).

Sattar, Babar. "Pakistan: Return to Praetorianism," in Alagappa, ed., *Coercion and Governance*, 385–412.

Sayigh, Yezid. "Security Sector Reform in the Arab Region," http.arab-reform.net, accessed December 14, 2007.

———. "'Fixing Broken Windows': Security Sector Reform in Palestine, Lebanon, and Yemen," *Carnegie Papers No. 17* (Washington, DC: Carnegie Endowment for International Peace, October 2009), 29 pp.

Schanzer, Jonathan. "Yemen's War on Terror," *Orbis*, 48:3 (Summer 2004): 517–31.

Schapera, Isaac. *The Tswana* (London: Kegan Paul, 1953).

Schedler, Andreas., ed. *Electoral Authoritarianism: The Dynamics of Unfree Competition* (Boulder, CO: Lynne Rienner, 2006).

Scheetz, Thomas. "The Evolution of Public Sector Expenditures: Changing Political Priorities in Argentina, Chile, Paraguay, and Peru," *Journal of Peace Research*, 29:2 (1992): 175–90.

Schiff, Rebecca L. "Concordance Theory: The Cases of India and Pakistan," in Mares, ed., 27–44.

Schirmer, Jennifer. "The Guatemalan Politico-Military Project," in Koonings and Kruijt, eds., 64–89.

Schlaffer, Rudolf J. *Der Wehrbeauftragte 1951 bis 1985: Aus Sorge um den Soldaten* (Munich: Oldenbourg, 2006).

Schlaffer, Rudolf J., and John Zimmermann. *Wo bitte geht's zur Schlacht? Kurioses aus dem deutschen Militär von A–Z* (Berlin: be.bra, 2009).

Schmitter, Philippe C. "Liberation by Golpe: Retrospective Thoughts on the Demise of Authoritarian Rule in Portugal," *Armed Forces & Society*, 2:1 (November 1975): 5–33.

Schofield, Julian. *Militarization and War* (New York: Palgrave Macmillan, 2007).

Schönbohm, Jörg. *Two Armies and One Fatherland: The End of the Nationale Volksarmee*. Translated by Peter and Elfi Johnson (Providence, RI: Berghahn Books, 1996).

———. *Wilde Schermut: Erinnerungen einer Unpolitischen* (Berlin: Landt-Verlag, 2010).

Schwartz, Thomas A. "Europe as the Solution: John J. McCloy and the Rearmament of Germany, 1949–1952" (Harvard University, April 28, 1986), unpublished paper, 19 pp.

Searle, Alaric. *Wehrmacht Generals, West German Society, and the Debate on Rearmament, 1949–1959* (Westport, CT: Praeger, 2003).

Seegers, Annette. *The Military in the Making of Modern South Africa* (London: I. B. Tauris, 1996).

Seligson, Mitchell. "Democracy on Ice: The Multiple Challenges of Guatemala's Peace Process," in Frances Hagopian and Scott Mainwaring, eds., *The Third Wave of Democratization in Latin America* (New York: Cambridge University Press, 2005), 202–33.

Serra, Narcís. "La Política Española de Defensa," *Revista Española de Investigaciones Sociológicas*, No. 36 (October–December 1986): 173–86.

———. *The Military Transition: Democratic Reform of the Armed Forces*. Translated by Peter Bush (Cambridge, UK: Cambridge University Press, 2010).

Shafqat, Saeed. *Civil-Military Relations in Pakistan: From Zulfikar Ali Bhutto to Benazir Bhutto* (Boulder, CO: Westview, 1997).

Shah, Aqil. "Praetorianism and Terrorism," *Journal of Democracy*, 19:4 (October 2008): 16–25.

Sharp, Paul, and Louis Fisher. "Inside the 'Crystal Ball': Understanding the Evolution of the Military in Botswana and the Challenges Ahead," in Rupiya, ed., *Evolutions and Revolutions*, 43–60.

Shemella, Paul. "The Spectrum of Roles and Missions of the Armed Forces," in Bruneau and Tollefson, eds., 122–42.

Shevtsova, Lilia. *Putin's Russia* (Washington, DC: Carnegie Endowment for International Peace, 2003).

Shields, Vanessa E., and Nicholas D. J. Baldwin, eds. *Beyond Settlement: Making Peace Last after Civil Conflict* (Teaneck, NJ: Fairleigh Dickinson University Press, 2008).

Shils, Edward A. "The Military in the Political Development of the New States," in Johnson, ed., 7–67.

Shils, Edward A., and Morris Janowitz. "Cohesion and Disintegration in the Wehrmacht in World War II," *Public Opinion Quarterly*, 12:2 (Summer 1948): 280–315.

Shlykov, Vitaly V. "Does Russia Need a General Staff?" *European Security*, 10:4 (Winter 2001): 45–83.

Siani-Davies, Peter. *The Romanian Revolution of December 1989* (Ithaca, NY: Cornell University Press, 2005).

Siddiqa, Ayesha. *Military Inc.: Inside Pakistan's Military Economy* (London: Pluto Press, 2007).

Sigmund, Paul. "Approaches to the Study of the Military in Latin America," *Comparative Politics*, 26:1 (October 1993): 111–22.

Sigur, Gaston J. "Power, Politics, and Defense," in Buck, ed., 181–95.

Silva, Eduardo. "Chile Past, Present and Future: The Long Road to National Reconciliation," *Journal of Interamerican Studies and World Affairs*, 33:4 (Winter 1991): 133–46.

———. "From Dictatorship to Democracy: The Business-State Nexus in Chile's Economic Transformation, 1975–1994," *Comparative Politics*, 28:3 (April 1996): 299–320.

———. "Chile," in Vanden and Prevost, eds., 432–67.

Silva, Patricio. "Searching for Civilian Supremacy: The Concertación Governments and the Military in Chile," *Bulletin of Latin American Research*, 21:3 (July 2002): 375–95.

———. "Between Autonomy and Subordination: Government-Military Relations in Post-Authoritarian Chile," in Cawthra and Luckham, eds., 102–22.

Singh, Depinder. *Field Marshal Sam Manekshaw: Soldiering with Dignity* (Delhi: Natraj, 2003).

Singh, Jaswant. *Jinnah: India, Partition, Independence* (New York: Oxford University Press, 2010).

Sklar, Richard. "On Democracy and Development in Botswana," in John Holm and Patrick Molutsi, eds., *Democracy in Botswana* (Athens, OH: Botswana Society and University Press, 1990), 273–79.

Smith, William Edgett. *Nyerere of Tanzania* (London: Gollancz, 1973).

Snyder, Jack. *From Voting to Violence: Democratization and Nationalist Conflict* (New York: Norton, 2000).

Spencer, Herbert. "Militancy and Industrialism," in J.D.Y. Peel, ed., *Herbert Spencer on Social Evolution: Selected Writings* (Chicago: University of Chicago Press, 1972), 149–66.

Stedman, Stephen John. *Implementing Peace Agreements in Civil Wars* (New York: International Peace Academy, 2001).

Steenkamp, Willem. *South Africa's Border War, 1966–1989* (Oxford, UK: African Books Collective, 1992).

Stepan, Alfred. *Rethinking Military Politics: Brazil and the Southern Cone* (Princeton, NJ: Princeton University Press, 1988).

Stewart, Rory. *The Places in Between* (New York: Harvest/Harcourt, 2006).

Suchit, Bunbongkarn. *The Military in Thai Politics, 1981–86* (Singapore: Institute of Southeast Asian Studies, 1987).

Sun Tzu. *The Art of War*. Translated by Samuel B. Griffin (Oxford: Oxford University Press, 1963).

Sun Tzu, II. *The Lost Art of War*. Translated by Thomas Cleary (New York: HarperCollins, 1996).

Surachart, Bamrungsuk. "Changing Patterns of Civil-Military Relations and Thailand's Regional Outlook," in Mares, ed., 187–205.

———. *Military Coups and Thai Politics* (in Thai) (Bangkok: The Predi Institute, 2008).

Švajncer, Janez. *Obranili Domovino: Teritorialna Obramba Republike Slovenije v Vojni za Svobodno in Samostojno Slovenijo, 1991* (Ljubljana: Viharnik, 1993).

Swai, F. "The Politicisation of the Tanzania Defence Forces," in Jeanette Hartman, ed., *Rethinking the Arusha Declaration* (Copenhagen: Centre for Developmental Research, 1991), 94–104.

Talbott, Strobe. *The Russia Hand* (New York: Random House, 2002).

Tanzania People's Defence Forces. *Tanganyika Rifles Mutiny, January 1964* (Dar es Salaam: Dar es Salaam University Press, 1993).

Taylor, Brian D. *Politics and the Russian Army: Civil-Military Relations, 1689–2000* (New York: Cambridge University Press, 2003).

———. *State-Building in Putin's Russia: Policing and Coercion after Communism* (New York: Cambridge University Press, 2011).

Thelen, Kathleen. "Historical Institutionalism in Comparative Politics," *Annual Review of Political Science*, 2 (June 1999): 369–404.

Thomas, Raju G. *Democracy, Security, and Development in India* (New York: St. Martin's Press, 1996).

Thucydides. *History of the Peloponnesian War*. Translated by Richard Crawley (London: Dent, 1993).

Tismaneanu, Vladimir, and Dorin Tudoran. "The Bucharest Syndrome," *Journal of Democracy*, 4:1 (January 1993): 41–52.

Trinkunas, Harold A. *Crafting Civilian Control of the Military in Venezuela: A Comparative Perspective* (Chapel Hill: University of North Carolina Press, 2005).

Tungaraza, Casta. "The Transformation of Civil-Military Relations in Tanzania," in Hutchful and Bathily, eds., 291–315.

Ukrist Pathmanand. "A Different Coup d'État?" *Journal of Contemporary Asia*, 38:1 (February 2008): 124–42.

Ungváry, Krisztián. *The Siege of Budapest: One Hundred Days in World War II* (New Haven, CT: Yale University Press, 2005).

United Kingdom Ministry of Defence. *Review of Parliamentary Oversight of the Romanian Ministry of National Defence and the Democratic Control of Its Armed Forces* (London: Ministry of Defence, February 1997).

Vacs, Aldo C. "Argentina," in Vanden and Prevost, eds., 396–431.

Vanden, Harry E., and Gary Prevost. eds. *Politics of Latin America* (New York: Oxford University Press, 2006).

Varshney, Ashutosh. "Why Democracy Survives," *Journal of Democracy*, 9:3 (July 1998): 36–50.

Veremis, Thanos. *The Military in Greek Politics: From Independence to Democracy* (Montréal: Black Rose Books, 1997).

Visser, Reidar. "Iraq's Partition Fantasy," www.openDemocracy.net, May 19, 2006.

Volkmann, Hans-Erich Volkmann. "Die innenpolitische Dimension Adenauerscher Sicherheitspolitik in der EVG-Phase," in *Die EVG-Phase: Anfänge westdeutsche Sicherheitspolitik 1945 bis 1956. Vol II.* (Munich: Oldenbourg, 1990), 235–604.

Wagner, Andrea. *Der argentinisch-chilenische Konflikt um den Beagle-Kanal: Ein Beitrag zu den Methoden friedlicher Streiterledigung* (Frankfurt: Peter Lang, 1992).

Waisbord, Silvio. "Politics and Identity in the Argentine Army: Cleavages and the Generational Factor," *Latin American Research Review*, 26:2 (1991): 157–70.

Waldmeir, Patti. *Anatomy of a Miracle: The End of Apartheid and the Birth of the New South Africa* (New Brunswick, NJ: Rutgers University Press, 1998).

Wallander, Celeste. *Mortal Friends, Best Enemies: German-Russian Cooperation after the Cold War* (Ithaca, NY: Cornell University Press, 1999).

Walt, Stephen M. *The Origins of Alliances* (Ithaca, NY: Cornell University Press, 1987).

Ware, Robert Bruce. "Will Southern Russian Studies Go the Way of Sovietology?" *Journal of Slavic Military Studies*, 16:4 (December 2003): 163–65.

Watanabe, Akio. "Japan's Postwar Constitution and Its Implications for Defense Policy," in Matthews and Matsuyama, eds., 35–49.

Watts, Larry L. "The Romanian Army in the December Revolution and Beyond," in Daniel N. Nelson, ed., *Romania After Tyranny* (Boulder, CO: Westview, 1992), 95–126.

———. "Reform and Crisis in Romanian Civil-Military Relations, 1989–1999," *Armed Forces & Society*, 27:4 (Summer 2001): 597–622.

Weber, Max. *The Theory of Social and Economic Organization* (New York: Free Press, 1964).

Wedeen, Lisa. *Peripheral Visions: Publics, Power, and Performance in Yemen* (Chicago: University of Chicago Press, 2008).

Weeks, Gregory. "A Preference for Deference: Reforming the Military's Intelligence Role in Argentina, Chile, and Peru," *Third World Quarterly*, 29:1 (February 2008): 45–61.

Weigley, Russell F. "The American Military and the Principle of Civilian Control from McClellan to Powell," *Journal of Military History*, 57:5 (October 1993): 27–58.

Weiner, Myron. "Empirical Democratic Theory" in Myron Weiner and Ergun Özbudun, eds., *Competitive Elections in Developing Countries* (Washington DC: American Enterprise Institute, 1987), 3–34.

Welch, Claude E., Jr. "Civilian Control of the Military: Myth and Reality," in Welch, ed., *Civilian Control of the Military*, 1–41.

———. "Two Strategies of Civilian Control: Some Concluding Observations," in Welch, ed., *Civilian Control of the Military*, 313–27.

———, ed. *Civilian Control of the Military: Theory and Cases from Developing Countries* (Albany: State University of New York Press, 1976).

Welsh, Helga. "Political Transition Processes in Central and Eastern Europe," *Comparative Politics*, 26:4 (July 1994): 385.

Wenzke, Rüdiger. *Staatsfeinde in Uniform?* (Berlin: Ch. Links Verlag, 2005).

Werlin, Herbert H. "Ghana and South Korea: Explaining Developmental Disparities," *Journal of Asian and African Studies*, 29 (April 1994): 205–25.

Whitehead, Laurence. "International Aspects of Democratization," in Guillermo O'Donnell, Philippe Schmitter, and Laurence Whitehead, eds., *Transitions from Authoritarian Rule: Comparative Perspectives* (Baltimore, MD: Johns Hopkins University Press, 1986), 3–46.

Wiarda, Howard. "The Corporatist Tradition and the Corporative System in Portugal: Structured, Evolving, Transcended, Persistent," in Lawrence S. Graham and Harry M. Makler, eds., *Contemporary Portugal: The Revolution and Its Antecedents* (Austin: University of Texas Press, 1979), 89–122.

Wiking, Staffan. *Military Coups in Sub-Saharan Africa* (Uppsala: Scandinavian Institute of African Studies, 1983).

Williams, David. *On the Border, 1965–1990: The While South African Military Experience* (Cape Town: Tafelberg, 2010).

Williams, Philip J., and Knut Walter. *Militarization and Demilitarization in El Salvador's Transition to Democracy* (Pittsburgh, PA: University of Pittsburgh Press, 1997).

Williams, Rocky, Gavin Cawthra, and Diane Abrahams, eds. *Ourselves To Know: Civil-Military Relations and Defence Transformation in Southern Africa* (Pretoria: Institute for Security Studies, 2003).

Wilson, David A. "The Military in Thai Politics," in Johnson, ed., 253–76.

Winter, Thomas N. "Cincinnatus and the Disbanding of Washington's Army," *Classical Bulletin*, 51:6 (April 1975): 81–86.

Wolf, Sonja. "Maras Transnacionales: Origins and Transformations of Central American Street Gangs," *Latin American Research Review*, 45:1(2010): 256–65.

Woo, Jongseok. *Security Challenges and Military Politics in East Asia: From State-Building to Post-Democratization* (New York: Continuum, 2011).

Woodward, Susan L. "Bosnia and Herzegovina: How Not to End Civil War," in Barbara F. Walter and Jack Snyder, eds., *Civil Wars, Insecurity, and Intervention* (New York: Columbia University Press, 1999), 73–145.

Worboys, Katherine J. "The Traumatic Journey from Dictatorship to Democracy: Peacekeeping Operations and Civil-Military Relations in Argentina, 1989–1999," *Armed Forces & Society*, 33:2 (January 2007): 149–68.

Wright, Thomas C. *State Terrorism in Latin America* (Lanham, MD: Rowman & Littlefield, 2007).

Yeltsin, Boris. *The View from the Kremlin* (London: HarperCollins, 1994).

Yoshida, Shigeru. *The Last Meiji Man*. Edited by Hiroshi Nara, translated by Yoshida Ken'ichi and Hiroshi Nara (Lahham, MD: Rowman & Littlefield, [1961] 2007).

Young, Thomas-Durrell. "Military Professionalism in a Democracy," in Bruneau and Tollefson, eds., 17–33.

Yudhoyono, Susilo Bambang. "The Democratic Instinct in the 21st Century," *Journal of Democracy*, 21:3 (July 2010): 5–10.

Zaffiro, James. "The Press and Political Opposition in an African Democracy: The Case of Botswana," *Journal of Commonwealth and Comparative Politics*, 27:1 (1989): 51–73.

Zágoni, Ernő. *Hadsereg, honvédelem* (Budapest: Zrínyi, 1968).

Zaverucha, Jorge. "The Degree of Military Political Autonomy during the Spanish, Argentine, and Brazilian Transitions," *Journal of Latin American Studies*, 25:2 (1993): 283–99.

Zilian, Frederick, Jr. *From Confrontation to Cooperation* (Westport, CT: Praeger, 1999).

INDEX

꿔 퓨